# COMPARATIVE ECONOMIC SYSTEMS

# COMPARATIVE ECONOMIC SYSTEMS

Heinz Kohler
*Amherst College*

Scott, Foresman and Company
Glenview, Illinois    London, England

## Acknowledgments

Unless otherwise acknowledged, all photos are the property of Scott, Foresman and Company.

**PAGE 28,** The Granger Collection, New York; **PAGE 119,** Courtesy Wassily W. Leontief; **PAGE 120,** UPI/Bettmann Newsphotos; **PAGE 192,** Historical Pictures Service, Chicago; **PAGE 194,** AP/Wide World; **PAGE 195,** AP/Wide World; **PAGE 196,** Sovfoto; **PAGE 234,** Sovfoto; **PAGE 259,** Y. Karsh/Woodfin Camp & Associates; **PAGE 298,** UPI/Bettmann Newsphotos; **PAGE 299,** The White House; **PAGE 300,** UPI/Bettmann Newsphotos; **PAGE 325T,** Sovfoto; **PAGE 325,** Sovfoto; **PAGE 433,** UPI/Bettmann Newsphotos; **PAGE 434,** UPI/Bettmann Newsphotos; **PAGE 436,** Reuters/UPI/Bettmann Newsphotos; **PAGE 452,** Brown Brothers.

## Library of Congress Cataloging-in-Publication Data

Kohler, Heinz, 1934–
    Comparative economic systems.

    Includes bibliographies and indexes.
    1. Comparative economics. I. Title.
HB90.K63  1989      330      88-33674
ISBN 0-673-38096-3

1 2 3 4 5 6-KPF-94 93 92 91 90 89

# *Preface*

The comparison of economic systems, in particular of Capitalism versus Socialism, is likely to draw a highly emotional response in most places on earth. Many people just *know* that their system is superior to any other or that any other is bound to be superior to theirs; and they hold such belief as a citadel to be defended, not as a hypothesis to be put to the test. Thus they have no room for discussion with the unbeliever. They are willing to preach but not to engage in dialogue. This book, however, was written to encourage dialogue. It was written for those who are less certain of all the answers, who wish to escape uncritical self-congratulation as well as the naive admiration of the unknown.

This book is intended for students who have had only an introductory course in economics, but for those students better prepared, there are optional sections of greater rigor. Additionally for those students less than ideally prepared for this course, there are optional review sections. Chapter 1 introduces the nature of the economic problem; Chapters 2–4 present possible goals that might be pursued in response to that problem; and Chapter 5 suggests major types of institutional arrangements to achieve these goals. These chapters show why reasonable people may well differ on the meaning of human welfare and, therefore, on the types of actions appropriate for its achievement. That is, of course, why one person's dream about the earthly paradise has always been another person's nightmare.

As the Table of Contents shows, the various possible economic systems introduced in Chapter 5 are then discussed in depth in the remaining chapters, and they are assessed in light of their ability to achieve the goals stated earlier. This does not mean that readers will find the ultimate answer, ready-made, about the best economic system. For one thing, your ideal society may pursue goals different from any of the goals specified in Chapters 2–4. For another, different systems are likely to perform differently with respect to different goals. Readers *will* find a framework for thinking about the major issues involved in the choice among economic systems. Therefore, they should be better able, in light of their own preferences, to make such a choice.

## Organization and Rationale for this Book

I have received a great deal of advice from potential users of this textbook, and am grateful for it. Unfortunately, but inevitably, some of this advice cannot be followed; instructors should know why this is so. The suggestions given to me mainly involved three issues: the order of presentation, the relative emphasis on description versus theory, and the role of Marxism. After pretesting this book in numerous classes at a small liberal arts college (Amherst College) and at a large state university (the University of Massachusetts), I have made choices on all of these matters on pedagogical grounds.

## The Order of Presentation

About half the instructors have urged me to treat capitalism before socialism, on the reasonable grounds that one should start where students are, moving from the familiar to the unfamiliar. The other half of instructors have suggested just the opposite; their advice has been followed here and for this reason: In my experience, students who have grown up in a capitalist country (probably the United States), who have just taken an introductory economics course focusing on capitalism exclusively (as is typical), and who have now signed up for a comparative systems course, are ready and eager to learn about *alternative* economic systems. If they are first asked to spend six weeks on capitalism, their eagerness vanishes, and they get bored. It pays to use their initial eagerness and to introduce various forms of socialism right away and *then* to have a final look back at the students' familiar world. Nevertheless, instructors who wish to do so can change the order of presentation. Parts 1–4 of this text are self-contained modules; instructors are free to teach Part 3 prior to Part 2, for example.

## Description Versus Theory

Many instructors have urged me to be thorough in describing the economies of various countries, detailing the evolution of their institutions and the history of their successes or failures. Indeed, numerous instructors have emphasized that a good comparative systems book must do more than cover the obvious (the United States and Japan? the Soviet Union and China?); there simply *must* be a chapter on Cuba and Sweden, they have said, on Yugoslavia and Hungary, on India and Brazil— the list goes on. Yet, even with the best of will, it is impossible to satisfy everyone on this issue. Neither the space available in a standard-size textbook nor my limited competence allows it.

On the other hand, just as many instructors have *complained* about the traditional country-by-country accounts of national economies that overwhelm students with institutional and historic detail (all of which is forgotten almost instantly) and that are often considerably less challenging than even introductory textbooks are. These instructors have urged me to forgo description and take a strong theoretical approach.

My personal preference lies with the latter suggestion. However, this book does not abandon description. Once again, for pedagogical reasons, the book develops a crucial core of theoretical material that students can make their own and that they can then use—now and in the future—to assess economic systems that are of interest to them. This book also demonstrates, with a number of case studies, how this process of assessment can be carried out. I have found that students are appreciative of the unifying conceptual frame employed in this book. In addition, this book also meets the typical student's desire to hear anecdotes and stories, to learn about everyday life on the farms and in the homes of ordinary people in other countries, to view candid snapshots of life in factories, offices, and shops. The biographies, close-ups, and analytical examples at the end of most chapters are designed precisely for the purpose of adding such touches of color to the basic theme pursued in this text.

## The Role of Marxism

Some instructors have urged this author to follow tradition in still another way, not only to discuss capitalism *before* socialism, but also to present an exposition of Marxist theory before any discussion of socialist economic systems. The reasoning is almost persuasive: There is, first, the chronological argument; in the Marxian scheme of things, history moves from capitalism to socialism (and on to communism), not the other way around. There is, second, the well-known fact that all real-world socialist revolutions have been fought in the name of Marx. Yet the suggestion to discuss Marxism before socialist systems has not been followed in this book, once again for pedagogical reasons. This book is meant to be neither a text on area studies (hence the rejection of the country-by-country approach) nor a text on the history of economic doctrines (such as those of Marx). Marx concentrated on criticizing capitalism; he had very little to say about the future socialist society he predicted. True enough, the leaders of real-world socialist countries always claim to be the executors of Marx's ideas, but this is a monstrous pretense. There is, in fact, little correspondence between the (few) Marxian pronouncements on socialism and the realities that are supposed to be their embodiment. So why should we ask students to study Marx first only to leave all this material behind as so much unclaimed baggage as we then proceed to study socialist economic systems? On the contrary, *after* having studied socialist systems, students are in a much better position to appreciate the (almost imperceptible) relationship between Marx and today's socialist realities. Accordingly, the last chapter of this book does summarize Marx's thought and assess its true role in today's world (which is not the provision of blueprints for socialist systems).

## Teaching Aids

A number of teaching aids have been built into the text: the figures made self-contained by carefully worded captions, chapter summaries, end-of-chapter listings of key terms (boldfaced in the text and also gathered in a glossary at the back of the book), end-of-chapter questions and problems (with detailed responses or answers at the back of the book), and lists of selected readings. Most importantly, note the availability of a personal-computer diskette, called SYSTEMS-1, designed to be used with IBM microcomputers and compatible machines. For each chapter of the text, this diskette contains a series of multiple-choice questions (along with instant responses to incorrect answers). In addition, there are mathematical programs (for inverting matrices, solving simultaneous-equations, linear-programming, or cash-flow problems, and much more). Instructors will find that they can use this diskette with great profit to supplement the text.

## Alternative Course Outlines

Instructors should note that the book is suitable for a great variety of student backgrounds. Certain chapters (such as Chapters 1 through 4) and certain sections within chapters have been identified by asterisks and footnotes as review material. This material covers relevant parts of the elementary course; it can be stressed for poorly prepared students, read rapidly by average students, and ignored by advanced students. More difficult sections of chapters are similarly identified by asterisks and footnotes as advanced material. Instructors teaching students with limited backgrounds in economics (or desiring to teach courses of more descriptive natures) can easily avoid the advanced sections without loss of continuity. The Chapter 6 sections on matrix inversion and simultaneous equations or the Chapter 11 section on linear programming provide examples. Instructors teaching advanced students can emphasize these sections as well as the more difficult end-of-chapter questions and problems. These instructors can also supplement the text with the computer programs noted at the end of various chapters. (For example, it is possible to work out numerous "central plans" with the matrix operations, simultaneous equations, or linear-programming modules and to do so in minutes.)

Finally, it should be noted that the end-of-chapter problems can serve two types of purposes. Some of them can be used to review material from the elementary economics course. Others are designed to take students beyond the chapter's material and to deal with issues that easily could have been taken up in a separate chapter (for example, the Chapter 14 problems that teach students about the pitfalls of international statistical comparisons). For both of these purposes, elaborate answers and solutions are needed, and they have been provided in the answer section at the back of the book.

## Acknowledgments

I would like to express my sincere gratitude to many who have helped me in the creation of this text. Many reviewers took the time to examine at least a part of the project and gave me good advice:

| | |
|---|---|
| J. C. Brada | Arizona State University |
| Helen H. Jensen | Iowa State University |
| Janet Mitchell | University of Southern California |
| Simon Power | Queen's University |
| Kazimierz Poznanski | University of Washington, Seattle |
| Louis Putterman | Brown University |
| Barbara N. Sands | University of Arizona |
| Peter Schran | University of Illinois at Urbana-Champaign |
| Larry T. Wimmer | Brigham Young University |

I am equally grateful to acquiring editor George Lobell, editors Ellen Silge and Colleen McCauley, and designer Beth Morrison. They have guided this project through the long process of production and have created, as most will agree, a beautiful book.

Heinz Kohler
Amherst College

# *To the Student*

The comparative study of economic systems is a fascinating subject because it makes us aware of the fact that the same economic problem—scarcity—can be tackled in so many different ways. A study of this subject, therefore, broadens our horizon beyond the here and now; it helps us avoid the all-too-common error of mistaking our own economy for the world at large and our own times for eternity. This book will help you escape narrow-minded self-righteousness; it will also disabuse you from the common view that the grass is *bound to be* greener on the other side. The book will not tell you what the best economic system is, but it will give you the ability to make up your own mind.

Students should note a number of study aids that have been built into the text: the graphs made self-contained by carefully worded captions, chapter summaries, end-of-chapter listings of key terms (boldfaced in the text and also gathered in a glossary at the back of the book), end-of-chapter questions and problems (with detailed responses or answers at the back of the book), and lists of selected readings. Most importantly, note the availability of a personal-computer diskette, called SYSTEMS-1, designed to be used with IBM microcomputers and compatible machines. For each chapter of the text, this diskette contains a series of multiple-choice questions (along with instant responses to incorrect answers). In addition, there are several useful mathematical programs.

## Using the SYSTEMS-1 Computer Diskette

A set of programs for IBM personal computers and compatible machines has been specifically designed to accompany this text. Although it is not required, a color display is preferable.

SYSTEMS-1 covers all aspects of the text. It contains:

1. Over 250 multiple-choice questions (along with numerous graphs and tables). For each question, the correct answer is identified and immediate comments are provided on incorrect responses.
2. A matrix operations program, allowing students to transpose, add, subtract, multiply, exponentiate, invert matrices, and more.
3. A simultaneous equations program, allowing students to solve a maximum of 12 simultaneous equations.
4. A capital budgeting program, allowing students
   a. to explore the relationships between present value, future value, interest rates, and time; and
   b. to investigate the profitability of (negative and positive) cash flows that extend over time.
5. A linear programming module, allowing students to solve all types of linear programming problems.

## Initial Start-Up Procedure

The SYSTEMS-1 diskette contains detailed operating instructions. For first-time-ever users, however, the following will be helpful:

1. Prior to loading SYSTEMS-1, in response to the DOS prompt, (e.g. A>), type: **BASICA/D** and press [ENTER].
   Note: Failure to type **BASICA** and typing **BASIC** instead will make it impossible to see graphs on the screen; failure to type **/D** will adversely affect the accuracy of calculations.
2. At this point, in response to the BASICA prompt (**OK**) (and assuming the diskette resides in Drive A), type: **RUN"A:SYSTEMS"**
   (Replace **A** with any other appropriate letter if the diskette resides in another drive.) Then press [ENTER].
3. Some program features are automatic. Do not press any key unless told.
4. You can escape any program at any time by pressing [CTRL] plus [BREAK], typing **SYSTEM**, and pressing [ENTER].
   (It may be necessary to escape for a variety of reasons, such as the occurrence of an overflow error when the computer's capacity is exceeded or the sudden realization that BASICA was not loaded initially.)
5. You can restart a program by the procedure noted in (1) and (2) above. You can also type **RUN** and press [ENTER] or simply press the F2 key.

# Brief Contents

**PART 4** *Special Topic*   441

# *Contents*

# COMPARATIVE ECONOMIC SYSTEMS

# PART 1

# *Basic Concepts*

The chapters of Part 1 lay the foundation for the comparative study of economic systems in the rest of the book. Some of them review key concepts of elementary economics and can be read rapidly. These chapters show that all present-day societies—whether rich or poor—face the identical problem of scarcity, that certain criteria can be employed universally to judge the success of those who would challenge scarcity, and that the inevitable choices that scarcity forces upon people can be made in distinctly different ways, which accounts for the alternative types of economic systems found in the world today.

# CHAPTER 1

# *The Scarcity Problem*

A universal problem exists. Small bands of African Bushmen face it, as do Amazon Indians and Greenland Eskimos. Peasants in China, Egypt, and Peru face the problem no less, and so do urban dwellers in Moscow, Paris, and New York. Everywhere and every day, people have to wrestle with the basic economic problem of *scarcity*. This chapter explains what is involved.

## An Immense Desire for Goods

Suppose a smiling genie popped out of a bottle and offered to be at your service. Suppose he was prepared to bring you, just for the asking, any object you desired and the devoted attention of any person you named. Wouldn't you be tempted to accept the genie's offer? Imagine the abundance of goods that could then be yours: If you were hungry, you could call for food, and it would be there, in the wink of an eye! And you could conjure up new clothes, too, or that fancy camera you had never been able to afford. Presents for family and friends? A flashy sports car for yourself? Of course. A house on your favorite island in the middle of the sea? A plane to get you there? A yacht to play with in the sun? They could be yours. Lessons to fly that plane, to gain all kinds of other skills? The best in medical care, concerts at night, visits to beautiful places? All of these you could enjoy.

Now imagine yourself as someone else—a business executive, perhaps, or government official. Surely, the genie's offer would quickly trigger an equally impressive set of wishful thoughts: You might then dream of a new fleet of trucks, a powerful new computer, an air-conditioned warehouse, a pollution control facility, a robot-driven assembly plant. Or you might wish for more police officers, teachers, and subway cars, for a new sewage-treatment plant, for better bridges, street lights, and roads, for cruise missiles, space satellites, and national parks. . . .

We need not belabor the point. We can return from our brief flights of fancy and consider the real world.

Over five billion people live on this earth, and they do not have genies ready to serve them. But they do spend their individual lives in the pursuit of happiness. To most of them, most of the time, happiness is an elusive goal indeed. Most of them, probably, could not name exact ingredients that would produce happiness for them. But, surely, the kinds of material things named above would be mentioned by many. Thus we can guess that most people, if given the chance offered by our genie (of getting all kinds of commodities and services in return for *nothing*), would not reject it. Most likely, they would be all too ready to prepare an impressive list of things to have and of things or people to use. And all these people would hope that somewhere hidden in *their* list would be at least some of the ingredients required for their happiness. It does not seem unreasonable, therefore, to start our journey into the world of alternative economic systems by accepting as fact this basic observation about people:

> *Most people on earth harbor desires for a truly staggering variety and quantity of commodities and services that they believe will enhance their welfare and, thus, be good for them.*

We will henceforth refer to these objects of desire simply as **goods,** and we will assume that the aggregate quantity of goods desired by all the people is immense in all of the world's nations today. If we have any lingering doubts about this fact, we need only imagine people all over the world—in their various capacities as family members, business executives, government officials, and so on—and contemplate the lengthy lists of wishes most people would surely prepare if they did meet the incredible kind of genie noted above who was ready to offer all goods at a zero price.

We conclude this section with two notes of caution: First, we must remember that the *goods* that people want include both tangible commodities and intangible services. As our brief thought experiment has illustrated so vividly, people clearly believe that their welfare can be promoted by the ownership of various **commodities**— physical objects, like food, clothes, or cars. But people also believe that their welfare can be enhanced by the provision of **services**—the temporary use of physical objects or other people: a house by the sea for the summer months, a seat for six hours on the New York–Paris jet, ten minutes of a doctor's time.

Second, we must never confuse people's *desire* for goods with their *demand* for goods. While the **desire for a good** is measured by the quantity of the good people would take in a period if they could have the good for nothing, the **demand for a good** refers to all the alternative quantities of the good people would buy in a period at all of the good's possible prices—all else being equal. In short, demand is a concept that refers to desire backed up by purchasing power, which enables people in our society to acquire goods that are for sale at *positive* prices.

Instead, desire refers to wishful thinking, to the quantities people would take if no purchasing power were needed because all goods were available at *zero* prices. It is desire for goods in this sense that we claim to be immense in most places on earth and certainly among the large groups of people that make up each one of the world's nations. This is not to deny that particular individuals, or even small groups of them, may have a sharply limited desire for goods (and would reject the genie's offer). For the time being, however, these are rare exceptions to the general rule.

## Resources—The Ingredients To Make Goods

People are not likely, of course, to meet our genie. In the real world, goods are not made by genies with the help of magic; on the contrary, goods are made by people with the help of productive ingredients called **resources.** They are put to work in the **process of production,** a set of activities deliberately designed to make goods available to people where and when they are wanted. Customarily, economists classify the productive ingredients used in this process into three major groups: human, natural, and capital.

**Human resources** are people able and willing to participate in the productive process, supplying their mental or physical labor. **Natural resources** are gifts of nature in their natural state; that is, productive ingredients not made by people and as yet untouched by them. Think of sunlight, wind, and ocean tides, of virgin land and the plants and animals upon it, of schools of fish in the ocean, or of minerals and fuels underground. **Capital resources,** finally, are all the productive ingredients made by people. They include all types of structures used by producers of goods— structures such as factory buildings, blast furnaces, warehouses, highways, or air-port control towers. They include equipment of producers, such as computers, milling machines, or fleets of trucks. And they include producer inventories of raw materials, semifinished goods, or even finished goods (such as boxes of shoes in the store) that have not yet reached their ultimate users.

Three things should be noted concerning the capital concept. First, many items considered by people in general to be natural resources are viewed as capital resources by economists. Consider animals that have been domesticated and specially bred; soil that has been cleared, irrigated, and fertilized; or oil that has been pumped from the ground and shipped far from its original place of deposit. None of these is in its natural state; all of them are in a sense made by people. So they are capital resources, as just defined.

Second, one is almost tempted to carry this reasoning a step further. Economists know that a healthy, educated, and trained labor force (like soil that has been cleared, irrigated, and fertilized) is more productive than it would be without these qualities. Thus one might wish to classify people who are in good physical condition, educated, and trained as produced capital, too! Nevertheless, economists do not classify people as capital resources. They recognize, however, that different people clearly possess different amounts of an invisible kind of **human capital,** consisting of the health care, general education, and training embodied in them. (Accordingly, the production of goods attributable to the use of human resources can sometimes be explained separately by the use of "raw" labor and of human capital.)

Finally, *capital resources,* as the term is used in this book, do not include **financial capital,** such as money, stocks, deeds, or bonds. For an individual in many societies such items are important indeed, but they are not directly productive. People could easily increase such paper claims a millionfold. Yet, if no corresponding increase occurred in the form of real resources (as defined above), people would not be richer at all. They could not produce more on that account. Just as a baker uses butter, eggs, flour, and milk (and not green dollar bills) to bake a cake, so the people in every society must mix *real* capital resources with natural and human ones to produce each and every good they do acquire.

## Technology—The Knowledge to Make Goods

In fact, the quantities of goods people are able to produce depend not only on the quantities of resources they have and put to use, but also on their **technology,** the set of known methods of production available to them. This knowledge of possible methods of production, like the recipe book available to the baker, sets limits on the quantity of goods that can be produced *per unit* of resources. Such limits are, of course, far from eternally fixed. Consider how, during the past century, people have discovered fertilizers, hormones, and high-yield crops and have used these discoveries, along with wonders of agricultural machinery, to raise incredibly the yield per acre of land. Before we run out of conventional fuel, people may well discover how to use solar power on a large scale. Should that happen, the quantities of goods produced per unit of this particular natural resource would increase dramatically. This would happen, furthermore, not because of any change in the quantity or quality of this resource (the sun radiates as much energy to us now as it will then). It would happen because of a new entry in our productive recipe book that would enable us to switch to a technique of production previously unavailable. (Such an advance in technical knowledge should not be confused with a switch, in response to changing circumstances, from one known technique of production to another. While the former is akin to discovering a new recipe, the latter is about selecting a different one from among those previously known.)

## Limited Resources and Limited Technology Yield Limited Goods

Just as a cake is limited in size by the quantities of ingredients and the possible recipes available to the baker, so the "pie" of goods produced by any society is limited by the resources and technology available to it. Obviously, no society has unlimited stocks of resources or of technical knowledge. At any one moment, there are only so many people able and willing to work in the productive process, and limited quantities of human capital are embodied in them. There are only so many acres of virgin timberland and so many known barrels of oil in the ground. There are only so many assembly plants and miles of highway in existence. There are only so many recipes of production from which to choose. Given the best techniques of production available, even the use of all resource stocks at the maximum possible rate (of 24 hours each day) would produce limited flows of resource services and, thus, of newly produced goods in a year. In fact, of course, some resources cannot be used at such a maximum rate. This is most obvious in the case of people.

Once again, a note of caution: To avoid confusion, we must clearly distinguish between stocks and flows of resources and of goods as well. The term **stock** always refers to a quantity at a given moment of time, such as 100 gallons of water sitting in a tub on June 1 at 8 A.M. or 100 million people being ready for work on January 2 at sunrise. (Note how a particular *moment* of time is specified in each instance.) The term **flow,** in contrast, always refers a quantity over some length of time, such as 10 gallons of water per day draining from our tub or 600 million hours per day being worked by our 100 million people. (Note how a particular *period* of time is specified in each of these examples.) You can easily see how talking about flows makes no sense without specifying a time dimension. While 600 million labor hours might be performed per day, they might also be performed per month or per century—with very different implications for the production of goods! If you are only told that 600 million hours are being worked, you are told nothing.

## Scarcity—The Basic Economic Problem

The fact that every society with limited resource stocks and limited technical knowledge will only come up with a limited flow of resource services and, ultimately, of goods in any given period creates no problem in itself. This is so because the limited flows of each and every good that can be produced in a given period might still be *larger* than the quantities needed to fulfill, in that period, the combined desire for goods by all the people. In that case, all goods would be **free goods;** if all people tried to take all that they wanted of each good (provided goods could be had for nothing), people would succeed. Indeed, something would be left over.

There are a few *individual* goods for which this is, in fact, true. Air to breathe (not necessarily pure air) is available at all times and everywhere on the surface of the earth in quantities greater than desired by all people. On earth (but not on the moon should people visit it) air is a free good. Navigable air space from 2 to 3 A.M. Tuesdays over New York City (but not from 5 to 6 P.M. Fridays) is similarly available in quantities greater than desired by all people. It is a free good too. But these are exceptions. The typical situation is different, and to that we now turn.

In all nations on earth today, the limited flows of each and every good that can be produced in a given period are *smaller* than the quantities needed to fulfill, in that period, the combined desire for goods by all the people. This makes for **scarce goods;** if all people tried to take all that they wanted of each good (provided goods could be had for nothing), people would *not* succeed. There would not be enough to go around. And, thus, the basic economic problem is the **scarcity problem:** It is impossible, in any nation today, to fulfill the combined desire for goods by all the people.

And note: The problem is not that some goods are available in small quantities only. What matters is the *relationship* between the desire for goods and opportunities to satisfy them. Consider, for instance, Frozen Glass Splinters. Each year, it is safe to say, very few packages of them come into the world. The same is true of cans of Shredded Bees' Wings or Number One Steamed Cherry Pits. In the entire world, their production is very low indeed. Yet this causes no problem at all because nobody desires these things. There is no scarcity of them.

On the other hand, every year huge quantities of automobiles come into the world—and huge quantities of honey and cherries too. Yet, there is a problem because people desire (that is, would take when offered free) even larger quantities.

Nor is the problem people's inability to produce whatever quantity of any *one* good all the people want. Nothing would be easier than that! If people only wanted any one good, such as a particular type of food, clothing, or car, or, for that matter, the services of doctors, musicians, or trans-Atlantic jets, all they would have to do is arrange for the production of that one good by setting aside and putting to work all their resources for this single purpose. Most likely, they could then produce more of this one good than all the people desired. Similarly, people could surely produce all the goods any *one person* desired by concentrating all resources on satisfying this one person. But this is decidedly not the problem. Although it is easy enough to find the resources needed for the production of the quantity of any one good all the people desire, or even of all the goods one person desires, we shall not find enough to produce the truly huge quantities of *all* the goods that *all* the people desire. This scarcity of resources in relation to a virtually infinite desire for goods is the ultimate reason why we often have to go without. Figure 1.1, ''The Scarcity Problem'' illustrates the point.

**Figure 1.1**   The Scarcity Problem

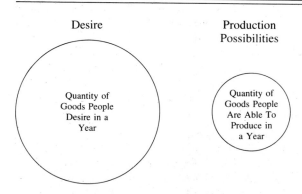

Desire

Production
Possibilities

Quantity of
Goods People
Desire in a
Year

Quantity of
Goods People
Are Able To
Produce in
a Year

Unlike in a world of make-believe filled with genies, in the real world people face the unpleasant fact of scarcity. In any nation today, the people's wish to satisfy all their desires for goods is frustrated by the unavailability of sufficient resources to produce a sufficiently large quantity of goods. While resources allow the production of the ''pie'' shown by the right-hand circle, people would like to consume the one shown by the left-hand circle.

Because economists are forever telling people that ours is a world of scarcity wherein people can never have all they want, economics is often called "the dismal science." Yet, actually, economists are far from content with being prophets of gloom. While they recognize that scarcity is a built-in fact of life—not only for isolated Bushmen and Eskimos, but also for so much richer Russians and Americans—the main concern of economists is to explore the exact implications of scarcity. This exploration can help people minimize the impact of scarcity. But that is the subject of the next chapters.

## Summary

1. Most people on earth harbor desires for a truly staggering variety and quantity of goods. One can appreciate the extent of this desire by imagining the quantities of goods people would take if all goods were available at zero prices.
2. Goods are produced with resources—human, natural, and capital.
3. Technology sets limits on the quantity of goods producible per unit of resources.
4. Limited resources and limited technology combine to yield limited quantities of goods in any given period.
5. In all nations today, the quantity of goods that can be produced in a given period with available resources and technology falls short of the quantity required to fulfill, simultaneously, the desire for goods by all the people. This condition constitutes the economic problem of scarcity.

## Key Terms

| | |
|---|---|
| capital resources | human resources |
| commodities | natural resources |
| demand for a good | process of production |
| desire for a good | resources |
| financial capital | scarce goods |
| flow | scarcity problem |
| free goods | services |
| goods | stock |
| human capital | technology |

## Questions and Problems

1. This chapter cautions the reader not to confuse the *desire* for a good with the *demand* for a good. Can you show the difference graphically?
2. Which of the following are *natural resources* as defined in this chapter: 100 cubic feet of coal, a highway, a cow, an acre of land, sand at a

beach not yet discovered by people, sunshine, a school of tuna in the ocean, a college building, a can of peas? (*Hint:* Of the nine correct answers, three will be *always,* three others *never,* and the remaining three *maybe.*) What reasons can you give for your answers?

3. Which of the following are *capital resources* as defined in this chapter: an automobile assembly plant, a toy truck, Ford Motor Company stock, a natural waterfall, unsold refrigerators held by an appliance dealer, an inventory of groceries held by a food store, a horse, a truck driver, a wristwatch? (*Hint:* Of the nine correct answers, three will be *always,* three others *never,* and the remaining three *maybe.*) What reasons can you give for your answers?

4. Reconsider Figure 1.1, "The Scarcity Problem."
    a. Redraw the graph for a society of abundance in which all goods are free goods.
    b. Redraw the graph for a society that is positioned precisely at the threshold between scarcity and abundance.

5. Elementary economics textbooks often make use of the *production possibilities frontier,* a graphical device showing all the combinations of two groups of goods (say, consumption goods and capital goods) that people in a society can produce in a period, given their current technology and the full and efficient use of all their resources. Use this graphical device to depict a society (a) suffering from scarcity, (b) enjoying abundance, and (c) being positioned at the very threshold between scarcity and abundance.

6. The *demand-and-supply* graph is a favorite diagram of elementary economics texts. Use this graphical device to depict (a) scarcity, (b) abundance, and (c) the threshold between scarcity and abundance.

7. Reconsider Problem 6, along with its solution (Figure 1.E) at the back of this book. Can you think of a real-world example to illustrate each of the three panels of Figure 1.E?

8. Comment on the following statement: "*Scarcity* is, in fact, just another word for *shortage; abundance* is simply another word for *surplus.*"

9. Can you think of goods that were once free but are now scarce? Goods that are now free at some times or places but scarce at other times or places? Explain.

10. Comment on the following statement: "Figure 1.1, "The Scarcity Problem," is highly misleading because it focuses on a brief and unusual time in mankind's history: the present century. In contrast, mankind's past and future are much longer periods and both of these are periods of abundance."

## Selected Readings

Boulding, Kenneth E. *Collected Papers,* vols. 1–4. (Boulder, CO: Associated University Press, 1971–75). A number of papers explore the scarcity issue. For example, vol. 3, chap. 20, "Is Scarcity Dead?" takes on critics who argue that it makes no sense to talk about scarcity in modern industrialized societies; vol. 4, chap. 20, "The Menace of Methuselah: Possible Consequences of Increased Life Expectancy," considers the effect of longer lifespans on scarcity.

Hamblin, Dora Jane. "Has the Garden of Eden Been Located at Last?" *Smithsonian,* May 1987, pp. 127–35. A fascinating discussion, in the light of modern science, of the possibility that mankind once lived a life of abundance rather than scarcity. The Biblical myth is analyzed with the help of archeology, linguistics, psychology, and even LANDSAT space images.

Keynes, John Maynard. "Economic Possibilities for Our Grandchildren," *Essays in Persuastion* (New York: Harcourt Brace Jovanovich, 1932), pp.358–73. Includes an argument that mankind is headed for a future of abundance in which the problem of scarcity will have withered away.

Kohler, Heinz. *Intermediate Microeconomics: Theory and Applications,* 2d ed. (Glenview, IL: Scott, Foresman and Co., 1986). Chapter 1 provides a more detailed discussion of the implications of scarcity, such as the need to make choices (that bring benefits and costs) and the desirability to optimize (by equating marginal benefit and marginal cost).

Linder, Staffan B. *The Harried Leisure Class* (New York: Columbia University Press, 1970). An amusing but important book on how the scarcity of time constrains people's consumption choices, even if the scarcity of goods does not. Note the symposium on this book in *Quarterly Journal of Economics,* November 1973, pp. 628–75.

Weisskopf, Walter A. *Alienation and Economics* (New York: Dutton, 1971). Argues that scarcity would persist even with unlimited resources and unlimited goods. This is so because life is not endless; hence, our ability to satisfy our desire for goods would still be limited by the scarcity of time.

## Computer Programs

The SYSTEMS personal computer diskette that accompanies this book contains one program of interest to this chapter: Program 1, "Scarcity," provides 20 multiple-choice questions about Chapter 1, along with immediate responses to incorrect answers.

# CHAPTER 2

# *Scarcity Challenged: Full Employment and Efficiency*

People dislike scarcity. This is not surprising. After all, when scarcity prevails, people have insufficient resources to produce all the goods they want. Hence, some of their desires for goods must remain unsatisfied and their material welfare must remain below the level they would like to achieve. So what are people to do?

One bit of advice is obvious enough: People should use their resources as carefully as possible; they should always *economize* them (and this idea suggests where *economics* got its name). Unfortunately, however, people who only receive the vague piece of advice just given are quite capable of making foolish choices with the resources at their disposal. People need more specific guidance than that. This chapter and the following two explore a number of specific actions people can take if they care to minimize the extent of scarcity. The list of possible actions found in these chapters is not meant to be an exhaustive one, but it does point to the most important criteria, commonly called **performance criteria** or **success criteria,** that can be used to assess the performance of economic systems and, thus, their success in dealing with the scarcity problem.

One possible set of actions against scarcity is suggested by the title of this chapter: People should avoid a less-than-full or inefficient utilization of their resources; otherwise the degree of scarcity prevailing in their society is bound to be more severe than necessary. Have another look at Figure 1.1, "The Scarcity Problem," and focus on the right-hand circle. It illustrates the quantity of goods the people of a society are able to produce in a year, if they use their resources fully and efficiently. Yet, they may in fact produce a smaller quantity of goods, if they do not utilize some of their resources at all or if they make inefficient use of the resources they do employ. Obviously, people who wish to conquer scarcity must, first of all, see to it that existing resources are employed fully and efficiently so that the actual production equals the potential production of goods shown by the right-hand circle in Figure 1.1. This chapter explores the meaning of full and efficient resource utilization.

## The Full Employment of Resources

It is easy enough to see why a less-than-full utilization of resources amounts to utter folly in the context of scarcity. It is equivalent to *not* baking a cake that is craved by hungry people even though all the necessary ingredients for the cake are available. Aside from such a general statement that is difficult to dispute, one should note, however, that there is room for debate on the proper meaning of ''full'' employment.

Consider human resources. Are they fully utilized only if every citizen is participating full time in the making of goods? Surely, this approach will not work; the very young, the very old, the very sick cannot possibly aid in the production of goods. But even when we focus only on *able-bodied adults,* questions remain. Should one allow some of these people (as we do in the United States) voluntarily not to participate at all in the productive process or to do so only part of the time? And how is one to define ''able-bodied adult''—by counting everyone aged 18 or above, 14 or above, by excluding people above 65 or 70 or 75? Again, how is one to define ''full time''—as working 18 hours every day of the year, or in some other way that supplies fewer labor hours to the productive process but gives people more leisure to enjoy?

Defining the full employment of natural and capital resources presents similar problems. Unlike people, these resources could, of course, be utilized at the rate of 24 hours a day each day of the year (being operated by people working in shifts). Yet, even here some may wish to opt for defining ''full'' utilization by a less intense rate, thereby extending the lifespan of the resources, particularly if they are non-renewable natural ones. Others may argue against ''too low'' a rate of resource use, against preserving nonhuman resources for the future, asking ''What has posterity ever done for us?''

Clearly, every society must find some way of answering these types of questions and of thus defining full employment. Equally clearly, only when given that definition, along with data on actual resource use, can one proceed to determine a society's success at achieving full employment and avoiding the unnecessary scarcity that the undesired unemployment of resources implies.

## The Efficient Employment of Resources

Just as human desires for goods can be unnecessarily frustrated by the less-than-full utilization of available resources, so they can be unnecessarily frustrated by their incorrect or *inefficient* utilization. Such inefficient utilization always involves situations in which resources are in fact being utilized (rather than kept unemployed), but they yield less human welfare than is possible. Depending on where the error is being made, we can distinguish two types of inefficiency, technical and economic.

## Technical Inefficiency

We can focus our attention narrowly on a single productive enterprise, such as a given orchard producing apples or a given factory producing cars. If we find that the inputs actually being employed by this enterprise could, under current technology, yield a larger quantity of output than is in fact being produced, **technical inefficiency** is said to exist. This situation (of actual output falling short of maximum possible output) implies that current technology allows the enterprise in question to produce its actual quantity of output with less of at least one input without having to increase other inputs. All this is illustrated in Figure 2.1, "Technical Inefficiency," which is a partial graph of an enterprise's **production function,** the technical relationship that shows the alternative *maximum* quantities of an output

**Figure 2.1** Technical Inefficiency

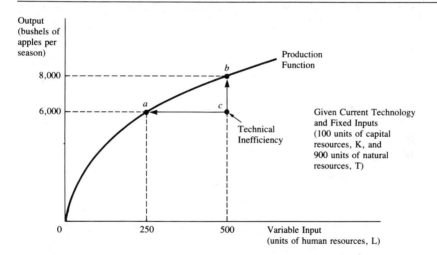

Let curved line *Ob* represent the production function of an apple orchard, showing alternative *maximum* outputs associated with various possible inputs of human resources, L—given current technology and fixed inputs of capital resources, K, and natural resources, T. If this orchard in fact uses 500L (along with the indicated 100K and 900T), but produces only 6,000 bushels per season (point *c*), *technical inefficiency* exists. It implies the two following possibilities (or combinations thereof): First, one could then increase output to 8,000 bushels, while keeping resource use unchanged (a move from point *c* to *b*). Second, one could instead decrease at least one input without the need to increase any other input, while keeping output unchanged (a move from *c* to *a*). Either way, scarcity would be reduced: People could have 2,000 more bushels of apples (distance *cb*) or they could produce other goods with the 250 units of labor saved (distance *ca*).

that are associated, under current technology, with all conceivable combinations of inputs.

Why would technical inefficiency ever occur? One possible answer is inadequate motivation of workers or managers to do their best. Consider the multitude of tasks involved in running even a simple enterprise, such as the apple orchard discussed in Figure 2.1: In the winter, the tree trunks must be wrapped to keep rodents away, branches must be pruned, and heavy limbs must be supported against wind, ice, and snow. In the spring, roots must be fertilized, and blossoms must be sprinkled lest they die in the early morning frost. In the summer, trees must be watered during times of drought; they must be sprayed lest pests eat leaves and fruit. In the fall, every last apple must be carefully picked by hand and placed in a cold-storage barn. And all along, someone must take care of the orchard-spraying machines, the trucks, the ladders, and much more. The list goes on. . . .What then if the people involved don't care? What if they fail to undertake some of the above tasks, perform them at the wrong time, work at a pace unreasonably slow, do a sloppy job? The effect on output can be disastrous. Trees improperly fertilized, pruned, or sprayed may yield half their potential crop. Apples carelessly picked may rot in a week.

One economist, Harvey Leibenstein, has paid particular attention to technical inefficiency, which he calls **X-inefficiency,** caused by people who are inadequately motivated to do a good job. Close-Up 2.1, ''A Tale of Two Ford Plants: X-Inefficiency,'' at the end of this chapter gives a real-world example of what he has in mind. The story speaks for itself.

We conclude: Those who wish to fight scarcity must do more than merely employ their resources *somehow.* They must see to it that each productive enterprise reaches a condition of **technical efficiency.** This is a situation in which the inputs actually being employed by an enterprise *cannot,* under current technology, yield a larger quantity of output than is in fact being produced. Such a situation (of actual output equalling maximum possible output) implies that current technology does *not* allow the enterprise in question to produce its actual quantity of output with less of at least one input without having to increase other inputs. In terms of Figure 2.1, each enterprise must be operating on (and not below) the production function—at points such as *a* or *b* (and not *c*).

## Economic Inefficiency

Even when resources are fully employed and every single enterprise that uses some of them manages to achieve technical efficiency, avoidable scarcity can still persist. This amazing fact becomes obvious once we step back from our narrow focus on individual productive enterprises and instead view the economy as a whole. As we *compare* the circumstances of two or more producers (or, for that matter, of two or more households), we can often discover further possibilities for improvement. We often discover economy-wide inefficiency, more simply called **economic inefficiency,** a situation in which it is possible, through some reallocation of resources or goods among different productive enterprises or households, to make some people better off (in their own judgment) without making others worse off (in *their* own judgment). Such a situation implies that the total welfare of people—defined as the sum of the welfares of all individuals—can be raised with certainty. Because the removal of such economic inefficiency always involves a reallocation of resources or goods among different productive enterprises or households, this type of inefficiency is also called **allocative inefficiency.** Once again, we can illustrate the concept graphically, as in Figure 2.2, ''Economic Inefficiency.'' Its caption tells the story, but, as the remainder of this chapter shows, it is by no means the whole story.

## Pareto's Marginal Conditions

At the turn of this century, the Italian economist Vilfredo Pareto (see Biography 2.1 at the end of this chapter) pointed to a large number of so-called **marginal**

**Figure 2.2**   Economic Inefficiency

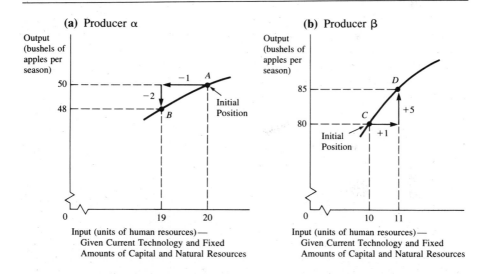

Let curved lines *BA* and *CD* represent, respectively, relevant portions of the production functions of two technically efficient orchardists, α and β. Initially, α uses 20 units of human resources, along with unspecified amounts of other resources, to produce 50 bushels of apples (point *A*). At the same time, β uses 10 units of human resources, along with unspecified and probably different amounts of other resources, to produce 80 bushels of apples (point *C*). Jointly, they use 20 + 10 = 30 units of human resources and produce 50 + 80 = 130 bushels of apples. By itself, neither producer can possibly do better. Yet, a simultaneous inspection of the two production functions in the vicinities of *A* and *C* reveals that *economic inefficiency* exists: It is possible to reallocate 1 unit of human resources from α to β (thereby moving α to *B* and β to *D*) and to raise society's apple output by 3 bushels (−2 bushels at α, +5 bushels at β). Thus, someone can be made better off (by the receipt of 3 extra bushels), while no one needs to have less. (Can you see how, at *B* and *D*, the joint use of *all* resources is unchanged, but total output has risen to 48 + 85 = 133 bushels?)

**conditions** all of which must be met if economic inefficiency is to be avoided and economic efficiency is to be achieved. To these conditions we now turn.

**Condition 1: The Optimum Allocation of a Resource among Producers of the Same Good.** One marginal condition of economic efficiency deals with the optimum allocation of a resource among producers of the same good:

> 1. Economic efficiency requires that the marginal rate of transformation (*MRT*) between any resource x and any good a be the same for any two producers, $\alpha$ and $\beta$, producing this good with that resource.

$$MRT^{\alpha}_{x,a} = MRT^{\beta}_{x,a}$$

Suppose we picked, from among millions of producers, $\alpha$ and $\beta$ (who might be orchardists in Vermont) and who are using an identical resource $x$ (a type of unskilled labor, perhaps) to produce an identical good $a$ (a type of apple, called Golden Delicious). We might find our two producers in the initial situation shown in part (A) of T2.1

**Initial Position.** Producer $\alpha$ is using in a year 20 units of labor to produce 50 units of apples. Producer $\beta$ is using in a year 10 units of identical labor to produce 80 units of identical apples. Both producers must, of course, also be using various amounts of other resources. These other resources (not shown in the table) will

**Table 2.1**   The Optimum Allocation of a Resource among Producers of the Same Good

| | Input and Output per Year | MRT | Assessment |
|---|---|---|---|
| **(A) Initial Situation** | | | |
| Producer $\alpha$ | 20$x$ make  50$a$ | 1$x$ for 2$a$ | |
| Producer $\beta$ | 10$x$ make  80$a$ | 1$x$ for 5$a$ | |
| | 30$x$ make 130$a$ | | Economic inefficiency exists; it is advisable to move a unit of the resource from producer $\alpha$ to producer $\beta$. |
| **(B) New Situation*** | | | |
| Producer $\alpha$ | 19$x$ make  48$a$ | 1$x$ for 2.1$a$ | |
| Producer $\beta$ | 11$x$ make  85$a$ | 1$x$ for 4.9$a$ | |
| | 30$x$ make 133$a$ | | |
| **(C) Final Situation*** | | | |
| Producer $\alpha$ | 9$x$ make  22$a$ | 1$x$ for 3.1$a$ | Economic efficiency has |
| Producer $\beta$ | 21$x$ make 128$a$ | 1$x$ for 3.1$a$ | been reached; no further |
| | 30$x$ make 150$a$ | | changes are desirable. |

*Subject to constraints noted in the text, all the numbers in sections (B) and (C) have been chosen arbitrarily in order to illustrate the process by which inefficiency might be turned into efficiency. These numbers cannot be derived uniquely from those given in section (A); other numbers might have served as well.

almost certainly differ in type and quantity between the two producers. Thus, $\alpha$'s workers may be working with 500 apple trees, 1 ton of fertilizer, and a season of bad weather, while $\beta$'s workers may be working with 1000 apple trees, 20 tons of fertilizer, 2 orchard-spraying machines, plenty of pesticides, and a season of perfect weather. Note in part (A) how our two producers are using initially a total of 30 units of labor, while producing 130 units of apples. Is the allocation of labor between them efficient?

We cannot answer this question, argued Vilfredo Pareto, until we consider how small (or marginal) changes in resource allocation would transform present circumstances. The **marginal rate of transformation,** or *MRT,* is the rate at which a producer is technically able to exchange, in the process of production, a little bit of one variable (say, labor) for a little bit of another variable (say, apples produced with the help of that labor). The data contained in the top circle in Table 2.1 indicate that $\alpha$ is technically able to exchange, in the initial circumstances just postulated, $1x$ for $2a$, which means that $\alpha$ could produce an extra 2 units of apples per year with an extra 1 unit of labor—assuming all of $\alpha$'s other inputs remained the same. This *MRT* also tells us that $\alpha$'s production would fall by 2 units of apples per year if 1 unit of its labor input were to be lost—again assuming that all of $\alpha$'s other inputs remained the same. Thus, the *MRT* of $1x$ for $2a$ indicates $\alpha$'s capability to move from the initial position of using $20x$ and making $50a$ each year to a new position *of either* using $21x$ and making $52a$ or using $19x$ and making $48a$ each year.

The top circle also indicates that $\beta$'s *MRT* differs from $\alpha$'s *MRT* and equals $1x$ for $5a$, which means that $\beta$ could move from its initial position of using $10x$ and making $80a$ each year to either using $11x$ and making $85a$ or using $9x$ and making $75a$ each year. (Caution: As these examples show, the *MRT* must never be confused with ratio of *total* output to input, such as $\alpha$'s initial $50a/20x$ or $\beta$'s $80a/10x$.)

The reason $\beta$'s *MRT* might differ from $\alpha$'s is that producer $\beta$'s endowment with natural and capital resources, as postulated above, might be so superior as to make its workers more productive than are identical workers employed by $\alpha$. Thus, an additional worker would add more to output at $\beta$ than at $\alpha$, while loss of a worker would reduce output more at $\beta$ than at $\alpha$.

**Worthwhile Change.**   The situation depicted by the data in the top circle clearly violates Pareto's first marginal condition stated above. This violation of an efficiency condition implies that economic inefficiency exists, which means it is possible to reorganize matters to make some people better off without making others worse off. Table 2.1 indicates what kind of change is required to escape inefficiency here: It clearly pays to move a unit of labor from where it is less productive (presently at $\alpha$) to where it is more productive (presently at $\beta$). The resulting new situation is shown in part (B) of Table 2.1. After a unit of labor has been moved from $\alpha$ to $\beta$, $\alpha$'s output is lower by 2 units of apples per year (just as $\alpha$'s initial *MRT* predicted) and $\beta$'s output is higher by 5 units of apples per year (just as $\beta$'s initial *MRT* predicted). But the sums reveal that output in society *as a whole* has risen from 130 to 133 units of apples per year, even though resource inputs have remained unchanged (at 30 units of labor plus unspecified amounts of other resources).

Clearly, someone in society can now receive an additional 3 units of apples per year, and no one need receive less because of it! The initial situation shown in Table 2.1 was economically inefficient. Even though both producers were technically efficient (we assume), people were getting a smaller quantity of goods from their resources than was necessary. Their *actual* production did not equal their *potential* production, depicted by the right-hand circle of Figure 1.1, ''The Scarcity Problem.''

But isn't the new situation depicted in part (B) still inefficient? Shouldn't one continue to move labor from α to β until all labor is employed by β? Not necessarily, Pareto tells us. If the marginal rates of transformation *in the new situation* continue to diverge, as they do in part (B), inefficiency still exists, and a further reallocation of labor is in order. But continuing along this route, the *MRT*s will eventually come to be equal, as they are in part (C) of Table 2.1, at which point economic efficiency will have been attained and a further reallocation of labor will serve no purpose. Such further reallocation would make the output of one producer rise exactly as much (by 3.1 units of apples per year) as it would reduce the output of the other producer.

**Converging MRTs.**    Why should the *MRT*s eventually come to equal each other? The key to answering that question is found in the famous **law of diminishing returns:** ''Given the quantities of all other inputs being used, and given technical knowledge, successive additions of equal units of a resource to the process of production eventually yield ever smaller additions to total output.'' This law teaches us that our *MRT* of resource *x* for good *a* cannot be expected to remain unchanged as circumstances change. The data in the circles of Table 2.1 indicate what is bound to happen as labor is moved from α to β: Initially an extra unit of labor is capable of adding 5 units to β's output (A), but subsequent extra units of labor can only add 4.9 units to output (B), then 4.8 units (not shown), and, eventually, 3.1 units (C). This progression reflects the fact that β's initially superior endowment with nonlabor resources is gradually eroding as it employs more labor. As more workers are used with unchanged natural and capital resources, less and less of the natural and capital resources are available *per worker;* hence the addition or loss of a worker has successively smaller impact on total output.

The very act of reallocating labor changes α's marginal rate of transformation, too. Initially the loss of a unit of labor costs only 2 units of output (A), but subsequent equal reductions in labor input reduce output by 2.1 units (B), then by 2.2 units (not shown), and, eventually, by 3.1 units (C). This progression reflects the fact that α's initially inferior endowment with nonlabor resources is gradually being overcome as α employs less labor. As fewer workers are used with unchanged natural and capital resources, more and more of the natural and capital resources are available *per worker;* hence the addition or loss of a worker has a successively greater impact on total output.

The reallocation of resources in the face of economic inefficiency, thus, changes circumstances in such a way as to limit the desirable degree of reallocation. Compare parts (A) and (C) of Table 2.1. Note how, in the end, only 11 of α's 20 labor units have been reallocated to β. Note also how, as a result, output from given resources, now differently employed, has risen by 15 percent from 130 to 150 units of apples per year. This increase in output shows the extent to which human desires were unnecessarily frustrated by the inefficient allocation of resources depicted in part (A).

**Wide Applicability.**   Although this example involved labor and apples, the first marginal condition is applicable to literally billions of situations. Resource *x* can be labor, but it can also be fertilizer or steel or turret lathes. Good *a* can be apples, but it can also be airplanes, haircuts, or residential houses. Even the term "producer" can refer to more than the ordinary productive enterprise; it might refer to a region or even a country! Suppose α meant "Oregon" (or even "China"), while β stood for "Vermont" (or the "United States"). It is easy to imagine circumstances under which the shift of at least some units of labor (or any resource) from Oregon to Vermont (or from China to the United States) would increase the world's output of goods. Artificial political boundaries that prevent such shifts make scarcity more severe than it has to be. The abolition of such boundaries (as within the United States or within a Common Market) helps raise the material welfare of people.

**Condition 2: The Optimum Specialization of Production among Producers of the Same Goods.\***   A second marginal condition of economic efficiency concerns the optimum specialization of production among producers of the same goods:

> 2. Economic efficiency requires that the marginal rate of transformation (*MRT*) between any two goods, *a* and *b*, be the same for any two producers, α and β, producing both goods.

$$MRT^{\alpha}_{a,b} = MRT^{\beta}_{a,b}$$

Consider Table 2.2 and imagine that producers α and β were farmers in Vermont, both producing apples (good *a*) as well as butter (good *b*).

**Initial Position.**   Initially, we find α using unspecified amounts of resources to produce 20 units of apples as well as 30 units of butter per year. Producer β produces 50 units of apples and 60 units of butter per year with similarly unspecified, but undoubtedly different, amounts of resources. We assume that both producers have achieved technical efficiency. Is the total annual production—of 70 units of apples and 90 units of butter—the largest possible output we can get from the resources employed by α and β?

The marginal rates of transformation given in the top circle of Table 2.2 help us answer this question in the negative: Under present circumstances, producer α is technically able to produce 1*a* less and, with the resources so released, to produce 2*b* more or to produce 1*a* more and 2*b* less. Producer β, on the other hand, endowed with different resources or different know-how, can presently exchange 1*a* for 5*b*

---

*Optional Section. This section explores the concept of *economic efficiency* in an alternative way.

**Table 2.2**   The Optimum Specialization of Production among Producers of the Same Goods

| | Outputs per year | MRT | Assessment |
|---|---|---|---|
| **(A) Initial Situation** | | | |
| Producer α | 20a and 30b | 1a for 2b | |
| Producer β | 50a and 60b | 1a for 5b | |
| | 70a and 90b | | Economic inefficiency exists; it is advisable for α to produce more a (and less b) and for β to produce more b (and less a). |
| **(B) New Situation*** | | | |
| Producer α | 21a and 28b | 1a for 2.1b | |
| Producer β | 49a and 65b | 1a for 4.9b | |
| | 70a and 93b | | |
| **(C) Final Situation*** | | | |
| Producer α | 27a and  11b | 1a for 3.6b | Economic efficiency has been reached; no further changes are desirable. |
| Producer β | 43a and  91b | 1a for 3.6b | |
| | 70a and 102b | | |

*Subject to constraints noted in the text, all the numbers in sections (B) and (C) have been chosen arbitrarily in order to illustrate the process by which inefficiency might be turned into efficiency. These numbers cannot be derived uniquely from those given in section (A); other numbers might have served as well.

in the process of production. Clearly, this violation of the second marginal condition stated above spells economic inefficiency.

Note how α is relatively better at producing apples, an extra unit of which can be had for the mere sacrifice of 2 units of butter, while β has to sacrifice 5 units of butter to produce another 1 unit of apples. Note also how β is relatively better at producing butter, 5 extra units of which can be had for the mere sacrifice of 1 unit of apples—as opposed to the gain of only 2 extra units of butter that α could achieve for an identical sacrifice of apples. Accordingly, it is advisable for α to produce more apples and for β to produce more butter.

**Worthwhile Change.**   Part (B) of Table 2.2 shows the effect of an initial reallocation of resources within each producing unit from the production of one good to the other. Note how this reallocation leaves overall apple production unchanged, while raising the overall production of butter by 3 units from 90 to 93 units per year. Thus, this reallocation makes it possible for someone to be better off without anyone else being worse off. Indeed, this process of specialization (of α producing more apples and β more butter) should be carried further as long as the *MRT*s continue to diverge, as they do in part (B) of our table. Eventually, though, these *MRT*s are also going to become equal, as shown in part (C).

**Converging MRTs.**   As α switches resources out of butter production to the production of apples, it is likely to switch first those resources least suitable for making butter and most suitable for making apples. As this process continues, it may have to switch into apple-production resources less suitable for making apples and more suitable for making butter, which will cause the sacrifice per extra unit of apples to rise from $2b$ in (A) to $2.1b$ in (B) to $2.9b$ (not shown) and, eventually, to $3.6b$ in (C). Producer $\beta$'s experience is bound to be similar. As $\beta$ takes successively out of apple production resources that are ever less suited to making butter, the gains per extra unit of apples sacrificed will decline from $5b$ in (A) to $4.9b$ in (B) to $4.3b$ (not shown) and, eventually, to $3.6b$ in (C). At that point, in our example, economic efficiency is reached. In the meantime, output from given resources, differently employed within each firm, has risen by 13 percent from 90 to 102 units of butter per year.

**Wide Applicability.**    As was true for the first marginal condition, so this second one is applicable to billions of situations. Not only can goods $a$ and $b$ represent any two goods, but $\alpha$ and $\beta$ can again refer to any two "producers," including regions or countries. Consider how international trading in goods might substitute for the international movement of resources should the latter prove impossible. If, in Table 2.2, $\alpha$ stood for China and $\beta$ for the United States, an *internal* shift of resources from the initial situation in part (A) to the final one in part (C) could be followed by trade: Given the new production volumes shown in part (C), China ($\alpha$) could export $7a$ to the United States ($\beta$) in return for $25b$, which would leave the Chinese with $27a$ (their production) minus $7a$ (their export), or $20a$ (as in the initial situation). This exchange would leave Americans with $43a$ (their production) plus $7a$ (their import), or $50a$ (as in the initial situation). This arrangement would also give the Chinese $11b$ (their production) plus $25b$ (their import), or $36b$ (a clear gain over their initial position in part (A) and would leave Americans with $91b$ (their production) minus $25b$ (their export), or $66b$ (also a clear gain over initial circumstances). Thus, the overall gain in output between the initial and final situations ($102b - 90b = 12b$) might be shared equally between the Chinese and the Americans (both of whom would gain $6b$). Close-Up 2.2, "Stalin and Comecon," at the end of this chapter, has more to say on the subject. ▬▬

**Condition 3: The Optimum Composition of Production and Consumption.***
Other Pareto conditions of economic efficiency are more subtle than the two just discussed. Economic welfare can possibly be increased, not because a greater quantity of goods could be made available, but because a different and preferred set of goods could be produced:

> 3. Economic efficiency requires that the marginal rate of transformation (*MRT*) between any two goods, $a$ and $b$, produced by any producer, $\alpha$, be equal to the marginal rate of substitution (*MRS*) between these two goods for any consumer, X, who consumes both.

$$MRT^{\alpha}_{a,b} = MRS^{X}_{a,b}$$

---

*Optional Section. This section explores the concept of *economic efficiency* in an alternative way.

Consider Table 2.3. Imagine picking, from among many millions of producers and consumers, α and X who have in common only that they produce and consume, respectively, apples (good *a*) and butter (good *b*).

**Initial Position.**    In part (A) of Table 2.3, we find α producing 20 units of apples and 30 units of butter per year, while X is consuming 10 units of apples and 20 units of butter per year. In the top circle, the marginal rate of transformation is assumed to be 1*a* for 2*b* for α. We must now introduce a new concept, a consumer's **marginal rate of substitution,** or *MRS*. It is the rate at which a consumer is willing to exchange, *as a matter of indifference,* a little bit of one variable (say, the consumption of apples) for a little bit of another variable (say the consumption of butter). Thus consumer X's *MRS* of 1*a* for 5*b* in the top circle indicates that person's willingness to move, as a matter of indifference, from the initial position of consuming each year 10*a* and 20*b* to a new position, consuming each year *either* 11*a* and 15*b or* 9*a* and 25*b*. The fact that the consumer is indifferent about this change implies that consumer X would feel *better off* if *more* than 5*b* could be procured for the sacrifice of 1*a* or if *more* than 1*a* could be procured for the sacrifice of 5*b*. The indicated *MRS* also implies that consumer X would feel *worse off* if *less* than 5*b* were to be received for the sacrifice of 1*a* or if less than 1*a* were received for the sacrifice of 5*b*.

The data inside the top circle of Table 2.3 show Pareto's third marginal condition to be violated because the producer's *MRT* does not equal the consumer's *MRS*. Consumer X is seen to value an extra unit of apples much more highly than such extra unit objectively costs. Note how X is *willing* to sacrifice 5 units of butter for a unit of apples that α is *able* to produce with resources released by sacrificing only

**Table 2.3**    The Optimum Composition of Production and Consumption

|  | Outputs Produced or Consumed per Year | MRT or MRS | Assessment |
|---|---|---|---|
| **(A) Initial Situation** | | | |
| Producer α | 20*a* and 30*b* | 1*a* for 2*b* | Economic inefficiency |
| Consumer X | 10*a* and 20*b* | 1*a* for 5*b* | exists; it is advisable for α to produce, and for X to consume, more *a* (and less *b*). |
| **(B) New Situation\*** | | | |
| Producer β | 21*a* and 28*b* | 1*a* for 2.1*b* | |
| Consumer X | 11*a* and 18*b* | 1*a* for 4.9*b* | |
| **(C) Final Situation\*** | | | |
| Producer α | 27*a* and 11*b* | 1*a* for 3.6*b* | Economic efficiency has |
| Consumer X | 17*a* and  1*b* | 1*a* for 3.6*b* | been reached; no further changes are desirable. |

\*Subject to constraints noted in the text, all the numbers in sections (B) and (C) have been chosen arbitrarily in order to illustrate the process by which inefficiency might be turned into efficiency. These numbers cannot be derived uniquely from those given in section (A); other numbers might have served as well.

2 units of butter. Thus, it is possible to make someone better off without making anyone worse off.

**Worthwhile Change.**   It is a matter of indifference (costing the same resources) for α to produce 2 units of butter less per year and 1 unit of apples more. As a result of this change in the composition of production, consumer X can consume 1 more unit of apples per year but must consume 2 less units of butter per year. *Since X would have been indifferent about sacrificing 5 units of butter for 1 unit of additional apples, X is now in fact better off.* Thus the new situation in part (B) implies that a greater economic welfare is being received than in the initial situation in part (A).

**Converging *MRT* and *MRS*.**   As in our previous example, this reallocation of resources should be continued as long as the marginal condition continues to be violated, as is the case in part (B). And as before, the marginal rates of transformation and substitution will converge as a result of the gradual shift in the composition of production and consumption; we noted above why producer α's *MRT* might change from 1*a* for 2*b* to 1*a* for 2.1*b*, 2.9*b*, and, eventually, 3.6*b*. The consumer's *MRS* will also change with the consumer's circumstances. As the consumer consumes more and more apples per year, consumption of additional units will be less and less capable of raising the consumer's welfare and will thus seem less and less urgent. (The reasoning involves the famous **law of declining marginal utility:** ''Given the quantities of all other goods being consumed, and given tastes, successive additions of equal units of a good to the process of consumption eventually yield ever smaller additions to total welfare or utility.''

At the same time, and for analogous reasons, as the consumer consumes less and less butter per year, sacrifices of additional units will be more and more capable of lowering the consumer's welfare and will thus seem less and less advisable. Hence the amount of (ever more precious) butter the consumer will be willing to sacrifice for an extra unit of (ever less precious) apples will decline; from 5*b* in (A) to 4.9*b* in (B), to 4.1*b* (not shown), and, eventually, to 3.6*b* in (C). At that point, economic efficiency will have been reached, and further changes in the composition of production and consumption will not be desirable.  ▬▬

**Condition 4: The Optimum Allocation of Goods among Consumers of the Same Goods.**\*   Given the overall quantity of production and even each person's share in this total, another important requirement of economic efficiency is that each person has the best combination of specific goods. According to Pareto:

> 4. Economic efficiency requires that the marginal rate of substitution (*MRS*) between any two goods, *a* and *b*, be the same for any two consumers, X and Y, consuming both goods.

$$MRS^X_{a,b} = MRS^Y_{a,b}$$

---

\*Optional Section. This section explores the concept of *economic efficiency* in an alternative way.

Consider Table 2.4. Imagine that we picked, from among millions of consumers, X and Y who had in common that they consumed apples (good *a*) and butter (good *b*).

**Initial Position.**   In part (A), we find consumer X consuming 10 units of apples and 20 units of butter per year, while Y is consuming 200*a* and 50*b* per year. The data inside the top circle indicate that Pareto's condition of efficiency is violated. There must be a way to squeeze a greater satisfaction from the 210 units of apples plus 70 units of butter being consumed per year by X and Y.

   Currently, X values the consumption of 1 unit of apples more highly than Y because X is willing, as a matter of indifference, to sacrifice 5 units of butter per year to get another unit of apples, while Y is indifferent about sacrificing 2*b* for 1*a*. Accordingly, it is advisable for X to consume more apples and for Y to consume more butter.

**Worthwhile Change.**   Part (B) of Table 2.4 shows the effect of an initial exchange of 1*a* for 3*b* between our two consumers. Both are better off because X, who would have been indifferent about giving up 5*b*, gave up only 3*b* for 1*a*. Y, who would have been indifferent about receiving only 2*b*, received 3*b* for 1*a*. Thus, this reallocation of an unchanged total of goods has clearly raised total economic welfare.

**Converging *MRS*s.**   This reallocation of goods, for reasons discussed in the previous section, has also changed the marginal rates of substitution. Note the first

**Table 2.4**   The Optimum Allocation of Goods among Consumers of the Same Goods

| | Goods Consumed per Year | MRS | Assessment |
|---|---|---|---|
| **(A) Initial Situation** | | | |
| Consumer X | 10*a* and 20*b* | 1*a* for 5*b* | Economic inefficiency |
| Consumer Y | 200*a* and 50*b* | 1*a* for 2*b* | exists; it is advisable for |
| | 210*a* and 70*b* | | X to consume more *a* |
| **(B) New Situation*** | | | (and less *b*) and for Y to |
| Consumer X | 11*a* and 17*b* | 1*a* for 4.8*b* | consume more *b* (and |
| Consumer Y | 199*a* and 53*b* | 1*a* for 2.1*b* | less *a*). |
| | 210*a* and 70*b* | | |
| **(C) Final Situation*** | | | |
| Consumer X | 20*a* and  2*b* | 1*a* for 2.9*b* | Economic efficiency has |
| Consumer Y | 190*a* and 68*b* | 1*a* for 2.9*b* | been reached; no further |
| | 210*a* and 70*b* | | changes are desirable. |

*Subject to constraints noted in the text, all the numbers in sections (B) and (C) have been chosen arbitrarily in order to illustrate the process by which inefficiency might be turned into efficiency. These numbers cannot be derived uniquely from those given in section (A); other numbers might have served as well.

signs of their convergence inside the second circle. Having more apples and less butter than before, X now values another unit of apples somewhat less (at 4.8 rather than 5 units of butter). Having fewer apples and more butter than before, Y values another unit of apples somewhat more (at 2.1 rather than 2 units of butter).

However, 4.8 is still different from 2.1; hence, situation (B) is still inefficient. Further reallocation is desirable until, as in situation (C), the two consumers' marginal rates of substitution have become equal. At that point of equality, the total utility derived by X and Y from the available set of goods is, of course, vastly higher than in the initial situation. Further changes in their consumption patterns would serve no purpose.

Close-Up 2.3, ''The POW Camp,'' at the end of this chapter provides another illustration of the lesson taught here.  ▬▬▬

## The Pareto Optimum

When all the marginal conditions of economic efficiency are fulfilled simultaneously, a society is said to have reached its **Pareto optimum.** One can, however, find efficiency conditions other than the four described above; as Pareto noted, a near infinite number exists. All such efficiency conditions, however, can be summarized by the following two propositions:

1. Whenever one can technically transform a little bit of one variable into a little bit of another, the marginal rate of technical transformation (the amount of one variable one can obtain objectively by sacrificing a unit of the other) must equal the marginal rate of indifferent substitution (the amount of one variable a person could substitute for a unit of the other without a feeling of gain or loss). That is, any *MRT* must equal any corresponding *MRS*.
2. All equivalent marginal rates of technical transformation or of indifferent substitution must be equal. That is, any *MRT* must equal anybody else's corresponding *MRT;* any *MRS* must equal anybody else's corresponding *MRS*.

Note how the third Pareto condition is described perfectly by proposition 1, while the first, second, and fourth conditions are covered by proposition 2. As long as these two propositions are not fulfilled and marginal inequalities persist, Pareto tells us, a reallocation of resources or goods is possible that raises total economic welfare with certainty.

We conclude: Those who wish to fight scarcity must, at the very least, employ their resources fully and in technically efficient ways. But they must also reach the Pareto optimum—a situation of **economic efficiency** or **allocative efficiency.** This is a situation in which it is *impossible,* through some reallocation of resources or goods among different productive enterprises or households, to make some people better off (in their own judgment) without making others worse off (in *their* own judgment). It is a situation, in short, in which all unambiguous ways of maximizing human welfare from a given stock of resources have been exhausted.

## A Tale of Two Ford Plants: X-Inefficiency

In the preface to his *Beyond Economic Man,* Harvard professor Harvey Leibenstein introduces his thoughts on X-efficiency with a quotation from Tolstoy's *War and Peace:*

> . . . *[M]ilitary science assumes the strength of an army to be identical with its numbers. Military science says that the more troops the greater the strength.* Les gros bataillons ont toujours raison *(Large battalions are always victorious).* . . .
>
> *In military affairs the strength of an army is the product of its mass and some unknown X. . . .*
>
> *That unknown quantity is the spirit of the army. . . .*
>
> *The spirit of an army is the factor which multiplied by the mass gives the resulting force. To define and express the significance of this unknown factor— the spirit of an army—is a problem for science.*
>
> *The problem is only solvable if we cease arbitrarily to substitute for the unknown X itself the conditions under which that force becomes apparent— such as the commands of the general, the equipment employed, and so on— mistaking these for the real significance of the factor, and if we recognize this unknown quantity in its entirety as being the greater or lesser desire to fight and to face danger.*

Leibenstein expands:

> *Without straining his meaning too much, Tolstoy's argument is similar to one of the central theses of this volume, despite the fact that his concern is the art of war, and mine economics, one of the arts of peace. To shift to the common language of economics, what Tolstoy is saying is that merely knowing the observable inputs (the number of guns, men, the commands of the generals, and so on) does not tell you the outcome, contrary to the claims of the "military scientists." Something else is involved, an X-factor that Tolstoy equates with "spirit." Similarly, in . . . this volume I argue that knowing the allocation of inputs and the state of the arts of production is not enough, there is also something else involved—what I have called the X-efficiency element.*

The recent experience of Ford Motor Company plants in Europe provides support for Leibenstein's contention. Two identical Ford plants were erected at Saarlouis, West Germany, and at Halewood, England. A casual visitor to the sleek gray buildings in either town finds them dominated by robot welders, vast automated presses, and shiny new cars rolling off the assembly line. Yet this is where the resemblance ends. Consider the accompanying data:

|  | *Germany* | *Britain* |
| --- | --- | --- |
| **Daily output** | | |
| anticipated | 1,015 cars | 1,015 cars |
| actual | 1,200 cars | 800 cars |
| **Workers employed** | 7,762 | 10,040 |
| Labor hours per identical car | 21 | 40 |

Ford officials in Europe say that the difference between the two plants comes down to the attitude of workers. In England, strikes are frequent; in Germany, unknown. In England, workers are visible everywhere, often reading, eating, or even kicking soccer balls; in Germany, the plant appears almost depopulated and workers always seem hard at work. In England, workers get twice as many quality demerits as in their German sister plant. In England, featherbedding is rampant (a doctor certified that it takes two men to lift the hood onto the car body, but in fact one man does it, while the other one watches); in Germany, featherbedding is absent. In England, visitors are jeered (and worse); in Germany, they are treated with extreme courtesy. In England, despite many union-made safety rules, the injury rate is high; in Germany, it is the lowest in Ford's European operations. . . .

*Sources:* Steven Rattner, "A Tale of Two Ford Plants: German Unit Far Outpaces One in Britain," *The New York Times,* October 13, 1981, pp. D1 and D4; Harvey Leibenstein, *Beyond Economic Man: A New Foundation for Microeconomics* (Cambridge, MA: Harvard University Press, 1976).

## CLOSE-UP 2.2

## Stalin and Comecon

Stalin's changing attitudes toward foreign trade provide an illustration of the second Pareto condition discussed in Table 2.2. Until the end of World War II, Stalin viewed foreign trade with suspicion. He looked upon it as a "safety valve" that would ensure the fulfillment of the national economic plan. Foreign trade allowed the import of essential items that could not be produced at home; exports were a necessary evil to pay for these imports. Ideally, though, a zero volume of foreign trade would ensure total independence from a hostile world surrounding the Soviet Union, while Stalin built "socialism in one country."

After 1945, other socialist countries emerged: Poland, Rumania, Bulgaria, Albania, Yugoslavia, Hungary, Czechoslovakia, East Germany—and in Asia others still. There is nothing wrong, argued Stalin's economists, with being dependent on friends. These economists urged abandonment of the old policy of minimizing foreign trade in favor of a grand international division of labor in "the socialist camp." Starting in 1949, the above-named countries joined the Soviet Union in the Council for Mutual Economic Aid (frequently abbreviated as Comecon or CMEA). They attempted to specialize in production in accordance with differences in their technical circumstances. The *MRT* data in parts (A) and (B) of Table 2.2 are an indication of such differences. For example, Albania would specialize in early potatoes, Bulgaria in industrial sewing machines, Czechoslovakia in sugar beet combines, East Germany in plastics, Hungary in aluminum products, Poland in horticultural tractors, Rumania in reed cellulose, and the Soviet Union in fishing vessels. In this way, given resources would yield higher output than a policy of national self-sufficiency would provide.[a]

[a]For a detailed listing of specialization decisions, see Heinz Kohler, *Economic Integration in the Soviet Bloc* (New York: Praeger, 1965), pp. 127–40.

## CLOSE-UP 2.3

## The POW Camp

World War II prisoner-of-war camps provide an illustration of the fourth Pareto condition of economic efficiency—the optimum allocation of goods among consumers of the same goods—discussed in Table 2.4. In these POW camps, almost no production occurred. Yet prisoners received many products, ranging from canned milk, beef, biscuits, butter, and jam to cigarettes, chocolate, sugar, clothing, razor blades, and writing paper. Like manna from heaven, these products came in the form of rations handed out by the detaining power, through Red Cross packages and private parcels. More often than not, everyone received almost identical quantities of all items. Yet, within seconds of receipt, widespread and spontaneous exchange of products occurred. People placed different personal evaluations on the items in their possession! The *MRS* data in parts (A) and (B) of Table 2.4 are an indication of such differences. Through exchange, the prisoners reallocated a given quantity of goods in such a way that the welfare of everyone was increased at the same time.

*Source:* R. A. Radford, "The Economic Organization of a POW Camp," *Economica,* November 1945, pp. 189–201.

## BIOGRAPHY 2.1    Vilfredo Pareto

Vilfredo Pareto (1848–1923) was born in Paris to an Italian father and a French mother. He studied in Italy, received a doctoral degree in engineering, and eventually became manager general of the Italian Iron Works. After years of industrial practice, he turned to economics. In 1893, he was appointed to succeed Léon Walras (see Biography 12.2) at the University of Lausanne, but he resigned that chair in 1906 and retired to Céligny on Lake Geneva. He devoted most of his later years to the study of sociology.

His major books on economics include *Cours d'Économie Politique,* vols. 1 and 2 (1896–97) and *Manuel d'Economie Politique* (1910). An Italian version of the latter work had appeared in 1906, and an English translation was published in 1971. Although he devoted no more than two decades of his long life to economics, by suggesting universal guidelines for the achievement of economic efficiency (the marginal conditions), Pareto has become one of the patron saints of the discipline.

From its early beginnings, thinkers in the field had attempted to specify which allocation of resources and goods would maximize social welfare. Unfortunately, this maximum was hard to identify because many conceivable changes in the current allocation of resources and goods would benefit some people while harming others, thus creating ambiguity as to the net effect. By the 18th century, however, certain ideas of British philosopher Jeremy Bentham became dominant. He suggested that people be guided by a "felicific calculus," which approves of any action if the pleasure it brings *outweighs* the pain it causes. He was prepared to measure cardinally the pleasure and pain of each action in units called *utils,* and he even believed it possible to add up these util numbers interpersonally so that +10 utils for John and −2 for Jane make a total of +8 for the pair. He identified the social total of utility produced by all actions as the common good, and he advocated that this total utility be maximized to achieve "the greatest happiness of the greatest number."

Pareto broke away decisively from these suggestions. He rejected the cardinal measurement of utility and any interpersonal comparisons thereof. He restricted economic science to welfare statements that require only intrapersonal comparisons (in which affected individuals themselves testified to the direction of change in their welfare). He insisted that economic science should make pronouncements only about *unambiguous* changes in social welfare, such as those found in this chapter's definition of economic inefficiency. If a reallocation of resources or goods left some individuals, in their own estimation, equally well off but others better off, social welfare had increased. (Such a reallocation, presumably, was desirable.) If a reallocation of resources or goods made some feel equally well off but others worse off, social welfare had decreased. (Such a reallocation, presumably, was not desirable.) Finally, if a reallocation of resources or goods left some people better off and others worse off, the situation could not be evaluated by economic science—unless, that is, the gainers actually compensated the losers to the losers' full satisfaction and were still better off. Such a case would, of course, be indistinguishable from one in which no one was worse off, but some people were better off. Thus, Pareto urged economists to concentrate on situations containing unambiguous possibilities for increasing human welfare and to channel their energies into making agreeable changes from which no one would lose, while turning away from ambiguous situations that inevitably give rise to conflicts from which some people are certain to lose.

## Summary

1. Scarcity may be unavoidable, but people who make foolish choices with the resources and goods at their disposal can make scarcity more intense than necessary. Economists identify the existence of avoidable scarcity with the help of so-called performance or success criteria.
2. One obvious performance criterion is the *full employment* of resources. Any society that tolerates undesired unemployment of resources also tolerates greater scarcity than necessary.
3. Those who wish to fight scarcity must, however, do more than merely employ their resources *somehow.* They must also see to it that each productive enterprise reaches a condition of *technical efficiency.* This is a situation in which the inputs actually being employed by an enterprise *cannot,* under current technology, yield a larger quantity of output than is in fact being produced.
4. Even when resources are fully employed and every single enterprise that uses some of them manages to achieve technical efficiency, avoidable scarcity can still persist. This amazing fact becomes obvious once we relinquish the narrow focus on individual productive enterprises and

instead view the economy as a whole. It is crucial to achieve *economic efficiency,* a situation in which it is *impossible,* through some reallocation of resources or goods among different productive enterprises or households, to make some people better off (in their own judgment) without making others worse off (in *their* own judgment).

5. Economic efficiency can be attained by fulfilling certain *marginal conditions* first stated by Pareto, including those concerning:
    a. The optimum allocation of a resource among producers of the same good
    b. The optimum specialization of production among producers of the same goods
    c. The optimum composition of production and consumption
    d. The optimum allocation of goods among consumers of the same goods

6. A general requirement for the achievement of the *Pareto optimum* is: Whenever one can technically transform a little bit of one variable into a little bit of another, the marginal rate of technical transformation must equal the marginal rate of indifferent substitution. All equivalent marginal rates of technical transformation or of indifferent substitution must be equal. When all of these equalities hold, all unambiguous ways of maximizing human welfare from a given stock of resources have been exhausted.

## Key Terms

| | |
|---|---|
| allocative efficiency | marginal rate of transformation (*MRT*) |
| allocative inefficiency | Pareto optimum |
| economic efficiency | performance criteria |
| economic inefficiency | production function |
| law of declining marginal utility | success criteria |
| law of diminishing returns | technical efficiency |
| marginal conditions | technical inefficiency |
| marginal rate of substitution (*MRS*) | X-inefficiency |

## Questions and Problems

1. Comment on the following statement: ''The involuntary unemployment of resources, this chapter notes, implies that people have fewer goods than they might. But the chapter fails to tell us that such unemployment has important other costs as well.''

2. To the extent that its existence can be traced to insufficient worker motivation, how, if at all, could one ever *eliminate* X-inefficiency? (*Hints:* Consider the possible role of external incentives, such as monetary rewards or public praise, or of internal incentives, such as

feelings of joy or guilt. Consider the possible role of worker participation in management.)

3. Review this chapter's discussion of Pareto condition 1. Illustrate it graphically.

4. Review this chapter's discussion of Pareto condition 2. Illustrate it graphically.

5. Invent a marginal rate of transformation between fishing vessels and sewing machines for the Soviet Union and another such *MRT* for Bulgaria so that it would pay the Soviet Union to specialize in producing fishing vessels, while Bulgaria specialized in sewing machines. Using your numbers, prove that specialization and trade could make everyone better off at the same time. Bonus point: Review Close-Up 2.2 and ask yourself what kind of data economic planners in Comecon would need to determine marginal rates of transformation.

6. Review this chapter's discussion of Pareto condition 3. Illustrate it graphically.

7. Review this chapter's discussion of Pareto condition 4. Illustrate it graphically.

8. The following is another marginal condition of economic efficiency: *Economic efficiency requires that the marginal rate of technical substitution,* MRTS, *between any two resources,* x *and* y, *be the same for any two producers,* α *and* β, *using both resources (to produce identical or different goods).* Explain this condition. (*Hints:* The *MRTS* refers to the rate at which a little bit of, say, labor can be exchanged for a little bit of, say, machine time in the process of production, while output remains unaffected. You might adapt Table 2.4 for your answer, imagining producers to "eat up" labor and machine time to produce visible products just as consumers eat apples and butter to produce invisible satisfaction.)

9. Review Problem 8 and its solution at the back of this book. Illustrate the condition graphically.

10. Can you think of any *criticisms* of Pareto's approach? (If you can't, look at the comments at the back of the book.)

## Selected Readings

Alessi, Louis de. "Property Rights, Transaction Costs, and X-Efficiency: An Essay in Economic Theory," *The American Economic Review,* March 1983, pp. 64–81. A sharp critique of the X-efficiency concept. For a reply, *see* Harvey Leibenstein, "Property Rights and X-Efficiency: Comment," *The American Economic Review,* September 1983, pp. 831–42.

Brenner, M. Harvey. "Influence of the Social Environment on Psychopathology: The Historical Perspective," in James E. Barrett et al., eds., *Stress and Mental Disorder* (New York: Raven Press, 1979), pp. 8–24. Estimates, among other things, that a 1-percentage-point rise in the U.S. unemployment rate—if sustained over a period of six years—would lead to 37,000 early deaths.

Kohler, Heinz. *Intermediate Microeconomics: Theory and Applications,* 2d ed. (Glenview, IL: Scott, Foresman and Co., 1986). Chapter 3 provides more detailed discussion of consumption indifference curves, chapter 5 of the production function and isoquants.

Leibenstein, Harvey. "Allocative Efficiency vs. 'X-Efficiency,'" *The American Economic Review,* June 1966, pp. 392–415. The original article on X-efficiency theory. It is reprinted in *idem. Beyond Economic Man: A New Foundation for Microeconomics* (Cambridge, MA: Harvard University Press, 1976), chap. 3. For elaborations, see the appendix to this book ("Toward a Mathematical Formalization of X-Efficiency Theory"), as well as *idem.* "Aspects of the X-Efficiency Theory of the Firm," *The Bell Journal of Economics and Management Science,* Autumn 1975, pp. 580–606; "On the Basic Proposition of X-Efficiency Theory," *The American Economic Review,* May 1978, pp. 328–34; and "A Branch of Economics Is Missing: Micro-Micro Theory," *Journal of Economic Literature,* June 1979, pp. 477–502.

Moore, John H. "Agency Costs, Technological Change, and Soviet Central Planning," *The Journal of Law and Economics,* October 1981, pp. 189–214. An interesting application of the X-efficiency concept to the Soviet economy—the largest hierarchical management system in the world. The attempt to run an entire economy like a single firm creates *agency costs* (less output and less technical innovation than possible) because agents (such as workers) who carry out activities on behalf of some principal (such as a boss or a central planning board), unless closely monitored, will maximize their own welfare and will behave nonoptimally from the principal's point of view.

Pareto, Vilfredo. *Manual of Political Economy.* (New York: Augustus M. Kelley, 1971). This is the only one of Pareto's works available in English. Note William Jaffé, "Pareto Translated: A Review Article," *Journal of Economic Literature,* December 1972, as well as the controversy elicited by this review (same journal, March 1974).

Stigler, George J. "The Xistence of X-Efficiency," *The American Economic Review,* March 1976, pp. 213–16. The 1982 winner of the Nobel Prize in economics criticizes the Leibenstein theory. For a reply, *see* Harvey Leibenstein, "X-Inefficiency Xists—Reply to an Xorcist," *The American Economic Review,* March 1978, pp. 203–11; and "Microeconomics and X-Efficiency Theory: If There Is No Crisis, There Ought to Be," *The Public Interest, Special Issue 1980: The Crisis in Economic Theory,* pp. 97–110.

## Computer Programs

The SYSTEMS personal computer diskette that accompanies this book contains one program of interest to this chapter: Program 2, *"Efficiency,"* provides 20 multiple-choice questions about Chapter 2, along with immediate responses to incorrect answers.

# CHAPTER 3

# *Scarcity Challenged: Growth and Equity*

If people dislike scarcity, as most of them do, it makes sense for them to aim, before all else, for the full and efficient employment of the limited resources that are available to them. Such was the story of the last chapter. In this one, we note how people can take the challenge to scarcity even further.

First, they can think about the *types* of goods being produced and give up any attempt to get the greatest possible set of goods for current consumption out of the limited resources currently available. They can divert some of these resources from the current production of consumption goods, *saving* them for another purpose. And they can turn to *investing* the resources so saved in the production of more resources or better methods of production or higher-quality resources. As a result of such action, people can, over time, increase their ability to produce goods—so much so, perhaps, that their production possibilities come to equal or exceed their desire for goods and scarcity gives way to abundance. All this is summarized in Figure 3.1, "One Path to Abundance: Enlarging the Ability to Produce."

Second, people can focus on how the goods they are producing are being apportioned among themselves. As long as there is scarcity, the matter of apportionment is bound to be a hotly debated issue in any society. This is so because it is always possible, given the overall degree of scarcity prevailing, to reduce the scarcity of any one person by increasing that of any other person. Conceivably, the welfare of the first person is raised more than that of the second person is reduced, and if this were true, the given annual flow of goods could be made to yield a greater welfare total. Yet, we can never know for sure (the welfare of the first person may, in fact, be raised by less than that of the second is reduced), which is why Pareto (Biography 2.1) was unwilling to make the requisite determination of who should be helped at the expense of whom. But others don't share his inhibitions.

**Figure 3.1**   One Path to Abundance: Enlarging the Ability to Produce

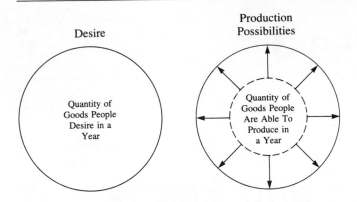

In any one year, people can divert some of their resources from the production of consumption goods and toward the production of more resources or better methods of production or higher-quality resources. Over time, this enlarges their ability to produce goods, as shown by the growth of the right-hand circle. Given unchanged material desires (shown by the left-hand circle) or less rapidly growing ones (not shown), this process might even replace scarcity by abundance (once the right-hand circle has grown sufficiently to equal or exceed the size of the left-hand circle).

Thus, the stage is set for intense conflict and for a never-ending discussion of what constitutes a fair, just, or equitable apportionment of the scarce goods society does manage to produce.

## Economic Growth

A sustained expansion over time in a society's ability to produce goods, such as that depicted in Figure 3.1, is called **economic growth.** We should note that economic growth comes in two forms, depending on the reasons behind its occurrence. An expansion of production possibilities resulting from the availability of more units of the very types of resources previously available, technology being unchanged, is called **extensive economic growth.** A similar expansion resulting from the availability of better methods of production and higher-quality resources is called **intensive economic growth.** The following sections explore each of these types of growth in turn.

### Extensive Economic Growth

Just as a baker who manages to acquire more butter, eggs, flour, and milk can bake a larger cake, so any society that manages to increase the stocks of its familiar resources thereby also enlarges its ability to produce goods. Given the three major classes of resources noted in Chapter 1, the policies that might be pursued to achieve extensive economic growth are fairly obvious.

People might set out deliberately to increase the size of their population so as to have available, eventually, a greater number of workers. This might involve a policy of encouraging births and immigration or discouraging (early) deaths and emigration. Once there are more people ready to work (at whatever full employment rate society established), more labor hours can be utilized in the process of production—yielding, presumably, each year a larger quantity of goods than before.

A word of warning, however, is in order: Consider Figure 3.1. Any increase in population is bound to increase the overall quantity of goods people desire (the left-hand circle) along with the production possibilities. Thus the degree of scarcity, which depends on the relationship between those two circles, may not be reduced at all by a population-raising policy. In fact, the degree of scarcity may rise should desire grow more rapidly than the ability to produce, as it well may. (Analytical Example 10.1, "The Chinese Population Bomb," on pp. 295 to 298 further discusses this issue.)

Thus, people seeking to increase the sheer quantities of their resources might be better advised to focus their attention on enlarging their stocks of nonhuman resources. Clearly, they could seek to discover new natural resources, such as deposits of fuels or minerals, and they could do so in familiar places or far away at the bottom of the sea and in outer space. They could also reclaim natural resources currently considered useless for producing goods, as by draining swamps, terracing mountainsides, or irrigating deserts. And they could make sure to more than replace the existing capital stock as it wears out so as to increase the great multitude of structures, equipment, and inventories usable in the productive process.

## Intensive Economic Growth

Just as a baker who manages to acquire a better recipe and the higher-quality ingredients it calls for can bake a superior cake, so any society that manages to enhance its technical know-how and to improve the quality of its resources thereby also enlarges its ability to produce goods. A society's most obvious inputs, such as labor hours worked or acres employed, may be unchanged; yet, total output (and, thus, the *ratio* of output to input or the quantity of output *per unit* of input) may rise. Sometimes societies manage to enhance their technical know-how by copying the advances made by other societies, of course, but let us consider what they must do to promote intensive growth on their own.

First of all, far removed from practical application, a society seeking to promote intensive economic growth on its own must provide an environment conducive to **basic research**—that is, scientific inquiry not directed toward any specific "useful" discovery. Its biologists may want to know why cells proliferate. Its chemists may wish to study the properties of fluids; its physicists, the laws of motion; its psychologists, basic human drives. People must be allowed to engage in such pure scientific inquiry for its own sake, not necessarily with any application in mind.

However, in a society that looks favorably upon free inquiry, experimentation, and the testing of hypotheses, such application is bound to come.

Sooner or later, some researcher will engage in **applied research,** the application to a particular problem of the knowledge gained in basic research. The general principles established by biologists, chemists, physicists, or psychologists will then be put to work toward the achievement of some well-defined goal. Think of the application of biological principles to the creation of specified varieties of plants and animals, to the production of food from sea water, or to medical techniques inhibiting the growth of undesirable cells. Think of the application of chemical principles to the creation of new drugs or fertilizers. Think of the application of physical principles to the design of electronic computers, electric power stations run by solar energy, factories run by robots, ships propelled by nuclear energy, and communications via artificial satellites. Think of the application of psychological principles to the design of workplaces or incentive systems in industry.

A society that seeks intensive economic growth must, in addition, tolerate—indeed, must encourage—**entrepreneurship,** risky, innovating activity in the very process of production itself. The innovators involved may indeed reduce to practice the new knowledge gained in systematic research, but they may also simply follow a mere personal intuition when they introduce new products (the railroad in place of the stagecoach, followed by automobile, airplane, or rocketship), when they try out new materials (from wood to steel to aluminum to plastics), or when they set up new forms of work organization (the assembly line there, the team concept here). Clearly, such innovating entrepreneurs must not be confused with manager-bureaucrats who keep established enterprises running in routine ways and who exhibit neither the imagination nor the daring of entrepreneurs who try out things that have never been done before.

Finally, innovations that show signs of raising the society's overall ability to produce goods must be supported by the production of appropriately improved types of resources, be they wonders of ever more sophisticated machinery or of workers who are abundantly endowed with *human capital*—generally well educated, kept in good health, and trained in important skills.

## The Optimum Rate of Growth

While the process of economic growth eventually can be of great benefit to those who are intent on conquering scarcity, it also imposes a cost while it is under way. Every single element of this process draws resources away from an obvious alternative use: the production of consumption goods now. When a society employs some of its currently available resources to grow more future workers, to engage in exploratory oil drilling and mineral surveys, to build more irrigation canals and dams, to create more harbors, railroads, highways, and factories, to endow and operate fancy research facilities, to set up hospitals and schools for the creation of human capital, and to construct more sophisticated pieces of equipment, that society loses the opportunity to employ these very resources in the immediate production of food, clothing, shelter, and other consumption goods. As a result, people must pay with a greater scarcity of consumption goods now for a lowered scarcity of consumption goods in the future. The fact that the former is temporary and the latter permanent may be of little consolation to the current generation of people called upon to make the sacrifice. It should not surprise us, therefore, to find that people differ in their opinions about the price that should be paid for the sake of economic growth. Three types of suggestions about the "optimum" rate of economic growth are often encountered.

*The maximum rate.* At one extreme, there are those who urge their fellows to make the maximum possible current sacrifice for future bliss. It is not difficult to establish the maximum amount of consumption goods any group of people is able to pay for economic growth: It is the difference between the maximum set of consumption goods they could enjoy now (if they had no economic growth at all) and the minimum set they must consume in order to survive.

*The minimum rate.* At the other extreme, there are those who wish to maximize consumption now. They do not want the future to "exploit" the present. They would prefer to have no economic growth or, better yet, negative growth. Note: A zero-growth policy requires *some* investment to replace the capital stock as it wears out. A policy that maximizes consumption in the sense of foregoing *any* investment will eventually yield a declining capital stock and *negative* economic growth.

*An intermediate rate.* Finally, there are those who suggest that each society find an acceptable rate of growth in between the extremes just discussed—perhaps a rate that is determined by whatever current sacrifice of consumption goods occurs when all individuals separately confront subjective *time preference* with objective *time productivity.* These new terms (and the accompanying argument) are explained easily enough.

Presumably, each individual consumer can, at any given moment, identify a subjectively felt marginal rate of substitution or **marginal rate of time preference** between current consumption goods, $C_c$, and future consumption goods, $C_f$. This rate shows the additional units of future consumption goods a consumer would have to get in order to be *indifferent* about a 1-unit sacrifice of current consumption goods. Economists postulate that this subjective rate of exchange is typically greater than unity and, in addition, tends to be larger the more units of current consumption goods have already been sacrificed. (A rate of 1.1 $C_f$ for 1 $C_c$, for example, indicates that the consumer would be equally well off—in the consumer's own opinion—if sacrificing 1 unit now were compensated by later repayment of 1.1 unit; that is, by repayment of "principal" plus 10 percent "interest.")

On the other hand, each producer can, at any given moment, identify an objectively determined marginal rate of transformation or **marginal rate of time productivity** between current and future consumption goods. This rate shows the additional units of future consumption goods a producer could produce if a 1-unit sacrifice of current consumption goods were made (and the resources thus saved were used for investment that made the added production of future consumption goods possible). Economists postulate that this objective rate of exchange is often greater than unity but tends to be smaller the more units of current consumption goods have already been sacrificed (and the more resources have already been channeled into the production of new capital goods).

We can easily see how a producer whose marginal rate of time productivity equaled 1 $C_c$ for 1.3 $C_f$ could make a welfare-raising deal with a consumer whose marginal rate of time preference was 1 $C_c$ for 1.1 $C_f$. If the consumer reduced current consumption by 1 unit ($-1$ $C_c$), the producer could reduce the production of consumption goods by 1 unit ($-1$ $C_c$). This would enable the producer to reallocate the saved resources to produce current capital goods that could help produce 1.3 units of consumption goods in the future ($+1.3$ $C_f$). Thus, the consumer (who would have been equally well off with an extra 1.1 $C_f$ later) could, in fact, consume 1.3 $C_f$ later (and would, thus, be better off).

We conclude: As long as some producer's marginal rate of time productivity (such as our 1.3 $C_f/1$ $C_c$) exceeds some consumer's marginal rate of time preference (such as our 1.1 $C_f/1$ $C_c$), increasing the rate of growth can raise welfare unambiguously. When the two rates have become equal (once increased investment has reduced the producer's rate and increased saving has raised the consumer's rate— to 1.2 $C_f/1$ $C_c$, for example), the rate of growth is optimal in the sense that all unambiguous possibilities for raising welfare have been exhausted. Clearly, if *further* investment reduced the marginal rate of time productivity even more (to, say, 1.1 $C_f/1$ $C_c$), while further saving raised the marginal rate of time preference even more (to, say, 1.3 $C_f/1$ $C_c$), *lowering* the rate of growth would raise welfare, according to this argument.

Thus, every society has to set up a mechanism by which this conflict about the "optimum" rate of growth is resolved and an actual rate is selected.


## Economic Equity

The concept of **economic equity** refers to a situation in which the apportionment of goods among people is considered fair. Two major arguments dominate the debate about the slice of the output pie that should properly go to any one person. One group of people seeks to promote *distributive* economic justice; another group, *commutative* economic justice. These two concepts will be discussed in turn.


### Notions of Distributive Justice

The advocates of **distributive justice** argue that goods should be apportioned among people by some authority seeking to act justly. This is said to be the case whenever the percentage of all goods going to any one person is determined by this authority with reference to some personal characteristic that establishes the recipient as meritorious. There is little agreement, however, as to who that authority should be or what characteristic it should consult. Should the latter be a person's IQ, race, or color of hair? Would a person's needs, humanity, or working time be more appropriate? Let us consider the last three, each of which has been a long-time favorite.

**Apportioning Goods According to Need.**    Some argue that equity is served best when all people receive goods in accordance with their needs. No one, probably, has popularized this idea more than Karl Marx (Biography 15.1). Marx thought that goods would be apportioned according to need after the establishment of communism, an event he predicted would occur at the end of a long period of historical development and after the demise of both capitalism and socialism. At that future time, Marx argued, scarcity will not exist because a new and selfless kind of person will have emerged (with a greatly reduced desire for goods), while a new and much more productive economy will have developed (with a greatly expanded ability to produce goods). In terms of Figure 1.1, ''The Scarcity Problem,'' by the time communism will have been established, the left-hand circle will have shrunk and the right-hand circle will have expanded to eliminate the scarcity problem.

Many of Marx's followers, however, argue that need could and should become the principle of apportioning goods *now*. The satisfaction of ''true material needs,'' they say, requires minimal amounts and simple types of food, clothing, and shelter, some medical care, and relatively little else. These amounts, it is argued, may differ among individuals: A sick person will require more drugs and medical care than a healthy one; a hardworking adult more food and clothing than a newborn infant; any person in Maine more fuel than any person in Florida. However, assert many of Marx's followers, all people can get exactly what they need the moment they learn to identify and reject material desires that are ''false.'' Who needs fancy cameras, private airplanes, houses on islands in the middle of the sea, jet trips to the far corners of the globe? People may think they need these things as long as parents and teachers, friends and neighbors, businesses and governments all conspire to enslave them to such ''false material desires.'' But if people are made conscious of this propaganda, it is said, if they are inspired to shed false desires, scarcity will vanish, allowing all people to get exactly what they truly need. Figure 3.2, ''Another Path to Abundance: Rejecting Material Desires That Are 'False','' illustrates the point.

Two implications of this proposal must be noted, however. First, those who would apportion goods according to need leave unclear who is to define ''true'' material needs and ''false'' material desires. Is bread, for example, always a ''true material need'' while a jet trip to Paris is always a ''false material desire''? Could the answer differ with circumstances? Who among the billions of people on earth can be trusted to give the correct answer? We clearly cannot let all persons decide for themselves, because if we did, we would return to the dilemma of scarcity illustrated in Chapter 1. Some people do consider cameras or jet trips to Paris to be true needs; all true needs, as defined by all people for themselves, add up, in the left-hand part of Figure 3.2, to the outer broken circle, not to the inner solid one. The proposal summarized in Figure 3.2, therefore, requires that some authority (who allegedly knows better) decides—contrary to their opinions—what all other people ''truly need'' and apportions available goods accordingly.

Second, when all people are assured of getting what they ''truly need'' (as defined by someone else), they have no incentive either to contribute to the process

**Figure 3.2** Another Path to Abundance: Rejecting Material Desires That Are "False"

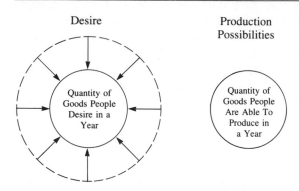

There are those who urge that people abandon their "false material desires," seeking satisfaction only of their "true material needs" (note the shrinking of the left-hand circle). This would eliminate scarcity, it is said, because the goods people are able to produce (right-hand circle) are sufficient to satisfy the "true material needs" of everyone. Thus, output could be apportioned according to need.

of production at all or to contribute in such a way as to produce just the types of goods that are "truly needed." Thus, it will also be necessary for someone— perhaps the same authority who gives people what they "truly need"—to draft people into the labor force and to tell them what kinds of goods they must produce. Otherwise, people might just go on an endless vacation, trusting that they will get in any case whatever someone else has decided they need. Even if the recipients of goods should feel impelled by conscience to work and to work hard (and if these people didn't have to be threatened with punishment for loafing), only if someone told them exactly what to produce would the composition of the set of goods produced equal the composition required for the satisfaction of what someone has defined as "true needs." Otherwise, the people who were working might be producing cars or satin sheets or television sets at the very time these had been defined as "false material desires." Under these circumstances, this production would be akin, in the eyes of authority, to producing totally useless things, such as cans of steamed cherry pits, jars of shredded bees' wings, or kegs of frozen glass splinters. Apportioning goods "according to needs" almost certainly implies a centralized definition of needs as well as a centralized direction of labor.

**Apportioning Goods Equally to All.** Then there are those who would give all people, as a basic human right, an exactly equal share of the total set of goods produced in any one year. When the argument is presented as a matter of moral judgment, little can be said about it. However, two of the more complex arguments for the equal apportionment of goods were presented by an economist, Abba P. Lerner, and by a philosopher, John Rawls.

    ***Abba Lerner.***   In order to illustrate Lerner's argument, let us suppose that a society's annual output of a multitude of goods were to be apportioned among 200 million persons. If the goods involved had freely flexible prices, one could distribute them most easily by apportioning among people an amount of, say, 2 trillion dollars and letting each person buy whatever quantities of whatever goods he or she could afford at whatever equilibrium prices emerged. Clearly, this method of distributing the available goods would work regardless of how much money income was given to any one person.

    However, argues Lerner, it would surely be desirable to apportion the dollars (and hence the goods they can buy) in such a way as to maximize the total satisfaction or utility people *as a group* derived from the goods available. For the sake of this desirable goal, says Lerner, one would have to give every person an exactly equal dollar amount (of $2 trillion divided by 200 million people, or of $10,000 per person in our example). This conclusion is based on Lerner's use of the law of declining marginal utility, first discussed in the Chapter 2 section on "Condition 3: The Optimum Composition of Production and Consumption." Consider the effect of giving money income to any one person: Presumably, the first dollar received would be spent to satisfy that person's most urgent material desire (as defined by that person), the second dollar would be spent on the next urgent desire, and so on. Each additional dollar of income would thus raise the person's overall satisfaction (or utility), but by less and less. In other words, while the person's *total* utility derived from income would rise with higher income, the person's *marginal* utility of income would fall with higher income. For any one person, A, the declining marginal utility of income is illustrated by line $MU_A$ in Figure 3.3, "The Equal Income Argument."

    The first dollar received by person A would bring utility represented by the thin column *la*. Additional dollars would bring smaller *extra* or marginal utility, even though total utility would rise. Thus, the 8,000th dollar received in a year would bring marginal utility of *mb* (which is smaller than *la*), but it would bring the total utility of all 8,000 dollars received up to area *lmba,* the *sum* of all those thin columns of marginal utility associated with the 1st, 2nd, 3rd, and, eventually, the 8,000th dollar received. Similarly, if person A were to receive 20,000 dollars per year, the 20,000th dollar would bring still lower marginal utility of *qf*, which would be but the last addition to a utility total then equalling *lqfa*.

    According to Lerner, a similar story could be told about any other person, B. The first dollar given to B would bring utility represented by thin column *qg*. If B received a 5,000th dollar (measured from right to left in the graph), B's marginal utility of income would be only *pe*, but B's total utility would then equal *qgep*. And if B received 20,000 dollars, marginal utility would be only *lk*, but total utility *qgkl*.

    How then, asks Lerner, can one possibly conclude that A and B and all others in this 200-million-person population should get an exactly equal $10,000 annual

**Figure 3.3** The Equal Income Argument

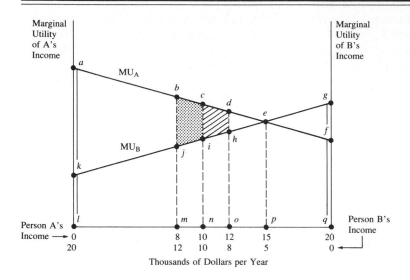

Thousands of Dollars per Year

All agree that one could hypothetically maximize the total welfare derived from a society's annual production of goods by apportioning the money income that can buy those goods in such a way (point *p*) as to equalize the marginal utility of money income among all persons (point *e*). Since one cannot in fact measure and compare people's marginal utility of income, however, it is argued by some that an absolutely equal income distribution (point *n*) is preferable to unequal distributions. This is said to be so because, in the face of uncertainty about the location of point *e,* equal dollar deviations from equality raise total welfare as often as they lower it, but each time total welfare is raised, it is raised by less (dashed area) than it is reduced (dotted area) when the total is lowered. This results from the operation of the law of declining marginal utility.

share of the 2 trillion dollars available (and of the goods they represent)? Surely, to squeeze the greatest possible amount of human welfare from the available goods would require, *in principle,* giving more income to those who could enjoy it more than to others who would enjoy it less. In our example, this principle seems to lead to a clear-cut conclusion: Because B's enjoyment at any given income level is always below A's, the total utility of $20,000 of income would be maximized if A (a more efficient pleasure machine) received $15,000 of income and B received only $5,000. (Note: If A and B received these amounts, their marginal utilities would be *pe* and equal to each other. Thus no reallocation of income could raise total utility.)

In real-life situations, however, we do not know people's marginal-utility-of-income lines, continues the argument. There exists no way to measure the satisfaction a person receives from the goods acquired by means of the spending of money income. One can measure a person's weight (as so many pounds), a person's height (as so many inches), and a person's temperature (as so many degrees), but one cannot measure a person's satisfaction (as so many "utils"?). Hence, a graph such as Figure 3.3 must forever remain hypothetical. One can only *imagine* measuring A's marginal utilities for a 1st, 8,000th, and 20,000th dollar, plotting them as distances *la, mb,* and *qf* and comparing them with similar data for B (such as *qg, oh,* and *lk*). Hence, one cannot know whether B's marginal utility line intersects A's marginal utility line at *e,* as in our example, or at some other point. One cannot know the true social utility maximizing apportionment of income.

If, however, each person received an identical income (of $10,000 in our example) corresponding to midpoint *n,* there would be a 50-50 chance that the distribution of income that would maximize utility in society (because A's and B's marginal utilities were equal to each other) was in fact to the right or to the left of our chosen point *n.* Every time the actual distribution of income deviated from the equal income distribution point *n* in the direction of the true (but unknown) point of equality of marginal utilities, total utility in society would go up. Thus, moving income distribution from *n* to *o* (closer to ideal point *p*) would give person A $2,000 of additional income at the expense of person B. As a result, A's total utility would rise by *ncdo,* but B's total utility would fall by *niho,* resulting in a social net gain in utility equal to dashed area *icdh.*

On the other hand, every time the actual distribution of income deviated from the equal income distribution point *n* in a direction away from the true but unknown point of equality of marginal utilities, total utility in society would go down. Thus, moving income distribution from *n* to *m* (farther from ideal point *p*) would give B $2000 of additional income at the expense of A. As a result, B's total utility would rise by *mjin,* but A's total utility would fall by more, namely *mbcn,* resulting in a social net loss in utility equal to dotted area *jbci.*

The argument concludes by noting that the *size* of the loss associated with an incorrect deviation from equality (the dotted area) would exceed the size of the gain associated with an equal correct deviation from equality (the dashed area). Since in a large population frequent deviations from equality can be expected to result in the same frequency of losses as of gains, such deviations would create a decline in social welfare *with certainty:* 100 million dashed-area gains would be overpowered by 100 million dotted-area losses. Thus, in the face of our inability to measure people's ability to enjoy income, a policy of absolute equality is preferable to a policy of inequality.

*Note:* The validity of the Lerner argument is by no means universally accepted. To name just one criticism, many economists have been troubled by the thought that different people's marginal-utility-of-income schedules may be interdependent and that the lines drawn in Figure 3.3 may shift during the very process of income redistribution.

**John Rawls.**    Rawls asks us to imagine people "in a state of nature" in which they all rely, individually, on their own efforts. Because these people realize that social cooperation could give everyone a better life, they decide to form a society. They meet in an assembly for the purpose of drawing up a "social contract" that is to govern their relations with one another, including the way the benefits of their cooperation are to be apportioned among them. What rule of division will they agree upon?

People in this "original position," Rawls argues, cannot know what kind of personal position they will have in the new society about to be formed. They cannot know whether they will end up as butchers, coal miners, deep sea divers, cleaners of sewers, judges, tax assessors, captains of industry, inventors of life-saving drugs, or pilots of jets. Therefore, they will consider the matter impartially, and they will reject income inequality. Each person will fear ending up with the lowest-paying job and will want to press for a "maximin" rule that makes as large as possible the lowest income any person can get.

Rawls concludes that impartial people who do not have an ax to grind (because they do not know what their position in society will be) would come to agree unanimously on income equality. According to Rawls, income equality would, therefore, be the proper rule for any society in which such a unanimous agreement cannot be reached because real people do know their actual positions in society. Those with above-average incomes will defend inequality because it is in their interest to do so. (Rawls recognizes, however, that everyone might agree on inequality of income, if, in comparison to an egalitarian division, it made possible an improvement of everyone's position at the same time.)

*Conclusion.*    Any policy that divides incomes equally among all people would have identical implications for incentives as a policy of apportionment according to need. If everyone were assured of the same income as everyone else no matter what, someone would have to make sure that people worked at all and also that they produced the types of goods people wanted. Income differentials (for example, between those who worked hard and others who loafed or between those who produced what people wanted and others who produced what people did not want) that could provide these incentives would be outlawed. Thus, some human authority, a type of economic commander-in-chief, would have to make people work and tell them what to make.

**Apportioning Goods According to Hours Worked.**    A third variant of distributive justice demands that each person receive a share of society's total output corresponding to the number of hours that person worked. This policy requires that someone keep track of hours of labor performed. If a janitor, a farmer, and a surgeon each worked 40 hours a week, it would only be fair according to this view to give the same income to each. Someone who worked 20 hours should then get half the amount given to the former three.

Unlike the previous two cases discussed above, this approach clearly has the advantage of providing a strong incentive to work, but it has at least two drawbacks. First, if strictly followed, unlike the "needs" and equality criteria, this criterion would give a zero share of goods to those who didn't work—even the very young, the disabled, or the very old who could not perform labor. Thus, exceptions would surely have to be made, requiring someone's definition of "inability to work."

Second, as in the other instances above, there would exist no incentive for people to produce the right kinds of goods. If the hours-worked criterion were to be strictly followed, a person working 40 hours producing apples would get the same share of society's output as would someone else spending 40 hours packing Mississippi river-bottom mud that nobody wanted. Don't assume either that the apple producer would be more meritorious than the mud packer! What if people didn't want apples either, but preferred refrigerators? If refrigerator making, compared with apple growing, was risky (as to life and health), dirty, dull, and tiring, involved great and unwanted responsibilities, and had to be performed at night and on holidays, no one might volunteer for such work. Consumers would have no way to encourage refrigerator making and discourage apple producing with the help of income differentials; if any apple producer spent 40 hours instead in refrigerator making, the same income share would be assigned as before, so why should he or she switch?

Once more, this method of creating distributive justice implies the need for a central human planner who would have to tell people what they should produce during the hours they worked. This recurring incentive problem is faced head-on by the advocates of a different type of economic justice.

## The Notion of Commutative Justice

All the advocates of distributive justice focus on some *human authority acting justly* by virtue of establishing a tight link between the output shares the authority allots to people and some personal characteristic of these people—their needs, their humanity, their industry. The advocates of **commutative justice** instead focus on the *just nature of an impersonal process,* that generates any given apportionment of output. To them, the output shares ultimately received by people would be fair (even if they should be highly unequal) as long as these shares had been determined by the free choices of all people, all of whom enjoyed as nearly equal opportunities as possible in the process of allocating resources to the production of goods.

For example, the advocates of commutative justice would be happy with a world in which all persons were given the chance, as far as possible, to own equal quantities of all resources and were given an equal freedom to use these resources to produce goods and to trade resources and goods with others. However, the advocates of commutative justice hasten to add, people so privileged should also be held responsible for the consequences of their choices. Consider what this involves.

Being given the chance to own the same amount of resources might require, first, a society that made free health care, general education, and vocational training available to all. These opportunities would serve the purpose of equalizing human resources owned insofar as it was possible and reasonable. (Any differences remaining among people's ability to sell labor services would then be traceable to such factors as their genetic makeup or their own choices. Presumably, one would not wish to equalize the skills of people by barring books from the intelligent until the retarded can catch up, or by dismembering the healthy until the crippled can be cured, or by forcing everyone to lead identical lives as a result of making identical choices on everything.)

Being given a chance to own the same amount of resources might require, second, a society that redistributed, at the time of each person's death, any accumulations of natural and capital resources so as to keep their ownership as equal as possible. Differences might then be allowed only to the extent that people acted differently during their lifetimes, as by being thriftier or more hardworking than others.

Finally, an equal freedom to use resources might imply a world in which no one was allowed to do anything with resources that all others were not also allowed to do, and an equal freedom to trade resources and goods might imply that everyone was allowed to trade with anyone else at whatever terms were agreeable to the parties involved.

In short, the advocates of commutative justice conceive of economic activity as something like a card game, and they intend to make it fair. As long as one distributes cards at the beginning of the game fairly (equal quantities of resources to all) and as long as one follows rules equally applicable to all (equal freedom to use resources, to trade resources and goods), the end result is seen as just. But in a fair card game, some win and others lose! Similarly, in a society aspiring to commutative justice the incomes of people (and, thus, their share of output) can be expected to differ in the end.

Person A may decide to be a hermit, to have nothing to do with the rest of the world, and to live on whatever goods her resources can produce in isolation. Person B may earn $10,000 a year for work as a baker of bread (even though he could have gone to school and made music his career); he may also take in $5,000 a year in rent for 100 acres of his land used by someone else to grow asparagus. Person C may forego income for a while, study music, and finally play in an orchestra for $30,000 a year, all the while growing lettuce on 100 acres of her land for a profit of $2,000 a year. Person D may go into the business of giving airplane rides, using owned resources as well as those hired from others—and incurring a $20,000 annual loss. And so it would go. . . .

Would the distribution of income be fair? Decidedly yes—the advocates of commutative justice would say—as long as each one of our friends could have done whatever any one of them did in fact do!

*Note:* A society that is commutatively just would not require any central planner defining "true needs" or making sure that people contributed to the process of production and did so by producing the right kinds of goods. Income recipients would decide for themselves what their needs were. If they spent money on symphony concerts and asparagus (rather than on bread, lettuce, and airplane rides), people producing the former would end up with higher incomes than others producing the latter. Thus, the system here contemplated would automatically see to it that high incomes (and large shares of output) would go only to those people who had allocated resources in ways pleasing to people. And it would give low incomes (and small shares of output) to those others who had allocated resources in ways not conducive to satisfying people's most urgent needs—*as defined by these people themselves.* This apportionment of income would happen regardless of how hard producers had worked or how good their intentions had been. The objective fact that people preferred concerts over airplane rides would show itself in higher income in the former than in the latter activity. Given equal opportunities, higher incomes for concert performers would be regarded as perfectly fair, for the producer of unwanted airplane rides (or any other low-income person) would be free to overcome his or her low income by redirecting resources from what people wanted less to what they obviously wanted more eagerly.

Naturally, there would be some people in any society who could not take advantage of opportunities even if they were available (the retarded) or who might become victims of unfortunate accidents (an earthquake). Here the advocates of commutative justice—just like the advocates of the labor-hour variant of distributive justice—suggest a humanitarian redistribution through government of some income from the more to the less fortunate.

## The Efficiency-Equity Distinction

In this final section, we reach back to the previous chapter's discussion of economic efficiency and highlight an important distinction: The question about the economic efficiency of any allocation of goods among people can be asked quite independently of the question of economic equity. Consider, for example, Table 2.4 on page 24. In this example, X is "poor" and Y is "rich" because X always has less, and Y always has more, of all goods. Whether this is considered fair depends, of course, on the principle of economic justice employed and the particular circumstances of this case. If the principle employed were the need or hours-worked version of distributive justice, the apportionment shown in Table 2.4 might be considered fair, if Y had greater need or had worked harder, respectively. And the opposite would be true should the reverse have been the case. Similarly, the apportionment would be considered fair or unfair by advocates of commutative justice depending on whether the initial apportionment shown in our table was generated under conditions of equal opportunity for X and Y. Yet, the important thing to understand is this: Regardless of whether one considered a given allocation of goods among people unfair (and one thought it possible, therefore, to raise social welfare by making person X better off *at the expense of* person Y), the allocation may in addition be inefficient (containing the possibility of making person X better off *without harming* person Y). Thus, there are always *two* possibilities for raising social welfare through a reallocation of goods among people. The elimination of economic inefficiency makes some people better off *without* making others worse off (or, as in Table 2.4, even while making others better off at the same time). The elimination of economic inequity makes some people better off *by* making others worse off (but it is argued that the former benefit exceeds the latter cost).

As a matter of fact, the mapping of preferences with the help of consumption indifference curves (see Chapter 2's problems 6 and 7, along with their answers at the back of this book) allows us to highlight the crucial distinction between economic efficiency and economic equity. Consider Figure 3.4, "The Edgeworth Box."

**Figure 3.4**  The Edgeworth Box

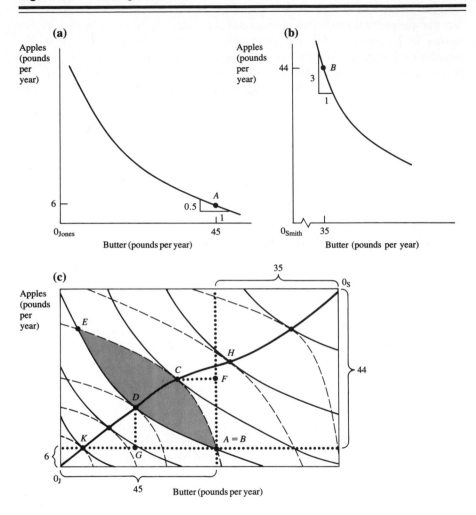

The Edgeworth box diagram* highlights the crucial distinctions between economic efficiency and economic inefficiency, and between economic efficiency and economic equity. Situations of inefficiency, evident by comparing panels (a) and (b), can be depicted as lying off a contract curve, as at point *A* (which equals *B*) in panel (c). Such situations of inefficiency can be removed through peaceful trading that can make everyone better off at one of the many efficient positions on the contract curve. Moves *along* this curve, however, affect the equity of the situation and inevitably cause conflict.

*Although it is named after him, this box diagram does not appear in any of Edgeworth's writings; it was first used by Pareto in 1893. See Vincent J. Tarascio, "A Correction: On the Genealogy of the So-Called Edgeworth-Bowley Diagram," *Western Economic Journal,* June 1972, pp. 193–97; and William Jaffé, "Edgeworth's Contract Curve," Parts I and II, *History of Political Economy,* Fall and Winter 1974, pp. 343–59 and 381–404.

Panel (a) of Figure 3.4 depicts the circumstances of Mr. Jones, who is consuming 6 pounds of apples and 45 pounds of butter per year (point $A$). The single indifference curve going through $A$, shows the marginal rate of substitution to be .5/1 in the vicinity of $A$. Panel (b) presents similar information for Ms. Smith. She consumes 44 pounds of apples and 35 pounds of butter per year (point $B$), but her *MRS* equals 3/1. The inequality of the two *MRS*'s spells economic inefficiency (see "Condition 4: The Optimum Allocation of Goods Among Consumers of the Same Goods" in Chapter 2).

The diagram in panel (c), called the **Edgeworth box,** depicts the same situation in a novel way. Jones's situation in panel (a) has been reproduced in the lower left-hand corner of the box, the origin of which is labeled $O_J$. The position of Jones is again shown at point $A$, but a whole family of Jones's indifference curves has been added to the curve going through point $A$ (see the solid lines convex with respect to $O_J$).

Smith's situation in panel (b) has also been reproduced in panel (c), but panel (b) has been rotated 180 degrees, and point $B$ of that graph has been positioned to coincide with point $A$. As a result, the origin of panel (b) now appears at the upper right-hand corner of the box, labeled $O_S$. The position of Smith is now also seen at $A$, but with respect to origin $O_S$; a whole family of Smith's indifference curves has been added to the one going through point $A$ (see the dashed lines convex with respect to $O_S$).

The dimensions of the box, it should be noted, correspond exactly to the total annual quantities consumed by the two people. The vertical distance measures 50 pounds of apples per year. As the brackets indicate, Jones consumes 6 of these (measured up from $O_J$), and Smith consumes 44 (measured down from $O_S$). The horizontal distance measures 80 pounds of butter per year. Jones consumes 45 of these (measured right from $O_J$); Smith consumes 35 (measured left from $O_S$).

The economic inefficiency of the situation is immediately evidenced by the obviously different slopes, at point $A$, of the two people's indifference curves. (Recall that the slope of an indifference curve equals the *MRS*.) Now notice the manifold possibilities for improvement: If Smith gave up, in favor of Jones, an amount of apples equal to $AF$ and received an amount of butter equal to $FC$ in return, both people would end up at point $C$. Smith would be equally well off (as evidenced by the fact that $C$ is found on the same dashed indifference curve as $A$), but Jones would be better off. (With respect to $0_J$, the solid indifference curve going through $C$ is higher than the one going through $A$.) At point $C$, the slopes of the two people's indifference curves are equal; therefore, their *MRS*s would be equal, and economic efficiency would prevail.

Another alternative to $A$, is found at point $D$: If Jones gave up, in favor of Smith, an amount of butter equal to $AG$ and received an amount of apples equal to $GD$ in return, both people would end up at point $D$. Jones would be equally well off (as evidenced by the fact that $D$ is found on the same solid indifference curve as $A$), but Smith would be better off. (With respect to $O_S$, the dashed indifference curve going through $D$ is higher than the one going through $A$.) At point $D$, the slopes of the two people's indifference curves are equal; therefore, their *MRS*s would again be equal, and economic efficiency would prevail.

As a matter of fact, if Jones and Smith traded with each other in such a way as to arrive at any point within the lens-shaped area *ADEC*, both would reach a higher indifference curve at the same time! As Pareto taught us, however, economic efficiency requires *equality* of the *MRS*s of different people. In the Edgeworth box, the two *MRS*s are equal wherever the two persons' indifference curves have the same slope. All such efficient points (including *K, D, C,* or *H*) have been linked by a heavy line, which economists call the **contract curve.** They use this term because people who find themselves in inefficient positions not on the curve (as at point *A*) can *contract* to trade with each other so that one or both can become better off at a position on the contract curve (as between *C* and *D* in our example). All positions that are not on the contract curve are economically inefficient; they make it possible for people to play a **positive-sum game,** in which no one wins utility at someone else's expense and the sum of (positive) winnings and (nonexisting negative) losses is positive.

The Edgeworth box diagram in panel (c) illustrates an important matter: Economic efficiency does not depict a single position, but a whole range of them. Any position on the contract curve is equally efficient. Once the *MRS*s are equalized, possibilities for simultaneous mutual gain are exhausted, regardless of the *total* quantities of goods consumed by the two individuals. Point *K* is efficient, as are *D, C,* and *H*.

Now note this: Once economic efficiency has been achieved by moving from positions off the contract curve to positions on it, any one person can become better off *only at the expense of another.* Quite possibly, people can then play only a **zero-sum game,** in which the winnings of utility of some are exactly matched by the losses of others and the sum of (positive) winnings and (negative) losses is zero. As long as we cannot measure and compare utilities, we can never be sure that winnings balance losses, but we can be sure of conflict all *along* the contract curve. The contract curve, therefore, can also be called a **conflict curve.** People who find themselves in positions on the curve (as at point *C*) find themselves fighting with one another about moving (as from *C* to *H* or *C* to *K*) because in such a case one person becomes better off only at the expense of the other. Note how at *H*, Jones's indifference curve is so much higher than at *C*, but that of Smith is so much lower. The opposite is the case at *K*. A move along the conflict curve raises the issue of *equity.*

The importance of the efficiency-equity distinction, which is brought out so clearly in the box diagram, cannot be overemphasized. In many potential conflict situations, which might give rise to divorces or strikes or even wars, there exist in fact possibilities for peaceful accommodation, for mutually beneficial trade, akin to a move from point *A* not on the contract curve to a point between *C* and *D* lying on it. Awareness of such possibilities can avoid many an unnecessary conflict, because conflict is inevitable only if one is already on the contract curve and determined to move.

# Summary

1. If people want to fight scarcity, they can do more than employ their resources fully and efficiently. They can also employ them in such a way as to bring about *economic growth,* a sustained expansion over time in the society's ability to produce goods.

2. Economic growth is said to be *extensive* if it results from the availability of more units of the very types of resources previously available, technology being unchanged.

3. Economic growth is said to be *intensive* if it results from the availability of better methods of production and higher-quality resources.

4. While economic growth eventually can be of great benefit to people, it also imposes a cost while it is under way: It draws resources away from the production of consumption goods now. Not surprisingly, people argue endlessly about the "optimum" rate of growth. Some argue it should be zero or even negative; others urge the maximum possible rate; still others would opt for a rate in between (possibly one that equates marginal rates of time preference and time productivity).

5. Conceivably, human welfare can be raised further by ensuring an equitable apportionment of the goods people do manage to produce. But the meaning of *economic equity* is hotly debated.

6. Some urge the creation of *distributive justice,* a situation in which goods are apportioned among people by some authority seeking to act justly, preferably by consulting some personal characteristic that measures the recipient's merit. This personal characteristic could be a person's "needs," a person's "basic human right to an equal output share," or the number of hours a person works. The use of "needs" or "basic human rights" as criteria of apportionment produces serious problems with incentives. Using the criterion of hours worked overcomes incentive problems only in part.

7. The incentive problems disappear when equity is viewed as *fairness of the process* that produces and distributes goods rather than as *fairness of the end result* of that process. The advocates of *commutative justice* aim to create a situation in which goods are apportioned among people as a result of free choices by all people, all of whom enjoy as nearly equal opportunities as possible in the process of allocating resources to the production of goods.

8. It is crucial to understand the distinction between economic efficiency and economic equity. The advocates of economic *efficiency* aim to raise total economic welfare by reallocating resources or goods whenever this results in some people feeling better off while nobody feels worse off. The advocates of economic *equity* (who do not accept the taboo against interpersonal comparisons of welfare) aim to raise total economic welfare by reallocating resources or goods whenever this results in some people

feeling better off, while others are judged to feel worse off *to a lesser degree*. All this can most clearly be seen with the help of the Edgeworth box diagram. Movements to its *contract curve* illustrate moves toward economic efficiency from which all can gain at the same time. Movements along its *conflict curve* illustrate alleged moves toward economic equity from which some people gain, while others lose.

## Key Terms

applied research
basic research
commutative justice
conflict curve
contract curve
distributive justice
economic equity
economic growth

Edgeworth box
entrepreneurship
extensive economic growth
intensive economic growth
marginal rate of time preference
marginal rate of time productivity
positive-sum game
zero-sum game

## Questions and Problems

1. If a government were interested in promoting *extensive* economic growth by increasing the flow of human resources to the process of production, what kinds of policies might it adopt? Can you think of actual cases?

2. The risk-taking entrepreneur is often cited as an important factor promoting *intensive* economic growth. Can you think of an example of how an entrepreneur may help increase productivity—that is, output per unit of input?

3. The Yugoslav economist Branko Horvat is among those who advocate *maximizing* the rate of economic growth (and who are willing to ignore, if necessary, people's obstinate preference for more consumption goods now. He would be willing to *force* saving up to some maximum near 40 percent of output). Table 3.1 illustrates his kind of reasoning: Growth Strategy I saves and invests a constant 15 percent of output in each plan period (which might represent a Five-Year Plan). Given the assumed marginal-output-to-investment ratio of $(\Delta\ Q_t/I_{t-1}) = 1/3$, output grows from 100 to 155 (and consumption from 85 to 132) between periods 1 and 10. Growth Strategy II saves and invests the same 15 percent of output initially but raises the percentage by 1 point in each period. Output now grows from 100 to 174 (and consumption from 85 to 132). Growth Strategy III is Horvat's favorite; it equals II, except that the saving/investment percentage is raised by 2 points in each period. Output now grows from 100 to 193 (and consumption from 85 to 129).

**Table 3.1**  Alternative Growth Strategies*

| | Strategy I | | | | Strategy II | | | | Strategy III | | | |
| | Output Q | Saving = Investment % of Q | Saving = Investment Amount S = I | Consumption C = Q − S | Output Q | Saving = Investment % of Q | Saving = Investment Amount S = I | Consumption C = Q − S | Output Q | Saving = Investment % of Q | Saving = Investment Amount S = I | Consumption C = Q − S |
| Period | | | | | | | | | | | | |
|---|---|---|---|---|---|---|---|---|---|---|---|---|
| 1 | 100 | 15 | 15 | 85 | 100 | 15 | 15 | 85 | 100 | 15 | 15 | 85 |
| 2 | 105 | 15 | 16 | 89 | 105 | 16 | 17 | 88 | 105 | 17 | 18 | 87 |
| 3 | 110 | 15 | 17 | 93 | 111 | 17 | 19 | 92 | 111 | 19 | 21 | 90 |
| 4 | 116 | 15 | 17 | 99 | 117 | 18 | 21 | 96 | 118 | 21 | 25 | 93 |
| 5 | 122 | 15 | 18 | 104 | 124 | 19 | 24 | 100 | 126 | 23 | 29 | 97 |
| 6 | 128 | 15 | 19 | 109 | 132 | 20 | 26 | 106 | 136 | 25 | 34 | 102 |
| 7 | 134 | 15 | 20 | 114 | 141 | 21 | 30 | 111 | 147 | 27 | 40 | 107 |
| 8 | 141 | 15 | 21 | 120 | 151 | 22 | 33 | 118 | 160 | 29 | 46 | 114 |
| 9 | 148 | 15 | 22 | 126 | 162 | 23 | 37 | 125 | 175 | 31 | 54 | 121 |
| 10 | 155 | 15 | 23 | 132 | 174 | 24 | 42 | 132 | 193 | 33 | 64 | 129 |

*Assuming output grows by $\frac{1}{3}$ of previous period's investment

Source: Adapted from Branko Horvat, *Towards a Theory of Planned Economy* (Belgrade: Yugoslav Institute of Economic Research, 1964), p. 190.

Continue the table for periods 11–15 (rounding each entry to a whole number). Then comment on Horvat's strategies.

4. Some economists, including the late Joseph Schumpeter, have argued that it may be worthwhile to sacrifice efficiency if this were to facilitate a more rapid rate of economic growth. What do you think?

5. **Mr. A:** Interpersonal comparisons of utility are impossible. No one can say with confidence, ''Your headache is worse than mine,'' or ''I enjoy apple pie more than you.'' Therefore, no one can ever tell which apportionment of goods among people is fair.
   **Ms. B:** I can. When some people can afford private planes and yachts, while others lack insulin or milk, economic injustice prevails.
   Evaluate these two positions.

6. **Mr. A:** Figure 3.3, ''The Equal Income Argument,'' presents Lerner's argument on the assumption of an initial deviation of actual income from equality of $no = nm$. Yet, the entire argument would be different if the assumed initial deviation were different; e.g., substantially larger.
   **Ms. B:** There are other problems with his argument, too. In fact, Lerner's income-equality argument is a farce. He argues for equality allegedly because we can't measure people's capacity to enjoy income, hence cannot justify departures from equality. Do you seriously think he would argue *against* equality, if we could make such measurement? Suppose we could prove someday that one person was an extremely efficient pleasure machine (was so much better than all other people at deriving utility from the consumption of goods). Suppose social welfare would be maximized if this person received 99 percent of output. Would Lerner agree with such inequality?
   Evaluate these two positions.

7. When discussing Rawls's argument (p. 44), the text argues that ''everyone might agree on inequality of income, if, in comparison to an egalitarian division, it made possible an improvement of everyone's position at the same time.'' Can you illustrate this possibility?

8. Consider panel (c) of Figure 3.4, ''The Edgeworth Box.''
   a. Indicate the positions to which Jones and Smith might move, without either of them becoming worse off, if their initial position was at $E$. What if their initial position was at *F* or *G?*
   b. Imagine that one could measure total utility in the third dimension above the diagram. What would the utility mountain look like above the contract curve?
   c. Imagine that Jones and Smith had identical tastes and, therefore, identical sets of indifference curves. Would mutually beneficial trade between them still be possible? Explain.

9. Comment on the following: ''There is one more thing this chapter should have discussed: the importance of avoiding inflation.''

10. Is there a *trade-off* between economic growth and economic equity?

## Selected Readings

Council on Environmental Quality and Department of State. *The Global 2000 Report to the President,* (Washington, D.C.: Government Printing Office, 1980). A reassertion of the doomsday theme first sounded by the Club of Rome and noted in the Meadows selection below.

Ehrlich, Paul R., and Anne H. Ehrlich. *The End of Affluence* (New York: Ballantine Books, 1974). Like the Meadows selection below, an argument that continued economic growth is impossible.

Hayek, Friedrich A. *The Mirage of Social Justice,* vol. 2 of *Law, Legislation and Liberty* (Chicago: University of Chicago Press, 1976), especially chaps. 8 and 9. The 1974 co-winner of the Nobel Prize in Economics discusses alternative concepts of equity and argues in favor of commutative justice.

Kohler, Heinz. *Intermediate Microeconomics: Theory and Applications.* 2d ed. (Glenview, IL: Scott, Foresman and Co., 1986). Chapter 15 discusses intertemporal decision making in detail.

Lerner, Abba P. *The Economics of Control: Principles of Welfare Economics* (New York: Macmillan, 1944). Chapter 3 presents the probabilistic argument for income equality noted in the text.

Meadows, Donella H., et al. *The Limits to Growth: A Report for the Club of Rome's Project on the Predicament of Mankind* (New York: Universe Books, 1972). The Club of Rome, a group of a hundred academicians, business executives, and scientists, uses an elaborate MIT computer model to show that growth paths of world population, output, and pollution are on a catastrophic collision course.

Nordhaus, William D. "World Dynamics: Measurement Without Data," *Economic Journal,* December 1973, pp. 1156–83. A sharp critique of the Meadows selection above.

Rawls, John. *A Theory of Justice* (Cambridge, MA: Harvard University Press, 1971). Presents the argument described in the text. See also Norman Daniels, ed., *Reading Rawls: Critical Studies on Rawls' "A Theory of Justice."* (New York: Basic Books, [1975]).

Simon, Julian L. *The Ultimate Resource* (Princeton, NJ: Princeton University Press, 1981).

Simon, Julian L., and Herman Kahn, eds. *The Resourceful Earth: A Response to Global 2000* (New York: Basil Blackwell, 1984). Critical assessments that show why the doomsday models noted above are wrong.

## Computer Programs

The SYSTEMS personal computer diskette that accompanies this book contains one program of interest to this chapter: Program 3, "Growth and Equity," provides 20 multiple-choice questions about Chapter 3, along with immediate responses to incorrect answers.

# CHAPTER 4

# *Scarcity Challenged: Beyond Economic Welfare*

The achievement of full employment, of technical or economic efficiency, or the promotion of economic growth and economic equity—all of these have one thing in common. They are concerned with improving the material welfare of people. But there are those who worry lest such concerns become an obsession and people forget that "man does not live by bread alone." They argue that the success of any society in promoting the welfare of its members must be judged by more than the quantity of goods it manages to produce and the way in which these goods are apportioned. In particular, they say, it must be judged by the degree to which all individuals are given the chance to develop during their lifetime the manifold creative potential dormant within them, to participate on an equal basis with others and free from coercion by others in all decisions affecting their lives, and to live in harmony with the natural world of which all human beings are a part. To the extent that these three important goals are sacrificed for the sake of getting more material things, a vital spiritual aspect of human welfare will be missing. Even if people should manage to reduce scarcity remarkably, it is argued, as long as they remain out of touch with or *alienated* from themselves, their fellow human beings, and the natural world, people's fight against scarcity will ultimately be recognized as a malign process. People will be overcome by a general feeling of frustration, of having won a hollow victory, of leading lives that are meaningless.

Unfortunately, the notion of **alienation**—people's estrangement from themselves, other people, and nature—is often bandied about in a manner resembling cant, the hypocritical expression of pious sentiments that are not really taken seriously. However, the annoying insincerity of many who moralize about the kinds of issues noted in the preceding paragraph should not blind us to the fact that alienation could correspond to a highly significant reality—a reality, furthermore, that might be strongly influenced by the prevailing type of economic system. This chapter, therefore, discusses the concept in some detail and considers, by implication, what the avoidance of alienation might entail.

## Avoiding Alienation from the Self

In order to understand what social critics have in mind when they talk of people's alienation from themselves, it helps to remember that people in all societies on earth have come to embrace the division of labor. True enough, theoretically, each and every good could be produced by the same people who consume it. Each family, for example, could be a totally self-sufficient unit of production and consumption. It could use whatever resources it had to produce its own food, clothing, shelter, and so on and, like Robinson Crusoe on his deserted island, be totally independent of the rest of humanity. In fact, this is the exception rather than the rule almost everywhere on earth. Except in the poorest of countries, most people consume little, if anything, of what they themselves produce, and they exchange most of what they produce with others who similarly specialize. The reason is obvious enough: All people can get more goods when the process of production is organized on the basis of specialization and exchange rather than self-sufficiency. This is so because people with different inherent talents can concentrate on what they do best. In addition, different skills can be created as each specializing person gains experience. "Practice makes perfect"—an advantage lost to the jack-of-all-trades. Specialization also stimulates the invention and use of machines to the extent that a person's work is reduced to a simple repetitive operation. What family, producing only for itself, would ever install an assembly line? Adam Smith (Biography 12.1) talked about the advantages of the division of labor 200 years ago when he pointed out how a pinmaker could not produce 20 pins in a day if he himself had to do everything that was required—drawing out the wire, straightening it, cutting it, pointing it, grinding it for receiving the head, making the head, and more. Yet Adam Smith observed that 10 people, only poorly equipped with machinery but with the proper division of labor among them, were able to make 48,000 pins in one day.

Thus, sooner or later, people in all societies come to embrace the division of labor as the supreme organizing principle of the productive process because it makes them so much richer than they would otherwise be. But beware, critics say. Such people may find themselves rewarded with an abundance of goods, but also enslaved to machines, in central work places, following rigid schedules.

Machines are admirably suited to perform the simple and repetitive movements required of people specializing in a small part of the productive process. But as human-sized tools give way to complex and giant machines, people become unskilled slaves tending them, it is said. Furthermore, once the task of producing each good is finely divided and supported by machines, work cannot be performed in many separate places. The unit of residence and workplace that artisans might enjoy must be sacrificed. Workers must meet in central workplaces. Naturally, this requires rigid schedules. People who closely work with others cannot work at their own time and pace; work 16 hours today and 3 tomorrow; work all winter, but take the summer off; work nights this week and mornings the next; work at a leisurely speed now and hurry things along later. They have to live by the clock.

Before long, it is said, individual workers will be spending their lives by filling some cubicle of office or factory space with their bodies and making repetitive motions designed by others: 40 times a minute, 2,400 times an hour, 16,800 times a day, every day. They will suffocate in boredom and meaninglessness. Their brains will turn to jelly, their muscles atrophy, their spirits be tormented. Work will be hated toil.

When will be the chance for such people to find themselves? Without the division of labor, it is imagined, they would have such a chance, for then work would be *creative*. Each person would produce a great variety of goods during the course of each year, each one of them from start to finish, and everyone would be able to point to a product in the end and say proudly, "*I* made *that.*" Thus, people would discover all kinds of abilities within them, would become knowledgeable, all-round experts during the course of their lives, would creatively use brain *and* hands and *simple* tools. They would work in their own homes, stand on their own feet, forever face new challenges and, thus, discover, develop, and exercise their talents. Work would be self-initiated, self-directed, and, thus, a prime means of self-expression. It would be a joy!

And, it is imagined, this joyful attitude would be reflected in people's other activities. Instead of surrounding themselves with more machines to tend during their leisure time (airplanes, boats, and cars; dishwashers, lawnmowers, and snow-mobiles), instead of engaging in further rounds of thoughtless activity (watching the moronizing tube, eating and drinking beyond any conceivable requirement), people would be in the *habit* of being creative. How could they fail to discover the joys of artistic, intellectual, and physical achievement? They would dance, master the piano, sculpt, or sing! They would read good books or write them. They would participate in rather than passively watch sports. Thus, they would meet themselves.

As Adam Smith also observed (rather bluntly), "The man whose whole life is spent in performing a few simple operations . . . has no occasion to exert his understanding or to exercise his invention. . . . He naturally loses, therefore, the habit of such exertion and generally becomes as stupid and ignorant as it is possible for a human creature to become. The torpor of his mind renders him not only incapable of relishing or bearing a part in any rational conversation, but of conceiving any generous, noble, or tender sentiment and, consequently, of forming any just judgement concerning many even of the ordinary duties of private life."[1]

Karl Marx (Biography 15.1), like Adam Smith, on the one hand extolled the virtues of economic growth and on the other hand expressed a similar fear:[2]

---

[1]Adam Smith, *An Inquiry into the Nature and Causes of the Wealth of Nations* (Homewood, IL: Richard D. Irwin, 1963), first published in 1776, vol. II, p. 284.

[2]Karl Marx and Friedrich Engels, *The Communist Manifesto* (New York: International Publishers, 1948), first published in 1848.

*The bourgeoisie . . . has been the first to show what man's activity can bring about.
It has accomplished wonders far surpassing Egyptian pyramids, Roman aqueducts, and
Gothic cathedrals. . . . The bourgeoisie, during its rule of scarce one hundred years,
has created more massive and more colossal productive forces than have all preceding
generations together.*

Yet, he thought "the production of too many useful things results in the creation
of too many useless people."[3]

Such is the warning voice of some to those who would challenge the scarcity
of material things. Pursue your goal, they say, but don't lose sight of people's deep-
seated need to develop themselves through a lifetime of creative activity. Should
one worry about this? Clearly, people in every society have to decide to what extent
they will push those aspects of the division of labor that raise productivity at the
expense of creating human wrecks and thwarting human creativity. But human
wrecks can also be created by extreme material deprivation that complete abandonment of specialization might entail. Furthermore, some people may positively
like what others call "moronizing" work because repetitive work may demand
little of their attention, and allow them to daydream and plan ahead for genuine
challenges in their leisure activities, challenges that may be difficult to pursue
without the leisure and the goods that the division of labor can deliver: flying or
even building one's own airplane, remodeling one's home, planting gardens, repairing complicated appliances, climbing mountains, playing instruments, participating in sports, and, perhaps, even taking evening courses in Chinese philosophy!

## Avoiding Alienation from Other People

There is something else people need, critics say, besides creative activity. To be
genuinely happy, people must also find a way to overcome their aloneness and to
establish loving relationships with other people. No possible quantity of material
things can satisfy that universal need. Yet, there is a great danger that a production
process based on the division of labor not only alienates people from themselves
but also from their fellow human beings.

True enough, critics continue, superficially a division of labor brings people
*together,* since they are engaging in a joint enterprise instead of trying to be self-
sufficient hermits. Yet, potential loving relationships are often nipped in the bud
by the way this vast joint enterprise is arranged. Often, for instance, people are
pressed into divisive social roles that make it impossible for them to participate,
on an equal basis with others, in the crucial decisions affecting their lives. Instead,
people become subject to manipulation and coercion by other people. Relationships
of domination and subordination, of rulers to subjects, develop, which clearly places
a barrier between people. Indeed, this is putting it mildly, for people who have

---

[3]Quoted in Erich Fromm, ed., *Socialist Humanism* (Garden City, NY: Doubleday, 1965), p. 237.

been manipulated or coerced (by threat of harm) into acting or not acting in specific ways chosen by others (and contrary to what they would have chosen voluntarily) have thereby been eliminated as thinking and valuing persons. They have ceased to be their own masters; they have become someone else's unwitting or unwilling tools; they have lost, as critics put it, their *sovereignty* as consumers, workers, and citizens alike. Let us consider each of these ideas in turn.

## The Concept of Consumer Sovereignty

Inevitably, all people everywhere are consumers of goods, but they need not necessarily share in the decisions about the types of goods being produced. Conceivably, such decisions are made by a central planning board or, perhaps in more subtle ways, by corporate boards of directors all across the land who engage an army of advertising people to persuade consumers into aligning their preferences with the production decisions that the directors in question have already made. If such should be the case, some people (the consumers) are said to be alienated from other people (those who coerce or manipulate them into consumption choices they would not otherwise have made).

In contrast, a state of affairs in which all consumers share the power to decide what types of goods are being produced (and consumed) is referred to as one of **consumer sovereignty.** In such a situation, the preferences of all consumers are respected—not only with respect to the broad division of output between current consumption goods and current investment goods (which, as Chapter 3 showed, in turn influences the rate of economic growth and, thus, the availability of future consumption goods), but also with respect to the detailed composition of the set of consumption goods that is currently being produced. Such power on the part of consumers requires: (a) that they have access to accurate and complete information about consumption goods; (b) that they can freely choose among such goods; and, (c) most importantly, that productive enterprises, taking their cue from these choices, passively comply with the consumers' wishes by allocating resources accordingly. In short, consumers, like sovereign kings, call the tune; productive enterprises, like obedient subjects, dance to it. As the saying goes, "The customer is always right."

## The Concept of Worker Sovereignty

Most people at one time or another come to be suppliers of labor to the process of production, but they need not necessarily share in the multitude of decisions connected with the supply and utilization of this labor. Conceivably, crucial decisions about the type of labor to be supplied and about the precise conditions under which it is rendered might be made by others than the workers themselves—by a distant central planning board, perhaps, or by an enterprise's complex hierarchy of overlookers who, as critics put it, rule workers' lives just as sergeants, captains, and generals in an army rule the lives of privates. The hierarchy in productive enterprises, these critics contend, will reduce the individual worker to a mere cog, to an inanimate piece of raw material that neither thinks nor judges, but is simply *used*. Money, command, the rule book—these will determine human relations; there won't be room for dignity or respect, much less for compassion or love. Isolated from decision making, enslaved by tyrants, the spirit of workers will once more be tormented, critics conclude.

The most extreme case of such alienation of some people (the workers) from other people (their overseers) is, of course, outright serfdom or slavery or a system of forced labor camps. In contrast, a state of affairs in which all workers share the power to decide what type of labor is being supplied and under what conditions it is rendered is referred to as one of **worker sovereignty.** In such a situation, the preferences of all workers are respected—not only with respect to the kinds of occupations they wish to enter, but also with respect to the manifold conditions under which their labor is performed. These conditions include their choice of geographic location and a specific productive enterprise in which to work as well as numerous details concerning the hours worked per day, the intensity of work, the organization of work, the provisions for health and safety, and more.

Are these matters important? Of course they are, but, once again, things are not as simple as some critics contend. True enough, impersonality *is* a common feature of large, specialized organizations associated with a complex division of labor, but it is an inevitable feature that need not have dreadful implications. It is inevitable for the simple reason that the human mind is incapable of handling complex relationships. Whenever hundreds, thousands, or millions of people co-operate with each other, it is impossible to have face-to-face discussions on every-thing that must be decided; it is even less possible to have discussions in which everyone participates as an equal, as one might in a small, loving family. It simply cannot be done. Hence, familial warmth has to give way in large groupings of people to something else, like the "cold cash nexus" or "bureaucratic commands" and, within each productive enterprise, to "impersonal rules" that specify who makes decisions and who follows them.

However, there is no reason why such arrangements must involve the tyranny of some people over other people. It is perfectly possible that those who are ruled assent to being ruled, that they are not unwilling but willing "tools" of others. Far from being robbed of all dignity as a result of their "enslavement" in the workplace, for example, workers may possess high self-esteem if they have participated in setting up exact procedures according to which those who would exercise power over them are selected, held to account, or both.

## The Concept of Citizen Sovereignty

In addition to being consumers and workers, all people are also citizens of their society. Again, however, they need not necessarily share in the political decisions that affect their common life. At one extreme, the arbitrary will of a single dictator might rule all aspects of people's lives—which would be another example yet of people's alienation from other people. And there are those who wonder: Might the type of economic system prevailing possibly be related to the existence of dictatorship or democracy and to the absence or presence of individual liberties that citizens would like to enjoy?

What is desirable, presumably, is **citizen sovereignty,** a state of affairs in which all citizens share the power to control their political leaders and, thus, to ensure themselves such precious individual liberties as the right to free speech and press, to peaceful assembly, to privacy in their homes, to habeas corpus, to a speedy trial by jury (while being innocent until found guilty), and more. In such a situation, the preferences of citizens are respected: All adults are free to choose among competing would-be leaders, to criticize these leaders, to form opposition parties, and, at not-too-infrequent intervals, to replace one government by another through peaceful voting.

## Conclusion

Social critics who worry about people's alienation from other people (and who would, ideally, have people relate lovingly to one another) insist that people, at the very least, do not coerce one another into choices they would not voluntarily make. This requires in their view an economic system in which consumer sovereignty and worker sovereignty prevail and a political system that accepts citizen sovereignty as well.

## Avoiding Alienation from Nature

There is a third danger inherent in the pursuit of material welfare, critics say. It involves the possibility that people treat the natural world, of which they are but a small and vulnerable part, as nothing more than a resource to be exploited and destroyed. Consider how the processes of production and consumption withdraw resources from nature and how many of these are irreplaceable. This is true not only of fossil fuels and minerals, but of the very space available on this planet. Is there no end to the acreage one can turn into cities, highways, and parking lots or cover with oil derricks, strip mines, and transmission wires? Doesn't the human spirit also crave the natural beauty, purity, and serenity of lakes, mountain valleys, ocean beaches, and woods?

Even when they do not totally eliminate it, critics continue, people do their best to ruin the natural world. Note how they dump millions of tons of carbon monoxide, fly ash, hydrocarbons, soot, and sulfur dioxide into the air; how incredible amounts of sewage, thermal wastes, inorganic chemicals, long-lived radionuclides, and debris find their way into rivers, lakes, and oceans; how trash of all kinds accumulates as fast as the goods people produce and consume.

The dangers involved clearly go beyond aesthetics. The earth is a single vast ecosystem, a system of interrelationships among plants and animals and people and climatic forces. As people cut down and pave over huge tracts of forests, as they turn fertile flood plains into suburbs, as they poison air, water, and land with numerous chemicals, they slowly kill off one species of plant and animal life after another. But each depends on the other, often in ways we do not even understand. Hence the danger. Since we know so little about the intricate living understructure supporting human life, we cannot risk losing any form of life. A single break in the planetary life-sustaining system can become fatal for all life. For example, all organisms build protein basically from carbon, hydrogen, nitrogen, oxygen, and sulfur. If people were to destroy any one of half a dozen types of bacteria involved in, say, the nitrogen cycle, all life on earth could end.

Thus, people cannot forever evade the truth that they are only part of nature. They must strive to live in harmony with nature by using renewable resources and by recycling wastes. In short, the highest possible output of goods is a reliable source of human welfare only if it is produced by people who have overcome their estrangement not only from themselves and their fellows but from nature as well, critics conclude.

## Summary

1.  There are those who argue that the success of any society in promoting the welfare of its members must be judged by more than the quantity of goods it manages to produce and the way in which these goods are apportioned. People must also take care to avoid *alienation,* their estrangement from themselves, their fellow human beings, and the natural world.
2.  To avoid alienation from themselves, individuals must be given the chance, as much as possible, to develop during their lifetime the manifold creative potential dormant within them. But social critics worry that people who covet too many goods and, for that purpose, embrace the division of labor will end up "enslaved" to machinery and rigidly scheduled work in centralized workplaces. This is said to turn work into a joyless activity and to rob people of a means of creative self-expression. Crippled in the work process, it is said, such people also fail to discover and develop their talents during their leisure time.
3.  To avoid alienation from their fellow human beings, individuals must be given a chance to participate on an equal basis with others, and free from coercion by others, in all decisions affecting their lives. This certainly requires, social critics contend, the achievement of consumer sovereignty, worker sovereignty, and citizen sovereignty. When *consumer sovereignty* prevails, all consumers share the power to decide what types of goods are being produced (and consumed). When *worker sovereignty* prevails, all workers share the power to decide what type of labor is being supplied and under what conditions it is rendered. When *citizen sovereignty* prevails, all citizens share the power to control their political leaders and, thus, to ensure themselves such precious individual liberties as the right to free speech and press, to peaceful assembly, to privacy in their homes, to habeas corpus, to speedy trial by jury, and more.

4. To avoid alienation from the natural world, people must learn to live in harmony with it. Critics point to the ever-growing size of the purely man-made world and to high levels of pollution of the natural world. The extent of people's disregard for nature is seen as so serious that it might cause the end of life on earth.

## Key Terms

alienation                                consumer sovereignty
citizen sovereignty                       worker sovereignty

## Questions and Problems

1. Comment on the following statement:
   "It is true that people in the rich, industrialized societies *are* alienated from themselves. Just compare an 'advanced' American with a 'primitive' Bushman of today."
2. Comment on the following statement:
   "The preferences of consumers in the United States (and many a similar society) are not worth respecting. This is so because people have been manipulated by an army of hidden and not-so-hidden persuaders (who peddle false and distorted information on behalf of business firms) into wanting things that are not good for them. And what a pathetic spectacle this is: Millions of adulterated, unneeded, and useless goods are being bought, reflecting faithfully the debased tastes instilled in people by the manipulators. Thus, people buy white bread and soft drinks and TV dinners, the nutritional values of which are pure fantasy. They waste money on deodorants, electric toothbrushes, liquor, and tobacco. And they suffocate themselves with gadgets they could do without. In short, American consumers are mere automatons, helpless puppets, marionettes, moved by strings behind their backs. They veritably sleepwalk through life, dominated by false material desires and the stupid belief that their satisfaction would bring happiness."
3. Comment on the following statement:
   "When a boss threatens employees with a reduction in pay unless they come to work on time, the boss is coercing the employees in the same way as a robber who yells, 'Your money or your life!' "
4. **Ms. A:** "I don't know about other countries, but American workers certainly do *not* hate their jobs. Why else would they work overtime and even moonlight? Why else would rates of absenteeism and labor turnover be so low, sabotage and strikes be so rare?"
   **Ms. B:** "They *do* hate their jobs. Why else would they gripe so much about them, daydream about other jobs or occupations, produce shoddy

products, and jam doctors' offices with fatigue, high blood pressure, insomnia, nervous tension, ulcers, and mental breakdowns?''
What do you think?

5. **Mr. A:** "The text admits that impersonality *is* a common feature in large, specialized organizations, but I don't go along with its claim that impersonality is an inevitable feature. With sufficient good will, even the people working in a giant enterprise like General Motors could cultivate an atmosphere of love and warmth and full participation of everyone in every decision."
**Ms. B:** "I doubt that. In a large enterprise, you can't do away with the hierarchy of command, and this will always make human relationships appear cold and businesslike. But I'll grant you this: The giant corporations of the world could be run in alternative ways than is presently the case and that might make life at the bottom of the hierarchy a lot more acceptable."
What do you think?

6. Comment on the following statement:
"The way the critics mentioned in this chapter describe human relationships within productive enterprises certainly does not describe the United States. American workers accept the authority of overlookers in centralized workplaces precisely because they get more goods by not trying to be medieval craftsmen. Yet, they are anything but slaves without self-esteem: Through labor unions they have established procedures that hold the exercise of power over them to account."

7. Since the 1820s, people have wanted to build a barge canal across Florida from Palatka (south of Jacksonville) to Yankeetown (on the Gulf of Mexico). In 1969, when it was 27 percent complete, someone sued to stop construction because the canal, by changing water flows, would destroy the Everglades. How would you decide if you were the judge? Explain.

8. Comment on the following statement:
"The whole antipollution crusade, at least in the United States, is an elitist thing, which is good mainly for the rich. Pollution avoidance requires a lower production of consumption goods so that either fewer wastes are produced in the first place or that resources can be diverted to making smokestack filters, treatment plants, and the like. The former approach hurts the poor by throwing them out of work; the latter hurts them by driving up the prices of consumption goods. Thus, well-to-do ecology crusaders are apt to drive the poor people right up the wall."

9. **Mr. A:** "Economic growth is a stupid idea: People seem to forget that the processes of production and consumption inevitably withdraw resources from nature and many of these (fossil fuels, minerals, and living space) are exhaustible and irreplaceable."
**Mr. B:** "I couldn't agree more. In addition, these same processes discard waste products into nature, and there are no unlimited reservoirs

to receive them. And waste disposal into the air, waters, or onto the land, which is so excessive as to make their subsequent uses harmful to life, becomes *pollution*. Economic growth accompanied by the exhaustion of irreplaceable resources and by pollution might better be regarded with shame rather than pride.''

Evaluate.

10. Suppose a government were determined to put an end to pollution. What kinds of policies could it pursue?

## Selected Readings

Fromm, Erich. *Escape from Freedom* (New York: Holt, Rinehart, & Winston, 1941), *Man for Himself* (New York: Holt, Rinehart, & Winston, 1947), *The Sane Society* (New York: Holt, Rinehart, & Winston, 1955), *Beyond the Chains of Illusion* (New York: Trident Press, 1962), *Socialist Humanism* (Garden City, NY: Doubleday, 1965), *You Shall Be As Gods* (New York: Holt, Rinehart, & Winston, 1966), *The Revolution of Hope* (New York: Harper & Row, 1968), and *The Crisis of Psychoanalysis* (Greenwich, CN: Fawcett, 1970). All these works deal with various forms of alienation.

Hayek, Friedrich. *The Constitution of Liberty* (Chicago: University of Chicago Press, 1960). A classic statement, by the 1974 co-winner of the Nobel Prize in Economics, of the meaning of liberty and coercion.

Kohler, Heinz. *Intermediate Microeconomics: Theory and Applications,* 2d ed. (Glenview, IL: Scott, Foresman and Co., 1986). Chapter 18 discusses alternative policies, in the context of the U.S. economy, designed to avoid the pollution of nature.

Marx, Karl. *Economic and Philosophical Manuscripts* (1844), most easily available in T. B. Bottomore, ed., *Karl Marx: Early Writings* (New York: McGraw-Hill, 1964), and in Erich Fromm, *Marx's Concept of Man* (New York: Frederick Ungar, 1961). Contains most of Marx's writings on alienation.

Weisskopf, Walter A. *Alienation and Economics* (New York: Dutton, 1971). A wide-ranging discussion of alienation.

## Computer Programs

The SYSTEMS personal computer diskette that accompanies this book contains one program of interest to this chapter: Program 4, ''Alienation,'' provides 12 multiple-choice questions about Chapter 4, along with immediate responses to incorrect answers.

# CHAPTER 5

# *Economic Systems: A Classification*

As the previous chapters have shown, all societies on earth face the problem of scarcity. Inevitably, therefore, people in all societies are engaged in a complicated process of making choices—choices by which they hope to achieve such goals as the full and efficient employment of their resources, an optimal rate of economic growth, an equitable and efficient allocation of goods, and, perhaps, even a state of affairs in which people have the greatest possible chance to develop their talents through creative work, to participate, on an equal basis with others, in all the major decisions affecting their lives, and to live in harmony with the natural world. The set of arrangements through which people in a society make choices about the allocation of their scarce resources and the apportionment of their scarce goods is called an **economic system.** One could also say that it is a social arrangement through which people cooperate with each other on matters affecting their economic welfare (which, inevitably, affects their noneconomic welfare as well).

It is not difficult to see that economic systems can take on innumerable forms. In the late 1980s, for example, over 150 independent nations existed on earth, and one could, in a sense, find a like number of economic systems because the arrangements people made concerning the allocation of resources and the apportionment of goods differed in many ways from one nation to the next. Indeed, were one to look into the past, one could find different economic systems still, now extinct. It is not the aim of this book, however, to study economic systems of the past (a matter more appropriately taken up by *economic history*), nor is it to study, one country at a time, the detailed variations of present-day economic systems (a matter typically covered by *economic area studies*). Instead, we seek to compare present-day economic systems, and for this purpose this chapter seeks to establish a limited number of abstract categories into which these systems might be placed. This will help us understand, in the remainder of the book, the essential nature of these systems more thoroughly than any detailed description ever could. The creation of such categories, however, is not an easy task.

## The Classification Problem

In principle, the classification of economic systems can be performed in the seemingly easy manner illustrated in Figure 5.1, "The Principle of Nested Sets." The most general category of economic systems, represented by the outermost $U$-shaped boundary in the graph, might be divided into two subcategories (such as socialist economic systems and capitalist economic systems), which are, in turn, represented by the two largest $U$-shaped figures nested just inside the outermost boundary. Each of these subcategories might then be divided further into sub-subcategories (such as centrally planned and market-directed socialist economic systems or perfectly competitive and government-regulated capitalist economic systems). Note the third layer of still smaller $U$-shaped figures. And the process can continue through further division of, say, the market-directed socialist economic system into one version with worker-managed enterprises and another one without that feature. Note the fourth layer of smallest $U$-shaped figures hinting at this possibility. When the classification process is completed, several actual economic systems might then be

**Figure 5.1**   The Principle of Nested Sets

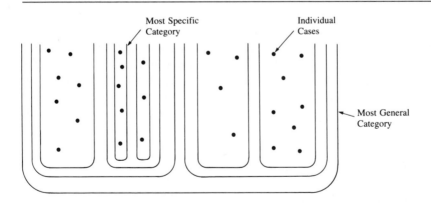

Most Specific
Category

Individual
Cases

Most General
Category

Real-world economic systems have many different attributes. Some of these are shared by most systems, others only by a few, and still others are unique to a single case. Yet, it is possible to create order from confusion by dividing existing systems into major categories, then subcategories, further sub-subcategories, and so on—taking care at each step that the new categories obtained by subdivision comprise all the individual cases contained in the previously existing broader category. In this graph, the various categories so obtained are shown by the $U$-shaped figures (also referred to as *nested sets*); the individual cases are represented by the large dots.

placed together (like the dots in Figure 5.1) into whatever specific category most closely resembles their particular features.

Unfortunately, economists—unlike other scientists with respect to *their* disciplines—have not been able to agree on a universally acceptable scheme of classifying the world's economic systems. Economists, it seems, are described well by this charming story of a little girl:[1]

> *Many dry river beds in central Arizona are filled with pebbles and rock fragments of infinite variety, resulting from earthcrust disturbances centuries ago. Once in such a spot I watched a little girl playing with attractive specimens selected from the millions of stones around her. She made little piles, first of all the white pebbles, then the red pebbles, the black pebbles, the multi-colored pebbles. But many were left which were of no dominant color. So she started again; she put the sharp-cornered pebbles in one pile and the round pebbles in another. Then she tried putting all the longish stones in one pile, the flat ones in a second pile, the chunky ones in a third pile. But this didn't work either, and by this time she was tired of playing and went into the house.*
>
> *Of course the little girl had no objective purpose in her classification; she merely was trying to comply with some inner demand for order which, like hope, seems to spring early as well as eternal in the human breast. Perhaps, too, she was attempting to gain some understanding of these little pieces of the universe by discovering classes in which individual specimens had membership. She was using common-sense methods to do this, and she was having the same difficulties which a more sophisticated person using scientific knowledge would have had. She knew nothing about mineralogy, or she might have sorted out the quartz, the obsidian, the calcite, the granite, the conglomerate; but she would still have been overwhelmed by the complexity of her task.*

Complex as it may be, we must attempt the task. As a matter of fact, among the many possibilities, two criteria have been employed quite often. These time-honored criteria classify economic systems by asking two crucial questions: Who effectively owns the resources and, therefore, has the power to make choices with them? What types of incentives are used to coordinate the choices of different resource owners? To these matters we turn in the following sections.

## Classification by Resource Ownership

As we noted in Chapter 1, all goods are produced with the help of three types of resources—human, natural, and capital. The ownership status of human resources, however, is not particularly helpful in differentiating present-day economic systems. Although it is possible for some people to own other people, as in a system of slavery or forced labor camps, such arrangements are absent or of negligible proportion in most countries at present. Hence, all the economic systems considered in this book will be ones in which most persons have exclusive control over their own labor power and in which, therefore, the ownership of human resources is widely dispersed over many individuals.

---

[1]Karl Menninger et al., *The Vital Balance* (New York: Viking, 1967), pp. 9–10.

So far as resource ownership is concerned, the major differences arising among the world's present economic systems concern natural and capital resources. (In some books, these nonhuman resources are simply referred to as the *means of production.*) Before classifying modern economic systems on the basis of property rights in natural and capital resources, it will be helpful, however, to clarify the concept of property rights itself.

A **property right** is the exclusive (but variously qualified) right to the use of something scarce. Such a right may be supported by tradition and accepted by voluntary consensus; more likely today it is established by law and protected by government force. For example, the formal holder of a property right to natural or capital resources can make choices concerning these resources and, with the help of government, can prevent all others from making such choices. This formal property right, however, has many components, called *substantive rights,* that indicate what kinds of choices can and cannot be made by the holder of the property right. Among the substantive rights are the custody right, the usufruct right, the alienation right, and more. The *custody right* to a resource is the right to hold it and do things with it. The custody right to a piece of land, for example, may include the right to keep it idle or to farm it or to mine the minerals below it, while excluding the right to fly over it, burn down its trees, build houses on it, or dam up the stream crossing it. Similarly, the custody right to a factory may include the right to produce all kinds of products in it, while excluding the right to burn the factory down or to operate machines and use materials in it that endanger the health and safety of workers and neighbors. The *usufruct right* is the right to claim the fruits of using a resource; for example, the right to appropriate the wheat grown on a piece of land, the coal mined from it, or the sewing machines produced in a factory. The *alienation right,* finally, is the right to transfer one's property right (or selected components of it) to someone else, either temporarily or permanently. Think of renting out a factory or piece of land, of putting a manager in charge of it, of selling it outright or giving it away, of bequeathing it at the time of death.

The foregoing discussion, brief as it is, clearly shows that property rights are anything but simple; additionally, they are not cast in stone for all time to come: They are extremely complex *bundles* of rights, typically created by and often modified by government. (Close-Ups 5.1 through 5.4 at the end of this chapter give examples of the emergence of new property rights in recent years.) Moreover, as time passes, the formal holders of property rights may effectively exercise their rights (directly or through managers), or they may find themselves sharing bits and pieces of their rights increasingly with other people and, perhaps, even losing components of their rights to others entirely. Then one can wonder: Who is the true owner—the formal holder of the property right or those others who have effectively appropriated some of the substantive rights? Consider how labor unions may strike a successful bargain or how government may pass a law that places worker representatives on the corporate board of directors; this certainly reduces the stockholders' (indirect) custody rights. Consider how corporate stockholders may even lose such indirect custody rights entirely to a self-perpetuating managerial group. Consider how corporate stockholders may come to share their usufruct right—

paying bonuses to hired managers, a profit share to workers, and taxes to the government. Examples such as these could be multiplied without end and for every society on earth. Like the pebbles in that dry Arizona river bed, the possibilities for sharing the numerous components of property rights to nonhuman resources are near infinite. How then can one possibly answer the question posed earlier: Who effectively owns these resources and, therefore, has the power to make choices with them? One approach, embodied in Table 5.1, is to focus on some of the major arrangements concerning nonhuman property rights in the world today, without even trying to cover every conceivable possibility.

As the left-hand column of Table 5.1 indicates, two major arrangements stand out: First, the total of natural and capital resources is divided into numerous subsets the formal ownership of which is widely dispersed among many private individuals. Second, the formal ownership of natural and capital resources is vested in groups of people, possibly even in all of a society's people as a group.

Now, focus on the right-hand column; it indicates some of the major alternatives concerning the effective control of nonhuman resources. Case 1a describes a situation in which private individuals are formal owners, while the same or other private individuals exercise effective control. Consider the owner-managed single proprietorship; consider the corporation run by a manager who has usurped most of the powers of individual stockholders. Case 1b describes a situation in which private individuals are formal owners, but they have joined their resources with those of other such individuals and are exercising control jointly as well. Consider the partnership (Elder Jones and Son; Cahillane Brothers; Blair, Kohler, Nicholson and Co.); consider the corporation run by a manager strictly controlled by individual stockholders. Case 2a describes a situation in which groups of people (or even all people as a group) are the formal owners, while a central government is in fact

**Table 5.1**    Classifying Modern Economic Systems: The Ownership of Natural and Capital Resources

| *The Formal Ownership of Natural and Capital Resources Resides in:* | *The Effective Control of Natural and Capital Resources Is Exercised by:* |
|---|---|
| 1. Private individuals | a. Private individuals <br> b. Self-selected small groups of private individuals |
| 2. Groups of people (possibly even in all of a society's people as a group) | a. A central government <br> b. Designated individuals or small groups <br> c. All group members jointly |

This table represents one possible (and admittedly imperfect) way of applying the lesson of Figure 5.1 to modern economic systems. True enough, no actual system will fit perfectly into any one classification shown here (1a, 1b, 2a, and so forth); each actual system is bound to exhibit a mixture of these features. However, economic systems in which arrangement (1) *predominates* may be called *capitalist;* those in which arrangement (2) predominates, *socialist.*

exercising control. Consider public enterprises (rare in the United States, more frequent in Western Europe, ubiquitous in Eastern Europe). Case 2b describes a situation in which groups of people (or even all people as a group) are the formal owners of nonhuman resources as well, while effective control over many subsets of these resources is exercised by designated individuals (such as appointed or elected managers) or small groups of people (such as all the people actually working with these resources). Consider the Soviet collective farm or the Yugoslav labor-managed firm. Case 2c, finally, describes a situation in which groups of people (or even all people as a group) are the formal owners of nonhuman resources, while the effective control is exercised by all group members jointly. Consider a commune.

Any actual economic system will undoubtedly encompass examples of several or even all of the cases just discussed, but usually case 1 or case 2 will *predominate.* In the rest of this book, we will follow common practice and refer to any economic system in which the formal ownership of natural and capital resources resides predominantly in private individuals as **capitalism.** We will similarly designate any economic system in which the formal ownership of natural and capital resources resides predominantly in groups of people, possibly even in all of a society's people as a group, as **socialism.**

Yet, just like the little girl in our earlier story, we may have all kinds of quarrels to pick with our first classification attempt. We may want to abandon that attempt and start all over again. Consider the next section.

## Classification by Incentives for Coordination

In every modern economy, the specialized activities of different people must somehow be integrated into a coherent, interlocking pattern. Yet, when different people own resources and independently make choices with them, it is possible for these choices to be inconsistent with each other. Suppose all the individual owners of human resources decided to employ them in the production of goods 5 days a week between 8 A.M. and 4 P.M., while the effective owners of nonhuman resources decided to employ these nonhuman resources 7 days a week, 24 hours a day. Since human resources typically have to be used together with nonhuman ones, this inconsistency must somehow be resolved.

Or suppose that some resource owners employed their resources to produce iron ore, while others wished to make steel into cars, but nobody was planning to turn ore into steel.

Or suppose that various resource owners managed to produce just the ore and steel needed to make cars, but people would much rather have shoes.

Clearly, there are billions of possibilities for separate choices thus not fitting into a well-coordinated whole. That is why every economic system needs some type of incentive to guide people into acting in such a way that their actions mesh with those of other people. Consider three major types of incentive.

## Money

One can try to arrange matters in such a way that people are always free to exchange for money any scarce resource or good that they own. Thus, owners of resources who wish to make choices requiring compatible choices by other owners of resources can approach those others with a conditional offer: "If you do something nice for me (namely, supply your human resources to work my nonhuman ones from 4 P.M. to midnight, or turn iron ore into steel or make shoes rather than cars), I will do something nice for you (namely, give you so many units of money)." As a result of billions of such conditional offers being made, people will come to learn about each others' preferences and capabilities (will come to learn, that is, about those marginal rates of substitution and transformation that we met in Chapter 2). As long as people's choices are inconsistent with each other, the units of money offered will change and people will adjust their behavior to these changing prices until, in the end, their choices fit together perfectly.

## Command

One can also try to arrange matters in such a way that some people have the right to give specific orders to other people, telling them what to do or not to do. In such a scheme, another motto is followed: "If you do something nice for me, I will refrain from doing something bad to you." By threatening others with harm for noncompliance, these others can be coerced into acting or not acting in specific ways that remove the type of inconsistencies noted above—by resolving them, of course, in favor of whoever issues the command.

## Love

One can, finally, try to make unnecessary the external incentives of money or command by promoting reliance on the internal incentive of good will or even love. Instead of being made aware of other people's wishes by their offers of money or their direct command (accompanied by threat of harm), the advocates of this arrangement suggest that people train themselves to be observant of all others and, when able, serve them voluntarily. "Because I love you, I will do something nice for you," they will say. With no strings attached, they will shift their resources into working from 4 P.M. to midnight, into making steel from iron ore, into making shoes rather than cars—or whatever else serving others "obviously" requires.

## Conclusion

We have, thus, discovered another possible approach to classifying economic systems. If we wished, we could abandon Table 5.1 and replace it with yet another table that classified economic systems on the basis of the three types of incentives just discussed that can help people fit their separate activities into a well-coordinated whole. We would have to recognize, of course, that each one of these incentives could be found in every actual economy. Consider how people in the United States continually exchange resources and goods for money in a multitude of markets and how their actions are always guided by the prices prevailing therein. Yet, in the same United States, the command principle is at work as well; consider the tax collector or the military draft. And the love principle can be found no less; consider volunteer work or the March of Dimes. The same sort of thing is true for all the other economic systems in the world. Nevertheless, the three types of incentives are often present to vastly different degrees. Accordingly, we could classify economic systems as *market economies* if the money incentive was predominant, as *command economies* if the command principle was most prevalent, and perhaps even as *economies of love* if the rule of love was the strongest of the three.

## Combining Ownership and Incentive Criteria

Now we are ready to discover the basic nature of the present world's major economic systems by considering possible combinations of the ownership and incentive criteria just discussed. Table 5.2 has been constructed to facilitate the discussion.

### Market Capitalism

Consider row 1 of Table 5.2 representing a state of affairs in which effective control over many subsets of a society's nonhuman resources is held by many separate individuals or groups (who may or may not be the formal owners). Clearly, their separate choices can be coordinated by voluntary exchanges, in markets of all sorts, for money (column A); this possibility has given rise to an economic system called **market capitalism.** Its idealized and actual versions, respectively, will be discussed in chapters 12 through 14 of this book.

On the other hand, it is unthinkable for command (column B) to play any significant role if the ownership of resources corresponds to the situation in row 1. This is so because the issuer of central commands, rather than many individuals or small groups, would exercise effective control over resources. Thus a row 1/column B combination is a logical impossibility, a fact shown by an *X* in the corresponding cell.

The row 1/column C combination, finally, is not logically impossible, but it would certainly be practically unworkable in any large group of people. The reason is simple: Once the size of any group expands much beyond the nuclear or extended family and comes to include many hundreds, thousands, and millions of people, it becomes impossible for any one member of the group to be aware of the preferences and capabilities of others. There is nothing sinister about this fact, nor has it anything to do with people not wanting to love others. One simply cannot love those whom one does not know! The relevant knowledge can, however, be supplied by the external incentive of money: As many unknown people who crave apples spend lots of money on them, they bid up the price of apples and thereby signal a multitude of unknown resource owners to use their resources to produce apples rather than

**Table 5.2** Classifying Modern Economic Systems: Resource Ownership versus Coordination Incentives

| *The Formal Ownership of Natural and Capital Resources Resides in:* | *The Major Incentive Used to Coordinate Choices Is:* | | |
| --- | --- | --- | --- |
| | *Money* (A) | *Command* (B) | *Love* (C) |
| 1. Private individuals, while effective control is exercised by private individuals also or by self-selected small groups of them | Market capitalism | ╳ | ? |
| 2. Groups of people, possibly even in all of a society's people as a group, while effective control is exercised by | | | |
| a. A central government | ? | Centralized socialism | ? |
| b. Designated individuals or small groups | Market socialism | ╳ | ? |
| c. All group members jointly | ? | ? | Communal socialism |

This table identifies general types or *models* of economic systems by combining the criteria of resource ownership and coordination incentives. No real-world economic system fits any of these categories perfectly, but all actual systems tend to come closer to one of these models than to the rest.

something else. In a large group of people, such knowledge cannot be gained by resource owners through personal observation of the daily lives of other people. In fact, no society has ever designed its economic system with the row 1/column C combination, even though one can imagine it working in a very small population. Hence the question mark.

## Centralized Socialism

Now consider row 2a, a state of affairs in which effective control over a society's nonhuman resources resides in a central government. Individuals still own their own human resources, but they own no other resources, and even the extent to which they receive education, health care, and vocational training depends on the government. It should not be surprising under the circumstances that exchange for money (A) will play a subordinated role (although it is not unthinkable), that the rule of love (C) will encounter the same difficulties discussed earlier (hence the question marks in row 2a, columns A and C), and that commands (B) issued by the central government will play a major role in coordinating choices. Indeed, the resultant economic system of **centralized socialism** has been an important one. Its idealized and actual versions, respectively, will be discussed in chapters 6 and 7 of this book (and, to some extent, in chapters 10 and 11 as well).

## Market Socialism

Now consider row 2b, a state of affairs in which effective control over many subsets of a society's nonhuman resources resides in individuals or small groups of individuals. This situation differs from that noted in row 1 only with respect to formal ownership. Hence, the results are the same as in row 1: The use of command would be logically inconsistent; the rule of love unlikely in any but the smallest society; the presence of exchange for money likely to be a powerful organizer of cooperation among people. The resultant economic system is called **market socialism.** Its idealized and actual versions, respectively, will be discussed in chapters 8 and 9 of this book (and, to some extent, in chapters 10 and 11 as well).

## Communal Socialism

There remains the state of affairs illustrated in row 2c, in which effective control over a society's nonhuman resources resides in the entire group of people making up the society. This must necessarily mean that everyone participates in all decisions about the use of nonhuman resources and that the society is a very small one. If it were not, everyone could not possibly participate in all decisions about nonhuman resources; hence, situation 2c would turn into 2b or 2a. Given a very small society and truly joint decisions about nonhuman resources, it is very unlikely that money or command will come to play major roles (hence the question marks in columns A and B), and it is very likely that joint decisions will also be made about the use of individually owned human resources and that love will rule supreme. Not surprisingly, examples of such **communal socialism** (column C) are rare. Chapter 10 will consider two examples, as well as two recent attempts to extend this type of system to larger societies.

## Alternative Classifications Rejected

Alternative classifications of economic systems abound but will be rejected here. Real-world economic systems, inevitably, are mixtures of the four general system types found in Table 5.2. Still, the classification of pure systems with the help of dominant ownership and incentive criteria will go a long way to explain the real world, for all real-world systems resemble closely one or the other of the four systems found in our table. It should be noted, however, that in the real world many alternative definitions of socialism abound. These have been rejected here because they contribute to confusion rather than understanding. Consider what is involved:

In the 1980s, the governments of over 50 of the world's nations called themselves socialist. Between them, these nations comprised about 40 percent of both the world's territory and the world's population. But what a strange group of countries was involved! They included Soviet-style dictatorships and U.S.-type democracies, constitutional republics and hereditary monarchies. Socialism, it seemed, ruled from the Soviet Union and its East European allies to Afghanistan, Mongolia, China, and North Korea; from Kampuchea, Laos, Vietnam, and Burma to Albania, Yugoslavia, Cuba, and Nicaragua; from Algeria, Libya, Syria, and Iraq to Yemen, Ethiopia, Zambia, and Angola. Indeed, depending on the party in power, the list has recently included Portugal, Spain, and Greece; France, West Germany, and Great Britain; Denmark, Norway, and Sweden. And this entire list could almost be doubled in length! Clearly, all these countries have only one thing in common: They have found it *convenient* to flaunt the socialist label. Beyond that, everyone defines socialism in a different way.

To some, indeed, the essence of socialism is the formal collective ownership of nonhuman resources (a definition accepted in this book), but there is no agreement as to which of the three forms of effective ownership (found in rows 2a through 2c of Table 5.2) represents "true" socialism. To others, socialism is the downgrading of markets and money ("a society based on cooperation instead of competition") and the adoption of centralized command as the prime organizing principle of economic life ("the rational organization of human society according to the most scientific, the most modern, and the most efficient methods"). To others still, the essence of socialism is the abolition of all bureaucracy and commands and the appearance of the rule of love ("socialism is love for your brother; socialism is linking hearts and hands, love and togetherness—that's what it means").

And then there are many who prefer to define socialism by neither the criterion of ownership nor by the type of incentive dominant in society, but by the type of goal to be pursued. "Socialism," they might say, "is the end of unemployment." Or, "It is rapid economic growth." Or, "It is the community of men in search of distributive justice," or, "Socialism is the end of alienation," or even, "Socialism is the end of scarcity."

Thus, everyone imagines socialism in his or her own way, frequently thinking nothing of combining features that are clearly incompatible with each other. Indeed, one favored definition of socialism, and of capitalism, comes to this: "Whenever something is good in a society, it is socialism; whenever something is bad, it is capitalism."

Obviously, no serious analysis of capitalism and socialism can adopt such a procedure. Hence, this book defines these systems not by their choice of goals or even by their success or failure in reaching specified goals, but by the major institutional features listed in Table 5.2: the effective control over natural and capital resources (which implies who makes choices with them) and the incentives used to coordinate the choices of different people. The remainder of the book considers to what extent which goals discussed in previous chapters are likely to be reached by various types of economic systems. Then the reader can decide which system he or she prefers—and can give it any name he or she likes!

CLOSE-UP 5.1

## The Painful Birth of Property Rights: The Law of the Sea

In the absence of a government that assigns property rights, the law of the jungle is likely to prevail; that is, the strong are likely to appropriate scarce resources. The world's oceans, which cover 70 percent of the earth's surface, are a case in point.

Because there has never been a world government, property rights in the ocean have been virtually nonexistent. Coastal nations used to claim sovereignty over a zone that extended 3 miles from the coast (the distance that a 17th century land-based cannon could shoot) and later claimed sovereignty over a 12-mile zone. Beyond that, "freedom of the seas" was the rule. Anyone was free to use the oceans as cheap routes of transport or for fishing, whaling, and the like.

During the 20th century, however, significant improvements in maritime technology have produced long-range fishing fleets that can even pinpoint schools of fish electronically. It did not take long for conflicts of interest to arise among the developed nations (the fishing fleets of which meet each other on the richest fishing grounds around the world) and between the developed nations and the poor nations (many of which are finding that the fish near their coasts are approaching extinction).

This conflict has been exacerbated by the discovery of oil and gas on the continental shelves and in the deep sea, and by the discovery of consolidated minerals, available in potato-sized nodules that lie scattered on the Pacific Ocean floor but at depths of 12,000 to 20,000 feet. Nodules of phosphate, ferromanganese, and manganese (with cobalt, copper, and nickel) have attracted particular interest. Additional conflicts have arisen about the uses of oceans as dumping sites, about the accidental pollution of coastal zones as a consequence of oil drilling, and about the uses of over 100 straits for merchant and naval transit.

Given the military and economic strength of the developed nations, some of these conflicts could easily be resolved in favor of the strong. For example, because certain developed nations (notably the United States, West Germany, and Japan) alone have the capability of mining deep-sea nodules, these nations possess de facto property rights. The poor countries, hoping for a share in the ocean's Eldorado-like riches, have, however, pressed for an international agreement on property rights in the sea. In 1970, a United Nations resolution declared that the resources of the deep sea are "the common heritage of mankind," not just hunting grounds for the developed nations. This resolution was interpreted to signify not that every nation had an equal right to stake a claim to a mineral site on the ocean floor, but that every nation had an equal right of ownership in the sea bed and, therefore, an equal claim on the financial proceeds from a mineral site regardless of who did the mining. Not surprisingly, a 158-nation U.N. conference on the Law of the Sea remained deadlocked for over a decade. In 1982, over U.S. opposition, a treaty was voted in, but many industrialized nations refused to sign it. (The treaty handed the sea bed, and thus more than two thirds of the earth's surface, over to an International Sea Bed Authority that could restrict access to would-be miners and also require them to share their technology and revenues with poor countries.)

In the meantime, coastal nations, in a sudden rush of unilateral declarations, have claimed exclusive rights to economic zones extending 200 nautical miles outward from their coasts. After initial challenges, this new limit of sovereignty has become the norm, at least for fishing and oil-drilling operations. However, even in these zones conflicts persist on such matters as shipping lanes, overflights, and marine scientific research.

*Sources:* Walter Berns, "Mining the Sea for a Brave New World," and Northcutt Ely, "One OPEC Is Enough," *Regulation,* November/December 1981, pp. 14–24; Stephen Chapman, "Underwater Plunder," *The Best of Business,* Fall 1982, pp. 105–8; Bernard H. Oxman, David D. Caron, and Charles L. O. Buderi, eds., *Law of the Sea: U.S. Policy Dilemma* (San Francisco: ICS Press, 1983).

## CLOSE-UP 5.2

## The Painful Birth of Property Rights: The Moon's Riches

In 1979, after seven years' labor, an international treaty on the exploitation of the moon's resources was approved by the 47-member United Nations Committee on Outer Space. The agreement seeks to ensure that smaller powers lacking the ability to explore space will have a stake in the mineral wealth of the moon and other celestial bodies by proclaiming these resources to be the "common heritage of mankind." Any commercial exploitation, however, is considered to be decades away.

Agreement on the new treaty was stalled for years because the Soviet Union was unwilling to accept the concept that the moon's resources should be a common heritage. The third world countries pressed for a commitment from the space powers similar to the one they sought on the mining of sea bed minerals.

The controversial article designating the moon and its resources as "a common heritage" stipulates that neither the surface nor subsurface shall become the property of any country, although countries retain the right to conduct lunar explorations. Once commercial exploitation "is about to become feasible," the treaty commits countries to establishing an international regime to see that the benefits of lunar exploitation are shared equitably.

*Source: The New York Times,* July 4, 1979.

## CLOSE-UP 5.3

## The Painful Birth of Property Rights: The Electromagnetic Spectrum

Like the air, the world's radio spectrum used to be taken for granted. But it is a very scarce resource now. If everyone who wished to just broadcast freely, there would be serious overcrowding and bad reception around the globe. As a result, property rights in radio frequencies (for voice communication, navigation, and data transmission) are sought by the military, by space agencies, by multinational manufacturing corporations and international banks, by airlines and ocean shippers, by radio and television broadcasters, by amateurs, and by many others.

In 1979, a 140-nation General World Administrative Radio Conference convened in Geneva to assign property rights in radio frequencies for the remainder of this century. A conflict emerged because nations wanted more frequencies than are available but also because nations had ideological differences. While Western, developed nations favored the free global flow of information, the poor and Soviet-bloc nations favored a "new world information order" that would enable them to control strictly all information flows within their borders. They linked agreement on the allocation of scarce frequencies to agreements restricting the flow of information. They argued that the beaming of radio and television broadcasts by one country to another should occur only with the latter's consent and that the transmission of news via satellite should occur only with the consent of the country in which the news originates.

*Source: The New York Times,* September 23, 1979, p. E8; September 15, 1979, p. A1.

## CLOSE-UP 5.4

## The Painful Birth of Property Rights: The Geostationary Arc

A precise orbit in space, positioned about 22,300 miles from earth and going around the equator, has been likened to a "mouth-watering delicacy" for the telecommunications industry. It is easy to see why. When a satellite occupies this orbit, its velocity not only perfectly offsets the earth's gravitational pull but also exactly matches the 24-hour rotation of the earth. As viewed from earth, the satellite appears to be stationary and can be seen from half the globe. Earth stations, therefore, need aim their antennae only once to be able to provide long-distance communications via satellite much more cheaply than by any other alternative. (The alternative to satellite telephone service, for instance, is a complex system of terrestrial microwave facilities that includes large numbers of transmitters, amplifiers, and relay stations.) Not surprisingly, telephone companies, television and radio broadcasters, weather forecasters, newspaper publishers, and many others want to own a piece of this galactic real estate.

Unfortunately, the arc can accommodate only a finite number of satellites. Given the worldwide desire to use the arc, scarcity has appeared. To deal with this scarcity, the United Nations International Telecommunications Union has divvied up the worldwide arc. The U.S. share of the arc has been further divided between governmental and private uses by the Commerce Department's National Telecommunications and Information Administration. The Federal Communications Commission, in turn, has allocated orbital slots among the many private would-be users. The latter division has been controversial, indeed. First, the FCC must decide on the number of slots it distributes, which involves the issue of the allowable spacing of satellites within the U.S. portion of the arc so as to avoid collisions and signal interference. Second, the FCC must decide on the method of distributing the slots. Should they be handed out as free gifts to a few lucky users (on a first-come, first-served basis, perhaps)? Should they be auctioned off to the highest bidder? At the time of this writing, the matter remained unresolved; a 1982 auction of seven satellite channels by one earlier recipient, RCA, was later invalidated by the FCC. (That auction had brought in $90.1 million.)

*Sources:* Molly K. Macauley and Paul R. Portney, "Property Rights in Orbit," *Regulation,* July/August 1984, pp. 14–18 and 51–52; *The New York Times,* December 1, 1981, p. D2, January 28, 1982, p. D4, January 29, 1982, p. 12.

## Summary

1. The set of arrangements through which people in a society make choices about the allocation of their scarce resources and the apportionment of their scarce goods is called an *economic system*. The present world contains a great diversity of such systems; classifying them according to a limited number of abstract categories helps us to escape a morass of descriptive detail and to focus on essential differences.
2. Such classification, however, is not an easy task, and economists have not been able to agree on a universally acceptable scheme of classifying the world's economic systems.
3. One possible classification scheme is based on this question: Who effectively owns the resources and, therefore, has the power to make choices with them? The distribution of property rights in *nonhuman* resources is particularly helpful in differentiating present-day economic systems. Two major arrangements stand out: First, *capitalism*—the total of natural and capital resources is divided into numerous subsets the formal ownership of which is widely dispersed among many private individuals, while the effective control is exercised by private individuals or self-selected small groups of them. Second, *socialism*—the formal ownership of natural and capital resources is vested in groups of people, possibly even in all of a society's people as a group, while the effective control is exercised either by a central government or by designated individuals or small groups or by all the group members jointly.
4. An alternative classification scheme is based on another question: What types of incentives are used to coordinate the choices of different resource owners? Three possible arrangements stand out in this case: the external incentives of money or command and the internal incentive of love.
5. One can also combine the ownership and incentive criteria. This procedure yields four pure types of model economic systems: market capitalism, centralized socialism, market socialism, and communal socialism. All of the world's actual economic systems approximate one of these four models more closely than the other three.

6. Alternative classifications of economic systems abound, as do alternative definitions of socialism. These alternatives are rejected; they often contribute to confusion rather than enlightenment.

## Key Terms

capitalism
centralized socialism
communal socialism
economic system

market capitalism
market socialism
property right
socialism

## Questions and Problems

1. Table 5.2 identifies four major classes of model economic systems into which present-day actual economic systems might be fit. Yet, were one to look into the past, one could find different economic systems still, now extinct. Can you think of any? Explain.

2. Economists seem to have trouble coming up with a universally accepted scheme of classifying the world's economic systems. Are other sciences doing any better in producing a taxonomy of their subject matter? Explain.

3. Comment on the following statement:
   "I have found an easy way to classify today's economic systems: When the government owns all the means of production—from farms, forests, and coal mines to factories, railroads, and telephone systems to hotels, houses, and stores—we have socialism. When all these things are privately owned, we have capitalism."

4. Comment on the following statement:
   "I have found an easy way to classify today's economic systems: When the economy is centrally planned by government, we have socialism; when people's activities are coordinated by markets, we have capitalism."

5. Comment on the following statement:
   "I have found an easy way to classify today's economic systems: When the level of government expenditures is high, we have socialism; when it is low, we have capitalism."

6. Comment on the following statement:
   "I have found an easy way to classify today's economic systems: When material incentives abound throughout society (wages, profits, bribes, in-kind subsidies, and the like), we have capitalism; when nonmaterial incentives abound (medals, praise, prison, ridicule, and the like), we have socialism."

7. **Mr. A:** "The comparative study of model economic systems, which are inspired by the real world but contain features that do not exist and are not likely ever to exist, can lead to nothing but bias."

   **Ms. B:** "The comparative study of actual economic systems, which are so complex that they differ from every model as well as every other existing system, can be just as biased."

   Evaluate this exchange.

8. **Mr. A:** "Although it is interesting to speculate about human relationships based solely on monetary incentives, in fact, such a system could not survive unless it contained islands within which command or love reigned supreme."

   **Ms. B:** "I would put it this way: Although it is interesting to speculate about human relationships based solely on command, in fact, a command system could not survive unless it was supplemented by love or monetary incentives."

   Evaluate this exchange.

9. Comment on the following statement:

   "Although it is interesting to speculate about human relationships based solely on love, in fact, a love system could not survive unless it was supplemented by monetary incentives or command."

10. **Mr. A:** "As the text notes, a large number of countries refer to themselves as socialist even though their economic systems differ as day does from night. Maybe we shouldn't apply the term *socialism* to any of them."

    **Ms. B:** "You've hit the nail on the head. Most countries in the world today are *capitalist* in the true Marxian sense of the term: While the means of production are controlled by a small percentage of the population, the vast majority of people have nothing but their labor to sell. In order to live, they must rent themselves out for wages to those who control natural and capital resources."

    Evaluate this exchange.

## Selected Readings

Baudin, Louis. *A Socialist Empire: The Incas of Peru* (Princeton, NJ: Van Nostrand, 1961). The story of an extinct economic system.

Boulding, Kenneth E. *The Economy of Love and Fear* (Belmont, CA: Wadsworth, 1973). Introduces the distinction, also used in this chapter, among the incentives of money, command, and love.

Dalton, George, ed. *Tribal and Peasant Economies* (Garden City, NY: Natural History Press, 1967). A discussion of "primitive" economies.

Eucken, Walter. "On the Theory of the Centrally Administered Economy: An Analysis of the German Experiment," *Economica*, May 1948, pp. 79–100, and

August 1948, pp. 173–93. A detailed analysis of the operation of the Nazi German economy.

Firth, Raymond. *The Elements of Social Organization* (London: Watts, 1951). A discussion of tribal economies.

Furubotn, Eirik and Svetozar Pejovich. "Property Rights and Economic Theory: A Survey of Recent Literature." *Journal of Economic Literature,* December 1972, pp. 1137–62. An extensive survey of the emerging economic theory of property rights. The same authors also edited *The Economics of Property Rights* (Cambridge, MA: Ballinger, 1974).

Holesovsky, Vaclav. "Revision of the Taxonomy of 'Socialism': A Radical Proposal," *Association for Comparative Economic Studies (ACES) Bulletin,* Winter 1974, pp. 19–40. Suggests, among other things, that Soviet-type economies be referred to as examples of state capitalism rather than socialism.

Laidler, Harry W. *History of Socialism* (New York: Crowell, 1968). A detailed comparative survey of all forms of socialism that were ever proposed or that ever existed. An excellent reference work.

Malinowski, Bronislaw. *The Argonauts of the Western Pacific* (London: Routledge, 1922). A discussion of tribal economies.

Montias, John Michael. *The Structure of Economic Systems* (New Haven, CT: Yale University Press, 1976). A sophisticated exposition of the modern approach to defining economic systems in terms of alternative series of characteristics, such as property ownership, incentives for coordination, and so on.

Pryor, Frederic L. *A Guidebook to the Comparative Study of Economic Systems* (Englewood Cliffs, NJ: Prentice-Hall, 1985). Contains an abundance of material that a would-be taxonomist could use to classify economic systems.

Wittvogel, Karl A. *Oriental Despotism: A Comparative Study in Total Power* (New Haven, CT: Yale University Press, 1957). A discussion of ancient economic systems, such as China, Egypt, and Peru.

## Computer Programs

The SYSTEMS personal computer diskette that accompanies this book contains one program of interest to this chapter: Program 5, "Classifying Economic Systems," provides 12 multiple-choice questions about Chapter 5, along with immediate responses to incorrect answers.

# PART 2

# Socialist Economic Systems

The chapters of Part 2 include two idealized versions of socialist economic systems: the models of centralized socialism and of market socialism. Each of these models, in turn, is contrasted with a real-world economy (of the Soviet Union and Yugoslavia, respectively) that is generally believed to resemble the model in question. In addition, the issue of whether communal socialism might be a viable alternative to both centralized and market socialism is addressed, and the current movements for economic reform in socialist countries throughout the world are studied as well.

# CHAPTER 6

# *Centralized Socialism: A Model*

As its title indicates, this chapter does not deal with an actual economic system. On the contrary, it engages us in a *thought experiment* wherein we imagine an idealized system that has never existed in the past, does not now exist, and is unlikely to exist in the future. Yet, a study of this chapter is far from pointless. As we imagine a nonexisting world strictly governed by the ideas of those who advocate centralized socialism—and as we assess this world by means of the performance criteria developed in Part 1 of this book—we come to understand the manifold implications of these ideas (which are rarely obvious). At the same time, we lay the foundation for understanding the nature of actual economic systems that are inspired by this type of model, yet are, to varying degrees, but imperfect copies thereof. The imaginary economic world we are about to enter has three major characteristics:

First, it is a world of pure socialism in which the formal ownership not of some or most, but of *all* natural and capital resources resides in different groups of people or even jointly in the single group of all the people making up society. (In real-world socialist economies, such group ownership predominates, but some private ownership exists as well.)

Second, we are imagining a world of perfectly centralized socialism in which the effective control over nonhuman resources is exercised exclusively by the central government. As a result, individual citizens who formally own their labor power, but who cannot produce a thing without the use of complementary natural and capital resources that the government controls, are pretty much obliged to do the government's bidding. Thus, all economic power is *concentrated* in government hands. It alone has the capacity to make and enforce decisions—from the most general to the most minute—on the allocation of scarce resources and the apportionment of scarce goods; there is no private decision making at all. (In real-world economies of centralized socialism, the economic power of the central government predominates, but some economic power is also exercised by private individuals and groups.)

Third, we are about to consider a world in which the central government, relying on a common plan that specifies everyone's future actions in detail, coordinates the separate economic activities of all people by verbal commands exclusively. The people to whom these commands are addressed, in turn, execute the government's will passively and obediently. (In real-world economies of centralized socialism, verbal commands may be common, but many actions of people are also determined by other types of incentives, especially monetary ones, that are set up by government or created in a variety of markets.)

While it is, thus, easy enough to outline the broad features of any economic system one cares to imagine, filling in the details is quite another matter. That task is much more complicated, as we shall see in the remainder of this chapter. We begin by noting a universal problem.

## The Coordination Problem

In every one of the world's nations today, individuals produce little, if anything, of what they consume; they consume little, if anything, of what they themselves produce. They are part of a grand division of labor. They exchange most or all of their own production with others who similarly specialize. These others, furthermore, are apt to be not a few identifiable persons, but literally hundreds of thousands of unknown people: farmers in Kansas or the Ukraine, factory workers in Georgia, Michigan, Sweden, tin miners in Bolivia, sheep ranchers in Australia, oil workers in the North Sea, typists in California. All these, in one way or another, help provide each of us with the goods we do consume.

Now consider this: As people interact in their economic activities, not only within each productive enterprise and nation, but also with people throughout the world, everything that one person does comes to intermingle with the actions of all others in an endless web. Any one decision is intricately bound up with all other decisions. Any one action requires, directly and indirectly, appropriate complementary actions by thousands of other people. To picture the incredible interdependence present in any modern economy, just think of a simple good—for example, a cake—and how it typically comes to you. Imagine the countless people and the countless types of natural and capital resources that are necessary to produce the ingredients of a cake. And trace in your mind the countless stages through which each of these ingredients must travel before they turn into a cake. Consider how many more resources are involved in bringing it to you. Then think of the many other goods you consume, every day. How easy it would be for something to go wrong in the complicated sets of events that create these goods and transport them through space and time!

All economic systems, therefore, must, first of all, see to it that things do not go wrong and that the activities of every specializing person mesh perfectly with those of all other such persons. Every economic system must somehow solve the **coordination problem,** the problem of fitting the specialized activities of all the people engaged in the division of labor into a well-coordinated whole. The solution we are about to discuss in this chapter is not the only conceivable one, but it is easiest to understand; it also tends to be the first solution that people consider who have never before confronted the coordination problem. Above all, it is also the solution the advocates of centralized socialism have in mind.

The separate economic activities of people engaged in a division of labor can be most easily coordinated, they say, by the deliberate application of reason on the part of a central planner or manager who then issues verbal directives to subordinates. This **managerial coordination** is also known as the system of the **Visible Hand.** Ideally, the central manager creates a **central plan,** a document that precisely specifies the economic activities to be performed by every individual in society during a future period. This social blueprint is supposed to account for the concrete actions of all individuals at every moment and to ensure that the separate activities of all people mesh perfectly. Thus, the document takes account of the fact that every output, by requiring inputs, affects other outputs, and so on in an ever dwindling chain. For example, if the central manager decided on producing locomotives, all the necessary inputs would be assigned to the assembly plant. But the manager would also assign just the right number of other people, raw materials, and machines to produce just the right amounts of iron ore needed to make just the right amount of steel to make the locomotives. And, similarly, the manager would order production of just the right amount of fuel to make just the right amount of electricity to run the furnaces that make the steel. . . . Once the plan was made, specific orders would be issued to all individuals, who would be expected to do nothing but obey. The entire economy would, thus, be run like one giant factory, by the visible hand of a manager.

Furthermore, argue the advocates of centralized socialism, reason and science would solve the coordination problem without undue strain. What seems infinitely complex at first sight could in fact be tackled easily with proper mathematical methods and an appropriate battery of electronic computers. Let us consider what they have in mind.

## Leontief's Input-Output Analysis

One way of solving the coordination problem is suggested by **input-output analysis,** a mathematical technique designed to visualize the internal structure of an economy and to study interdependencies in it. This type of analysis was first introduced some 50 years ago by Wassily Leontief (see Biography 6.1 at the end of this chapter). However, as Analytical Example 6.1, "The Economic Effects of Disarmament," and Example 6.2, "The Structure of Development" also at the end of this chapter, illustrate, Leontief's technique can be applied to any type of economic system; its use as a central-planning tool, which is illustrated here, represents but one of many possible applications.

## The Input-Output Table

Central planners could begin their task, argue the advocates of centralized socialism, by gathering accurate and detailed information on the economic activity of the year preceding the one for which a central plan was to be drawn up. The result might be presented in a huge **input-output table,** listing the flows of all newly produced goods and of resource services between all their suppliers and recipients and, thus, illustrating the web of interrelationships in the economy. Table 6.1, "The Input-Output Table," represents a highly simplified version of such a table. Its *columns* show *inputs* (that is, flows of newly produced goods and of resource services) received, during the year for which the table has been drawn up, by the parties listed on top from the parties listed on the left. The *rows* tell us about *outputs:* Each row shows how the total flow (column [8]) of any newly produced good or resource service (which came from the party listed on the left) was distributed during the year among the various recipients listed on the top.

Obviously, any input-output table that was to be used for actual centralized economic planning would have to contain millions of rows and columns. Besides the electric power, steel, and corn listed in rows A to C of our table, there would have to be separate rows for all other newly produced goods—from milk and shoes and electric motors to turret lathes and office buildings and super-highways! Indeed, different types of any one product would have to be listed separately, too, right down to such detail as boys' tennis shoes size 10 and color blue. This is so because in this economy everything would have to be *thought* through before the action started. There would be no one casting monetary votes for boys' tennis shoes (size 10 and color blue), thereby telling private resource owners to produce these instead of ladies' evening shoes (size 9 and color white). Production in this economy would take place in government enterprises exclusively; their managers would be waiting for verbal orders from the central mastermind, and just being told to produce "shoes" would not be good enough.

A realistic table, similarly, would have to specify in detail the types of resource services required. The large categories listed in rows D to F would have to be broken down into all their different components. This is so because in this economy enterprise managers would not be free to acquire the particular resource services they needed by casting monetary votes. They would be allotted the proper inputs by the central planners. Therefore, central planners could not just allocate such vague categories as 900 labor hours or 5,000 acre hours or 100 machine hours to their enterprises. Electric power producers would require quite a different type of labor than steel producers; the type of natural resources used by the latter would surely vary from that needed by corn producers; and the types of machines used by corn producers would have little resemblance to those needed by the makers of shoes. In addition, the quality of any worker would vary with age, skill, and health;

**Table 6.1**    The Input-Output Table

| Recipients / Suppliers | Of Intermediate Goods and Primary Resources | | | Of Final Goods and Primary Resources | | | | Total |
|---|---|---|---|---|---|---|---|---|
| | Electric Power Producers (1) | Steel Producers (2) | Corn Producers (3) | Domestic House-holds (4) | Domestic Producers (5) | Domestic Govern-ment (6) | Foreigners (7) | (8) |
| (A) **Electric Power Producers** (millions of megawatt hours) | 40 | 120 | 20 | 160 | | 50 | 10 | 400 |
| (B) **Steel Producers** (millions of tons) | 80 | 200 | 5 | 0 | 400 | 0 | 115 | 800 |
| (C) **Corn Producers** (millions of tons) | 40 | 80 | 100 | 500 | − 120 | 200 | − 300 | 500 |
| (D) **Owners of Human Resources** (millions of labor hours) | 4 | 800 | 500 | 50 | | 400 | 96 | 1,850 |
| (E) **Owners of Natural Resources** (millions of acre hours) | 4 | 200 | 2,500 | 200 | | 600 | 0 | 3,504 |
| (F) **Owners of Capital Resources** (millions of machine hours) | 100 | 400 | 100 | 0 | | 100 | 0 | 700 |

An input-output table is like a map of an economy. It gives an overview of the flows of commodities and services during a period between their suppliers (listed on the left) and their recipients (listed on top). The entries in columns (4) to (7) constitute what in many countries is referred to as the economy's (real) *gross national product.*

the quality of any piece of land with the weather; and that of a machine with its wear and tear. All this would have to be accounted for.

Nevertheless, for purposes of illustration only, we must remain with the over-simplified picture of Table 6.1, and we shall assume that it represents a complete picture of an economy in which only three goods were produced (rows A to C) and in which only three types of homogeneous resources were utilized (rows D to F).

**The Rows.** It is easy to interpret the meaning of each row of our table. Row A, column (8) indicates that electric power producers were producing, during the year in question, some 400 million megawatt hours. Some 180 million of these megawatt hours were delivered to domestic producers, in columns (1) to (3), and *completely used up* in the making of other goods. This portion of electric power output, therefore, is placed in the category of **intermediate goods,** or goods produced by domestic producers during a period and then used up by the same or other domestic producers during the same period in the making of other goods. Another 220 million megawatt hours, however, listed in columns (4), (6), and (7), were not used up domestically in the making of other goods. These hours are placed among **final goods,** or goods produced by domestic producers during a period and *not* used up (as intermediate goods are) by the same or other domestic producers during the same period in the making of other goods.

*Note:* In general, final goods may well have been used up (by households, government, or foreigners) or, in the case of durable goods such as steel or corn, they may have been added by domestic producers to their capital stock for *future* use. But goods can never be called final goods if they have been used up by *domestic producers* during the *same period* they were produced because that situation defines intermediate goods.

Row B, column (8) shows that 800 million tons of steel were produced this year. Of this total, some 285 million tons were completely used up by the makers of electric power (1), steel (2), and corn (3), leaving 515 million tons for final recipients. Of these 515 million tons, 400 million tons were received by domestic producers but not yet used up in the making of other goods (5), and 115 million tons were exported (7).

Row C, column (8) shows that 500 million tons of corn were produced this year. However, another 300 million tons were imported from abroad—the negative entry in column (7)—while 120 million more tons were taken out of storage by domestic producers—the negative entry in column (5). Thus, domestic supplies came to 500 + 300 + 120 = 920 million tons. Of this total, 220 million tons were completely used up by the makers of electric power (1), steel (2), and corn (3), perhaps in the production of plastic parts used in electric generators and blast furnaces and, of course, as seed. The remaining 700 million tons were delivered to domestic households (4) and government agencies (6).

Row D shows that 1,850 million labor hours were performed during the year. Some 1,304 million of these were used in the making of electric power (1), steel (2), and corn (3). The remaining 546 million hours were directly used by domestic households (4), government agencies (6), and foreigners (7), perhaps in the form of services provided by barbers, typists, or technical advisers, respectively. *Note:* It is no accident that an *X* appears in row D, column (5). Labor hours delivered to domestic producers must have been used up by them during the year in question in the making of goods; hence, they appear in columns (1) to (3). Unlike steel or corn received (which might be used up *or* stored for future use), labor (just like acre hours, machine hours, and megawatt hours) cannot be stored for use in some future year.

Rows E and F, similarly, list the totals of acre hours and machine hours used during the year as well as the purposes to which they were put.

**The Columns.**   The columns of our table have, of course, been discussed by implication. Columns (1) to (3) show all the inputs used by our three types of producers while producing the output totals given in column (8) of rows A to C. Electric power producers, for instance, produced this year 400 million megawatt hours—row A, column (8)—by completely using up the newly produced goods and primary resource services listed in column (1): 40 million megawatt hours (electric power used to run electric generators), 80 million tons of steel (to build transmission towers), 40 million tons of corn (to make plastic parts used in generators), 4 million labor hours (which might have involved 1,515 workers working 8 hours a day for slightly over 11 months), 4 million acre hours (which might have involved using slightly under 457 acres year round as sites for electric power stations and transmission facilities), and 100 million machine hours (which might have involved using 11,416 machines year round to generate electricity). Columns (2) and (3) can be similarly interpreted.

Column (4) lists all the goods received for private consumption by households (electricity, corn, services of barbers and of garden plots). Column (5) shows the change in the country's capital stock, or its annual investment (inventories of steel went up; inventories of corn went down). Column (6) lists goods received by government agencies and, thus, by people for collective consumption (electric light and heat for government offices, public schools, and hospitals; corn for the meals of soldiers; the services of clerks, doctors, and police officers; land used for parks and highways; and so on). Column (7), finally, lists the country's foreign trade (exports of electric power, steel, and labor services; imports of corn).

## Planning the Future Gross National Product

It is easy to imagine how central planners might utilize an input-output table describing the economic activity of the past to plan that of the future. Indeed, argue the advocates of centralized socialism, the ability to build on the past enormously simplifies the central planners' task. They do not have to plan from scratch; they can merely modify what happened in the recent past. Thus, planners might look at last year's gross national product—the entries in columns (4) to (7)—and they might dislike what they see. They might wish to give households 80 million megawatt hours of electric power less next year, but government agencies (in charge of street lighting and important research) some 120 million megawatt hours more. They might wish to decrease steel exports by 55 million tons per year, while providing government agencies (in charge of a new space program) with 95 million additional tons. They might wish to stop importing corn and to increase corn inventories by 100 million tons per year (instead of drawing them down at a rate of 120 million tons). And they might be willing to release 400 million acre hours from government land uses to enlarge the area set aside for household gardening.

Thus, they might prepare a new input-output table, such as Table 6.2, "The Plan Document," incorporating all these changes. At first, the reader must imagine,

**Table 6.2**   The Plan Document

| Recipients ⟍ Suppliers | Of Intermediate Goods and Primary Resources | | | Of Final Goods and Primary Resources | | | | Total |
|---|---|---|---|---|---|---|---|---|
| | Electric Power Producers (1) | Steel Producers (2) | Corn Producers (3) | Domestic House-holds (4) | Domestic Producers (5) | Domestic Govern-ment (6) | Foreigners (7) | (8) |
| (A) **Electric Power Producers** (millions of megawatt hours) | 48.862 | 132.889 | 46.873 | (80) | | (170) | 10 | 304.685 134.638 49.301 488.624 |
| (B) **Steel Producers** (millions of tons) | 97.725 | 221.481 | 11.718 | 0 | 400 | (95) | (60) | 81.894 777.423 26.607 885.924 |
| (C) **Corn Producers** (millions of tons) | 48.862 | 88.592 | 234.364 | 500 | (100) | 200 | (0) | 48.322 114.008 1,009.488 1,171.818 |
| (D) **Owners of Human Resources** (millions of labor hours) | 4.886 | 885.924 | 1,171.818 | 50 | | 400 | 96 | 2,608.628 |
| (E) **Owners of Natural Resources** (millions of acre hours) | 4.886 | 221.481 | 5,859.09 | (600) | | (200) | 0 | 6,885.457 |
| (F) **Owners of Capital Resources** (millions of machine hours) | 122.156 | 442.962 | 234.364 | 0 | | 100 | 0 | 899.482 |

This new input-output table shows the effects, throughout our hypothetical economy, of the planners' revision of some desired output targets. Revised targets in columns (4) to (7) have been highlighted by the encircled numbers. As a comparison with Table 6.1 indicates, the revision leaves no part of the economy untouched.

this table would be completely blank—except, of course, for the central planners' vision of the future composition of the gross national product, GNP. The changes contemplated above (which planners might make in the composition of the GNP) give rise to various new entries in columns (4) to (7); these have been highlighted by the circled numbers. Obviously, each of these changes would require other changes.

The increase by 40 million megawatt hours a year of the row A, columns (4) to (7) entries from 220 to 260, for instance, would require at the very least a corresponding increase from 400 to 440 in the *total* (intermediate plus final) output of electric power in column (8) of row A. That increase in total electric power output, in turn, would require increases in all the inputs used by electric power producers in column (1), which would raise all the totals in column (8) and, in due course, all the other table entries! This chain reaction explains why central economic planners would quickly have to educate themselves about the technical facts of life.

## Technical Coefficients

Central planners could use the type of information found in columns (1) to (3) and (8) of Table 6.1 to calculate **technical coefficients** for all goods they might wish to have produced. Technical coefficients are numbers showing the quantities of inputs producers in an industry require on the average per unit of output. Table 6.3, "Technical Coefficients," has been derived from Table 6.1, "The Input-Output Table." Every entry in column (1) of Table 6.1, for instance, has been divided by the 400-million-megawatt-hour total of electric power output shown in row A, column (8). This division yielded column (1) of the new table: Because it took 40 million megawatt hours to produce 400 million megawatt hours, it took on the average .10 megawatt hour to produce 1 megawatt hour. Because it took 80 million tons of steel to produce 400 million megawatt hours, it took on the average .20 ton to produce 1 megawatt hour. And so on. Columns (2) and (3) of Table 6.3 have been similarly derived.

Now we are ready to see how central planners, armed with technical coefficients, might set out to explore the implications of their desired changes in the GNP. They might figure, to begin with, that increasing annual electric power output by 40 million megawatt hours to accommodate the changes contemplated in row A, columns (4) to (7) requires extra inputs equal to 40 million times all the entries in column (1) of Table 6.3. But increasing inputs in this way would only be a first approximation of the truth. As one can see in the very first entry in column (1) of Table 6.3, in this economy electric power requires electric power for its production! Thus, any 40-million-megawatt-hour increase in electric power output requires *another* 40 million times .10, or another 4-million-megawatt-hour increase in electric power production; this, in turn, requires another 4 million times .10, or a .4-million-megawatt-hour increase; and so on in an ever dwindling chain. Even *further* electric power is needed to help produce the additional steel and corn!

It is easy to see how this sort of computation would quickly get out of hand if it were to be pursued by mentally following chains of reasoning such as the one above. Fortunately, however, the mathematical technique of *matrix inversion* enables planners to acquire a tool with which to calculate speedily all the effects, direct and indirect, of the types of changes envisioned in the example above. Matrix inversion produces, from the technical coefficients for intermediate goods (the top half of our Table 6.3) the so-called **Leontief inverse matrix.** It is yet another table, showing, for those goods of which a portion of output is used up in the process of

**Table 6.3**   Technical Coefficients

| | Inputs Required on the Average to Make: | | |
|---|---|---|---|
| | *1 Megawatt Hour of Electric Power* *(1)* | *1 Ton of Steel* *(2)* | *1 Ton of Corn* *(3)* |
| (A) **Electric Power** (megawatt hours) | $\dfrac{40}{400} = 0.10$ | $\dfrac{120}{800} = 0.15$ | $\dfrac{20}{500} = 0.04$ |
| (B) **Steel** (tons) | $\dfrac{80}{400} = 0.20$ | $\dfrac{200}{800} = 0.25$ | $\dfrac{5}{500} = 0.01$ |
| (C) **Corn** (tons) | $\dfrac{40}{400} = 0.10$ | $\dfrac{80}{800} = 0.10$ | $\dfrac{100}{500} = 0.20$ |
| (D) **Human Resources** (labor hours) | $\dfrac{4}{400} = 0.01$ | $\dfrac{800}{800} = 1.00$ | $\dfrac{500}{500} = 1.00$ |
| (E) **Natural Resources** (acre hours) | $\dfrac{4}{400} = 0.01$ | $\dfrac{200}{800} = 0.25$ | $\dfrac{2500}{500} = 5.00$ |
| (F) **Capital Resources** (machine hours) | $\dfrac{100}{400} = 0.25$ | $\dfrac{400}{800} = 0.50$ | $\dfrac{100}{500} = 0.20$ |

Technical coefficients can be calculated from an input-output table. The figures shown here are based on Table 6.1, columns (1) to (3) and (8). They are akin to a recipe in a cookbook. No attempt has been made to depict realistic production functions.

production itself (electric power, steel, and corn in our example), the total outputs ultimately required if one unit of such a good is to be delivered to final users. For serious central planners, the Leontief inverse matrix would be an indispensable planning tool. We will consider how it is derived.

## Deriving the Leontief Inverse Matrix*

To begin with, we must define a **matrix** as any rectangular array of numbers. The above set of technical coefficients for intermediate goods could, for instance, be symbolized by the capital letter $T$ and written in matrix form as follows:

$$T = \begin{bmatrix} .10 & .15 & .04 \\ .20 & .25 & .01 \\ .10 & .10 & .20 \end{bmatrix}$$

This matrix happens to be a square one, and the **main diagonal** of a square matrix is defined as all elements running from the upper left to the lower right corner. A

*Optional Section. This section contains advanced material that can be skipped without loss of continuity. Those who wish to pursue the mathematics involved, however, may also like to try out the relevant computer program noted at the end of this chapter. The "Matrix Operations" program enables the interested reader to invert any matrix instantly without having to go through the complicated calculations found on the following pages.

matrix that consists of ones along the main diagonal, all other elements being zero, is called an **identity matrix.** We will symbolize it by $I$, and write

$$I = \begin{bmatrix} 1 & 0 & 0 \\ 0 & 1 & 0 \\ 0 & 0 & 1 \end{bmatrix}$$

One matrix can be subtracted from another if both have identical numbers of rows and columns. Subtraction involves, as the example below shows, taking the difference of corresponding elements.

$$I - T = L$$

$$\begin{bmatrix} 1 & 0 & 0 \\ 0 & 1 & 0 \\ 0 & 0 & 1 \end{bmatrix} - \begin{bmatrix} .10 & .15 & .04 \\ .20 & .25 & .01 \\ .10 & .10 & .20 \end{bmatrix} = \begin{bmatrix} .90 & -.15 & -.04 \\ -.20 & .75 & -.01 \\ -.10 & -.10 & .80 \end{bmatrix}$$

Matrix L, resulting from subtracting our technical coefficients matrix from an identity matrix, is called a **Leontief matrix.** It is this matrix that has to be inverted.

An **inverse matrix** is a matrix that when multiplied by an original matrix yields an identity matrix. Labeling the inverse of the Leontief matrix $L$ by $L^{-1}$, we can say that $L \cdot L^{-1} = I$. Before we can find $L^{-1}$, however, we have to introduce additional concepts, namely, those of a *determinant,* a *minor,* and a *cofactor.* At first sight, it is easy to confuse a determinant with a matrix because a **determinant** is a number of elements arranged in rows and columns to form a square, such as

$$D = \begin{vmatrix} x_{11} & x_{12} \\ x_{21} & x_{22} \end{vmatrix}$$

wherein the subscripts identify rows and columns.

A visual distinction used is that a determinant is enclosed in straight lines, a matrix in square brackets. A more basic distinction is, however, that a determinant *can be evaluated, yielding a single number.* The type of determinant illustrated above is always equal to

$$D = (x_{11} \cdot x_{22}) - (x_{21} \cdot x_{12})$$

The above determinant, having two rows and two columns, is called a second-order determinant. The elements of a higher-order determinant can be expressed as minors and cofactors. Let us look at a third-order determinant, such as

$$D' = \begin{vmatrix} x_{11} & x_{12} & x_{13} \\ x_{21} & x_{22} & x_{23} \\ x_{31} & x_{32} & x_{33} \end{vmatrix}$$

The **minor** of any element of a third-order determinant consists of the second-order determinant remaining when the row and column of the element in question are deleted. Indicating minors by the symbol $m$, we can write the minor of $x_{11}$ as

$$m_{11} = \begin{vmatrix} x_{22} & x_{23} \\ x_{32} & x_{33} \end{vmatrix}$$

Similarly, the minor of $x_{23}$ would be

$$m_{23} = \begin{vmatrix} x_{11} & x_{12} \\ x_{31} & x_{32} \end{vmatrix}$$

The **cofactor** of an element, which we shall label $C$, equals the element's minor with an appropriate sign. If the sum of the subscripts of the element is *even*, as for $x_{11}$, where $1 + 1 = 2$, the cofactor has a *plus* sign; if it is *odd*, as for $x_{23}$, where $2 + 3 = 5$, a *minus* sign. Hence, the cofactors of $x_{11}$ and $x_{23}$ are

$$C_{11} = + \begin{vmatrix} x_{22} & x_{23} \\ x_{32} & x_{33} \end{vmatrix} \quad \text{and} \quad C_{23} = - \begin{vmatrix} x_{11} & x_{12} \\ x_{31} & x_{32} \end{vmatrix}$$

Each of the cofactors can, of course, be evaluated as was determinant $D$, giving us

$$C_{11} = + [(x_{22} \cdot x_{33}) - (x_{32} \cdot x_{23})] \quad \text{and} \quad C_{23} = - [(x_{11} \cdot x_{32}) - (x_{31} \cdot x_{12})]$$

A third-order determinant will obviously, then, have nine such cofactors. A third-order determinant is evaluated with the help of the minors of the first row, so that

$$D' = (x_{11} \cdot m_{11}) - (x_{12} \cdot m_{12}) + (x_{13} \cdot m_{13})$$

Now we are ready to proceed with the inversion of our matrix $L$. Six steps are involved.

(1) Writing the matrix as a determinant and evaluating it.

$$D = \begin{vmatrix} .90 & -.15 & -.04 \\ -.20 & .75 & -.01 \\ -.10 & -.10 & .80 \end{vmatrix}$$

$$= .90 \begin{vmatrix} .75 & -.01 \\ -.10 & .80 \end{vmatrix} - (-.15) \begin{vmatrix} -.20 & -.01 \\ -.10 & .80 \end{vmatrix} + (-.04) \begin{vmatrix} -.20 & .75 \\ -.10 & -.10 \end{vmatrix}$$

$$= .90 \{.75(.80) - [(-.10)(-.01)]\} + .15\{-.20(.80) - [(-.10)(-.01)]\}$$
$$- .04\{-.20(-.10) - [(-.10)(.75)]\}$$

$$= .90(.599) + .15(-.161) - .04(.095)$$

$$= .5391 - .02415 - .0038 = .51115$$

(2) Identifying all cofactors of the determinant.

$$C_{11} = + \begin{vmatrix} .75 & -.01 \\ -.10 & .80 \end{vmatrix} = .599$$

$$C_{12} = - \begin{vmatrix} -.20 & -.01 \\ -.10 & .80 \end{vmatrix} = .161$$

$$C_{13} = + \begin{vmatrix} -.20 & .75 \\ -.10 & -.10 \end{vmatrix} = .095$$

$$C_{21} = - \begin{vmatrix} -.15 & -.04 \\ -.10 & .80 \end{vmatrix} = .124$$

$$C_{22} = + \begin{vmatrix} .90 & -.04 \\ -.10 & .80 \end{vmatrix} = .716$$

$$C_{23} = - \begin{vmatrix} .90 & -.15 \\ -.10 & -.10 \end{vmatrix} = .105$$

$$C_{31} = + \begin{vmatrix} -.15 & -.04 \\ .75 & -.01 \end{vmatrix} = .0315$$

$$C_{32} = - \begin{vmatrix} .90 & -.04 \\ -.20 & -.01 \end{vmatrix} = .017$$

$$C_{33} = + \begin{vmatrix} .90 & -.15 \\ -.20 & .75 \end{vmatrix} = .645$$

(3) Arranging the cofactors in matrix form.

$$C = \begin{bmatrix} .599 & .161 & .095 \\ .124 & .716 & .105 \\ .0315 & .017 & .645 \end{bmatrix}$$

(4) Finding the **adjoint matrix,** which is the matrix of cofactors transposed— that is, with rows and columns interchanged.

$$A = \begin{bmatrix} .599 & .124 & .0315 \\ .161 & .716 & .017 \\ .095 & .105 & .645 \end{bmatrix}$$

(5) Finding the Leontief inverted matrix by dividing each element in the adjoint matrix by the value of the determinant found in step 1.

$$L^{-1} = \begin{bmatrix} 1.1718673 & .2425902 & .0616257 \\ .314976 & 1.4007629 & .0332583 \\ .1858554 & .2054191 & 1.2618605 \end{bmatrix}$$

(6) Checking the result by multiplying the original matrix $L$ by its inverse $L^{-1}$, which should yield an identity matrix $I$. Matrices can be multiplied only if they are *conformable;* that is, if the number of columns of the first equals the number of rows of the second. This is, of course, the case here with $L$ and $L^{-1}$. The product will have as many rows as the first and as many columns as the second. The rule for multiplication can easily be derived from the detail that follows. It involves finding each element of the product matrix by cumulative multiplication of the elements of the first row of the first matrix by those of the first, second, and third column of the second matrix, and so on.

$$L \cdot L^{-1} = I$$

$$
\begin{bmatrix}
.90 & -.15 & -.04 \\
-.20 & .75 & -.01 \\
-.10 & -.10 & .80
\end{bmatrix}
\cdot
\begin{bmatrix}
1.1718673 & .2425902 & .0616257 \\
.314976 & 1.4007629 & .0332583 \\
.1858554 & .2054191 & 1.2618605
\end{bmatrix}
=
$$

$$
\begin{bmatrix}
(\ .90 \cdot 1.1718673) + (-.15 \cdot .314976) + (-.04 \cdot .1858554) \\
(-.20 \cdot 1.1718673) + (\ .75 \cdot .314976) + (-.01 \cdot .1858554) \\
(-.10 \cdot 1.1718673) + (-.10 \cdot .314976) + (\ .80 \cdot .1858554)
\end{bmatrix}
$$

$$
\begin{matrix}
(\ .90 \cdot .2425902) + (-.15 \cdot 1.4007629) + (-.04 \cdot .2054191) \\
(-.20 \cdot .2425902) + (\ .75 \cdot 1.4007629) + (-.01 \cdot .2054191) \\
(-.10 \cdot .2425902) + (-.10 \cdot 1.4007629) + (\ .80 \cdot .2054191)
\end{matrix}
$$

$$
\begin{bmatrix}
(\ .90 \cdot .0616257) + (-.15 \cdot .0332583) + (-.04 \cdot 1.2618605) \\
(-.20 \cdot .0616257) + (\ .75 \cdot .0332583) + (-.01 \cdot 1.2618605) \\
(-.10 \cdot .0616257) + (-.10 \cdot .0332583) + (\ .80 \cdot 1.2618605)
\end{bmatrix}
=
$$

$$
\begin{bmatrix}
1 & 0 & 0 \\
0 & 1 & 0 \\
0 & 0 & 1
\end{bmatrix}
$$

This proves our calculation of the inverse as correct. It can now be presented as in Table 6.4, "The Leontief Inverse Matrix." ▬▬

## Interpreting the Leontief Inverse Matrix

Consider Table 6.4, "The Leontief Inverse Matrix." Its interpretation is considerably easier than its derivation. Column (1), for example, indicates that the recipients of final goods in our hypothetical economy could get 1 megawatt hour of electric power provided total electric power output equaled 1.1718673 megawatt hours, total steel output equaled .314976 tons, and total corn output equaled .1858554 tons. These production levels would ensure sufficient raw materials throughout the economy to accommodate the ultimate delivery of 1 megawatt hour to a final user. In addition, of course, the services of human, natural, and capital resources would also be needed.

Note how easily a central planner looking only at the technical coefficients table could have come to incorrect conclusions. Providing some final user with 1 extra megawatt hour of power, such a planner might have figured, would *directly* require the production of 1 extra megawatt hour (a matter of common sense), and would *indirectly* require the raw material production of another .10 megawatt hour of power, .20 ton of steel, and .10 ton of corn, as the entries in column (1) of Table 6.3 seem to indicate. But this conclusion would be wrong! As column (1) of the Leontief inverse tells us, providing a final user with 1 extra megawatt hour of power requires extra total output of not 1.1 but 1.1718673 megawatt hours of power; of not .20 but .314976 ton of steel; and of not .10 but .1858554 ton of corn! The inverse makes us aware not only of the direct extra output requirements

**Table 6.4**    The Leontief Inverse Matrix

| | Total Output Required If Delivery to Final Users Is to Equal: | | |
|---|---|---|---|
| | *1 Megawatt Hour of Electric Power (1)* | *1 Ton of Steel (2)* | *1 Ton of Corn (3)* |
| (A) **Electric Power** (megawatt hours) | 1.1718673 | 0.2425902 | 0.0616257 |
| (B) **Steel** (tons) | 0.314976 | 1.4007629 | 0.0332583 |
| (C) **Corn** (tons) | 0.1858554 | 0.2054191 | 1.2618605 |

The Leontief inverse can be calculated from a table of technical coefficients with the help of matrix algebra. This table is based on Table 6.3 and, ultimately, on Table 6.1. All figures are rounded.

(which common sense indicates) and not only of the most obvious indirect ones (which the technical coefficients point out), but also of those that are far from obvious (and which are too complex to be grasped by any human mind).

## Completing the New Input-Output Table

The advocates of centralized socialism argue that it would be easy for a central planner to use the Leontief inverse to work out all the implications of producing any desired GNP, such as the column (4) to (7) entries in Table 6.2, "The Plan Document." Three steps would be involved: planning total output requirements (rows A to C of column [8]), planning input requirements of intermediate goods (rows A to C of columns [1] to [3]), and planning input requirements of primary resource services (rows D to F of columns [1] to [3] and [8]).

**Planning Total Output Requirements.**    Return to Table 6.2, "The Plan Document," on page 93, and imagine that columns (1) to (3) plus (8) were still empty. Using the Leontief inverse, central planners could then fill in the top three entries in column (8):

Noting how they wished to deliver next year 80 + 170 + 10 = 260 million megawatt hours to final users (row A, columns 4 to 7), they could simply multiply each of the Table 6.4 column (1) entries by 260 million. This would yield the total production levels of electric power, steel, and corn that would accommodate this goal. The resultant figures, rounded to three decimals, are shown in column (8) of Table 6.2: 304.68549 million megawatt hours of power, 81.89376 million tons of steel, and 48.322404 million tons of corn.

However, this would not be the end of the story. Our planners had another goal of delivering 400 + 95 + 60 = 555 million tons of steel to final users. Thus, they would have to multiply each of the Table 6.4 column (2) entries by 555 million in order to find the *additional* total output of electric power, steel, and corn required to accommodate this additional goal. The resultant figures of 134.63756 million megawatt hours of power, 777.4234 million tons of steel, and 114.0076 million tons of corn are also shown in Table 6.2.

Finally, our planners had a third goal of delivering $500 + 100 + 200 = 800$ million tons of corn to final users. Multiplying each of the Table 6.4 column (3) entries by 800 million reveals further total output requirements for the three goods put out by this economy. The results, 49.30056 million megawatt hours of power, 26.60664 million tons of steel, and 1,009.4884 million tons of corn, are shown in column (8) of Table 6.2, along with the totals of the entries we have just imagined ourselves making in its top three rows.

**Planning Input Requirements of Intermediate Goods.** At this point, you must imagine, columns (1) to (3) of Table 6.2, "The Plan Document," as well as the lower half of column (8), would still be blank. But planners would now be ready to fill in the rest of the table. Knowing the total output requirements of all goods produced by the economy (rows A to C, column [8]), planners could simply use Table 6.3, "The Technical Coefficients," to calculate all the inputs required by each type of producer—assuming, of course, that the technical relationships between inputs and outputs that were observed in the past would also hold in the future (even if the volume of production, and, thus, perhaps even the number of producers should be different).

Multiplying the 488.624-million-megawatt-hour total output of electric power by all the entries in column (1) of Table 6.3 yields the entries in column (1) of Table 6.2. Similar multiplications of the 885.924-million-ton total output of steel by the Table 6.3 column (2) entries, and of the 1,171.818-million-ton total output of corn by the Table 6.3 column (3) entries yields all the data for columns (2) and (3) of Table 6.2.

At this point, a quick accuracy check can be made. Do the column (8) totals of rows A to C, which were independently arrived at with the help of the Leontief inverse, equal the sum of all the entries in their respective rows? They do.

**Planning Input Requirements of Primary Resource Services.** At this point, only three cells in our plan table would be blank: the column (8) totals of rows D to F. They could be found, of course, by simple addition of all the entries in these three rows, yielding the three boxed numbers in column (8). If planners could come up with the flows of resource services represented by these boxes, they would have in their hands a feasible as well as a coordinated plan of future economic activities that would have to be performed to accommodate the production of the newly desired GNP.

But note: As a comparison of the entries in rows D to F, column (8) between tables 6.1 and 6.2 shows, the new economic plan just worked out calls for con- siderably larger resource flows than the assumed earlier level of economic activity. Thus, central planners would have to ask themselves where such resources could possibly come from. If there had been much unemployment of human, natural, and capital resources earlier, the higher resource flows might easily be procured from households and the socialist administrators of natural and capital resources. If there had been full employment before, difficulties would exist. Planners would have to enforce a higher utilization of resource stocks than earlier (as by making each person work more hours per year), or they would have to slash some of their ambitious output goals. After reducing their original entries in columns (4) to (7) of Table 6.2, they could calculate a new economic plan that, in the end, utilized no more resources than were in fact available. Thus, ideally, any internal inconsistency of the plan would be ironed out (on paper or in the bowels of a giant computer) by changing prospective government decrees prior to the plan's implementation. Only after that point would central planners turn into commanders and begin to supervise the execution of their plan.

## Simultaneous Equations*

Central economic planning is sometimes likened to the "solving of millions of equations." This section will show that the solving of simultaneous equations is, indeed, an alternative to deriving Table 6.2, "The Plan Document," with the help of matrix algebra.

Consider Table 6.5, "The Input-Output Table Revisited." This table is a copy of Table 6.1, "The Input-Output Table," except that earlier numerical entries have given way to symbolic expressions. For example, the Table 6.1 totals of rows A to F— 400 million megawatt hours, 800 million tons of steel, and so on—have now been designated as $T_A$, $T_B$, . . . $T_F$. Similarly, the (combined) final uses in each Table 6.1 row—220 million megawatt hours, 515 million tons of steel, and so on— have been designated as $F_A$, $F_B$, . . . $F_F$. Finally, each of the Table 6.1 intermediate uses has been expressed as the mathematical product of a relevant technical coefficient and an appropriate row total. Note how the Table 6.3 technical coefficients appear in Table 6.5 as $t_{A1}$, $t_{A2}$, . . . $t_{F3}$, the subscripts denoting row and column. Thus, the row A, column (1) entry of Table 6.1 (which was 40) appears symbolically in Table 6.5 as $t_{A1} \cdot T_A$ (which in our example would equal $.10 \times 400 = 40$ as well).

We are now ready to discard our input-output table and write down the information contained in it as the following set of six simultaneous equations:

$$1. \quad (t_{A1} \cdot T_A) + (t_{A2} \cdot T_B) + (t_{A3} \cdot T_C) + F_A = T_A$$
$$2. \quad (t_{B1} \cdot T_A) + (t_{B2} \cdot T_B) + (t_{B3} \cdot T_C) + F_B = T_B$$
$$3. \quad (t_{C1} \cdot T_A) + (t_{C2} \cdot T_B) + (t_{C3} \cdot T_C) + F_C = T_C$$
$$4. \quad (t_{D1} \cdot T_A) + (t_{D2} \cdot T_B) + (t_{D3} \cdot T_C) + F_D = T_D$$
$$5. \quad (t_{E1} \cdot T_A) + (t_{E2} \cdot T_B) + (t_{E3} \cdot T_C) + F_E = T_E$$
$$6. \quad (t_{F1} \cdot T_A) + (t_{F2} \cdot T_B) + (t_{F3} \cdot T_C) + F_F = T_F$$

---

*Optional Section. Those who wish to consider the plan execution phase now are free to skip the following section without loss of continuity. (This section introduces an approach to plan formulation that is an alternative to Leontief's matrix approach. Once again, those who wish to pursue the equation-solving approach will find a computer program for this purpose noted at the end of this chapter.)

**Table 6.5**   The Input-Output Table Revisited

| Recipients / Suppliers | Of Intermediate Goods and Primary Resources | | | Of Final Goods and Primary Resources | | | | Total |
|---|---|---|---|---|---|---|---|---|
| | Electric Power Producers (1) | Steel Producers (2) | Corn Producers (3) | Domestic House-holds (4) | Domestic Producers (5) | Domestic Govern-ment (6) | Foreigners (7) | (8) |
| (A) **Electric Power Producers** (millions of megawatt hours) | $t_{A1} \cdot T_A$ | $t_{A2} \cdot T_B$ | $t_{A3} \cdot T_C$ | $F_A$ | | | | $T_A$ |
| (B) **Steel Producers** (millions of tons) | $t_{B1} \cdot T_A$ | $t_{B2} \cdot T_B$ | $t_{B3} \cdot T_C$ | $F_B$ | | | | $T_B$ |
| (C) **Corn Producers** (millions of tons) | $t_{C1} \cdot T_A$ | $t_{C2} \cdot T_B$ | $t_{C3} \cdot T_C$ | $F_C$ | | | | $T_C$ |
| (D) **Owners of Human Resources** (millions of labor hours) | $t_{D1} \cdot T_A$ | $t_{D2} \cdot T_B$ | $t_{D3} \cdot T_C$ | $F_D$ | | | | $T_D$ |
| (E) **Owners of Natural Resources** (millions of acre hours) | $t_{E1} \cdot T_A$ | $t_{E2} \cdot T_B$ | $t_{E3} \cdot T_C$ | $F_E$ | | | | $T_E$ |
| (F) **Owners of Capital Resources** (millions of machine hours) | $t_{F1} \cdot T_A$ | $t_{F2} \cdot T_B$ | $t_{F3} \cdot T_C$ | $F_F$ | | | | $T_F$ |

The input-output table can also be viewed as a system of simultaneous equations. The separate column (1) to (7) entries in each row always add to the column (8) total; thus each row can be written as a different equation. If Table 6.5 were a realistic table, containing millions of rows and columns, millions of equations would be involved as well.

If a central planner designated desired values for $F_A$ through $F_F$ (the targeted composition of the future GNP) and possessed (presumably from past experience) a set of technical coefficients ($t_{A1}$ through $t_{F3}$), there would remain precisely six unknowns ($T_A$ through $T_F$), along with our six independent equations. These could be solved by any conventional method, yielding precisely the information needed to set up, once again, the plan document of Table 6.2.

Note: The equation-solving computer program noted at the end of this chapter asks the user to recast each equation in such a fashion that all the unknowns appear in each equation and do so in the same order and all the known constants appear on the right-hand side. Thus, equations (1) to (6) would have to be rewritten as (7) to (12).

7. $[(t_{A1} - 1) \cdot T_A] + (t_{A2} \cdot T_B) \quad\quad + (t_{A3} \cdot T_C) \quad\quad\quad + 0T_D + 0T_E + 0T_F \quad = -F_A$
8. $(t_{B1} \cdot T_A) \quad\quad + [(t_{B2} - 1) \cdot T_B] + (t_{B3} \cdot T_C) \quad\quad + 0T_D + 0T_E + 0T_F \quad = -F_B$
9. $(t_{C1} \cdot T_A) \quad\quad + (t_{C2} \cdot T_B) \quad\quad + [(t_{C3} - 1) \cdot T_C] + 0T_D + 0T_E + 0T_F \quad = -F_C$
10. $(t_{D1} \cdot T_A) \quad\quad + (t_{D2} \cdot T_B) \quad\quad + (t_{D3} \cdot T_C) \quad\quad\quad - 1T_D + 0T_E + 0T_F \quad = -F_D$
11. $(t_{E1} \cdot T_A) \quad\quad + (t_{E2} \cdot T_B) \quad\quad + (t_{E3} \cdot T_C) \quad\quad\quad + 0T_D - 1T_E + 0T_F \quad = -F_E$
12. $(t_{F1} \cdot T_A) \quad\quad + (t_{F2} \cdot T_B) \quad\quad + (t_{F3} \cdot T_C) \quad\quad\quad + 0T_D - 0T_E - 1T_F \quad = -F_F$

Given the technical coefficients of Table 6.3 and the central planner's desired GNP embodied in columns (4) to (7) of Table 6.2, these equations would become equations (13) to (18):

13. $-.90T_A + .15T_B + .04T_C + 0T_D + 0T_E + 0T_F \quad = -260$
14. $.20T_A - .75T_B + .01T_C + 0T_D + 0T_E + 0T_F \quad = -555$
15. $.10T_A + .10T_B - .80T_C + 0T_D + 0T_E + 0T_F \quad = -800$
16. $.01T_A + 1.00T_B + 1.00T_C - 1T_D + 0T_E + 0T_F \quad = -546$
17. $.01T_A + .25T_B + 5.00T_C + 0T_D - 1T_E + 0T_F \quad = -800$
18. $.25T_A + .50T_B + .20T_C + 0T_D + 0T_E - 1T_F \quad = -100$

If one solves these six equations for the six unknowns, one derives almost precisely the row A to F totals given in Table 6.2, "The Plan Document" (slight differences being due to rounding):

$$T_A = \quad 488.624 \quad\quad\quad T_D = 2,608.629$$
$$T_B = \quad 885.924 \quad\quad\quad T_E = 6,885.460$$
$$T_C = 1,171.819 \quad\quad\quad T_F = \quad 899.482$$

Central planners who had used the equation-solving approach and had then calculated the total outputs and inputs required for the achievement of the planners' desired GNP could use technical coefficients to work out the Table 6.5 column (1) to (3) detail. Provided the $T_D$ to $T_F$ resource flows were available, the planners could once again turn to the task of executing the plan. ▬▬

## Plan Execution

Once central planners had worked out a well-coordinated plan of future economic activities that they considered feasible (in that it did not require larger resource flows than could be made available), they could issue a variety of "marching orders" to all those from whom action was required.

## Output Quotas

First, argue the advocates of centralized socialism, central administrators would issue **output quotas.** These would be verbal commands—addressed to each producing enterprise, household, and administrator of the means of production—to supply, during a given period, designated minimum quantities of goods or resource services, respectively, to designated recipients. In our example, these commands would involve the following: Electric power producers as a group would be *ordered* to produce 488.624 million megawatt hours of electricity next year and deliver them to various recipients as specified in row A. Steel producers would be ordered to produce 885.924 million tons of steel next year and deliver them to the recipients specified in row B. And corn producers would be ordered to produce 1,171.818 million tons of corn next year and deliver them to the recipients specified in row C.

At the same time, households as a group would be *commanded* (without any intervention of wages or labor markets) to provide 2,608.628 million hours of labor next year and distribute themselves among various users of labor as shown in row D. Since natural and capital resources would be collectively owned in our socialist state, government administrators of these resources would be ordered, similarly, to provide the services specified in rows E and F to the recipients designated there. Here again, the central authorities would have to specify all the details, telling, say, each specific household how many hours to work in which firm.

## Input Norms

In addition, central administrators would set **input norms.** These would be verbal commands—addressed to the manager of each productive enterprise—to use designated maximum quantities of various inputs per unit of designated outputs. Obviously, if producers did not adhere closely to the technical coefficients listed in Table 6.3 but used, say, more inputs per unit of product than listed there, input shortages would arise and the entire process of executing the plan (which was based on the above technical coefficients table) would break down.

## Incentives

The most perfectly computed plan would be nothing but a beautiful piece of paper if people did not obey it. Thus, central planners would also have to ask themselves how they could get individual households and government officials to obey the output quotas and input norms issued to them. Various possibilities would exist, including negative and positive incentives and these could be moral or material in nature. Negative incentives could include castigating, fining, or even jailing and shooting people for noncompliance with the orders of central planners. More likely, though, central planners would want to use positive incentives, such as praise, medals, or tying the distribution of consumption goods (the output of which is shown in column [4] of Table 6.2) to the proper performance of assigned tasks. Thus, people who went willingly to their designated places of employment and worked hard might get a larger share of consumption goods than others who were less obedient. And a similar distinction might be made between administrators of publicly owned nonhuman resources and managers of public enterprises who did or did not please central planners. In this way, the great questions of every economic system (of what to produce, and how, and for whom) might be answered by central planners without any use whatsoever of money and markets. The often alleged chaos of the Invisible Hand would be replaced by the deliberately arranged order of the Visible Hand! How would such an economy perform with respect to the goals discussed earlier in this book? We turn to that question in the remainder of this chapter.

## Performance Assessed

Having outlined a model of centralized socialism, we can now make an assessment of its likely performance by applying to it the various success criteria introduced in earlier chapters. Because an economy with the precise features we have postulated has never existed, we can only speculate about its performance. While such speculation is open to possible bias, we shall try to arrive at a reasoned assessment. The reader is free to agree or to dissent.

### Full Employment

The advocates of the model just described imagine that this economy would produce a full utilization of resources, the meaning of full employment being defined, of course, by the central government. Full employment would be achieved easily, it is believed, because central planners would simply try about on paper (or rework their computer programs) until they had drawn up a plan the execution of which would utilize the available flows of resources precisely. (The plan would be changed, that is, until the boxed row D to F, column [8] entries in Table 6.2 just equaled the full-employment flow of resources.) Then, as long as everyone followed central commands, all resources would end up working at the full-employment rate.

Critics of this model, on the other hand, are not so sure, saying that even if one were to accept the centralized definition of full employment and the centralized allocation of all resources in accordance with the plan, too many things might go wrong, so that the expected outcome cannot be ensured. The thought of being able to design centrally an intricate plan of a society's future economic activity is, of course, very pleasing to human vanity. But, argue critics, the advocates of centralized socialism are intoxicated by the cult of reason. They are propagating a myth of human omniscience and omnipotence according to which something that is logically conceivable is also practically possible. True enough, these critics continue, the type of central planning described earlier in this chapter is possible as a matter of pure logic. But in practice central planners could never acquire the infinite mass of information that would in the first instance be dispersed in the minds of countless individuals, but would have to be gathered in one place prior to setting up a *realistic* plan document such as Table 6.2 (with millions of rows and columns). This information would have to include up-to-date sets of technical coefficients for all possible production volumes for all conceivable goods, as well as detailed data about the availability of all imaginable subcategories of resources. Even if central planners did manage to gather all this information, critics think, they might then not be able to handle the computations required (modern high-speed computers notwithstanding), much less the load of communications involved in issuing billions of specific commands and verifying their execution. As a result, millions of mistakes would be made by planners (because of their lack of omniscience and omnipotence), and certainly some available resources would remain unemployed. Some of them would never be assigned to a place of employment, and others would be so assigned but be unable to work for lack of complementary inputs that a faulty plan (or its faulty execution) would fail to provide at the right time and place.

Critics note, for example, that the mathematical techniques introduced earlier assume constant technical coefficients: Whatever the technical coefficients were in the recent past, it is assumed that they will also hold in the future—even if the volume of production should change dramatically, up or down. For every product, the planning technique described earlier in fact assumes **constant returns to scale,** a characteristic of the production function such that a simultaneous and equal percentage change in the use of all physical inputs leads to an *identical* percentage change of physical output. If 10 workers, 100 tons of iron ore, 30 tons of coal, etc., can produce 25 tons of steel, then, it is assumed, doubling all inputs (to 20 workers, 200 tons of iron ore, 60 tons of coal, 2 etc.) will also double output (to 50 tons of steel). Similarly, halving all inputs (to 5 workers, 50 tons of iron ore, 15 tons of coal, and one half etc.) will halve output (to 12.5 tons of steel). All this may, in fact, not be true, critics fear. Many production functions exhibit **decreasing returns to scale** such that a simultaneous and equal percentage change in the use of all physical inputs leads to a *smaller* percentage change in physical output. Other production functions are characterized by **increasing returns to scale** instead and, in that case, a simultaneous and equal percentage change in the use of all physical inputs leads to a *larger* percentage change in physical output. Thus, it is not inconceivable that a plan that called for the production of, say, 50 million tons of steel instead of last year's 25 million tons and that carefully doubled all steel industry inputs nevertheless would deliver only 39 million tons (if decreasing rather than constant returns to scale prevailed). This single error alone might adversely affect every other economic activity: Because of the lack of steel, workers and machines in the truck industry might be idled. Because there would be fewer trucks than expected, seed and fertilizer might not get to the fields in time for planting corn, leaving precious acreage and farm workers idle as well. The list goes on. . . . Furthermore, critics contend, the knowledge of such unemployment (and the resultant lower-than-possible output) might be kept from central planners by fearful workers and enterprise managers who did not want to be punished for not having fulfilled their output quotas. They might *simulate* plan fulfillment, sending in false performance reports ("we did produce 50 million tons of steel, as planned") and, thus, give the impression that all was fine. Alternatively, bureaucrats on the planning board who *were* told about basic flaws in their plan might be reluctant or slow to acknowledge this fact and might obstinately cling to the initial commands. In the meantime, unemployment would persist.

Naturally, we cannot measure the extent of unemployment that might be caused by such conceivable imperfections in centralized planning or management, but we should be aware that full employment, however defined, would not be a matter of certainty under centralized socialism.

## Technical Efficiency

The advocates of centralized socialism find it easy to imagine that central planners would know the production function for each good and, thus, know the maximum quantity of output associated with any given combination of inputs. Naturally, this knowledge would be incorporated in a perfectly computed plan that obedient citizens—filled with moral fervor or in search of material rewards—would then execute with precision. There would be no technical inefficiency at all.

Critics are not so sure. They wonder, in particular, about the reaction of people to a system in which central planners enforced their decisions by commands. If the commands were backed up by threats, might the workers and enterprise managers not lie to central planners when initially questioned about the production functions they know most about? Might they not, for example, pretend that it took 0.2 tons of seed and 1 labor hour to produce 1 ton of corn (as in Table 6.3, "Technical Coefficients") when the true numbers were 0.1 tons of seed and 0.5 labor hour, respectively? This misinforming of planners would stack the deck in favor of workers and enterprise managers and make it less likely for them to be punished later for having missed their input norms and output quotas. At the same time, of course, corn output from given inputs would not be as high as was possible; workers might just *eat* some of the seed and goof off on the job, while producing one ton of corn instead of two.

Or consider the possibility, critics say, of central commands being backed up by rewards designed by central planners to create "distributive justice." Central planners might then divorce people's income from their contribution to production. But if people were told, for example, that they would get the same income as everyone else no matter what they did, they might just decide to work less than otherwise and produce less than the maximum possible output. People might just go through the motions, putting in a minimum effort, barely doing what was required and never doing more. The kind of problem reported in Close-Up 2.1, "A Tale of Two Ford Plants: X-Inefficiency," might be widespread, indeed.

Once more, we cannot be certain about any of this. Central planners might succeed, in one way or another, in motivating people admirably and in stamping out every trace of technical inefficiency. However, we certainly should not claim that such success would be a foregone conclusion.

## Economic Efficiency

If central planners were omniscient, they would, of course, make sure that their resources were employed in economically efficient ways. They would then be aware of the situations of economic inefficiency described in tables 2.1 to 2.4 of Chapter 2, and they would take immediate steps to achieve economic efficiency.

Even the most ardent advocates of centralized socialism, however, do not claim that it would ensure an economically efficient employment of resources or allocation of goods. Consider how, under the best of circumstances, resources and goods would be allocated in this system: Every enterprise manager would be told by the central planners how much to produce of each good (and to whom to deliver what quantities) and what combination of inputs to use to achieve this result. Other enterprise managers and households and public administrators of nonhuman re- sources would be told, in turn, to deliver specific quantities of specific inputs to specific enterprises. And households would be given specified quantities of con- sumption goods in return for their obedient execution of central commands. If the plan were perfect, the actions of all would fit perfectly into a well-coordinated whole. Thus, central planners would be completely absorbed in the coordination effort; they would be perfectly happy with a plan that called, say, for the production of 1,171.818 million tons of corn on the one hand—a figure noted in row C, column (8) of Table 6.2, "The Plan Document"—and that called for the allocation to various users of corn of precisely the same quantity on the other hand—as do the various entries in row C, columns (1) to (7) of our table. Yet, even a perfectly coordinated central plan that was perfectly executed could be an economically inefficient plan! No one has explained the reason for this more eloquently than Friedrich von Hayek (Biography 6.2 at the end of this chapter). As Hayek has put it, any large group of people who try to achieve economic efficiency inevitably encounter the **knowledge problem,** the difficulty of making use jointly of all the knowledge relevant to the achievement of economic efficiency, given the fact that this knowledge is not available to a single mind in its totality but is found, in billions of dispersed fragments, in the minds of countless separate individuals. This knowledge, furthermore, is not only *scientific* knowledge, of general applicability— for example, the technical knowledge about which chemicals must be combined in what proportions to make plastics. Such scientific knowledge could conceivably be gathered in one central place. The knowledge about which Hayek is concerned is primarily *unorganized* knowledge of particular applicability, the fleeting knowledge of the particular circumstances of place and time. Consider knowledge of *production possibilities* and *preferences* that refers only to particular places and people and moments. Each individual inevitably possesses unique bits of such knowledge.

As we already learned in Chapter 2, this type of knowledge may concern a *marginal rate of transformation (MRT),* the rate at which a producer is technically able to exchange, in the process of production, a little bit of one variable (say, labor or butter) for a little bit of another variable (say, apples produced with the help of that labor or produced in place of that butter). Or the information may be about a *marginal rate of substitution (MRS),* the rate at which a consumer is willing to exchange, as a matter of indifference, a little bit of one variable (say, the consumption of leisure or butter) for a little bit of another variable (say, the consumption of apples received for the sacrifice of leisure or butter). If we simply refer to these bits of information as *MRT*s (production possibilities) and *MRS*s (preferences), we can outline Hayek's argument thusly:

Consider, Hayek suggests, the enormous volume of this information. In the area of production possibilities, imagine the set of billions of *MRT*s. One *MRT* might be that of a farmer who could turn an extra day's worth of labor into 10 extra tons of wheat (given, of course, that farm's current levels and types of output, its current employment of particular people, land, and capital, and currently available technical knowledge). Another *MRT* might be the rate of a different farmer whose quite different circumstances allowed only a yield of 2 extra tons of wheat for an extra day of labor applied. Clearly, any one person who possessed knowledge of both of these *MRT*s would realize that it would be more effective to allocate extra labor to the first farm rather than to the second one, if extra wheat was to be produced. Yet, there might be another farmer still whose *MRT* was even more favorable. And all these *MRT*s would be conditional upon current circumstances. Every change in the volume of inputs and outputs, in technical knowledge, in the quality of people or machines, the weather, and a million other circumstances would change these objective possibilities.

The same is true for people's preferences. Imagine the nearly infinite set of *MRS*s: One *MRS* might be that of a man willing to exchange, indifferently, an extra hour of work for the equivalent of an extra bushel of apples. Another person might be delighted to give up income equivalent to two bushels of apples for an extra hour of leisure. Once more, a person knowing both could arrange for a mutually advantageous deal. And, once more, such a person would realize that there were billions of *MRS*s to consult, if the best allocation of resources and goods were to be achieved, and that each of these *MRS*s would be conditional upon current circumstances as well.

How could all this *dispersed* knowledge be utilized *jointly?* Sure enough, argues Hayek, if the mind (or the computer) of a national central planner contained all this knowledge about the ever changing circumstances of all individuals, that planner might search systematically for violations of Pareto's marginal conditions and, as we did in Chapter 2, could point out remedial actions to be taken that would raise the welfare of people. But such would not be the case. No central planner ever could gather together this unorganized type of knowledge. It would always remain dispersed. The central planner would always be ignorant of most of what was known to all others taken together. Indeed, the kind of economic system contemplated in this chapter contains no mechanism for centralizing the knowledge in question. Consider an example.

**The First Pareto Condition.**    Given a perfectly computed central plan of the type discussed earlier in this chapter, it would be quite possible for producer α to be told to use 20 units of input *x* (among other inputs) to produce 50 units of output *a;* and for β to be told to use 10*x* to make 80*a*. If it so happened that their *MRT*s diverged (as in part A of Table 2.1, "The Optimum Allocation of a Resource among Producers of the Same Good"), economic inefficiency would exist. The central planners (concerned solely with the internal consistency of their commands) would not know, and the managers of $\alpha$ and $\beta$ (concerned solely with obeying commands) would have no right to reallocate resources contrary to central orders, even if they should know about their divergent *MRT*s and the implied possibilities for higher output. The unique (and "unscientific") knowledge of people on the spot about their peculiar circumstances would therefore escape the central planners (whose general and "scientific" knowledge of technical coefficients would represent nationwide *average* rates of transformation, and not the marginal rates of transformation of particular producers). Since decisions would be made without the active cooperation of the people on the spot, their intimate knowledge would go unused, and output would end up smaller than necessary.

**The Other Pareto Conditions.** The same conclusion can be reached about other Pareto conditions of economic efficiency. If central planning worked perfectly, as envisioned in our model, producer $\alpha$ might receive output quotas for the production of 20$a$ and 30$b$, and producer $\beta$ for the production of 50$a$ and 60$b$ (as in part A of Table 2.2, "The Optimum Specialization of Production among Producers of the Same Goods"). If they fulfilled their targets exactly, the central planners would be happy, indeed, for the output of every enterprise would mesh neatly with that of all others. Yet, there would be no incentive for anyone to inquire whether the *MRT*s differed as in Table 2.2. The central planners would not know; the enterprise managers would only be concerned with doing as they were told.

The same can be said about the situation of part A, Table 2.3, "The Optimum Composition of Production and Consumption." If producer $\alpha$ was told to produce 20$a$ and 30$b$, and if consumer X was assigned 10$a$ and 20$b$, the central planners would be all too happy if things worked out exactly as specified in the plan. The central planners would have no knowledge of the (divergent) *MRT* and *MRS*. And producer $\alpha$ and consumer X would have no right, even if they could reveal this fact to each other, to arrange a private reordering of production. In this moneyless centralized economy, the Invisible Hand, by which people might signal to each other bits of information about their peculiar capabilities and preferences, would be quite dead.

Finally, it is equally likely that the allocation of goods in the model economy envisioned here would be inefficient as well. Since people would be assigned consumption goods by the central planners (in accordance with whatever criterion was considered fair), the type of situation depicted in part A of Table 2.4, "The Optimum Allocation of Goods among Consumers of the Same Goods," could easily arise. The central planners would neither know nor care about the peculiar and momentary preferences of consumers (that can be expressed by the *MRS*).

The likely inefficiency of a direct assignment of consumption goods could be removed, however, if the central planners allowed households to trade their rations freely with one another. Then a private market would arise (similar to the one described in Close-Up 2.3, "The POW Camp"), and the inefficient situation depicted in part A of Table 2.4 would quickly turn into the efficient one depicted in part C. Even if central planners did not allow such exchanges (because they wanted households to consume exactly the quantities of each good central planners considered best for them), illegal black markets would almost certainly arise and help remove the inefficiency.

We conclude: There is nothing in the design of the model of centralized socialism that would bring about economic efficiency. If such a state of affairs were to be achieved, it would be the consequence of human activities *outside* the central plan, as in black markets among enterprise managers or households who happened to be aware of possibilities for mutually beneficial transactions.

## Economic Growth

The advocates of centralized socialism believe that their favorite economic system would be particularly well suited to the promotion of an ''optimum'' rate of economic growth—optimum growth being typically defined as *rapid* growth. Such rapid economic growth would be achieved easily, it is believed, because central planners would have total control over the composition of the set of final goods produced. By reducing entries in column (4) of Table 6.2, ''The Plan Document,'' to whatever low levels were feasible, central planners could *force* households to save (that is, release resources from the production of consumption goods) at the ''proper'' rate. And planners could allocate these resources, in turn, to growth-promoting activities by making appropriate high entries in columns (5), (6), or (7), it is said. Let us consider the two types of economic growth noted in Chapter 3.

**Extensive Growth.**   Given the enormous economic power of the central planners, entries in columns (5) to (7) could be arranged to ensure the acquisition of capital goods—in the form of new airports, blast furnaces, fleets of trucks, stockpiles of steel, superhighways, and more. As long as this acquisition of capital (through direct domestic production or through imports paid for by exports) exceeded that needed to replace depreciating old capital or the drawing down of inventories, the stock of society's capital could be made to grow.

In addition, planners would have total control over the hours worked by people and over the rate at which existing stocks of nonhuman resources were utilized. Thus, extensive growth could be promoted by forcing people to work harder, as well as by forcing them to save harder.

Critics, however, are not so sure of the system's success in promoting growth. Although they are willing to admit all of the above, they wonder whether errors in planning or plan execution would not offset the growth-promoting potential inherent in centralized economic power. What, they say, if the plan failed to specify the production of the proper type of ball bearings? Or what if they were sent to the wrong place? That might bring to a halt the production of railroad freight cars (and be one cause of unemployment in that industry). That, in turn, might make it impossible to ship iron ore from the mines to steel mills; and the lack of steel might make a shambles out of all kinds of grand investment projects. Before long, unfinished factories, blast furnaces, and bridges would be strewn across the land, and that wouldn't do much for the rate of economic growth. And people who were forced to work at an exhausting pace all year (perhaps even at occupations and in locations they despised) might not exactly bubble over with productivity. Thus, throwing more hours into the productive process would not be an assurance of a corresponding increase in output, critics conclude.

**Intensive Growth.**   The resources saved from the production of consumption goods could also be allocated, by proper entries in columns (5) to (7) of the Plan Document, to the production of hospitals, schools, and research facilities—all designed to improve the quality of resources and to advance technical know-how—and, thus, create intensive growth.

Critics, however, wonder whether the rate of innovation in the centrally planned economy might not suffer severely. They point out how technical progress would be hampered by the central planners' insistence on giving detailed instructions to all enterprise managers (remember the output quotas and input norms). Who, therefore, would ever dare take the risk of trying out a new way of producing? Such action would involve going against specific instructions! To undertake such innovative activity with permission, on the other hand, would require, critics suspect, endless rounds of approval and clearances, and that would surely slow things down. Thus, in the end, no one but the central planners themselves would take the risks of innovating; and central planners might be reluctant to engage in the kind of continuous experimentation that occurs in a decentralized capitalist economy. (In such an economy, many independent entrepreneurs continually try out new ways of doing things on a small scale; failures are therefore localized, but successes are quickly imitated and spread throughout the economy.)

We conclude: Like full employment and technical efficiency, rapid economic growth under centralized socialism, though possible, is not a certainty. Central economic planners have the power to enforce any desired division of the GNP between consumption and investment. If they were so inclined, they could, in fact, maximize the current production of consumption goods at the expense of investment goods, which would do little for the rate of economic growth. Or, they could, on the contrary, maximize the current production of investment goods at the expense of consumption goods, which would tend to raise the rate of economic growth. Yet there would be possible offsetting factors: errors in planning or plan execution that wasted resources saved from consumption, or the stifling of entrepreneurship, to name just two of the possibilities.

## Equity

It is easy to see that the model economy described earlier in this chapter would not produce *commutative* justice. All the necessary ingredients for such a state of affairs would be missing—by design.

The advocates of centralized socialism argue, however, that theirs would be a system of perfect *distributive* justice. This would be so because consumption goods would be directly allocated by the central government to all the people—with a view, of course, to fairness (as defined by the central government). Thus, inequalities, should they arise, would be deliberately arranged for good reasons; they would not emerge from the "blind forces" of the market economy.

Critics, naturally, are worried about the absolute power resting in the hands of the central government. It clearly could apportion goods among people in *any* fashion it chose—and call the result fair.

## Alienation

Would people encounter alienation in the model world of centralized socialism? The answer is almost certainly "yes" with respect to the first two forms of it.

**Alienation from the Self.**  Surely the centralized socialist economy, like any modern economy, would be filled with machines, centralized workplaces, rigid schedules, and such. Thus, it would have its share of "moronizing" work, but would individuals, nevertheless, be able to live their own lives freely, and to develop their talents in whatever ways they considered best? Critics think not, because the advocates of centralized socialism, above all else, champion collectivism and reject individualism. As they see it, there is something incredibly crass about millions of separate individuals seeking their own happiness in a multitude of different (and unpredictable) ways. How much nobler would be a society in which all people embraced the same dream and then acted in selfless devotion to achieve this all-embracing common purpose! Therefore, argue the collectivists, a central government should define the meaning of that dream (variously referred to as "the common good," "the general interest," or "the social welfare") and then specify the actions required by everyone to achieve it. (Recall Table 6.2, "The Plan Document.") This implies that individuals would have to submit to the will of the central planners, whose decisions, made "for the people's own good," could not be open to compromise. And this is the chief reason, critics fear, why centralized socialism would be likely to keep people from leading their own lives in their own ways. Should people find themselves in situations that stunted the development of their talents, they would have precious little chance to escape them.

**Alienation from Other People.**  The model of centralized socialism implies the presence of an all-powerful bureaucracy that claims supreme wisdom and, thus, the right to impose its will upon all. By design, there would be no room for consumer sovereignty or worker sovereignty or citizen sovereignty (concepts discussed at length in Chapter 4). Consider, for example, central planners who had just worked out a plan like Table 6.2. Then imagine the consequences if central planners discovered that their people would prefer having fewer goods and working fewer hours (because their happiness as defined by them would be greater if they could have leisure time to play the violin or sit under trees thinking about the meaning of life). Imagine the consequences if central planners discovered that their people would prefer producing and consuming more airplane trips and restaurant meals and less electric power and corn (because their happiness as defined by them would be greater if they could travel and see the world). Imagine the consequences if central planners discovered that their people would prefer consuming more now and less in the future (because their happiness as defined by them would be greater if they could have books and oil paints and tennis rackets and washing machines now rather than more blast furnaces and highways now and more housing and medical care later). Central planners would really only have this choice: Give up central planning based on planners' preferences or force the people to accept the planners' preferences. They are bound to choose the latter, critics think.

Along with consumer sovereignty, critics continue, worker sovereignty would be lost as well. Unless the whole plan was to be abandoned, for example, 885.924 million labor hours would have to be worked in the steel industry (Table 6.2, row D, column [2]) even if only 200 million labor hours were forthcoming voluntarily or if, for that matter, people would prefer to supply 1,110 million labor hours to that industry. Thus, many people would have to be coerced into working, though they might prefer leisure, or be coerced into working in one place though they might prefer working in another. Throughout their lives, all workers would be totally dependent on a single employer, the central government. What are the chances, critics ask, that this single central government employer who was already channeling people into occupations as well as specific places of employment would grant workers the right to control their working conditions, perhaps with the help of genuine labor unions? Critics do not consider them high.

And critics are equally pessimistic with respect to citizen sovereignty. As we have seen, except by abandoning their power, central planners could not leave people a choice on matters contained in the central plan, such as work versus leisure, this occupation or that one, consumption versus investment, this consumption good or another—unless, of course, people's own wishes happened to fit into the central plan. To the extent that their wishes did not fit (and the plan was not abandoned), people's actions would have to be *made* to fit into the plan. Is it far-fetched to suppose that central planners would surround themselves with population groups willing to support their choices? That a loyal army, party, secret police, and labor union might be created for the sole purpose of forcing others to submit to the planners' choices or of inducing them to accept a common creed and make these choices their own? Is it far-fetched to suppose that coercion and propaganda, first designed to free central planners from constant criticism and griping, would soon spread to all areas of life? Thus, critics fear, central planners would soon come to suppress any expression of dissent and abolish the political freedoms of individuals along with their economic ones.

**Alienation from the Natural World.**  It is impossible to predict how our model world of centralized socialism would affect people's relations to the natural world. Central planners with complete economic power could clearly indulge a great variety of preferences. If they happened to be nature enthusiasts, they might spare no resources to preserve the natural world; and they might even force extreme material deprivation upon their people to achieve this goal.

Yet, the opposite would be equally possible. If the planners had no use for nature except as a resource to be exploited to the fullest, they might not hesitate in the least to foul up the air, or bodies of water, or the land with agricultural and industrial wastes. They might freely scar the landscape with oil derricks, strip mines, and transmission wires; construct nuclear power plants with abandon; and hunt whales till they were extinct. They might always opt for more goods now—no matter what the cost.

## Analytical Example 6.1

### The Economic Effects of Disarmament

Input-output analysis can be used for more than central economic planning. It has been used to answer questions about the U.S. economy; for example, about the major economic effects certain to follow an international agreement to disarm. The accompanying table, based on 1958 U.S. data, shows some of the predicted results. For example, the 1958 military expenditures on food and kindred products in fact equaled $536 million (at 1947 prices). Yet, a complete cessation of military spending would have reduced demand in that industry by $1513 million because other industries, depending on military demand, would also reduce their demands for food and kindred products. All other entries can be similarly interpreted.

| Industry (1) | Military Demand (millions of 1947 dollars) | |
|---|---|---|
| | Direct (2) | Direct and Indirect (3) |
| Food and kindred products | 536 | 1,513 |
| Apparel and textile-mill products | 143 | 575 |
| Leather products | 24 | 116 |
| Paper and allied products | — | 788 |
| Chemicals and allied products | 85 | 877 |
| Fuel and power | 991 | 2,633 |
| Rubber and rubber products | 6 | 244 |
| Lumber and wood products | 19 | 451 |
| Nonmetallic minerals and products | — | 337 |
| Primary metals | — | 3,384 |
| Fabricated metal products | 106 | 1,281 |
| Machinery (except electrical) | 166 | 823 |
| Electrical machinery | 915 | 3,110 |
| Transportation equipment and ordnance | 9,478 | 10,609 |
| Instruments and allied products | 22 | 370 |

| Industry | Military Demand (millions of 1947 dollars) | |
| (1) | Direct (2) | Direct and Indirect (3) |
| --- | --- | --- |
| Miscellaneous manufacturing industries | — | 119 |
| Transportation | 730 | 1,486 |
| Trade | 78 | 735 |
| Service and finance | 705 | 1,886 |
| Construction | 967 | 967 |
| Unallocated and waste products | 742 | 2,144 |

*Source:* Wassily W. Leontief and Marvin Hoffenberg, ''The Economic Effects of Disarmament,'' *Scientific American,* April 1961, pp. 47–55. Copyright © 1961 by Scientific American, Inc. All rights reserved. Reprinted by permission.

Clearly, disarmament by itself would produce massive but differential cuts in industry sales, as indicated in column (3) of the accompanying table and, therefore, cuts in output and employment. Yet, the same analysis can be used to indicate the opposite effects of any increase in nonmilitary demands and can help guide policy makers toward actions that minimize adjustment effects.

*Note:* Regional aspects of the same issue are explored by Walter Isard and Eugene W. Schooler in "An Economic Analysis of Local and Regional Impacts of Reduction of Military Expenditures," *Peace Research Society Papers,* 1 (1964), pp. 15–45. International impacts are investigated in Emile Benoit, editor, *Disarmament and World Economic Interdependence* (New York: Columbia University Press, 1967).

## Analytical Example 6.2

## The Structure of Development

Input-output analysis, by facilitating comparisons of the internal structures of developed and undeveloped economies, can help map out paths to economic development. The input-output tables in Figure 6.1 indicate internal structures of model economies symbolically. Each number (at the head of a column or row) represents a different economic sector, and $O$ stands for "output," $I$ for "input," $D$ for "final demand," $T$ for "total output," and $H$ for "household-supplied resource services." The filled-in squares represent numerical entries in the various cells of the table.

Panel (a) shows a completely interdependent economy. Each sector supplies outputs to all others and draws inputs from all others. Panel (b), on the other hand, shows a random pattern of interindustry transactions. Some boxes are empty because no transactions occur between the affected sectors. In panel (c), panel (b) reappears with sectors rearranged (note the sequence of sector "call numbers"). This rearrangement, called *triangulation,* reveals a hierarchical pattern of interindustry transactions. Note how sector 9 delivers its entire output to itself or to final

**Figure 6.1**    Input-Output Tables

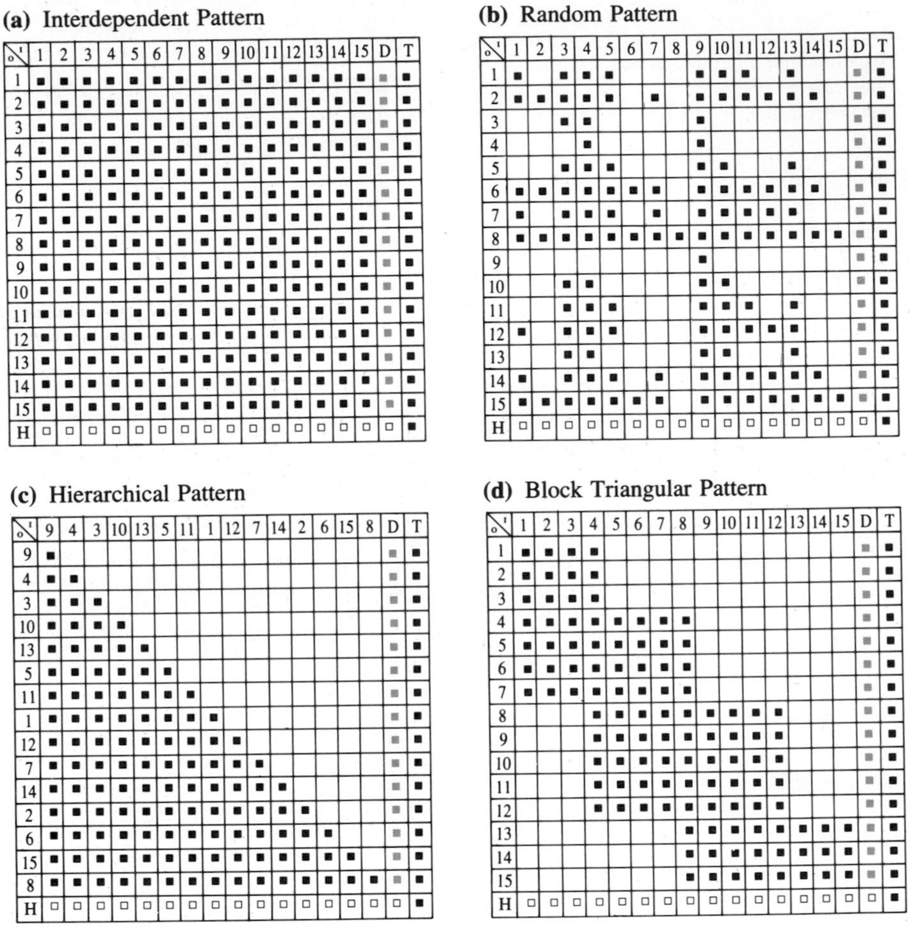

**(a) Interdependent Pattern**

| o\ | 1 | 2 | 3 | 4 | 5 | 6 | 7 | 8 | 9 | 10 | 11 | 12 | 13 | 14 | 15 | D | T |
|---|---|---|---|---|---|---|---|---|---|---|---|---|---|---|---|---|---|

**(b) Random Pattern**

| o\ | 1 | 2 | 3 | 4 | 5 | 6 | 7 | 8 | 9 | 10 | 11 | 12 | 13 | 14 | 15 | D | T |
|---|---|---|---|---|---|---|---|---|---|---|---|---|---|---|---|---|---|

**(c) Hierarchical Pattern**

| o\ | 9 | 4 | 3 | 10 | 13 | 5 | 11 | 1 | 12 | 7 | 14 | 2 | 6 | 15 | 8 | D | T |
|---|---|---|---|---|---|---|---|---|---|---|---|---|---|---|---|---|---|

**(d) Block Triangular Pattern**

| o\ | 1 | 2 | 3 | 4 | 5 | 6 | 7 | 8 | 9 | 10 | 11 | 12 | 13 | 14 | 15 | D | T |
|---|---|---|---|---|---|---|---|---|---|---|---|---|---|---|---|---|---|

*Source:* Wassily W. Leontief, "The Structure of Development," *Scientific American,* September 1963, pp. 148–66. Copyright © 1963 by Scientific American, Inc. All rights reserved. Recently, Leontief has developed the first input-output model of the world economy. Interested readers may wish to study his associated discussion of the economic prospects of the less developed nations. *See* "The World Economy of the Year 2000," *Scientific American,* September 1980, pp. 207–31.

demand but absorbs inputs from all sectors. Sector 8, on the other hand, delivers output to everyone but uses as inputs only its own output and household-supplied resource services. The sectors above a given row in panel (c) are that row's customers; the sectors below a given row are suppliers. Thus, any increase in final demand for a sector generates indirect demands that cascade down the diagonal slope of the matrix and leave the sectors above unaffected.

Panel (d), finally, shows a "block triangular" economy with interdependence of industries within blocks and hierarchical relationships among them. The analysis of such tables shows development planners in economically less developed countries which "working parts" typically found in developed economies are lacking in their country and also the sequence in which sectors must be developed.

## Biography 6.1    Wassily W. Leontief

Wassily W. Leontief (1906– ) was born in St. Petersburg, Russia (now Leningrad), where his father taught economics and his mother art history. He studied at the universities of Leningrad and Berlin, did postgraduate research at the University of Kiel, and advised the Chinese government in Nanking. In 1931, he joined the National Bureau of Economic Research and soon thereafter the faculty of Harvard. He stayed at Harvard until his retirement and subsequent move to New York University. While at Harvard, in 1970, he served as president of the American Economic Association. In 1973, "for his input-output methods of quantifying interdependencies in an economy and using them to predict large-scale trends," he was awarded the Nobel Memorial Prize in Economic Science.

Even though Leontief had experimented with primitive chessboard balances of the Soviet economy in the 1920s while at Leningrad, his major work on input-output analysis appeared much later as *The Structure of [the] American Economy: 1919– 1939: An Empirical Application of Equilibrium Analysis* (1941). Other important works include *Studies in the Structure of the American Economy: Theoretical and Empirical Explorations in Input-Output Analysis* (1953); *Input-Output Economics* (1966); *Essays in Economics,* vol. 1: *Theories and Theorizing* (1966), vol. 2: *Theories, Facts, and Policies* (1977); and *The Future of the World Economy: A United Nations Study* (1977).

During World War II, the U.S. government was the first to develop input-output tables; today such tables are commonly used around the world. But everywhere analysts have run into the problem of having insufficient data that advancing theoretical knowledge and high-speed computers are ready to use. Said Leontief in his presidential address to the American Economic Association:[a]

*Economics today rides the crest of intellectual respectability and popular acclaim. . . . But I submit that the consistently indifferent performance in practical applications is in fact a symptom of a fundamental imbalance in the present state of our discipline. The weak and all too slowly growing empirical foundation clearly cannot support the proliferating superstructure of pure, or should I say, speculative economic theory. . . . The task of securing a massive flow of primary economic data can be compared to that of providing the high energy physicists with a gigantic accelerator. The scientists have their machines while the economists are still waiting for their data. In our case not only must the society be willing to provide year after year the millions of dollars required for maintenance of a vast statistical machine, but a large number of citizens must be prepared to play, at least, a passive and occasionally even an active part in actual fact-*

*finding operations. It is as if the electrons and protons had to be persuaded to cooperate with the physicist. . . . Economists should be prepared to take a leading role in shaping this major social enterprise. . . . [The] public has amply demonstrated its readiness to back the pursuit of knowledge. It will lend its generous support to our venture, too, if we take the trouble to explain what it is all about.*

[a]Wassily Leontief, "Theoretical Assumptions and Nonobserved Facts," *The American Economic Review,* March 1971, pp. 1–7.

## Biography 6.2　Friedrich A. von Hayek

Friedrich August von Hayek (1899– ) was born and educated in Vienna. He began his career as director of the Austrian Institute for Economic Research and lecturer in economics at the University of Vienna. Starting in 1931, he served as professor first at the London School of Economics, then at the University of Chicago, and finally at the University of Freiburg in Germany. In 1974, while serving as visiting professor at the University of Salzburg in Austria, von Hayek was awarded the Nobel Memorial Prize in Economic Science (jointly with Sweden's Gunnar Myrdal). Von Hayek's greatest insight, perhaps, is that markets, above all else, are mechanisms for utilizing knowledge. He considered the question of what institutional arrangement could best enable large numbers of people—each possessing only bits of knowledge—to cooperate with each other so as to achieve the best use of resources. He rejected the notion that one could put at the disposal of some center all the knowledge that ought to be used but that was initially dispersed among many. The relevant knowledge is made up of elements of such number, diversity, and variety, he argued, that its explicit, conscious combination in a single mind is impossible. Yet, the spontaneous interaction of people in free markets can bring about that which could be achieved by deliberate action only by someone possessing the combined knowledge of all. Consider his own words.[a]

*It is worth contemplating for a moment a very simple and commonplace instance of the action of the price system to see what precisely it accomplishes. Assume that somewhere in the world a new opportunity for the use of some raw material, say tin, has arisen, or that one of the sources of supply of tin has been eliminated. It does not matter for our purpose—and it is very significant that it does not matter—which of these two causes has made tin more scarce. All that the users of tin need to know is that some of the tin they used to consume is now more profitably employed elsewhere. . . . There is no need for the great majority of them even to know where the more urgent need has arisen. . . . If only some of them know directly of the new demand, and switch resources over to it, and if the people who are aware of the new gap thus created in turn fill it from still*

[a]Friedrich A. von Hayek, "The Use of Knowledge in Society," *The American Economic Review,* September 1945, pp. 519–30.

*other sources, the effect will rapidly spread throughout the whole economic system and influence not only all the uses of tin, but also those of its substitutes and the substitutes of these substitutes, the supply of all the things made of tin, and their substitutes. . . .*

*The most significant fact about this system is the economy of knowledge with which it operates. . . . In abbreviated form, by a kind of symbol, only the most essential information is passed on, and passed on only to those concerned. . . . The marvel is that in a case like that of a scarcity of one raw material, without an order being issued, without more than perhaps a handful of people knowing the cause, tens of thousands of people whose identity could not be ascertained by months of investigation, are made to use the material or its products more sparingly. . . .*

*I have deliberately used the word "marvel" to shock the reader out of the complacency with which we often take the working of this mechanism for granted. I am convinced that if it were the result of deliberate human design, and if the people guided by the price changes understood that their decisions have significance far beyond their immediate aim, this mechanism would have been acclaimed as one of the greatest triumphs of the human mind. . . . But those who clamor for "conscious direction"—and who cannot believe that anything which has evolved without design (and even without our understanding it) should solve problems which we should not be able to solve consciously—should remember this: The problem is precisely how to extend the span of our utilization of resources beyond the span of the control of any one mind; and, therefore, how to dispense with the need of conscious control and how to provide inducements which will make the individuals do the desirable things without anyone having to tell them what to do.*

Von Hayek is more than an economist. He is also an eminent political and legal theorist. He is convinced that markets do the best job of solving the problem of resource allocation, but only if they are free from any distortions introduced by ill-advised governments. In a best-selling book, *The Road to Serfdom* (1944), von Hayek warns that the enthusiasm of governments for intervening in the market leads us down a path that ends in central planning and totalitarianism. Government intervention will, thus, cause the end of the free society, humanity's highest social achievement.

Von Hayek's most recent books from the University of Chicago Press are magnificent statements of all these themes: *The Constitution of Liberty* (1960); and *Law, Legislation, and Liberty,* vol. 1, *Rules and Order* (1973), vol. 2, *The Mirage of Social Justice* (1976), and vol. 3, *The Political Order of a Free Society* (1979).

## Summary

1. In this chapter, we perform a thought experiment and imagine an idealized economic system of *centralized socialism*. This economic model has three features: (a) It is a world of pure socialism in which the formal ownership not of some or most but of *all* natural and capital resources resides in different groups of people or even jointly in the single group of

all the people making up society. (b) It is a world of perfectly centralized socialism in which the effective control over nonhuman resources is exercised exclusively by the central government. (c) It is a world in which the central government, relying on a common plan that specifies everyone's future action in detail, coordinates the separate economic activities of all people by verbal commands exclusively.

2. Modern economies are characterized by an incredible degree of interdependence because millions of households and productive enterprises participate in an intricate system of specialization and exchange. This interdependence makes central economic planning difficult because the decision to employ resources in one direction inevitably requires decisions to employ them in other directions as well, for each output, by requiring inputs, affects other outputs. Before all else, therefore, central planners must solve the *coordination problem* and see to it that the specialized activities of all the people engaged in the division of labor fit into a well-coordinated whole.

3. One approach to solving the coordination problem makes use of *input-output analysis,* a mathematical technique designed to visualize the internal structure of an economy and to study interdependencies in it. An input-output table for a recent time period might be used as a basis for the central planning of economic activity to be performed in a future period. Such planning is bound to go through several stages: the selection of a desired set of final goods, the calculation of technical coefficients, the calculation (perhaps with the help of the Leontief inverse) of future total output requirements, and the calculation of future input requirements of intermediate goods and primary resource services.

4. An alternative approach to solving the coordination problem expresses each input-output table row as an independent linear equation and then solves the set of simultaneous equations for the unknown future flows of goods to be produced and resources to be utilized—given a knowledge of technical coefficients and an arbitrarily designated composition of the future GNP.

5. Once central planners have worked out a well-coordinated plan that is also feasible, they can turn it into reality by issuing appropriate commands (output quotas and input norms) to all those from whom action is required. Obedience to such commands can be ensured through negative incentives or positive incentives (moral or material).

6. It is interesting to speculate about the likely performance of the model of centralized socialism. Such speculation is provided by applying the various success criteria introduced in chapters 2 through 4.

## Key Terms

| | |
|---|---|
| adjoint matrix | cofactor |
| central plan | constant returns to scale |

coordination problem
decreasing returns to scale
determinant
final goods
identity matrix
increasing returns to scale
input norms
input-output analysis
input-output table
intermediate goods
inverse matrix

knowledge problem
Leontief inverse matrix
Leontief matrix
main diagonal
managerial coordination
matrix
minor
technical coefficients
output quotas
Visible Hand

## Questions and Problems*

1. Consider an input-output table, such as Table 6.1, "The Input-Output Table," or 6.2, "The Plan Document."
   a. Could a column (4) entry be negative? What would a negative entry there mean?
   b. Suppose the table applied not to the moneyless model economy of centralized socialism, but to the actual U.S. economy and that all entries were in monetary terms. What would be the meaning of the *sums* of the various rows and columns?
2. Consider the accompanying input-output table, Table 6.6. Interpret the meaning of (a) the various rows and (b) the various columns.
3. Once again, consider Table 6.6. Use it to calculate a table of technical coefficients like Table 6.3.
* 4. Consider the answer to problem 3 (which is Table 6.A at the back of this book). Use it to derive the Leontief inverse. Interpret the meaning of columns (1) and (2) of that inverse.
5. Consider the answers to problems 3 and 4 (Tables 6.A and 6.B at the back of the book). Use these answers to set up a complete central plan for producing the desired GNP given in Table 6.7. Explain how one can get such an answer.
6. What would happen to the kind of central planning described in this chapter if constant returns to scale did *not* prevail? Explain.
* 7. Write down the central plan contemplated in problem 5 in the form of six equations analogous to equations (13) to (18) in the text (page 104). Then solve the equations and compare your answer to Table 6.C, "The New Plan," at the back of the book.
8. Comment on the following statement:
   "Central planners often fail to appreciate the fact that scientific knowledge is not the only knowledge relevant to the best use of

---

*Questions marked with an asterisk utilize advanced material presented in optional sections.

**Table 6.6**

| Recipients / Suppliers | Of Intermediate Goods and Primary Resources | | | Of Final Goods and Primary Resources | | | | Total |
|---|---|---|---|---|---|---|---|---|
| | Truck Producers (1) | Fuel Oil Producers (2) | Corn Producers (3) | Domestic Households (4) | Domestic Producers (5) | Domestic Government (6) | Foreigners (7) | (8) |
| (A) Truck Producers (millions of trucks) | 1 | 2 | 3 | 0 | 7 | 2 | 5 | 20 |
| (B) Fuel Oil Producers (millions of barrels of oil) | 2 | 5 | 6 | 400 | 200 | 100 | −663 | 50 |
| (C) Corn Producers (millions of tons of corn) | 1 | 0 | 30 | 20 | −261 | 10 | 500 | 300 |
| (D) Labor Owners (millions of labor hours) | 200 | 1 | 30 | 100 | | 300 | 69 | 700 |
| (E) Land Owners (millions of acre hours) | 800 | 550 | 930 | 100 | | 500 | 20 | 2,900 |
| (F) Capital Owners (millions of machine hours) | 400 | 50 | 150 | 200 | | 20 | 80 | 900 |

resources. Knowing the specific circumstances of producers at particular times and places (such as the age of their machines, the state of health of their workers, and even the weather) can be just as productive.''

9. Comment on the following statement:

   ''Under centralized socialism, economic inefficiency might well persist even if, by some miracle, central planners could gather together all the relevant knowledge about *MRT*s and *MRS*s that should be used but that was, in the first instance, held by others.''

10. Comment on the following statement:

   ''I am confused. The caption to Table 6.3, ''Technical Coefficients,'' says that the figures 'are based on Table 6.1, columns (1) to (3) and (8).' Yet when I calculate technical coefficients from Table 6.2, I get the same answer.''

**Table 6.7**

| Recipients / Suppliers | Of Intermediate Goods and Primary Resources | | | Of Final Goods and Primary Resources | | | | Total |
|---|---|---|---|---|---|---|---|---|
| | Truck Producers (1) | Fuel oil Producers (2) | Corn Producers (3) | Domestic House-holds (4) | Domestic Producers (5) | Domestic Govern-ment (6) | Foreigners (7) | (8) |
| (A) **Truck Producers** (millions of trucks) | | | | 0 | 7 | 20 | 5 | |
| (B) **Fuel Oil Producers** (millions of barrels of oil) | | | | 400 | 200 | 100 | − 100 | |
| (C) **Corn Producers** (millions of tons of corn) | | | | 20 | 100 | 10 | 500 | |
| (D) **Labor Owners** (millions of labor hours) | | | | 100 | | 300 | 0 | |
| (E) **Land Owners** (millions of acre hours) | | | | 100 | | 500 | 0 | |
| (F) **Capital Owners** (millions of machine hours) | | | | 200 | | 20 | 0 | |

# Selected Readings

Chenery, Hollis B., and Paul G. Clark. *Interindustry Economics* (New York: Wiley, 1962). A text on input-output analysis.

Hayek, Friedrich A. *The Road to Serfdom* (Chicago: University of Chicago Press, 1944). The 1974 co-winner of the Nobel Prize for Economics argues that central economic planning leads to dictatorship because dictatorship is the most effective instrument of coercion, which is essential to such planning.

Leontief, Wassily W. *The Structure of [the] American Economy, 1919–1939: An Empirical Application of Equilibrium Analysis*, 2nd ed. (New York: Oxford University Press, 1951). The first major work on input-output analysis, by the 1973 winner of the Nobel Prize in economics.

Leontief, Wassily W. *Input-Output Economics* (New York: Oxford University Press, 1985). A text on input-output analysis.

Miernyk, William H. *The Elements of Input-Output Analysis* (New York: Random House, 1965). A text on input-output analysis.

Miller, Ronald E., and Peter D. Blair. *Input-Output Analysis: Foundations and Extensions.* (Englewood Cliffs, NJ: Prentice-Hall, 1985). A comprehensive text, including applications and the U.S. input-output tables for 1947–77.

U.S. Department of Commerce, Interindustry Economics Division. "The Input-Output Structure of the U.S. Economy, 1977," *Survey of Current Business,* May 1984, pp. 42–84. An actual input-output table, complete with technical coefficients and inverse. Contains also an excellent bibliography of U.S.-government publications on input-output.

Wiles, P. J. D. *Economic Institutions Compared* (New York: Wiley, 1977). Chapter 17 discusses the connection between political and economic freedom (and disagrees with the Hayek view noted above).

## Computer Programs

The SYSTEMS personal computer diskette that accompanies this book contains three programs of interest to this chapter:

**a.** Program 6, "Centralized Socialism: A Model," provides 20 multiple-choice questions about Chapter 6, along with immediate responses to incorrect answers.

**b.** Module A, "Matrix Operations," allows you to perform numerous types of matrix operations, including transposing a matrix, adding or subtracting matrices, multiplying matrices by a scalar or with one another, exponentiating a matrix, finding the determinant of a matrix, and inverting a matrix.

**c.** Module B, "Simultaneous Equations," allows you to solve up to 12 simultaneous linear equations.

# CHAPTER 7

# *Centralized Socialism: The Soviet Case*

The Soviet Revolution of 1917 launched the first large-scale experiment in socialism. Its leaders were inspired by Karl Marx (Biography 15.1), but, as we will note in the last chapter of this book, he had concentrated on criticizing capitalism and left no blueprint for the future socialist society he predicted. So the early Soviet leaders engaged in lengthy debates and experiments concerning the best institutional arrangements for dealing with the economic problem. By the late 1920s, a special brand of *centralized* socialism emerged that ever since has been closely identified with the name of Stalin. His system dominated the Soviet Union until far beyond his death in 1953, and, in somewhat modified form, survives there even today. Indeed, as the Soviet sphere of influence has expanded, Stalin's system has been copied widely—in Poland and East Germany, in Czechoslovakia and Hungary, in Bulgaria and Rumania, in Albania and Yugoslavia, even in China, North Korea, Vietnam, and Cuba. As we will see in chapters 9 through 11, all of these countries, to different degrees, have modified Stalin's system. In the present chapter, however, we focus on its role in the Soviet Union itself.

## The Historical Background

Karl Marx expected socialism to arrive first in the most industrialized capitalist countries. As he saw it, their population at that time would consist almost entirely of fairly sophisticated industrial workers, members of an urbanized, class-conscious proletariat. They would be using the world's most advanced production methods, applying their efforts to the most centralized means of production ever assembled and belonging to but a handful of capitalists. None of these predictions was to come true.

True enough, Russia had been put on the path to industrialization by Peter the Great (who reigned from 1689 to 1725), more than two centuries before the Soviet Revolution, but progress had always been slow and its pace had not quickened until after 1861, the year the serfs were freed. By World War I, czarist Russia did have a modest machine industry, moderate numbers of skilled technicians, and a tradition of excellence in mathematics and pure science. A substantial stock of "overhead" capital, such as housing, communications, and transportation facilities, which could, in turn, support industrial activity, had been accumulated. Nevertheless, when the Soviet Revolution was fought in the name of Marx, 80 percent of the Russian population was still composed of illiterate peasants. The industrial proletariat was rather small. By the standards of Western Europe, Russia's production methods were backward. So was her capital stock.

## The Revolutionary Period

In October 1917 (according to the old Russian calendar), an alliance of soldiers, peasants, and workers, searching for "peace, land, and bread" and led by Lenin (Biography 7.1), overthrew the Provisional Government that had taken over from the Czar, who had been forced to abdicate earlier that year. Lenin's government extricated Russia from World War I. The landed estates of aristocrats, church, and government were expropriated, divided, and made available, on an egalitarian basis, to 25 million peasant families for private use. (Buying and selling of the newly acquired land and the hiring of outside labor, however, were forbidden.) In urban areas, many factories were taken over spontaneously by the workers employed in them. More often than not, they ejected owners and managers alike, abolished all income differentials among types of workers, and elected new managers from their own ranks. The central government's attitude toward such matters, however, was cautious and restrained. Nationalization was supported only on a limited basis, involving banks, the grain trade, communications, transportation, and the oil and armament industries. Beyond that, private management was to be retained—supervised, within limits, by worker councils (*Soviets*). And the activities of all producers and consumers continued to be coordinated by markets. All this changed, however, as Lenin's new government became embroiled in a bitter civil war.

## War Communism

As its name suggests, the ensuing period of **War Communism** (from mid-1918 to early 1921) was characterized by two events, not unrelated: a civil war and an apparent attempt to establish communism. Undoubtedly, however, the new regime's fight for survival was of primary importance. The Red Army, organized by Leon Trotsky, was battling the White Armies loyal to the Czar as well as numerous expeditionary forces sent by Britain, France, Japan, Poland, and the United States.

The threat to the new Soviet regime was serious, indeed; at one point, the counterrevolutionary forces held three-quarters of Soviet territory. In the end, the Red Army prevailed, but the path to victory was not an easy one.

In order to fight the civil war, the Soviet government above all else required supplies: food for the soldiers and urban workers, raw materials for industry, arms for the military. In the existing chaos, these supplies could hardly be financed by taxes.

For a while, the revolutionary leaders expected an outbreak of similar revolutions in the advanced industrialized countries of Western Europe. They looked forward to economic aid from the victorious workers abroad. When foreign revolutions failed to materialize, they realized that they had to make it on their own. So the government turned to the liberal printing of money to finance requisite purchases from peasants and industrial enterprises. In the process, a hyperinflation was born. As prices soared, money became almost worthless. Exchange deteriorated into barter; the economy was effectively demonetized. Some of Lenin's followers, notably members of the Trotsky faction of the Bolshevik Party—now renamed Communist Party—were elated at this (unintended) result. Evgenii Preobrazhensky, a prominent economist, for example, likened the printing presses to a machine gun that had brought down the bourgeois market economy by forcing the replacement of monetary exchanges (so many rubles for a bushel of grain or so many rubles for a day's work) by in-kind exchanges that involved natural units only (yards of cloth for bushels of grain, loaves of bread for hours of work). To Preobrazhensky this ''naturalization'' of the economy was a welcome sign of things to come: the entry of Soviet society into the moneyless world of communism. ''Honor to our printing presses,'' he said.

Indeed, many revolutionaries shared a vague vision of a future economy without money and markets, but they had not worked out the details. Consider these ideas circulating at the time:

> The factories, workshops, mines and other productive institutions will all be subdivisions, as it were, of one vast people's workshop, which will embrace the entire national economy of production. . . . Everything must be precisely calculated. We must know in advance how much labour to assign to the various branches of industry; what products are required and how much of each it is necessary to produce; how and where machines must be provided. . . . The communist system of production presupposes in addition that production is not for the market, but for use. . . . The work of production will be effected by the giant cooperative as a whole. In consequence of this change, we will no longer have commodities, only products. These products are not exchanged for one another; they are neither bought nor sold.[1]
>
> Every member of society, performing a certain part of socially-necessary work, receives a certificate from society to the effect that he has done such and such a quantity

[1]Nikolai I. Bukharin and Evgenii A. Preobrazhensky, *The ABC of Communism* (Harmondsworth, England: Penguin, 1969), pp. 114 and 116. (Marxists distinguish goods produced for market sale, which they call *commodities,* from goods produced for direct use and not to be sold, which they call *products.*)

*of work. According to this certificate, he receives from the public warehouses, where articles of consumption are stored, a corresponding quantity of products.*[2]

Around 1919, the Soviet economy seemed to move in the direction just noted. Monetary transactions having broken down, but determined to win the civil war, Lenin's government took a number of steps that gave the appearance of a deliberate effort to establish **communism**—the perfect society that Marx expected to emerge at the end of a long historic development, after the demise of both capitalism and socialism. It would be a moneyless society in which all resources would be owned in common and selfless people would, as Marxists had long put it, contribute to the best of their ability to the process of production, while only taking according to their needs.[3] The steps in question involved the following:

1. The establishment of a centralized system of "requisitioning" (read *confiscating*) agricultural produce from the peasants (*prodrazverstka*) and of allocating the supplies so obtained to the tasks considered most urgent.
2. The nationalization of almost all industrial enterprises, no matter how small, and the centralized allocation of their output. (In part, this legalized the prior unauthorized takeovers of firms by workers; also, this action was designed to remove owners and managers who were sympathetic to the other side in the civil war.)
3. The complete nationalization of all enterprises engaged in wholesale and retail trade (but black markets did, in fact, continue to flourish).
4. The universal conscription (under the leadership of Leon Trotsky) of all able-bodied persons into labor armies and their allocation to tasks specified by the central government. Severe penalties were instituted for deserters.
5. The establishment of a centralized system of rationing by which available consumer goods were allocated directly to all individuals.

Missing, however, was any mechanism for *coordinating* the interdependent activities of 25 million peasant households and some 37,000 enterprises that had just been nationalized. The market system had been destroyed, and a central-planning alternative (such as the input-output technique discussed in Chapter 6) had not been invented. The economy was one of "planless command."

Not surprisingly, the new policies alienated the peasants from the new regime. The peasants resented and resisted the widespread use of brutal force by the Soviet authorities. Many peasants reduced their production to their own consumption needs. Others hid stocks and crop surpluses alike from the confiscating agents of the state so as to sell them in black markets instead. (By 1920, agricultural production had fallen to 64 percent of the prewar 1913 level.)

Enterprises outside agriculture, in turn, were frequently paralyzed by lack of workers, equipment, and raw materials as well as by the absence of directives on

---

[2]Vladimir I. Lenin, *State and Revolution* (New York: International Publishers, 1971), p. 76.
[3]See, for example, Karl Marx, *Selected Works*, vol. 2 (New York: International Publishers, 1932), p. 566.

what to do. As workers went to the countryside in search of food, the urban labor force declined from 2.6 million in 1917 to 1.2 million in 1920. Morale was low; strikes were frequent. (By 1920, industrial production had fallen to 20 percent of the 1913 level.)

While the civil war was won, the economy was in chaos. In 1921, Kronstadt sailors joined Petrograd workers in open revolt; after a bloody battle, Lenin decided that it was time for a change.

## The New Economic Policy

Lenin called it a "strategic retreat" and "a step backwards"; Bukharin referred to it as the "collapse of our illusions." The **New Economic Policy,** or **NEP,** initiated by Lenin in 1921 (and destined to last to 1928), yanked the Soviet economy out of the paralysis brought about by War Communism. It permitted a heavy dose of "capitalism *under communism*"; that is, under the political rule of the Communist Party. The following measures were involved:

1. An immediate end to the system of requisitioning agricultural products (*prodrazverstka*) and its replacement by a fixed tax in kind (*prodnalog*) expressed as a percentage of the peasants' production above subsistence.
2. A currency reform aimed at restoring the role of money and markets.
3. The denationalization of light industry and retail trade, private owners being free to hire up to 20 workers.
4. Major administrative changes in government enterprises. While the government retained the "commanding heights" of the economy (notably banks, communications, transportation, foreign trade, and heavy industry), most government enterprises were made operationally and financially independent. That is, they could make their own input and output decisions and had to cover their costs from sales revenues or bank credits (rather than relying on grants from the government budget). Quite a number of these enterprises were even leased to private managers, often their former owners.
5. An end to all restrictions on labor mobility; wages were to be determined by the market.

By thus sanctioning widespread private ownership in the means of production and providing incentives for private initiative in agriculture, small industry, and trade, Lenin hoped to get the economy moving again. For example, he imagined that the peasants now owning the land would produce a maximum of output in the context of free markets. Whatever they did not need for their own consumption or the new tax in kind would presumably be offered for sale, providing both industrial raw materials and food for the urban population. With the income received, peasants would demand industrial goods wanted as inputs in agriculture or for personal consumption, and this would set the wheels of industry into motion again. As before the war, Lenin speculated, the population was likely to refrain from consuming all its income. The aggregate saving would allow a corresponding use of some resources for investment, stimulating economic growth.

Indeed, this "natural" process of economic growth seemed to work. Industrial output grew at record rates and (by 1927) the prewar level of GNP was regained. But Lenin had never envisioned that his "capitalism under communism" would last forever. He argued, for instance, that rural capitalism would, in the long run, be eliminated by the wholesale introduction of tractors and the electrification of the countryside. As one of his slogans put it, socialism *meant* "Soviet power plus electrification." After Lenin's death, therefore, a serious debate arose within the Communist Party about the advisability of continuing the NEP. Many party leaders wondered how wise it was to rely on the "petty bourgeois" activities of the "NEP men," as the newly sanctioned private entrepreneurs were called, to determine the country's rate of economic growth.

## The Great Industrialization Debate

By 1925, Soviet leaders were united in their belief that industrialization was the country's foremost economic task, but they were divided on how to achieve this goal.

**The Rightists.**    The so-called right wing of the Party, led by Nikolai Bukharin, Mikhail Tomsky, and Alexei Rykov, proposed an indefinite continuation of Lenin's New Economic Policy. The rightists noted how things had worked out just as Lenin had predicted: The end of agricultural requisitioning had induced peasants to raise mightily the flow of agricultural products to the industrial sector (and the flow of money income to themselves). The subsequent increase in peasant demand had, in turn, encouraged production by denationalized small-scale industry of consumption goods and capital goods wanted by the peasants. Moreover, the more successful peasants (or *kulaks*) had begun to save some of their income, making it available to other investors, private and public. Indeed, the collection of Lenin's tax in kind had provided further materials (food for workers, raw materials to be processed) that had made possible the running of nationalized large-scale industries or the promotion of exports in exchange for foreign machinery. In short, Lenin's policy had enabled gradual and simultaneous expansion of all sectors of the economy (balanced growth), all based on voluntary peasant activities. Why not continue a good thing?

Bukharin strongly opposed any "monopolistic parasitism" of nationalized industry; that is, any attempt to speed up this "natural" process of industrialization at the expense of the peasants' standard of living. The best policy toward the peasants (who, after all, constituted the vast majority of the population), argued Bukharin, was to make it possible for them to become rich by working hard. The rest would follow: High peasant income would lead to high saving, high investment, and (balanced) economic growth. The more prosperous were the peasants, the faster would be the pace of economic growth. Indeed, Bukharin borrowed a slogan used in France during the 1840's: "Enrichissez vous," he said the peasants. "Enrich yourselves."

Tomsky, who was a trade union leader, argued similarly with respect to industrial workers. He stressed positive incentives (the carrot rather than the stick) to make them do their best: Higher real income, better working conditions, even worker control of industry—all these would raise worker morale and, ultimately, raise labor productivity and economic growth.

**The Leftists.**   The left wing of the Party, led by Leon Trotsky, Lev Kamenev, and Grigori Zinoviev (and supported by Evgenii Preobrazhensky, the economist), had other ideas. They regarded Lenin's compromise with an individualist peasantry, even if unavoidable at the time, as a bitter defeat, which was to be reversed as quickly as possible. They pointed out (correctly) that the success of the New Economic Policy was by nature not sustainable. The reason for the initial rapid rise in industrial output up to 1925 was simple: Large reserves of human, natural, and capital resources, unemployed in the confusion of War Communism, had finally been put to work again. The country was only regaining the 1913 level of economic activity. Continuing the New Economic Policy, they argued, would at best *maintain* the new (and old) level of output. In fact, it might reduce it, they asserted, because the existing capital stock was then very old, and more and more of each year's investment was needed just to replace it and keep it from falling. As the left-wingers saw it, as long as the average level of income per head was just barely above subsistence, resources released for growth by right-wing policies would be few. Peasants would save too little voluntarily, and the government could not be too forceful in pushing taxation. If it was, Russia would slip right back into War Communism; peasants would again blackmail the government by threatening to produce nothing but subsistence for themselves. Thus, concluded the left-wingers, continued *rapid* growth of industrial output and GNP required more than the New Economic Policy could provide. This could only be achieved by *drastically* reducing consumption while using the resources so released, *in accordance with a national economic plan,* for purposes conducive to growth. And that would have to be forced upon the uncooperative peasants by harsh dictatorial methods, they argued.

The left-wingers similarly opposed any concessions to industrial workers, whether in the form of direct worker control of industry or increased trade union activity. As Trotsky put it (italics added),

> *Without* compulsory *labor, without the right to give orders and demand their implementation, the trade unions would become a mere form without content, since the process of building a socialist society needs trade unions not for the struggle for better working conditions—that is the task of social and state organs as a whole—but to organize the working class for production, to educate, to discipline, to group, to attach specific categories and individual workers to their posts; i.e. hand-in-hand with the government, to* coerce *the workers into the framework of a unified plan.*[4]

Trotsky similarly dismissed as sheer nonsense all that ''babble'' about proletarian democracy. Such impulses had to give way to the historic task of enforcing an unpopular policy: a rapid increase in the production of capital goods rather than consumption goods wanted by peasants and workers alike. Under the circumstances,

---

[4]Leon Trotsky, *Sochineniya,* vol. 12 (Moscow, 1925), p. 126.

**Figure 7.1**    The Road to Riches: The Rightest Versus the Leftist View

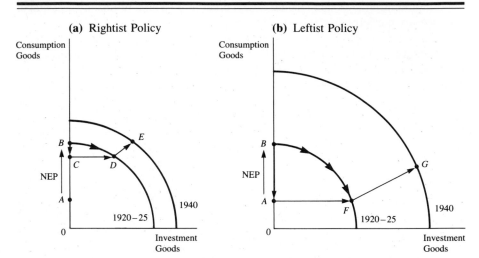

The production possibilities frontiers shown here help contrast the initial effects of Lenin's New Economic Policy (a move from *A* to *B*) with those expected by rightists (a) and leftists (b). By continuing the NEP and making only moderate and largely voluntary sacrifices in consumption, the rightists expected to move from *B* to *D* and, ultimately, to *E*. By abandoning the NEP and imposing massive and involuntary sacrifices in consumption, the leftists expected to move from *B* to *F* and, ultimately, to *G*.

said Trotsky, the state "takes the form of the dictatorship of the proletariat, i.e. of the most pitiless state, which coercively controls the life of citizens in all its aspects."[5]

**An Illustration.**    This debate is summarized in Figure 7.1, "The Road to Riches: The Rightist Versus the Leftist View." The lower production possibilities frontier in either panel might refer to the Soviet Union in the early 1920s. Actual 1920 production may have been occurring at point *A*, signifying production of a minimal quantity of consumption goods and almost no investment goods, along with massive unemployment of resources due to the chaos of War Communism. Lenin's New Economic Policy is represented by a move from *A* to *B* between 1920 and 1925. Although the country's capacity to produce (the frontier itself) had not changed, actual output grew mightily (to point *B*).

Now focus on panel (a). As the rightists saw it, people were then rich enough to assent to a small sacrifice of potential consumption goods (*BC*), either through voluntary saving or a moderate amount of taxation. This would allow a moderate amount of investment (*CD*). A continuation of the New Economic Policy would, thus, move the composition of output to point *D*. Over time, the formation of new

---

[5]*Ibid.*, p. 161.

capital would expand production possibilities. The frontier might reach the outer line in panel (a) by, say, 1940. Thus, 1940 production might occur at point $E$ (or at any other point on that line).

The leftist ideas, on the other hand, are represented by panel (b). The leftists were ready to enforce a much larger sacrifice of consumption goods (shown, perhaps, by distance $BA$). This would make possible a correspondingly larger volume of new capital formation (equal to $AF$ rather than $CD$). As a result, the country's production possibilities frontier might expand more rapidly, shifting out to the outer line in panel (b). Thus, 1940 production might occur at any point on *that* line, such as $G$.

## Stalin's Decision

The great industrialization debate (along with Lenin's New Economic Policy) ultimately came to an end through the intervention of Stalin (Biography 7.2). Early on, Stalin had lashed out against the "superindustrializers" of the left who wanted to force the peasantry into making such massive sacrifices of consumption (distance $BA$ in panel [b] of Figure 7.1). He argued against a policy that treated the peasants as if they were "internal colonies" to be exploited, and he generally sided with the arguments of the right. By 1926, following a series of shrewd political moves, he had managed to remove the left-wingers from all positions of power and had put his own supporters in their places. But then Stalin turned against the rightists, who were similarly ousted, and he proceeded to adopt as his own the very program of the left! By 1928, Stalin was ready to make up for Lenin's "step backward" and to impose a "revolution from above." A series of decrees spelled the end of the NEP and the birth of the Stalinist economic system. His system will be discussed in detail in the following sections of this chapter. Three major features characterized it:

1. With minor exceptions, the private ownership and management of natural and capital resources was abolished and replaced by state-run enterprises. (Outside agriculture, enterprises were simply nationalized and put under the control of managers appointed by the state. Within agriculture, the same happened to some extent, but most peasants were made to pool their land in favor of nominally cooperative ownership, while their capital equipment was nationalized.)
2. With minor exceptions, the role of markets was abolished and replaced by a hierarchically organized system of central planning. (Decision-making power was concentrated at the top; interenterprise relations were arranged "vertically" through the administrative hierarchy, not "horizontally" by direct contacts between enterprise managers.)
3. The role of money, while not abolished, was reduced to passive functions designed to facilitate the implementation of the predetermined central plan. (The plan specified inputs and outputs in physical units whenever possible; prices were set subsequently—not by supply and demand, but by administrators aiming to help along the execution of the plan.)

Stalin argued that these institutional changes would promote the most rapid pace of industrialization possible. Like the leftists, he wanted to shift the composition of the country's GNP away from consumer goods and toward investment goods. Moreover, he was determined not to invest much in agriculture, housing, or light industries. (Such investment, had it been undertaken, might relatively soon have provided increased flows of the types of goods consumers crave.) Instead, Stalin wanted to concentrate investment in *heavy* industries, such as coal mining, machine tools, and *steel* (note Stalin's chosen name). Such investment does next to nothing for consumers in the short run, but can lay the foundation for an all-round attack on scarcity—eventually.

## Stalin's Economic System

As was noted in the previous section, Stalin was determined to put the Soviet Union on a path of rapid (unbalanced) economic growth, favoring heavy industry above all else. Like the leftists he had removed, Stalin argued that "something like a tribute" had to be imposed on the peasantry in order to carry out such a policy. Yet, 25 million independent peasants, who had received their land at the time of the revolution, were hard to control. They would surely resist the collection of that tribute (represented by distance *BA* in panel [b] of Figure 7.1). Accordingly, Stalin proceeded to destroy the basis for peasant resistance: the private property of land, buildings, equipment, inventories, and livestock.

### The Collectivization of Agriculture

Unlike Lenin who gave in to them, Stalin decided to make all-out war on the peasants. Starting in 1928, he initiated what a year later became a sweeping program of **collectivization.** It involved the forced elimination of agricultural private property and its transferral to three new types of government-controlled institutions: state farms, collective farms, and machine-tractor stations.

**State farms** (*sovkhozy*) were huge farms owned by the people as a whole. They had an openly authoritarian structure, like any other nationalized enterprise: On each farm, a government-appointed manager commandeered large numbers of farm workers; the farm's output, just like that of a steel mill, naturally belonged to the government, which disposed of it. By 1940, there were 4,200 such state farms, averaging over 30,000 acres in size and covering about 8 percent of the country's sown area. By the mid-1980s, their numbers had grown to over 22,000, averaging over 41,000 acres and covering over 53 percent of the sown area.

**Collective farms** (*kolkhozy*) were large farms as well—officially formed by the voluntary pooling of the separate land and livestock holdings of numerous peasant households. In fact, these "voluntary" collectives were compulsory producer cooperatives; as Stalin put it, "he who does not join a kolkhoz is an enemy of Soviet power." In addition, the peasants' capital equipment was taken away from them and concentrated in government hands; until 1958, even the new collectives were not allowed to own it.

To be sure, the collective farms were endowed with the outer trappings of democratic organs and procedures: A General Meeting of members elected a chairman, an executive management board, an auditing commission; it also debated and approved an annual production plan. In fact, however, those "elected" came from a single slate of Party nominees, were responsible to the central government rather than the members, and transmitted to the collective farmers governmental production and delivery quotas that could neither be rejected nor revised in any meaningful way.

By 1940, there were 237,000 such collective farms, averaging over 3,500 acres in size and covering 78 percent of the country's sown area. By the mid-1980s, their numbers had shrunk to 25,000, but their average size had grown to over 16,000 acres, covering 44 percent of the sown area.

**Machine-tractor stations** (MTS) were state-owned enterprises, run by Party faithfuls, which held all the agricultural implements of the formerly independent peasants and, upon request, provided services of plowing, sowing, harvesting, and the like to the collective farms that now lacked such equipment. By this institutional device Stalin protected the agricultural capital stock from damage that peasants might inflict upon it, whether out of ignorance or malice. More importantly, by threatening to withhold crucial working tools from disobedient peasants, Stalin could use the MTS to force his production and delivery quotas on the collectivized peasants. Never again, he argued, would peasants be able to cripple the urban economy by cutting production to practically nil. The new institutions would ensure continued agricultural production at a high level because individual peasants would be reduced to the dependent status of factory workers, supervised by loyal managers, and threatened with severe punishment for "sabotage." Thus, the state would get most of the agricultural output and could turn it into capital goods either by exporting it (and importing foreign machinery in return) or by feeding it to the urban population (engaged in producing investment goods domestically).

Not surprisingly, peasants were not impressed by the official presentation to them of state and collective farms as "vehicles for the introduction of mass production methods into agriculture." In fact, rebellious peasants responded to collectivization with the destruction of buildings and inventories and a wholesale slaughter of livestock that was not to be made up for over 20 years. From 1928 to 1933, in millions of heads, the numbers of cattle dropped from 60.1 to 33.5; of hogs, from 22.0 to 9.9; of sheep and goats, from 107.0 to 37.3; of horses, from 32.1 to 17.3.

And yet, Stalin's scheme worked! From 1928 to 1937, the percentage of peasant households collectivized rose from 2 to 93. Agricultural output at first fell, but despite a terrible famine in the countryside, agricultural *collections* by the state increased. In the case of grain, they rose from 12 million short tons in 1928 to 32 million in 1937. At the same time, industrial consumption goods became all but unavailable. Tensions mounted and social relations came to the point of explosion, but Stalin was absolutely pitiless in carrying out his policy. He answered peasant resistance by exiling or exterminating 5 million peasants. He responded to worker demands for higher consumption by purging union leaders. And he built an efficient terror machine to discourage any further criticism of his policy to promote maximum growth. As he put it at the time,[6]

> *To slacken the tempo would mean falling behind. And those who fall behind get beaten. But we do not want to be beaten. No, we refuse to be beaten! One feature of the history of old Russia was the continual beatings she suffered for falling behind, for her back- wardness. She was beaten by the Mongol khans. She was beaten by the Turkish beys. She was beaten by the Swedish feudal lords. She was beaten by the Polish and Lithuanian gentry. She was beaten by the British and French capitalists. She was beaten by the Japanese barons. All beat her—for her backwardness: for military backwardness, for cultural backwardness, for industrial backwardness, for political backwardness. . . . Do you want our socialist fatherland to be beaten and lose its independence? If you don't want this, you must liquidate our backwardness and develop a real Bolshevik tempo in building our socialist economy. There is no other road. . . . We lag behind the advanced countries by 50 to 100 years.* We must make good this distance in ten years.

## The Central Planning Process

Along with the new institutions that would let the central government take control of the nation's economic surplus (the difference between potential consumption $B$ and minimum necessary consumption $A$ in either panel of Figure 7.1), Stalin in- troduced central economic planning. As a result, Soviet economic activity has been carried out, ever since 1928, on the basis of a series of multiyear plans. First came a Five-Year Plan that covered the October 1928 to December 1932 period; it was followed by a second Five-Year Plan for 1933–1937, and so on right to the present (minor exceptions being the years of World War II and an abortive Seven-Year Plan).

Each of the **central plans** has been a systematic program of allocating resources and apportioning output, designed to achieve objectives chosen by the government. To this day, the planning is performed by a State Planning Commission, called **Gosplan.** The agency had in fact been created as early as 1921 (out of an even earlier State Commission for Electrification), but, during the NEP period, Gosplan's activities had been rather limited. Stalin changed all that; by the late 1920s, Gos- plan's work took on central importance. The agency's procedures, however, are not correctly described by the model of Chapter 6; in fact, Stalin showed great hostility to such careful mathematical planning. While Trotsky had referred to Soviet forerunners of input-output analysis as "the glorious historical music of growing socialism," Stalin dismissed them contemptuously as "but a game with figures." Nevertheless, as will be shown presently, the input-output model is ideally suited to help us understand Stalin's approach. Consider the work of Gosplan during a

---

[6]Joseph Stalin, *Voprosy Leninizma* (Moscow, 1952), pp. 362–63. Italics added.

typical year in which a portion of the current long-term plan is being formulated in detail. A number of steps are involved.

**Data Collection.**   During the first half of the planning year, Gosplan collects data on the past performance of the economy. These include data on inputs and outputs of the previous year and estimates for the first half of the current year. With these data, naturally imprecise, Gosplan makes projections for the second half of the current year. All these data provide the basis for constructing next year's plan. (Although these data are not set up in this form, they correspond to our Table 6.1, "The Input-Output Table," on page 90.)

**Party Directives.**   The estimated data about the economy's past performance are sent by Gosplan to the leaders of the Communist Party. These are the people who hold all economic and political power in their hands: members of the Party's Politbureau and the Secretariat of its Central Committee. (See Close-Up 7.1, "The Locus of Power in the U.S.S.R.," for a description of the major bodies that have governed the Soviet Union ever since Stalin's early days.) After studying the information so obtained, the Party leaders determine the major objectives to be sought during the following year. These are sent to Gosplan and are usually cast in very general terms: "Increase the share of resources devoted to capital formation from 15 to 21 percent" or "Reduce the importance of road building in favor of school construction" or "Cease expanding the coal industry and rapidly enlarge chemicals production with emphasis on plastics." This, of course, amounts to giving general directives as to the desired makeup of the GNP. Indeed, these instructions are called **Party directives.** (They can be viewed as general instructions for filling in columns [4] to [7] of Table 6.2, "The Plan Document," on page 93.)

**Tentative Plan Formulation at the Top.**   The Party directives are used by Gosplan in the second half of the planning year to specify in physical terms, for thousands of "important" commodities (but certainly not for millions of them), the exact output targets, the distribution of output, and the major inputs required. (The setting of output targets can be viewed as equivalent to calculating total outputs—our row A to C, column [8] entries in Table 6.2. The calculation of output distribution and input requirements corresponds to our earlier calculation, on the basis of total outputs and technical coefficients, of the column [1] to [3] entries in Table 6.2.) But note: Although it can be explained by reference to it, Stalin's economic plan for "important" goods was not set up in the form of an input-output table, but rather as a collection of separate material balances. Any one **material balance** lists, in physical units (such as tons or hours), all the prospective sources and uses of a given "material" (such as steel or labor), making certain that these sources and uses are equal to each other and, thus, "balance." In fact, any one material balance corresponds precisely to a single row of an input-output table.

Consider the information of Table 7.1, "A Material Balance for Steel"; it corresponds to row B of Table 6.2, "The Plan Document," but contains some additional information: The fact that steel inventories both decreased and increased was hidden

**Table 7.1**   A Material Balance for Steel (in millions of tons)

| Sources | | Uses | | |
|---|---|---|---|---|
| Production | 885.924 | Industry | | ⎫ |
| Inventory decrease | 52.000 | (a) electric power | | |
| Imports | 13.100 |    producers | 97.725 | Intermediate |
| | | (b) steel producers | 221.481 | uses |
| | | Agriculture | | |
| | | (c) corn producers | 11.718 | ⎭ |
| | | Households | — | ⎫ |
| | | Inventory increase | 452.000 | Final |
| | | Government | 95.000 | uses |
| | | Exports | 73.100 | ⎭ |
| Total sources | 951.024 | Total uses | 951.024 | |

A material balance shows all the sources from which a given ''material'' (commodity or service) will
   be received and all the uses to which it will be put, making sure the two categories ''balance''
   (are equal to one another).

*Source:* Row B, Table 6.2.

in row B, column (5) of Table 6.2, which showed a 400-million-ton net increase only.
Similarly, the sizes of imports and exports shown in Table 7.1 were hidden in the
60-million-ton net export entry of row B, column (7) of Table 6.2.

    Gosplan's setting up of a series of material balances can, thus, be viewed as
the formulation of an input-output plan *in disaggregated form.* (Each balance, set
up by different groups of people, in different offices, at different times during the
planning process, is in effect a different input-output table row.) However, because
Gosplan sets up a rather limited number of material balances only—it focuses on
''important'' goods and neglects ''unimportant'' ones as defined by the Party
leadership—its procedure is equivalent to leaving many input-output tables rows
(and columns) completely blank! Without question, therefore, Gosplan's initial set
of material balances constitutes an economic plan that contains innumerable gaps
and inconsistencies.

**Tentative Plan Movement Down the Hierarchy.**   The tentative material balances
of Gosplan are called **control figures.** Gosplan is well aware that they are far from
perfect. (At this point in the planning process, nobody, for example, has yet checked
whether all the separate material balances fit together: What if steel producers are
planning to deliver 97.725 million tons to the electric power industry, as Table 7.1
shows, while electric power producers are planning projects requiring 123 million
tons of steel?)

    To improve the workability of the national economic plan, Gosplan proceeds
to generate additional information by inviting widespread study, evaluation, and
criticism of the plan. (The criticism, however, is confined to the control figures set
up by Gosplan; the initial Party directives are exempt from scrutiny.) Accordingly,

the tentative control figures are passed down the administrative hierarchy to various ministries. The Ministry of Metallurgy, for instance, might be told that it is expected next year to produce 885.924 million tons of steel; the Foreign Trade Ministry, that it is to import 13.1, while exporting 73.1 million tons of steel; the Agriculture Ministry that it can expect delivery of 11.718 million tons of steel; and so on.

As a next step, each ministry splits up the aggregate into subtotals. The Ministry of Metallurgy might tentatively allocate the production of 885.924 million tons of steel among the planning agencies of the various Soviet Republics. They, in turn, pass the plan down to smaller geographic administrations and, ultimately, to individual enterprises. Finally, the management of a steel plant in Irkutsk has before it tentative control figures for next year, telling it to produce 77,000 tons of steel, to deliver them as specified, and to produce them with so many units of coal, iron ore, labor, and more. At this point, the planning process is reversed.

**Tentative Plan Movement Up the Hierarchy.**   Next, given their intimate knowledge of local conditions, enterprise officials who foresee problems or see untapped opportunities are supposed to suggest changes in the control figures; superior agencies who find such suggestions well taken make appropriate adjustments and, in turn, pass on the adjusted control figures to *their* superiors. Eventually, moving back up the hierarchy, the control figures become more and more aggregative and return to the hands of Gosplan itself.

In the meantime, the feedback from workers and managers, perhaps, has made the plan less imperfect than it once was. Originally, for example, steel plant X might have been assigned too much labor and too little iron ore and (by mistake) cabbage-planting machines. Steel plant Y might have been assigned too little labor and too much coal. And state farm Z might not have received much needed cabbage-planting machines! Such mistakes would now be ironed out. Loyal managers would have reported to their superior planning agencies the projected receipt of inputs not needed (here labor and cabbage-planting machines for X and coal for Y), while also reporting projected deficiencies in inputs required to fulfill the plan (here iron ore for X, labor for Y, and cabbage-planting machines for Z). Planners would then have reassigned inputs until everybody had exactly what was needed to fulfill the output target.

**Plan Becomes Law.**   After the plan has traveled down and back up the hierarchy, Gosplan makes a final revision of the control figures, creating a **draft plan** ready to be approved by the Party and then submitted to the Supreme Soviet of the U.S.S.R.—a rubber-stamp parliament. (Once again, see Close-Up 7.1, ''The Locus of Power in the U.S.S.R.'') The result is the **plan law,** a set of revised control figures destined to be passed down the hierarchy one more time—as *commands* to be obeyed.

**The Priority Principle.**   Even the ultimate plan emerging from the year-long process just described is always flawed, in innumerable ways. To ensure that, nevertheless, the Party's wishes prevail, Stalin introduced the **priority principle,** which still rules supreme. Different production targets are assigned different levels of priority, and, if it becomes necessary during plan execution, low-priority targets are sacrificed for high-priority targets. So-called "leading links" (such as the production of steel, machine tools, or military goods) are designated as high-priority goods; others (such as the production of automobiles, clothing, or housing) are given low-priority status. If any problems arise during the execution phase of the plan, resources are simply shifted from low-priority to high-priority sectors. As a result, low-priority output plans are rarely fulfilled; high-priority tasks are almost always fulfilled. Thus, Stalin made sure—despite his imperfect system of planning—that the things he cared most about were produced, exactly as he had decided.

## The Agency Problem and Incentives

The Soviet Union is a vast country. It covers one sixth of the earth's surface and stretches across eleven of its time zones. Setting up a central economic plan that treats all of the country's enterprises as if they were part of one giant factory, therefore, is difficult enough. Getting people to obey the central will, however, is equally problematic. Stalin certainly was not ready to sit back and merely *hope* that the plan law would be obediently implemented. He was well aware of the **agency problem** of getting *agents* (who are supposed to implement decisions made at the top) to obey *principals* (who are in charge). This becomes a problem whenever any organization grows beyond the stage at which the principals can possibly know all that is going on; at that point, the agents have the power to subvert the principals' will. Being free from minute-by-minute supervision and having, perhaps, had no voice in the decision they are asked to carry out on the principals' behalf, the agents may well perform the assigned tasks reluctantly or sloppily or at a pace unreasonably slow; they may even perform entirely different tasks. How then, Stalin asked, can the Party leadership get the country's peasants, managers, and workers to act precisely as specified in the plan? Stalin answered his own question by noting that agents must be given a personal interest in the tasks chosen by principals. He introduced a mixture of the command-love-money incentives first noted in Chapter 5. With minor exceptions, these incentives have continued to motivate Soviet citizens to the present.

**Command.**    To begin with, central planners issue output quotas to the managers of collective farms, state farms, and all other enterprises. These quotas command the production of *minimum* quantities of corn, sugar beets, steel, tractors, and the like—these being the quantities specified on the left-hand sides of the relevant material balances. In addition, the central planners indicate the parties to whom this output is to be delivered, in accordance with entries on the right-hand sides of material balances. By implication, this procedure rations key raw material inputs to prospective users. Similar assignments are commanded for other inputs, such as capital and natural resources and, to some extent, labor. Until 1975, for example, collective farmers were tied to their kolkhoz and were not free to leave it. Graduates of educational institutions are typically *assigned* to their first job, which they are not free to leave for four years. And, in the long run, labor is channeled into the fields and locations desired by Gosplan by a variety of other devices, such as the governmental determination of openings in educational and vocational programs or the selective construction of housing (and a corresponding issuing of residence permits).

The proper execution of all these commands is verified with the help of multiple lines of communication into each enterprise: There is the chief accountant, who is responsible not to the enterprise manager but to superior planning agencies; additional reports are sent up the hierarchy by Party representatives who are found in each enterprise and by secret police officials who are attached to the more important ones. Workers are encouraged to keep their eyes and ears open and send in malfeasance reports.

Under Stalin, punishment for disobeying the central plan was often severe. It could involve relatively mild measures, such as the demotion of a manager to the rank of ordinary worker or the manager's reassignment to a less desirable job in a less desirable location. More often than not, it meant criminal prosecution for mishandling the people's property and a long sentence to a forced labor camp. Indeed, between 1937 and 1953 (the year of Stalin's death), some 17 million people were sent to such camps, which held between 8 and 9 million inmates on the average.[7] More than that! People who disobeyed Gosplan commands knew too well that punishment could also be extended to their parents, spouses, and children, their more distant relatives, even their neighbors and fellow workers. Thus, there were good reasons to obey. As will be shown later in this chapter, some of the "excessive" actions Stalin took to ensure plan fulfillment have since been branded as "enormous and unforgivable" crimes against the Soviet people.[8] Nevertheless, many of Stalin's negative incentives survive even today.

**Love.**  Central planners in the Soviet Union do not confine themselves to the external incentive of commands, backed up by threats for disobedience. They also mount a massive propaganda effort that envelops people from cradle to grave and tries to instill in them an inner need to *serve* their fellow citizens, their country, the cause of socialism. Peasants, managers, workers—all of them are continually exhorted to be self-critical, to look into themselves, to drive out selfishness, to open themselves to the revolutionary spirit, to be guided by the love of others. How can such people possibly disobey the central plan?

Thus had Lenin shown great enthusiasm for the *subbotniks,* workers who would forgo all selfishness and perform volunteer labor on Saturdays. And Stalin dramatized the production record set by Aleksei G. Stakhanov, who, filled with revolutionary spirit, reportedly mined 102 tons of coal in a single shift. Ever since,

---

[7]These numbers were recently confirmed by Nikolai Shmelyov, a senior staff member of the Soviet Institute of USA and Canada Studies. See the *Daily Hampshire Gazette,* June 17, 1987, p. 19.

[8]For example, in Mikhail Gorbachev's speech on the occasion of the 70th anniversary of the Bolshevik Revolution. See *The New York Times,* November 3, 1987, pp. 1 and 10.

groups of "Stakhanovites" have been pitted against one another in socialist competitions and emulation contests.

By now, a comprehensive system of awards and decorations exists. They are available to individuals and groups who follow the central planners' guidance with the greatest of enthusiasm. When workers are urgently needed in the Far East, for example, Gosplan does not have to command people to move there as long as young Muscovites respond to a "Go East, young man" campaign. Those who do may become "Heroes of Socialist Labor" or even members of the "Order of Lenin," enjoying fame and prestige.

**Money.**    Monetary incentives to carry out the Soviet central plan are, however, of primary importance. Under Stalin's guidance, early dreams of a moneyless economy were decisively put to rest. Such dreams quickly gave way to the widespread use of money and prices as devices to implement the predetermined central plan. In the worlds of peasants, managers, and workers alike, monetary magnitudes play a crucial role to this day in motivating behavior. We will consider each of these groups in turn.

## Monetary Incentives and the Peasants

Consider any group of collective farmers. They must deliver governmentally set quotas of beef, corn, wheat, and the like to the government, but, at the time of delivery, each farm is *paid* for its delivery at **agricultural procurement prices** that are set not by supply and demand in free markets, but by government administrators. Thus, a farm delivering 50,000 bales of cotton (as commanded) may face a procurement price of 2 rubles per bale (which it is unable to influence) and would, thus, receive 100,000 rubles in "sales revenue." At the same time, the farm may receive a variety of inputs, such as fertilizer, as specified by the central plan. These prescribed inputs have to be *purchased,* but again at prices set by the government. The government sets **enterprise wholesale prices,** for interenterprise transactions involving nonagricultural products, on the basis of an industry branch's planned average total cost plus (typically) a 5-percent planned profit. Until recently, the only major costs recognized were wages, raw material costs, and depreciation of capital equipment. Thus, if the chemicals industry is expected to produce 50 million tons of nitrogen fertilizer, while incurring planned wage, raw material, and depreciation costs of 100, 350, and 50 million rubles, respectively, the government might add a 25-million-ruble planned profit and set a price of 525 million rubles divided by 50 million tons, or 105 rubles per ton. If the collective farm noted above received 800 tons of this fertilizer (and nothing else), it would have to pay $800 \times 105 = 84,000$ rubles for it. Deducting these "costs" from its "sales revenue," the collective farm would have $100,000 - 84,000 = 16,000$ rubles of "residual income." Such residual income is divided among the collective farmers at the end of the year (in accordance with "labor-day" points accumulated by them during the year), and this dividend becomes their personal reward for working on the collectively owned land. By manipulating the prices involved, Stalin saw to it that the collective farmers' personal income was extremely small, which made it impossible for them to buy any significant quantities of industrial consumer goods. Thus, as Stalin put it, the peasants were "effectively selling without purchasing."

Not surprisingly, the collective farm residual income has been a poor incentive to induce collective farmers to do their best. In fact, until 1966, when low but guaranteed wages were introduced on the collective farms, the individual farmer's share has not only been extremely low, but it has also varied capriciously and unpredictably from farm to farm and from one year to the next. Given two farmers, one attached to a farm with fertile soil or blessed by good weather would benefit from the resultant larger crop, larger sales revenue, and larger residual income, while the other farmer *working equally hard* but cursed with poor soil or bad weather would get much lower income. No wonder that collective farmers, ever since the 1930s, have been malingering on the collectively owned land. Their relations with the state have remained strained. They have gone through the motions of carrying out the central plan, but their hearts have not been in it. "The state pretends to pay us, we pretend to work," they have said. "Why work all year to get (perhaps) enough income to buy a bicycle?"

Yet, perhaps inadvertently, Stalin did introduce another set of incentives in Soviet agriculture; these turned out to be powerful indeed. Millions of acres of land were made available to collective farm households, state farm workers, and certain others (such as factories, hospitals, and schools) as private garden plots. Each of these plots is less than 1 acre in size. Their owners are free to grow anything they like on these plots; they can even hold some animals privately, such as a cow, some pigs, chickens, or geese. More than that! They are free to sell their privately produced output on so-called **collective farm markets** to anybody at any price, freely determined by supply and demand. The consequences have been amazing. Although the private plots contain only 3 percent of the country's agricultural land, about a third of total agricultural output is being produced on them: 60 percent of honey and potatoes, 40 percent of berries, fruits, and eggs, 30 percent of milk, meat, and vegetables. . . . (State farms and collective farms produce roughly another third each of agricultural output, using the remaining 97 percent of agricultural land.)

## Monetary Incentives and Enterprise Managers

The behavior of enterprise managers is also being monitored and guided by the existence of money and prices.

**Internal Auditing.**　For one thing, each enterprise is subject to an ongoing process of internal auditing. It is known as the **system of economic accountability** (*khozraschet*). Each manager is asked to engage in "businesslike behavior": In addition to fulfilling the central planners' physical output quotas and input norms, the manager is to keep monetary accounts, at governmentally set prices, of the gross value of output, input costs, and profits. (These accounts look very much like the income statement of an American firm.) The manager is supposed to maximize profit by making the gross value of output as large as possible and costs as small as possible.

Given the fact that the manager has no control over prices, is given a minimum physical output target, and receives maximum physical input allocations (with no substitutions allowed), all this amounts to asking managers to achieve technical efficiency (a concept illustrated in Figure 2.1 on page 13): Given the full use of the inputs assigned to them, managers are to maximize physical output; given any physical output, they are to minimize—separately—the consumption of each input.

**External Auditing.**   In addition, each enterprise is also subject to a form of external auditing. It is called **control by the ruble** and involves the State Bank (*Gosbank*). This monopoly bank, with thousands of branches throughout the country, is in a unique position to monitor interenterprise transactions and, thus, to keep a running account of plan execution. The reason is as follows.

Except for wage payments to households and their purchases of goods from retailers, the use of cash in the economy is severely restricted. Typically, enterprises have to deposit cash receipts (from households) immediately and cannot get cash (for wage payments) except under strict rules. To avoid black market cash transactions (which cannot be traced), payment for all transactions not involving households are to go through the State Bank. At the time of plan formulation, firms are to make contracts with each other, stated in monetary units and promising to ''sell'' to and ''buy'' from each other the quantities specified in the central plan (and valued at the enterprise wholesale prices noted above). Such monetary transactions among firms are to be made via the **acceptance method.** Instead of the buyer writing a check, the seller initiates the process by billing the State Bank. The State Bank delivers the order to pay to the buyer, who by signing it ''accepts,'' thereby gaining legal title to the goods. Then the buyer's account at the State Bank is reduced and the seller's account increased, just as if a check had been written.

Consider a tractor plant. The physical plan may call for the production of 5,000 tractors and their delivery to designated recipients. The plan may also call for the delivery of 1,000 tons of steel to the plant from a designated steel producer. If the government has mandated enterprise wholesale prices of 500 rubles per tractor and 90 rubles per ton of steel, the State Bank would expect the tractor plant to ''sell'' $5,000 \times 500 = 2.5$ million rubles worth of tractors during the year (a lower figure would point to underfulfillment of the output quota). The bank would also expect the tractor plant to ''buy'' $1,000 \times 90 = 90,000$ rubles worth of steel (a higher figure would point to a violation of input norms). The purpose of this whole exercise is that the State Bank can theoretically check the purpose, timing, and size of every transaction, preventing it unless it fits into the plan. In fact, the State Bank has at its disposal stern sanctions, ranging from the expropriation of a firm's deposits to a full-scale Party investigation into enterprise affairs. Yet, the burdens of surveying details of economic activity on the scale ideally required are too enormous. The State Bank frequently only engages in ''formalistic'' controls, using sanctions sparingly and failing in its role of overseer. For that reason, Stalin introduced what to this day has remained the most powerful incentive determining enterprise behavior: the managerial bonus system.

**The Bonus System.** Enterprise managers receive monetary salaries, but also bonuses for fulfilling and overfulfilling various components of the central plan. The basis for bonuses ranges widely from the output quota, expressed in physical units or as the gross value of output (*val*), to input norms, sales, profit, and even to keeping the factory yard clean. Not surprisingly, self-interested managers have chosen to respond to the bonus, among the numerous possible ones, that is most capable of raising their personal income: the bonus derived from comparing actual output with the output quota. And there has long existed an extremely sharp dividing line between success and failure: A manager might receive as a bonus up to 50 percent of basic salary for plan fulfillment alone and up to 4 percent more for each percentage point of overfulfillment. Thus, the difference between 99- and 100-percent plan fulfillment could mean up to a 50-percent difference in the incomes of managers. A manager overfulfilling the plan by 5 percent could receive up to 70 percent above basic salary. Thus, output plan fulfillment receives the managers' undivided attention. And this is where trouble enters the planning process itself.

To begin with, managers figure, the lower their output quotas, the easier their fulfillment. Hence, they do their best to hide the true productive capabilities of their enterprises from central planners so as to get low output quotas from them. To the extent that they succeed, they can, perhaps, underutilize their available resources, while still overfulfilling output targets (and being personally rewarded for it by the payment of bonuses).

The same incentive makes managers operating under the Stalinist system overstate input requirements when government statisticians come around to collect data for those technical coefficients discussed in the previous chapter and on which input norms and input allocations are based. Any manager who claims that more equipment, raw materials, or workers are needed to produce a unit of output than is in fact the case might receive more from central planners. If necessary, the manager can always accumulate hoards of equipment and raw materials in the warehouse and keep even idle workers on the payroll. This "stacks the deck" beforehand, enabling the manager, when the need arises, to overfulfill planned targets of output, or to fulfill them at all at times when truly needed inputs do not arrive.

The greed for bonuses leads similarly to undesirable consequences during the process of plan execution. Managers do their best to *simulate* good performance, to create the appearance of it even if there is little substance behind the impression. Since the output target (on which the bonus depends) typically is stated in quantity terms, managers frequently condone the production of low-quality output, thereby causing untold trouble for other managers. If a manager's output target is stated in tons of steel, for example, one can guess what the manager does when the available resources could produce 100 tons of perfect steel or 110 tons of brittle steel. Similarly, fewer screws or thinner parts on machines do not affect the number of machines counted as output, but this does free some inputs to raise output. And this phenomenon pervades all sectors of the economy: In agriculture, the managers of farm equipment (who are rewarded for area plowed) have urged their workers to plow shallowly; this increases the area plowed per day (and the bonus)—it is bad for agricultural production. In the mining industry, managers in charge of oil exploration (who are rewarded for meters drilled) have urged their teams to drill many shallow holes rather than fewer deep holes; because drilling is a slower process at greater depth, this increases the meters drilled per day (and the bonus)—it is bad for discovering oil. In the construction industry, managers (who are rewarded for number of bricks laid) have found it to their advantage to concentrate on putting up brick walls, but not on finishing buildings; as a result, the average completion time of new buildings exceeds a decade. In the transportation industry, managers (who are rewarded for ton miles) have found it desirable to make drivers take the longest possible routes; a ton of freight driven from A to B along a 150-mile route, rather than a 111-mile route, produces 150 ton miles rather than 111 ton miles (and a higher bonus).

The managerial bonus system is also responsible for persistent and ubiquitous complaints in the Soviet economy about shortages of spare parts and lack of servicing. It is easy to see why. If the production decision involves a choice between 500 tractors with spare parts and a good service organization to back up their future operation or 550 tractors without spare parts and without service, one does not have to guess about the manager's choices.

A related problem is the **assortment problem,** the disregard of the wishes of customers as to the composition of output. This problem arises in part because central planners are simply unable to break down their commands into infinite detail covering every possible category and subcategory of goods and resources. Thus, they may construct a single material balance for steel, rather than hundreds of such balances for 1-inch sheet steel, ¼-inch sheet steel, tube steel, and so on. The disaggregation of large aggregates into subcategories, therefore, is often left to others, such as the managers of producing enterprises. They, however, have no reason to ask their customers about the preferred assortment of output or to heed their pleas should such advice be offered. After all, the managers of enterprises are induced to act or not to act in specific ways by bonuses promised them by central planners for the fulfillment or overfulfillment of the centrally set output quota (which is to be delivered in accordance with the central plan to designated and, therefore, captive customers who do not have alternatives). Thus, managers need not worry about their making *sales* to customers (who are free to spend their money as they like and able to turn to other suppliers when dissatisfied). Hence, if steel users are clamoring for ¼-inch sheet steel, but 1-inch sheet steel is more easily produced and the producer's bonus depends simply on *tons of steel* produced, we should not be surprised that only 1-inch sheet steel is produced. If small nails are needed, but the producing enterprise's output plan is stated in tons, only huge nails are produced (if that frees some resources to overfulfill the plan and raise that bonus). If the output plan is stated in numbers, only the tiniest nails are made, and no large ones at all. Again, if the output plan is stated in tons, only thick glass is made; when stated in square meters, only thin glass is produced, even if all of it breaks on the way to the construction site.

The same problem arises when output quotas are stated in terms of *val*, the gross value of output. Given the way enterprise wholesale prices are set, the use of more raw material raises the official price of the product containing that raw material. Thus, a foundry commanded to produce 100 castings but judged by *val* will rather use 200 pounds of metal per casting than 100 pounds because bigger and heavier castings will translate into a larger ruble figure. No matter that users might prefer lighter castings and have to machine away all that excess metal! Private household users of output are, of course, similarly affected. Fewer stitches on each garment enable managers to save yarn and labor and to raise overall output. So might producing only shoes for little boys, if the output target is stated in number of shoes; or producing nothing but knives, if the output plan called for tons of kitchen utensils, and knives are more easily produced than pots, pans, and can openers.

Nor can central planners possibly specify the precise timing of production and deliveries for millions of goods. Even if the total quantity of ball bearings produced in a year equals the quantity needed by and promised to the makers of railroad freight cars, trouble may be at hand if production and deliveries do not occur on a regular basis. Although some ball bearings are needed in January, in February, in March, and so on, producers may ignore the (captive) customers' needs and focus on their own convenience. As long as the planned quantity is produced at *some* time during the first quarter of the year, say, the bonus is ensured, and that alone determines a manager's behavior. In fact, it is typical in the Soviet economy to produce at a fairly leisurely pace during the early part of any calendar quarter, but later the pace of activities quickens and turns into a furious tempo as the date of reckoning approaches. These regular seasonal spurts in production activity, designed to fulfill or overfulfill the output plan by, say, the quarterly accounting deadline are referred to as **storming** (*shturmovchina*) and seem to account for the fact that goods produced early in a quarter are generally of higher quality than others that have been slapped together at a frantic pace later on. This problem affects all types of customers, be they enterprises or households. (Households shopping in state retail stores for durable goods, such as TV sets, routinely check labels indicating the date of production. They reject March 28 in favor of January 10.)

## Monetary Incentives and Workers

Stalin also rejected early revolutionary notions about workers under socialism being drafted into labor armies, assigned to places of work, and rewarded by in-kind distributions of consumer goods. He introduced a system still prevalent today of paying workers money wages for labor performed and letting them spend their income freely on consumer goods, either at state retail stores or in the collective farm market.

These money wages are highly differentiated by type of work and geographic location so as to channel the necessary numbers of workers into the various occupations and regions that the central plan requires. Additional wage differentials are designed to make workers do their best once they are at work. (In a recent year, only 12 percent of Soviet workers received straight hourly pay; some 46 percent did piecework, and another 42 percent shared group bonuses.)

Although workers enjoy free consumer choice (they can spend their money income as they like), the central planners decide on the types and amounts of goods among which this choice can be exercised in state retail stores. At the same time, a government agency, not demand and supply, determines the **state retail prices** at which consumer goods produced by state enterprises are offered for sale. As a result, shortages and surpluses are common; this phenomenon is illustrated in Figure 7.2, "The Governmental Distribution of Consumer Goods." The graph pictures a situation in which 16,000 units of a good are offered for sale in state retail stores and an official price of 10 rubles per unit has been set. If consumer demand just happens to equal $D_2$, equilibrium exists (point $e$). Such a coincidence, however, is unlikely. More likely than not, demand is more or less intense. If demand equals $D_3$, a shortage of $ec$ units per year emerges. This sort of situation is quite common throughout the Soviet Union and is attested to by the fact that members of the typical urban household spend a combined total of 40 hours *per week* standing in long lines in front of retail stores, and more hours prowling the streets to discover purchase opportunities, not always with success. Often people absent themselves from work in order to queue, and when people do find what they have long been

**Figure 7.2** The Governmental Distribution of Consumer Goods

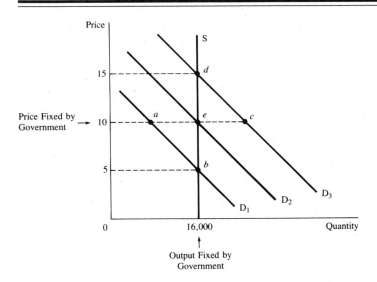

Soviet central planners determine the supply of any given consumer good that is offered in state retail stores; for example, at 16,000 units a year, as in this graph. The government, however, also fixes the good's price, often for years at a time; for example, at 10 rubles per unit as shown here. Workers are free to spend their money income as they like; therefore, one of three situations is bound to emerge: If governmental supply and private demand just happen to meet at the official price (which would happen if demand equaled $D_2$), all is well (point $e$). If demand is stronger ($D_3$), a shortage emerges (distance $ec$). If demand is weaker ($D_1$), a surplus exists instead (distance $ae$).

looking for, they are apt to buy 18 units, not 3; the rest is hoarded or resold to family and friends. Thus, shortage items always sell out in a flash. For certain items, such as apartments and cars, there are decade-long waiting lists. The ubiquitous rude behavior of sales personnel toward household buyers is another indication of significance.

On the other hand, if demand equals $D_1$, a surplus of $ae$ units per year prevails. This type of situation is also common. Frequent press reports complain of unwanted, unsold goods—ranging from accordions to cross-country skis to radios—accumulating in ever growing quantities in warehouses.

Note that shortages and surpluses could be eliminated quickly by flexible pricing. In our example, raising the 10-ruble price to 15 rubles would eliminate the shortage because quantity demanded would fall along $cd;$ lowering the 10-ruble price to 5 rubles would eliminate the surplus because quantity demanded would rise along $ab$. Soviet price setters, however, are not inclined to follow such a policy. They prefer to keep prices constant for long periods of time (and never fail to point out how their brand of socialism has produced price stability).

Similarly, central planners are not inclined quickly to raise supply in the face of shortages (as from $e$ to $c$), nor are they quick to cut supply in the face of surpluses (as from $e$ to $a$).

Households that face persistent shortages (and are unwilling to buy surplus goods instead) do, however, have a way out. They can spend their money in the free collective farm market, bidding the prices of fruit, meat, vegetables, and the like to whatever high levels will clear the market. All this then enables the government to point out how (open) inflation occurs only in the economy's capitalist sector! In the past, the money acquired in this way by peasants has, in turn, been "mopped up" by a variety of means, including currency reforms (exchanging 10 old monetary units for 5 new ones), higher taxes, forced bond purchases, decreases in prices for output deliveries to the state, increases in prices of industrial farm inputs, and the production of more industrial consumption goods wanted by peasants.

## The Underground Economy

Neither Stalin nor his successors have been able to solve the agency problem. As a result, there exists a second economy—beyond the official economy described in the previous sections and outside the control of Gosplan. In one way or another, the majority of the Soviet population is involved in it. This **underground economy** comprises a wide spectrum of semilegal and clearly illegal activities through which people enhance their own welfare by allocating resources and acquiring goods in ways not sanctioned by the central plan. It is easy to see why this underground economy exists.

Participants in the official economy everywhere are plagued by the ubiquitous "supply problem," the inability to obtain the types of goods they want. Because the central plan inevitably reflects the will of central planners (rather than that of enterprise and household consumers) and because it is in any case less than perfect (it is not as comprehensive as it should be, and it is internally inconsistent), certain goods are simply not provided by the official economy at all. Other goods never seem to be available at the right time or in the right amounts or in the right quality. Thus, enterprise managers who have output quotas to fulfill (and whose bonus depends on their doing so) may find that they cannot get the right kind of ball bearings they need to finish the machine tools they are to produce. Or they may be unable to find the crates they need for shipping their output or they may simply lack the nails to nail down the covers onto the crates. Households, similarly, may find state retail stores devoid of certain goods they crave: linen fabrics, socks, and thread; vacuum cleaners and soap; pineapples and sunflower oil; brass locks, silver spoons, and toothpaste; rock music records and films; blue jeans, chewing gum, and rugs—the list goes on. Even if they do find the type of products they seek, households may dislike their quality: There may be plenty of pots and pans made of aluminum zinc (which leaves a bad taste in food); households may wish for enamelware, stainless steel pots, copper and nonstick pans. And households may be fed up with endless waiting lists: for apartments and cars, for the services of painters and plumbers, carpenters and TV repairers, dentists and doctors. . . . Is it difficult to understand why enterprise managers and households thus frustrated will turn to extralegal means to get what they really want?

## The Semilegal Behavior of Enterprise Managers

Soviet enterprise managers who are frustrated by the supply problem routinely engage in a variety of activities that employ illegal means to achieve legal ends (the fulfillment of output quotas). These activities are officially deplored and denounced; yet they are often tolerated precisely because they help achieve an end result of which central planners approve. They make an imperfect plan workable. Let us consider just three examples of the managerial behavior in question.

**Connections.**    Enterprise managers create and carefully nourish a delicate network of people whose personal influence (*blat*) can get things done that cannot be accomplished in any other way. Often the controllers and the controlled at the bottom of the planning hierarchy find it in their mutual interest to support each other, rather than to be at each other's throats. Before long, a friendly "family relation" develops, which becomes an alliance against the central planners. These managers often succeed in getting the very Party and banking officials and chief accountants who are to watch *them* to use their personal connections with the higher authorities to make life easier for the enterprise, as by having input allocations raised or output targets cut. Central planners, however, dislike losing their grip. They have a number of defenses against the kind of lobbying just described: They "flush out reserves" by routinely slashing what they suspect to be padded input requests or by arbitrarily raising output quotas. And they frequently move managers from one job to another. This disrupts the "family relation" among the controllers and the controlled and introduces an air of uncertainty among those who would do illegal things.

**Black Markets.**   Most enterprise managers surreptitiously employ special kinds of "expediters" or "pushers" (*tolkachi*) who scour the economy for needed supplies and arrange illegal exchanges of equipment and raw materials among enterprises. Thus, the manager of a tractor plant who has received cabbage-planting machines by mistake or whose padded input requests for steel were granted may hoard these items for years. Eventually, though, they may become the means of payment in a black market barter deal involving the acquisition of milling machines and boxes of nails that had been similarly hoarded by other managers.

**Empire Building.**   Many officials in charge of ministries, regions, or enterprises engage in **empire building;** they try to solve the "supply problem" by becoming self-sufficient and, thus, independent of others who might not supply the right types of inputs at the right time. The ministry in charge of chemicals, for example, having been stung in the past by the unavailability of the right kinds of railroad freight cars, may set up facilities for freight car production. It may even produce its own iron ore and fuel so as to be able to make the steel needed for freight car production, a practice officially condemned as "departmentalism" (*vedomstvennost*). Planning officials in the Ukraine, after years of bad experiences with deliveries from other regions, may similarly turn to producing everything within their own jurisdiction. Thus, they may see to it that machine tools made in the Ukraine are delivered to Ukrainian plants in preference to plants in other geographic regions, a practice condemned as "localism" (*mestnichestvo*). The managers of individual enterprises, similarly, try their best to avoid linkages with other enterprises and to become as self-sufficient as possible by producing as many of their own inputs as possible.

## The Illegal Enterprise Sector

All types of inputs (human, natural, and capital) that have been assigned to the official economy are routinely stolen and diverted for use in a wide range of illegal enterprises. It is taken for granted that many workers who are on the state payroll nevertheless are engaged in *private* activities, either at their official places of employment or while away from them pretending to be sick. These workers are, in effect, stealing labor services from the state. And stories abound about the theft of socialist property: In a recent year, state farmers diverted fertilizer to their private plots and grain to their private animals, state doctors diverted medicine to their private practices, state retailers raised private cows and pigs on bread and rolls stolen at a bakery, a million rubles worth of fashionable fabric disappeared from a textile factory, so did all the batteries, tires, and radios from cars being shipped through a railroad yard, so did millions of bricks and plates of glass at a construction site—the list goes on. All these inputs and more fuel a thriving private economy; consider some of the major types of private firms.

**Operations Behind an Official Facade.**   Some private firms conveniently operate behind the facade of an official state enterprise. When watched, workers perform their official duties; otherwise, they use company time, raw materials, and equipment, along with other inputs smuggled in, to produce commodities that are then smuggled out. Among other things, such private entrepreneurs have produced American-style cigarettes, (forbidden) books, chewing gum, disposable diapers, duplicating devices, religious articles (such as candles and icons), short-wave accessories for radio receivers, and tape recorders. Even services can be produced in this way: Private car repair facilities operate at state garages; bus drivers carry ticketless passengers, called "hares," for a private fee.

**Putting Out.**   Some private entrepreneurs engage large numbers of workers all of whom do piecework in their own living quarters. The boss provides raw material, collects the product, and markets it. The large-scale production of American-style blue jeans is a case in point.

**Home-Based Operations.**   Many private producers are headquartered in and when possible carry out most of their operations in their own homes. They produce commodities as well as services. These operations may be illegal, involving, perhaps, the production of lipstick or *samogon* (a type of moonshine made from cheap Cuban sugar). The production, however, is often quite legal in principle but illegal in the sense that it is performed without a license, to avoid taxes. Consider plumbers and tailors, dentists and doctors, people who repair appliances or transport freight and passengers in their private cars. Consider people who simply sell information (the availability of apartments, the imminent arrival of imported pantyhose at a certain department store). Consider construction teams who transform stolen building materials into private houses (a dangerous type of operation that was once financed by Yekaterina A. Furtseva, Minister of Culture, now deposed). Consider the middlemen, called "speculators," who market commodities produced in the underground economy or stolen from the official economy. (Employees of state retail stores are one major source of these stolen goods; such goods can be acquired in innumerable ways besides outright theft—for example, by misweighing, adulteration, writing off as spoilage, and more.)

## Bribery and Corruption

Bribes, monetary or in-kind, are a way of life in the Soviet Union. In a recent year, for example, 2 rubles would make a police officer forget about the running of a red light (or make a hospital nurse bring you a thermometer or change the sheets), 80 rubles could make a retail clerk find under-the-counter imported shoes, 100 rubles would get a patient into a *clean* hospital ward (or schedule a patient for surgery *now*), 300 rubles would procure a "00" license plate (a useful status symbol of the higher-ups), 2,000 rubles would eliminate the 10-year waiting period for a new car, 10,000 rubles and more would procure a permit to live in Moscow or a coveted college admission.[9] Bribes in kind are equally ubiquitous and equally necessary to move things along: A case of vodka will get an apartment redone now

---

[9]See *The New York Times*, May 7, 1978, pp. 1 and 22.

(rather than 4 years hence), that new faucet will be found instantly in return for tickets to the ballet, a car repair can produce a doctor's appointment right away, four bottles of cognac can produce access to one's spouse in a hospital otherwise off-limits to visitors, and an author who can arrange for an editor to meet a top Party official can have an article published next month.

Lenin called bribery "the worst enemy of the revolution." Khrushchev tried to stamp out "this disgraceful survival of the past" by the death penalty. Yet, the taking of bribes by corrupt officials up and down the entire central planning hierarchy remains commonplace. And it is the ultimate reason why the underground economy can thrive. Auditors, court officials, inspectors, managers, police officers, top Party officials—all of them are involved in a complex network of bribetaking, extortion, kickbacks, shakedowns, tribute-taking. When properly compensated, they can be induced to look the other way. Consider Close-Up 7.2, "Russia's Underground Millionaires," at the end of this chapter.

# An Overall Assessment

Given the broad features of the Soviet economy described so far, we are ready to ask how well it has performed with respect to the criteria introduced in chapters 2 to 4.

## Full Employment

According to the Soviet government, unemployment was abolished way back in 1930 during Stalin's first Five-Year Plan and a full utilization of all resources has been maintained ever since. Indeed, statistics on unemployed labor or idle nonhuman resources are not even gathered, and there is no such thing as paying people unemployment benefits. Having replaced the chaos of the market system by science and reason, it is said, involuntary unemployment of resources is a logical impossibility! Close-Up 7.3, "What About Unemployment?," presents the official point of view. In fact, however, unemployment, in hidden form, is all too common.

**Seasonal Unemployment.**   There is plenty of seasonal unemployment. Consider agricultural and construction workers during the winter. Unlike in the United States, their forced idleness is not reflected in unemployment statistics; they are kept on the payroll, sometimes at 50-percent wages, which makes these wages take on the role played by unemployment benefits elsewhere. Or consider teenagers looking for jobs during school vacations. There are plenty of them unable to find jobs because managers avoid hiring teenagers, being constrained by law to grant them 8 hours' pay for 4 to 6 hours' work, as well as generous leaves for part-time study. Such involuntary idleness, however, is simply not measured in the Soviet Union.

**Frictional Unemployment.**   There is also plenty of frictional unemployment, mainly as a result of long delays between leaving school and taking a first job and also due to voluntary quits, which have been allowed without penalties since the mid-1950s. (Earlier decrees forbade anyone from quitting or being absent from a job without permission of the enterprise director, and there were penalties even for quitting with permission, such as denial of sick leave for 6 months, loss of bonuses, and more.) Despite a vigorous campaign against "rolling stones" (workers who hop from job to job), Soviet labor turnover nowadays is huge. While about 4 percent of American industrial workers change jobs in a typical year, it is not unusual for 20 percent of Soviet industrial workers to do so. Although systematic Soviet statistics on the subject do not exist, it is inevitable that much labor time is thus lost between jobs. (In 1964, when 33 percent of all Soviet industrial workers changed jobs, it took 24 days on the average to be reemployed. In a more recent year, 9 percent of those who had quit were still without a job a year later.)

**Systemic Unemployment.**    Even more serious, but equally unmeasured, is unemployment caused by errors in plan formulation and execution. Central planners have found themselves incapable of setting up the billions of carefully coordinated material balances that would be required to specify everyone's future economic activity with precision. The task is inherently too complex; the fact that enterprise managers, when consulted by central planners, also have an incentive to overstate input needs and understate productive capacity does not help. As a result, imperfectly formulated central plans often maldistribute labor, causing de facto unemployment. For example, there have been frequent shortages of labor in large industrial centers and in Siberia, but *surpluses* in small towns and in European Russia. And enterprise managers, whose padded input requests are accepted, hoard labor, raw materials, and equipment for the day when they will come in handy, causing, in the meantime, "unemployment on the job" (*prostoy*). While being idle much of the time, these inputs can be used during the next "storming" episode, in the black market, or in emergencies (as when the government suddenly orders industrial workers into the fields to help with the harvest). Most importantly, much unemployment is caused by the ubiquitous "supply problem" discussed earlier in this chapter. When raw materials arrive at the wrong time or in wrong assortments, complementary workers and machines will be idled. (In the United States, there would be layoffs, and this would be reflected in unemployment statistics; in the Soviet Union, workers remain on the payroll.) Similarly, workers without proper equipment are often idle for long periods of time; consider the frequent breakdown of low-quality capital goods that are not backed up by the manufacturer with the availability of spare parts or servicing. (As a result, the number of equipment repair workers in the Soviet economy greatly exceeds that of production workers making *new* equipment.)

**Conclusion.**    Given ambitious output quotas, the Soviet economy has been spared massive general unemployment of resources, such as that associated with the Great Depression. Nevertheless, unemployment does exist, although its extent cannot be reliably measured. In the Soviet press, anecdotal evidence abounds. In a recent year, Gosplan complained that the equivalent of 2.5 million full-time workers was being hoarded by enterprises and that among workers who were not redundant 25 percent of potential working time was being lost because of the "supply problem."

## Technical Efficiency

The kind of problem summarized in Figure 2.1, "Technical Inefficiency" (page 13), and illustrated in Close-Up 2.1, "A Tale of Two Ford Plants: X-Inefficiency" (pp. 26–27), is common throughout the Soviet economy. In part, it results from actions taken by managers who deliberately hoard labor and other inputs as "insurance" against unforeseen contingencies that could threaten the steady flow of bonuses. As a result, all kinds of resources are "employed" but, in fact, redundant. Thus, foreign observers never cease to marvel at the large numbers of workers employed in Soviet factories that were imported from the West and that were designed to use hardly any workers at all. (In one case, an automated chemicals plant using 91 workers abroad used 723 workers in the U.S.S.R.) And foreign visitors to Soviet department stores are equally amazed at the awkward way in which sales are handled: A customer stands in one line to find out from a clerk whether the displayed item is in stock and stands in another line to find out from another clerk what the price is. There follows a third line leading to a cashier and a fourth one to a clerk who exchanges the cashier's receipt for the item in question. Such examples of bad management could be multiplied without end.

But technical inefficiency is also the result of a widespread lack of labor discipline. Working at a snail's pace, being absent for hours at a time, and being drunk on the job are commonplace. Consequently, output is much smaller than it might be with a more disciplined labor force. The seriousness of the problem is underlined by the fact that two Soviet leaders, Andropov and Gorbachev, have recently mounted major campaigns against absenteeism and alcoholism, respectively. Under Andropov, police would routinely raid mid-day crowds—in movie theaters, retail stores, public bathhouses, and even in the streets—looking for those who should be at work. Under Gorbachev, the production of alcohol was severely curtailed, alcohol prices were raised, and liquor store hours were curtailed, while a temperance campaign was being waged.

## Economic Efficiency

The discussion in the previous chapter has indicated why centralized socialism, even under the best of circumstances, cannot be expected to produce an efficient allocation of resources and goods. That discussion applies fully to the Soviet case. The knowledge of billions of marginal rates of transformation or substitution surely is not available in a Gosplan computer or any other central place. Nor can it possibly be gathered there. Consider agricultural land and how it varies—even within a few hundred yards—in chemical composition, physical contours, rockiness, water availability, and more. Only a few individuals on the spot will know how many extra heads of lettuce can be expected from another application of fertilizer or what the likely trade-off currently is between fertilizer and tender loving care. Or consider the Soviet machine tool industry, which alone produces over 125,000 types of products. Only a few individuals on the spot can possibly know about the currently available trade-off between the production of milling machines and turret lathes;

thousands of others, similarly, only know a tiny segment of the millions of *MRT*s that might be relevant for an efficient allocation of resources. Consider, finally, the millions of consumers who might, if the opportunity arose, better their lot by trading a bicycle for a stove, a refrigerator for furniture, a TV set for fruit and meat. Only each individual can possibly articulate the *MRS*s that currently apply to that individual's circumstances. Let us review some of the Pareto conditions in the context of the Soviet economy.

**The First Pareto Condition.**  It is easy to see why Pareto's first condition (summarized in Table 2.1 on page 16 and Figure 2.2 on page 15 is likely to be violated on a large scale. There simply is no mechanism in the Soviet economy to ensure that a unit of human, natural, or capital resources is released by one enterprise if it can produce more of the same output in another. On the contrary, for reasons noted earlier, enterprise managers in the Soviet economy have all the reason in the world to hold on to whatever resources have been assigned to them. Managers want to increase their own output; they do not care whether some other manager could raise output more. Indeed, managers want to hold on to resources even if their productivity should be zero at the moment. Resources that are idle now might well be used in the future to fulfill or overfulfill output targets, or they might be traded in the black market for different types of resources should deliveries promised by planners fail to materialize.

**The Second Pareto Condition.**  Similarly, Soviet managers all too often find themselves in the process of producing the same goods as other managers with obviously divergent *MRT*s. Thus, Pareto's second condition (summarized in Table 2.2 on page 20 and Figure 2.A on page 475) is likely to be violated as well. Yet, even if managers were aware of this, they could not contract to specialize and trade with each other. Their obligation is to the central planner, not to each other.

Indeed, as we have seen, managers do not trust one another, and specialization in production is discouraged by the ever present "supply problem" that has given rise to the (understandable) tendency of different ministries or regions or even enterprises to create a miniature of the national economy in their own bailiwick. Such "empire building" runs counter to Pareto's insight.

This costly tendency toward autarchy has been equally evident on the national level. Stalin had an isolationist point of view; he distrusted foreigners. (It is significant that he placed foreign visitors in walled-in compounds and that he concentrated railroad construction on north-south lines. East-west lines that might forge a link to Western Europe were built last and even then had a wider gauge than other European railroads, which discouraged transport across the border.) Stalin disliked the idea of the Soviet Union becoming dependent on what he considered untrustworthy foreigners. He disliked national dependence in the same way as the manager of a machine tool plant dislikes dependence on other domestic enterprises (which are to deliver a varied assortment of steel) or as the Ministry of Chemicals Production dislikes dependence on other ministries (which are to deliver the freight cars and trucks needed to transport chemicals). Stalin had an aversion to foreign trade; he wanted to import as little as possible and export only the minimum amount necessary to pay for unavoidable imports. Accordingly, he saw to it that neither individual enterprises nor their superior ministries had any dealings with foreigners. They could neither shop abroad for imports nor search for foreign customers in order to export. All contacts with the outside world were monopolized by the Ministry of Foreign Trade, which implemented the foreign trade portion of material balances by taking deliveries of exportables from domestic enterprises and allocating imported goods among them. Until the late 1940s, the Ministry of Foreign Trade paid no attention to the manifold efficiency-enhancing possibilities inherent in a large-scale international division of labor, based on divergent marginal rates of transformation in the Soviet Union and abroad.

To be sure, the 1949 formation of CMEA, the Council for Mutual Economic Assistance, among the Soviet Union and its East European satellites was associated with much *talk* about improving economic efficiency. (See Close-Up 2.2, "Stalin and Comecon," on page 27.) But, in fact, the Soviet economic relations with Eastern Europe since World War II are better viewed as a form of **economic imperialism** by which the dominant country obtained involuntary favors from weaker countries. Until the mid-1950s, for example, the Soviet Union forced its satellites to add to the Soviet capital stock through a massive net flow of goods into the Soviet Union, especially war reparations. (The size of this flow from Eastern Europe to the Soviet Union equaled U.S. Marshall Plan aid to Western Europe.) Simultaneously, and ever since, the Soviet Union has insisted that its East European satellites give up efficiency-enhancing opportunities to trade with the West, while enlarging their own capital stock as a prelude to trade with the U.S.S.R. The goal has been to create area-wide autarchy by making satellites into industrial workshops that process imported Soviet raw materials into manufactured goods then exported to the Soviet Union. More recently, the satellite countries have also been induced to enter a number of "barter-over-time" deals whereby they contribute to capital formation on Soviet soil now (constructing steel mills, oil and gas pipelines, and more) while receiving as payment a portion of the new facilities' output later. Yet, despite these types of arrangements, barriers to a full-scale division of labor among the Soviet Union and Eastern Europe remain high. (In a recent and not unusual year, the CMEA countries' share in world trade was only one third as high as their share in world industrial output; in contrast, the Common Market countries of Western Europe had a trade share two and a half times as high.)

**The Third Pareto Condition.**    Pareto's third condition (summarized in Table 2.3 on page 22 and Figure 2.B on page 477) is violated no less than the others. Consider, for example, the crucial intertemporal decision that allocates resources between current consumption and, via investment, future consumption. If we interpret good *a* as a consumption good available now and good *b* as the same type of consumption good available in the future, we can view the $MRT^{\alpha}_{a,b}$ as a producer's marginal rate of time productivity. (Thus, an $MRT^{\alpha}_{a,b}$ of $1a = 2b$ indicates producer $\alpha$'s ability to produce 1 unit less of the good now, channel the saved resources into capital formation, and, because of the new capital, produce an extra 2 units of the good in the future. It also indicates that α can produce 1 more unit of the good now as long as less is invested now, which requires sacrificing 2 units of the good in the future when the capital stock is not as large as it might have been.) Similarly, we can view the $MRS^X_{a,b}$ as a consumer's marginal rate of time preference. (Thus, an $MRS^X_{a,b}$ of $1a = 7b$ indicates consumer X's indifference about consuming 1 unit less of the good now as long as 7 units more become available in the future. It also indicates an indifference toward consuming 1 unit more of the good now, while having to reduce future consumption by 7 units.) Clearly, there is no mechanism in the Soviet economy that determines an optimum amount of investment by taking account jointly of consumers' marginal rates of time preference and producers' marginal rates of time productivity. By design, the decision about the overall volume of investment has been taken out of the hands of consumers and is made by Party leaders. They are quite capable of promoting investment beyond the point of Pareto efficiency. (In the example just discussed, the producer can transform $-1a$ into $+2b$ only, the consumer would consent to an intertemporal exchange of $-1a$ for at least $7b$ only; yet Gosplan may insist on the $-1a$ current sacrifice nevertheless.)

In addition, there are strong indications that Gosplan has not managed to allocate investment resources in the best possible way. Still using the previous example, it is as if Gosplan added insult to injury by taking the resources released from not producing $1a$ and handing them to producer α whose investment will one day yield $2b$, while ignoring producer β whose investment could have yielded $4b$. For example, Gosplan has concentrated investment in heavy industry, while ignoring investment in agriculture. Quite likely, this strategy has neglected the most productive investment projects. For example, a Soviet lathe exported to Brazil may yield the funds needed to buy 1,000 bushels of American wheat, but shifting Soviet investment from the machinery industry to agriculture might have lowered lathe production by one, while yielding an extra 3,000 bushels of *Ukrainian* wheat. Nor is this speculation only. Soviet agriculture has suffered greatly from Stalin-inspired neglect. (Under Stalin, only 12 percent of investment went into agriculture.) As a result, in many parts of the country there are no hard-surface roads. Most villages are cut off from each other and from urban areas for months at a time—by snow drifts in the winter, mud in the spring, deep ruts in the summer. (Half of all tractor time is used not to harvest or plow, but to tow trucks!) In addition, storage facilities on farms (barns, silos, tool sheds, and the like)) are often lacking entirely or highly inadequate; more often than not, the nearest warehousing facilities are hundreds of miles away. Is it surprising that up to a quarter of many crops (grain, fruits, potatoes, vegetables, and so on) are regularly left in the fields to rot? That cows and pigs die regularly from exposure to the weather? That equipment becomes unusable because of rust?

**All Other Pareto Conditions.**    It is equally doubtful that the other Pareto conditions will be fulfilled. Consider, for example, the fourth and fifth conditions (summarized, respectively, in Table 2.4 and Figure 2.C on pages 24 and 477 and in Table 2.A and Figure 2.D on pages 478 and 479). They deal with the efficient allocation of goods among consumers and of resources among producers. Given the way such allocation is accomplished in the Soviet economy, the inefficient situations depicted in the earlier examples could easily arise. On the other hand, the all-pervasive system of private trading—among enterprises and among households—in the underground economy is likely to remove some of these inefficiencies and improve the overall welfare derived from available consumption goods and the output derived from available resources. Nevertheless, in 1959, the Soviet economist L. V. Kantorovich (Biography 11.1) suggested that Soviet industrial output could be increased by 50 percent without the use of any additional inputs, if existing inputs were allocated efficiently. An American economist, Abram Bergson, computed 1960 indexes of output per unit of combined labor and capital inputs for the Soviet Union and for the United States. The overall Soviet index stood at 41, compared to 100 for the U.S.; the indexes for industry were 58 and 100, respectively.

## Economic Growth

Ever since 1928, when central economic planning was initiated, rapid economic growth has been a major goal of Soviet leaders. Table 7.2, "Average Annual Rates of Growth in the U.S.S.R.," brings together some of the relevant data for selected periods from 1928 to the recent past. Column (6) presents the big picture: With the understandable exception of the World War II years, the Soviet real GNP until the late 1950s grew at impressive annual rates of roughly 6 to 7 percent. Since then, however, the overall rate of growth has steadily declined. Let us consider some of the detail.

**The 1928–1940 Period.** The early Five-Year Plans clearly established two precedents that have effectively survived to the present. First, central planners placed primary emphasis on the growth of industry rather than agriculture; note the growth rates of 8.1 versus 1.6 percent given in Table 7.2 (along with a similar differential in future periods). Second, central planners decisively opted for a strategy of extensive rather than intensive growth; note the 1928–1940 growth rates of labor and capital versus the lack of any increase in productivity (again a situation that has persisted in later years).

Thus, in the 1930s, many of Stalin's favorite industries—ranging from coal, iron, and steel to electric power, locomotives, and tractors—achieved manifold increases in output, typically through manifold increases in inputs. (Electric power output, for example, increased seven-fold after the completion of various construction projects, such as the giant Dnieper Dam.)

Steady increases in labor input (the number of hours worked) were achieved in a variety of ways. First of all, the government exerted tremendous pressure on all adults to participate in the labor force and not to remain voluntarily unemployed and, thus, lead an "antisocial parasitic way of life." Indeed, Article 12 of Stalin's 1936 Constitution states: "Work in the U.S.S.R. is a duty and a matter of honor for every able-bodied citizen, in accordance with the principle: He who does not work, neither shall he eat." As a result, the Soviet Union achieved labor force participation rates higher than anywhere else in the world (close to 90 percent for

**Table 7.2**   Average Annual Rates of Growth in the U.S.S.R. (percentage change)*

| Period | Labor Input (1) | Capital Input (2) | Land Input (3) | Combined Inputs (4) | Productivity (Output per Unit of Combined Inputs) (5) | Real GNP (6) | Industrial Output (7) | Agricultural Output (8) |
|---|---|---|---|---|---|---|---|---|
| 1928–1940 | | | | | | 7.2 | | |
| agriculture | 1.2 | 3.2 | | | −.1 | | — | 1.6 |
| industry | 8.5 | 14.1 | | | −2.1 | | 8.1 | — |
| 1940–1950 | .6 | .2 | | .6 | 1.4 | 2.0 | | |
| 1950–1955 | 1.9 | 9.0 | 4.0 | 4.5 | 1.4 | 6.0 | 11.3 | 4.1 |
| 1955–1960 | .6 | 9.8 | 1.3 | 3.9 | 1.8 | 5.8 | 8.7 | 4.1 |
| 1960–1965 | 1.6 | 8.7 | .6 | 4.1 | .9 | 5.0 | 7.0 | 2.4 |
| 1965–1970 | 2.0 | 7.4 | 0 | 4.4 | .5 | 4.9 | 6.0 | 3.4 |
| 1970–1975 | 1.7 | 8.0 | .1 | 4.5 | −1.4 | 3.1 | 5.7 | −.4 |
| 1975–1980 | 1.2 | 6.9 | −.1 | 3.7 | −1.4 | 2.3 | 2.7 | 1.0 |
| 1980–1985 | .7 | 6.3 | 0 | 3.2 | −1.0 | 2.2 | 2.3 | 2.2 |

*All growth rates refer to the official economy only. Systematic data on the underground economy do not exist.

Sources: Data, only roughly accurate and roughly comparable, have been derived from Norman M. Kaplan, "Retardation in Soviet Growth," *Review of Economics and Statistics,* August 1968, pp. 293–303; Stanley H. Cohn, "The Soviet Economy: Performance and Growth," in Marshall I. Goldman, editor, *Comparative Economic Systems: A Reader,* 2d ed. (New York: Random House, 1971), pp. 342, 346, and 348; Joint Economic Committee, Congress of the United States, *Soviet Economy in a New Perspective* (Washington, D.C.: U.S. Government Printing Office, 1976), pp. 272 and 279; idem, *Allocation of Resources in the Soviet Union and China, 1985* (Washington, D.C.: U.S. Government Printing Office, 1986), pp. 30, 41, 80, and 81.

men and close to 80 percent for women aged 16 to 60). In addition, central planners shifted people from agricultural part-time employment into urban full-time employment and were able to take advantage of favorable demographic developments (which increased the percentage of working-age adults in the population).

Above all, central planners changed drastically the composition of output, away from the production of consumption goods and toward the production of capital goods. (In 1928, only 8 percent of output consisted of capital goods; by 1937 it was 21 percent, by 1958, and ever since, about 33 percent. At the same time, per capita consumption declined after 1928 and did not regain the 1928 level for three decades. Since 1958, per capita consumption has been rising—slowly.)

Finally, the early central plans promoted the discovery and development of significant quantities of new natural resources or "land"—ranging from bauxite, copper, nickel, phosphate, and tin mines to oil fields and newly cultivated agricultural areas.

**The 1940–1950 Period.**   The decade of the 1940s was, of course, dominated by World War II, which not only put a temporary halt to Stalin's industrialization drive but set it back considerably. Even during the initial phase of the war in mid-1941, the Soviets lost to the Germans half of their productive capacity in aluminum, coal, and steel and a third of their grain-producing territories and railroad lines. Later, the Soviets lost more, and when the Germans finally retreated, they pursued a policy of systematic devastation: wrecking and flooding mine shafts, blowing up factories and railroad lines, destroying all farm animals and buildings. Although 10 million people had been evacuated to the Urals, Siberia, and Central Asia (along with a thousand large-scale enterprises), much of the Soviet Union in 1945 was a wasteland and 20 million Russians were dead.

**The 1950s and Beyond.**   The most significant (and much lamented) fact about Soviet economic growth since the 1950s has been the steady decline in the rate of growth. This can be explained by two factors in turn: (a) fewer opportunities to pursue the favored strategy of extensive growth and (b) an inability of central planners to harness the potential of the alternative strategy of intensive growth. Let us consider each of these cases in some detail.

   *Fewer opportunities for extensive growth: labor resources.*   In the case of labor, past increases in hours utilized, for instance, are harder and harder to repeat. Once labor force participation rates for men and women have been pushed to their practical limits, this source of increased labor supply is closed. Similarly, because most underemployed agricultural labor has now been drawn to the industrial sector, this source of additional labor is drying up as well. In addition, Stalin's iron fist is gone—he was willing to force people to work *more* hours per week; his successors have reduced weekly hours. Worst of all, since the late 1950s, demographic trends have turned against central planners: The great disasters of the Soviet past (emigration, famine, purges, and World War II) have decreased the ratio of males to females in the population and now produce a remarkably slower annual increase in the potential labor force. (The labor force in the more industrialized areas, such as the Baltic, White Russian, and Ukrainian republics, is actually declining; it is rising in peripheral areas, such as Central Asia, Kazakhstan, and the Transcaucasus.)

   *Fewer opportunities for extensive growth: capital resources.*   In the case of capital, prospects for extensive growth are equally declining. This is true despite the fact that Stalin's successors continue to impose heavy sacrifices in consumption goods in order to ensure that a large percentage of each year's GNP consists of new capital (or investment) goods. There are two reasons: (1) For a given production of new capital goods, past increases in the capital stock are impossible to repeat to the extent that an ever greater percentage of each year's new capital goods now just replaces the wear and tear of a much larger (and older) capital stock. (2) Unlike in the past, when investment was stressed in sectors with high marginal output-to-capital ratios, more of it is now channeled into sectors with low marginal output-to-capital ratios; therefore, a given increase in the capital stock (which is so much harder to achieve in the first place) also yields less of an output increase than in the past. Consider a numerical example.

Suppose the Soviet Union had a small but young capital stock of 200 million rubles and used it to produce 100 million rubles of output in a year. If 25 percent of the new output was invested, **gross investment,** the addition of new buildings and equipment to the capital stock, plus the change in producer inventories, would come to 25 million rubles in that year. Suppose that **depreciation,** the shrinkage through wear and tear of buildings and equipment from the capital stock, came to only 2.5 percent of the stock, or 5 million rubles—given that the existing capital stock was small and young. The $25 - 5 = 20$ million rubles of the new capital goods would measure the extent of **net investment,** or the net change in the capital stock in that year. Thus, the capital stock would grow from 200 to 220 million rubles, or by 10 percent that year. Now picture the country some 30 years hence. The capital stock may have grown to 3,000 million rubles, annual output to 500 million rubles. Let gross investment remain at 25 percent of the GNP, now equaling 125 million rubles. Let depreciation equal 3 percent of the capital stock, or 90 million rubles—given a capital stock that is not only larger but also older. Then $125 - 90 = 35$ million rubles would equal net investment. The capital stock would only grow from 3,000 to 3,035 million rubles, or by 1.2 percent that year.

We can similarly illustrate the second problem noted earlier. Given a larger capital stock, the economy can produce a higher output, but exactly how much higher depends on the exact *form* the new capital goods take. Consider the original case of a 20-million-ruble net change in the capital stock. If this addition consisted of residential houses for 1,200 new families and, as is customary in a GNP calculation, the output of residential houses was evaluated by their rental value (of, say, 1,500 rubles per year each), the GNP would rise by 1,200 times 1,500 rubles, or 1.8 million rubles. The extra output produced with the help of extra capital, divided by that extra capital, is the **marginal output-to-capital ratio.** In this case, it would equal 1.8 million rubles divided by 20 million rubles, or .09, and it would be associated with a GNP growth from 100 to 101.8 million rubles, or 1.8 percent that year.

The marginal output-to-capital ratio, however, differs widely among economic sectors. The same 20-million-ruble net investment, had it consisted of new chemical plants, might have raised the GNP by 13 million rubles (in the form of new chemical output). Then the marginal output-to-capital ratio would have equaled 13 million rubles divided by 20 million rubles, or .65, and this higher ratio would have been associated with a higher GNP growth from 100 to 113 million rubles, or 13 percent that year.

It so happens that Stalin concentrated investment in sectors with high marginal output-to-capital ratios; his successors have had to direct their (harder-to-achieve) increases in the capital stock to sectors with lower marginal output-to-capital ratios.

*Fewer opportunities for extensive growth: natural resources.* In the past, increases in agricultural output were made possible by drawing new lands into cultivation. (The most spectacular example was Khrushchev's ''virgin lands campaign'' in the 1950s.) The practical limits of this policy have now been reached. Further increases in agricultural output require increases in yield per acre. And such increases are much more resource-absorbing. As the law of diminishing returns implies, if a certain amount of resources added to an area of new land produces a certain amount of extra output, only a larger amount of resources will raise output equally on an equal area of old land already under cultivation. Thus, given sacrifices in consumption goods (to make given amounts of, say, machinery and chemicals) yield smaller increases in agricultural output now than in Stalin's days.

The same problem has arisen in the exploitation of minerals and fuels. Those of the highest grade and those nearest industrial centers have been mined first. As the Soviets resort to lower grades or mines that are farther away, more resources are needed to obtain identical results. If, previously, 10 machines mined 100 tons of iron ore per day (with 60 percent pure iron content) and 10 freight cars used for one day could transport them to the steel mill, the same amount of pure iron can be obtained now only if 20 machines mine 200 tons of ore (with 30 percent content) and 20 freight cars are used for two days to transport them a distance twice as long. Given sacrifices in consumption goods (to make mining machinery and freight cars) yield smaller increases in industrial output now than in Stalin's days. Indeed, there was a time when almost all energy raw materials (coal, gas, oil, hydropower) originated west of the Urals; in the 1980s, almost 90 percent of them came from Siberia, Central Asia, and the Far East.

*The missed potential of intensive growth.*    The Soviets have not been unaware of the fact that qualitative improvements of resources or technical advance could promote intensive growth. Yet, as column (5) of Table 7.2 so clearly indicates, their policies to improve output *per unit* of input have been a failure to far.

Consider *education*. The number of educational institutions and enrollment in them has skyrocketed under Soviet rule. In 1939, only 12 percent of working inhabitants of the Soviet Union had any education beyond elementary school. By 1975, the percentage was 75. Experts, furthermore, have found the quality of Soviet education to be excellent, both with regard to curricular content and the level of achievement by students. Also, the Soviets have closely integrated educational policies with economic objectives. They have trained people as needed by the economy rather than let them pursue any education that suited their personal fancy. Hence, there are now relatively large numbers of people trained in mathematics, engineering, and the sciences (rather than in the liberal arts). This sort of improvement in the quality of labor might be expected to yield a substantial harvest of output. On the other hand, there is an offsetting factor. The Soviet labor force in the 1980s was thoroughly demoralized after many decades of broken promises about the future consumer paradise. Alcoholism on the job was rampant; so were absenteeism and malingering.

Consider *health care*. Although spectacular improvements in health care since 1928 have been much heralded by Soviet propaganda, reality leaves much to be desired. In 1987, after decades of rising death rates and falling life expectancy, the Soviet press decided on a public airing:[10] In rural areas, 17 percent of hospitals still had no running water, 27 percent had no sewer system, 35 percent had no hot

---

[10]As reported by *The New York Times*, August 18, 1987, pp. 1 and 27.

water. Even in Moscow, over a third of maternity hospitals failed to meet the most basic sanitary standards; there were no sterile bandages, no disposable needles, no diapers; infections were common, infant mortality was rising (and put the Soviet Union in 50th place worldwide). And everywhere, doctors had norms to meet; 8 patients per hour with two thirds of the time spent on paper work. . . .

Consider *technical advance*. Under Stalin, the Soviets organized the wholesale copying of the most advanced production techniques from the West. While ignoring the international patent conventions, this skillfully executed policy enabled the Soviet economy to leap in a few decades over a long period of research and development that had preceded economic growth in the West. (Even today, the Soviets are running the most elaborate information-gathering organization in the world, which systematically monitors all scientific and technical progress abroad.) Instead of simply producing on a large scale more capital of the same kind found in czarist Russia, the Soviets installed, on a large scale, more capital *of a completely different kind,* embodying the latest scientific discoveries and technical advances. (However, their copying typically produced a standard design for a production process that was then relied upon for decades rather than updated continuously.)

In addition, Stalin laid the groundwork for domestic technical advance by establishing an extended system of scientific research institutions, culminating in the Academy of Sciences of the U.S.S.R. Soviet leaders have been most eager to supply the research institutions lavishly with resources and, with few exceptions, have provided scientists with all the perquisites conducive to creative thinking. As Soviet progress in rocket technology has shown, they are quite capable of making advances on their own.

Notwithstanding all of the above, a major weakness exists in the field of Soviet technology. It concerns the lack of something that has proven in the long run to be the most important source of growth in most of the world's economies: innovative activity at the level of the enterprise (with failure being localized and successes being quickly imitated by all). In contrast to their Western colleagues, Soviet enterprise managers have been notoriously uninterested in experimenting on a small scale and continuously with new improved methods of production. It is not difficult to see why: Since central planners give them inputs for the express purpose of producing designated quantities of output (and fulfillment of output quotas, in turn, produces managerial bonuses), any diversion of inputs to experimentation with the productive process not only is contrary to specific commands (and exposes the manager to criminal prosecution for misuse of the people's property), but it also endangers the managerial bonus (and, thus, the manager's personal standard of living). Thus, managers have unanimously resisted the temptation to produce technological change on their own. Indeed, they have even resisted technological innovations commanded by central planners (because their introduction inevitably upsets the smooth flow of production at the very time that central planners are tempted to raise output targets in accordance with the improved methods of production). Hence, technological changes spell at least a temporary loss of bonuses. As Secretary Brezhnev put it, Soviet enterprise managers shy away from innovating activity ''as the devil shies away from incense.''

At the same time, it has become obvious that innovation decided upon and commanded by central planners is a slow and possibly disastrous sort of thing. Consider the slow Soviet changeover from coal to oil and gas as major energy sources. For all too many years, human, natural, and capital resources that could have produced a vastly greater amount of energy had they been producing oil and gas instead were wasted on coal production. Yet, nothing happened until central planners finally ordered the switchover nationwide. When all decisions are big decisions (involving entire industries or the whole nation), mistakes become big mistakes, too. The most infamous of these was Stalin's support of Lysenko, whose unscientific approach to biological science cost the Soviet Union dearly in agricultural output. Close-Up 7.4, "The Lysenko Tragedy," tells the story.

## Economic Equity

As was noted in the previous chapter, a system of centralized socialism can never produce *commutative* justice; the necessary ingredients for such a state of affairs are missing by design. In principle, such a system could, however, produce *distributive* justice; the central government does have the power to define the meaning of fairness and to apportion goods among people accordingly. The Soviet Union is a perfect case in point. To be sure, goods are not distributed among people in accordance with any of the distributive justice criteria discussed in Chapter 3 (need, equality, or hours worked), yet the Soviet government maintains that equity is achieved because (a) no one receives income from the private ownership of capital and natural resources and (b) admittedly large differences in people's labor income are government-determined with a view to what people deserve—they are not the result of "blind" market forces. You may not wish to agree, but, according to the Soviet government, the distribution of goods among the Soviet people is fair simply because their government says it's fair!

**The Rejection of Income Equality.**   Whatever one's personal view about the alleged fairness, the Soviets certainly have managed to create enormous differences in the incomes of people. This is true with respect to money income as well as income in kind. And it is the consequence of both the hierarchical organization of the economy "as one large factory" (with corresponding income differences reflecting the status of recipients) and the pervasive use of material incentives, ranging from the deliberately set occupational and regional wage differentials to piece rates and bonuses designed to affect performance on the job. This situation of inequality certainly contradicts the vision of perfect equality held by early revolutionaries. Even Lenin had moved away from that egalitarian vision by the time he initiated the NEP, but he still endorsed the "party maximum," a rule that the income of party officials should under no circumstances exceed that of skilled workers. In the 1930s, Stalin put an end to all that (Trotskyite) "equality mongering," as he called it. "Marxism is an enemy of equalization," he said. In his view the wish to have all workers pool their wages in a common fund and then share equally was dreamed up by "leftist blockheads"; it was a "reactionary, petty-bourgeois absurdity worthy of a primitive sect of ascetics, but not of a Socialist society organized on Marxian lines.''[11] Accordingly, Stalin created wide income gaps between peasants and urban workers, unskilled and skilled workers, ordinary workers and Stakhanovite record-breakers, and, in general, all kinds of subordinates and higher-level officials. Some 50 years later, Party Chairman Gorbachev expressed similar hostility toward income equality. ''Work, and work alone,'' he said, ''should be the criterion for determining a person's value, his social prestige and his material status. Some will come off badly—the slacker, the drunkard, the slovenly. Let them not take offense—they are getting what they deserve. And we will elevate, both materially and morally, the diligent, those who are putting all their strength and resources into their work.''[12]

**The Income Pyramid.**    At the top of the Soviet income pyramid are the political and economic leaders, followed by the military brass, the professional-managerial elite, and superstars in arts and sports. Below them, in turn, are industrial workers, followed by the peasants at the very bottom. In the mid-1970s, Party Chairman Brezhnev was officially earning 2,900 rubles a month, a full-fledged member of the Academy of Sciences 2,000 rubles a month. The director of a scientific research institute or an enterprise manager was earning 700 rubles a month, the average industrial worker 141 rubles, a doctor, policeman, or state farm worker 100 rubles, an office clerk 75, and the average collective farmer 50 rubles.

By themselves, such figures, however, are misleading. To see why this is so, we must learn about the **nomenklatura system,** the appointment system operated by the Central Committee of the Communist Party that is used to fill the most significant jobs throughout society. The system was introduced by Stalin but has been used by all of his successors right to the present. Stalin was distrustful of his associates; he wanted to reduce the likelihood of ''betrayal.'' So he reserved for himself the task of staffing all the top jobs in society. First, he drew up a list of key posts to be filled: People's Commissar of War (later Minister of Defense), deputy to the Supreme Soviet, provincial party secretary, head of Gosplan, district military commander, research institute director, editor of *Pravda,* and the like. Then he drew up another list of persons (*nomenklaturnye rabotniki*) who were deemed loyal and, therefore, eligible to fill the aforementioned posts. And he made ap-pointments accordingly. Thus, all power emanated not from the bottom up, but from the top down. (By a particularly creative use of language, this is referred to as ''democratic centralism.'') Along with the nomenklatura system, the special rewards Stalin provided to his elite supporters have survived to the present. Thus, Party Chairman Brezhnev received not only the 2,900 rubles a month noted above—he also managed to acquire a personal fleet of foreign cars that included a Mercedes, Cadillac, Rolls Royce, Lincoln Continental, Monte Carlo, French Matra, and Lancia

---

[11]Quoted by John G. Gurley, *Challengers to Capitalism,* 2d ed. (New York: Norton, 1979), p. 112.

[12]*The New York Times,* March 8, 1987, p. 8.

Beta. And the other 227,000 people on his nomenklatura list[13] were equally insulated from the intense scarcity that was and is a basic part of Soviet life. They received part of their salaries in so-called certificate rubles, which, along with special passes, opened the guarded doors of special windowless stores stocked with otherwise unavailable imported goods, with Soviet-made durables at 20 percent of normal price, and with a cornucopia of fruits, meats, and vegetables. Such special rubles and passes also provided access to city mansions, better apartment houses, and country *dachas* (''cottages''), to theater boxes, luxury vacation resorts, and foreign travel, to fine restaurants and special medical clinics, to chauffeured cars and large gasoline allowances, and to special schools for one's children. And we have not even mentioned the additional advantages of connections within the elite class (which could, for example, procure the right job for one's spouse or child). Many of these privileges are, of course, not susceptible to precise numerical measurement, but they are certainly enormous and not included in official income statistics.

It is difficult to believe that the low money income of industrial workers and the even lower money income of peasants was correspondingly increased by their receipt from underground economic activities or by their access to agricultural produce in kind from work on collective farms or private garden plots. In fact, peasants fared worse than even ordinary urban industrial workers in such matters as access to child care, medical care, and education.

**Available Data.**   Given all that has been said, it is clear that summary statistics on the Soviet distribution of money income must be interpreted with the greatest caution. In fact, comprehensive data of this type do not exist. Fragmentary data, pieced together by Western scholars, corroborate the fact of inequality. During the 1972–1974 period, for example, the ,(official) after-tax money income of Soviet urban households was distributed as follows: The poorest 10 percent of households received 3.4 percent of the total; the richest 10 percent, 24.1 percent of the total. The poorest and richest 20 percent received respectively, 8.7 and 38.5 percent of the total.[14]

## Alienation

All that has been said on the subject of alienation in the previous chapter (which dealt with a *model* of centralized socialism) can be said about the Soviet Union as well. Consider the three types of alienation introduced in Chapter 4.

---

[13]In the 1970s, a tiny fraction of 1 percent of the Soviet population was on the list. It included 80,000 Party officials, 60,000 government and trade union officials, 40,000 members of the ''intelligentsia'' (academicians, university and research institute directors, senior editors and journalists, top artists, and so on), 30,000 military, police, and diplomatic personnel, and 17,000 top enterprise directors. See Abram Bergson, ''Income Inequality under Soviet Socialism,'' *Journal of Economic Literature,* September 1984, p. 1086.

[14]Abram Bergson, *op. cit.,* p. 1070.

**From the Self.**    All the alleged causes of people's alienation from themselves surely exist in the Soviet Union no less than in other industrialized countries: the division of labor and "enslavement" of people to machines, to work outside the home, to rigid schedules, to mammoth workplaces. True enough, Soviet citizens are considerably less "enslaved" to fancy gadgets in private homes in sprawling suburbs. But that is true only because their government has so far refused to provide them with sufficient quantities of such consumption goods. Having an abundance of such goods is, however, the great dream of Soviet citizens as well as the pronounced goal of their government. And note: In Soviet society, should people wish to escape the division of labor and all it implies, they rarely have the option to go off and live by themselves, in their own way, even if they are willing to pay the price in terms of goods foregone. People are taught to submerge their individuality in the community at large, to be a willing cog in the great central plan, not to go off and do their own thing. Consider these stories: In 1974, Soviet authorities used bulldozers, dump trucks, and water-spraying machines to break up an outdoor exhibition of "unofficial" art being held on a vacant lot in Moscow. Young vigilantes beat the artists and burned, ripped up, or trampled their paintings. "Why do you paint old houses under dark skies and hazy moons?" they said. "Why not big houses being built by happy workers in sunlight?" Later the artists were fined or imprisoned for not conforming to "socialist realism." In 1987, police brutally beat loitering "hippies" and motorcycle "rockers" in a Moscow park, sending them to the hospital. Punks in rainbow hair sporting electric guitars and playing "decadent" Western music were no more acceptable than the painters of "incorrect" art.

These anecdotes tell much about the ability of individuals to be themselves in a society where conforming to the Party line has the highest priority. In this society, should people wish to develop their inherent talents by painting pictures or playing music, by reading books or writing them, or by doing a million similar things commanded by an inner voice, they do not have the option, unless they act in ways approved by central planners. One cannot read or write just any book; one cannot paint just any picture. If one insists on doing so, one must face the secret police, jail, or the insane asylum (at worst) or demotion, loss of job, or harassment of family and friends (at best).

**From Other People.**    Can the Soviet people be described, as early revolutionaries predicted, as one vast community of loving brothers and sisters who participate as equals in all crucial decisions affecting their lives? Hardly.

In Soviet society, the fears expressed in the corresponding section of the previous chapter have been abundantly realized. More than any other factor, the all-embracing presence of a bureaucracy that combines all economic and political power is responsible for a severe alienation of people from their fellows.

*Consumer sovereignty* does not exist. The major decision about current versus future consumption is made by the Party leadership; even decisions about the detailed make-up of the annual basket of consumption goods are made by the planning hierarchy. Ultimate consumers, far from participating as equals, have no choice but to accept what is offered them or go without. All this does not occur by accident but by design. The Party leadership has always doubted the validity of consumer preferences, referring to them as arbitrary, irrational, subjective, even vulgar. Naturally, the leadership knows best. Its preferences are seen as rational, objective, and, therefore, correct. At best, consumers can assert themselves through passive resistance. They can and do protest their low real income (which is occasioned by the high investment rates central planners prefer) by working at the slowest possible pace. And they protest an undesirable assortment of consumption goods by not buying the goods offered, letting the inventories of state retail stores build up, and turning to the underground economy instead.

*Worker sovereignty* is equally limited, despite the official description of the Soviet economy as one of *nationwide* worker self-management. The truth is that the Party leadership pretends to speak for and act in the name of the workers, but the workers have no real control over those who exercise the "dictatorship of the proletariat." Although workers enjoy all kinds of statutory guarantees in their places of work (as do citizens at large), they have no procedure for enforcing them should they be violated by enterprise managers (or the central government). The labor unions to which virtually all Soviet workers belong do not represent the workers' interests in any meaningful way. They are not authentic unions responsible to workers but pseudo-unions controlled by the government; their primary task is to "strengthen labor discipline"—that is, to encourage hard work by the workers so as to fulfill the central plan. This primary task of unions is pursued in a variety of ways, including the provision of medals or vacation trips for the meritorious or the pillorying of the slothful by "comrades' courts" that can dock workers' pay as well as send them on to prisons and forced labor camps. (Labor unions do have some subordinate tasks as well, such as administering health and pension programs, cultural programs, and the like.) Certainly, Soviet unions do not engage in collective bargaining about wages or working conditions, and labor's ultimate weapon, the strike, is illegal. Soviet ideology views strikes as meaningless because all enterprises "belong to the workers." What sense is there in workers striking against themselves?

Almost all the ingredients for *citizen sovereignty* are absent as well. There is an extreme concentration of power in the hands of the Party leadership, and it exercises this power over all aspects of life, denying citizens most of the individual liberties enjoyed in the West. Having formulated the central plan for the good of all, the central planners are determined to defend that plan by any means required, be it force or persuasion. Therefore, public criticism of the government and expressions of doubt about its infinite wisdom are suppressed whenever possible and treated as acts of disloyalty, treachery, sabotage. The governmental monopoly of education, movies, newspapers, radio, television, and all other means of spreading knowledge ensures that only those views are publicized that strengthen the belief in the rightness of the leaders' decisions.

We conclude that Soviet society is far removed from the revolutionary vision of a land inhabited by loving brothers and sisters. But we should also note that this is not only so because the government for decades on end has oppressed its people. Somehow, the government's attitude has permeated all of society. Like bicyclists who bow to the world above and trample that below, Soviet citizens everywhere, no matter how lowly their status, are apt to butter up those who have power over them, while treating abysmally those others who don't. Perhaps it is no accident that there is an incredible abrasiveness in everyday encounters, an unbelievable level of shouting in stores, a common disdain (among Muscovites) for the "un-cultured" peasants and the "uncouth" Asians who (unlike European Russians) multiply like rats in a barn (and threaten the purity of the race).

**From Nature.**    Although they hold the power to preserve nature, Soviet central planners have, in fact, not shown themselves particularly sensitive to nature. Any horror story about the pollution of the environment that one can tell about the United States, one can tell also about the Soviet Union. Indeed, Soviet bureaucrats have shown considerably less concern with the problem. While Americans worried about the environmental impact of the Alaska pipeline, the Soviets were boasting of having constructed the world's longest pipeline; while Americans agonize over the con-struction of every nuclear power station, the Soviets build them freely; while Amer-icans rejected the building of the supersonic transport, the Soviets were among the first to build it.

Soviet pollution of air, rivers, lakes, and oceans is ubiquitous. In light of the managerial incentive system discussed earlier, it is easy to see why: Producing, installing, and operating antipollution devices, or changing production processes to recycle wastes otherwise dumped, amounts to wasting resources from the point of view of managers who are rewarded for fulfilling output targets. Every bit of human, natural, and capital resources used to produce antipollution devices can also be used to produce more output (and, thus, to get a higher bonus). Changing production processes to recapture wastes amounts to the same thing. Like technological change, it upsets the applecart by interrupting the smooth, ongoing process of producing. It is as simple as that. Thus, the ugly byproducts of production—foul air, noise, poisoned water, despoiled land—can be found as easily in a land run by party bureaucrats as in one run by capitalist "tycoons."

One final note: As have the governments of real-world capitalist countries, the Soviet government has been taking notice of this problem increasingly. As in the West, laws have been passed "to preserve flora and fauna"; as in the West, they have not always been enforced. Reports indicate how resources allocated in the central plan for antipollution devices have not been used, how waste-treatment equipment always seems to be out of order, to be working intermittently or below capacity. Considering the existing incentive system, this is not surprising. Every resource saved from preserving the natural world is a resource saved for raising output and someone's bonus!

## The Call for Reform

The Stalinist economic system has been plagued by a great variety of problems, as the previous sections of this chapter have made abundantly clear. The inherent complexity of the task of setting up a comprehensive national plan of economic activity that is perfectly coordinated and feasible would be sufficient by itself to account for this fact. Thus, it is not surprising that Soviet plans have consistently failed to meet that standard of perfection. The perverse system of incentives guiding peasants, enterprise managers, and workers has not helped. It has induced peasants to malinger on the collectively owned land and to concentrate their efforts on tiny private plots. It has induced managers to corrupt the crucial flow of information to central planners, to resist technical innovations, to pollute the natural environment with abandon, and, above all, to ignore the wishes of their customers (with respect to the proper assortment of goods, their quality, their timely delivery, and the availability of spare parts and servicing). The Stalinist incentive system has contributed to a widespread lack of labor discipline and induced workers who cannot find what they want in state retail stores to focus their attention on the underground economy. It has blanketed the entire society with a network of bribery and corruption.

The results of these factors have been hidden unemployment of resources, ubiquitous inefficiency, declining rates of economic growth, a widely shared perception of economic inequity, and a severe degree of alienation. During Stalin's lifetime, however, few dared openly criticize the system associated with his name or the results it produced. People were caught in a deepfreeze of tongues, if not of thought. All this changed after Stalin's death, with the coming to power of Nikita Khrushchev (Biography 7.3). His famous speech at the 20th Congress of the Soviet Communist Party in 1956 (secret at the time) was a turning point. Eventually, it freed people from the need to accept Stalin's teachings with admiration and blind credulity. Soviet publications, which had languished in oppressive sterility since 1928, turned into an exciting forum for debate. All kinds of new ideas were born.

## Radical Ideas: An Overview

There was the idea that a wholesale dismantling was in order of the bureaucratic superstructure engaged in physical central planning and the issuing of detailed administrative directives. This having been accomplished, some thought, diverse forms of ownership in nonhuman resources might be recognized, giving rise, perhaps, to a mixture of state-owned, worker-owned, and private enterprise. Given the well-known experience with private plots in agriculture and with the underground economy in general, many thought that private enterprises would be particularly useful in agriculture, light industry, and services. In other sectors of the economy, they thought, the time was ripe for full financial independence of self-governing enterprises that would make all input and output decisions with a view toward maximizing *profit* and that would, perhaps, even be run by workers' councils. These, in turn, would invest any profit or distribute it among the workers at their discretion. And the actions of all enterprises would then be coordinated not by a vertical structure of command with the central planners at the top, but by horizontal relations among suppliers and demanders in free markets for all resources and goods. In these markets, equilibrium prices would be established through competition among buyers or sellers, be they private or socialist, domestic or foreign. Indeed, there might even be markets for loanable funds in which households or enterprises could offer voluntary savings for interest-bearing certificates of indebtedness, such as bonds, issued by private or socialist firms aware of potential investment projects yielding returns equal to the market interest rate or more. If carried to its logical conclusion, as the next section explains, this most radical innovation would restore consumer sovereignty with respect to the overall volume of investment as well as its apportionment among competing projects.

## Interest under Socialism? An Example

Throughout history, there were those who looked upon interest as something immoral. This view was shared by Moses and Aristotle, by Mohammed and medieval scholastics, and, eventually, by Karl Marx. Marx traced the existence of interest under capitalism to the fact that a small number of capitalists owned all of society's capital resources, that workers could produce very little without these productive tools, and that capitalists allowed workers to use these crucial tools only in return for a portion of output, which was called the capitalists' "interest." Thus, interest in Marx's view was akin to a forced payment of blackmail; it was a payment by workers to the idle rich, destined to disappear at the socialist revolution when the workers would chase away the capitalists and take over the means of production as their own. The Soviets, accordingly, claimed for decades that interest played no role in *their* system.

**The Sources of Interest.**   Yet, long before the Soviet Revolution, an Austrian economist and statesman, Eugen von Böhm-Bawerk (1851–1914), propounded a different view. His view is now generally accepted as correct, and it is beginning to be accepted even in the Communist world. Böhm-Bawerk denied that interest was a phenomenon of the class struggle between the haves and the have-nots. Rather, he looked upon interest as a phenomenon of *barter across time*—a phenomenon that will manifest itself in all societies, among Amazon Indians, Kalahari Bushmen, and Greenland Eskimos as much as among modern-day Americans, Russians, and Chinese. Interest, Böhm-Bawerk argued, arises in all societies from two sources.

First, interest arises because of *consumer time preference:* Consumers everywhere are impatient to consume *now.* They do not care to undertake the unpleasant task of abstinence and waiting. Subjectively, they value current goods more than future goods of like kind and number. When asked, they may be willing to sacrifice a unit of current consumption goods $(-1C_c)$, but only if compensated by more than one unit of future consumption goods (such as $+1.2C_f$). Thus, a consumer's indifferent rate of exchange of $-1C_c$ now for $+1.2C_f$ a year later denotes an insistence on being paid a minimum 20-percent interest premium, and this phenomenon simply reflects the impatience of mortal men and women. (Clearly, the interest premium required to make consumers give up goods now can differ among consumers, and it can be expected to rise for any one consumer with the amount of goods already sacrificed.)

Second, interest arises because of *producer time productivity:* Producers everywhere know that time-consuming, indirect, roundabout methods of production—methods that are capitalistic in the literal sense of being capital-using—are superior in the long run to instant, direct methods that simply apply raw labor to natural resources. Objectively, the sacrifice of current goods can yield a greater quantity of future goods. By not producing a unit of current consumption goods $(-1C_c)$ and channeling the resources so saved into the production of investment goods $(+1I_c)$, future labor and natural resources, together with the new capital goods, may be able to produce more than one unit of future consumption goods (such as $+1.5C_f$). Thus, a producer may be able to reap an interest return of 50 percent, and in this case the phenomenon simply reflects the technical superiority of roundabout methods of production. (Clearly, the interest premium that can be earned in this way can differ among producers because they face different investment opportunities, and it can be expected to fall for any one producer with the number of such opportunities already realized).

A single example can drive home Böhm-Bawerk's point that the technological interest premium, just like the impatience premium, is unrelated to the nature of the economic system. Consider Robinson Crusoe. Surrounded by nothing but natural resources, and using his bare hands only, he might catch 5 fishes a day. Over time, his daily food production would equal the series 5 . . . 5 . . . 5 . . . 5 . . . and so on, forever. Now suppose that Crusoe went hungry for a day and sacrificed the five fishes he might have caught. He might use his time to make a net and even build a canoe. Starting the next day, he might catch 10 fishes per day, and he might do so in half the time previously spent. He might spend the remainder of the time each day repairing net and canoe, thereby making his capital goods last as long as he lives. As a result, his daily food production would equal the series 0 . . . 10 . . . 10 . . . 10 and so on, forever. A 5-fish sacrifice on day 1 would, thus, yield a 5-fish increase in output on all future days—a real interest return of 100 percent per day! In this way, Böhm-Bawerk noted, the sacrifice of present consumption goods (like the 5 fishes sacrificed by Crusoe on day 1) can be productively transformed in every society through capital formation (like Crusoe's production and subsequent maintenance of net and canoe) into a *permanently* larger flow of future consumption goods.

**A Loanable Funds Market.**   If one accepts interest as a universal phenomenon, one can easily derive a number of implications, which is precisely what the most daring would-be reformers in the Communist world have done: With the help of a market in which loanable funds are traded for interest-bearing certificates of indebtedness (such as bonds), the equilibrium interest rate can be used: (a) to determine an optimal volume of investment and (b) to channel the available investment funds to the most productive projects. Consider Figure 7.3, ''A Loanable Funds Market.'' Let consumers be free to determine their own sacrifices of current consumption goods by lending funds in this market. The more they have already saved and lent, the more reluctant are they to save and lend even more; only higher interest rates

**Figure 7.3**   A Loanable Funds Market

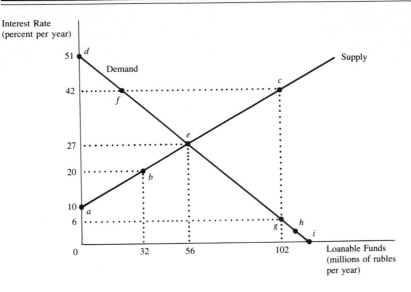

A loanable funds market can be used to determine the optimum volume of investment (from the point of view of consumers). In this example, an equilibrium interest rate of 27 percent per year yields voluntary saving equal to lending and borrowing equal to investment of 56 million rubles per year. The volume is optimal because no consumers whose impatience requires higher rates (along *ec*) than available investment projects can procure (along *ei*) are forced to save against their will.

The market also ensures an efficient allocation of the investment funds so determined. In this example, *all* investment projects yielding a return of 27 percent per year or more (along *de*) are carried out; *none* of the projects (along *ei*) that yield less than the equilibrium rate is funded.

*Note:* The supply of loanable funds here can also be viewed as a demand for bonds; the demand for loanable funds, as a supply of bonds.

can induce them to do so, and this accounts for the positive slope of the supply line. Thus, the supply of loanable funds is zero at 10 percent (point *a*), 32 million rubles at 20 percent (point *b*), 56 million rubles at 27 percent (point *e*), and 102 million rubles at 42 percent (point *c*). Let producers, similarly, be free to determine their own investment programs by borrowing funds in this market. The more they have already borrowed and invested, the more the high-productivity projects are gone, and the less able are they to pay high interest rates. Only lower interest rates can induce them to borrow more and tackle the remaining and less productive projects, and this accounts for the negative slope of the demand line. Thus, the demand for loanable funds is zero at 51 percent (point *d*), 56 millions rubles at 27 percent (point *e*), and 102 million rubles at 6 percent (point *g*).

**The Optimal Volume of Investment.**   The interaction of lenders and borrowers will establish an equilibrium interest rate, here of 27 percent per year. The corresponding volume of voluntary saving and lending, borrowing and investing will equal 56 million rubles per year (point *e*). The ratio of this voluntary sacrifice (of 56 million rubles) to the GNP (of, say, 200 million rubles) thus determines the percentage of resources devoted to capital formation (here 28 percent). And note: Every single ruble saved and invested brings a clear net gain to both parties involved. Lenders in fact receive 27 percent interest per year, but would have been willing to accept (along segment *ae*) lower rates ranging from just above 10 percent to 27 percent (reflecting the varying degrees of their impatience). Borrowers, in fact, pay 27 percent interest per year, but would have been willing to pay (along segment *de*) higher rates ranging from just below 51 percent to 27 percent (reflecting the varying productivities of their projects). Under Stalin's system, however, central planners might well have *enforced* saving and investment of 102 million rubles per year (or 51 percent of our hypothetical GNP), thus creating economic inefficiency: The last ruble saved would have been sacrificed voluntarily only for a 42-percent return (point *c*); when invested, it yielded only a 6-percent return (point *g*).

**The Efficient Allocation of Investment.**   The market allocation of investment funds can also be counted upon to channel the available funds (here 56 million rubles) to the most productive projects. In our example, when the equilibrium interest rate equals 27 percent per year, *all* of the projects along segment *de* (which earn real returns between 51 and 27 percent) are funded and carried out; *none* of the projects along segment *ei* (which earn real returns below 27 percent) are carried out. The reason is simple: An enterprise with an investment project promising a return below the equilibrium interest rate, such as 6 percent (point *g*) could not afford to borrow the requisite funds at the equilibrium rate. Under Stalin's system, central planners, however, were free to act otherwise and often did. Given 102 million rubles of funds, they might have foregone a project (such as building roads and barns in the countryside) that yielded a return of 42 percent (point *f*), while authorizing another one (such as building a steel mill) that yielded less than 6 percent (point *h*). Analytical Example 7.1, "Soviet Investment Criteria," explains.

## The Actual Reforms

As the previous sections have shown, Stalin's death brought into the open plenty of ideas for reform. But there is a big difference between airing new ideas and implementing them. In the Soviet Union, at least, a coherent blueprint for radical change that was acceptable to the Party never emerged. Instead, there has been an endless series of *limited* reforms, and even these have often not been implemented fully. Each new reform has tinkered with minor aspects of the Stalinist system without touching its most fundamental features, the physical allocation system and the administrative setting of prices. By thus retaining the essence of the old system, the Soviets have repeatedly managed to cripple the impact of the new.

**The Khrushchev Era.**    Nikita Khrushchev (Biography 7.3) emerged in the 1950s as Stalin's successor, and he had plenty to criticize about Stalin's way of doing things. Consider the amazing story he told about Stalin's indifference to careful central planning.

> *I will mention a fact to show how plans were approved at that time. This happened shortly before Stalin's death. The Council of Ministers met to approve the annual plan and Stalin came to the meeting. Ordinarily he did not preside over the Council of Ministers. This time, however, he presided. He picked up the folder containing the draft plan and said: "Here is the plan. Who is against it?" The ministers looked at each other and said nothing. "Then it is accepted," Stalin said, and the meeting ended. As we left the meeting he said: "Let's go to a movie." He arrived at the movie theatre and said: "We took them for a good ride!" Who had been taken for a ride? It was the ministers.*
>
> *The plan went awry. Great miscalculations were made in it because the ministers had had no real hand in its preparation and did not agree with it. Other officials who had read it also disagreed with it. But Stalin himself did not pay much attention to questions of planning, and he was not anxious for others to pay much attention to these questions. (Pravda, June 29, 1963)*

Khrushchev tried to improve the *organizational structure* of central planning by abolishing the central ministries and replacing them by about 100 **regional economic councils** (*sovnarkhozy*). The idea was to cut down on cumbersome communication lines typified by a steel mill in the Donets Basin that could communicate with a next door coal mine only via the Moscow Ministry of Metallurgy that, in turn, contacted the Ministry of Coal Mining. By eliminating the Moscow middlemen, and letting enterprises within a region communicate through their regional council, Khrushchev hoped, many errors of planning and management would be avoided.

Khrushchev was similarly concerned with the *incentive system*. He abolished the machine-tractor stations and let collective farmers own their equipment. He abolished many restrictions on labor mobility and tried to improve labor incentives by raising the per capita production of consumer goods. Above all, he attacked the bonus system that made managers embrace technical inefficiency and reject technical innovations. Said Khrushchev:

> *It has become the tradition to produce not beautiful chandeliers to adorn homes, but the heaviest chandeliers possible. This is because the heavier the chandeliers produced, the more a factory gets since its output is calculated in tons. So the factories make chandeliers weighing hundreds of kilograms and fulfill the plan. But who needs such a plan? . . . The plan for furniture factories is stated in rubles. Consequently the furniture factories find it more advantageous to make a massive armchair, since the heavier the chair the more expensive it is. Formally the plan is thus fulfilled since the furniture makers add this and that to the armchair and make it cost more money. But who needs such armchairs? (Pravda, July 2, 1959)*

And again,

> *Steel production is like a much-used road with deep ruts; even a blind horse will not lose its way. . . . Some officials have put on steel blinkers; they do everything as they*

*were taught in their day. A material appears which is superior to steel and is cheaper, but they keep on shouting 'steel, steel.'* (*Pravda*, November 20, 1962)

Thus, it was no coincidence that Yevsei Liberman, Professor at Kharkov University and Director of the Economic Research Unit of the Kharkov Economic Council, was allowed to publish his ideas for reform in the 1962 pages of *Pravda*. Khrushchev highly approved of Liberman's thoughts:

1. Prices should be "rationalized." Liberman noted that Soviet relative prices reflected neither relative costs nor relative utilities. Thus, it was possible and indeed common for material A to be priced at 10 rubles per pound and material B at 20 rubles per pound despite the fact that it took five times as many resources to produce a pound of A as a pound of B. Anyone "minimizing cost" by using A instead of B was, thus, making a wrong decision. (Collective farmers often fed bread to their livestock because it was cheaper—in rubles—than the grain contained in it!) Similarly, it was possible for materials C and D each to be priced at 50 rubles per unit, while C was twice as useful as D. Any buyer using these prices as a guide and showing indifference between C and D was making a mistake. (Tires with different service lives were often priced identically, as were different fuels with different energy contents.) At a minimum, Liberman suggested, Soviet price setters should include in their cost calculations not only the traditional Marxian categories of wages, raw materials, and depreciation, but also charges of *interest* and *rent* to reflect the use of scarce capital and natural resources during the process of production. (Liberman stopped short of suggesting that his goals could be achieved by letting free markets set prices.)

2. Planning should occur "from the bottom up." On the basis of "rationalized" prices, and after consulting its customers, each enterprise should make a proposal as to what, how, and when it wants to produce and pass it on to higher authorities for approval. (Liberman expected central planners to disapprove proposals if they were inconsistent with other proposals or violated "the public interest" in such matters as the investment share of the GNP, the allocation of investment funds, and even the output of "principal" products.)

3. The bonus system should be revised. Managers should be judged not on the basis of gross output but on the basis of *profitability*, the ratio of profit made to capital held. As a result, argued Liberman, many things would change: Managers would think twice before holding on to idle buildings, unused equipment, or inventories of raw materials because they would now have to pay interest for that privilege (hence, they would have higher costs and lower profits). For the same reason, they would think twice about holding on to idle natural resources because they would have to pay rent for that privilege. And they would suddenly care a great deal about the *productivity* of their labor, capital, and natural resources, getting rid of them if the value of their output did not cover

their wage, interest, and rental costs. Finally, managers would think twice before producing the wrong types of goods, shoddy goods, goods without spare parts or servicing, or goods delivered at the wrong time, for profits would not materialize until satisfied customers had voluntarily bought what was produced.

4.  Enterprises should be free to spend their profit—on managerial or worker bonuses, on social consumption (such as worker housing), or on research and investment. (The latter possibility, Liberman hoped, would encourage technical innovations.)

Despite all the verbal fanfare, little happened while Khrushchev was in charge. A 1963 price reform was carried out by the old-line economists and resulted, as one might expect, in a complete victory for the traditionalists, such as Maizenberg (Deputy Chief of the Gosplan Price Bureau) and Ostrovitianov (outstanding member of the U.S.S.R. Academy of Sciences). The goat having been appointed gardener, the so-called reform left completely unchanged the old principle of price setting. Agricultural and retail prices were not even touched at all. Industrial wholesale prices were only revised *on the basis of the old formula.* To take account of uneven changes in wage and material costs over the past years and of a revision of depreciation allowances, prices were changed to restore desired profit margins. And in 1964, just before Khrushchev's fall, the Central Committee authorized an experiment to test the Liberman proposals in precisely *two* enterprises.

**The Treadmill of Reforms: 1965–1985.** Almost immediately after Khrushchev's ouster, his regional economic councils were abolished and Stalin's ministerial system of planning and management was reestablished. All Soviet leaders during the subsequent two decades, however, continued to pay lip service to the *idea* of reform. Their actions continued to be insignificant in that they left the essentials of Stalin's system unchanged. For example, the much heralded 1965 law ''On Improving the Management of Industry, Perfecting Planning, and Strengthening Economic Incentives in Industrial Production'' was supposed to usher in the most significant changes since 1928 by applying the Liberman suggestions nationwide. In fact, the ''increased authority'' of enterprise managers was quickly eroded by the continued authority of the upper echelons of the not-yet-dismantled planning hierarchy. (How, for example, could an enterprise produce nylon craved by its customers if the requisite machinery could not be gotten out of the Moscow Machinery Ministry?) In addition, there was widespread ministerial interference with even the most minute enterprise decisions. (This practice was often condemned as ''petty tutelage,'' but it continued, nevertheless.) Despite the alleged emphasis on profit (derived from sales to pleased customers), managers continued to reap the most crucial bonuses from fulfilling targets of output (delivered to customers whether they liked it or not).

All kinds of newfangled changes designed to cure specific problems were introduced—piecemeal—and failed. For example, in 1973, to cure autarchic tendencies by enterprises, so-called **production associations** were formed, cartel-like groupings of enterprises based on product-relatedness or geographic proximity.

Among other things, this organizational change was designed to increase output by encouraging proper specialization among the once-independent enterprises. Yet, the old practice of empire-building remained alive and well. (Of 100 machine plants later surveyed, 84 were producing their own forgings, 71 their own cast iron, 61 their own clamps, 57 their own nonferrous castings, 27 even their own steel. So much for subcontracting.) Again, in 1979, to cure the managerial behavior problems of long standing, a new value-added success indicator, called **measure of net normative output,** was introduced along with price reform. But it had little effect on managers because Gosplan continued to set physical targets for 20,000 key products, while *Goskomtsen,* the State Committee on Prices, continued to set over a million prices, some 200,000 prices annually. Again, in 1982, a new **brigade contract system** was introduced to raise the level of effort on collective farms: Each farm would be divided into brigades of 10 (unrelated) workers who would commit themselves to produce a designated crop on a designated piece of land and whose personal income would depend on their contract performance. The idea was resisted fiercely.

**The Gorbachev Era.**   Since the mid-1980s and the coming to power of Mikhail Gorbachev (Biography 7.4), the rhetoric about economic reform, now called *restructuring (perestroika),* has become louder. Experiments of one kind or another abound, and new laws have been passed—but their ultimate impact is far from certain. Consider what *has* happened:

Since 1985, groups ranging from 5 to 50 workers have been allowed to set up *private cooperative enterprises.* Many of them operate out of buildings rented from the government for a set fee and distribute profits among the workers involved. Others must share a percentage of their profit with the government. Such enterprises have sprung up to satisfy consumer demand typically neglected by the state (and traditionally satisfied by the underground economy), in such fields as hairdressing, recycling, restaurants, and television repair.

Since 1987, numerous types of *private individual and family enterprises* have also been authorized in principle. However, their operations are restricted in a number of ways: The family members involved may not withdraw their labor from the state sector (thus, they must be students or pensioners or they must devote their spare time only to the family business), they may not hire nonfamily workers, they must acquire supplies from the state sector rather than from other private businesses, they may not be involved in middlemen activities (such as merely selling someone else's product), and more. Each of these enterprises must be duly registered with the government and pay a profit tax. Such enterprises have also sprung up in traditionally underground-economy areas. Early registrations involved some commodity production (designer clothing, postcards, shoes), but mostly services, including apartment and auto repair, building demolition, cafés, consumer referral (to babysitters, doctors, plumbers), dog hairdressing, horsedrawn carriage rides, interior design, locksmithing, matchmaking, pay toilets, plumbing, stand-up meat pie restaurants, tailoring, taxis, tombstone engraving, watch repair, and more.

Since 1987, numerous experiments involving *state enterprises* have been authorized. As with past reforms that have quickly failed, *selected* enterprise managers once again are to be given all kinds of discretionary powers previously reserved to higher authorities: the right to retain a portion of profits and spend it on bonuses, increased wages or investment projects; the right to fire workers, while using the wages then saved to increase the wages of the remaining workers; the right to defy the stifling monopoly of the Foreign Trade Ministry, to retain a portion of convertible foreign currency export earnings (such as dollars), and to use these coveted funds for purchases, at home or abroad, of otherwise unavailable supplies; and even the right to engage in joint ventures with foreign firms either on Soviet soil or abroad. (See Close-Up 7.5, ''Gorbachev's Joint Ventures.'') And again, as so often in the past, a joint resolution of the Communist Party's Central Committee and the Council of Ministers called for all kinds of other market-oriented changes, ranging from the freeing of a third of all prices from central control to the introduction of wholesale trade among state enterprises (as an alternative to the Gosplan distribution of material supplies) to the creation of a network of banks that would *lend* investment funds at interest to state enterprises (as an alternative to their distribution as free gifts by Gosplan). As usual, a comprehensive implementation was planned for the future, affecting all 48,000 state enterprises by 1991.

Simultaneously with the above measures (which make for good newspaper headlines in the West[15] but have hardly changed the basic nature of the Soviet economic system), Gorbachev has promoted a policy of greater openness, called *glasnost,* in the discussion of troublesome subjects. It has given rise to a number of amazing phenomena that could never have happened in the Stalinist past:

Thus, Gorbachev has urged an honest and open look back, arguing that there should be ''no blank pages in Soviet history,'' that it is wrong to hide names. He himself referred to Stalin's ''enormous and unforgivable crimes'' and restored such nonpersons as Bukharin and Khrushchev to respectability.

The Soviet press has touched topics long taboo: It has published convicts' letters about the poor quality of rehabilitation work in forced labor colonies; about their sufferings from isolation, petty indignities, biting cold or hunger, frequent beatings. It has dealt with police brutality, court injustice, the execution of innocent people, the Chernobyl nuclear disaster, anti-Russian rioting in Alma-Ata, and abuses in psychiatry.[16] The press has admitted the presence of alienated youths, drug addiction, environmental pollution, prostitution, rampant alcoholism, street crime, suicide. It has discussed the pros and cons of the death penalty and foreign travel curbs.

---

[15]Consider *The New York Times,* May 1, 1987, p. 1: *In Soviet, Capitalism.*

[16]The Soviet psychiatrist Andrei V. Snezhnevsky designed a system of diagnosis that equates nonconformity with illness. For example, ''an obsessive desire to seek social justice'' is called ''sluggish schizophrenia'' and its victims are treated with psychotropic drugs that cause fever, slurred speech, and an inability to lie, sit, or stand comfortably. See *The New York Times,* October 21, 1987, pp. A1 and 7.

Long-forbidden books have been published, including Boris Pasternak's *Doctor Zhivago*, Andrei Platonov's *The Foundation Pit* (an irreverent fable about the building of communism), Anatoly Rybakov's *Children of the Arbat* (an unflinching look at Stalin's terror), and Aleksandr Tvardovsky's poetry (about Stalin's "rampage of evil").

All kinds of unofficial journals have been allowed to appear, including Sergei Grigoryants' *Glasnost,* the *Bulletin of Christian Opinion,* and *Mercury* (a Leningrad magazine devoted to ecology and the preservation of historic monuments).

Incredible movies have been released: *Repentance* (an honest look at Stalin's purges) and *Is It Easy to Be Young?* (a powerful look at disaffected Afghanistan vets).

To a limited extent, there has been toleration of even abstract art, dissonant music, experimental theater. (At one point, the Young Communist League, *Komsomol,* better known for its character-building summer camps in mosquito-infested Siberia, has sponsored heavy metal music clubs, but later referred to them as "ugly phenomena that are alien to the socialist way of life.") Famous emigrés have been allowed to visit: Mikhail Baryshnikov (the dancer), Yuri Lyubimov (former director of Moscow's Taganka Theater). Even open demonstrations—not organized by the Party—have been tolerated, although grudgingly. Thus, in August 1987, on the 48th anniversary of the Hitler-Stalin pact that led to the Soviet annexation of the three Baltic states, thousands gathered in the capitals of Lithuania, Latvia, and Estonia, defiantly singing anthems of independence. In 1988, similar nationalist striving emerged in Soviet Armenia and Azerbaijan.

**The Resistance Movement.**     It would be a great mistake, however, to conclude that the Soviet economy and political system are about to undergo radical and irreversible changes. For every one of the examples of *glasnost* cited earlier, one can also find counter examples of continued repression.[17] This is not surprising. There are many who oppose reforms of the system.

First of all, the entrenched bureaucracy of central planners counsels against reform. Since human beings always like to see themselves as eternally indispensable, and the central planners are being asked by would-be reformers to give up their power, their negative reaction is not surprising. They have a strong personal interest in digging in their heels and saving their jobs and privileges. They pretend, however, to oppose reform for ideological reasons. Thus, they accuse would-be reformers of lacking confidence in the power of reason and science and of denigrating central planning, while worshipping and romanticizing the spontaneous regulation of pro-

---

[17]A major Soviet newspaper, *Isvestia,* for example, has bitterly complained about the recent tolerance of nongovernment publications. In an article entitled "Backward Toward Tarzan," it referred to private publications as "a primitive activity not necessary in a country where the Communist party has proven superior wisdom on intellectual matters." (*The Wall Street Journal,* September 9, 1987, p. 29.) And in 1988, the publisher of *Glasnost* magazine was arrested, his files were trashed, and his printing equipment was confiscated. (*The New York Times,* May 20, 1988, p. A30.)

duction by the Invisible Hand. Adoption of the reform proposals, they argue, would put an end to the ''solidarity society.'' The general interest would cease to be defined by Party leaders (with their unique understanding of the Holy Writ). It would cease to be embodied in the central plan; it would no more be served by multitudes of unselfish people eager to act as they were told. Adoption of the reform proposals would instead invite the splintering of the social interest: In the place of one common ownership of nonhuman resources, there would be multitudes of owners; in the place of cooperation toward one common goal, there would be conflict among groups pursuing different goals. The old concepts of rent, interest, and profit (long looked upon as arch-symbols of capitalist exploitation) would once more be resurrected. Competition would once more come to dominate people's lives. One group of workers would fight other groups of workers to gain profit for themselves; or unions of workers would fight managers and their own government over the range of issues they could decide. Economic reform would spill over into political reform, socialism be destroyed by ''creeping capitalism.'' Thus argue the central planners. They are far from alone.

Many enterprise managers also doubt the desirability of reform. They are not used to being cost-conscious business executives, to buying and selling in competitive markets. They are used to being production engineers who put together sets of inputs provided by the planners to produce sets of outputs designated by the planners. What would happen, they worry, if they had to pay rent and interest for the use of natural and capital resources (as well as wages for the use of labor), and if receipt of such inputs was not ensured by order of central planners, but all these inputs could be snapped up by other enterprises offering higher prices for them? What would happen if disposition of their output was not ensured by order of central planners, but potential recipients were free to reject it and buy the output of other enterprises (domestic or foreign) who might provide lower prices, better assortments, higher quality, or better service? What would happen if they failed to meet such unaccustomed challenges? Would they sustain losses and face bankruptcy—a situation unheard of in the old system?

Even workers are fearful of the new. Might suddenly cost-conscious managers refuse to pay them for mere attendance and lay off unproductive workers, speed up work, or lower wages when their output was insufficient to recoup their wages? Might managers neglect safety devices to cut costs further? Might they go bankrupt and dismiss workers altogether? Might managers everywhere attempt to raise revenues by raising prices—including those of food, clothing, housing, and all the other things workers buy? Such are the questions raised. Thus, the workers' fear of unemployment and inflation adds fuel to the arguments of planners and managers who would rather not tamper with the system.

The Yeltsin affair of 1987, perhaps more than any other event, highlighted the enormous resistance to economic and political reform: Boris N. Yeltsin, Moscow Party Chief, had been one of the most outspoken supporters of the Gorbachev reforms, but he was impatient—he wanted to hurry things along. So he took on the central planning bureaucracy, calling it ''an inert layer of time servers who think they work so hard that they actually deserve their special stores, clinics, cars, and other comforts denied ordinary Muscovites.'' He challenged them to get out of their limousines, forsake their privileges, ride the buses as the masses do. He even invited the public ''to root out the S.O.B.'s languishing on the public payroll.'' And he permitted ''reconstruction groups'' to hold a national convention in Moscow—independently of Party and Komsomol—and let them issue a call for a multiparty system.[18]

The reaction of the Politbureau was fierce. In a secret meeting reminiscent of the days of Stalin, two dozen top Party officials, rising one after the other, savagely denounced Yeltsin's adventurism, intolerance, lack of ethics, pretensions of infallibility, wrathful speech, and more. Having made an abject confession of guilt, Yeltsin was stripped of his position but, unlike in Stalin's days when he would have been shot, put to work as a senior official in the construction industry.

Stalin's name has now been removed from factories, parks, streets, cities, and mountain tops. Yet, Soviet society is still possessed by his legacy, infected by a profound ambivalence about him. His name triggers the dread of mass terror but also a sense of pride that *there* was a man who got things done, whose iron fist, however brutally, pulled Russia into the industrial age and won the Great Patriotic War. What can would-be reformers, who let dissidents and defilers of the motherland run loose, possibly do to match that?

## CLOSE-UP 7.1

## The Locus of Power in the U.S.S.R.

The Communist Party of the Soviet Union (A) holds all political power; the Government (B) is subordinate to it and lacks independent power.

A. The Party

### Communist Party Congress

Theoretically the highest body. Consists of delegates elected by party organizations around the country and meets once in five years. The congress elects:

### The Central Committee

Consists of several hundred members picked from among congress delegates. Acts for the congress between sessions and meets about twice a year to discuss and approve policies. It elects what are, in effect, the two highest party bodies:

### The Politbureau

Sets the overall policy of the country on foreign, economic, and social affairs. Consists of about a dozen full (voting) members and about nine candidate (nonvoting) members, all of whom are the country's leading political figures.

### The Secretariat

Actually runs the day-to-day affairs of the country. Is headed by the General Secretary, assisted by other secretaries and a large permanent staff.

---

[18]*The New York Times,* November 18, 1987, p. 35; November 22, 1987, p. 27; and November 23, 1987, p. 3.

B. The Government

*Supreme Soviet of the U.S.S.R.*

Counterpart of the Party congress, this nominal parliament is "elected" every five years from a single slate of candidates handpicked by the Party leadership. Meets perfunctorily twice a year to approve legislation drafted by that leadership and selects two government bodies:

↓

*Council of Ministers*

The actual government, headed by the Prime Minister and consisting of numerous ministers and agency chairs.

↓

*Presidium of the Supreme Soviet*

A chairman and deputies perform functions as the nation's president and vice-presidents.

Note: In late 1988, Secretary Gorbachev proposed to change the government structure by creating a new supreme body (*Congress of People's Deputies*) that would elect a new powerful president (*Chairman of the Supreme Soviet*) and a legislative body (*Supreme Soviet*). The latter, in turn, would elect a *Council of Ministers*. These changes were to go into effect in 1989.

*Source: The New York Times,* February 12, 1984; October 1, 1988, p. 5; and October 2, 1988, p. 14.

## CLOSE-UP 7.2

## Russia's Underground Millionaires

Sometimes a small scene can shed a sharp light on a hidden reality:

Picture a sprawling, 11-room apartment in Moscow, with a single kitchen and a single bathroom, shared by seven families. It is the sort of place that houses families of workers, doctors, engineers. In the huge kitchen stand seven tables and two gas ranges on which the women take turns cooking dinners and breakfasts. There are no secrets; everyone knows everything there is to know about everyone else, who eats what and who buys what. Maybe . . .

There is the foreman of a small hosiery mill, always dressed in an old suit and shoddy shoes, who does not stand out from the other six families in the apartment. The neighbors see his wife preparing meals from the cheapest of materials: curd pancakes, potatoes, soup from scraps of meat. . . . Yet, the humble foreman is a millionaire—an underground businessman in a land where private enterprise is a crime.

The neighbors do not see his family later, when everyone else is asleep, flushing these meals down the toilet or tossing them into the garbage pail. They do not know that the foreman's refrigerator is packed with expensive delicacies—smoked salmon, caviar, sturgeon—that none of them can afford. They do not see into the foreman's back room, where another meal is prepared on a small electric hot plate hidden under the table, which is draped with a long tablecloth to smother telltale odors.

When the family of the foreman dines, they eat behind closed doors. Two meals are set on the table: the meal cooked in the kitchen in full view of the neighbors and the one prepared in the back room. . . .

Konstantin Simis, a former Soviet lawyer who defended underground businessmen (and who told the above story), reports of the amazing tenacity of the entrepreneurial impulse in the Soviet Union—despite the threat of harsh penalties, even capital punishment. To be sure, private entrepreneurs cannot manufacture automobiles in secret, but tens of thousands of them do manage to produce a vast array of consumer goods, ranging from hosiery, leather jackets, and sweaters to handbags, sunglasses, and recordings of Western music. Typically, a private enterprise will coexist, under the same name and the same roof, with a state factory. Alongside "official" goods destined to be marketed by the state retail stores, the factory will produce "left-hand" goods—not registered in documents, produced on the same equipment and by the same personnel as the official goods, and marketed privately. (While it may take years before a state enterprise obtains permission from the administrative hierarchy to produce a new product, a private entrepreneur can follow consumer demand instantly.) Many private entrepreneurs "own" dozens of factories in a number of cities—Moscow, Odessa, Riga, Tiflis—and have established a national network of personal connections and sales. Many amass millions of rubles of assets (200 million rubles in one case) and have personal incomes of several hundred thousand rubles per year. What can they do with it? In most cases, the choices are limited.

Unlike high-paid individuals in the official economy, who might spend 15,000 rubles on a co-op apartment or 10,000 rubles on a Volga car or even 150,000 rubles on a private house, underground businessmen must be careful. They must be able to justify their expenses by their legal income or find some unusual way to protect themselves: Some have laundered their money by buying up winning state lottery tickets at a premium. Some have paid monthly bribes to government officials to look the other way. (As a result, a Georgian businessman could live openly in two magnificent houses, luxuriously furnished, and host huge banquets on regular occasions.) Others still have bought themselves high government positions. (In Azerbaidzhan, the going price has ranged up to 250,000 rubles.) Others are found out, are tried, and die in labor camps. One of those arrested, when asked why he didn't retire rich many years before, said: "Don't you understand? Do you really think I need the money? I need my life! And my life is my business."

*Source:* Konstantin Simis, "Russia's Underground Millionaires," *Fortune,* June 29, 1981, pp. 36–50.

## CLOSE-UP 7.3

## What about Unemployment?

The following is an official Soviet commentary on the subject of unemployment.

"We have none. The Soviet Constitution has it down in black and white that every citizen has the right to work. People avail themselves of this right. There is no basis for unemployment, since the economy progresses rapidly, according to a state plan, with no crises or depressions. Wherever you go in the Soviet Union you see plenty of "Situations Vacant" notices. Jobs are advertised in the papers, over the radio, and on special boards. Anyone seeking work may also turn to the Executive Committee of the local Soviets, which always has precise information as to which enterprises require hands. Finally, every town and region has a type of Labor Exchange which can provide jobs in various parts of the country. Anyone going to work in another area receives, as a rule, an allowance: a grant based on monthly wages, traveling expenses and money for six days settling in, a daily allowance, free transport plus baggage.

As economic development is planned, it is possible to foresee manpower needs some time ahead and therefore spread employment over the country in a rational way. This especially applies to specialists and workers graduating from trade schools, technical schools, and colleges. Naturally, we cannot plan for every contingency say, for some reason or other a worker decides to change his workplace. Every citizen enjoys this right by law. In such cases the worker has no trouble at all in finding other employment."

*Source:* Novosti Press Agency, *U.S.S.R. Questions and Answers* (Moscow: Novosti Press Agency Publishing House, 1965), p. 146.

## CLOSE-UP 7.4

### The Lysenko Tragedy

By supporting the establishment of a nationwide network of scientific research institutions, Stalin provided a key ingredient for technical advance. By insisting on "infusing science with the aims and methods of the Communist Party," however, he negated much of the potential for economic growth he had thus created. Consider his appointment of Trofim D. Lysenko (1898–1976) as president of the Academy of Agricultural Sciences. Lysenko hypothesized that a changed environment could cause hereditary changes in plants (a line of thinking that was in line with Marxism and, thus, pleasing to Stalin). The idea promised short-cuts to bigger harvests in that one might: (a) raise crops in a shorter growing period and (b) transform the nature of seed, adapting it to climatic conditions for which it was not originally suited. Among Lysenko's fantastic claims were the following:

1. Preheating winter wheat seeds would turn them into spring wheat. Such "vernalization" of grain would increase yields 40 percent; it would allow the reaping of five crops per year in some areas.
2. Tropical plants can be taught to flower in the Arctic.
3. Pine trees can be turned into spruce; wheat into barley, oats into rye.

Lysenko falsified evidence to support his claims and suppressed evidence to the contrary. As scientific overlord, he disapproved research along other lines; he repressed and terrorized his opponents, many of whom were exiled or killed. Indeed, with Stalin's blessing his influence spread from biology to related fields (such as medicine), and before long Lysenko imitators appeared in all branches of science.

The end results were tragic for a country beset by intense scarcity. Planting "preseasoned" winter wheat in spring wheat areas, in fact, reduced crop yield. Counting on the alleged advantages of "vernalized" wheat delayed the introduction of high-yield corn for decades. Even in the 1980s, the Lysenko legacy is present: Compared to American cows, Soviet cows have an extremely low milk yield; to produce the same quantity of milk, more cows are needed, more grain is used up to feed the cows, and less grain is available to keep up herds for beef production.

Compared to American grain, Soviet grain has a low protein content; 5 tons of American grain produces a ton of meat, while it takes 8 tons of Soviet grain to do the same.

*Sources: The New York Times,* November 24, 1976, p. 36, and Marshall I. Goldman, *Gorbachev's Challenge: Economic Reform in the Age of High Technology* (New York: Norton, 1987), pp. 39–40.

## CLOSE-UP 7.5

## Gorbachev's Joint Ventures

For many years, the Soviet Union has borne the brunt of American jokes about the poor quality of consumer goods. Consider the 1985 Wendy's commercial that ridiculed Soviet fashions by featuring a matronly Soviet woman in a drab dress that looked like a potato sack.

Recently Mr. Gorbachev has turned to a new strategy to improve the quality of Soviet goods: joint ventures with Western firms. One of these involved the production of fashionable clothes. Shortly after his wife visited the Paris fashion houses of Pierre Cardin and Yves St. Laurent, an agreement was reached for Pierre Cardin to design a new line of clothes for the Russians, to be made in Soviet plants and sold in Moscow boutiques. At the same time, a Soviet-American venture was born. It involved the Moscow designer Vyacheslav Zaitsev (who is known for his designs of the Bolshoi Ballet costumes) and Intertorg of California, a company specializing in trade with the Soviet Union. The Zaitsev collection is to be produced in North Carolina and marketed in the United States. The first showing of his collection of dresses, suits, coats, evening and holiday attire at New York's Waldorf-Astoria Hotel took place in 1987 and elicited an enthusiastic response.

Numerous other ventures are in the works, involving RJR-Nabisco, Eastman Kodak, Johnson and Johnson, Chevron, Ford, and many other firms in capitalist America, Europe, and Japan. Get ready to see Pizza Hut restaurants within sight of Lenin's Tomb!

*Sources: The New York Times,* September 13, 1987, p. F3; November 19, 1987, p. D2; April 10, 1988, pp. F1 and 13; July 31, 1988, p. F4.

## ANALYTICAL EXAMPLE 7.1

## *Soviet Investment Criteria**

There can be little doubt, given Stalin's resolution of the great industrialization debate and his determination to carry out the program of the left, that Soviet central planners ever since 1928 have forced upon their people larger sacrifices of consumption goods than they would have voluntarily made. Unfortunately, central planners have

---

*Optional Section involving advanced material.

added insult to injury by badly allocating the resources diverted from consumption. Marxist ideology (concerning the inapplicability of interest to socialism) prevented Soviet planners from identifying, with the help of an equilibrium interest rate, the most productive investment projects. Therefore, they had no way to direct the limited resources released from present consumption to the most productive investment projects first, and their rate of economic growth was less than it might have been.

**The Correct Procedure.**  Consider what might have happened if central planners had been willing to utilize the interest concept. Table A presents hypothetical investment projects that might have to vie for the inevitably limited investment funds, limited even in a Stalinist country wherein consumers are forced to save more than they wish. Each investment project is described by a sequence of dated cash flows; negative numbers denote net expenditures, positive numbers net receipts. Thus, the light industry project (A) involves net spending of 300 million rubles now, followed by net receipts of 50 million rubles in one year, 60 million rubles in two years, and so on, with the project terminating in 5 years when a 210-million-ruble net receipt is made. Projects B through E are similarly interpreted, but C and D continue beyond year 5, as indicated.

Now it is possible to calculate, for each investment project, an **internal rate of return,** which is the average annual rate of return on the initial investment expenditure over the years of the project. (It is also the maximum interest rate designated by points such as *d, f,* or *g* on the demand line in Figure 7.3, "A Loanable Funds Market," that a borrower of investment funds could afford to pay.) Table B shows the internal rates of return for the Table A projects. The internal rates of return of Table B are interpreted easily enough. Consider the 13.3-percent rate of project A. It tells us that 300 million rubles invested at 13.3 percent per year make possible the flow of receipts shown in the first row of Table A: 300 growing at 13.3 percent turns into 339.9 by year 1. Taking out 50 leaves 289.9, which turns into 328.5 by year 2. Taking out 60 leaves 268.5, which turns into 304.2 by year 3. Taking out 70 leaves 234.2, which turns into 265.3 by year 4. Taking out 80 leaves 185.3, which turns into 210 by year 5. Taking out 210 exhausts the project.

It is also clear what the internal rates of return advise us to do: A central planner seeking to maximize economic growth would be well advised to fund projects in the order E, C, A, D, and B—until funds run out. If the equilibrium interest rate were 10 percent, funds would run out by the time projects E, C, and A had been authorized.

As an alternative (which would yield the same result), central planners could compute the "net present value" of each potential investment project at the equilib-

**Table A**  Selected Investment Opportunities (net cash flows in million rubles)

| Project \ Year | 0 | 1 | 2 | 3 | 4 | 5 | |
|---|---|---|---|---|---|---|---|
| A. Light industry | − 300 | + 50 | + 60 | + 70 | + 80 | + 210 | |
| B. Chemicals industry | − 100 | + 10 | + 12 | + 15 | + 20 | + 50 | |
| C. Rural roads | − 33 | + 2 | + 5 | + 8 | + 10 | + 10 | + 10 to year 10 |
| D. Steel industry | − 550 | + 50 | + 50 | + 50 | + 50 | + 50 | + 50 to year 20 |
| E. Farm storage facilities | − 65 | + 20 | + 20 | + 20 | + 20 | + 50 | |

**Table B**    Selected Data on Investment Projects

| Project | Internal Rate of Return (percent per year) | Net Present Value (millions of rubles) at 10% interest | Net Present Value (millions of rubles) at 0% interest |
|---|---|---|---|
| A. Light industry | 13.30 | + 32.67 | 170 |
| B. Chemicals industry | 1.79 | − 25.02 | 7 |
| C. Rural roads | 18.25 | + 15.54 | 52 |
| D. Steel industry | 6.52 | − 124.32 | 450 |
| E. Farm storage facilities | 24.09 | + 29.44 | 65 |

rium interest rate, such as our hypothetical 10 percent. By authorizing all projects with positive net present values (see the 10-percent column of Table B), planners would also allocate all available investment funds, once again to the most productive projects.

The **net present value** of an investment project is the sum of the present values of all its negative and positive components, each year $t$ future value, $FV_t$, being converted to an equivalent year 0 present value, $PV_0$, by the formula

$$PV_0 = \frac{FV_t}{(1 + r)^t}$$

where $r$ is the equilibrium interest rate, such as our hypothetical 10 percent = (10/100) = .1. Thus, the year 0 present value of the year 1 net receipts from project A equals

$$PV_0 = \frac{50}{(1.1)^1} = 45.45$$

indicating that a year 0 amount of 45.45 would grow to the year 1 amount of 50, if the interest rate were 10 percent and is, therefore, equivalent to the year 1 amount of 50. By the same token, the net present value of the entire project A equals

$$NPV_A = -300 + \frac{50}{(1.1)^1} + \frac{60}{(1.1)^2} + \frac{70}{(1.1)^3} + \frac{80}{(1.1)^4} + \frac{210}{(1.1)^5} =$$

$$-300 + 45.45 + 49.59 + 52.59 + 54.64 + 130.39 = 32.67$$

**The Actual Procedure.**    Being constrained *not* to use interest calculations, Soviet planners long added outlays to receipts without regard to their timing and calculated, in effect, the net present values of investment projects at a zero interest rate (akin to the zero-interest column of Table B). As a result, planners found many more projects worthwhile than could possibly be carried out with the resources that could be spared from current consumption.

To choose among all these "worthwhile" investment projects, the planners calculated for each project a **payback period,** the number of years it takes for initial investment outlays to be paid back by (undiscounted) future receipts. (Thus, a project with annual cash flows of − 100, + 30, + 30, + 30, + 30 has a payback period of 3.33 years.) The planners then compared actual payback periods with an *arbitrary* *norm* (such as "4 years or sooner") and thereby reduced the potential number of projects to a feasible one.

This **payback method** that rejects all projects the undiscounted returns of which require more than a predetermined length of time to repay the initial investment outlay involves, of course, the crude application of an interest rate without mentioning the term. (In medieval times, people similarly talked of making a "4-year purchase," instead of lending a sum at 25-percent interest per year, because four annual 25-unit payments of money returned an initial 100-unit sum.)

Indeed, Soviet planners have at times also calculated the *reciprocal* of the payback period (1/3.33 in our earlier example, or .30), and they have called this reciprocal the **coefficient of relative effectiveness.** Planners compared it to an arbitrary **norm of relative effectiveness** (such as ".25 or more") to weed out investment projects. Note: These planners were, in effect, comparing something like an internal rate of return (of, say, 30 percent per year) with an interest rate (of, say, 25 percent per year).

Yet, the Soviets utilized different norms of relative effectiveness for different industries. As a result, they rejected investment projects in some industries in favor of those in others, although the former could have contributed much more to net present value and hence economic growth. (Consider Table B. Let the economy's equilibrium rate of interest be 10 percent per year. Now imagine applying a "norm of relative effectiveness" of .05 to projects A and B, of .15 to projects C and D, and of .25 to project E. If you recognize the given "norms" as code words for interest rates of 5 percent, 15 percent, and 25 percent per year, you see from Table B that projects A and C will be accepted but that projects B, D, and E will be rejected. Yet, this is not the correct decision, as the 10-percent column reveals.) According to Soviet Nobel Prize winner L. V. Kantorovich (Biography 11.1) the Soviet Union could have gotten, around 1960, from 30 percent to 50 percent more output from its existing resources. He attributed this fact in part to the planners' failure to make investment decisions with the help of an undisguised and uniform equilibrium interest rate. Perhaps his numbers were exaggerated to emphasize the importance of finally recognizing the crucial role of interest, even under socialism.[a]

[a]An alternative calculation was made by Judith Thornton, "Differential Capital Charges and Resource Allocation in Soviet Industry," *Journal of Political Economy,* May/June 1971, pp. 545–61. Her calculations were confined to Soviet industry for 1960–1964. They suggested possible increases in value added of 3 to 4 percent if differential capital charges were eliminated.

## BIOGRAPHY 7.1    Vladimir I. Lenin

Vladimir Ilyich Ulyanov (1870–1924)—now known as Lenin—was born in Simbirsk, Russia. His father was a councillor of state who later became a nobleman. Lenin's older brother, on the other hand, was a Marxist who was later hanged for complicity in an attempt on the life of Czar Alexander III. This led Lenin to study Marx in addition to his law books at the University of Kazan. He was expelled, but still passed the bar exam. By the time he became an assistant to a St. Petersburg attorney, he was a revolutionary at heart.

Lenin was deeply influenced by G. V. Plekhanov, who organized the first Russian Marxist group (The Emancipation of Labor). The group argued against the Narodniks, who were promoting the view that the Russian peasant commune (*mir*) was an ideal foundation on which socialism could be built. (Land in the mir was held in common, but periodically redistributed among the peasants for individual family cultivation.) Lenin joined Plekhanov's (and Marx's) view that socialism must be built by industrial workers. Accordingly, in 1895 in St. Petersburg, Lenin founded the League of Struggle for the Liberation of the Working Class and edited an underground journal (*Labor's Work*). He was arrested, convicted of revolutionary activities, and exiled to Siberia. (In his absence, in 1898, the 1st Congress of the Russian Social Democratic Labor Party was held in Minsk; all the delegates were arrested as well.)

Released in 1900, Lenin visited Plekhanov and other revolutionary exiles in Western Europe. He launched a Marxist paper and magazine (*The Spark* and *The Dawn*) to be smuggled into Russia. And he wrote a book, *What Is to Be Done* (1902), in which he developed a remarkable new argument: Workers, left to themselves, only develop a *trade-union* consciousness; that is, they become aware of the need to fight employers for better wages and working conditions, but that is it. By themselves workers do not develop a *socialist* consciousness; they never come to recognize their possible role in abolishing the entire wage *system*. That realization is reached by intellectuals who are trained to view the broad sweep of history. Therefore, concluded Lenin, the intellectuals in question must raise the consciousness of the working class above the day-to-day bread-and-butter issues; this can be done best by forming a highly centralized and secretive party, a professional vanguard of highly disciplined and dedicated revolutionaries who would lead the workers to socialism.

Lenin's ideas were discussed at a stormy 2nd Congress of the Russian Social Democratic Labor Party, held in London in 1903. The delegates split into a majority (the Bolsheviks) supporting Lenin and a minority (the Mensheviks) opposing him. The latter group charged Lenin with advocating an elite dictatorship, not *of* but *over* the proletariat as well as over the party itself. By the time the party held its 3rd Congress (in London in 1905), it was an exclusively Bolshevik affair.

Except for visiting Russia briefly after the abortive revolution of 1905, Lenin spent the years until 1917 in Switzerland. Overwhelmed by boredom, he watched, waited, and wrote, including *Imperialism: The Highest Stage of Capitalism* and *The State and Revolution.*

In early 1917, when the Czar abdicated, Lenin returned to St. Petersburg—just renamed Petrograd—and propounded the April Theses: The bourgeois-democratic revolution that had just taken place must quickly be followed by a socialist revolution establishing the dictatorship of the proletariat. In October, in an almost bloodless coup, Lenin took power from the Provisional Government and became President of the Soviet of People's Commissars. The rest is history: War Communism, followed by the New Economic Policy, discussed in this chapter. Lenin died at a relatively young age, following a series of increasingly debilitating strokes, but not before warning the Party against Stalin, whose "coarseness, intolerance, capriciousness, and rudeness" Lenin deplored. In contrast, he referred to Bukharin as "the favorite of the whole Party."

*Source:* John G. Gurley. *Challengers to Capitalism,* 2d ed. (New York: Norton, 1979), pp. 63–95; *The New York Times,* September 29, 1977, p. A18.

## BIOGRAPHY 7.2    Yossif V. Stalin

 Yossif Vissarionovich Dzhugashvili (1879–1953)—now known as Stalin—was born in Gori, Georgia. His parents had just been freed from serfdom and lived in abject poverty; his three brothers died in childhood. Stalin entered the Tiflis theological seminary, but was expelled for dangerous ideas and uncooperative behavior. He joined a secret socialist organization, helped organize strikes and raids on government institutions, and wrote for a Marxist journal (*Fight of the Proletariat*). Repeatedly, he was arrested, jailed, exiled to Siberia; repeatedly, he escaped.

In 1905, in Finland, he first met Lenin; by 1912, he was on the Central Committee of the Bolshevik Party; soon he was involved in putting out the first issue of *Pravda* (later to become the major Soviet newspaper). In 1917, after the overthrow of the Czar and until Lenin's return from Switzerland, Stalin even led the Party. A day after the October Revolution, Lenin made Stalin Commissar for Nationalities, a post that gave him control over almost half the population. Before long, Stalin also became Commissar of the Workers' and Peasants' Inspectorate, a position that allowed him to supervise every branch of the government and to build up his personal authority. And in 1922, he was appointed to the new office of Secretary General of the Central Committee and, thus, came to manage the daily affairs of the Party. By the time Lenin issued his warning about Stalin (see Biography 7.1), Stalin already held much of the political power in the new Soviet state. In the following years, he moved to get all of it.

In 1923, after Lenin's third stroke, Stalin formed a triumvirate with Kamenev and Zinoviev within the Politbureau (the other members being Bukharin, Rykov, Tomsky, and Trotsky) to prevent Trotsky from succeeding Lenin. And Stalin faced the issue of Lenin's "will" head-on. "It is said," Stalin noted boldly, "that in that 'will' Comrade Lenin suggested to the congress that in view of Stalin's 'rudeness' it should consider the question of putting another comrade in Stalin's place as General Secretary. That is quite true. Yes, comrades, I am rude to those who grossly and perfidiously wreck and split the Party. I have never concealed this and do not conceal it now. . . . It is characteristic that there is not a word, not a hint in the 'will' about Stalin having made mistakes. It refers only to Stalin's rudeness. But rudeness is not and cannot be counted as a defect in Stalin's *political* line or position."

Skillfully, Stalin managed to eliminate all who might challenge his power. Between 1925 and 1929, for example, Trotsky was dismissed as Commissar of War, then from the Politbureau, then from the Party. He was exiled to Alma-Ata, then deported to Turkey. Finally, in 1940, he was murdered by a Stalin emissary in Mexico. The other superstars of the Bolshevik Revolution (and participants in the great industrialization debate discussed in this chapter) did not fare better; they all became victims of the great purge trials of the 1930s: Kamenev and Zinoviev were tried in 1936 (and executed), Tomsky committed suicide in the same year, Bukharin and Rykov were tried in 1938 (and executed). All of them vanished even from official histories of the revolution! And then Stalin was the supreme master of the Soviet Union. All aspects of Soviet life were under his control, and he used his power ruthlessly to carry forward his program of industrialization (also discussed in this chapter). In addition, he encouraged an attitude of extreme adulation toward his person, his pronouncements, his writings. His major works include *Marxism and the National Question* (1913), *The Foundations of Leninism* (1924), and *Economic Problems of Socialism in the U.S.S.R.* (1952).

*Source:* John G. Gurley, *Challengers to Capitalism,* 2d ed. (New York: Norton, 1979), pp. 97–131.

## BIOGRAPHY 7.3     Nikita S. Khrushchev

Nikita Sergeyevich Khrushchev (1894–1971) was born at Kalmkova, a small village at the Russian-Ukrainian border. His father was a miner; Nikita became a shepherd boy, a metalworker, and a miner as well. He joined the Bolsheviks in 1918, attended a new Party technical college, and became a full-time political leader by the mid-1920s. In the 1930s, already a member of the Central Committee of the Communist Party, he organized the construction of the Moscow Metro (and received the Order of Lenin). Like everyone else, he dutifully adored Stalin, who was "the best that humanity possesses. For Stalin is hope; he is expectation; he is the beacon that guides all progressive mankind. Stalin is our banner! Stalin is our will! Stalin is our victory!" (*Pravda*, January 31, 1937).

In 1938, at Stalin's request, Khrushchev conducted a merciless purge in the Ukraine. There were thousands of victims. Said Khrushchev: "Our work is holy. He whose hand will shake or who will falter half-way—the person whose knees give way beneath him when he has to kill ten or a hundred enemies—that person exposes the revolution to danger." By 1939, he was a member of the Politbureau; during World War II, he directed guerrilla warfare behind the German lines, then fought in the battle of Stalingrad as a lieutenant general. He became First Secretary of the Communist Party shortly after Stalin died in 1953 and, thus, the first Soviet leader who had not participated personally in the revolution.

The world remembers him as an ebullient figure, full of earthy humor, given to tempestuous moods, disdainful of diplomatic subtleties, yet canny and tough. He is remembered for his stress on "peaceful coexistence" with the capitalist world and his boastful pledge (inspired by the 1957 Soviet launching of Sputnik, the world's first artificial satellite) of "burying" the United States economically by outproducing her in everything. (In fact, the ratio of Soviet to U.S. GNP, which was 27 percent in 1928, 42 percent in 1940, and 29 percent in 1948, rose from 39 to 44 percent between 1957 and 1958, remained there till the mid-1960s, and had risen to 53 percent by the mid-1980s. Given the recent slowdown in Soviet rates of economic growth, the "burial" may never take place.)

More important than all this, however, has been Khrushchev's reversal of Stalinism, his passionate search for checks and balances that could forestall any future attempt at personal tyranny. In 1956, in his now famous but then secret speech to the 20th Congress of the Communist Party of the U.S.S.R., Khrushchev attacked Stalin's personality cult, along with the wholesale torture and murder of millions of innocent people. Said Khrushchev:

*We are concerned with a question which has immense importance . . . for the future—with how the cult of the person of Stalin has been gradually growing, the cult which became . . . the source of a whole series of exceedingly serious and grave perversions of . . . revolutionary legality. . . . When we analyze the practice of Stalin . . . we must be convinced that Lenin's fears were justified. The negative characteristics of Stalin, which, in Lenin's time, were only incipient, transformed themselves during the last years into a grave abuse of power by Stalin which caused untold harm. . . . Stalin acted not through persuasion, explanation, and patient cooperation with people, but by imposing his concepts and demanding absolute submission to his opinion. Whoever opposed this concept . . . was doomed to removal from the leading collective and to subsequent moral and physical annihilation. . . . Stalin originated the concept "enemy of the people" . . . ; many . . . who were branded . . . as "enemies" were actually never enemies, spies, wreckers, etc., but were always honest Communists; they were only so stigmatized and often, no longer able to bear barbaric tortures, they charged themselves . . . with all kinds of grave and unlikely crimes.*

The effects of this denunciation filtered throughout Eastern Europe and encouraged uprisings against Stalin's nominees, still ruling. (In Poland, the moderate Gomulka came to power; in Hungary, the Red Army moved in.) But Khrushchev's days were numbered. In 1964, he was ousted, for "failure to consult with colleagues," for "unpredictable high-handed actions," and for the promotion of "hare-brained schemes" (such as the failed "virgin lands" campaign in Kazakhstan and the failed attempt to place Soviet missiles in Cuba). Khrushchev was pensioned off; his name promptly disappeared from all Soviet publications. (In 1970, however, his smuggled memoirs appeared in the West as *Khrushchev Remembers*).

Yet, in 1987, another Soviet leader concerned with Stalin's crimes restored official respectability to Khrushchev (along with Nikolai Bukharin). Said Mikhail Gorbachev, referring to the Khrushchev years, "A wind of change swept the country, the people's spirits rose. . . . It required no small courage to criticize the personality cult and its consequences and to re-establish socialist legality."

*Sources:* United States Information Agency, "Pages from the Past: A Garland of Stalinisms," *Problems of Communism,* March-April 1963, p. 87; *Obituaries From the Times, 1971–1975* (Reading, England: Newspaper Archive Developments, 1978), pp. 283–86; Philip Taubman, "Gorbachev Assails Crimes of Stalin, Lauds Khrushchev," *The New York Times,* November 3, 1987, pp. 1 and 10.

---

### BIOGRAPHY 7.4    Mikhail S. Gorbachev

Mikhail Sergeyevich Gorbachev (1931–    ) was born in Privolnoye, a small village in Russia's grain-growing area between the Don and Volga rivers. It was this very region that blossomed under Lenin's NEP (when private farming was encouraged in the 1920s) and that was severely brutalized under Stalin's collectivization drive (when repression and famine reigned in the 1930s). Gorbachev's father was a combine operator on a collective farm, but his son attended Moscow State University and received a law degree in 1955. At Moscow, he shared a college room with Z. Mlynar, a liberal-minded Czech who later was to be a leader of the Prague Spring. Gorbachev worked his way up the political ladder as organizer of the Party's youth arm (Komsomol)

and as a local Party official (in Stavropol), and then earned a second university degree as an agronomist-economist. A protégé of Yuri V. Andropov, Gorbachev became national agricultural chief, a member of the Central Committee, the Polit-bureau, and then General Secretary of the Communist Party.

The world at large knows him as a winning showman who likes to wear tailored pinstripe suits and up-to-date felt hats and who dazzles the public with talk of abolishing all nuclear weapons, restructuring the economy (*perestroika*), and promoting openness (*glasnost*). Indeed, much of this has been more than mere talk. In 1988, a special Communist Party Conference saw some 4,991 delegates approve the Gorbachev program and involve the Soviet Union in an intoxicating swirl of political debate and cultural and economic experimentation. The Conference voted to remove the Party from the day-to-day control of nearly all aspects of Soviet life, to expand the authority of popularly elected legislatures, to establish a powerful new presidency (with a maximum term of 10 years), to revise the criminal code and increase civil liberties, to introduce democratic procedures in the selection of Party officials, and even to erect a monument to the victims of Stalin's tyranny.

Gorbachev himself even recommended increasing private control of state-owned farms and factories. He offered a Chinese-style farm-leasing program (see pp. 282) as well as the transfer of some factories to private entrepreneurs. In late 1988, Gorbachev was also made President, then still a largely ceremonial post, but scheduled to be invested with real power in 1989.

*Sources: The New York Times,* December 7, 1987, pp. A1 and A19; July 2, 1988, pp. 1, 6, and 7; October 2, 1988, p. 1.

## Summary

1. When the first socialist revolution was fought in the name of Marx, contrary to his prediction, the event did not occur in one of the world's most industrialized countries. The Soviet Revolution led by Lenin involved a country mostly inhabited by illiterate peasants. No wonder that after the chaos of revolution and civil war had subsided Soviet leaders were concerned most with charting a path to industrialization. By instituting his New Economic Policy, Lenin replaced the "planless command" of War Communism by "capitalism *under communism*," but his successors debated whether this policy, successful as it was in the short run, could possibly succeed in the long run. The leadership of the Communist Party split between "rightists" and "leftists." While the rightists (such as Bukharin) wanted to promote gradual economic growth by continuing the NEP indefinitely, the leftists (such as Trotsky) wanted to speed up the growth process by a different policy that would accelerate investment by imposing drastic and involuntary sacrifices of consumption on the peasantry. After a series of shrewd political moves that eliminated all the original revolutionary leaders, Stalin assumed absolute power and promptly proceeded to enact the program of the left.

2. Stalin was determined to put the Soviet Union on a path of rapid economic growth, favoring heavy industry above all else. In order to

forestall likely peasant resistance to drastic reductions in consumption, he collectivized agriculture, creating state farms, collective farms, and machine-tractor stations. Along with these new institutions, designed to let the central government take control of the nation's economic surplus, Stalin introduced central economic planning. Such planning involved the setting up of a large number of material balances—a procedure that can be viewed as the formulation of an (incomplete) input-output plan in disaggregated form. Stalin, however, was not ready to sit back and merely hope that his plans would be obediently implemented. He was well aware of the agency problem and the implied power of agents to subvert the will of principals. Accordingly, he introduced a wide range of incentives designed to motivate people to carry out the central plans. These included and continue to include commands backed up by severe threats, exhortations to lay aside selfishness, and, above all, monetary rewards for peasants, industrial managers, and workers alike. The nature of the monetary rewards has given rise to a large number of perverse behavior problems: Peasants (who have an eye on opportunities in the free collective farm markets) malinger on the collective land, but produce almost a third of agricultural output on their private plots. Enterprise managers (who seek to raise their income through bonuses) routinely misinform central planners about their productive capacity and exaggerate input needs for given output targets. They also fail to produce high-quality output, to back up their products with spare parts and service, or to satisfy their customers with respect to assortment and timing. They resist technical innovations and pollute the environment. Finally, household members spend an inordinate amount of time queuing for consumer goods in short supply, while ever larger inventories of unwanted goods accumulate in warehouses.

**3.** Beyond the official economy, and outside the control of Gosplan, there exists a second and underground economy. It covers a wide spectrum of semilegal and clearly illegal activities through which people enhance their own welfare by allocating resources and acquiring goods in ways not sanctioned by the central plan. Thus, state enterprise managers make use of "connections," deal in black markets, and engage in "empire building." In addition, numerous types of private enterprises carry on operations throughout the country. And all these activities are made possible by a vast network of bribery and corruption.

**4.** A careful assessment of the Soviet economy's overall performance suggests the following:

Contrary to official propaganda, continuous full employment does not exist. There is seasonal unemployment (due to weather) and frictional unemployment (due to high labor turnover). Above all, there is widespread hidden unemployment caused by errors in plan formulation and execution (the "supply problem").

Technical inefficiency is widespread, in part the result of managerial input hoarding, in part caused by a general lack of labor discipline.

Economic inefficiency is ubiquitous, as a careful analysis of various Pareto conditions in the context of Soviet conditions suggest.

Economic growth has been impressive until the late 1950s, but the overall rate of growth has steadily declined since. This can be explained by vanishing opportunities for extensive growth and an inability of central planners to harness the potential for intensive growth (especially through technical advance).

By design, the Soviet Union cannot produce commutative justice; whether distributive justice exists is a matter of value judgment. Certainly, such is not the case with respect to the distributive justice criteria introduced in Chapter 3. Nevertheless, the Soviet government claims that its highly unequal distribution of income is just.

As to alienation, whether from the self, from other people, or from nature, Soviet society scores poorly on all counts.

5. Given the severe problems just noted, it is not surprising that a call for economic reform was heard following Stalin's death. Many critics of Stalin's system argued for a dismantling of the bureaucratic superstructure engaged in physical central planning and for a more market-oriented system in which enterprises would be guided by the profit motive. Some of the ideas on the subject were radical indeed, suggesting even the resurrection of the concept of interest and its use to determine the overall volume of investment as well as its optimal apportionment among competing projects. (This proposal thus accepted Böhm-Bawerk's view that interest is a universal phenomenon concerned with barter across time that does not become obsolete with the advent of socialism.) There is a big difference, however, between airing new ideas and implementing them. A coherent blueprint for radical change that was acceptable to the party never emerged. Instead, there has been an endless series of limited reforms—reaching from Khrushchev to Gorbachev—and even these limited reforms have often not been implemented fully.

## Key Terms

acceptance method
agency problem
agricultural procurement prices
assortment problem
brigade contract system
central plans
coefficient of relative effectiveness
collective farm markets
collective farms (*kolkhozy*)
collectivization
communism
control by the ruble

control figures
depreciation
draft plan
economic imperialism
empire building
enterprise wholesale prices
Gosplan
gross investment
internal rate of return
machine-tractor stations (*MTS*)
marginal-output-to-capital ratio
material balance

measure of net normative output
net investment
net present value
New Economic Policy (*NEP*)
nomenklatura system
norm of relative effectiveness
Party directives
payback method
payback period
plan law
priority principle

production associations
regional economic councils
  (*sovnarkhozy*)
state farms (*sovkhozy*)
state retail prices
storming
system of economic accountability
  (*khozraschet*)
underground economy
War Communism

## Questions and Problems*

1. Consider Table 6.2, "The Plan Document," on page 93.
   a. Write down row C as a *material balance,* making use of all the categories given in Table 7.1, "A Material Balance for Steel," on page 140.
   b. To the extent possible, repeat the process for row D of Table 6.2.
2. Consider the following events, all of which occurred in the Soviet Union; can you explain them?
   a. In one year, a quarter of all window glass produced broke before it could be installed because it was excessively thin. In another year, all window glass was excessively thick and no thin glass could be found.
   b. On a vacant lot near the city of Baku stands a long, high fence made of expensive materials. It serves absolutely no purpose.
   c. An engine plant in Kharkov made 30-kg parts out of 200-kg slabs of metal, discarding the 170 kg not needed. It could have used 50-kg slabs as well, saving material and labor.
   d. A group of peasants weeded a field of sugar beet plants, all of which had died.
3. **Mr. A:** "People say a lot of mean things about the Soviet economy, but there is one thing on which you can't fault it: There is no inflation."
   **Ms. B:** "You are wrong."
      Arbitrate this exchange by searching through the literature noted in this chapter's "Selected Readings."
4. **Mr. A:** "In recent years, the Soviets have shown great interest in trade with the West; we should deny them that opportunity. Let's not forget

---

*Question marked with an asterisk utilizes advanced material presented in Analytical Example 7.1 and computer Module C.

what Lenin said, 'The capitalists will compete with one another to sell
the communists the rope on which to be hanged.' ''
**Ms. B:** ''Your strategy would be counterproductive.''
   What do you think and why?

5. In 1950, a 10-percent increase in capital by itself would have increased
the output of Soviet industry (mining, manufacturing, power) by almost
9 percent; by 1969, the output response to a 10-percent increase in
capital had dropped to only 4 percent. Can you explain this?

6. Reconsider the text section ''Fewer opportunities for extensive growth:
capital resources'' on pages 163 to 164. Given the hypothetical
marginal output-to-capital ratios of residential housing and chemicals
noted there, what would be the rate of growth of GNP in the 30-years-
hence case if investment were channeled into these two sectors,
respectively?

7. ''For every example of pollution in the capitalist U.S.A. (say, Lake
Superior), one can find an example in the socialist U.S.S.R. (say, Lake
Baikal).''
   Make use of the ''Selected Readings'' at the end of this chapter to
find out about Lake Baikal.

\* 8. Consider the following electric power investment projects and rank them
by: (a) simply adding expenditures and receipts without regard to
interest (as the Soviets often did), (b) the payback method, (c) the net
present value criterion—given 9-percent interest, and (d) the internal
rate of return. (The data represent net cash flows in million rubles; the
capital-budgeting computer program noted at the end of the chapter can
help you.)

| Project \ Year | 0 | 1 | 2 | 3 | 4 | 5 | |
|---|---|---|---|---|---|---|---|
| A. Hydroelectric plant | − 500 | 90 | 90 | 90 | 90 | 90 | → Continues to year 40 |
| B. Conventional steam plant (oil) | − 100 | 80 | 80 | 80 | 80 | 80 | → Continues to year 25 |
| C. Conventional steam plant (coal) | − 100 | 90 | 90 | 90 | 90 | 90 | → Continues to year 20 |
| D. Nuclear plant | − 800 | 50 | 50 | 50 | 50 | 50 | → Continues to year 50 |

9. ''Considering the existence of the underground economy, the Soviets are
going to get their economic reforms, even if the official reforms fail.''
Comment.

10. ''It is unfair to accuse Stalin's followers of crimes; after all, they only
followed Stalin's orders, they were cogs in a machine, they had no
choice but to obey.'' Comment.

## Selected Readings

Bergson, Abram. *The Real National Income of Soviet Russia Since 1928* (Cambridge, MA: Harvard University Press, 1961). A pioneering study of Soviet economic growth.

Bergson, Abram. "Income Inequality under Soviet Socialism," *Journal of Economic Literature*, September 1984, pp. 1052–99.

Bergson, Abram, and Herbert S. Levine, eds. *The Soviet Economy: Toward the Year 2000* (London: Allen and Unwin, 1983). An appraisal of the future course of the Soviet economy.

Bukharin, Nikolai I. "Notes of an Economist at the Beginning of a New Economic Year," in Nicolas Spulber, ed., *Foundations of Soviet Strategy for Economic Growth: Selected Soviet Essays* (Bloomington, IN: Indiana University Press, 1964). Contains the anti-collectivization argument of the famous Soviet industrialization debate.

Erlich, Alexander. *The Soviet Industrialization Debate, 1924–1928*. (Cambridge, MA: Harvard University Press, 1962).

Goldman, Marshall I. *The Spoils of Progress: Environmental Pollution in the Soviet Union*. (Cambridge, MA: MIT Press, 1972). The best study available on Soviet environmental problems. Discusses Soviet environmental protection laws, the extent of their enforcement, and all types of pollution. Includes a comprehensive bibliography (pp. 333–57).

Goldman, Marshall I. *Gorbachev's Challenge: Economic Reform in the Age of High Technology* (New York: Norton, 1987). Chapters 4 and 5, in particular, deal with the Soviet system's inability (exceptions in the military and space sectors notwithstanding) to develop new technology or even to adopt Western technology in an effective way.

Green, Donald W., and Christopher I. Higgins, *SOVMOD I: A Macroeconomic Model of the Soviet Union* (New York: Academic Press, 1977). The first of a series of econometric models of the Soviet economy, an impressive and innovative achievement.

Hewett, Ed A. *Reforming the Soviet Economy: Equality versus Efficiency* (Washington, D.C.: Brookings Institution, 1988). A superb analysis of the challenge facing Gorbachev.

Joint Economic Committee, Congress of the United States (Washington, D.C.: U.S. Government Printing Office). Numerous publications deal with all aspects of the Soviet economy:

a. *Soviet Economic Growth: A Comparison With the United States*, 1957.
b. *Comparisons of the United States and Soviet Economies*, 1959.
c. *Dimensions of Soviet Economic Power*, 1962.
d. *New Directions in the Soviet Economy*, 1966.
e. *Soviet Economic Outlook*, 1973.
f. *Soviet Economic Prospects for the Seventies*, 1973.
g. *Soviet Economy in a New Perspective*, 1976.

**h.** *Soviet Economy in a Time of Change,* 1979.

**i.** *Soviet Economy in the 1980's: Problems and Prospects,* 1982.

**j.** *USSR: Measures of Economic Growth and Development, 1950–80,* 1982.

**k.** *East European Economies: Slow Growth in the 1980's,* 1986.

**l.** *Allocation of Resources in the Soviet Union and China—1985,* 1986.

Kohler, Heinz. *Intermediate Microeconomics: Theory and Applications,* 2d ed. (Glenview, IL: Scott, Foresman and Co., 1986). Chapter 15 deals with capital and interest.

Liberman, Evsei G. *Economic Methods and the Effectiveness of Production* (Garden City, NY: Doubleday, 1973). The "architect" of the 1965 Soviet economic reforms provides an incisive and colorful criticism of central planning and delineates the major characteristics of the reform (which, ultimately, never was).

Nove, Alec. *An Economic History of the U.S.S.R.,* rev. ed. (London: Penguin Books, 1982).

Ofer, Gur. "Soviet Economic Growth: 1928–1985," *Journal of Economic Literature,* December 1987, pp. 1767–1833. A superb survey of the Western literature on the subject. Discusses the kinds of data found in this Chapter's Table 7.2 and more.

Smith, Hedrick. *The Russians,* rev. ed. (New York: Ballantine, 1984). The New York Times bureau chief in Moscow reports on the personal lives of the Russian people.

Ulam, Adam B. *Stalin: The Man and His Era* (Boston: Beacon Press, 1973). An impressive description and analysis of Stalin's dictatorship.

## Computer Programs

The SYSTEMS personal computer diskette that accompanies this book contains two programs of interest to this chapter:

**a.** Program 7, "Centralized Socialism: The Soviet Case," provides 20 multiple-choice questions about Chapter 7, along with immediate responses to incorrect answers.

**b.** Module C, "Capital-Budgeting," allows you to perform numerous types of operations with present and future values, including the determination, in cash-flow problems, of internal rates of return and net present values (at numerous discount rates).

# CHAPTER 8

# *Market Socialism: A Model*

Long before the Soviet Revolution launched the modern world's first nationwide experiment in socialism (as discussed in the preceding chapter), economists were fascinated by this question: How would a future socialist government—which presumably would own all the capital and natural resources of a country—have to allocate these nonhuman resources, along with human labor, if it cared to produce a welfare-maximizing set of goods and, thus, to minimize scarcity? The Italian economist Enrico Barone, for example, writing in 1908, pointed to the *theoretical* possibility of a centralized direction of such an economy.[1] As he saw it, the millions of interactions among households and enterprises in any economy can be expressed as a vast system of independent equations with an equal number of unknowns. These demand and supply equations for resources and goods would look precisely the same whether they expressed relationships in an economy of market capitalism or of centralized socialism. The *formal* solution to the resource allocation problem, Barone argued, was independent of *who* owned the resources available and even *whose* preferences were being satisfied by their allocation. Barone, however, was the first to recognize the impracticability of a centralized mathematical solution of this kind. Even if one could centrally collect the necessary information on continually changing demands and supplies, and even if one were willing to employ an army of officials for this gigantic task, it would still be necessary to solve the equations on paper and to ensure that the price and quantity solutions so derived would be faithfully executed. That would be impossible in practice.

---

[1]Enrico Barone, "The Ministry of Production in the Collectivist State," reprinted in F. A. Hayek, ed., *Collectivist Economic Planning* (London: Routledge and Kegan Paul, 1963), Appendix A.

## A Famous Debate

The Soviet Revolution of 1917 rekindled the earlier interest of economists in the socialist economy. In light of the economic chaos evident in the young Soviet state, one question, in particular, was raised: Could an actual socialist economy ever hope to allocate its resources efficiently and, thus, to achieve maximum welfare from given resources? An Austrian economist, Ludwig von Mises, writing in 1920, initiated a lively debate on the subject by denying this possibility.[2] Under socialism, argued von Mises, there would be no genuine markets for the stocks or services of capital and natural resources. Because these resources would be collectively owned and used, they would never be bought and sold; thus, there would be no occasion to discover their relative worth. In the absence of market prices for these crucial inputs, it would be impossible to make rational calculations of the benefits and costs of alternative courses of action. There could be no economizing (no careful minimizing of inputs to achieve any given end); there could only be groping in the dark. Thus, concluded von Mises, every departure from the private ownership of the means of production is a step away from rational economics. "Socialism is the abolition of rational economy," he said. To be sure, von Mises did not deny that socialism was *workable,* but he believed to have shown conclusively that *rational* socialism—socialism that allocated resources efficiently—was a contradiction in terms, that a socialist economy must necessarily be less successful in the creation of welfare than a capitalist competitive market economy (in which self-interested private resource owners meet one another in markets and thereby create and diffuse information crucial to economizing).

Along came a Polish economist, Oskar Lange (Biography 8.1). Writing in the mid-1930s, he presented what he regarded as a practical way of combining real-world socialism and economic rationality.[3] True enough, he argued, Barone's mathematical solution of millions of equations was impractical. Still, equilibrium prices and quantities of goods and resources could be found and economic efficiency could be ensured, even under socialism. Building on the ideas of an American economist, Fred M. Taylor, Lange developed a blueprint of such an economically efficient socialist economy. It is generally referred to as the "competitive solution" and is presented and assessed in the remainder of this chapter.

## The Lange Model

Oskar Lange asked us to imagine a world in which the formal ownership of capital and natural resources would reside in the people as a whole. The effective control

---

[2]Ludwig von Mises, "Economic Calculation in the Socialist Commonwealth," reprinted in F. A. Hayek, ed., *op. cit.,* chap. 3.

[3]Oskar Lange, "On the Economic Theory of Socialism," *Review of Economic Studies,* October 1936, pp. 53–71, and February 1937, pp. 123–42. Some of Lange's ideas were anticipated by Fred M. Taylor, "The Guidance of Production in a Socialist State," *The American Economic Review,* March 1929, pp. 1–8. All these articles have been reprinted in Oskar Lange and Fred M. Taylor, *On the Economic Theory of Socialism* (New York: McGraw-Hill, 1964).

of these resources, however, would not lie in the hands of a central planning board that issued verbal commands (as in the Soviet Union), but would be shared by numerous individuals throughout the economy. Their actions would be coordinated by markets in which all resources as well as goods would be bought and sold. Figure 8.1, "The Socialist Market Economy," presents an overview. Consider the major types of actors involved.

## The Major Actors

Four major types of actors would make decisions in Lange's economy: a central planning board, private households, enterprise managers, and industry managers.

**The Central Planning Board.** There would be, Lange imagined, a central planning board overseeing the economy, but it would not be engaged in setting up and executing a physical input-output plan. The board would neither allocate physical

**Figure 8.1** The Socialist Market Economy

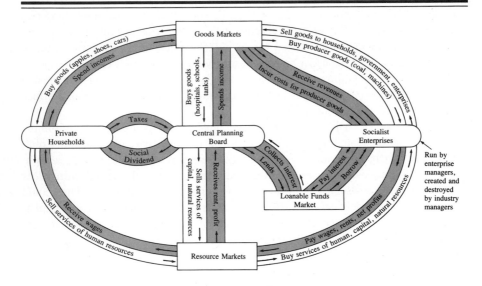

This circular-flow diagram provides a bird's-eye view of the most important exchange relations in Lange's model of market socialism. While real flows of resources and goods are shown in white, monetary flows are shaded. Note how *private households* are expected to sell labor services for wages, to receive (perhaps) a social dividend from the government, and to spend their after-tax income on consumer goods (such as apples, shoes, and cars). The *central planning board* makes collectively owned capital and natural resources available to socialist enterprises in return for rental payments, lends them investment funds at interest, and collects taxes from households and net profits from enterprises. It also buys collective consumption goods (such as hospitals, schools, and tanks). *Socialist enterprises*, finally, pay wages and rents to acquire the services of all types of resources (of people, blast furnaces, pastureland), buy producer goods (coal, iron ore, milling machines), from other enterprises and sell output to households, government, and other enterprises. They can also borrow investment funds from the government at interest; their net profit becomes government revenue.

input quantities nor specify physical output targets; its tasks would be of a different nature entirely.

First, the board would appoint tens of thousands of **enterprise managers** (one for each producing unit throughout the economy), as well as a small number of **industry managers** (one for each industry), and all of these managers would be expected to follow certain general rules of behavior (to be discussed below).

Second, the board would determine the percentage of the GNP devoted to investment by making an appropriate amount of investment funds available in a loanable funds market in which managers could acquire such funds in return for interest payments.

Third, the board would supply the available services of existing stocks of capital and natural resources (so many blast furnace hours per year, so many acre hours per year, and the like) in resource markets; managers would demand these services and pay rent for them.

Fourth, the board would supplement its interest and rental income just noted by taxing households and collecting the net profits of enterprises (collecting the profits of some and making up the losses of others). This total income would be disposed of through the aforementioned lending in the loanable funds market, through regular government spending (on defense, health care, education, and the like), and, perhaps, the payment to all citizens of a **social dividend,** representing their share in the interest, rent, and profit income generated by the collectively owned means of production.

Fifth, the board would be intimately involved in the process of setting prices. Except for the prices of labor and private consumption goods (which would be established in free markets), the board would set the prices of all other inputs and outputs: the interest rate on loanable funds; rental rates on blast furnaces and acres of pastureland; prices of coal, iron ore, and steel; of milling machines, turret lathes, and a million other producer goods. In doing so, the board would follow a rule of its own, also to be discussed below.

**Private Households.**   The members of private households, Lange imagined, would be quick to take advantage of ample opportunities for health care, general education, and vocational training provided by the government. They would be free to dispose of their labor as they saw fit: They could stay home or look for a job; they could enter whatever occupation they liked, and live wherever they chose. If they worked, they would receive money wages. Unlike in capitalism, individual households would not own natural and capital resources. These would be owned by households as a group, but be made available to socialist enterprises by government administrators, as was noted in the previous section. Nevertheless, households might benefit from their joint ownership of nonhuman resources through the receipt of a social dividend *if* the government decided to distribute its interest, rent and profit income (rather than channel it toward investment or collective consumption projects). Lange imagined that the social dividend would be the same for all individuals, whose income would, thus, equal wages plus social dividend minus taxes. Households would be free to dispose of their after-tax money income by spending it on any consumer goods they liked. They could not, of course, acquire natural or capital resources.

**Socialist Enterprise Managers.**   The government-appointed managers of enterprises—all of which would be owned by the people as a whole—would be expected to make their own input and output decisions on the basis of certain general rules of behavior (to be discussed shortly). These managers, too, would be oriented toward markets. For example, they would buy the services of human, capital, and natural resources in resource markets, buy producer goods in goods markets, borrow investment funds in a loanable funds market and, thus, incur monetary costs in the form of wages, rents, interest, and raw material and equipment expenditures. Enterprise managers would, in turn, supply goods in goods markets to households, other enterprises, and government, thereby deriving monetary receipts. Their profits would become government revenue; their losses would be covered by the government.

**Socialist Industry Managers.**   In this economy, productive enterprises would not be set up as a result of private initiative. As we have seen, the central planning board would appoint *enterprise managers* to all existing enterprises; it would also appoint a separate group of *industry managers* whose task it would be to expand, contract, or liquidate existing enterprises, or to create new ones. Once again, those managers would be following certain rules of behavior (to be discussed shortly); these rules would, in fact, eliminate profits as well as losses in the long run.

## The Price-Setting Process

Figure 8.1 highlights the three major types of markets found in Lange's model economy: markets for goods, resources, and loanable funds. In some of these markets, equilibrium prices would be established by the interaction of multitudes of buyers and sellers; in others, the central planning board would set prices by a procedure of trial and error with the aim of equating demand and supply.

**Market Competition.**   In markets for consumer goods and human labor, Lange imagined, equilibrium prices would be established by the interaction of numerous buyers and sellers. Figure 8.2, ''Price Setting In Free Markets,'' illustrates the process. Imagine, for example, that the graph referred to the apple market. Undoubtedly, there would be many buyers and many sellers in such a market and, as a result, no one person would buy or sell a significant percentage of the total traded. Given all other factors that might influence people's decision to buy or sell, buyers would probably demand a larger quantity at lower prices than at higher ones, and (given the rules of behavior to be discussed shortly) sellers would supply a larger quantity at higher prices than at lower ones. This is illustrated by the sloping lines labeled *demand* and *supply* in our graph. And that graph tells us something else. One can expect that the interaction of many buyers and sellers in this market would come to establish an *equilibrium price* of $5 per unit at which the quantities demanded and supplied would be just equal to each other at 34 million units per year. It is easy to see why.

If the market price were higher than its equilibrium value of $5 per unit, an inconsistency would exist between the choices of buyers and sellers. At $7 per

**Figure 8.2**   Price Setting in Free Markets

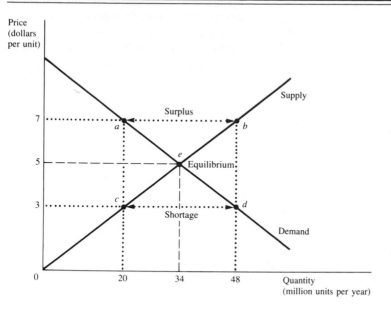

Markets for consumer goods (apples and shoes, haircuts and cars) would be free markets, as would be those for different types of human labor (the services of apple pickers and shoemakers, of barbers and autoworkers). In each market, the interaction of multitudes of buyers and sellers would establish an equilibrium price (here $5 per unit) at which quantity demanded would just equal quantity supplied (here 34 million units per year).

unit, for instance, buyers as a group would wish to buy 20 million units per year (as noted by point *a* in our graph), while sellers as a group would want to sell 48 million units per year (as noted by point *b*). Thus, a surplus would emerge of 48 − 20 = 28 million units per year (distance *ab*), and many would-be sellers would be very frustrated. Before long, at least some of them would probably offer to sell the item in question for a somewhat lower price. Immediately, the surplus would diminish: Buyers, moving from *a* toward *e*, would buy a larger quantity at the lower price; sellers, moving from *b* toward *e*, would offer a lower quantity. This process of competition among frustrated sellers would continue until price and quantity corresponded to their equilibrium values at point *e*.

If the market price were lower than its equilibrium value of $5 per unit, a similar inconsistency would exist between the choices of buyers and sellers. At $3 per unit, for instance, buyers as a group would wish to buy 48 million units per year (as noted by point *d* in our graph), while sellers as a group would want to sell only 20 million units per year (as noted by point *c*). This time a *shortage* would emerge of 48 − 20 = 28 million units per year (distance *cd*), and many would-be *buyers* would be frustrated. Before long, at least some of them would probably offer to buy the item in question for a somewhat higher price. Immediately, the shortage would diminish. Sellers, moving from *c* toward *e,* would supply a larger quantity at the higher price; buyers, moving from *d* toward *e,* would demand a lower quantity. This process of competition among frustrated buyers would continue until price and quantity corresponded to their equilibrium value at *e.*

A similar story could be told if we imagined our graph to refer to any other consumer good or if it referred to any one of a thousand types of human labor. In every one of these markets—be it for apples or shoes, haircuts or airplane rides, the services of barbers or engineers—an important piece of information would emerge: the equilibrium price at which any buyer could be sure to find a seller and any seller could be sure to find a buyer.

**Trial and Error.**   In markets for producer goods, loanable funds, or the services of capital and natural resources, Lange imagined, appropriate prices would be set by the central planning board. In doing so, the board would follow a simple rule of its own (which in fact would imitate the behavior of a competitive market): Whenever there was a surplus (as shown by distance *ab* in Figure 8.2), the board would lower the price. Whenever there was a shortage (as shown by distance *cd* in Figure 8.2), the board would raise the price. Thus, it would find the equilibrium price by trial and error. Figure 8.3, "Price Setting by Trial and Error," illustrates some of the possible outcomes.

The managers of socialist enterprises would be instructed, in turn, to base all their decisions on the prices established in the manner just discussed.

## Behavioral Rules for Enterprise Managers

Enterprise managers would be given strict rules of behavior with which to determine optimum input and output quantities. These rules would, in fact, simulate their maximization of profit on the basis of given prices.

**Optimum Input Quantities.**   Enterprise managers about to make decisions would be asked to accept as given the current prices of labor and consumption goods, set by competition in markets, and all the other prices of inputs and outputs, set by trial and error in the offices of the central planning board. Acting *as if* these prices were never going to change, each manager would be asked to determine, for any given production period, the optimum quantity of any input in this fashion:

> *Use a quantity such that the input's falling marginal value product just equals the input's price.*

Let us consider what would be involved with the help of a numerical example. A socialist manager might be running an apple orchard, presently endowed with 1,000 apple trees, 1 truck, 2 warehouses, 3 pesticide spraying machines, various stocks of fertilizer and pesticides, and so on. What would be the best number of workers to be hired for the season? The technical facts of life might be those given in columns (1) to (3) of Table 8.1, "Crucial Data for the Input Decision." That is, the manager might know from experience what maximum output levels might be

**Figure 8.3** Price Setting by Trial and Error

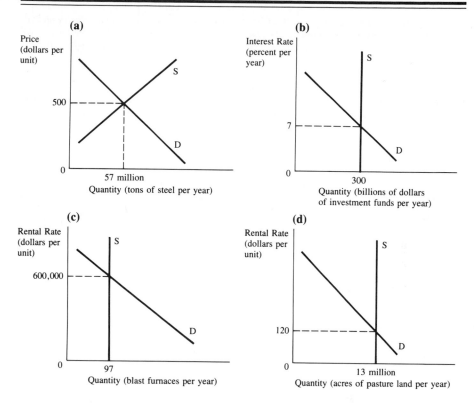

By a procedure of trial and error (which lowered prices in the face of surpluses but raised them in the face of shortages) the central planning board would find equilibrium prices for producer goods, loanable funds, capital resource services, and natural resource services, as shown in panels (a) through (d), respectively. The board would not be expected to have any knowledge of the demand curves involved nor of the supply curves of producer goods; it would only respond to reports of surpluses and shortages, finding, in this example, the equilibrium price of $500 per ton of steel, the equilibrium interest rate of 7 percent per year (given the government's decision that a $300-billion share of the GNP should consist of new capital goods), the equilibrium rental rate of $600,000 per blast furnace per year (given the availability of 97 such units), and the equilibrium rental rate of $120 per acre of pastureland per year (given the availability of 13 million such acres).

achieved (col. [3]) for various combinations (A to H) of the above inputs (col. [1]) and human labor (col. [2]). If one worker only was used (combination A), many potential apples might never appear on the trees (as it would be impossible for this one person to do all the fertilizing, pruning, spraying, watering, and so forth that might be undertaken to raise output from the given number of trees to the biological maximum). Or many actual apples might go unharvested due to lack of time or might spoil in warehouses due to lack of attention. Thus, salable output might only

**Table 8.1**   Crucial Data for the Input Decision

| | Fixed Inputs Used (1,000 apple trees, 1 truck, etc. per season) | Variable Inputs Used (workers per season) | Maximum Total Output (bushels of apples per season) | Marginal Physical Product of Variable Input, $MPP_i$ (bushels of apples per worker per season) | Marginal Value Product of Variable Input $MVP_i = MPP_i \cdot P_o$ (dollars per worker per season) | Price of Variable Input, $P_i$ |
|---|---|---|---|---|---|---|
| | (1) | (2) | (3) | (4) | (5) | (6) |
| A. | 1 | 1 | 1,000 | | | |
| | | | | 2,000 | 10,000 | 5,000 |
| B. | 1 | 2 | 3,000 | | | |
| | | | | 3,000 | 15,000 | 5,000 |
| C. | 1 | 3 | 6,000 | | | |
| | | | | 2,000 | 10,000 | 5,000 |
| D. | 1 | 4 | 8,000 | | | |
| | | | | 1,000 | 5,000 | 5,000 |
| E. | 1 | 5 | 9,000 | | | |
| | | | | 500 | 2,500 | 5,000 |
| F. | 1 | 6 | 9,500 | | | |
| | | | | 300 | 1,500 | 5,000 |
| G. | 1 | 7 | 9,800 | | | |
| | | | | 200 | 1,000 | 5,000 |
| H. | 1 | 8 | 10,000 | | | |

be 1,000 bushels for the season. If two workers were hired (combination B), on the other hand, overall output might rise to 3,000 bushels as some of the otherwise neglected tasks could be performed. Thus, a second worker might add to output a physical quantity of 2,000 bushels, and that change in total physical product associated with a one-unit change in labor input (all other inputs and technology being held constant) would be called the worker's **marginal physical product** (col. [4]). Further additions of human labor (col. [2]) might raise total output even more (col. [3]), though (after the hiring of the third worker) by less and less (col. [4]). It is easy to see why the law of diminishing returns would eventually take hold: The more workers were being used already, the more of the above-named output-raising tasks would already be done, and the less chance an (equally bright and hardworking) additional worker would have to raise output even further. Eventually, no additional apples might be had at all from additional labor, because the orchard might be saturated with tender loving care.

Lange imagined that each socialist enterprise manager could be trusted to know the technical circumstances just noted—certainly central planners wouldn't know them unless these facts were first communicated to them by the very people on the spot. And each manager would be provided, by the market or by the central planning board, with the prices of all inputs and outputs; in our case, perhaps, with a price of $5 per bushel of apples and $5,000 per orchard worker per season of work. Thus, a manager could figure what the output of each additional unit of input (shown in col. [4]) would be worth by simply multiplying the marginal physical product per unit of input ($MPP_i$) by the price of output ($P_o$). This would yield (col. [5]) the **marginal value product** per unit of input ($MVP_i$). And the manager could compare the resultant figure with the price of the input ($P_i$), shown in column (6). Under the rule of behavior stated above, an obedient manager of our orchard would employ five workers (note the boxed numbers in cols. [5] and [6]).

And note one other thing: Since the particular circumstances of different enterprises (represented by the data in cols. [1] to [3] above) would surely differ, different enterprise managers would surely make different input decisions even though they would face identical input and output prices. This is just what Lange wanted, and we will see the reason for that in the discussion of economic efficiency that follows. At the moment, simply note the fact just stated. It is illustrated in Figure 8.4, "The Input Decision."

**Figure 8.4** The Input Decision: $MVP_i = P_i$

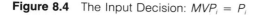

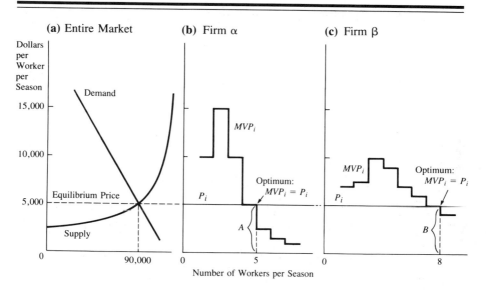

Number of Workers per Season

In Oskar Lange's world of market socialism, market forces (in the case of labor) or central planning board trial and error (in the case of other inputs) would be expected to establish equilibrium prices for all inputs, such as the $5,000-per-worker price shown in panel (a). All enterprise managers would be expected to buy quantities of any input such that the input's falling marginal value product just equalled its price. Since the former would reflect the peculiar technical circumstances of enterprises and would almost certainly differ among enterprises, managers following the same rule would most likely make different input-buying decisions. This is shown in panel (b) for firm α facing the technical data of Table 8.1, and in panel (c) for firm β facing different technical data.

**Optimum Output Quantities.**  Enterprise managers would also be asked to determine, for any given production period, the optimum quantity of any output in this fashion:

> Produce a quantity such that the output's rising marginal cost of production just equals the output's price.

This rule is actually implied by the input rule, noted in the previous section, but we can illustrate it separately using the same numerical example. Our socialist enterprise manager, faced with the $5,000 price per worker per season and the $5 price per bushel of apples assumed earlier, could construct Table 8.2, "Crucial Data for the Output Decision." The first three columns are already familiar to us from the previous section. The fourth one would be derived by multiplying each of the input quantities assumed fixed (the 1,000 apple trees, 1 truck, etc.) by the prices current for their use. The socialist enterprise manager may be authorized to pay himself or herself a $10,000 salary, while having to pay the central planning board $1,000 rent per season for the privilege of using 1,000 apple trees belonging to all the people, $500 rent for the use of 1 truck, and so forth. All this may come to $15,000 per season (as shown in col. [4]). Given the assumed $5,000 wage per worker per season, the use of 1, 2, 3, or more workers would cost the manager $5,000, $10,000, $15,000, or more (as shown in col. [5]). Thus, the manager could calculate the total production cost (in col. [6]) by adding the fixed and variable cost associated with every possible combination of inputs (A to H).

**Table 8.2**  Crucial Data for the Output Decision

| | Fixed Inputs Used (1,000 apple trees, 1 truck, etc. per season) | Variable Inputs Used (workers per season) | Maximum Total Output (bushels of apples per season) | Fixed Cost | Variable Cost | Total Cost | Marginal Cost, MC | Price of Output, $P_o$ |
|---|---|---|---|---|---|---|---|---|
| | | | | (dollars per season) | | | (dollars per bushel) | |
| | (1) | (2) | (3) | (4) | (5) | (6) | (7) | (8) |
| A. | 1 | 1 | 1,000 | 15,000 | 5,000 | 20,000 | 2,50 | 5.00 |
| B. | 1 | 2 | 3,000 | 15,000 | 10,000 | 25,000 | 1.67 | 5.00 |
| C. | 1 | 3 | 6,000 | 15,000 | 15,000 | 30,000 | 2.50 | 5.00 |
| D. | 1 | 4 | 8,000 | 15,000 | 20,000 | 35,000 | 5.00 | 5.00 |
| E. | 1 | 5 | 9,000 | 15,000 | 25,000 | 40,000 | 10.00 | 5.00 |
| F. | 1 | 6 | 9,500 | 15,000 | 30,000 | 45,000 | 16.67 | 5.00 |
| G. | 1 | 7 | 9,800 | 15,000 | 35,000 | 50,000 | 25.00 | 5.00 |
| H. | 1 | 8 | 10,000 | 15,000 | 40,000 | 55,000 | | |

From the data in columns (3) and (6), the manager could calculate the cost of producing extra bushels of apples. This **marginal cost,** *MC,* is nothing else but the change in total cost (between any two adjacent figures in col. [6]) divided by the associated change in total output (between any two adjacent figures in col. [3]). Thus, the hiring of a second worker (moving from row A to row B) would raise total cost by $5,000 (which is $25,000 − $20,000 in col. [6]), while raising total output by 2,000 bushels (which is 3,000 − 1,000 bushels in col. [3]). But $5,000 divided by 2,000 bushels is $2.50 per bushel, and that is the first marginal cost entry in column (7). It tells the manager that each one of the extra bushels that could be acquired via the hiring of a second worker would in effect cost $2.50 to produce.

Under the rule of behavior stated at the beginning of this section, an obedient manager of our orchard would produce 9,000 bushels of apples per season because this quantity would be associated with an equality of rising marginal cost and output price (note the boxed numbers in cols. [7] and [8]). It is no accident, of course, that 9,000 bushels could be produced by using 5 workers, the very number derived earlier when discussing the input decision. Producing 9,000 bushels in our example implies the use of 5 workers, just as the use of 5 workers implies the production of 9,000 bushels.

And note: Since the particular circumstances of different enterprises (represented by the data in cols. [1] to [3] of Table 8.2) would surely differ, different enterprise managers would surely make different output decisions, even though they would face identical input and output prices. This is just what Oskar Lange wanted, and we will again see the reason for that in the discussion of economic efficiency below. At the moment, simply note the fact just stated. It is illustrated in Figure 8.5, "The Output Decision."

## Behavioral Rules for Industry Managers

Industry managers would serve the function of determining the optimum size of their industries. Accordingly, the central planning board would provide another set of rules for each manager of an industry:

> *Expand the size of existing firms, or establish new ones, when the typical firm in the industry is making profits; contract the size of existing firms, or abolish them, when the typical firm in the industry is making losses.*

This is also illustrated easily with the help of our example. Consider Table 8.3, "Crucial Data for the Industry Size Decision." All columns except the last one repeat data from Table 8.2. The last column, however, brings in new data of particular interest to the socialist industry manager. They show firm α's **average total cost** of producing each conceivable output volume, each number in column (6) being nothing else but the total cost (col. [4]) divided by the corresponding total output (col. [3]). Thus, the industry manager could see that firm α, were it to produce its 9,000 bushel optimal output volume, would have an average total cost of $4.44 per bushel (the number is rounded), while selling each bushel for $5

**Figure 8.5** The Output Decision: $MC_o = P_o$

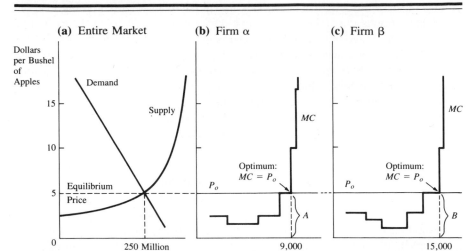

In Oskar Lange's world of market socialism, market forces (in the case of consumer goods) or central planning board trial and error (in the case of other outputs) would be expected to establish equilibrium prices for all outputs, such as the $5 per bushel price shown in panel (a). All enterprise managers would be expected to produce quantities of any output such that the output's rising marginal cost of production just equaled its price. Since the former would reflect the peculiar technical circumstances of enterprises and would almost certainly differ among enterprises, managers following the same rule would most likely make different output-producing decisions. This is shown in panel (b) for firm α facing the technical data of Table 8.2, and in panel (c) for firm β facing different technical data.

(boxed numbers). Thus, α would make an average profit of 56¢ per bushel (the number is rounded), or a total profit of about 56¢ times 9,000 bushels, equal to exactly $5,000 for the season. (The accuracy is easy to check: Firm α would have total revenues of 9,000 bushels times $5 per bushel, or $45,000. It would pay out $15,000 as manager salary, apple tree rental, and so on, while paying 5 orchard workers a total of $25,000 in wages.) The profit, along with any interest and rental payments, it should be remembered, would flow to the central planning board and become part of the fund from which the social dividend would be paid, collective consumption goods be purchased, or investment funds be lent.

**Profits and Industry Expansion.**   Now consider the manager of the apple industry under the behavioral rule stated at the beginning of this section. Assuming firm α's profit-making position was typical, the manager would be expected to expand the size of the apple industry. This would imitate the effect of free entry of new firms into a profitable industry under capitalism. Before long, the supply of industry output would rise, creating a surplus at the old equilibrium price. Then market forces or central planning board action, respectively, would lower the price of

**Table 8.3**  Crucial Data for the Industry Size Decision (typical firm α)

| | Fixed Inputs Used (1,000 apple trees, 1 truck, etc, per season) | Variable Inputs Used (workers per season) | Maximum Total Output (bushels of apples per season) | Total Cost (dollars per season) | Price of Output | Average Total Cost |
|---|---|---|---|---|---|---|
| | | | | | (dollars per bushel) | |
| | (1) | (2) | (3) | (4) | (5) | (6) |
| A. | 1 | 1 | 1,000 | 20,000 | 5.00 | 20.00 |
| B. | 1 | 2 | 3,000 | 25,000 | 5.00 | 8.33 |
| C. | 1 | 3 | 6,000 | 30,000 | 5.00 | 5.00 |
| D. | 1 | 4 | 8,000 | 35,000 | 5.00 | 4.38 |
| E. | 1 | 5 | 9,000 | 40,000 | 5.00 | 4.44 |
| F. | 1 | 6 | 9,500 | 45,000 | 5.00 | 4.74 |
| G. | 1 | 7 | 9,800 | 50,000 | 5.00 | 5.10 |
| H. | 1 | 8 | 10,000 | 55,000 | 5.00 | 5.50 |

output. Simultaneously, profits would fall. Eventually, they would disappear altogether (when output price had fallen to equal the minimum average total cost of production).

**Losses and Industry Contraction.**   Analogously, an industry manager who discovered that the typical enterprise in the industry was making losses would be expected to contract the size of the industry. This would imitate the effect of free exit of existing firms from an unprofitable industry under capitalism. Before long, the supply of industry output would fall, creating a shortage at the old equilibrium price. Then market forces or central planning board action, respectively, would raise the price of output. Simultaneously, losses would fall. Eventually, they would disappear altogether (when output price had risen to equal the minimum average total cost of production).

**Summary.**   All this is summarized in Figure 8.6, "The Task of Industry Managers." Part (a) shows the situation of a profit-making industry. At the equilibrium price of $5 per bushel of apples, the typical firm would be making profits when enterprise managers followed the rule of behavior laid down for them. Firm α, for instance, as noted in our earlier numerical examples, would produce 9,000 bushels per season (where the output's marginal cost, $MC$, would equal its price, $P_o$). Yet, average total cost, $ATC$, would then only come to $4.44 per bushel (point a), yielding an average profit of about 56¢ per bushel (distance ab) and a total profit of $5,000 (shown by the shaded area).

**Figure 8.6** The Task of Industry Managers: $P_o$ = minimum $ATC$

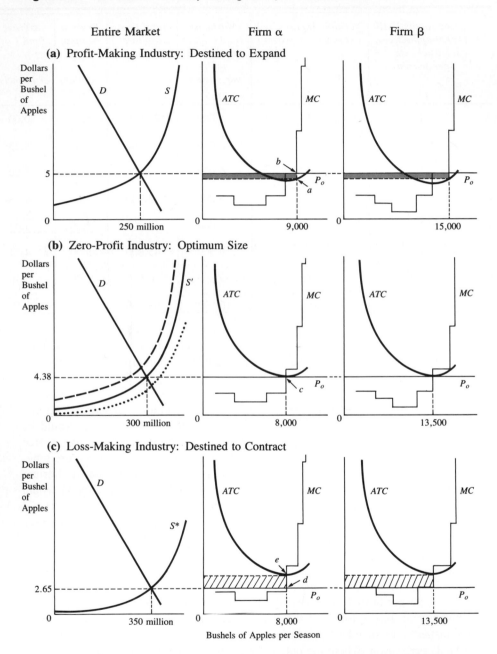

Entire Market        Firm α        Firm β

**(a)** Profit-Making Industry: Destined to Expand

**(b)** Zero-Profit Industry: Optimum Size

**(c)** Loss-Making Industry: Destined to Contract

Bushels of Apples per Season

In Oskar Lange's world of market socialism, especially designated industry managers would expand any profit-making industry (part a), and contract any loss-making one (part c), until the price of the industry's output just equaled its minimum average total cost of production (part b).

As industry managers expanded existing apple orchards and created new ones, market supply would rise to S' in Part (b) (the old supply S is shown by the dashed line for comparison). So the output's equilibrium price would fall to $4.38 per bushel. Although the managers of $\alpha$ and $\beta$ would adjust their outputs downward to 8,000 and 13,500 bushels, respectively (to keep $MC = P_o$), there would be so many more firms that industry output would rise from 250 to 300 million bushels per season. Note how the typical firm would be producing an output volume at which minimum $ATC$ just equaled $P_o$ (as at point $c$); thus, profit would be zero.

We can also imagine, by looking at part (c), what would have happened if the equilibrium price originally had been $2.65 per bushel. The manager of $\alpha$, for example, would have selected to produce 8,000 bushels per season (where $MC = P_o$). Given an average total cost at that volume of output of about $4.38 per bushel (point $e$), an average loss of about $1.73 per bushel would have been made (distance $de$), and a total loss of $13,800 (shown by the cross-hatched area).

An industry manager would have decreased the size of some existing apple orchards and shut down others, market supply would have fallen to S' in part (b) (the old supply S* is shown by the dotted line for comparison). So equilibrium price would have risen to $4.38 per bushel. Although the managers of $\alpha$ and $\beta$ would not have adjusted their outputs in this case, other enterprises might have reduced theirs, there would have been fewer firms in the industry, and industry output would have fallen from 350 to 300 million bushels per season. Once more, the end result would have been the zero-profit industry shown in part (b).

## An Illustration

Consider an example that illustrates how resources would be allocated and reallocated in the Lange model without the use of verbal commands by the central planning board. Imagine that households increased their demand for bicycles, while decreasing their demand for refrigerators.

### Increased Demand

Figure 8.7, "An Increased Demand for Bicycles," tells part of the story. In part (a), we picture an original long-run equilibrium. Market forces have established an equilibrium price of $200 per bicycle in accordance with intersection $a$ where demand, D, equals supply, S. A total of 500,000 bicycles are produced and sold annually. There are numerous firms in the industry; we picture the situation of two of them. Following the rules of behavior in the Lange model, the manager of firm A adjusts the volume of output so as to equate (at $b$) the marginal cost of producing a bicycle, $MC$, with the market-determined output price, $P$. Firm A produces 10,000 bicycles per year. At that output level, its average total cost, $ATC$, equals price as well; thus, its profit is zero. For analogous reasons, the manager of firm B chooses to produce 31,000 bicycles per year. Once again, profit is zero. Given similar circumstances in other firms (not shown), the *industry manager* does nothing at all.

**Figure 8.7**   An Increased Demand for Bicycles

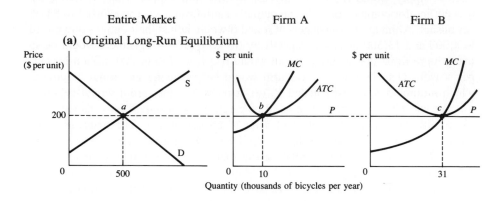

Entire Market                    Firm A                    Firm B

**(a)** Original Long-Run Equilibrium

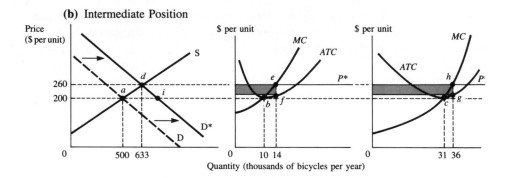

**(b)** Intermediate Position

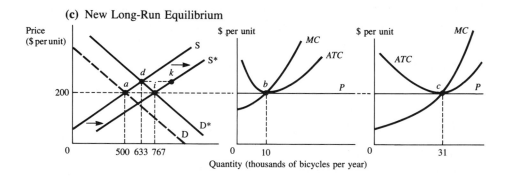

**(c)** New Long-Run Equilibrium

This set of graphs depicts the process of industry expansion in response to an increased demand for bicycles, when enterprise managers and industry manager follow the rules of behavior laid down for them. It is assumed that the industry in question is a constant-cost industry.

In part (b), we picture the situation soon after demand has risen to D\*. A potential shortage of *ai* is averted by price rising to $260 per bicycle. According to intersection *d* of new demand, D\*, and old supply, S, annual production and sales now total 633,000 bicycles. Following the rules of behavior laid down for them, the managers of firms A and B adjust output volume to 14,000 and 36,000 bicycles per year, respectively, equating (at *e* and *h,* respectively) marginal cost, *MC,* with new output price, *P\*.* But there is one other change: The typical firm in the industry is now making positive profits (shaded). For firm A, for example, output price exceeds average total cost by *ef;* for firm B, a similar gap has appeared equal to *hg.* This is where the *industry* manager comes in and creates new firms. As a result, a new zero-profit, long-run equilibrium is reached.

In part (c), the entry of new firms into the industry raises supply from S to S\*. A potential surplus of *dk* is averted by price falling to $200 per bicycle. According to intersection *i* of new demand, D\*, and new supply, S\*, annual production and sales now total 767,000 bicycles. Following the rules of behavior laid down for them, the managers of firms A and B revert to their original positions (part [c] = part [a]). Their profit disappears. Still, industry output is *up* because there are more firms (not shown). Note: The example given here illustrates the case of a **constant-cost industry** the long-run supply curve of which is horizontal (going through points *a* and *i*). In such an industry, the output price is unchanged after the industry has ceased to expand (in response to higher demand and temporary profits) or has ceased to contract (in response to lower demand and temporary losses). An industry could, however, also exhibit an upward-sloping or downward-sloping long-run supply curve. In an **increasing-cost industry,** the output price is higher after the industry has ceased to expand and lower after it has ceased to contract, typically because profit is squeezed away not only by falling output price as firms enter (as in our example), but also by rising input prices (as firms demand more inputs). Similarly, losses are eliminated not only by rising output prices as firms leave, but also by falling input prices (as they demand fewer inputs). Thus, unlike in our example, the *MC* and *ATC* curves of all firms shift up in the process of industry expansion and down in the process of industry contraction. Finally, in a **decreasing-cost industry,** the output price is lower after the industry has ceased to expand and higher after it has ceased to contract, typically because profit is squeezed away by falling output price as firms enter, but partially restored by *falling* input prices (as firms demand more inputs), while losses are eliminated by rising output prices as firms leave but partially restored by *rising* input prices (as firms demand fewer inputs). Thus, the *MC* and *ATC* curves of all firms shift *down* in the process of industry expansion and *up* in the process of industry contraction.

## Decreased Demand

Figure 8.8, "A Decreased Demand for Refrigerators," tells another part of our story. In part (a), we picture once again an original long-run equilibrium. Market forces have established an equilibrium price of $500 per refrigerator in accordance with intersection *a* where demand, D, equals supply, S. A total of 300,000

**Figure 8.8**    A Decreased Demand for Refrigerators

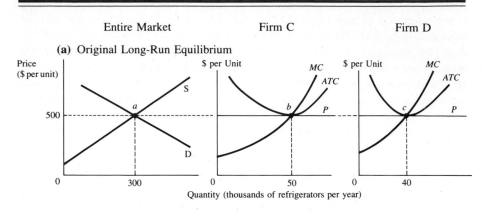

Entire Market          Firm C          Firm D

**(a)** Original Long-Run Equilibrium

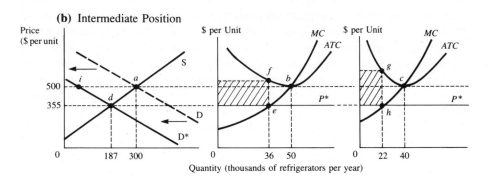

**(b)** Intermediate Position

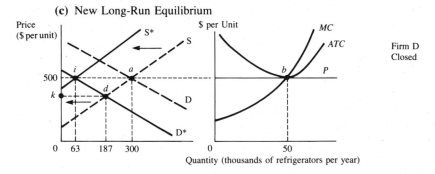

**(c)** New Long-Run Equilibrium

This set of graphs depicts the process of industry contraction in response to a decreased demand for refrigerators when enterprise manager and industry manager follow the rules of behavior laid down for them. It is assumed that the industry in question is a constant-cost industry.

refrigerators are produced and sold annually. There are numerous firms in the industry; we picture the situation of two of them. Following the rules of behavior in the Lange model, the manager of firm C adjusts the volume of output so as to equate (at *b*) the marginal cost of producing a refrigerator, *MC*, with the market-determined output price, *P*. Firm C produces 50,000 refrigerators per year. At that output level, its average total cost, *ATC*, equals price as well; thus, its profit is zero. For analogous reasons, the manager of firm D chooses to produce 40,000 refrigerators per year. Once again, profit is zero. Given similar circumstances in other firms (not shown), the *industry* manager does nothing at all.

In part (b), we picture the situation soon after demand has fallen to D*. A potential surplus of *ia* is averted by price falling to $355 per refrigerator. According to intersection *d* of new demand, D*, and old supply, S, annual production and sales now total 187,000 refrigerators. Following the rules of behavior laid down for them, the managers of firms C and D adjust their total output volumes to 36,000 and 22,000 refrigerators per year, respectively, equating (at *e* and *h,* respectively) marginal cost, *MC,* with new output price, *P\**. But there is one other change: The typical firm in the industry is now sustaining losses (cross-hatched). For firm C, average total cost exceeds output price by *fe;* for firm D, a similar gap has appeared equal to *gh.* This is where the *industry* manager comes in and closes down some firms. As a result, a new zero-profit, long-run equilibrium is reached.

In part (c), the exit of firms from the industry (such as that of firm D) lowers supply from S to S*. A potential shortage of *kd* is averted by price rising to $500 per refrigerator. According to intersection *i* of new demand, D*, and new supply, S*, annual production and sales now total 63,000 refrigerators. Following the rules of behavior laid down for its manager, firm C reverts to its original position (part [c] = part [a]). Its loss disappears. Industry output is down because there are fewer firms.

Note: Once again, the example given here illustrates the case of a constant-cost industry; its horizontal long-run supply curve goes through points *i* and *a*. Also note that other consequences of the shift in demand toward bicycles and away from refrigerators are not shown in figures 8.7 and 8.8. These might include increased demands for labor, aluminum, and machinery by bicycle manufacturers and similar decreases in demands for inputs used by the makers of refrigerators. In the end, resources are reallocated through the intervention of markets in accordance with the initial shifts in demand and quite without any Soviet-style centralized input-output plan.

# An Assessment

Having studied the major features of Lange's model of market socialism, we are ready to speculate about its likely performance. We consider each of the criteria introduced in chapters 2 through 4.

## Full Employment

Oskar Lange envisioned that his type of socialist economy would produce full employment of resources—by whatever definition the suppliers of resources would care to give to that term. These suppliers would, of course, be private households in the case of human resources, and they would be government administrators in the case of nonhuman ones. Given the supply of any resource so determined, and given the demand for it by enterprise managers (who would be following the input rule discussed earlier), an equilibrium price for the resource would be found (by competition among buyers and sellers in the case of labor; by the central planning board's trial and error procedure otherwise). At that equilibrium price, whatever quantity was offered by suppliers would be utilized, as was shown earlier in figures 8.2, "Price Setting in Free Markets," and 8.3, "Price Setting by Trial and Error."

Recall, for instance, Figure 8.2 on page 209 and imagine it applied to a labor market. Competition among buyers or sellers would then establish the equilibrium price of $5 per labor hour. Anyone who wished to sell that particular type of labor at that price could find employment. Involuntary unemployment could only be a temporary phenomenon, one can argue, since it would represent a surplus of the resource on the market. If, in Figure 8.2, the price of labor were $7 per hour, people would indeed offer 48 million hours for sale (point *b*), but firms would hire only 20 million hours (point *a*). The suppliers of some 28 million labor hours could find no job (distance *ab*). A fall in the price of labor to $5 per hour, however, would quickly eliminate this unemployment. As the price fell, firms following the input rule would hire more labor (a movement from *a* toward *e*), and households would voluntarily withdraw some of the labor previously offered (a movement from *b* toward *e*). The same type of adjustment would occur in all other resource markets.

And note: This proposition does not depend on the particular slope of the supply line given in Figure 8.2. If people, for example, insisted on working 48 million labor hours per year regardless of the price of labor (making the labor supply line vertical through points *b* and *d*), a different equilibrium wage would be established (at $3 per hour), but full employment would still come to prevail. Permanent unemployment of a resource could be imagined only if the resource was not scarce; that is, the demand for it, even at a zero price, fell short of its supply. This situation would imply that all firms had so much of the resource in question that use of another unit of it would add nothing to output; hence, its use would not even be worth a penny! Indeed, argued Lange, should anything go wrong with this procedure (should the adjustment process be too slow, for example), the central planning board would also have the option (as governments in real-world capitalism do) of fighting unemployment by using the familiar Keynesian fiscal and monetary policy tools.

## Technical Efficiency

Oskar Lange imagined that enterprise managers would loyally follow the input rule, minimizing the use of inputs for any given level of output and, thus, maximizing output for any given set of inputs. Critics wonder about the managers' incentives to do so, which Lange did not specify.

## Economic Efficiency

Lange argued, similarly, that his type of socialist economy would produce economic efficiency. What the desire for profit by self-interested private owners of firms would accomplish in capitalism, the rules of behavior imposed on socialist enterprise managers would accomplish here.

**The First Pareto Condition.**   Recall, for instance, Figure 8.4, "The Input Decision," on page 213. It illustrates the responsibility of each manager to choose an input volume such that falling $MVP_i = P_i$. Since the price of the input, $P_i$, would be the same for all ($5,000 per worker per season in the earlier example), the marginal value product of the input, $MVP_i$, would be the same in all enterprises using this input, argued Lange. (Note the equality of distances $A$ and $B$ in Figure 8.4.) The marginal value product being nothing else but marginal physical product multiplied by output price, and the latter being also the same for all ($5 per bushel of apples in the earlier example), each enterprise's marginal physical product would end up alike (1,000 bushels of apples per worker in the earlier example). The marginal physical product, however, is nothing else but the $MRT_{x.a}$ first discussed in Chapter 2.

Oskar Lange noted how superior this result would be to that probably achieved under centralized socialism. The central planning board in that other world, not being omniscient, would have assigned 5 units of labor to firm $\alpha$ and 8 to $\beta$ only by the sheerest of coincidences. In fact, its input distribution plan (such as row D of Table 6.2, "The Plan Document," on page 93) might have given 7 units to $\alpha$ and 6 to $\beta$, and (as a look at Figure 8.4 shows) that would have implied different marginal value products (less than $A$ for $\alpha$ and more than $B$ for $\beta$); hence, different marginal physical products or $MRTs$,—hence, economic inefficiency.

Critics of the Lange model wonder, on the other hand, whether such an inefficient result might not also occur in a scheme of market socialism. What might happen, they argue, is this: The central planning board, like all bureaucracies, might turn out to be a cumbersome machine. It might find it impossible to use the trial and error procedure at all for infrequently traded items that are unique (such as buildings, giant generators, or ships), and it might find itself unable to respond quickly to continual changes in the demand for or supply of many categories of nonhuman inputs. Before it could raise the price in the face of a shortage, for instance, it would have to be told about the shortage by someone; it would have to verify the report, clear up contradictions, decide on the required price increase, communicate it to managers, possibly revise the change if it was not of the right magnitude, and so on. Before long, the board would be buried in an avalanche of paperwork. It might begin to revise prices less frequently than circumstances actually justified; and it might set uniform prices for large categories of inputs ("steel" and "trucks" and "land") rather than millions of finer subdivisions that take account of differences in quality and other circumstances of time and place ("#10 tube steel" and "10-year-old 5-ton trucks" and "Vermont pastureland"). As a result, surpluses and shortages might be permanent rather than fleeting events, and that might spell economic inefficiency!

Just consider, in Figure 8.4, what would have happened if the input in question had been something other than labor and its price had been set incorrectly at $2,000 per unit. This would have caused a shortage, and here is why: Following their rules of behavior, the managers of $\alpha$, $\beta$, and of all other enterprises would then have wished to use more than the 5, 8, or whatever number of units they would have used with the $5,000 price. Yet, the quantity of the input supplied would have been smaller than before, as shown in part (a). Thus, managers could not have achieved what the rule required of them. The manager of $\alpha$ might have wished to use 6 units but only have been able to buy 3 units; the manager of $\beta$ might have wished to use 13 units but only have been able to buy 6. As a result, marginal value products, and therefore marginal physical products, would have diverged; the first Pareto condition would not have been fulfilled.

Friedrich von Hayek has been particularly suspicious of the alleged capability of the socialist central planning board to escape the immense task of computation (discussed in Chapter 6) and to imitate the competition of the marketplace via the Langean trial and error price setting procedure:[4]

> *This seems to be much the same thing as if it were suggested that a system of equations which was too complex to be solved by calculation within reasonable time and whose values were constantly changing could be effectively tackled by arbitrarily inserting tentative values and then trying about till the proper solution was found. Or . . . the difference between such a system of regimented prices and a system of prices determined by the market seems to be about the same as that between an attacking army where every unit and every man could only move by special command and by the exact distance ordered by headquarters and an army where every unit and every man can take advantage of every opportunity offered to them.*

**The Second Pareto Condition.** Oskar Lange was equally optimistic, and his critics are equally pessimistic, about the likely fulfillment of the second Pareto condition. Recall, for instance, Figure 8.5, "The Output Decision," on page 216. It illustrates the responsibility of each manager to choose an output volume such that rising $MC = P_o$. Since the price of the output, $P_o$, would be the same for all ($5 per bushel of apples in the earlier example), the marginal cost of producing the output, $MC$, would also be the same for all enterprises producing this output, argued Lange. (Note the equality of distances $A$ and $B$ in Figure 8.5).

Hence, the ratio of the marginal costs of any two outputs produced by any one enterprise would be the same as the corresponding ratio of any other enterprise producing these two outputs. Equality of these ratios, in turn, would mean equality of the $MRT_{a,b}$ first discussed in Chapter 2. (If $\alpha$'s marginal cost of producing a unit of apples were $5 and its marginal cost of producing a unit of butter were $10, $\alpha$ would have a marginal rate of transformation of $2a$ for $1b$. If $\beta$ had the same $MCs$, it would have the same $MRT$.)

---

[4]Friedrich von Hayek, "Socialist Calculation: The Competitive 'Solution,' " *Economica,* May 1940, pp. 130–131.

Yet, critics have wondered about the possibility of this result being spoiled not only by an incompetent central planning board (and the appearance of disequilibrium prices), but perhaps also by disloyal enterprise managers (and their cheating on the rules). How would managers, they have wondered, be rewarded? Solely by payment of salary? Critics have doubted this possibility, fearing that managers who knew that they would receive the same personal reward no matter what they did (and who were not saints) might make life easy for themselves and not carry out the careful calculations required for strict adherence to the rules. Therefore, critics have speculated, Lange's socialist managers would probably be rewarded (as are their counterparts in capitalism's corporations) by salary plus bonus—the latter being a percentage of enterprise profit. This would be likely because the Lange rules for enterprise managers amount to rules for profit maximization:

As long as $MVP_i$ exceeds $P_i$, each extra input unit used adds more to revenue than to cost; thus, it raises profit, and it is exactly under these circumstances that enterprise managers are advised to use more of the input involved. Whenever $P_i$ exceeds $MVP_i$, however, each extra input unit used adds more to cost than to revenue; thus, it reduces profit, and it is exactly under these circumstances that enterprise managers are advised to use less of the input involved. The same holds for the output rule. As long as $P_o$ exceeds $MC$, each extra output unit produced adds more to revenue than to cost; thus, it raises profit, and it is exactly under these circumstances that enterprise managers are advised to produce more of the output in question. Whenever $MC$ exceeds $P_o$, however, each extra output unit produced adds more to cost than to revenue; thus, it reduces profit, and it is exactly under these circumstances that enterprise managers are advised to produce less of the output in question.

Hence, it would be eminently reasonable for a central planning board (that wanted its managers to be diligent followers of its rules) to pay these managers a bonus based on profit achieved. The closer the rules are followed, the board might reason, the greater would be profit and, thus, the manager's bonus. Hence, managers promised a bonus based on profit would follow the rules.

Yet, critics contend, there would also exist the possibility for some managers to raise profit (and personal bonus) by cheating on the rules! Managers who were in charge of enterprises supplying a large percentage of the market might act just like a capitalist monopoly: restricting output to raise price and profit. This is how:

Imagine that $\alpha$ and $\beta$ in Figure 8.5, "The Output Decision," were the only enterprises in the industry (and were producing not 9,000 and 15,000 bushels, respectively, but 100 million and 150 million bushels). If $\alpha$ and $\beta$ were to cut output in half (quite illegally), a shortage would develop in the market at the $5-per-bushel price. Through competition among frustrated apple buyers (or, in the case of a good such as steel, through the central planning board's trial and error procedure) price would rise to some higher equilibrium level of, say $13 per unit. As a result, $\alpha$ and $\beta$ might well have higher profit, and in our case they would. (Their combined revenues would go from 250 million bushels times $5 per bushel, or $1,250 million, to 125 million bushels times $13 per bushel, or $1,625 million. Their costs would surely be lower as a result of producing so much less.) The two managers would get higher bonuses than before!

Also as a result, and this is the crucial point, the marginal costs of production would be the same in α and β only by sheer accident (*MC* would be less than *A* for α and less than *B* for β). Hence, the marginal cost ratios (and the *MRT*s) between any two goods produced would only be identical by accident. Thus, economic efficiency could not be counted on as a sure thing in circumstances wherein the number of producers was small enough to give each of them the power to affect market supply noticeably. Yet, the central planning board would be powerless to prevent such cheating; it could not possibly check the accuracy of billions of calculations made daily in all enterprise offices, critics conclude.

**All Other Pareto Conditions.**    The story is the same with respect to all other Pareto conditions. Lange expressed fond hopes that economic efficiency would be achieved. Critics wonder whether the central planning board's price-setting procedure or the professional ethic of socialist managers might not fail in the task assigned them.

Nevertheless, it seems likely that Lange was correct in situations in which prices are determined by free markets (rather than the central planning board) and in which the number of buyers as well as sellers is large (so as to preclude monopsonistic behavior of buyers or monopolistic behavior of sellers). Take the allocation of consumer goods, first discussed in Chapter 2 as the fourth Pareto condition. In Lange's model, households would be free to spend their money income as they liked, and all of them would face identical equilibrium prices. Consider the case of the two consumers depicted in Table 2.4, "The Optimum Allocation of Goods among Consumers of the Same Goods," on page 24. Suppose they faced equilibrium prices of $2.90 per unit of apples and $1 per unit of butter. Under the circumstances, neither of them would remain in the position indicated in Part (A) of Table 2.4. Given A's *MRS* of 1*a* for 5*b,* A could clearly save $2.10 by consuming 1 more unit of apples (spending an extra $2.90), while consuming 5 units of butter less (spending 5 × $1, or $5 less). Since 1 unit of apples, by assumption, yielded the same welfare as 5 units of butter, A's overall satisfaction would be unaffected. But A could then spend the saved $2.10 on anything and be better off. Thus, self-interest would drive A to do just what Table 2.4 demanded: consume more apples and less butter!

Given B's *MRS* of 1*a* for 2*b,* B could save 90¢ by consuming 1 less unit of apples (saving $2.90), while consuming 2 units of butter more (spending 2 × $1, or $2 more). Since 1 unit of apples, by assumption, yielded for B the same welfare as 2 units of butter, B's overall satisfaction would be unaffected. But B could then spend the saved 90¢ on anything and be better off. Thus, self-interest would also drive B to do just what Table 2.4 demanded: consume more butter and fewer apples!

Clearly, these changes would continue until the *MRS* of both consumers was 1*a* for 2.9*b* (both quantities being worth $2.90). Then further reallocations of their budgets would be of no interest to the two consumers involved. Obviously, the two consumers would not have to get together and exchange goods with each other. They would only have to be free to spend their money incomes as they liked and be faced with identical prices. Both of these conditions would be met in Lange's model economy.

## Economic Growth

Oskar Lange also imagined that his market socialist model would produce optimal economic growth.

**Extensive Growth.**    Above all, he argued, the investment share of the GNP would be determined by the central planning board rather than by individual households (with their unacceptable myopic view that makes them prefer things now to things tomorrow). The central planners would simply tax away whatever portion of national income they thought people should save; and the planners would adjust the rate of interest until industry managers just demanded a corresponding amount of investment funds. (Recall panel [b] of Figure 8.3.)

**Intensive Growth.**    In addition, central planners would, of course, contribute to growth by their own spending on health care, education, and training—similarly financed from taxes. If necessary, all of the social dividend might be taken right back in taxes, along with additional taxes on wages, to finance whatever growth-producing expenditures were deemed "proper" by the planners.

Critics admit the above possibilities, but they wonder about the likely effect of stifled entrepreneurship. From where, they say, would innovation spring in Lange's world of market socialism? Might his enterprise managers not prefer to get bonuses from easy profits reaped by cheating on the rules rather than to undertake the risky business of committing resources to experiments that may not pay off and would reduce profits if they failed? Unlike in capitalism, there would be no room for outsiders to an industry to acquire nonhuman resources with funds provided by banks, to establish an enterprise in that industry, to apply a better method of production, to prove the fact to existing firms by undercutting their prices, and to force them, finally, to adopt the new as well. The private ownership of nonhuman resources that has been so successful in making possible such innovation in capitalism would be ruled out by design. Thus, all innovation would have to come from insiders, most likely industry managers. What could possibly convince them to unleash anything equivalent to the "gale of creative destruction" that newcomers in the capitalist economy continuously inflict upon existing firms? Except in spectacular instances that might involve glamour and prestige (such as the introduction of a space program), the industry managers might have little incentive to innovate. Who, therefore, would produce the millions of small improvements in production processes and products that are not very exciting by themselves (such as a better frying pan), but that improve the living standard of the masses so spectacularly in the long run? Critics have not heard a convincing answer. Thus, they fear that technical innovation, the most powerful stimulus to growth, might be lacking in the Lange world.

## Economic Equity

Oskar Lange argued that his model would produce a good mixture of commutative and distributive justice in the apportionment of goods among people. First, all people would be equally free to avail themselves of the supposedly generous opportunities for health care, education, and training, and they would be free to choose their jobs and change them as they pleased. Second, people would receive, via the social dividend, an equal share of property income; and they would receive transfer payments should they be unable to take advantage of opportunities to gain and use skills. Any persisting income differences would, therefore, be deserved— the result of unwillingness to use opportunities.

Critics, predictably, wonder whether a growth-minded central planning board would *have* any social dividend to distribute. In addition, the government would have the power to set positive and negative taxes on wages and, thus, to fashion the after-tax income distribution in any way it liked. As always, we cannot predict what such a government would in fact do and whether the result would be ''fair'' by any of the possible standards discussed in Chapter 3.

## Alienation

How, finally, would Oskar Lange's model perform with respect to the broader aspects of welfare first noted in Chapter 4?

**From the Self.**  People would have somewhat less of a chance than in the world of market capitalism to experiment with different ways of living. Since all non-human resources would be owned jointly, for instance, people would be forced to become part of the division of labor. They could not go off and live by themselves, if they cared to. Nor could they set up enterprises of their own.

**From One's Fellows.**  In some ways, the Lange model would ensure *consumer sovereignty,* as indicated by the earlier discussion surrounding Figure 8.7, ''An Increased Demand for Bicycles,'' and Figure 8.8, ''A Decreased Demand for Refrigerators.'' If consumers wanted more bicycles and fewer refrigerators, prices would change in a manner discussed in that earlier section. Following their rules of behavior, enterprise managers would produce more of the former, less of the latter (and change their demands for inputs correspondingly). And industry managers would create more enterprises in the profitable bicycle industry, while liquidating others in the refrigerator industry.

On the other hand, the consumers' sovereignty would be severely restricted so far as the question of saving and investing is concerned. Indeed, there would be a danger, as Lange himself suggested, of an uncomfortable bureaucratization of economic life: A central planning board that determined the share of national production devoted to investment, that was setting a multitude of prices, that was appointing and supposedly supervising all the managers of enterprises and industries, might inevitably be frustrated by the complexity of these tasks. Then it might well imagine that it could improve the system's performance by taking on more power and making detailed input and output decisions directly at the center rather than making general rules and accommodating (through the setting of equilibrium prices) the decentralized decisions made by others. Thus, it might be tempted to give up this "anemic" type of socialism (as some socialist critics have called it) and become a *real* board of planners (like the one discussed in Chapter 6). Such a trend, in the end, might engulf the individual once more in a sea of bureaucracy, as discussed in that earlier chapter on centralized socialism.

A similar argument can be made with respect to *worker sovereignty* and *citizen sovereignty.* The Lange model has room for both; a deterioration of the model into centralized socialism could easily eliminate both.

**From the Natural World.** Oskar Lange was optimistic about saving the natural environment because government administrators, rather than private owners, would hold all natural resources in the name of all the people. Just as socialist enterprises that wanted to use 1,000 apple trees would have to pay the equilibrium rental fee to the government, so others wishing to dump wastes into the environment or take fish out of a lake would have to pay such a fee. Thus, the government could limit the use of all aspects of the natural environment to whatever levels it considered proper. For political reasons, rationing of nature by price would be much easier to accomplish, he argued, for a government in socialism than in capitalism. Analytical Example 8.1, "A Market for Pollution Rights," illustrates what Lange had in mind.

Critics cannot quite follow that argument, however. Might a socialist government, they say, if it should be obsessed with economic growth, not be just as willing as any other government to trade off the quality of the natural environment for more material goods?

## Other Models

Although this chapter has focused on the most famous model of market socialism, Lange's is by no means the only one. As the "Selected Readings" indicate, a number of other models, associated with names such as Dickinson, Lerner, and Vanek, exist. The most distinctive and also the most recent of these is Vanek's model of the **participatory economy** or **labor-managed market economy.** It emphasizes democratic decision making within firms and envisions all firms operating within a competitive market environment. The highest authority in each firm is the full working staff. (Although there are no state-appointed managers, the workers may elect a manager to perform executive tasks.) The workers are expected to maximize *value added per worker* (profit as a category distinct from wages is gone). An interesting feature is the fact that the self-employed workers do not own the means of production, nor are these owned by the state or the people as a whole. The means of production are in a sense owned by creditors— they are supposed to be financed by continuous short-term borrowing and re-borrowing in a well-developed capital market wherein funds supplied by banks, households, and the government are exchanged for interest-bearing IOUs issued by groups of workers. In fact, workers are not allowed to invest their own income in their firm; thus, workers need not struggle with their consciences about the division of their value added between reinvestment in the firm and the payment of wages, nor need they worry about losing their investment should they ever leave their firm. The incentives are clear and simple: As long as they can afford to pay the equilibrium interest rate, groups of workers can acquire and keep control over capital and natural resources by borrowing requisite investment funds in the capital market; whatever portion of their sales revenue is not needed to pay this interest or to purchase raw materials from other firms and pay taxes is their *private* income; whatever portion of this income they care to save, they can privately supply to the capital market at large.

Most importantly, Vanek argues, the juxtaposition of employer and employee will be gone. Therefore, workers will work longer, more intensively, with more enthusiasm. Their effort will increase manifold and scarcity be reduced mightily.

## ANALYTICAL EXAMPLE 8.1

## A Market for Pollution Rights

It is easy to see how environmental pollution in the Lange model might be restricted with the help of market forces. Consider the accompanying figure. A large number of firms in the economy might be creating a certain type of waste during their production process; in the absence of any governmental action, these wastes would be dumped into the natural environment: Firm A would dump 8,000 units (point *a*), firm B an equal amount (point *b*), and other firms other amounts (not shown). Suppose, however, that firms were technically able to treat the wastes and avoid dumping them; the marginal costs of abatement, *MCA*, for our two firms are shown by the heights of the vertical blocks. Picture firm B at point *b*, currently dumping 8,000 units of wastes per year into a river. By incurring a cost of $1 per unit, it could treat 1,000 units of its wastes and dump only 7,000 units (moving to point *c*). By incurring further abatement costs of $1, $1, $2, $2, $7, $7, and $7 per unit,

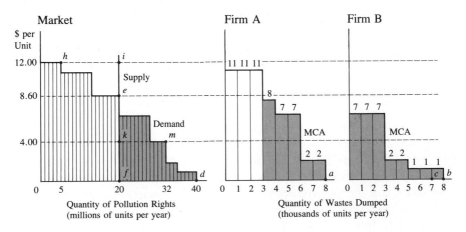

respectively, waste dumping could be further reduced by successive 1,000 units—all the way down to zero. (The rising marginal cost of abatement shown here is typical of the real world; it is often fairly easy to treat a portion of wastes; it becomes increasingly difficult and costly to treat additional portions.) The middle graph tells a similar story about firm A. Again read the graph from right to left. By starting at point *a* and incurring even higher marginal costs of abatement (which differ from those of firm B), firm A could also treat its wastes. Yet, neither firm would do so unless an appropriate incentive was provided.

Now focus on the left-hand graph. Suppose the central planning board was determined to reduce the nationwide waste dumping into waterways from an annual 40 million units (point *d*) to 20 million units (point *f*). It could make all dumping illegal except to holders of **pollution rights**—transferable certificates each of which allows the holder to dump one unit of specified wastes into a specified environment. Accordingly, the central planning board could supply 20 million such rights to a market, and this is shown in the left-hand graph by the vertical line from *f* to *i* and beyond. (This limited supply of nature's waste absorption capacity would correspond to the analogous supply of blast furnaces or pastureland depicted in Figure 8.3, "Price Setting by Trial and Error.") Enterprise managers, in turn, would have to buy such rights before they could do any dumping at all. Their demand, however, would clearly be related to their marginal abatement costs noted earlier. If the price of a pollution right were $12, for instance, neither the manager of firm A nor the manager of firm B would care to buy any of these rights. If properly motivated to keep costs to a minimum, each of them would rather treat wastes at costs of $1, $2, $7, $8, or even $11 per unit than to pay $12 for the right simply to dump the wastes. Nevertheless, other firms with marginal abatement costs above $12 may well demand pollution rights; as our graph indicates, at the $12 price some 5 million rights would be demanded (point *h*). Because 20 million rights would be supplied (point *i*), a surplus of *hi* would exist, and the central planning board would lower the price.

At a lower price, the quantity of pollution rights demanded would be larger; at a price of $4, for instance, some 32 million rights would be demanded (point *m*). In that case, firm A would wish to buy 6,000 rights and dump 6,000 units, while abating 2,000 units of wastes. This is so because the abatement of the first 2,000 units from initial point *a* would cost only $2 per unit (while it would cost $4 per unit just to acquire the right to dump them). On the other hand, the remaining 6,000 units could only be abated at marginal costs of $7, $8, and $11, and it would be cheaper just to dump these units after paying the $4-per-unit fee. For analogous reasons, firm B would abate 5,000 units and dump 3,000 units if the dumping fee were $4 per unit. That fee, however, would not persist. Because 32 million rights would then be demanded (point *m*), but only 20 million rights be supplied (point *k*), a shortage of *km* would exist, and the central planning board would raise the price.

As the point *e* intersection of supply and demand indicates, a possible equilibrium price of $8.60 per pollution right might emerge from the central planning board's trial-and-error procedure. At that price, overall demand would just equal the 20 million rights supplied. Firm A would buy 3,000 such rights at $8.60 each and then dump the 3,000 units of waste that could only be abated at a cost of $11 each. It would also abate 5,000 units of waste at a total cost of $26,000 (shaded): $2 (1,000) + $2 (1,000) + $7 (1,000) + $7 (1,000) + $8 (1,000), which would be cheaper than paying $8.60 (5,000) for the right just to dump these units. Firm B in our example would abate all of its wastes at a total cost of $28,000 (shaded) because all its marginal abatement costs lie below the $8.60 equilibrium price for a pollution right.

As this example shows, a governmental auctioning off of a limited quantity of pollution rights could achieve two things: (a) the reduction of overall waste dumping to any amount considered acceptable and (b) the abatement of a given amount of wastes at minimum total cost (shaded) because nature's limited waste absorption capacity would inevitably be used for the dumping of those wastes that are costliest to abate.

## BIOGRAPHY 8.1    Oskar R. Lange

Oskar Richard Lange (1904–1965) was born in Tomaszow Mazowieckj, Poland, the son of a textile manufacturer. He graduated from the University of Cracow in the late 1920s and soon acquired an international reputation for his writings on the economic theory of socialism. They were widely acclaimed as a powerful refutation of the contentions of von Mises on the impossibility of an efficient allocation of resources under socialism. Said Lange in 1936:[a]

*Socialists have certainly good reason to be grateful to Professor Mises, the great advocatus diaboli of their cause. For it was his powerful challenge that forced the socialists to recognize the importance of an adequate system of economic accounting to guide the allocation of resources in a socialist economy. . . . Both as an expression of recognition for the great service rendered by him and as a memento of the prime importance of sound economic accounting, a statue of Professor Mises ought to occupy an honorable place in the great hall of the Ministry of Socialization or of the Central Planning Board of the socialist state.*

Before long, Lange taught at various American universities, then became a Professor of Economics at the University of Chicago and also an American citizen. While at Chicago, he was regarded as "the best teacher of economics in America." He was also a pioneer in mathematical economics (and one of the founders of the Econometric Society) and a strong protagonist of the new Keynesian macroeconomics. These interests remained with him throughout his life and are reflected in such works as *Price Flexibility and Full Employment* (1944), *Introduction to Cybernetics* (1970), and *Optimal Decisions: Principles of Programming* (1971).

But Lange had not only a distinguished academic career; he was also a highly respected public servant in his native Poland. From early on, he had been a member of the Polish Democratic Party. As such, he published a famous letter in the *New*

---

[a]Oskar Lange and Fred M. Taylor, *On the Economic Theory of Socialism* (New York: McGraw-Hill, 1964), pp. 57 and 58.

*York Herald Tribune* in 1943 in which he urged his Polish ex-countrymen not to be victimized by anti-Russian propaganda. He argued that the survival of Poland as an independent nation after World War II was indissolubly linked with the maintenance of friendly relations with the Soviet Union. As a result of this letter, Lange received a personal invitation from Stalin to visit Moscow in 1944 and to discuss the future of Poland. Lange decided to support the provisional government of Poland established in Moscow and, in 1945, renounced his U.S. citizenship to become the first ambassador of postwar Poland in Washington. Later, he became chief Polish delegate at the United Nations and (to the dismay of his American friends) staunchly supported the Stalinist line in the Security Council.

In the post-Stalin era, Lange became chairman of the Polish State Economic Council and Vice-Chairman of the Polish Council of State. In addition, he lectured widely in Western universities and acted as a consultant in many underdeveloped countries.

What of the Lange model discussed in this chapter? Toward the end of his life, Lange was keenly interested in electronic computers and cybernetics. When asked to reconcile his earlier views on market socialism with Poland's Soviet-style central planning, he described his trial-and-error method of finding equilibrium prices as quaintly out of date in the computer age:

> Were I to rewrite my essay [On the Economic Theory of Socialism] today, my task would be much simpler. My answer to [critics] would be: So what's the trouble? Let us put the simultaneous equations on an electronic computer and we shall obtain the solution in less than a second. . . . The trial and error procedure proposed in my essay really played the role of a computing device for solving a system of simultaneous equations. . . . The computer has the undoubted advantage of much greater speed. The market is a cumbersome and slow-working servo-mechanism.

However, given the limited capacity of even the most powerful electronic computers, Lange argued, computers should be used in combination with, rather than in place of, markets under socialism. He saw their most important contribution in long-term development planning in which the computer "fulfills a function which the market never was able to perform."[b] Indeed, in his final work Lange proposed a mixture of central control and decentralization for the advanced socialist economy. Central authorities, aided by computers, should continue to determine the basic proportions of the GNP, he thought, but give up detailed, day-to-day management to the market. In addition, central planners should give up verbal commands in favor of "economic means"; that is, monetary incentives that induce rather than command households and enterprises to act in ways desired by the socialist government.[c]

[b]Oskar Lange, "The Computer and the Market," in C. H. Feinstein, ed., *Socialism, Capitalism and Economic Growth: Essays Presented to Maurice Dobb* (Cambridge, England: Cambridge University Press, 1967), pp. 158–61.

[c]Oskar Lange, *The Political Economy of Socialism* (The Hague: Institute of Social Studies, 1958).

*Source: Obituaries from the Times 1961–1970* (Reading, England: Newspaper Archive Developments, 1975), pp. 461–62.

# Summary

1. In light of the economic chaos evident in the young Soviet state, a famous debate arose among economists in the West on whether an actual (as opposed to hypothetical) socialist economy could ever allocate resources efficiently. This possibility was denied in the 1920s by von Mises and others; their challenge, in turn, led to Lange's construction in the 1930s of a model economy that combined socialism and a market system.

2. In Lange's model, the formal ownership of capital and natural resources resides in the people as a whole, but decision-making power is spread among a number of economic actors, notably a central planning board, private households, enterprise managers, and industry managers. Their separate actions are coordinated by numerous markets.

    The *central planning board* appoints all managers, determines the percentage of GNP devoted to investment, rents out the services of publicly owned capital and natural resources, collects taxes from households and all enterprise profits, purchases collective consumption goods, pays social dividends, and sets all prices except those for labor and private consumption goods. In doing so, the board follows a trial-and-error procedure, lowering prices in the face of surpluses and raising them in the face of shortages.

    *Private households* supply their labor in free labor markets in return for wages that may be supplemented by a social dividend or reduced by taxes. They demand consumer goods in free markets as well.

    *Socialist enterprise managers* are also oriented toward markets; they are expected to make their own input and output decisions on the basis of certain general rules of behavior: (a) adjust any input quantity until the input's falling marginal value product just equals the input's price and (b) adjust any output quantity until the output's rising marginal cost of production just equals the output's price.

    *Socialist industry managers* have the task of creating new enterprises in profitable industries and closing down existing enterprises in loss-sustaining industries.

3. An extended example about a shift in consumer demand from bicycles to refrigerators illustrates how resources are allocated and reallocated in the Lange model.

4. The likely performance of the Lange model is assessed with respect to the set of criteria first introduced in chapters 2 through 4. Oskar Lange was confident that his socialist market economy would perform superbly with respect to all of these criteria; his critics are not so sure.

5. A number of alternative market-socialist models exist. The most distinctive and most recent of these is Vanek's labor-managed market economy.

## Key Terms

average total cost
constant-cost industry
decreasing-cost industry
enterprise managers
increasing-cost industry
industry managers
labor-managed market economy

marginal cost
marginal physical product
marginal value product
social dividend
participatory economy
pollution right

## Questions and Problems

1. "The behavioral input rule for Lange's enterprise managers is in effect a rule for profit maximization." Have a look at Table 8.1 and show why input combinations A and H (both of which were rejected) would not maximize profit. (Hint: As a rereading of the text would show, fixed inputs were assumed to cost $15,000 per season; the price per unit of variable input was $5,000 per season, and the price per unit of output was $5.)

2. "The behavioral output rule for Lange's enterprise managers is in effect a rule for profit maximization." Have a look at Table 8.2 and show why output levels B and G (both of which were rejected) would not maximize profit.

3. How would a simultaneous increase in household taxes and government purchases of collective consumption goods affect the Lange economy?

4. How would an increase in population and, therefore, labor supply affect the Lange economy?

5. One of the Pareto conditions of economic efficiency demands an equality of the marginal rate of transformation between any two outputs, *a* and *b*, both of which are produced by any two producers. Illustrate graphically how this condition might be fulfilled in Lange's socialist market economy.

6. One of the Pareto conditions of economic efficiency demands an equality of the marginal rate of technical substitution between any two inputs, *x* and *y*, both of which are used by any two producers. Illustrate graphically how this condition might be fulfilled in Lange's socialist market economy.

7. "The rules of Lange's model economy would surely break down in the case of *natural monopolies* the average total costs of which are declining throughout the range of quantities that might conceivably be demanded." Comment.

8. The text discussion of "the second Pareto condition" contains a section speculating about possible managerial cheating on the rules. Illustrate the possibility graphically.

9. **Ms. A:** "Lange's argument for a socialist rather than capitalist market economy makes no sense to me. If a government can collect the interest, rent, and profit flowing from socialist enterprises and then distribute these to all citizens as a 'social dividend,' it surely can just as easily tax away the interest, rent, and profit income of private capitalists and redistribute it to all."

   **Ms. B:** "You are so right. And if all citizens would benefit indirectly if a few socialist government officials invested most of this income (except for a portion used to pay high salaries to themselves), so they would benefit indirectly if a few private capitalists invested most of this income (except for a portion used to finance high consumption levels for themselves). Why *bother* with all this socialist charade?"

   What do you think?

10. Review Biography 8.1 and ponder (and comment on) Lange's statement: "So what's the trouble? Let us put the simultaneous equations on an electronic computer and we shall obtain the solution in less than a second."

## Selected Readings

Dickinson, H. D. *Economics of Socialism* (London: Oxford University Press, 1939). Another market-socialist model.

Hayek, Friedrich A., ed. *Collectivist Economic Planning,* 6th ed. (London: Routledge and Kegan Paul, 1963). Critical studies on the possibilities of socialism, including essays by Barone, Halm, Hayek, von Mises, and Pierson.

Hayek, Friedrich A. "Socialist Calculation: The Competitive 'Solution,' " *Economica,* May 1940, pp. 125–49. A scathing criticism of the Lange model.

Lange, Oskar, and Fred M. Taylor. *On the Economic Theory of Socialism* (New York: McGraw-Hill, 1964). The Lange model plus essays by Taylor and Lippincott.

Lavoie, Don. *Rivalry and Central Planning: The Socialist Calculation Debate Reconsidered* (Cambridge, England: Cambridge University Press, 1985). A careful rethinking of the classic debate involving von Mises, Lange, and others, about socialism and economic rationality. Claims that the standard accounts of the debate are seriously flawed.

Lerner, Abba P. *The Economics of Control: Principles of Welfare Economics* (New York: Macmillan, 1944). Another model economy designed to serve the "social interest." It emphasizes Keynesian stabilization policies and, unlike the Lange model, is not dogmatic about the ownership of the means of production: Private and public ownership are equally acceptable as long as governmental aims are achieved.

Mises, Ludwig von. *Socialism: An Economic and Sociological Analysis* (New Haven, CT: Yale University Press, 1951). An elaboration of the 1920 article (noted in the footnote on page 205) on rational economic calculation and socialism.

Vanek, Jaroslav. *The General Theory of Labor-Managed Market Economies* (Ithaca, NY: Cornell University Press, 1970).

Vanek, Jaroslav. *The Participatory Economy: An Evolutionary Hypothesis and a Strategy for Development* (Ithaca, NY: Cornell University Press, 1971).

Vanek, Jaroslav, ed. *Self-Management: Economic Liberation of Man* (Harmondsworth, England: Penguin, 1975).

## Computer Programs

The SYSTEMS personal computer diskette that accompanies this book contains one program of interest to this chapter:

Program 8, "Market Socialism: A Model," provides 20 multiple-choice questions about Chapter 8, along with immediate responses to incorrect answers.

# CHAPTER 9

# *Market Socialism: The Yugoslav Case*

The first socialist market economy did not come into existence until the 1950s. Even then, its appearance was a gradual process that had nothing to do with any conscious desire to try out the Lange model discussed in the previous chapter. It happened in Yugoslavia; this chapter tells the story.

## The Historical Background

Yugoslavia, Land of the South Slavs, first came into being in 1918, as a kingdom formed from various fragments of the disintegrated Austro-Hungarian and Turkish Ottoman empires. The country was then, as it is now, the home of numerous ethnic groups with a long history of bloody conflicts among themselves. There were Slovenes and Croats, Bosnians and Serbs, Montenegrins and Macedonians; and among them lived Germans, Hungarians, Czechs, Ruthenians, Romanians, Bulgarians, Turks, Albanians, Italians, even gypsies and others still. These groups had no chance to amalgamate into a united whole prior to the German-Italian onslaught of World War II. Not surprisingly, the royal army collapsed at once, and various German allies within and without sliced up Yugoslavia like a cake. Nevertheless, from the wildly beautiful and forbidding mountains along the Adriatic coast, a National Liberation Movement emerged. Led by Tito (Biography 9.1 at the end of this chapter) and against all odds, the ill-equipped and outnumbered partisans eventually threw off the invaders and, in 1945, with widespread popular support established the socialist republic we know today. The event was unique: There were few Soviet troops on Yugoslav soil. The League of Communists of Yugoslavia had come to power almost entirely on its own.

Yugoslavia now consists of six constituent republics. A northern tier, including Slovenia, Croatia, and Serbia (plus the autonomous province of Vojvodina) is relatively well-to-do; a southern group of Bosnia-Herzegovina, Montenegro, and Macedonia (plus the autonomous province of Kosovo) is fairly poor. As in the past, there are numerous ethnic minorities. The people continue to be separated by ancestral bitterness, five major languages (Serbo-Croatian, Slovenian, Macedonian, Hungarian, and Albanian), two alphabets (Latin and Cyrillic), and three religions (Roman Catholic, Eastern Orthodox, and Islamic). During his lifetime, however, Tito's charisma and popularity managed to hold all these people together and got them started on building a modern nation.

## Tito's Road to Socialism

Just like the Soviet Union, Yugoslavia emerged from World War II a devastated country. Its industry lay in ruins, its railroads were destroyed, its cities bombed, its farms without life. Over 10 percent of the population was dead; the rest was scarred by memories of all too many atrocities committed not only by the Nazi invaders but even by Yugoslavs against Yugoslavs. But Tito was determined to overcome destruction and poverty. Unlike the rest of Eastern Europe where the Red Army imposed it, Tito turned to the Stalinist example by choice.

### The Stalinist Model: Tried and Abandoned

Initially, Tito adopted full-scale central planning of the Soviet type (discussed in Chapter 7 of this book). A first Five-Year Plan, scheduled to run from 1947 to 1951, called for rapid industrialization by raising the investment share of the GNP to 33 percent. In their exuberance to outdo the Russians, the Yugoslavs set up a central plan of unparalleled completeness and detail. The plan document itself weighed over 3,000 pounds, and it provided for 217 federal ministers giving verbal instructions on everything to government-appointed managers of all the country's enterprises. Indeed, the Yugoslavs outdid Stalin also in brutality when collectivizing agriculture and ridding the country of internal ''enemies'' who were opposed to establishing a one-party state. And Tito's hostility to the capitalist West could hardly have been surpassed.

Yet, the ambitious economic plan was error-riddled. Numerous parts did not fit together, which caused other parts to fail as well. Before long, unfinished projects were strewn across the land. But things got worse in 1948 when a proud Tito rejected Stalin's meddling in Yugoslav affairs. Tito insisted on being treated as a sovereign equal; he accused Stalin of attempting to dominate the Yugoslav army and Communist Party, of exploiting the Yugoslav economy through ''joint companies,'' of trying to direct Yugoslav investment toward light industry only (in order to preserve Soviet dominance in heavy industry), of blackmailing prominent Yugoslavs into becoming Soviet agents, and more. Stalin rejected Tito's "slander," and for "boundless ambition, arrogance, and conceit" the "Tito clique" was cast out of the Cominform (a precursor of the Warsaw Pact). Tito responded to the threat of a Soviet invasion with full mobilization and a determination to resist the Russians, like the Nazis, with a drawn-out guerrilla war. As a result, the Soviet-bloc nations withdrew their technicians and cut off all trade. By 1950, Tito abandoned the Five-Year Plan.[1]

## The Introduction of Worker Self-Management: 1950–1965

Having stood up to Stalin earned Tito great admiration and respect throughout the world as well as at home. Tito grasped the opportunity implied thereby. Internationally, Yugoslavia accepted a considerable amount of Western economic aid; in return she abandoned her anti-Western foreign policy stance in favor of a policy of nonalignment between the two superpower blocs. Domestically, Yugoslavia abandoned the Stalinist economic system, which most concerns us here.

In a famous 1950 speech, Tito adopted ideas previously offered him by his erstwhile partisan comrades, Milovan Djilas and Edvard Kardelj:

1. The first idea focused on the Marxian precept that *workers* were to run the economy under socialism. Stalin's interpretation of Marx was wrong, argued Tito. The Soviets had introduced state capitalism, not socialism. Their practice of "nationwide worker management," according to which workers allegedly elected the Communist Party elite which then managed the economy in the workers' name and for their benefit was a farce, Tito said. What Marx surely meant was for the workers of each enterprise to manage collectively the enterprise in which they were employed; hence, Yugoslavia would institute an appropriate system of **worker self-management.** "The factories to the workers," Tito proclaimed.

2. The second idea focused on the role of the government in economic affairs. Marx had predicted the eventual *withering away* of the state; in the Soviet Union, argued Tito, the state had been immeasurably strengthened instead and had simply taken over the private capitalists' role of exploiting workers. As a result, as even Boris Kidrič (head of Yugoslavia's Fed-

---

[1]After 1948, Soviet-Yugoslav relations have never been quite the same. In 1955, Khrushchev (Biography 7.3) came to Belgrade to apologize for 1948; Tito could hardly conceal his contempt, and he felt vindicated in his suspicions when the Soviets intervened in the Hungarian uprising a year later and executed "the Hungarian Tito," Imre Nagy. In 1971, Brezhnev made a similar pilgrimage to Belgrade and reassured Tito about the 1968 Soviet-bloc invasion of Czechoslovakia. In 1972, Tito even visited Moscow and accepted the Order of Lenin, but suspicions remained, and Tito persisted to the end in his fiercely independent path at home and abroad. Long after Tito's death, in 1988, Gorbachev (Biography 7.4) accepted Soviet blame for the 1948 rift. (*The New York Times,* March 17, 1988, p. A5.)

eral Planning Commission) admitted, the centralized state machine was killing people's enthusiasm for hard work. Accordingly, Tito initiated the withering away of the Yugoslav state. The process would begin, promised Tito, with a gradual dismantling of the central planning bureaucracy in favor of free markets; it would continue with the shifting of political power from the central government to the republican governments and further to local governments (called *communes*) of villages and towns.[2]

During the next 15 years, Tito's new course was gradually implemented. The central government slowly withdrew from economic decision making; the decision making of households and enterprises, coordinated by markets, was promoted instead. By 1953, the collectivization drive was abandoned and private farms with a maximum of 25 acres were legalized. Before long, well over 80 percent of the arable land and over 90 percent of the livestock belonged to such private farms. Over 90 percent of the agricultural labor force worked on them. Outside agriculture, private enterprises with a maximum of five employees were legalized as well. Such businesses soon flourished in construction and handicrafts, in retail trade and the service sector.

While private tailors and barbers, doctors and plumbers, restaurants and taxis were acceptable, private steel plants and auto plants were another matter. In fact, all enterprises with a staff exceeding five individuals had to remain socialist; the capital and natural resources in their possession belonged to the people as a whole. But unlike in the Soviet Union, the state did not substitute itself for the capitalist class in its role as overseer, telling the workers what to do. On the contrary, Yugoslav socialist enterprises were to be run like democracies, not as autocracies. The full-time staff of such enterprises (henceforth simply referred to as ''the workers'') was to be the ultimate enterprise authority. The workers were given the role of trustees, responsible to society for the preservation of the means of production under their immediate control, but free to make all the decisions involved in their utilization. Thus, the workers on the spot (and neither a private capitalist nor a state central planning board) were to decide what other inputs to combine with capital and natural resources, what types of products to produce, where to buy inputs and sell outputs, what prices to pay or charge, whether to innovate, whether to borrow from the banks, and how to dispose of their net revenue: via investment in their enterprise, via collective consumption (such as housing construction for workers), or via personal income payments to workers.

In fact, however, all these decisions were not made by all the workers as a group. The Yugoslav socialist enterprise in the 1950s became a *representative* democracy, akin to the U.S. democracy in which all power emanates from the people as a whole, but basic policy decisions are made by elected representatives of the people and are then implemented by other elected officials still. In the larger

---

[2]A few years later, Milovan Djilas carried the argument even further: As an antidote to the privileged living style of the Party elite, he recommended the withering away of the Party as well. He was arrested for excessive liberalism and given nine years in jail.

socialist enterprises, Yugoslav workers elected from their midst a **workers' council**—a group of worker representatives numbering anywhere from 15 to 120 persons (depending on the size of the full-time staff) and responsible for basic policy decisions. The workers' council, in turn, delegated authority to a smaller (3- to 11-person) **management board.** In very small enterprises, workers elected the management board directly. In either case, the board—together with certain officials from the local government and the industry trade association—appointed an **enterprise director.** The latter was responsible for carrying out the day-to-day management of the enterprise under the immediate supervision of the management board.

The central government, meanwhile, dismantled the central planning board and confined itself to intervention in a few selected areas; by the mid-1960s, this intervention had ceased taking the form of direct physical controls and consisted instead of generalized fiscal and monetary policies. In particular, the central government was concerned with five issues:

1. Controlling the overall division of the GNP between investment goods and consumption goods (a high investment-to-GNP ratio was desired to promote rapid economic growth)
2. Influencing the geographic distribution of investment (a "fair" distribution among the republics was desired, especially one that promoted the development of the poorer regions of the south)
3. Determining the volume and direction of foreign trade
4. Ensuring a "fair" distribution of income among population groups
5. Providing collective consumption goods (defense, education, research, and the like)

## The Self-Managed Firm: 1965–1971

Since the mid-1960s, Tito's socialist market economy has been fully in place. Its centerpiece is the self-managed firm. It is important to analyze its nature in some detail, for it differs in many respects from the autocratic type of firm traditionally investigated by economists. A number of characteristics are of particular interest and will help us understand, in a later section, the performance of the Yugoslav economy.

**The Separation of Founders from Subsequent Decision Making.**   Self-managed firms come into being by the initiative of governmental units, social organizations, existing enterprises, or groups of individuals. These decide what kind of firm to establish and where to locate it. They provide the initial buildings and equipment and recruit the initial labor force, but then—unlike in any other type of firm—the founders relinquish all control of the firm to the workers! This fact often reduces the willingness to establish new firms. It also leads to the establishment of so-called **political factories,** firms that are established as a result of political pressure with the aim of providing local employment or prestige, but that are economic mistakes, being designed to produce the wrong product in the wrong place with the wrong technology. (Consider placing a steel mill in an inaccessible mountainous region that contains neither iron ore nor coal and is, perhaps, even set up to use an outdated production technique.)

**The Objectives of the Workers.**  Once they are in charge, the firm's workers as a group carry out all the entrepreneurial functions—subject only to the restriction that they must preserve the means of production under their care. (Thus, they cannot create personal income for themselves by selling off the capital equipment or refusing to replace it as it wears out.) What goal are workers likely to pursue when they make any one of the numerous daily decisions noted earlier that running an enterprise entails? Analysts think it likely that the worker collective will want to maximize the firm's *residual income per worker* because this amount represents the potential personal income of each worker.

Consider the finances of the worker-managed firm. Like any firm, it acquires revenue from the sale of its output. The nature of its cost, however, differs from other types of firms in that the category of wages is gone. The worker-managed firm pays for raw materials and services bought from other firms, it incurs depreciation costs (to replace its capital stock), it pays interest to banks, taxes to the government. The rest is its **residual income,** akin to profit in a firm that doesn't pay wages and destined to be disposed of by a joint decision of the workers. Thus

$$\text{Revenue} - \text{Cost} = \text{Residual Income}$$

but

$$\text{Cost} = \text{Purchases from Other Firms} + \text{Depreciation} + \text{Interest} + \text{Taxes}$$

(There are no wages.) The residual income, in short, contains, in undifferentiated form, the collective income of workers from their labor services and their entrepreneurial services.

**The Disposition of Residual Income.**  How are workers likely to dispose of the residual income? Three major possibilities exist:

1. The residual can be used for reinvestment, to purchase *new* capital equipment beyond the replacement of the old. As a result, the firm's capital stock grows, and workers may become more productive and get higher revenue and residual income in the future.
2. The residual can be used for collective consumption, such as the construction of housing or swimming pools or tennis courts.
3. The residual can be distributed as personal income among the workers—on an equal or unequal basis, whatever the workers decide. (Indeed, the central government requires that workers receive no less than a set minimum hourly "wage" in this way. If the residual income is insufficient to pay it, the enterprise must borrow the necessary funds from the banks.)

It is not difficult to guess (and Yugoslav experience bears it out) what workers are likely to do when the time comes to vote on the issue: Workers will try to minimize disposal options (1) and (2), while maximizing option (3).

Consider why any given worker would want to minimize option (1). Every dinar of residual income reinvested in the enterprise is a dinar lost from the personal-income-distribution pool. Even if a worker was willing to refrain from consumption now, saving and investing privately (*following* option [3]) would be preferred to saving and investing collectively (via option [1]). This is so because private investment (for example, in a savings account, a piece of land, an artisan shop, a taxi, or even education) will not only yield a future return (such as interest and other types of revenue), but will also preserve the worker's right to the principal. How different with the collective investment! For one thing, its future return is uncertain.

If the enterprise uses the investment funds to introduce a technical innovation, say, and the project fails, there will be no future increase in productivity, no increased revenue, no increased pool of residual income to be shared. Even if there is more physical output, market conditions could change. More physical output at lower prices per unit may still yield no change in revenue and, again, no higher personal income at all. In short, workers choosing option (1), like any entrepreneur, are in effect taking a *risk,* and, as surveys show, Yugoslav workers typically have no interest in doing so.

More than that! Workers choosing option (1) are fully aware of the fact that they can never retrieve the principal involved. They do not get a savings bank passbook when they reinvest residual income in their enterprise. Nor do they get bonds or stock certificates. Like the founders of the firm, workers who reinvest *lose* their principal; it becomes the property of the Yugoslav people as a whole. (The loss is irretrievable because workers have the legal obligation to maintain the firm's capital stock forever; they cannot invest now and disinvest later.) Indeed, should workers ever leave the firm (through retirement or dismissal or in order to take up employment elsewhere), they lose the right to a return on their investment as well. The residual income belongs to the workers on the spot, currently employed, not to those who were there in the past, even if they did help acquire the firm's capital stock.

For similar reasons, workers are often reluctant to vote for option (2). They can think of plenty of things to do with money that is wholly their own. Why should they sacrifice the potential private consumption made possible by option (3)? This is especially so if the kinds of collective consumption goods contemplated are of differential interest to different workers. Unlike the young, for example, older workers close to retirement may not be interested in tennis courts or fancy improvements in working conditions. Unlike the old, the very young (who consider themselves immortal) may not care to pay for a nursing home for retired workers.

## The Bargaining Society: 1971 to the Present

In the early 1970s, just as he had once before changed his view of the central planning bureaucracy, Tito changed his mind about the role of markets as coordinating devices. He argued that less emphasis should be placed on "impersonal and uncontrolled" market forces as means of coordinating the independent decisions of private households, private enterprises, socialist enterprises, and governmental units. At the same time, he favored an extension of the self-management principle to smaller units of workers within each enterprise on the one hand and beyond the enterprise sector (to social and political groupings of people) on the other hand. And he set out to create an extended system of intraenterprise, interenterprise, and interregional *bargaining* that would coordinate the separate activities of people by establishing a consensus. These ideas were ultimately embodied in a new 1974 Constitution.

**The Extension of Self-Management Within Enterprises.**  Within each socialist enterprise, small groups of workers who could be distinguished from other such groups by the nature of their tasks and whose output was, thus, distinguishable from that of such other groups were designated as **basic organizations of associated labor** or **BOALs.** (In an integrated steel company, for example, a BOAL might be established for all the workers mining iron ore, a second one for the workers transporting the ore, a third one for workers mining coal, a fourth one for workers making raw steel, a fifth one for workers producing sheet steel, a sixth one for workers engaged in the selling of steel, and so on for possibly hundreds of groups. Similarly, the workers in an auto plant might be subdivided by numerous stages of production and assembly.) Each BOAL was put in charge of its own equipment, told to elect its own workers' council or management board, was to appoint its own manager, and was authorized, within its narrow realm, to make all the entrepreneurial decisions previously made at the enterprise level. Thus, the enterprise as a whole was transformed into an *association of independent BOALs,* and it became necessary to coordinate their separately planned activities.

**The Coordination of Activities Within Enterprises.**  After each BOAL has drawn up its own input and output plan, it is to share the information with the other affected parties in the enterprise. (Obviously, the iron ore input to be used by the raw steel BOAL must correspond to the iron ore output planned by the iron ore transportation BOAL. Similarly, the installation of new equipment by the tire-producing BOAL must be synchronized with the increased demand for tires by the tire-assembling BOAL.) After the sharing of information, plans are to be adjusted by mutual consultation, and different BOALs are to draw up **self-management agreements** or **SMAs** that spell out their mutual obligations to one another. Typically, the SMAs are legally binding five-year contracts specifying quantities to be delivered, "transfer prices" to be paid by one BOAL to the other, or pricing formulas to be applied at the time of delivery. Thus, each BOAL has its own revenue and costs and, consequently, its own residual income that it can allocate according to the three options discussed in an earlier section.

**The Coordination of Activities among Enterprises.**  Enterprises, in turn, reach similar SMAs with other enterprises after a similar process of information sharing and bargaining. Besides fixing the deliveries of products, such agreements might involve profit-sharing joint ventures, interenterprise loans, mergers, joint research, and more.

**The Extension of Self-Management Beyond Enterprises.** As already noted, the principle of self-management was extended to other groupings of people, such as those working in hospitals, post offices, schools, or government offices in general. They also acquire inputs and supply outputs that can be arranged through bargaining. An example is voluntary organizations of producers and consumers that provide all kinds of public goods and that are called **communities of interest.**

**The Pursuit of Macroeconomic Goals.** Even the pursuit of macroeconomic goals has been linked with the national network of bargaining. Consider balance of payments or inflation targets, matters of income distribution among the republics or ethnic groups, the geographic placement of new investments, or the relative growth of the private versus the public sector. The central government has effectively abdicated its power to make and enforce laws or regulations on these matters. Perhaps because of his fear that any *imposed* solution to sensitive issues of this type would tear apart the nation, especially after his death, Tito suggested that interested economic, social, and political groups negotiate **social compacts** or **SCs** with one another. These SCs are consensual statements on macroeconomic policy objectives that establish people's mutual obligations if specified goals are to be reached. For example, the League of Communists might arrange for a meeting of local and republican government officials with representatives of large enterprises, industry associations (which are groups of enterprises), and economic chambers (which are groups of industry associations) to hammer out a way to hold next year's inflation to 10 percent. Only upon unanimous agreement by all involved would such a compact be signed and become law. Thus, the Communist Party, Tito figured, might become the "institutional glue" to hold the country together. Analytical Example 9.1, "An Incomes Policy," provides an example of what Tito had in mind.

# An Assessment

We can once again employ the criteria of chapters 2 through 4 to assess the performance of the Yugoslav economy.

## Full Employment

The Yugoslavs have confirmed the worst fears of the Soviet enemies of reform that the income-maximizing behavior of independent socialist firms in a market economy might turn hidden unemployment into open unemployment. The official unemployment rate has in fact steadily risen over time: from 2.2 percent in 1952 to 7.6 percent in 1967 to 12 percent in 1980 and higher still. In addition, anywhere from half a million to a million Yugoslavs have been employed in Western Europe. Had they been home, the statistics would have been worse.

Although exacerbated by the peculiar ethnic frictions within Yugoslavia (which make it next to impossible for an unemployed Croat to fill an available job in Macedonia, for example), much of this unemployment seems to have resulted from the type of incentives associated with the worker-managed firm. As has been noted earlier, workers in Yugoslavia's socialist firms do not receive wages, but are free to distribute the firm's residual income in whatever fashion they like. Whatever the actual distribution turns out to be, they have an incentive to maximize the residual income *per worker,* and that desire can easily lead them into a policy of not replacing workers who have quit, retired, or died.

To see what is involved, consider again Table 8.1, "Crucial Data for the Input Decision," on page 212. A capitalist firm run for the benefit of its owner, as well as a socialist firm following the Lange rules of behavior, would attempt to maximize *total profit.* Thus, it would hire a number of workers that would equate the falling marginal value product of labor with the wage of labor. That came to five workers in our earlier example and produced (for the capitalist owner or the people as a whole, respectively) a total profit of $5,000 a season: 9,000 bushels times $5 per bushel yielded $45,000 of total revenue; fixed costs of $15,000 plus variable costs of $25,000 (five workers times $5,000 per season) came to $40,000 of total cost. Thus, the five workers employed, should they have found themselves in a Yugoslav socialist firm, could have paid to each one of themselves (in place of the $5,000 in wages) a residual income share of $45,000 − $15,000 = $30,000, divided by 5, or $6,000. Now note what would happen if one of the workers retired: Output would fall to 8,000 bushels, hence revenue to $40,000. Fixed input costs would remain at $15,000, making for a residual income of $25,000 and a per-worker share of $25,000 divided by 4, or $6,250. This is a $250 gain for each of the remaining workers. Surely, the remaining workers would not care to replace their retired colleague. Something like this, perhaps, has happened in Yugoslavia over the years. The possibility is illustrated in Figure 9.1, "Employment Levels in the Democratic Versus Autocratic Firm."

## Technical Efficiency

The incidence of technical inefficiency has been high. For example, as a result of an extreme fragmentation of the land (the average private farm holds eight acres in nine separate plots), productivity in Yugoslavia's private agriculture has been unusually low. It has been estimated that 30 percent of the agricultural labor force could easily be withdrawn without any loss in output.

Since the reforms of the 1970s (which carried decentralization to its outer limits), a similar problem has been widely noted in the socialist nonagricultural sector. The system of BOALs and SMAs has absorbed enormous amounts of time and energy and has led to an incredible duplication of administrative personnel. Without doubt, there has occurred a significant trade-off of more democracy for fewer goods. Close-Up 9.1, "A Change of Hearts," provides a fascinating glance into a Yugoslav factory that confronted the issue.

**Figure 9.1** Employment Levels in the Democratic Versus Autocratic Firm

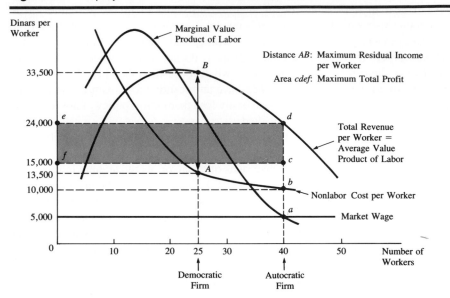

This graph depicts a firm in the short run, similar to the one discussed in Table 8.1 on page 212. It employs a fixed quantity of nonlabor inputs but can use varying numbers of workers. Given eventually diminishing returns to labor and a market-determined output price, the average and marginal value product of labor curves can be derived as shown. Given the market prices of the fixed inputs, the curve of nonlabor costs per worker can be derived as well. Given these identical circumstances, the number of workers employed would differ, depending on managerial incentives:

(1) Let the firm be run autocratically by an appointed manager who is charged by private owners (under capitalism) or by a central planning board (under Lange's socialism) to hire labor at the market wage and to maximize *total profit*. The marginal value product of labor will be equated with the market wage at *a*, 40 workers will be employed, and the maximum total profit will equal shaded area *cdef*. (Point *c* shows the sum of labor plus nonlabor costs per worker.)

(2) Let the firm be self-managed by workers. They will wish to maximize *residual income per worker*. This occurs when 25 workers are employed, which will maximize the difference between per-worker total revenue and per-worker nonlabor cost (as *AB*). Should the firm have 40 workers in it initially, it would over time reduce its workforce to 25.

## Economic Efficiency

So far as economic efficiency is concerned, the situation is far removed from that depicted in the Lange model of market socialism. Consider this: The Yugoslav worker-managed firm tends to maximize residual income per worker, rather than total profit (a matter illustrated in Figure 9.1). Hence, the Yugoslav socialist firm cannot be relied upon to employ a number of workers such that the declining marginal value product of labor equals the market price of labor (there is no such thing). Therefore, the mechanism envisioned by Oskar Lange, and applied in the

Chapter 8 discussion of the first Pareto condition, does not operate in Yugoslavia. Hence, the marginal physical product of labor producing a given good in one firm is equal to that of identical labor used in any other such firm only by the sheerest of coincidences. One firm, as in our earlier example, might maximize residual income per worker (at $6,250 each) by employing 4 workers with a marginal physical product of 1,000 bushels per season; another may be employing 41 workers with a residual income per worker of $500 and a marginal physical product of 600 bushels. Even though transfer of 1 worker from the second firm to the first would raise national output by 400 bushels, the workers of the first firm, as we saw, would have no reason to hire the newcomer (since per-worker residual income would then fall to $6,000). Nevertheless, the second firm, if it had the chance, might be delighted to dismiss a worker (into unemployment), for this might increase the residual income available for each of the remaining workers.

Figure 9.2, "Economic Inefficiency in a System of Worker-Managed Firms," illustrates the problem with a different example. This sort of situation has been

**Figure 9.2**　Economic Inefficiency in a System of Worker-Managed Firms

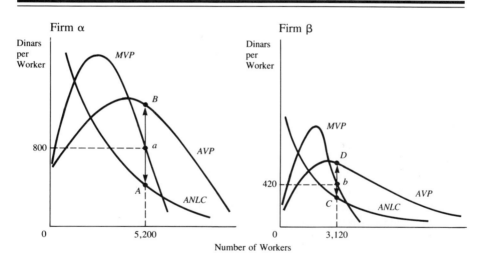

This graph illustrates the behavior of two Yugoslav firms producing the same product. They are endowed with different amounts of capital and natural resources; each is trying to maximize *residual income per worker* (the difference between the average value product of labor, AVP, and the average nonlabor cost, ANLC). Thus, firm α maximizes *AB* by employing 5,200 workers; firm β maximizes *CD* with 3,120 workers. Neither firm has an incentive to use more or less labor. Yet, economic inefficiency prevails: Labor's marginal value product (which is of no interest to either firm) equals 800 dinar in α (according to point *a*); it equals 420 dinar in β (point *b*). Given a product price of, say, 20 dinars, the marginal physical products of labor equal (800/20) equals 40 units of output and (420/20) equals 21 units of output, respectively. According to Pareto's first condition, one could move a worker from β to α and raise overall output by 40 − 21 equals 19 units.

widespread. Labor mobility inside Yugoslavia has been incredibly low, equaling at most 1 percent of the labor force annually.

The same peculiar incentives, as well as ethnic frictions, have produced a similar immobility of capital. As we have seen, workers lose ownership of their principal when they invest in their own firms, but they can at least hope to gain future additions to income. If they invested in *another* firm (where the return might be much higher), they would lose all rights to a return (because it would belong to the workers of *that* firm). This problem could conceivably be overcome by income-sharing joint ventures with other firms, but such SMAs have been rare, indeed.

Many other Pareto conditions have been violated as well. The recent system of social compacts in particular seems to have encouraged regional self-sufficiency. As a result, many output-raising opportunities that involve interrepublican or international trade have been missed. Indeed, in the early 1980s, a government *Commission for Problems of Economic Stabilization,* headed by Central Committee member Sergej Kraigher, issued a series of reports. It complained of the inefficiency caused by regional barriers to resource mobility and even argued for a replacement of the inefficient system of all-sided bargaining by a unified market system.

## Economic Growth

The Yugoslavs have managed to achieve fairly high rates of economic growth, but, as in the Soviet Union, these have been declining. The real GNP rose at rates close to 7 percent per year in the 1950–1965 period, at around 5 percent per year till 1980, and at anywhere from $-1$ to $+2$ percent per year since. The strategy has been one of extensive growth, almost entirely due to heavy investment. For many years, some 30 percent of the GNP consisted of investment goods; after the reforms of the 1970s, the percentage was pushed even higher. The reluctance of workers to reinvest their residual income has been overcome by a variety of devices, notably government intervention in local decision making and the pursuit of appropriate macroeconomic policies. These have involved heavy taxes (on the firms' capital endowment, their sales, the residual income, and the workers' personal income) and easy money (banks have linked the availability of investment funds to the workers' own reinvestment).

## Economic Equity

Opinion surveys indicate that egalitarianism is of great importance to Yugoslavs. This is not surprising given the peasant origin of most Yugoslavs and the long-standing egalitarian ethos of the traditional Yugoslav village. At the same time, and despite the marketization of the economy, the League of Communists has continued to preach the Marxian virtues of ''giving to the best of one's ability'' and of ''taking only according to one's need.'' Not so long ago, a Yugoslav leader recalled how Marx had looked upon socialism as a period of transition, during which a new type of selfless human being would be formed. He recalled Lenin's enthusiasm about the *subbotniks,* workers who would forego material incentives and perform volunteer labor on Saturdays. He noted Lenin's warning that the socialist revolution against the bourgeoisie had to be followed by another one, much more difficult, but much more important, in which all people turned into subbotniks, overcame the habits left by accursed capitalism, and achieved victory over their own selfishness. Only when *that* revolution was won would reversion to capitalism be impossible, would the revolution be invincible. Thus, even after three decades of market socialism, Party leaders were promoting a major expansion of youth brigades. In these, young people, aged 16 to 26, would voluntarily perform heavy manual labor for the state. To develop the spirit of unity and socio-political consciousness, they said, the traditional virtues of collective sacrifice and hard labor must be kept alive.

Yet, how different reality has been! The actual distribution of income has been anything but equal and certainly has not reflected need. There have been significant income differentials within firms, based on "contribution." There have been enormous income differentials among enterprises, based in part on their different historical endowment with capital and natural resources. (As another look at Figure 9.2 confirms, the lucky workers of firm $\alpha$ receive a residual income of $AB$; the unlucky workers of $\beta$ receive $CD$.) Additional differentials have arisen among industries, based on market conditions: Workers whose enterprises happen to have been favored by rising demand or that hold monopoly power have gained higher income (through higher prices) than other workers not so favored.

As a result, there are now significant income differentials within enterprises, among enterprises, among industries, among regions. (Incomes in the north are above the national average; incomes in the south, below it. In 1975, a per-capita income index ranged from 33 in Kosovo to 100 for Yugoslavia as a whole to 202 in Slovenia.)

Given a general perception of injustice, it is not surprising that workers' councils have attempted to improve the relative income position of workers in their firms by: (a) pushing for higher prices of their firms' products (which might raise total revenue and, thus, the residual income) and (b) financing investment with bank loans to the maximum extent possible (which allows the residual income to become personal income).

As a result of this type of behavior, Yugoslavia has experienced increasingly serious rates of inflation. The annual inflation rate has risen from a mere 1.5 percent in 1956 to about 10 percent in the late 1960s and about 15 percent in the late 1970s. By 1980, it was 80 percent; by 1987, 140 percent. So far, an attempt to stem the problem with social compacts has not been successful. See Analytical Example 9.1, "An Incomes Policy."

## Alienation

We consider, finally, the major forms of alienation first introduced in Chapter 4.

**From the Self.**  Yugoslavs, in contrast to their Soviet brethren, seem to have considerably more freedom to shape the nature of their personal lives. For one thing, a significant private sector exists in the economy. Therefore, substantially wider opportunities exist for individuals to live their lives according to their own preferences. This liberal attitude toward individualism has also been reflected in other aspects of life: Most significant among these is the fact that virtually all Yugoslav citizens—unlike the citizens of any other East European country—are free to travel abroad and to return at will. Not unrelated is their freedom to read Western publications and to enjoy art and music of their own choice.

**From Other People.**   When it comes to people's relations with one another, the record is mixed, but undoubtedly superior to that of the Soviet Union. *Consumer sovereignty* is fairly complete so far as the *make-up* of the consumption portion of the GNP is concerned. Firms cater to the wishes of consumers as expressed in market demand. So far as the *size* of the consumption portion is concerned, individual consumers have considerably less power. On the one hand, governmental units at various levels have consistently pushed for an extremely high rate of saving and investment, using taxation and persuasion for the purpose. Even beyond that, any individual can easily be forced—through the majority vote of fellow workers— to save more or to save less than is preferred. There is no unified national loanable funds market through which the marginal time preferences of savers can be equated with the marginal time productivities of investors.

*Worker sovereignty,* argue the advocates of Yugoslavia's system of worker self-management, is more complete here than anywhere else in the world. Critics disagree and argue that this is nothing but a myth, that the "mass participation" of workers in management is a sham. Significantly, they say, the self-management system has not emerged as a result of worker initiative; it has been imposed upon workers from above. More than anything else, it is a symbol of national independence that was erected by Tito in order to differentiate himself from Stalin. (Interestingly, to this day worker self-management is anathema to Soviet and all other East European leaders.)

Furthermore, critics argue, it didn't take Yugoslav workers long to realize the inherent *impossibility* of an entire firm's workforce exercising direct control over everything. As a result, Yugoslav workers do *not* manage; management is exercised by professional executives, by what Milovan Djilas has called "the new class." Most ordinary workers do nothing more than vote on occasion; some serve a stint on the workers' council, but these delegates only intervene—selectively, intermittently, and unimportantly—in the management of the director.

Why should this be so? For one thing, the enterprise director has the information necessary to make decisions; it is generated by the director's professional staff of accountants, engineers, lawyers, marketing experts, and more. Council members have to be given information by the director before they can be co-managers. Secondly, the director is professionally qualified to use the information in question; the typical council member is not suited, by education or experience, to interpret the information even if it is made available. Thirdly, the director's position tends to be durable (although appointed for a four-year term, directors are almost always reappointed); the typical worker serves a single two-year term on the council. Fourth, the director is paid to manage and does so full time; the council member is not paid and serves part time.

Is it surprising that director and staff attend all the council meetings at which decisions are made, while many worker delegates are absent? (Workers often feel incompetent or they have other interests, such as family, soccer, do-it-yourself electronics, or playing the cello.) Is it surprising, as a survey showed, that council meetings are dominated by the director, who talks 39 minutes for every 1 minute workers talk? (Workers can't become interested in questions of accounting, engineering, law, or marketing, but they are concerned about their personal income, working conditions, and clean towels in the washroom.) A rare survey (although not a scientific random sample) is fascinating: When asked to rank the degree of power of each, Yugoslav workers ranked top executives first, then the management board, then the chiefs of economic units, then the workers' council, then the foremen, *then* the workers.[3]

In conclusion, critics say, the typical enterprise director is not constrained by the will of the workers, but listens just as much to government, the industry's trade association, the League of Communists, and the secret police as to the workers on the spot. That's why workers so often disagree with the policies of the "worker-managed" firm, gripe continually about "unrepresentative workers' councils," and routinely go out on wildcat strikes!

*Citizen sovereignty* is considerably more extensive in Yugoslavia than in the rest of Eastern Europe. It is true that Yugoslavia is a one-party state and political criticism is taboo. (In 1986, there were some 8,000 political prisoners, including secessionists, pro-Soviet Communists, and a wide range of "anarcho-liberal" film directors, newspaper editors, professors, and writers.) At the same time, there are considerably fewer signs of an all-devouring bureaucracy and the secret police. Note again how Yugoslavs are the only socialist citizens in Eastern Europe who can travel to the West in large numbers—an indicator that is hardly insignificant. Contrast that with the Berlin Wall, and, surely, one must agree that man's alienation from man, if such there be, has reached an entirely different (and more acceptable) order of magnitude in Yugoslavia.

Note also that Tito, as one of his last acts, sought to alleviate future concentrations of power by establishing two collective leadership bodies, the State Presidency and the Communist Party Leadership; in each, the leadership now rotates annually among the six republics and two autonomous provinces.

**From Nature.** Yugoslavia has not particularly distinguished herself by policies to protect the natural environment. Pollution is widespread.

---

[3]Egon Neuberger and Estelle James, "The Yugoslav Self-Managed Enterprise: A Systemic Approach," in Morris Bornstein, ed., *Plan and Market: Economic Reform in Eastern Europe* (New Haven, CT: Yale University Press, 1973), p. 276.

Analytical Example 9.1

## An Incomes Policy

Consider the kind of *social compact* that might put an end to Yugoslavia's inflation. Realizing that, say, a 10-percent increase in everybody's money income accompanied by, say, a mere 3-percent increase in real GNP is a recipe for failure (in that the subsequent inflation is bound to cancel most of people's raises), everyone in the nation might agree to this:

> *Henceforth, each year and in every industry, personal income (called* wages *for short) will be raised only to the extent of the long-run growth in labor productivity in the nation as a whole. In addition, output prices in every industry will be adjusted up or down to ensure that each year the ratio of the industry's contribution to the GNP at current prices to its employment also rises at that long-run trend. This formula will force industries in which labor productivity is rising more rapidly than the long-run national trend to lower prices, while forcing others in which labor productivity is rising at that trend (or less rapidly) to leave their prices unchanged (or to raise them).*

**The Compact Explained.**    Consider Table A, which illustrates a possible social compact of this kind. We assume a goal of stopping inflation at a time when labor productivity in the nation as a whole grows at 3 percent per year. Row 1 lists average annual "wages" paid the workers of three industries in 1987. It also lists their average wages in 1988 if everyone obeys the social compact and receives a 3-percent raise. Row 2 records the hypothetical development of labor productivity for 1987 to 1988.

Evaluating the output per worker at unchanged 1987 prices (to measure real changes), we find the average worker in industry A producing 20 percent more; in industry B, 3 percent more; in industry C, 1 percent more. Thus, the performance of industry B in this year corresponds to the long-run national trend, while industry A is doing better and industry C, much worse.

Row 2 also shows what the average worker's output in 1988 would sell for if the firms involved did not change their 1987 prices. But the social compact requires that labor productivity in each industry (when measured in current prices) rise by 3 percent also. Thus, the 1988 output of the average worker of industry A must sell for 3 percent more than in 1987; that is, for 10,300 dinars, not for 12,000 dinars. This requires a cut in output price. Similarly, the 1988 output of the average employee of industry B or C must sell for 3 percent more than in 1987, and this requires the price policies indicated. Thus, some prices fall, some remain unchanged, and others rise when people follow the social compact. If the 3-percent long-run rise in productivity persists, adherence to such a rule could avoid inflation.

**Problems.**    The hammering out of such a social compact and its subsequent enforcement, however, are difficult. Some groups of workers insist on wage hikes far above the percentage given in row 1; others disagree violently with the price policy percentage given in row 1; others disagree violently with the price policy noted in

**Table A**  A Social Compact to Stop Inflation

| | Industry A 1987 | Industry A 1988 | Industry B 1987 | Industry B 1988 | Industry C 1987 | Industry C 1988 |
|---|---|---|---|---|---|---|
| 1. Wages per worker (*dinars per year*) | 5,000 | 5,150 +3% | 10,000 | 10,300 +3% | 20,000 | 20,600 +3% |
| 2. Contribution to real GNP per worker (*dinars per year at* constant *1987 prices*) | 10,000 | 12,000 +20% | 15,000 | 15,450 +3% | 30,000 | 30,300 +1% |
| | | Prices cut | | Prices unchanged | | Prices raised |
| 3. Contribution to nominal GNP per worker (*dinars per year at* current *prices*) | 10,000 | 10,300 +3% | 15,000 | 15,450 +3% | 30,000 | 30,900 +3% |
| 4. Work force (*thousands*) | 5 | 10 | 30 | 30 | 20 | 21 |
| 5. Total contribution to GNP (*millions of dinars per year at current prices*) = (3) × (4) | 50 | 103 | 450 | 463.5 | 600 | 648.9 |
| 6. Total wages (*millions of dinars per year*) = (1) × (4) | 25 | 51.5 | 300 | 309 | 400 | 432.6 |
| 7. Total nonwage income (*millions of dinars per year*) = (5) − (6) | 25 | 51.5 | 150 | 154.5 | 200 | 216.3 |

noted in row 2. We should not be surprised. Workers do not really want to share equally in the fruits of progress, but that is what the type of social compact discussed here would bring about. Consider rows 4 to 7 of Table A. The entries in row 4 are arbitrary; the rest follow logically. A comparison of the row 6 and 7 entries shows how adherence to the proposed compact would leave the relative shares of wage and nonwage income (that is, workers' personal income versus collective consumption and investment) unchanged over time: In industries B and C, wages are double the amount of nonwage income in both years; in A, they remain equal to the latter. Similarly, as row 1 shows, relative wage rates remain the same among industries: Industry A workers earn half of what industry B workers earn, and a quarter of what industry C workers earn, in both years.

But the existence of Yugoslav inflation stems exactly from the fact that workers are using economic power to *change* relative shares. Therefore, no group of workers that could get a 20-percent wage boost is likely to settle for 3 percent by lowering the prices of its products. In fact, this is the fun of the whole game. On the average, everyone's real income can only rise by 3 percent if the real GNP rises by 3 percent. Yet, everyone can (legitimately) hope to get more by raising money income by more, and by then letting the subsequent inflation decide *whose* excessive claim to a nonexistent part of the real GNP must be canceled.

In fact, the making of social compacts in Yugoslavia is a tortuous process. Since the compacts require unanimity, all bargainers try to hold out for what's best for them. More often than not, the time for action is up before an agreement can be reached. Increasingly, angry workers simply go on strike, but it is unclear against whom they are striking since they are their own bosses! In 1986, some 80,000 workers struck for higher pay; they included bus drivers and coal miners, doctors and school teachers, shipyard workers and vegetable vendors. Even the staff of the Parliament walked off. In 1987, when Prime Minister Branko Mikulic imposed a freeze on worker income, 150,000 workers in 1,000 enterprises walked off the job and asked for his resignation. In 1988, when the inflation rate reached 200 percent, ethnic tensions went from simmer to boil. Yugoslavia became almost unglued as a wave of mass rallies swept the country and Serbian Party Chief Slobodan Milosevic emerged as a potential strongman.

*Sources: The Wall Street Journal,* March 25, 1987, p. 1; *The New York Times,* March 23, 1987, p. A6, November 16, 1987, p. A3, and October 11, 1988, pp. A1 and A12.

## CLOSE-UP 9.1

## A Change of Heart

Ever since the 1970s when decentralization was carried to its outer limits with the creation of intraenterprise BOALs, the 5,000 workers of the Rakovica Motor Works in Belgrade had inhabited a federation made up of 10 duchies. One duchy built engines, another chassis, another transmissions. Maintenance was a duchy, too. So were the accountants and lawyers. So was the mountain resort run by the workers for their holidays. Each BOAL elected its own workers' council but also sent delegates to a central council.

Now consider the general manager trying to draw up a budget. It had to go to the central council, which amended it. Then it went to the other 10 councils, each one of which could veto it. When all the councils had finally passed it, the budget went to a vote of the entire workforce. The process was only slightly more involved than amending the U.S. Constitution.

Any one of the 10 councils had the right to veto any other project as well, whether the building of a new type of tractor or the installation of new machinery. And for every one of these projects, each council had to negotiate a joint-venture deal with all the other councils. Rakovica had 78 such "self-management agreements." When things went smoothly, it took a mere 18,000 man hours a year to negotiate them. In other years, it took much longer, and when workers lost patience with other workers, there were strikes. In 1987, the Rakovica workers had had enough. They voted to scrap their BOALs, the basic building blocks of self-management. Self-management, they complained, had given everyone the capacity to impede and no one the strength to implement. They were hungry for discipline, and they handed their powers to the general manager.

*Source:* Barry Newman, "Change of Heart: Yugoslavia's Workers Find Self-Management Doesn't Make Paradise," *The Wall Street Journal,* March 25, 1987, pp. 1 and 25.

## BIOGRAPHY 9.1   Josip Tito

Josip Broz (1892–1980), later to be known as Tito, was born in Kumrovec, a small village in Croatia, then part of the Austro-Hungarian Empire. His father owned a small farm specializing in cattle, hay, and horses, but reportedly spent most of his time drinking in neighborhood inns. There were 14 other children and, as was customary, Josip was put to work tending cattle at age 12. He moved on to be a waiter in a restaurant, then was apprenticed to a locksmith and metalworker, learning to repair machinery and do fancy ironwork. (A railing Josip made is still part of a staircase proudly shown off in a local district court.)

From age 18 to 21, he traveled widely in the old tradition of wandering journeymen—from Zagreb to Pilsen, from Munich to Vienna. He ended up as a skilled mechanic at a Daimler auto factory. By then he was fluent in German, a member of the metal workers union and of the Social Democratic Party. Drafted during World War I, Josip rose to the rank of sergeant in the Imperial Army, fighting the Russians on the Galician front. Badly wounded and taken prisoner, he ended up in the depths of Russia, working as a POW village mechanic, learning Russian, and taking a Russian wife (the first of many). In 1917, he escaped to join the street fighting in Petrograd—on the side of the Bolsheviks.

He returned to a new Kingdom of Yugoslavia and joined the newly created but illegal Communist Party. Working as a metal worker, he agitated for labor unions, fomented strikes, and distributed Communist literature. It was then, in the 1920s, upon visiting his home village, that he first shaped a vision of a future socialist society of abundance in which each region and nationality would have an equal stake. As he later put it,

> I thought of the day when Kumrovec and thousands of other towns and villages all over Yugoslavia would rouse themselves from backwardness, when young people would at last have a chance in life, a chance to live in peace and happiness and to bring up their families. I did not know when that would happen. But I knew very well that it was worth making every effort and sacrifice to insure that it did happen.

But the police caught up with him; his underground activities brought a five-year jail sentence in 1929. Tito promptly organized a Communist Party unit among the prisoners and spent much of his time reading: Shakespeare, John Stuart Mill, Greek philosophy, and, of course, Marx and Engels. "It was," he recalled, "just like being at a university."

In 1934, Tito moved to Moscow to work for the Comintern, the Communist International. Along with other Communist leaders (G. Dimitrov of Bulgaria, O. Kuusinen of Finland, and P. Togliatti of Italy), he narrowly escaped Stalin's purges. Deeply disillusioned and suspicious of the Russians, he returned to his homeland in 1937 to become Secretary General of Yugoslavia's Communists. Before long, he had built an underground party of some 12,000 members. When World War II broke out, Tito set up headquarters in the mountains of Bosnia and Montenegro, called himself Marshal, and organized his followers—outnumbered and ill-equipped as they were— for what was to be a bitter and protracted guerrilla war against the German invaders and their numerous allies. Tito proved to be a man of great courage; he was ready to die for his beliefs. And from the start he saw the struggle of his partisans as an ideal opportunity "to seize power and to seize it in such a way that the bourgeoisie would never regain it." So it came to be. In 1945, the victorious partisans established a Communist state, and their leader was the only one in Eastern Europe who held something resembling a popular mandate.

Tito used his power with the confident air of a king born to the throne. He governed like a monarch and eventually had himself proclaimed President for Life. Strong-willed and proud, Tito was determined to go his own way, unbending before his opponents. Unlike anyone else in Eastern Europe, he openly defied Stalin during the latter's lifetime and got away with it. As a result, Yugoslavia became the only East European nation to follow its own road to socialism. Domestically, it embraced the system of worker self-management discussed in this chapter. In foreign affairs, it pursued a policy of nonalignment with respect to the two superpower blocs, making Tito, along with Egypt's Nasser and India's Nehru, an influential leader of the third world movement. (Even late in his life, after successive Soviet leaders had tried in vain to lure Yugoslavia back into the Soviet bloc, Tito worked hard to counter Castro's attempts to tilt the third world movement toward the Soviet Union.)

Tito lived like a monarch, too. He owned numerous palaces, a personal island, the famous Blue Train. He was always surrounded by an awed retinue, and he was ruthless to those who defied him. (Even his closest partisan comrades were not immune from his wrath. Milovan Djilas and Aleksandr Rankovic, upon criticizing Tito, promptly lost their freedom and their posts, but not their lives.) Tito was quite vain (he dyed his hair) and he was drawn to smart clothes, fine food, and other touches of stylish living. Thus, he loved to wear imperial uniforms with white gloves and gold braid, go to black-tie dinners, and drive luxury cars. He took pleasure in smoking large cigars, sipping Chivas Regal, and dancing with beautiful women. (In 1986, his last wife was suing the government for Tito's estate that had been declared public property: his cars and yachts, his houses and vineyards, his horses and medals.)

Yet, Comrade Tito, the peasant son, never lost the ability to empathize with ordinary people. Life, he argued, should be a pleasurable experience; people should not be made to suffer endlessly for a distant vision of a better life. And so he transformed Yugoslavia into a little bright spot amid the general grayness of Eastern Europe. Throughout his life, he bound together Yugoslavia's diverse and rivalrous ethnic groups with his sheer charisma and the old partisan slogan "Brotherhood and Unity."

*Sources: Who's Who in the Socialist Countries* (New York: K. G. Saur, 1978), p. 624; *The New York Times,* May 5, 1980, pp. 1, 12, and 13; *The Wall Street Journal,* May 8, 1986, p. 1.

# Summary

1. The first socialist market economy came into existence in the 1950s, in Yugoslavia, following a brief and unhappy experiment with Stalin's economic model. Following his rift with Stalin, Tito reinterpreted the Marxian meaning of "workers running the economy under Socialism" and of the "eventual withering away of the state." Outside agriculture (which he privatized) and apart from tiny firms, Tito instituted a system of socialist enterprises separately managed by the workers employed therein and facing one another in markets. He abolished the central planning board and initiated a process of shifting political power from the central government toward lower-level governments.

    Before long, each socialist firm became a representative democracy: Power emanated from the workers as a group, who appointed and supervised managers via elected workers' councils and management boards.

    A number of characteristics distinguish the Yugoslav worker-managed firms from autocratically run firms: (a) Founders are separated from subsequent decision making, (b) the workers in charge are likely to maximize the residual income per worker, and (c) the workers in charge are reluctant to use the residual income for reinvestment or collective consumption; they prefer its distribution as personal income.

    Starting in the 1970s, Tito moved to downgrade markets as coordinating devices, just as he had once before downgraded central planning. He set out to create an extended system of intraenterprise, interenterprise, and interregional bargaining that would coordinate the separate activities of people by establishing a consensus.

2. An assessment of the Yugoslav economy shows the following: Unemployment has been severe, possibly exacerbated by incentives peculiar to worker collectives. Technical inefficiency has been high, especially in agriculture and, elsewhere, as a result of the bargaining society reforms of the 1970s. Economic inefficiency has been rampant, once again as a result of the incentives peculiar to the worker-managed firm (which erect insurmountable barriers to resource mobility). This has been exacerbated by ethnic frictions and, lately, the replacement of market relations by bargaining. There have been fairly high rates of economic growth (mainly due to heavy investment), but they have been declining. Despite a professed commitment to egalitarianism, income differentials have been enormous. Attempts to correct them have led to increasingly serious rates of inflation. Alienation undoubtedly has been reduced relative to, say, the Soviet Union, but it has hardly been abolished. Even the unique feature of the Yugoslav economy, worker self-management, may not provide as much worker sovereignty as is alleged.

## Key Terms

basic organizations of associated labor
  (BOALs)
communities of interest
enterprise director
management board
political factories

residual income
self-management agreements (SMAs)
social compacts (SCs)
workers' council
worker self-management

## Questions and Problems

1. "Most *new* firms in Yugoslavia are founded by communes (the local governments). This is not surprising because communes (unlike such other potential founders as existing enterprises or groups of individuals) *do* get a return on their investment."
   What do you think?
2. Have another look at Table 8.1, "Crucial Data for the Input Decision," on page 212. Imagine the firm involved were a worker-managed Yugoslav firm. Derive the kinds of data needed to determine the maximum residual income per worker.
3. Using the data derived in problem 2, illustrate the workers' ideal employment level graphically.
4. Consider Figure 9.1, "Employment Levels in the Democratic Versus Autocratic Firm," on page 250. Determine:
   a. The size of the autocratic firm's maximum total profit.
   b. The collective labor income in the democratic firm if it has 25 workers.
   c. The collective labor income in the democratic firm if it has 40 workers.
5. Consider Figure 9.2, "Economic Inefficiency in a System of Worker-Managed Firms," on page 251. It has been argued: (a) that the inefficiency argument (based on labor immobility) may well be wrong and (b) that the income disparity shown (*AB* versus *CD*) may grow over time. What do you think?
6. "In a capitalist system of enterprise autocracy, workers are used by capital for the sake of profit. In a socialist system of enterprise democracy, capital is used by workers to serve the community."
   What do you think?
7. "An increase in product price will have a different effect on employment in the autocratic firm than in the democratic firm."
   What do you think?
8. "The Yugoslav worker-managed firm vindicates a fear expressed long ago by von Mises: Socialism is the abolition of rational economy" (see page 205).
   What do you think?

9. "There is a great inequity between old-timers and new workers in the Yugoslav worker-managed firm."

What do you think?

10. "The whole idea that Yugoslav workers try to maximize *residual income per worker* is absurd. Workers have a whole range of goals, and different workers in a given firm have different goals."

What do you think?

## Selected Readings

Cole, G. D. H. *Guild Socialism Restated* (London: Leonard Parsons, 1920). Advocates worker control of all economic, social, and political organizations.

Dirlam, Joel, and James Plummer. *An Introduction to the Yugoslav Economy* (Columbus: Merrill, 1973). A textbook.

Djilas, Milovan. *The New Class: An Analysis of the Communist System* (New York: Praeger, 1957).

Djilas, Milovan. *The Unperfect Society: Beyond the New Class* (New York: Harcourt Brace Jovanovich, 1969).

Djilas, Milovan. *Tito: The Story from the Inside* (New York: Harcourt Brace Jovanovich, 1980). The one-time guerrilla fighter and co-founder of socialist Yugoslavia becomes one of Tito's most severe critics.

Fusfeld, Daniel R. "Labor-Managed and Participatory Firms: A Review Article," *Journal of Economic Issues,* September 1983, pp. 769–89. A thorough review of the literature, extending beyond Yugoslavia to the worldwide experience.

Horvat, Branko. *Self-Governing Socialism,* 2 vols. (White Plains, NY: International Arts and Sciences Press, 1975).

Horvat, Branko. *The Yugoslav Economic System: The First Labor-Managed Economy in the Making* (White Plains, NY: International Arts and Sciences Press, 1976).

Horvat, Branko. *The Political Economy of Socialism* (Armonk, NY: M. E. Sharpe, 1982).

Johansen, Leif. "The Bargaining Society and the Inefficiency of Bargaining," *Kyklos,* 3, 1979, pp. 497–522. Shows that bargaining leads to worse allocations of resources than does central planning or the competitive market system.

Joint Economic Committee. U.S. Congress (Washington, D.C.: U.S. Government Printing Office). Numerous essays deal with all aspects of the Yugoslav economy.

   a. *Economic Developments in Countries of Eastern Europe: A Compendium of Papers* (1970), especially pp. 608–34.

   b. *Reorientation and Commercial Relations of the Economies of Eastern Europe* (1974), especially pp. 725–43.

   c. *East European Economies Post-Helsinki* (1977), especially pp. 479–502 and 941–96.

   d. *East European Economies: Slow Growth in the 1980's* (1986), especially volume 3.

Pejovich, Svetozar. *The Market-Planned Economy of Yugoslavia* (Minneapolis, MN: University of Minnesota Press, 1966). A textbook.

Singleton, Fred. *A Short History of the Yugoslav Peoples* (Cambridge, England: Cambridge University Press, 1985).

Tawney, R. H. *The Radical Tradition* (New York: Random House, 1964). First published in 1918; advocates the replacement of industrial autocracy by industrial democracy.

Ward, Benjamin N. "The Firm in Illyria: Market Syndicalism," *American Economic Review,* September 1958, pp. 566–89. The first serious theoretical treatment of the self-managed enterprise. See also his *The Socialist Economy* (New York: Random House, 1967).

Zaniovich, George M. *The Development of Socialist Yugoslavia* (Baltimore, MD: Johns Hopkins University Press, 1968). Contains a history of the Yugoslav break with the Soviet bloc.

Županov, Josip. "The Yugoslav Enterprise," in Morris Bornstein, *Comparative Economic Systems: Models and Cases,* 3d ed. (Homewood, IL: Irwin, 1974), pp. 172–92. A leading Yugoslav industrial sociologist compares the performance of the self-managed Yugoslav enterprise in theory to that in reality.

## Computer Programs

The SYSTEMS personal computer diskette that accompanies this book contains one program of interest to this chapter: Program 9, "Market Socialism: The Yugoslav Case," provides 12 multiple-choice questions about Chapter 9, along with immediate responses to incorrect answers.

# CHAPTER 10

# *Communal Socialism: An Alternative?*

In this chapter, a fascinating question is explored: Might there be a viable alternative to both the economy dominated by the central plan and the economy held together by a network of markets? Could the actions of large numbers of people be coordinated by neither the threat of punishment nor the lure of money rewards but by something altogether different, perhaps even love? There are certainly some who claim this is so. They reject as unbearable a society in which government bureaucracy, central plans, and a hierarchical command structure dominate people's lives, and they reject equally a society in which market exchange and the pursuit of monetary gain play any significant role. They abhor Stalin's type of world but Tito's as well; theirs is a vision of a different kind.

Theirs is a vision of an **intentional community,** a voluntary and deliberate association of a people who value togetherness above all and seek to extend intimate, sharing relationships beyond the immediate family. They want to establish a whole new way of life in which all barriers among people are broken down and individuals merge with other individuals to become as one. Two significant obstacles to such a union are usually identified: the institutional barrier of private property in the means of production *as well as consumption* and the psychological barrier surrounding the ego steeped in the "deadly sin" of selfishness.

Ask these people for a blueprint of their society and never will you get one. They will talk about "mass participation in all production decisions" when the means of production are collectively owned and about everyone "taking according to need" when the means of consumption are collectively owned. They will talk about people with transformed egos "contributing to the maximum of their ability" to the creation of goods, but "not needing very much" in the way of goods. They will talk of people being guided by **internal incentives** (stimuli arising within, such as feelings of joy or guilt) that compel everyone in the new society continually to serve the social body with which they become one. They will assure us of the absence of **external incentives** (stimuli coming from other people, such as criticism and punishment or praise and money rewards) that ordinarily motivate people to take or not to take an action. And they will paint an idyllic but vague picture of a new world inhabited by loving brothers and sisters who live happy and joyful lives of creative leisure and work. These new-world people, it is often imagined, will not have ugly cities and highways and parking lots, nor strip mines and oil derricks and transmission lines, nor developments of ticky-tacky houses and endless commercial strips, nor will they pollute the world and kill off species of animals. They will live in the country surrounded by fields and gardens, and they will work where they live. They will be self-reliant, producing a whole variety of goods in small workshops, at their own pace, with hands *and* brain and *simple* tools. Thus they will develop themselves—physically, intellectually, artistically. Their days will be filled with happy song!

Often those who are ready to live in this way have been inspired by the writings of others who have also dreamed of **utopia,** the good place that is no place, in which people would lead a perfectly fulfilling existence, in which human welfare would be higher and longer lasting than ever before. Among these inspirational writings have been those about the Hebrew prophets (Amos, Hosea, Isaiah, Jeremiah, Ezekiel, and, finally, Jesus), those of Greek philosophers (such as Plato's *Republic*), and others by the fathers of the Christian church (such as St. Augustine's *City of God*). They have included More's *Utopia* (1516), Campanella's *City of the Sun* (1602), Andreae's *Christianopolis* (1619), Bacon's *New Atlantis* (1624), and Harrington's *Oceana* (1656). In more recent times, an equally strong influence has been exercised by the 19th century writings of François Babeuf, Louis Blanc, Etienne Cabet, Charles Fourier, Robert Owen (who invented the term *socialism*), and, above all, "the last of the Hebrew prophets," Karl Marx (Biography 15.1).

While some of these writers have imagined the perfect society in faraway places—above the clouds, on inaccessible islands, in lost valleys, or in outer space—others have suggested the possibility of creating it right here among ourselves. And they or their followers have set out to put such dreams into effect. There have been many hundreds of such attempts. To name a few, consider the Hutterite communities (founded in 1528 in Moravia and still surviving in the Dakotas and Western Canada today), or the True Inspirationists of the Amanas (1842–1932), or the Perfectionists of Oneida (1848–1880), or the kibbutzim of Israel, Japan, and Tanzania (all founded during this century). More often than not, however, the founders of such communities have ended up sadder, but wiser, with their dreams in ruins. Few intentional communities survive for long, for they often attempt the impossible: to create their new world with the unchanged human material of the old. It is easy to find hundreds of examples of failure. The next section, however, presents two counterexamples of small-scale intentional communities that have survived, even though they have not realized each and every one of the features just described.

# Small-Scale Communal Experiments

America's Bruderhof and Israel's kibbutz represent two successful examples of communal socialism on a small scale. We consider each of them in turn.

## The Bruderhof

The Bruderhof is an intentional community held together by a fundamental Anabaptist type of Christianity. In the 1980s, it had a population of 750 persons who lived in three federated "colonies" in rural Connecticut, New York, and Pennsylvania. The community was founded in Germany in 1920 and has survived migration to the United Kingdom, Paraguay, and Uruguay and, finally, the United States. The unifying belief of its members concerns a world gripped by a death struggle between good and evil. God leads the forces of good and will win. Humans can help by emptying themselves of ego (symbolized through crucifixion and death), allowing themselves to be filled by the Holy Spirit (symbolized through resurrection) and bearing witness in every one of their acts, however commonplace, to the spirit of goodness. The members consider themselves bound together by virtue of having a common Father in heaven and, thus, love each other as brothers and sisters. Theirs is one large family: They own all things together, they make all decisions together, they have their meals together, they work together, they raise their children together, they meet almost every night together, they spend their entire lives together—within the geographic confines of their estate (their *hof* ).

**All Things in Common.**    When people become full members, they sign over all their property to the community irrevocably. Even the smallest piece of *personal* property! And they get nothing back should they ever leave. Except for a few individuals, members never see money again. (A visitor noted that a nine-year-old child did not recognize a dime.) Everyone's material needs (as defined by the membership) are freely provided, regardless of whether the recipient is of working age or too young or too old to work. People live in family units and are assigned their own apartments within the hof. The community is not self-reliant in the production of food but buys food from the outside world (not all of it). But this is done in bulk by one member. The rest simply take supplies from a communal kitchen for breakfast, snacks, and two suppers a week, which they have in their apartments (but, as they say, "we never take much"). All lunches and five suppers a week are held jointly in a communal dining room. They are festive, joyful, and leisurely occasions. Tables are beautifully bedecked with tablecloths, china, candles, and flowers. Songs are sung; music is played by members.

Clothes are made by members or bought communally in bulk, like food. Individual members make up a "necessity list" twice a year and are assigned used clothing. Once a year, they make up a "birthday list" and get new clothing. Other items, ranging from bobby pins and books to craft and school supplies to shampoo and toys, are also bought on the outside by a communal purchaser and handed to individuals upon request.

Pre–high school education is provided within the community. High schoolers are sent by bus to public high schools nearby. For selected individuals, the community also pays for outside college education.

The means of production are, of course, also jointly owned. Members own a large piece of land in a beautiful setting. They do some farming, but their major activities involve two small industries located on the premises, Community Playthings and Plough Publishing. The former is a highly successful enterprise that turns out children's furniture and large wooden toys, widely sold to kindergartens. Sales went from $45,000 in 1954 to well over $1 million per year in the early 1960s. At that time, the membership decided it was getting too rich and too much involved in business; so production has been cut deliberately since 1965. Characteristically, not believing in private property and competition, the community did not patent its highly successful products. As a result, other firms have made exact copies of them. The publishing business is low key. It produces only two to three religious books per year, as well as a few Christmas and children's books.

**Destroying the Old Self.**    When people become members, they must give up more than their material possessions. Most importantly, they must commit themselves to a lifelong struggle against their old selves by submitting, without qualification, to the will of the community forever. Such loyalty to the community must come above that even to one's own family. This alone, it is said, can open up the individual to a crucial death and rebirth experience: The old ego must die, a new creature must be born. This is likened to the process of drying walnuts in preparation for shelling. When a walnut is green, it is impossible to remove its shell without causing serious damage to the kernel. Shell and kernel form an inseparable whole. After drying out, however, the shell becomes brittle and separates from the kernel. A light tap will split it, revealing the kernel in perfection. The community is there to help individuals get rid of the shell of attitudes that reveal the presence of "seven deadly sins" of pride and covetousness, lust and anger, gluttony, envy, and sloth. And then the community is ready to let the kernel of the new self merge with the community. This merging of identities is seen as a glorious moment, releasing intense feelings of enthusiasm and joy and peace and uniting the individual not only with present-day brothers and sisters, but also with all the apostles and saints throughout history!

To achieve this goal of ego loss and ego merging, the community relies heavily on "thought reform." People are kept from outside influences as much as possible. There is no TV; only on rare occasions does one visit outside movies or concerts. Once a year, there is an open house; otherwise, outside friendships are strongly discouraged. One doesn't normally take political stands; one doesn't vote in the world at large. (Some members did participate in nonviolent antiwar and civil rights demonstrations, however.) And within the community, everyone is supposed to watch the words, gestures, and mannerisms of everyone, including one's own. Criticism, including self-criticism, is encouraged, but there are strict rules: No gossiping ever behind a person's back. When pride, covetousness, lust, anger, gluttony, envy, or sloth show themselves in a person, it is the duty of others to discuss this face to face. The critics are to be humble; the criticized are to be thankful and repentant. Repentance is to be followed by forgiveness, and the incident is never to be mentioned again. For persistent behavior problems of this type, there are other methods: intensive counseling, a change in work assignment to minimize contact with others, physical isolation, and even expulsion. Ideally, long before expulsion, the offender is moved to public confession, met by forgiveness. In spite of confession and forgiveness, lapses occur. So the same battle has to be fought again and again. The Holy Spirit, alas, is not a possession or a permanent resident, but only a visitor who comes to see those who are worthy, it is said.

**The "Dictatorship of the Holy Spirit."**   Ultimate decision-making powers rest with an assembly of full members in good standing, the Brotherhood. (It excludes seriously ill or senile members, members excluded for punishment, and novices who have not taken their full membership vows, as well as children, teenagers, and guests.) The Brotherhood meets almost every evening for two to three hours. Factionalism, interest groups, and majority votes are not allowed. It is assumed that "one right decision" preexists on all matters (God's will) and the problem is only to find it. No single person can find it. Therefore, each person must be involved in each decision and must speak his or her mind even if all others are contradicted. Only unanimous decisions are made.

More often than not, however, people are tired after a day's work. Sometimes they hate to express opinions that might ultimately not agree with the "right" decision (thereby proving how out of touch they were with the Holy Spirit!). Thus, they gladly delegate authority and end up giving near dictatorial powers to various executives: a Chief Servant, two Servants of the Word, a Steward, six Witness Brothers, and six Housemothers. These executives typically make the decisions about housing, food, clothing, and education. They do the spiritual counseling. And they assign people to work, 48 hours a week, including everyone capable, even short-term guests.

Men are usually assigned for months or years; women are frequently changed around. Jobs considered unpleasant (waiting on tables and washing dishes) are rotated among all. Some jobs mostly go to men: working in the woodshop and maintaining buildings and grounds. Some jobs mostly go to women: apportioning clothes and other supplies, cooking, laundering, sewing, cleaning public areas, and minding babies in the "Baby House" (where all babies go for about eight hours each day). Other jobs go to both men and women: working in the publishing office, the archives, and the school. Only parents with a newborn child are exempt from work for six weeks, as are mothers for one hour in the morning (to clean their apartments) and for one hour in the afternoon (to visit the children).

**Assessment.**   How does the Bruderhof compare with the vague vision noted earlier in this chapter? Clearly, it displays some of the features dreamed about, but not all. In fact, even if not in theory, there is a lot of hierarchical decision making about consumption and production within the community. And even though it does not use money within, the community is integrated with the market economy that surrounds it, selling its own products to it and buying others from it.

It is also true that people are humble and selfless when it comes to taking consumption goods. But do they give according to ability, without external incentives? Internal ones are, indeed, encouraged, as we have seen. The "new person" always seeks to bear witness, even when digging potatoes or arranging the dinner table! Such a person always does a good and perfect job and looks for even better ways. But external incentives have not died out. True enough, no one gets money, and even praise is not allowed (in that it fosters pride), but some people have high status by virtue of their offices. People are also punished by temporary exclusion from various functions, and they can even be expelled (during a "great crisis" from 1959 to 1962, half the membership was lost in this way).

We can also note that people do work in small workshops in the middle of woods, fields, and gardens right where they live. They do work with hands and brains (there is a mystique about everyone taking turns at mental and practical work: The doctor often sands blocks in the woodshop). They do work at their own pace while at work, and supervision is rather casual. (But their life as a whole follows a rigid schedule indeed: Bells ring to wake everyone for work or school, and they ring for lunch and supper.) And people do spend their leisure creatively: There is lots of folk dancing, hiking, making music, writing poetry, and putting on puppet shows.

Why, finally, has this community managed to survive three quarters of a century while most others quickly die? Most important no doubt, is the Bruderhof's success in assembling a selfless group of people by letting go those who cannot be transformed. Unlike other such communities, where children become members automatically (and where second generation enthusiasm inevitably wanes), the Bruderhof has deliberately exposed teenagers and college-age youngsters to the world at large and then given them the choice between it or the closed community. Three quarters of them have returned as full members. Of those, and of other novices, only individuals able and willing to go through the process of ego loss and ego merging again and again survive as members. In addition, there is a strong incentive to lay aside one's selfishness. Those who do not must leave, because "a single rotten apple can spoil the whole barrel." And members have much to lose when leaving the community: All the people who matter to them, many of them lifelong friends, possibly even their own spouses and children, will be cut off *forever,* not to mention the fact that those who leave will enter the larger world without a cent's worth of material possessions. These factors have helped assemble a selfless group of people with radically reduced needs for goods and with a radically increased inner drive to submit to a strict discipline of hard work. In addition, unlike other such experiments, the Bruderhof is successfully integrated with the world at large. Thus, it is able to provide its members with many more goods than total self-sufficiency could procure.

## The Israeli Kibbutz

Israel's *kibbutz* (the word means "group" in Hebrew) provides another example of a successful intentional community. This voluntary grouping of people has been around for a long time, predating the formation of the Israeli state by many years. The first kibbutz (Degania Aleph) was founded in 1909; by 1987, there were 280 kibbutzim, containing a mere 3 percent of the Israeli population, but producing 10 percent of the country's GNP.

From the beginning, all the kibbutzim have been engaged in nation building; only a few have a strong religious orientation. Nevertheless, the similarities to the Bruderhof are striking. Again, most consumption is collective: Housing is assigned to people (but children live in separate quarters), meals are eaten in communal dining halls (except for tea at home), work clothes are replaced as they wear out, and dress clothes are strictly rationed. Communal cars are allocated for private use on evenings, weekends, and holidays; for selected individuals, higher education on the outside is community-financed (but repaid by the recipients should they decide not to return). Members receive a small amount of pocket money only.

The means of production are owned jointly. Economic activity in the past was overwhelmingly agricultural (involving production of cattle, citrus fruit, fish, and poultry), but as of late has switched to small, highly capital-intensive, high-technology industry (involving anything from electronics to armaments). Output is sold in the rest of the economy in competition with private firms. Revenues are used for investment or the communal consumption just referred to.

Ultimate decision-making power rests in a General Assembly of members. They elect executives such as a Secretary, a Treasurer, and a Work Coordinator, as well as an Economic Committee. The latter draws up plans for production, consumption, and investment that the General Assembly must approve.

Everyone capable works; even children work part time (and spend time with their parents only on evenings and weekends). Senior members hold jobs more or less permanently; only newer members move about among occupations and tasks. Jobs are assigned by the Work Coordinator, who tries to meet people's preferences. Everyone, however, takes turns at unpleasant jobs, such as cleaning toilets, dishwashing, disposing of garbage, and waiting on tables. An effort is made to eliminate unpleasant jobs when possible (as by switching to cafeteria-style self-service) or letting machines do them (as in the case of garbage disposal).

Incentives are mainly external, but not monetary. Probably the strongest one is praise or disapproval by the closely knit community. Nothing is more highly valued than being regarded as a good, selfless worker. By the same token, nothing is more feared than being considered a laggard or a parasite. Occasionally, such people are expelled. More often, they leave by themselves. (In recent years, much to the chagrin of old-timers and contrary to the original intentions, one half of kibbutz nonagricultural workers have been outsiders hired for wages.)

In many ways, life is like the dream: in the country, near the home, in small workplaces. There, as in the Bruderhof, success seems to be closely related to the ability to select for membership only those few who have passed suitability tests, to get rid of selfish people by sending them back into society at large, and to maintain a close economic integration with a larger society, which produces the usual gains from specialization and trade.

## Nationwide Experiments

Not all experiments with communal socialism, however, have been small-scale. Some communalists have imagined that intentional communities could succeed on a large scale, encompassing, perhaps, all the people of a nation and, eventually, of the world. As they have seen it (quite correctly, it seems), this would require a major revolution—not only of human institutions, but above all *within* human beings. All people would have to empty themselves of individual longings, die to the self, and be reborn as cells in the social body they would then serve.

Karl Marx, the patron saint of all socialists, predicted, for example, that the course of history would lead, inevitably, to such a communal utopia. It would be a society without scarcity, but also one *without egoism*. While Stalin and Tito and all the other East European socialists have been eager to usher in the world without scarcity, they have been in no hurry at all about creating the new kind of human being envisioned by Marx. They have only paid lip service to the goal of forging a loving community of brothers and sisters who have shed self-centeredness and are driven by inner necessity to serve their fellows and to do so to the best of their ability. China's Mao Zedong and Cuba's Fidel Castro, on the other hand, have not been content with fighting scarcity now and egoism in the distant future. However, as the remaining sections of this chapter show, they have also found, to their chagrin, that any determined effort to destroy egoism interferes with the creation of abundance, while any determined effort to create abundance interferes with the destruction of egoism. As a result, neither one of the nationwide experiments that they initiated survives today.

## China under Mao

Ever since 1949, when Mao Zedong came to power (see Biography 10.1 at the end of this chapter), economic policies in mainland China have followed a zig-zag course that has mirrored an internal struggle between so-called ''experts'' or ''pragmatists'' on the one hand and so-called ''reds'' or ''revolutionary zealots'' on the other. While the former have been interested in fighting scarcity, the main concern of the latter has been the destruction of egoism. Let us consider the major phases of their struggle in turn.

**The Recovery: 1949–1952.**   There was, first, a period of recovery from the disruptions of the Sino-Japanese war and the civil war. Similarly to Lenin, and for similar reasons, Mao made a number of compromises with capitalism. ''We must learn to do economic work from all who know how, no matter who they are,'' he said. As with Lenin, the results were spectacular. The Chinese real GNP during this period grew by leaps and bounds, possibly at an average annual rate of almost 18 percent. However, this only reflected the end of total chaos. As in the early 1920s in the Soviet Union, production levels were regained that had already been attained earlier in China proper during the 1930s and in Manchuria during the

1940s. This laid the groundwork for the determined program of industrialization that was to follow.

**The First Five-Year Plan: 1952–1957.**    Before long, Mao turned to Stalin. "The Communist Party of the Soviet Union is our best teacher," he said. "We must learn from it." So he adopted Stalin's system of planning and managing the economy (discussed in Chapter 7). In good Stalinist fashion, peasants were collectivized and made to work harder and for less. Labor was shifted on a large scale from agriculture to industry. The agricultural surplus collected by the state from the collectives was used in three ways: (1) to provide raw materials and food for industrial workers, (2) to provide food for workers in the fields of education, health care, and research, and (3) to earn foreign exchange by exports. Industrial workers, of course, were used mainly to produce capital rather than consumption goods. The foreign exchange earned from exports went to pay for the import of additional capital goods; and still more capital goods were acquired abroad as a result of friendly relations with the Soviets, who provided large loans to their new socialist brother. Thus, all the major ingredients for economic growth were provided for: more real capital, more education, more health care, and more knowledge.

Indeed, throughout the first plan period, capital formation equaled between 19 and 23 percent of GNP, which was a solid, even though painful, achievement for a country with such a low per-capita GNP. During this period, the Chinese produced their first power-generating equipment and their first motor vehicles ever. But about 40 percent of their real capital formation consisted of imported goods. Soviet aid alone helped carry out 156 major projects, involving the construction of plants to manufacture automobiles, aircraft, chemicals, electric power, steel and trucks, and the erection of facilities for mining, oil refining, and transportation.

Together with real capital formation, education was pushed hard. The number of young people going to full-time educational institutions multiplied rapidly. Before long, all urban and the majority of rural children went to primary schools. Secondary school enrollment rose by millions in this period, and that in institutions of higher education rose from a mere handful to a million. Additional educational efforts were made in many study groups on a part-time or spare-time basis, wherever people worked. (By 1970, half of all Chinese adults were literate, as opposed to fewer than 10 percent in 1950. The 1982 census showed 76 percent to be literate.) Education, however, was directed to more than basic skills, such as learning to read and write. Scientific and engineering education was greatly favored, partly to dispel myths and superstitions that stood in the way of the new, partly to train the type of manpower required by a modern economy.

China's remarkable gains in the field of health were attested to by a number of expert visitors. Most startling was the control of infectious and parasitic diseases that had ravaged China for centuries. Through intensive radio propaganda, the general environmental sanitation in cities and rural areas was phenomenally improved.

Finally, although most poor countries seem to devote only a tiny fraction of 1 percent of GNP to research and development, the Chinese figure was pushed to well above 1 percent. This relatively strong showing reflected the determination of the Chinese government to achieve great-power status. Eventually, as we now know, it made China the first country among the poor ones to possess the atomic bomb and to put satellites into earth orbit.

All this effort led to a significant increase, at an estimated average annual rate of 6.5 percent, of the Chinese real GNP during this period. But to Mao this remarkable result of the Five-Year Plan was unsatisfactory.

**The "Great Leap Forward": 1957–1962.**   Mao was unhappy because a step had been taken toward abundance, but not a step away from egoism. He noted how people's attitudes had not changed considering the selfish ways in which they were being motivated to work. These ways, too, had been copied from Stalin. Workers and peasants alike, as in the Soviet Union, worked on the basis of external incentives established by the state. Hourly wages, piecework rates, bonus payments, and the like were stressed for industrial workers and managers, while private plots of land, together with some private animal holdings and sale of the product in free markets, kept peasant interest up. In addition to these material incentives, nonmaterial ones, like banners, commendations, and medals won in emulation contests, and, of course, all kinds of privileges connected with status in the hierarchy of command had also been developed. Professional managers and engineers, who were running the show during the first Five-Year Plan, had fashioned the kinds of incentives they thought would make human self-interest work for the programs of the state.

But Mao feared that this approach would engulf China, as it had engulfed the Soviet Union, in crass materialism. He insisted on drawing up a radically different program for the second Five-Year Plan, from 1957 to 1962. It would create abundance by the very device of destroying egoism! Industrialization was to make a **Great Leap Forward.** Output throughout the economy was to increase 100 percent in 1 year. Counting on such breakneck speed of industrialization, the Chinese leaders announced their intention to surpass the United Kingdom in industrial output within 15 years.

The Russians advised against even trying, but Mao, like Tito before him, insisted on demonstrating his independence. True enough, he argued, the Great Leap could never be achieved by relying on people's material self-interest, on such capitalist and Soviet devices as piecework rates, bonuses, and private plots of land. People's motives would have to be *pure*; people would have to be filled with revolutionary enthusiasm (as were his guerrilla fighters earlier) to work for the good of their fellows. Then anything would become possible.

Correspondingly, the Chinese government initiated the second Five-Year Plan by putting on the pressure to increase output at exceedingly high rates. At the same time, many material incentives were abolished. Mao was confident in his ability to motivate the masses, as he had his guerrilla fighters earlier, by revolutionary fervor and not by "grimy pay." The new policies were pursued with a ruthlessness and a disregard of the individual that would have put even Stalin to shame: In agriculture, an army of 100 million peasants was organized on "mass irrigation projects," building canals, dikes, and reservoirs in ceaseless day and night shifts under unbelievably harsh conditions. The irrigated area was doubled, and the land was worked under a new "deep-plowing and close-planting policy." Close-Up 10.1, "The Great Leap Forward," provides a fascinating glance into the spirit of the times.

Ninety-nine percent of all peasants were forced into **communes,** institutions in which they were to live and work together and to own jointly all the means of production and consumption. Peasants lost title to their private family plots and with it the age-old hope for independence. The free private farm markets (which had previously provided significant percentages of butter, eggs, meat, milk, and vegetables) were closed. All private property was abolished. Peasants were made to work more and harder on the collective land, and for less, and they were virtually treated like draft animals. Even the individual family unit was abolished. Women were forced to work at all jobs as equals with men. Children were raised in government nurseries. People ate in common mess halls and slept in common barracks. Wages were mostly received in kind and in no way related to the amount of work performed: "From each according to his ability, to each according to his need" was to be put into practice here and now; and "need" was defined as physical subsistence.

Outside agriculture, the same principle of mass mobilization of labor was used. Organized by military principles and driven to the limit of their endurance, 60 million students and women were to supplement the new modern industrial complexes by producing "steel" (actually pig iron) in "backyard furnaces." Others set up numerous tiny and widely dispersed factories to make fertilizer and agricultural tools. They, too, worked in night and day shifts.

The new efforts were successful at first. From 1957 to 1958, real GNP grew at a rate of over 15 percent. The share of investment was raised to an unprecedented one third of GNP. Yet, seeds of disaster had also been sown. The utopian neglect of labor incentives, the exhausting pace of work, the excessive regimentation of all of life (imposing, among other things, unrealistic farming practices), and two years of thoroughly bad weather combined to take their toll. Agricultural output began to fall in 1959. This, in turn, caused a fall in industrial output and in GNP as well. The severity of the downturn can, in addition, be blamed on the increasingly bitter Sino-Soviet rift. Mao quarreled with Khrushchev (Biography 7.3) over who was then the true leader of international communism; the mounting political tension between the two nations led to a sudden withdrawal of Russian aid and a diversion of Chinese resources from investment to military pursuits.

The "Great Leap Forward" turned into the "Great Crisis." In 1959, the Chinese ceased to release economic data, they retreated substantially from their commune policy (some land was even returned to private ownership), the "backyard furnaces" died, and industrialization plans were scaled down. But it was too late. By 1962, real GNP was 13 percent below its 1958 peak and exactly equal to the 1957 level. Thus, the Great Leap Forward had produced a zero rate of economic growth! This was very serious, for China's population had continued to rise. A severe 1960–1961 food crisis during which millions died pointed to a potential disaster on a scale unheard of in human history. Analytical Example 10.1, "The Chinese Population Bomb," tells more of that story.

**"Consolidation and Readjustment": 1962–1966.**  Starting in 1962, "anti-Mao forces" under the leadership of Liu Shaoqi (then China's head of state, deputy leader of the Communist Party, and Mao's successor-to-be) proceeded to restrain the revolutionary fervor. The government bureaucracy either refused to cooperate further with Mao or subtly altered his directives. "Selfishness" once more replaced Mao's "purism" in the realm of incentives. Investment was pushed less, though not necessarily by choice. Massive crop failures and the disruptions of the Great Leap, which continued to be felt, forced massive food imports at the expense of imports of capital goods. Though they had taken only 2 percent of total imports during the first Five-Year Plan, food imports (mainly from the West) took up to 40 percent annually. Gradually, the economy recovered. Real GNP, growing at an average annual rate of 8.4 percent during this period, shot above its previous 1958 peak by 1964. Thus, China had lost six full years of economic growth.

But Mao was not concerned with material things. He wanted to create a new type of human being. So he unleashed a new revolution.

**The "Great Proletarian Cultural Revolution": 1966–1969.**  When the government bureaucracy would not cooperate with Mao's drive to abolish external incentives and create a new human being who would serve the national family from inner necessity, Mao decided to destroy that bureaucracy. In 1966, Mao instigated the **Great Proletarian Cultural Revolution**. And what a masterstroke it was! Unlike Stalin, who operated with forced confessions, rigged trials, and bloody purges, Mao simply called upon the youth of his country to come and see him. Imagine that gigantic dawn rally in 1966, packing a million youngsters aged 13 to 22 into Beijing's Great Square, singing "The East Is Red." Picture the speakers, whipping their audience into a frenzy about the young and the pure winning over the old and the impure, telling them of a new generation willing to deny itself on behalf of a higher cause that would outlast the lives of individuals, urging them to eliminate those "five black people": landlords, rich peasants, counterrevolutionaries, bad elements (such as criminals and the lazy), and rightists! So an army of wandering zealots was forged that August morning, unified by the transcendent vision of the immortal racial substance of the Chinese blending with the immortality of the Communist revolution.

And the Red Guards, as they called themselves, went out "to clear the path for Mao-thought." Commandeering food and lodging, trucks, and public address systems, they fanned out through the country, "dragging out the power holders" and chanting, "We will crush your dog heads!" Wherever they went, they harassed and tormented the bureaucrats, parading them through the streets in dunce caps and publicly beating them. Liu Shaoqi was vilified as "China's Khrushchev," toppled in disgrace, and later died in prison. He was replaced by Red Guard leader Chen Pota. As the Red Guards explained to everyone:

> *To become one large family, people would have to conquer self-centeredness and become pure in heart. That would require serving the people without external stimuli. Therefore, differences would have to be abolished not only in pay, but also in status. All that stood*

*in the way of a classless society would have to go: all differences between males and females, the old and the young, leaders and followers, experts and laymen, the skilled and the unskilled, mental and physical work, worker and manager, urban worker and peasant, the rich and the poor, teachers and students. But if everyone participated in everything on an equal basis, a miracle would occur, for it is from participation that ability is born. People would suddenly realize the manifold creative powers slumbering within them. An "atom bomb of talent" would be released once everyone was made as able as possible. Then they could give according to ability, and abundance would be ensured as an added dividend to the joy of all being one loving family!*

With that message, the Red Guards moved through cities and countryside and turned student into teacher, teacher into worker, worker into manager, manager into peasant, and peasant into doctor. And they abolished all differences in pay.

Meanwhile, as everyone crammed the writings of Chairman Mao, production stood still. But there were those practical-minded technicians who agreed with the "revisionist" Russians and their acceptance of human self-centeredness. They proposed to work through human nature (as they understood it), not to change human nature. They argued that Mao's ideological extremism was conducive to economic crisis, not to economic growth. They recalled with horror the disastrous Great Leap. They did not care to repeat it. They called off the political indoctrination sessions and reintroduced the old piecework rates.

The struggle between Maoists and the anti-Mao forces was intense. Their confrontation was more than verbal. Large groups of people, even troops, moved within and between the cities and around the countryside to emphasize the importance of their beliefs. "Let there be a civil war," cried the Red Guards. As they struggled over military weapons, public buildings, the news media, transport facilities, and water supply, agricultural and industrial output and GNP again began to fall in 1967.

In 1968, the struggle came to a head. With the help of the military, the power of the unruly and fanatical Red Guards was reduced by the removal of their leader, Chen Pota. Defense minister Lin Biao was newly designated as Mao's successor-to-be. In 1969, he formed a new government to restore order (and get production going again). This time, Red Guards and party members became the object of a giant purge, being sent off by the millions to the countryside ("the largest classroom with the best teachers") to "labor on the front line of agriculture" and to "receive reeducation humbly from poor peasants." For the peasants, said Mao, are "after all the cleanest persons . . . even though their hands are soiled and their feet smeared with cow dung." Mao announced that he would completely reconstruct the party organization, filling it with "new blood," mostly workers and soldiers.

Thus, the Great Cultural Revolution came to an end. During this period, real GNP had once more slowed to a creep, growing at an average annual rate of 2.8 percent from 1966 to 1969.

**Normalization: 1970–1976.**  Lin Biao did not stay in power long. In 1971, it is alleged, having mobilized warships, bombers, and flame throwers for the purpose, he attempted to depose and assassinate Mao, the coup was aborted, and Lin Biao died in a plane crash in Mongolia, trying to flee to the Soviet Union. Subsequently, Zhou Enlai headed a ''government of reconciliation.'' He tried to relax tensions within the country, notably between the leftists (or ''reds'') who wanted to crush egoism (like Mao's wife Jiang Qing) and the pragmatists (or ''experts'') who wanted to create abundance (like the military leaders). He was able to restore enough calm to allow the adoption of a new Party constitution (in 1973) and of a new state constitution (in 1975). He also relaxed international tensions, as evidenced by China's renewed contacts with the United States and her entry into the United Nations. Meanwhile, Chinese real GNP again resumed its faster climb, at an average annual rate of 6.6 percent from 1969 to 1976.

## China at the Time of Mao's Death

What was the nature of China's economic institutions at the time of Mao's death in 1976? Overshadowing all else were the communes.

**Communes.** Some 80 percent of China's population lived in 70,000 rural communes, holding between 1,000 and 50,000 people each. Families lived in their own houses with their children; unmarried adults lived in dormitories. About 7 percent of agricultural land was divided into private plots held by commune members to produce goods for their own consumption or for sale in free markets. But the focus was on working with the communal land, owned jointly, together with animals and simple tools, by groups of about 50 families called **production teams.** Groups of 10 teams were organized into **production brigades.** They jointly owned forests and larger pieces of equipment, such as threshing machines, tractors, and water pumps. They also made annual production decisions, allocated labor, and distributed the output. Finally, groups of 10 brigades were organized into communes. They owned hospitals and schools, cultural and recreational facilities, flood control and irrigation facilities, roads, and smaller industrial plants. Team and brigade leaders were elected by their members. Communes were run by ''revolutionary committees'' elected by a commune members' congress.

Some 60 percent of the output of each commune was distributed as income to the members, either in kind or, after sale, in cash. The other 40 percent was sold, and the receipts were used to buy inputs, such as fertilizer or machines, and to finance public consumption, such as education and health care. Sales of major crops, such as cotton, rice, sugar, wheat, and vegetable oils, were made at fixed and nationally uniform prices to the central government. Sales of other products, such as fish, fruit, meat, milk, and vegetables, were made to local governments at prices locally negotiated.

Industrial enterprises were owned by various levels of government, depending on the type of enterprise. Heavy industry was owned by the national government; small industry, by communes or cooperatives; most other industry, by local and provincial governments. Revolutionary committees of managers, technicians, and workers were in charge. Workers were typically attached to an enterprise for life, although they could leave for ''good'' reasons, such as joining a new plant or going into a newly developing region. New labor force entrants were assigned by the government to enterprises.

How far had China come in destroying egoism? Were people driven to serve others by inner necessity? Were they giving according to their ability, regardless of what they were receiving? Had distinctions in pay and status been abolished as unnecessary for the new type of human beings Mao had hoped to create? Not quite.

**The Destruction of Egoism: Equalizing Incomes.**   Consider how income was apportioned within the communes. The portion of total commune income to be distributed was apportioned according to "work points" held by members. Members received "work points" for work on the collective land, and these varied with the nature of the work, the number of days worked by a person, and the worker's effort and political attitude (as assessed by teammates). Thus, there were plenty of reasons for family incomes to differ drastically within a commune. However, the actual differences were rather small. In addition, and most importantly, all commune members received equal quantities of such public consumption goods as child care, education, health care, retirement benefits, and vacations.

There were, however, significant income differences among communes rather than within them. Members of some communes, lucky enough to have such things as more fertile soil, better equipment, more water, a better climate, or better access to markets, were earning four times as much as members of less lucky communes.

In addition, the urban population was earning significantly better incomes than the rural one, and within the former group an "eight-grade wage system" saw to it that some people (such as factory managers, top civil servants, and university professors) were earning, officially, five times as much cash (but, in fact, ten times as much) as the lowest-paid workers. These cash differences allowed some urban residents more than others to buy such things as bicycles, clothing, furniture, radios, railroad travel, sewing machines, television sets, and wristwatches. Yet, everybody was receiving equal quantities of the public consumption goods referred to earlier. In addition, all urban residents received equal rations of grain (40 to 50 pounds per month), of vegetable oil and soy sauce (⅔ pound per month of each), and of cotton cloth (enough for about two suits per year). Finally, there was equality in the receipt of low-priced (but old and crowded) housing and city transit.

One thing is certain. Unlike other poor countries, China had no one who was very rich and no one who was very poor. One could find neither families owning large houses with many servants, driving personal cars, dining in splendor, and enjoying foreign travel; nor could one find hordes of diseased, homeless, and starving addicts, beggars, or prostitutes in the city streets. Nevertheless, just before his death Mao was quite unhappy about the income differentials that remained. The eight-grade wage system, he said in 1975, was scarcely different from the old society, and he urged factory meetings to discuss such "revisionist black goods" as bonuses and overtime pay. In addition, he urged continued pursuit of a policy of increasing, at intervals, the lowest industrial wages only, as well as state agricultural procurement prices. Obviously, this would, over time, narrow intraurban as well as rural-urban income differentials.

**The Destruction of Egoism: Equalizing Status.**   Differences in status, as in cash income, could also be found in the China of the mid-1970s. But Mao had not given up the goal, once so forcefully promoted by the Red Guards, of crushing elitism. In 1974, Mao unleashed another "anti-reactionary campaign," holding before the people the examples of "bourgeois careerist conspirators and counterrevolutionary double-dealers" like Liu Shaoqi and Lin Biao. He even accused the ancient Chinese sage Confucius (who lived from 551–479 B.C.) of having blood ties with the latterday renegades. "Although Confucius has been dead for over 2,000 years," he said, "his corpse continues to emit its stench among us today. Its poison is deep, its influence extensive." He compared Confucian proverbs to "poisonous weeds," for they teach people to accept fate instead of urging them to struggle against oppressors without as well as within. He encouraged mass rallies to arouse people to create a huge contingent of "Marxist theoretical workers" who would join all the workshops and teams and expose the "sham Marxism" of the Soviets with the help of "Marx-Lenin-Mao straight-thinking."

Everyone was to watch continually for the bourgeois devil of self-centeredness, in themselves and in others. Thus, youngsters who deliberately failed high school exams (so as not to be sent to the countryside as "educated young workers"); youngsters who ran away from assignments in backward areas to return to the city (trafficking in forged resident permits and ration cards); party officials who pulled strings to get their children into the university or used public cars for private trips; overbearing managers who put production first and worker attitudes second; parents who wanted to marry off their daughters against their will; former landlords who talked approvingly of capitalism; peasants who showed crude, ironic, and sarcastic attitudes toward the "educated young persons" sent to them; scientists who did research for the sake of research (instead of practical work of benefit to the people)— all these were to be exposed or were to expose themselves. That was the purpose of giant wall posters and of "struggle meetings" and of flag-waving rallies. Those criticized were to thank their "clear-thinking" critics for arousing them from their "revisionist reveries." And, whenever possible, people were to expose on their own "the evil influence of Lin Biao's line and the doctrine of Confucius" within themselves. Thus, a university professor stepped before a mass rally and confessed to a "mandarin-style of acting," a student confessed having entered the university "via the back door" (with father's influence), and both were sent off by cheering crowds to the countryside, complete with gifts of hoes, sandals, straw hats, and the works of Mao!

As Mao saw it, there would have to be many more wars "against the old ideology, culture, customs, and habits of the exploiting classes," against the "four olds" that predispose people into taking privilege for themselves. Until the new human being has emerged, said Mao, the class struggle continues even under socialism. For there are always lapses. "People who integrate themselves with the masses of workers and peasants today are revolutionary," said Mao. "But the judgment is never final! If tomorrow they cease to do so or turn around and oppress the common people, then they become nonrevolutionary or counterrevolutionary." Then another death and rebirth experience is called for!

# China after Mao

It is instructive to see what has happened to Mao's great experiment in communal socialism since his death in 1976. Although Mao had handpicked a successor, Hua Guofeng, who presumably was to carry on the struggle against egoism and for equality and do so at any cost, when Mao died the days of the Maoist zealots were numbered. Before long, it became clear that real power had fallen into the hands of a pragmatist, Deng Xiaoping (Biography 10.2), who declared that Mao's single-minded pursuit of ideological purity had been a serious blunder because it had come at the cost of the material well-being of the masses. Even before Hua Guofeng was officially ousted as Prime Minister (1980) and Party Chairman (1981), Deng proceeded to dismantle the Maoist policies.

**The Gang of Four.**   Before all else, the most powerful leftist leaders, soon to be known as "the Gang of Four," were arrested and put on trial. In 1981, they were duly convicted of having tried to usurp power after Mao's death and having persecuted Party and government leaders who did not agree with them during the Great Proletarian Cultural Revolution. Thus, Yao Wenyuan, propaganda chief and editor of the Party journal, *Red Flag,* was sentenced to 20 years in jail. (The journal itself ceased publication in 1988.) Wang Hongwen, Deputy Party Chairman, received a life sentence. Zhang Chunqiao, Senior Deputy Prime Minister, and Jiang Qing, Mao's wife, were sentenced to death, but their sentences were later commuted to life in prison.

**The Four Modernizations.**   On the positive side, Deng put into motion a long-range development plan that would make China "rich and strong" and allow it to catch up with the advanced capitalist countries by the middle of the 21st century. The modernization focused on four areas: agriculture, industry, the military, and science/technology. Said Hu Yaobang, General Secretary of the Communist Party, in reference to Mao's Great Leap and the Cultural Revolution: "We have wasted 20 years. . . . In the 1980s, we must constantly remind ourselves— moreover we must tell the next generation—that from now on we cannot afford to mess things up, we can never again undertake such radical, leftist nonsense as 'take class struggle as the key link' and 'better to have socialist weeds than capitalist seedlings.' We can never again afford internal chaos, as we will cause our own collapse and poverty."[1] Deng himself referred to his development plan facetiously as "the Great Leap Backward"—backward, that is, from the economically disastrous policies of Mao.

**Economic Reforms.**   As the next section indicates in greater detail, Deng also introduced an important set of market-oriented economic reforms designed to enhance individual enterprise at the expense of centralized direction. The reforms

---

[1]*The New York Times,* February 21, 1985, p. A7.

were quite successful; the Chinese real GNP grew at an average annual rate of 8 percent per year from 1979 to 1987. Moreover, in a brilliant 1987 coup, Deng neutralized the opposition to his reforms. At the 13th Congress of the Chinese Communist Party, Deng installed his reform-minded protégé, Zhao Ziyang, as the Party's General Secretary, while he himself retired from most of his positions and took with him into retirement the entire generation of senior leaders who had opposed the reforms. Mindful of Mao's dictum that ''political power grows out of the barrel of a gun,'' Deng retained only one post, the chairmanship of the Party's Central Military Commission. (Close-Up 10.2, ''The Locus of Power in China,'' is of special interest here.)

## Deng's Market-Oriented Reforms

By the time the Chinese Communist Party held its 13th Congress in 1987, not even a dozen years after Mao's death, a number of reforms had thoroughly transformed the economic landscape. Mao's dream of a moral community of men and women— each of whom was driven by an inner voice to ''serve the masses'' and to do so without regard to material reward—that dream was no more. Within sight of Beijing's Forbidden City (where Mao had lived), his slogans had been replaced by ''Things Go Better with Coke,'' while portraits of Marx, Lenin, Stalin, and Mao had given way to the beaming face of ''Comrade'' Sanders (of Kentucky Fried Chicken fame). What had happened?

**Agricultural Reform.**   Ever since 1978, when Deng Xiaoping emerged as China's paramount leader, the agricultural communes have been effectively decollectivized by the introduction of the **household contract and responsibility system.** The system abolished communal work on the communal land, along with the equal sharing of the results (which had proven to be disastrous for incentives). Under the new system, the legal title to the land remained with the commune, but each household was given a specific plot of land to farm for a specified period (ranging from 3 to 50 years). In return, the household contracted with the production team to deliver specified quantities of specified products at governmentally set prices (akin to the payment of a rental fee or tax). The household was free to sell the remainder of these products as well as any other products in free markets at any price. (The production team made similar contracts with the brigade, and the brigade with the commune, which had to meet an overall government delivery quota.) The results were amazing. Between 1978 and 1984 (when 98 percent of all peasants had joined the new system), overall agricultural output grew by 55 percent, but the growth equaled 63 percent for wheat, 89 percent for oil seeds, 101 percent for sugar, and 186 percent for cotton. By the late 1980s, the privatization of agriculture had been carried even further: Peasants were free to hire between 7 and 100 workers and could even sell their land utilization rights to others. Thus, it was possible for successful peasants to assemble large farms on which machinery might be employed. Contrast that with not so many years ago when a furious Mao ordered commune leaders to chop down fruit trees and rip out melon patches peasants had planted to get some private income. Nevertheless, the Maoist urge toward equality at any cost has not died out entirely. See Close-Up 10.3, "The Great Leap Backward."

**Industrial Reforms.** Ever since 1978, a similar shift of decision-making power from central planners to enterprise managers has occurred outside agriculture. As under Lenin's NEP (discussed in Chapter 7), a mixture of state, cooperative, and private enterprises was allowed, and their activities were increasingly coordinated by markets. State-owned firms still received government output quotas, to be delivered to the government at fixed prices, but all of them were free to sell additional quantities of the same or other products in open markets. (In 1985, for example, China's #2 Auto Plant delivered 55,000 trucks to the government, but sold an additional 36,500 trucks in the market.) State enterprises also ceased to get investment funds as a grant from the government budget. They could borrow funds from banks or the public through the sale of bonds. They were free to allocate above-plan profits (as in Yugoslavia) to investment and collective consumption projects or to pay them out as worker bonuses. And, unlike ever before, they could even go bankrupt.

Private individuals could join with others to set up cooperative enterprises, or they could set up firms of their own. The individuals involved could use their own funds, but were also free to sell bonds and stocks to the public. They could even lease state enterprises from the government. Individually owned private firms could hire a maximum of 7 nonfamily employees, but the rule was often ignored. (In one 1987 case, a private firm had over 900 employees.) The number of private firms grew rapidly, from 140,000 in 1978 to 20 million in 1988.

By 1986, a bond market had emerged in Shenyang and a stock market in Shanghai; in 1987, with much fanfare, a stock market was opened in Beijing. (The market started off slowly, with the sale of 1,200 shares of the Tianqiao Department Store Company, and then nothing happened for seven months. In addition, unlike elsewhere in the world, Chinese stocks, like bonds, mature in a specified number of years and pay a predetermined annual divided until the principal is repaid.)

**Open-Door Policy.** A third feature of the post-Mao reforms has been a reversal of Mao's policy on national self-reliance, which has increased China's volume of foreign trade fivefold between 1978 and 1986. Joint ventures with and foreign investment by Western firms in China have been encouraged in order to promote the import of modern technology and management techniques. To attract foreign firms, "special economic zones" (with low rents, wages, utility rates, and taxes) were established (which the enemies of reform quickly labeled "a return to the open-treaty-port concessions made Western imperialists in the 19th century"). Nevertheless, by 1986, some 2,500 joint ventures were underway and over $18 billion of foreign investment had been made. Involved were mainly Japan, Western Europe, and the United States; projects ranged widely from 120 complete Japanese factories to French nuclear power stations, satellite communications, and clothes (Pierre Cardin) to Swedish railroads, Danish port facilities, and even a chain of 1,000 American hotels.

Note: In 1988, loud complaints were heard from interior regions about the unfair concentration of foreign investments in the coastal regions. In addition, the dismantling of government price controls produced an inflation rate of 50 percent. Accordingly, the Communist Party Central Committee voted to slow down the pace of marketization, thereby weakening the hand of Zhao Ziyang, the reform-minded General Secretary, and strengthening that of Li Peng, the more cautious Prime Minister.

**Political and Cultural Liberalization.**    The economic reforms just described have been accompanied by a considerable degree of liberalization in other areas of life, although not consistently so. Soon after his death, the official description of Mao was downgraded from a veritable god to a great man. (Deng Xiaoping called him ''70 percent good, 30 percent bad.'') In a symbolic gesture, the Beijing Mao mausoleum was ''closed for repairs,'' and on the city's ''democracy wall,'' the most remarkable wall posters appeared and were tolerated:

> *''Let the people say what they wish. The heavens will not fall. The modernization program depends on the talent, initiative, and enthusiasm of the entire population. If a person is to be punished for saying wrong things, no one will say what he thinks. The suffocation of democracy produces bad results.''*

> *''Marxism has become just another religion. The Communist Party taught us not to believe in religion—Christianity or Buddhism—so why should we believe in Marxism?''*

> *''Capitalism and socialism are just names. The important thing is we want happiness, freedom, and an advanced economy. Whichever system achieves that, that's what we want.''*

Before long, there also appeared criticisms of arbitrary legal practices, condemnations of the systematic torture of political prisoners, and demands for a *fifth* modernization (democracy). One wall poster even reproduced the Bill of Rights of the U.S. Constitution!

Gradually, the limits of the permissible have been pushed out in all areas of life: Women could suddenly wear skirts and colorful clothes, even curl their hair. Writers and poets could publish material far removed from Maoist dogma. Painters could abandon ''socialist realism'' and create abstract, impressionist works. . . .

To be sure, the wind of freedom has alternated, blowing warm, then cold. In the mid-1980s, hard-liners even mounted a campaign against ''spiritual pollution,'' forced the resignation of Deng's protégé, Hu Yaobang, from the Party leadership, and arranged the arrest of many who had called for genuine political democracy. (In 1987, Wei Jingsheng died in prison while being punished for his ''counterrevolutionary crime,'' the demand for a fifth modernization, democracy.) Still, unlike in the Mao years, the one-party state allowed some room for a diversity of lifestyles and views, for intellectual curiosity and artistic creativity. There were no more executions of dissidents, no more public beatings of ''enemies'' in stadiums full of hysterical fanatics, no more mass shipments of state enemies to labor camps. And in 1988, workmen at Beijing University toppled the towering statue of Mao that the Red Guards had made and hauled away the fragments.

# Cuba under Castro

There are many parallels between China and Cuba. Among them are pendulum-like swings in economic policies. In the end, however, there is a major difference: Unlike China, which gave up on communal socialism and adopted market-oriented reforms, Cuba gave up on the ideas as well, but embraced the rigid Soviet model of central planning instead.

**Transition to Socialism: 1959–1961.**   There was first a period of transition to socialism. In keeping with promises made prior to the revolution, Fidel Castro (Biography 10.3) did not introduce full-fledged socialism at the time of his victory in 1959. A limited nationalization program touched only electric power and telephone companies, large landed estates owned by absentee landlords, and sugar mills. Even then, compensation payments were made to owners. There was much stress on democracy; and widespread popular discussion occurred on the percentage of GNP to be invested and the allocation of investment among branches of the economy. The market economy was retained. Fiscal and monetary policies were used to accomplish the goals chosen. Real GNP rose rapidly.

**Sucrophobia and Superplanning: 1961–1964.**   By the early 1960s, the effects of the western hemisphere's trade embargo, imposed after the earlier nationalization of U.S. assets, began to be felt seriously. Spare parts ran out on everything, from cars to trucks, from industrial machinery to elevators, from air conditioners to refrigerators. And all of them said "Made in U.S.A." At about the same time, the Cuban leaders succumbed to **sucrophobia**; that is, they decided that they really disliked an economy so very much dependent on the production and export of one crop, sugar. This conjured up memories of colonialism and slavery. So they concluded that it was time to industrialize, and to do it fast. Following the advice given by American Marxist economists, the Cuban leaders turned to Stalin's model, but with one modification. They adopted Stalin's method of planning but rejected his ways of motivating workers.

In 1961, all the means of production, with one exception, were made collective property. The exception concerned a third of the agricultural economy, containing some 250,000 small peasants hiring no outside labor and producing mostly coffee and tobacco. At the same time, democracy came to an end. The leadership made the decisions. With the help of Czech, Polish, and Russian technicians, short-term and long-term material balances were worked out to plan the entire economy "as one giant enterprise." In good Stalinist fashion, the plan called for a high rate of investment to be channeled into heavy industry, education, and health care. Contrary to Stalinist practice, the plan called for everyone getting the same income. Che Guevara insisted that people be motivated by inner desire to serve others and not by external incentives. Like Mao in China, he envisioned the Cuban people as one vast guerrilla team, single-mindedly pursuing their common objective of creating one large, loving family living in material abundance. Like a band of guerrillas, they would be self-disciplined, hard working, conscientious, and incorruptible. Each member would be dedicated not to serving the self but to sacrificing the self for the welfare of the team.

Thus, the dice were loaded in favor of disaster. The planners had started with inadequate statistical data and set grossly over-optimistic output targets. They had produced an internally inconsistent plan that would ask people to do the impossible. They had, finally, assumed that the "new type of human being" could be created almost overnight. Before long, the inevitable consequences appeared.

Inability to carry out central output commands (because they were contradictory or failed to provide the necessary inputs) and unwillingness of undisciplined workers and managers to follow commands caused failure to plant many crops or to harvest them or to transport them where they were needed. In addition, bad weather reduced the agricultural yield, and bad marketing (the attempt to charge higher than world market prices) reduced export sales. As a result, imports of capital goods did not materialize as planned, further interrupting plan fulfillment. By 1964, Cuba's sugar crop had declined to three quarters of its prerevolutionary level. Half completed, empty factories were strewn about the land. "Superplanning" had produced a negative rate of GNP growth. So it was abandoned.

**Sucrophilia and Miniplans: 1964–1970.** The East European advisers were sent home, and a new team arrived from France. They suggested that a small country like Cuba, lacking most minerals and fuels needed for industrialization and having just lost hundreds of thousands of its professionals by emigration, would be well advised, like Denmark and New Zealand, to concentrate on agriculture and foreign trade. And being thus dependent on weather, on world markets, and on the hard work of geographically dispersed laborers (all factors hard to control by central planners), she would be better run by a market economy. They held up Oskar Lange's model for imitation (discussed in Chapter 8). Promptly, Lange's works were translated and widely discussed. But, eventually, only the first part of the advice given was followed.

The Cuban leaders gave up their phobia of sugar and decided to love it! They would follow the advice of Figure 10.1, "The Road to Riches: Foreign Trade." Exports would be agricultural, mainly sugar, but would also include cattle, coffee, tobacco, and tropical fruits. Embracing **sucrophilia,** Castro set a 1970 output target of 10 million tons of sugar, double the prerevolutionary peak. The export revenues would be used to support agriculture by importing farm machinery, fertilizer, pesticides, and transportation and milling equipment. In addition, internally, sugar-using activities would be developed, such as cattle raising (using molasses as fodder) and chemicals, paper, plywood, and textile production (using bagasse and sugar). Beyond that, only a few other activities would be built up, such as education, health care, and fishing.

But Castro would not stomach an economy guided by money and material incentives. The economy would be guided from the center, Castro decided, and people would receive equal incomes. The former would not be done by drawing up a superplan to cover the whole economy, but with the help of "miniplans" designed to draw into a given smaller project whatever resources were needed for

**Figure 10.1**  The Road to Riches: Foreign Trade

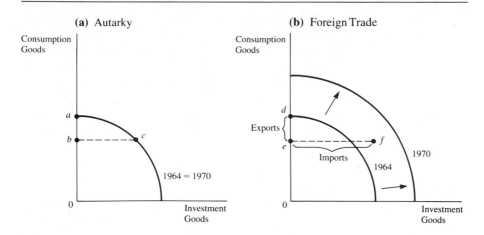

The production possibilities frontiers shown here help contrast the effects of a move from national economic self-sufficiency (panel a) to a policy embracing foreign trade (panel b). Initially, a country may "go it alone" and produce combination *c*, sacrificing *ab* of potential consumption goods in order to produce *bc* of investment goods. If these investment goods are just sufficient to replace the depreciation of the capital stock, the production possibilities frontier remains stationary over time.

Let the country specialize according to comparative advantage and produce combination *d*. By exporting *de*, it may be able to import *ef* which exceeds *bc*. As a result, the set of goods available to the country (point *f*) exceeds what it could have produced by itself and, over time, the country's production possibilities may expand as shown.

its accomplishment. The latter would be supplemented, if need be, by the forceful commandeering of labor.

The latter proved indeed necessary. To accomplish its egalitarian income goals, the Cuban government introduced free food service at all places of work. It provided equal rations of food, clothing, and other goods in state stores. It made education and medical care and even buses and public phones available free of charge (and housing almost free). And it provided all Cubans with free vacations at beach resorts. The rate of absenteeism on the job soared. Productivity on the job and the quality of work done plummeted. So Castro provided every adult citizen with a "work force control card," and a "labor history file" was set up by all enterprises for every worker. Students and housewives and workers and peasants were organized along military lines into "battalions" and "brigades" and *assigned* to jobs. They could not leave their jobs without government approval. All infractions of labor discipline (coming late to work, disobeying a superior, damaging the means of production, doing shoddy work, and even showing the wrong political attitude) were recorded in the file. People absent from work without a valid excuse for more than 15 days were sent to labor farms.

But, as in 1961 to 1964, the results were far from the expected. Market relations having been destroyed, everyone was awaiting central commands. Yet the miniplans provided no *coordinated* set of activities for the economy as a whole. Again and again, production came to a halt for lack of materials, transport equipment, and so on. Industrial output, a tiny proportion of the GNP, increased slightly each year, but agricultural output was usually lower than in prerevolutionary days. In 1970, to be sure, sugar output reached a record high of 8.5 million tons. But it was 15 percent below the target and was accompanied by a plummeting of world sugar prices. Exports were the least profitable in history! Thus, planned imports did not materialize, and all other targets were missed by far. This was reinforced by the fact that a million people were commandeered to harvest sugar, and their diversion from other pursuits slowed other activities to a creep. Overall, the rate of real GNP growth from 1964 to 1970 was zero. Castro offered to resign, but, in the end, he remained, sadder but wiser.

**Pragmatism: 1970 and Beyond.**   By 1970, Castro had learned two lessons: (1) If there was to be no market economy, central planning had to be comprehensive and careful, and (2) for the time being, humans were still imperfect and had to be stimulated to give their best by external incentives. Said Castro rather sadly: ''We've had formulas and schemes, some of which have been presented as full-fledged miracles, as miraculous remedies for solving problems, but what happened? Things got worse. And some of those inventions called for superperfect planning. . . . Perhaps our greatest idealism lies in having believed that a society . . . could, all of a sudden, be turned into a society in which everybody behaved in an ethical moral way. . . .''[2] So Castro postponed the realization of some of his dreams. He turned to making patient improvements, with good management, all the while being aware of the moral limitations of people.

Once more, the Cubans turned to Soviet methods of central planning, but this time they introduced many material incentives as well. Plans called for the continued pursuit of the overall strategy of agricultural exports (especially sugar), but exports of mining products (mainly nickel) and the export of services (tourism) were also stressed. Most of this trade was to be directed toward Eastern Europe from whence oil, capital goods, and industrial consumption goods would be received. By buying sugar at highly inflated prices and selling oil at bargain rates, the Russians have provided Cuba with enormous amounts of aid, putting Cuba on the path described in Figure 10.2, ''The Road to Riches: Foreign Trade Plus Aid.''

So far as incentives go, internal ones were still encouraged, but a variety of external ones were being stressed. Although there were about 1,000 ''microbrigades'' selflessly building housing, schools, and shopping centers voluntarily on evenings and Sundays, most people were driven by external incentives, negative and positive. Thus, a 1971 ''antiloafing law'' promised two years of labor camp to all able-bodied men (aged 17 to 60) who were not on a job or did not stay there.

---

[2]*Granma Weekly Review,* Sept. 20, 1970.

**Figure 10.2**    The Road to Riches: Foreign Trade Plus Aid

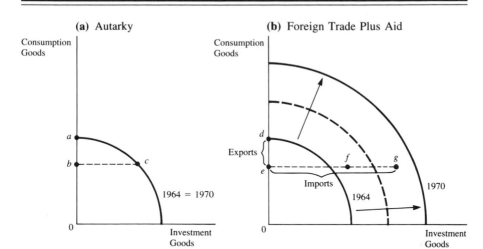

The production possibilities frontiers shown here help contrast the effects of a move from national economic self-sufficiency (panel a) to a policy embracing foreign trade plus aid (panel b). Initially, a country may "go it alone" and produce combination *c*, sacrificing *ab* of potential consumption goods in order to produce *bc* of investment goods. If these investment goods are just sufficient to replace the depreciation of the capital stock, the production possibilities frontier remains stationary over time.

Let the country specialize according to comparative advantage and produce combination *d*. By exporting *de*, it may be able to import *ef* which exceeds *bc*. By also accepting foreign aid of *fg*, it may be able to raise imports from *ef* to *eg*. As a result, the set of goods available to the country (point *g*) exceeds by far what the country could have produced by itself. Over time, the country's production possibilities may expand not to the dashed line (which foreign trade alone would have made possible), but to the solid outer line (which reflects the effect of foreign aid as well).

As a result, 100,000 "*mongollones*" (lazy birds) straggled forward to take jobs. In addition, positive forms of external incentives were introduced, ranging from flags, medallions, and pennants given to the winners of "fraternal competitions" to extra vacations, personal meetings with Castro, better housing, cash prizes, and higher wages given to "vanguard workers" who did more than the ordinary share of labor. The latter types of income could be translated in state stores into East European consumer durables, such as cameras, pressure cookers, radios, records, refrigerators, and television sets.

At long last, Cuban real GNP began to grow (at an estimated rate of 8 percent a year from 1970 to 1975). For a while, Cuban plans were also helped greatly by a rise in world sugar prices from 2 cents per pound in 1970 to 53 cents per pound in 1975, but the increases were temporary. Cuba's first Five-Year Plan, from 1976 to 1980, accomplished much less than had been hoped. And nobody mentioned Castro's promises of the early 1960s, according to which, by 1980, every Cuban family would own a house, an automobile or motorcycle, and a refrigerator full of the most varied food stuffs, while workers would be tilling the land in air-conditioned cabins of tractors for only a few hours each day.

## Cuba in the Late 1980s

By the late 1980s, what had become of the goal of creating a new breed of human beings, filled with esprit de corps, dedicated to their fellows? Castro, unlike the Chinese, certainly had not given up on achieving this goal, and he showed great hostility to the Soviet as well as Chinese economic reforms. While markets and private enterprise expanded in the latter two countries, Castro closed Cuba's free farm markets in 1986 because "neocapitalist elements" had become too rich. He initiated a "rectification campaign" that once again stressed moral over material incentives.

**The Destruction of Egoism: Equalizing Income.** By the late 1980s, although vanguard workers were better off when it came to housing and consumer durables, all Cubans received equal rations of many important items (food, clothing), and they had equal access to many others (education, health care). This was a phenomenal change from prerevolutionary days when differences were stark, especially between the residents of Havana and of the countryside. Consider the fact that hundreds of thousands of volunteer reading and writing teachers (*"alfabetizadores"*) have chopped the illiteracy rate from 24 percent to under 4 percent, making it the lowest in Latin America. Consider how only half of school-aged children went to school in 1958, but 98 percent did by 1985. Consider how Cuba had 59 hospitals and clinics in 1958, mostly in Havana, but there were hundreds of them by 1985, spread out over the whole island. As a result, Cubans got the best medical care in Latin America. They had the lowest infant mortality, and they had conquered malaria and polio.

As in China, the very poor and the very rich alike had disappeared from the scene in Cuba. Havana, once the playground of the Americas, had a rather rundown look: cracked and peeling buildings, stores empty of consumption goods, and a fleet of American cars from the 1950s driving through the streets (along with more recent Russian and Polish cars). But the ragged barefooted children and the beggars and the pimps were gone, along with the ostentatious rich. And the once forgotten cane cutters and fishermen in the interior had better housing, new equipment, guaranteed food rations, and, for the first time, education and health care.

**The Destruction of Egoism: Equalizing Status.** Mass participation in decision making was largely laid aside in 1961 in favor of centralized authoritarian rule. (There were massive rallies during which people shouted "Si" or "'No," but the eight-member Central Committee of the Communist Party made the decisions.) This led to privilege taking by government, military, and Party leaders who helped themselves to cars, special foods, and better housing. Since the mid-1970s, however, Castro has shown greater interest in eliminating such privileges by dismantling the centralized bureaucracy and providing a more democratic process of decision making. In late 1974, he announced project "popular power," designed to transfer power from the top-heavy Havana bureaucracy to the grass roots. An "experiment" was initiated in Matanzas province, the smallest of Cuba's six provinces, holding only half a million people. They were to elect a provincial general assembly and set up their own local government to take control of hospitals, schools, stores, and, eventually, production enterprises.

At the same time, a massive propaganda campaign utilized a variety of mass organizations (the Committees for the Defense of the Revolution, the Federation of Small Farmers, the Federation of Women, the Young Pioneers, and others) to tell people that power belonged to them, but its exercise required selflessness, always putting oneself at the service of the people.

## Conclusion

The question mark contained in this chapter's title is not a printing error. Considering the experience of hundreds of small communal experiments throughout the world, as well as that of the only two (and limited) larger-scale experiments in Mao's China and Castro's Cuba, one can doubt that communal socialism is a viable alternative to centralized or market socialism.

Most small-scale communal experiments have failed because people were not selfless enough: First, when everyone was free to take consumption goods "according to need," people took too much and there was not enough to go around. Then rationing by money or command became inevitable. (In addition, the sharing of spouses, children, and even pets has caused no end of troubles.) Second, when internal incentives were relied upon to make people contribute "according to ability," such contribution fell in an environment wherein real income could be had for nothing. Thus, people had to be induced to work by money or command. Third, when living in cities and working in large workplaces and the like were replaced by working in small workplaces in the countryside (and perhaps even self-sufficient ones), the inevitable fall in output (and the total unavailability of some goods, such as, perhaps, penicillin) caused dissatisfaction and abandonment of the scheme.

All this surely holds for nationwide communalism as well. More than that! Among larger groups of people, it becomes physically impossible to have everyone participate directly in all decisions. Any attempt to do so leads to a massive waste of resources and a fall in output that causes people to abandon the scheme by reintroducing markets or central planning.

Since most small-scale experiments have demonstrated the near impossibility of assembling or creating even a *small* group of selfless people (willing to take little and give much and to do so out of an inner drive to serve humanity), there is no reason to believe that it is easier to assemble or create *large* groups of such selfless creatures any time soon. The truth of this has been amply demonstrated by the Chinese and Cuban examples.

CLOSE-UP 10.1

## The Great Leap Forward

Consider these eyewitness accounts of what happened in China when Mao unleashed the "fervor of the masses":

> The countryside was in convulsion. Marching in columns and working in dense crowds, immense peasant masses were spending their over-spilling energy. As in some fabulous pantomine, innumerable men, women and adolescents were on the move, perpetually purposeful and with apparently precise missions. Enormous crowds were carrying sand to swell embankments along rivers. Innumerable little figures were swinging their shovels to dig new canals. Marchers in formation were following coloured flags on bamboo poles, on their way to replace teams laying railway tracks. Monumental ant-heaps were busy on the sites of future reservoirs. Endless lines of blue-clad men and women were filling up mountain-sides like some unnatural stream changing course. In the background, scattered all over the fields, multitudes of people were moving around with two buckets hanging from their shoulder poles. All together, they recalled the rhythmic breathing of some mythological colossus, suddenly awakened and flexing its milliard muscles in a supreme effort to change the face of the earth. . . . Literally millions of [backyard furnaces] were built around villages, along railway lines or even in the gardens of schools and houses in the towns. Like innumerable glow-worms they shone in China's night. Seeing them all over the country one had the haunting impression of fanatical alchemists feeding the flames in desperation to turn into gold the rocks they had carted from the mountains.[a]

And again:

> All the peasants—men and women, old and young—are busy at work. They dig canals and repair dams; they level mountains to bring them under the plough; they change the nights into days, the moon into the sun, and the slack season into busy season. On the work sites are red flags everywhere in the daytime, and lights everywhere at night. In work all vie with one another in fortitude and courage. . . .
>
> The peasants created devices as they worked. At a steep cliff the peasants worked in mid-air, being suspended with a rope let down from the top of the precipice. Picks were so worn that only 4 or 5 inches of their 2-foot heads was left. When the workers had no more tools they went home for more. At night they would light torches so as to enable them to continue their work.[b]

What made people do it? An intense propaganda campaign, entitled "Give Your Heart to the Party," was designed to whip up people's enthusiasm to do unselfish things. This was reflected in an explosion of *tatze-pao*, or newspapers of large ideograms, each paper usually consisting of two or three sheets prominently dis-

---

[a]Tibor Mende, *China and Her Shadow* (New York: Coward-McCann, 1962), pp. 70–71.
[b]*China's Big Leap in Water Conservancy* (Peking: Foreign Languages Press, 1958), pp. i, 3, and 4.

played on walls of buildings, in corridors, on improvised frames of stalks out in the fields, and wherever space could be found.

Everyone was expected to contribute slogans and poems to invigorate the masses, but also to engage in criticism of others and oneself. Thus, the *tatze-pao* recounted stories of revolutionary endeavor and were also filled with personal recriminations of laggards. As one poem put it,

> Thousand threads were used
> In mending my clothes.
> But my grandmother's concern for me
> Means much more than all this:
> I won't go home
> Until the reservoir is completed
> So as to repay my grandmother's kindness.

*Source*: Jan S. Prybyla. *The Political Economy of Communist China* (Scranton, PA: International Textbook Company, 1970), pp. 256–59.

## CLOSE-UP 10.2

## The Locus of Power in China

The Communist Party of China (with 46 million members in 1987) holds all political power; the government is subordinate to it and lacks independent power.

### *Communist Party Congress*
Theoretically the highest body. Consists of delegates elected by Party organizations around the country and meets every few years. (At the 13th Congress in 1987, there were 1,936 delegates.) The Congress elects:

### *The Central Committee*
Consists of 175 members picked from among Congress delegates. Members have other full-time jobs; they act for the Congress between sessions and meet periodically to discuss and approve policies. (There are various commissions, such as the Central Military Commission that controls the armed forces and the Central Advisory Commission that contains retired elders.) The Central Committee elects what are in effect the two highest Party bodies:

### *The Politbureau*
Sets the overall policy of the country—on foreign, economic, and social affairs. Consists of 18 members chosen from the Central Committee, all of whom are the country's leading political figures. Five senior members make up an inner-circle Standing Committee.

### *The Secretariat*
Actually runs the day-to-day affairs of the country. Is headed by the General Secretary, assisted by other secretaries and a large permanent staff.

*Source: The New York Times,* November 3, 1987, p. A8.

CLOSE-UP 10.3

## The Great Leap Backward

Mao urged his people to conquer their selfishness and serve the masses, and output stagnated. Deng made it possible for people to follow their self-interest, and output soared. In many places, life changed remarkably. Consider these typical stories:

1. In the North China village of Liuqiying, Yin Yongcheng used to grow paddy rice, corn, cotton, and peanuts on the collective land. Regardless of how hard he worked, he got the same income as everyone else. Under Mao's system of "the big pot," everyone shared equally in what the community produced, and it wasn't much. (It took almost 18 months' income to buy a bicycle.) One day, Yin heard of the economic reforms, and he had an idea. He asked the village committee to let him use 11 acres of unused land on the side of the mountain, and they gave him a 10-year contract. Then Yin got a local bank loan, hired 12 workers, and planted orange saplings and grape vines. In 1987, he got his first crop, and it was a good one. His income soared and before long he built himself a nice red brick house on the mountainside. It had 5 rooms and real window glass. He left behind his windowless 2-room apartment in the long row of communal hovels, made with baked mud and lacking water as well as light.

    Then Yin had an even better idea: He could multiply his yield if he had an irrigation pond. He applied for another bank loan, but it was denied. There was a lot of ill-disguised envy among his neighbors; they resented his good fortune.

2. Li Sigai lives in the village of Lolam in the Yunkai mountains. His father was a policeman, but he was murdered as a "Taiwan spy" during the Great Proletarian Cultural Revolution. Recently, Li built two small factories. One of them employs 160 workers; they make glass vials for medicines. The other one employs 40 workers; they make plastic bottle caps for the glass vials. Workers are paid by the piece; they can earn between 1,200 and 2,000 yuan per year. That is a lot in a place where the average income is 370 yuan per year, and it has brought radios, television sets, and electric fans into his workers' homes. Li's own income is much higher still: 120,000 yuan per year, and it shows—Li built himself a 38-room house, made with bluish-gray bricks and charcoal roof tiles and built in the style of prerevolutionary mansions. There is a huge entry hall, and rooms have 25-foot ceilings supported by big beams. The house stands on a hillside, overlooking the paddy fields and rows of mud houses across the valley.

    Li has become the effective leader of the village. People come to him for advice or to borrow money for their son's wedding or a TV set. Says Li, "If the big river is full of water, then the small rivers will also be full."

    In the meantime, the village Party committee has nothing to do; no one applies to join the Party. But there are complaints: Li Wasai (who grows rice on a third of an acre and lives in a 3-room mud house) has enough to eat but no cash and he can't find the time to work in the factory. He thinks all this is highly unfair.

The stories just told could be multiplied without end. In the mid-1980s, 50 percent of peasant households had a watch, 40 percent a bicycle, 30 percent a foot-powered sewing machine. More and more had new houses; some even had stereo sets and soft beds. Some got "rich" by growing chives, garlic, and lettuce on tiny plots of land or by raising ducks for their eggs, others by converting a corner of their house into a sty and raising half a dozen pigs. Others still wrote best-selling books with titles such as "Raising Angora Rabbits" or "The Scientific Cultivation of Mushrooms."

*Sources: The New York Times,* July 26, 1987, p. 12; November 7, 1987, p. 27; and December 1, 1987, p. 4.

## ANALYTICAL EXAMPLE 10.1

## The Chinese Population Bomb

"China has stood up." Such were the proud words of Mao Zedong in 1949 when his revolution had put an end to a century of national humiliation at the hands of foreign powers. Presumably, China was on its way to becoming "rich and strong." But despite the general optimism then prevailing, there were those who worried about a time bomb silently ticking away. As they saw it, the relentless growth of China's population—a mere 538 million in 1949—could easily push China into the abyss of permanent poverty. The problem had been spelled out by Thomas Robert Malthus, a British economist, way back in 1798. His thoughts are summarized in Figure A.

Take any country with a given set of natural and capital resources, a given technical knowledge, and a population of 100 million. Let its population and, there-fore, its labor force grow. Its food output will also grow, but along a curved line such as *OX* in the upper graph, depicting diminishing returns to labor. As a result, labor's average product, shown in the lower graph, will decline over time, falling to and then below the minimum of subsistence. In the end, population growth will be controlled: by mass starvation and death.

But it is clear that the evil day can be postponed by one of two events: (1) An increase in the quantity or quality of natural and capital resources, along with im-provements in technology, would shift up line *OX* as well as line *abc* and would, thus, move into the future the day of reckoning (point *b*); (2) a voluntary decrease of population growth would lengthen the time it takes for the day of reckoning to appear—a complete cessation of population growth (at, say, 100 million) could even ensure a permanent per-capita food output (point *a*) in excess of the subsistence minimum.

It is fascinating to note that the zig-zag course of China's economic policies since 1949 has been reflected in her population policy as well. Whenever the "reds" were in charge, population growth was seen as no problem at all, but when the "experts" were in charge, population control was given serious attention.

**Doctrinaire Marxism: 1949–1954.**   In an early period of boundless optimism, birth control was rejected as a capitalist trick, designed to kill off the Chinese people. Said Mao:

**Figure A**    The Malthusian Doctrine

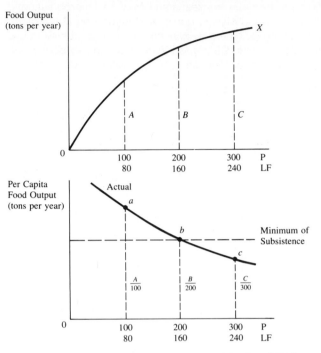

Food Output
(tons per year)

X

A              B              C

0

| 100 | 200 | 300 | P |
| 80  | 160 | 240 | LF |

Per Capita
Food Output
(tons per year)

Actual

a

b

Minimum of
Subsistence

c

$\frac{A}{100}$          $\frac{B}{200}$          $\frac{C}{300}$

0

| 100 | 200 | 300 | P |
| 80  | 160 | 240 | LF |

Millions of people in population, P, or labor force, LF (given
quantity and quality of natural resources, capital resources,
technical knowledge)

It is a very good thing that China has a big population. Even if China's population multiplies many times, she is fully capable of finding a solution; the solution is production. The absurd argument of Western bourgeois economists like Malthus that increases in food cannot keep pace with increases in population was not only thoroughly refuted by Marxists long ago, but has also been completely exploded by the realities in the Soviet Union and the Liberated Areas of China after their revolutions. . . .

Of all things in the world, people are the most precious. Under the leadership of the Communist Party, as long as there are people, every kind of miracle can be performed. . . . We believe that revolution can change everything, and that before long there will arise a new China with a big population and a great wealth of products, where life will be abundant and culture will flourish. All pessimistic views are utterly groundless.

**Family Limitation Campaign #1: 1954–1957.**    Then came a time when Mao promoted free discussion among people. "Let a hundred flowers bloom and a hundred schools of thought contend," he said. Before long, the vilified Malthusian doctrine became a "scented flower" even to Mao, who urged abortion, sterilization, late marriage, and contraception on his people to ward off the Malthusian danger. As a Beijing doctor put it:

> The wise directive of Chairman Mao concerning the need for planned birth control to regulate the population of China is deeply touching to all the intellectuals in the medical and public health circles. This highly creative directive is of great political, economic, historical, and international significance. We medical workers must respond warmly to the call of Chairman Mao along with all the people of the country. We must take action so that this glorious and great task can be well carried out. . . . There can be no doubt that under the leadership of the Party and Chairman Mao the Chinese people will have both the determination and confidence in their ability to carry out the glorious task of first class political significance entrusted to us by Chairman Mao. . . . The wise directive of Chairman Mao in this connection is exactly what all the people in China want because it conforms to the highest interests of the Chinese people.

**The Great Leap Forward: 1957–1962.**    The spirit of the Great Leap changed everything. As one official put it,

> A large population is a good, not an undesirable, thing. A larger population means greater manpower. This is simple logic. . . . Man is the most precious treasure and the determining factor in our great undertakings. . . . The force of 600 million liberated people is tens of thousands of times stronger than a nuclear explosion. Such a force is capable of creating wonders which our enemies cannot even imagine. Facts since the "big leap forward" movement have sufficiently proved this point.

And Mao said:

> The decisive factor, besides leadership by the Party, is the 600 million people. The more people, the more views and suggestions, and the more intense the fervor and the greater the energy. Never before have the masses been so spirited, with such high morale and so strongly determined. . . . Apart from their other characteristics, China's 600 million people are, first of all, poor, and secondly "blank." This seems a bad thing, but in fact it is a good thing. Poor people want change, want to do things, want revolution. A clean sheet of paper has nothing on it and so the newest and most beautiful words can be written and the newest and most beautiful pictures painted on it.

Still other officials echoed Mao's thoughts:

> Peasants have proven that the potentiality of the land is unlimited and the wisdom and strength of the people are inexhaustible. . . . The doubling of grain production shows the superiority of man in having not only a mouth but also hands. . . . The creativity of the masses is limitless, one leap will follow another year after year, miracle after miracle will happen, the soil will yield in proportion to man's audacity. . . . The incredibly high food grain harvest of 1958 has smashed the idealistic theory of diminishing returns from land and put the final nail in the

Malthusian coffin. . . . The vaunted reactionary bourgeois theory of population has been dealt a destructive blow by iron-clad facts.

**Family Limitation Campaign #2: 1962–1966.**   The end of the Great Leap brought another flip-flop in population policy. Officials emphasized the "horrid effects" of early marriage on family health, including a decrease in reasoning power (caused by decreased cell formation in the cerebral cortex), calcium loss from bones, the *torture* of birth, and much more. Above all, they noted, "having love affairs, looking at girls in pretty dresses, strolling with them in the street" was a form of *unhappiness* in that it wasted time and energy that should be devoted to working, studying, and serving one's fellow men.

**The Great Proletarian Cultural Revolution: 1966–1969.**   As the Red Guards "dragged out the power holders," the second birth control campaign, as all other policies, came to an end, amid utter confusion.

**Family Limitation Campaign #3: 1970–Present.**   Since 1970, population limitation has been urged rather consistently. This has included a vigorous campaign for the one-child family, accompanied with monetary subsidies and extra allocations of land for private garden plots. On the other hand, heavy fines have been levied against those having a second child and even heavier ones for third children. Forced abortions have also been performed. And the government has maintained detailed dossiers on all women of child-bearing age, listing their methods of birth control as well as rewards and punishments in connection with child-bearing behavior. Nevertheless, the Chinese population has continued to grow. In 1982, the largest census ever undertaken in human history counted 1,008,175,288 people. In 1988, when the national population growth rate itself rose, experts predicted 1.5 billion Chinese by 2010.

*Sources*: John S. Aird, "Population Policy and Demographic Prospects in the People's Republic of China," Joint Economic Committee, U.S. Congress, *People's Republic of China: An Economic Assessment* (Washington, D.C.: U.S. Government Printing Office, 1972), pp. 220–331; *The New York Times*, October 28, 1982, p. 1; *The Wall Street Journal*, July 18, 1983, p. 14, and July 14, 1988, p. 1.

## BIOGRAPHY 10.1   Mao Zedong

Mao Zedong (1893–1976) was born in Shaoshan, a small village in China's Hunan province. His father was a peasant who put Mao to work at age six, but also let him attend primary school.

In 1911, Mao joined the revolutionary army that overthrew the Ch'ing dynasty, and then attended the Chansha Teachers Training College. Upon graduation, he worked at Beijing University as a library assistant under Li Tachao. Li introduced Mao to a Marxist study group and, in 1921, along with Mao and others, founded the Communist Party of China. Mao became Party Secretary for Hunan province and a full-time revolutionary. By 1924, Mao realized the enormous revolutionary potential of the *peasants* as opposed to that of the small urban proletariat on which other Marxists were counting. He actively supported the Communists' alliance with the Nationalists (Kuomintang), organized labor unions and strikes and, in 1927, an autumn harvest uprising in Hunan. At the same time, the Nationalists under Chiang Kaishek turned against the Communists. After years of fighting, a critical moment arrived in 1934. Mao's forces—some 90,000 strong—broke through a Nationalist encirclement and retreated from southern China. They proceeded on the now famous Long March to the country's northwest, across 6,000 miles of mountains, rivers, and wastelands. Two years later, a mere 20,000 men, women, and children arrived to settle in the caves of Yenan. (In future years, participation in the Long March became a political litmus test of a person's revolutionary zeal.)

In Yenan, Mao ran a Party School and, from his mountain base, he organized the Communist fight against both the Nationalists and the Japanese invaders who had attacked China in 1937. A dozen years later, in 1949, a victorious Mao stood in Beijing, proclaiming the People's Republic of China.

Perhaps as many as 3 million "class enemies" were executed in the early 1950s. Then Mao, the impatient and romantic dreamer, launched the sweeping and convulsive campaigns noted in this chapter, which were designed to transform a semifeudal, backward, agricultural society into a socialist, egalitarian utopia and do so almost overnight. Mao was determined to achieve his dream by mass enthusiasm alone. "I have witnessed the tremendous energy of the masses. On this foundation it is possible to accomplish any task whatsoever," Mao said. "At no time and in no circumstances should a Communist place his personal interests first; he should subordinate them to the interests of the nation and of the masses. Hence selfishness, slacking, corruption, seeking the limelight, and so on, are most contemptible, while selflessness, working with all one's energy, whole-hearted devotion to public duty, and quiet hard work will command respect." Yet, Mao himself rose to be a living god to his people. His words were the doctrine of state. Printed in millions of little red books, the "Quotations from Chairman Mao Zedong" were taken to possess almost invincible magic properties.

*Sources: Quotations from Chairman Mao Tse-Tung* (Peking: Foreign Language Press, 1967), p. 269; *The New York Times,* September 10, 1976, pp. A1 and 13–17; *Who's Who in the Socialist Countries* (New York: K. G. Saur, 1978), pp. 380–81.

## BIOGRAPHY 10.2    Deng Xiaoping

Deng Xiaoping (1904–    ) was born in Guangan, Szechuan, the son of a prosperous landlord. He was educated at the French School in Chongqink, where he won a scholarship to France. In Paris, he met Zhou Enlai, China's future Prime Minister and Deng supporter but then editor of the *Red Light,* a communist publication. Deng joined the Chinese Communist Party in 1925 and continued his studies at Moscow's Far Eastern (Sun Yatsen) University.

Upon his return to China, he became Dean of Education at Zhongshan Military Academy. By 1930, he was Chief of Staff of the Red Army, then participated in the Long March and the subsequent Sino-Japanese War. After the Revolution of 1949, he held numerous high-level positions in Party, army, and government, ranging from membership in the Politbureau to Chief of Staff of the People's Liberation Army to Minister of Finance, Deputy Prime Minister, and more. Twice, in 1966 and again in 1976, he was purged from all his posts for his advocacy of pragmatic policies. During the Great Proletarian Cultural Revolution, at the urging of Mao's wife, who despised him, Deng was paraded through the streets of Beijing with a dunce cap, and he was given a menial job. (His daughter was assaulted and crippled at a Maoist rally.) Wall posters attacked him as an "unrepentant capitalist-roader" who emphasized production, saying, "I do not care whether a cat is black or white; the important thing is whether she catches mice." Said Mao: "This person does not grasp class struggle. He has never referred to this key link. He knows nothing of Marxism-Leninism. He represents the bourgeoisie."

But Deng returned with a vengeance. Quite likely, Deng has put an end to China's continuous series of 180-degree policy flip-flops. As this chapter's discussion of post-Mao reforms indicates, Deng eradicated Mao worship and put the country firmly back on the track of careful development planning, guided by a strong dose of material incentives. Unlike Mao, who had described them as being on the verge of collapse, Deng pictured his neighbors (Japan, Taiwan, Hong Kong, and South Korea) as gleaming citadels of wealth to be emulated. Unlike the Soviets whose economic reforms he characterized as "99 percent talk and 1 percent deeds," he pushed the Chinese reforms with "1 percent talk and 99 percent deeds."

Also unlike Mao before him, the aging Deng insisted in 1987 on stepping down "before my mind becomes confused." With this remark, he made it clear that he did not care to repeat Mao's last mistake: In his later years, Mao had refused to emerge from seclusion and quickly acquired a distorted view of the world, being surrounded by self-serving associates who sought to find out what Mao wanted to hear and then told it to him. As a result, Mao lost all contact with reality and had no notion that China had edged so close to economic catastrophe.

*Sources: Who's Who in the Socialist Countries* (New York: K. G. Saur, 1978), p. 619; *Time,* January 1, 1979, pp. 22 and 25; *The International Who's Who, 1982–83* (London: Europa Publications, 1982), p. 315; *The New York Times,* November 14, 1987, p. 27.

## BIOGRAPHY 10.3 Fidel Castro Ruz

Fidel Castro Ruz (1927–    ) was born in Birán, Cuba. He was educated in Jesuit schools in Santiago and Havana, graduated with a Doctor of Law degree from the University of Havana, and practiced law in Havana.

In 1953, he began his active opposition to the Batista regime with an attack on the Moncada barracks at Santiago. Sentenced to 15 years in prison but amnestied 3 years later, he went into exile in Mexico to plot armed rebellion. After landing with a small force in Oriente Province, he carried on the fight that displaced Batista in 1959. Ever since, Castro has held the leading positions in Party and government. During internal struggles in the 1960s between advocates of "economic rationality" like Carlos Rodriguez (who wanted to use monetary incentives to create wealth) and advocates of "revolutionary ethics" like Che Guevara (who wanted to abolish money and use political awareness to create wealth), Castro sided with the latter group. Consider some of his thoughts:

No human society has yet reached communism. The ways along which a superior form of society is reached are very difficult. A communist society means that man will have reached the highest degree of social awareness ever achieved; a communist society means that the human being will have been able to achieve the degree of understanding and brotherhood which man has sometimes achieved within the close circle of his family. To live in a communist society is to live in a real society of brothers; to live in a communist society is to live without selfishness, to live among the people and with the people, as if every one of our fellow citizens were really our brother.

Man comes from capitalism full of selfishness; man is educated under capitalism amidst the most vicious selfishness, as an enemy of other men, as a wolf to other men. . . .

And one of the first battles in the march toward communism is . . . lessening income inequalities, moving toward income egalitarianism. . . .

And we should not use money or wealth to create political awareness. We must use political awareness to create wealth. . . .

Some day we will all have to receive the same. Why? Some will ask: Will a cane-cutter earn as much as an engineer? Yes. Does that mean that an engineer will receive less? No. But some day a cane-cutter—and I say cane-cutter symbolically, because in the future we won't have any cane-cutters—let us say, the driver of a harvest combine or a truck, will earn as much as an engineer today.

And why? The thing is clear, very logical. The Revolution has thousands of young students in the universities. The Revolution has thousands of young people studying abroad, dedicated to studying, to becoming engineers, chemists, specializing in different fields. Who pays for their expenses? The people.

If the Revolution needs to send many young people to study in Europe and others in universities, all right; . . . but that doesn't mean they are privileged. It is important to the Revolution that they study, that they prepare themselves. But at the same time that thousands of our young people study abroad, thousands of others have to go into the fields to plant cane, to weed cane, to do very hard work. Within a few years there will be much more wealth in our country. The former will have finished three, five years of studies and will have become technicians, engineers; and the latter will have been working those years in the fields and they will not become engineers, but they will develop our economy, they will be building the future of our country.

Under what concept and in what way would it be just for us to tell these young people after a few years, in a more prosperous country, in a country with much more wealth: You are earning one fourth of an engineer's wages? Would it be just, would it be basically just, that those whom the country called on not to go to the university but to work to win the battle of the economy, to make the effort which at this time we cannot make with chemistry or with the machines which we do not have, but must make with our hands, with our sweat—would it be just, whenever the nation is able to enjoy the riches which they are creating now, for us to treat them as fourth- or fifth-class citizens, entitled to receive from society an insignificant part of what in the future will be received by those who are in the universities, those who are studying abroad?

No! Not at all. Communist conscience means that in the future the wealth that we create through everybody's effort should be equally shared by all. That is communism; that is communist conscience!

Indeed, in the late 1980s, Castro made it clear that he wanted no part of Soviet experiments with "capitalism." He shut down Cuba's independent farmers' markets and eliminated bonuses. A new campaign of "rectification" was to revive the dream of a selfless Cuba and to provide an ideological defense against everything that threatened "fundamental socialist principles."

*Sources: The International Who's Who,* 46th ed. (London: Europa Publications, 1982), p. 216; Fidel Castro, "To Create Wealth with Social Conscience," in Bertram Silverman, ed., *Man and Socialism in Cuba: The Great Debate* (New York: Atheneum, 1971), pp. 362–63 and 377–79; *The New York Times,* July 28, 1988, p. A13, and July 31, 1988, p. E3.

## Summary

1. Some people reject as equally unbearable a society dominated by the central plan and a society dominated by markets. They envision an alternative: the *intentional community* wherein people are united by love and where the institutional barrier of private property as well as the psychological barrier of selfishness is gone. In such a society of communal socialism, they imagine, people will serve one another driven by internal incentives alone; they will contribute to the best of their abilities and take only according to their needs.

2. Many attempts have been made to establish intentional communities on a small scale. Most of these attempts have ended in failure. Two successful experiments are described in detail: America's Bruderhof and Israel's kibbutz. The similarities are striking.

3. Two nationwide experiments with communal socialism have been made as well, by Mao Zedong in China and by Fidel Castro in Cuba. Both experiments foundered on the same dilemma: Any determined effort to destroy egoism interferes with the creation of abundance, while any determined effort to create abundance interferes with the destruction of egoism. Interestingly, China's experiment ended up with a decisive turn toward market-oriented reforms, while Cuba's experiment led to an embrace of orthodox Stalinist central planning.

4. Considering the experience of hundreds of small communal experiments throughout the world, as well as that of the only two (and limited) larger-scale experiments in Mao's China and Castro's Cuba, one can doubt that communal socialism is a viable alternative to centralized or market socialism. Thus, the question mark contained in this chapter's title is not a printing error.

## Key Terms

communes
external incentives
Great Leap Forward

Great Proletarian Cultural Revolution
household contract and responsibility
  system

intentional community
internal incentives
production brigades
production teams

sucrophilia
sucrophobia
utopia

## Questions and Problems

1. **Ms. A**: "Utopian visionaries are smart fellows. They always refuse to give a blueprint of their vision. Then all followers can imagine that exactly what *they* want is, in fact, being sought, while in truth the various visions of different followers are totally inconsistent with each other."
   **Ms. B**: "Of course. Unless all people are exactly alike, there is no such thing as utopia, *the* best of all possible worlds. There is a different utopia for each person!"
   What do you think?

2. **Mr. A**: "The Bruderhof is a perfect example of spiritual tyranny."
   **Mr. B**: "Small communities like the Bruderhof cannot possibly be dictatorial because would-be dictators (a) would have nothing to gain from being dictators, and (b) would not succeed because people would simply leave."
   What do you think?

3. "More often than not, those who want to make everybody do everything for love end up making everybody do everything out of fear." Evaluate.

4. Have a look at some of the "Selected Readings" and find out what American communes of the 1960s were trying to achieve.

5. In 1966, Kuo Mojo, chairman of China's Academy of Sciences, made the following public confession: "In the past score of years, a pen was always in my hand, writing and translating works amounting to many millions of words. However, in the light of present-day standards, what I have written, strictly speaking, should all be burned. It has no value— none whatsoever." Note: he continued in his job. Can you explain this?

6. Do you see any parallels between happenings in Mao's China and happenings in the Bruderhof? Make a list and explain.

7. Have a look at some of the "Selected Readings" and investigate the claim that much of the feverish effort put forth during China's Great Leap was wasted.

8. Have a look at some of the "Selected Readings" and investigate the claim that the alleged income equality between the leadership and the masses even in Mao's China was a myth.

9. Have a look at some of the "Selected Readings" and investigate the Chinese attitude toward the preservation of nature.

10. At one point Castro argued that it was morally wrong to let some people (like professional cane-cutters) do all the heavy or dirty work for

other people. So he decided that all people must take turns doing such work. Later, he considered it perfectly fine for some people only to do such work, provided they got extra rewards (more money or longer vacations). What do *you* think about this subject?

## Selected Readings

### Communes and Utopias

Andrews, E., *The People Called Shakers* (New York: Oxford University Press, 1953).

Armytage, W. H. G., *Heavens Below: Utopian Experiments in England, 1560–1960* (London: Routledge and Kegan Paul, 1961). A fascinating history, ranging from Diggers, Quakers, and Moravians to Owenites and Tolstoyans.

Arrington, Leonard J., *Great Basin Kingdom: An Economic History of the Latter-Day Saints, 1830–1900* (Cambridge, MA: Harvard University Press, 1958).

Bestor, A. E., Jr., *Backwoods Utopias: The Sectarian and Owenite Phases of Communitarian Socialism in America, 1663–1829* (Philadelphia: University of Pennsylvania Press, 1950).

Bouvard, Marguerite. *The Intentional Community Movement: Building a New Moral World* (Port Washington, NY: Kennikat Press, 1975). A superb discussion of numerous types of communes: free-church, rural-anarchist, and behaviorist.

Carden, Maren Lockwood, *Oneida: Utopian Community to Modern Corporation* (Baltimore, MD: Johns Hopkins Press, 1969).

Diamond, Stephen, *What the Trees Said: Life on a New Age Farm* (New York: Delta, 1971).

Fairfield, Richard, *Communes USA: A Personal Tour* (Baltimore, MD: Penguin Books, 1972).

Hertzler, Joyce O., *The History of Utopian Thought* (New York: Macmillan, 1923). A history from the eighth century B.C. to modern times.

Kanovsky, Eliyahu, *The Economy of the Israeli Kibbutz* (Cambridge, MA: Harvard University Press, 1966).

Kanter, Rosabeth M., *Communes: Creating and Managing the Collective Life* (New York: Harper and Row, 1973). A collection of articles describing different types of communes (religious, political, psychological) in many places (Japan, Israel, Tanzania, the United States).

Kateb, George, *Utopia and Its Enemies* (Glencoe: Free Press, 1963). An analysis of Utopia as heaven and utopia as hell.

Kinkade, Kathleen, *A Walden Two Experiment: The First Five Years of Twin Oaks Community* (New York: William Morrow, 1973). A frank and fascinating discussion of the joys and problems encountered by a Virginia commune.

Leon, Dan, *The Kibbutz: A New Way of Life* (Oxford: Pergamon Press, 1969).

Nordhoff, Charles, *The Communistic Societies of the United States* (New York: Harper, 1875). Discusses numerous communes, including the Amana, Harmony, Separatist, Shaker, Perfectionist, Aurora, Bethel, and Icarian societies.

North, Robert C., *The World That Could Be* (New York: Norton, 1976). A comprehensive discussion of literary utopias and experimental model settlements.

Peters, Victor, *All Things Common: The Hutterian Way of Life* (Minneapolis, MN: University of Minnesota Press, 1965).

Sugihara, Yoshi, and Plath, David W., *Sensei and His People: The Building of a Japanese Commune* (Berkeley, CA: University of California Press, 1969).

Walsh, Chad, *From Utopia to Nightmare* (New York: Harper and Row, 1962). A superb analysis of the utopian dream; what is utopia: a heaven? a hell? a bore?

Webber, Everett, *Escape to Utopia: The Communal Movement in America* (New York: Hastings House, 1959). A superb discussion of Shakers, Rappists, Owenites, Fourierists, Icarians, and many more.

Wilson, William E., *The Angel and the Serpent: The Story of New Harmony* (Bloomington, IN: University of Indiana Press, 1964).

Yablonsky, Lewis, *The Hippie Trip* (New York: Pegasus Press, 1968).

Yambura, Barbara, *A Change and a Parting: My Story of Amana* (Ames, IA: Iowa State University Press, 1960).

Zablocki, Benjamin, *The Joyful Community* (Baltimore, MD: Penguin Books, 1971). This chapter's account of the Bruderhof is based on this book.

## China

Chow, Gregory C., *The Chinese Economy* (New York: Harper and Row, 1985). A sophisticated textbook stressing mathematical model building.

Eckstein, Alexander, *China's Economic Development: The Interplay of Scarcity and Ideology* (Ann Arbor, MI: University of Michigan Press, 1975).

Eckstein, Alexander, *China's Economic Revolution* (Cambridge, MA: Harvard University Press, 1977).

Goodstadt, Leo, *China's Search for Plenty: The Economics of Mao Tse-Tung* (New York: Weatherhill, 1973).

Harding, Harry, *China's Second Revolution: Reform After Mao* (Washington, DC: The Brookings Institution, 1987).

Joint Economic Committee, U.S. Congress (Washington, DC: U.S. Government Printing Office). The following volumes contain numerous articles on all aspects of the Chinese economy.

a. *An Economic Profile of Mainland China.* 4 volumes (1967)

b. *Mainland China in the World Economy* (1967)

c. *Economic Developments in Mainland China* (1972)

d. *People's Republic of China: An Economic Assessment* (1972)

e. *Allocation of Resources in the Soviet Union and China* (1974)

f. *China: A Reassessment of the Economy* (1975)

g. *Chinese Economy Post-Mao* (1978)

h. *China under the Four Modernizations*, parts 1 and 2 (1982)

i. *Allocation of Resources in the Soviet Union and China* (1985)

*Journal of Comparative Economics,* September 1987. The entire issue is devoted to "Chinese Economic Reform: How Far, How Fast?"

Lifton, Robert J., *Revolutionary Immortality: Mao Tse-Tung and the Chinese Cultural Revolution* (New York: Vintage Books, 1968).

Prybyla, Jan S., *The Political Economy of Communist China* (Scranton, PA: International Textbook Company, 1970). A superbly written textbook full of unusual and fascinating detail about the Mao years.

Shapiro, Judith, and Liang Heng, *Cold Winds, Warm Winds: Intellectual Life in China Today* (Middletown, CN: Wesleyan University Press, 1986). Presents the dramatic story of the evolving but fragile freedoms of speech, belief, art, literature in the post-Mao years.

Wheelwright, E. L., and Bruce McFarlane, *The Chinese Road to Socialism: Economics of the Cultural Revolution* (New York: Monthly Review Press, 1970).

## Cuba

Draper, Theodore, *Castroism: Theory and Practice* (New York: Praeger, 1965). A superb treatment of the ideological and experimental aspects of Castro's revolution.

Mesa-Lago, Carmelo, *Cuba in the 1970s: Pragmatism and Institutionalization* (Albuquerque, NM: University of New Mexico Press, 1974).

Mesa-Lago, Carmelo, *Revolutionary Change in Cuba* (Pittsburgh, PA: University of Pittsburgh Press, 1971).

Ritter, Archibald, *The Economic Development of Revolutionary Cuba: Strategy and Performance* (New York: Praeger, 1974).

Silverman, Bertram, *Man and Socialism in Cuba: The Great Debate* (New York: Atheneum, 1971).

## Computer Programs

The SYSTEMS personal computer diskette that accompanies this book contains one program of interest to this chapter: Program 10, "Communal Socialism: An Alternative?" provides 20 multiple-choice questions about Chapter 10, along with immediate responses to incorrect answers.

# CHAPTER 11

# *Economic Reform: Variations on a Theme*

Consider these words from Chapter 7 of this book (which dealt with the *Soviet economy*):

> The Stalinist economic system has been plagued by a great variety of problems. . . . The inherent complexity of the task of setting up a comprehensive national plan of economic activity that is perfectly coordinated and feasible would be sufficient by itself to account for this fact. Thus, it is not surprising that Soviet plans have consistently failed to meet that standard of perfection. The perverse system of incentives guiding peasants, enterprise managers, and workers has not helped. It has induced peasants to malinger on the collectively owned land and to concentrate their efforts on tiny private plots. It has induced managers to corrupt the crucial flow of information to central planners, to resist technical innovations, to pollute the natural environment with abandon, and, above all, to ignore the wishes of their customers (with respect to the proper assortment of goods, their quality, their timely delivery, and the availability of spare parts and servicing). The Stalinist incentive system has contributed to a widespread lack of labor discipline and induced workers who cannot find what they want in state retail stores to focus their attention on the underground economy. It has blanketed the entire society with a network of bribery and corruption.
>
> The results of these factors have been hidden unemployment of resources, ubiquitous inefficiency, declining rates of economic growth, a widely shared perception of economic inequity, and a severe degree of alienation. During Stalin's lifetime, however, few dared openly criticize the system associated with his name or the results it produced.

One could write precisely the same words with respect to any one of the East European nations that fell into the Soviet orbit after World War II and on which the Stalinist economic system was imposed. Albania, Bulgaria, Czechoslovakia, East Germany, Hungary, Poland, Rumania—all of these eventually came to experience deep dissatisfaction with Stalin's centralized system of planning and managing the economy. And just as the Soviet Union herself—from Khrushchev to Gorbachev—has embarked on a seemingly endless series of economic reforms, so has the economic history of all these countries since Stalin's death been dominated by a single theme: *economic reform.*

To be sure, the type, timing, pace, and reversibility of reform have differed among the countries in question, but the various national leaders have been united in their desire to improve upon the Stalinist system. While this chapter does not aim to describe each country's economic history in detail, it will provide a general overview of the post-Stalin movement for reform. Within that movement, three ideas have emerged concerning the central planning bureaucracy: (1) that it might be replaced by markets, (2) that it might be improved by a judicious dose of administrative decentralization, and (3) that it might be strengthened through improvements in mathematics and computer technology. In the remainder of this chapter, each of these ideas will be explored in turn.

## Marketization

In at least two countries, Czechoslovakia and Hungary, there surfaced the idea that much of the central planning bureaucracy could simply be dismantled. There was no need at all, it was argued, to have any centralized input-output planning followed by the issuing of detailed verbal directives couched in physical terms. With a view to Lange's model (Chapter 8) and Tito's experience (Chapter 9), it was considered quite possible to coordinate the actions of households and enterprises not by a vertical structure of command with the central planners at the top, but by horizontal relations among suppliers and demanders in free markets for resources and goods. Given the well-known experience with private plots in agriculture and with the underground economy, it was even argued that private and cooperative firms might be legitimized and allowed to compete with state-owned enterprises and that the latter might be made financially independent and self-governing.

There is always a big step, of course, between thoughts tentatively expressed and actions actually taken. Consider what did happen.

## Czechoslovakia

In Czechoslovakia, a blueprint for reform was first published in 1964. It was endorsed by Communist Party Secretary Alexander Dubček and Deputy Premier Ota Šik (Biography 11.1 at the end of this chapter). And it was implemented between 1966 and 1968. The power of central planners was substantially reduced: As in

Yugoslavia earlier, most of the centralized physical command system was abolished; central planners were to guide a market economy with an array of "economic regulators." These were to involve monetary and fiscal policies, the setting of exchange rates, and various levels of price control (the outright fixing of prices for some goods, the setting of maximum prices for others and of price ranges for others still). The direct operative intervention of central authorities in enterprises was to be exceptional. Eventually, all prices were to be set by competition in markets that would be open to free international trade, even with the West.

The right to make input and output decisions was transferred to the enterprises themselves, and there was even talk of worker self-management in the future. In any case, enterprises were to buy inputs in markets, sell outputs in markets, and engage in strict financial accounting. They were to follow the profit motive. Profits were to be taxed in part, the remainder being distributed among a reserve fund, a sharing fund (for bonuses), and a development fund (to finance investment, along with depreciation allowances and bank credits). As in Yugoslavia, private initiative was encouraged, even the hiring of some employees by private firms. (Before long, private agricultural enterprises flourished; so did private housing construction and apartment rental, and a host of small businesses, ranging from bakeries, electric repair, and garages to laundries, restaurants, and tailor shops.)

Alexander Dubček, First Secretary of the Czechoslovak Communist Party, even argued that these economic reforms stood no chance of ultimate success unless coupled with a revamping of the political system—in particular, the abandonment of the systematic use of terror as an instrument of governance. The free market in goods must eventually be extended to a free market in ideas, he said. He proposed a pluralistic, participatory democracy (within the framework of the one-party system) based on free speech and a free press. Everyone should have the right to criticize the government, he argued, so that the best blend of centralized and decentralized direction of the economy could be discovered from discussion. There was no advantage, he argued, in always persecuting critics, dismissing them from their jobs, denying them educational opportunities, evicting them from their apartments, punishing even their relatives, and, finally, exiling them or locking them up in prisons or mental hospitals. The "Prague spring" had arrived.

Yet, it was not to last. The Czech reformers had deeply offended the Soviets with their Titoist talk of worker self-management, with their announced intention to achieve economic integration with the West, and with their linkage of economic and political reforms. Thus, in the summer of 1968, and at the invitation of a self-appointed group of Czech conservatives, Soviet tanks rolled into Prague. The invasion of Czechoslovakia by five Warsaw Pact countries was later justified by the Brezhnev doctrine: "It is the duty of socialist states to intervene in other such states to protect the socialist system from revisionism." At the time, Czechoslovakia's Deputy Premier, Ota Šik, came under special attack by the occupying powers. They charged him with counterrevolution, having tried to "restore capitalism under the vulgar economic slogan of confrontation between the enterprises and the market." His ideas were characterized as "devilishly resembling the capitalist wolves' law of the free play of market forces." He was pictured as having engaged in a variety of "intrigues" against the people, including the sponsorship of unemployment, the elimination of the state monopoly on foreign trade, and the teaching of a course on the principles of capitalism to high economic functionaries. All this was to have created "chaos" in the economy. Thus, the Czech economic reforms were halted and reversed. Even in later years, when many Communist parties in Europe differed openly with the Soviets, the Czechs under Communist Party Secretaries Gustav Husak (until 1987) and Milos Jakes (since 1987) persisted in a stance of extreme adulation toward the Soviet Union. And within Czechoslovakia, people longed in vain for the fleeting moments that had been the Prague spring. (Charter 77, a much harassed human rights group, issued a manifesto in 1987 that strongly criticized the repressive regime as well as "the special and mysterious incomes" of the Party elite. A year later, on the 20th anniversary of the invasion, it called upon Secretary Gorbachev "to provide an open space for a factual assessment of the events of 1968 and to reach the appropriate conclusions.")[1]

## Hungary

In Hungary, under Premier Imre Nagy, a market-oriented economic reform had been on the drawing board ever since 1953. The uprising of 1956, which was smashed by Soviet troops and led to the execution of Nagy, seemed to put an end to all the reformist talk. Yet, the Soviet-installed leadership under János Kádár, while realizing that any anti-Soviet policy was suicidal, was united in its desire to improve the performance of the Hungarian economy through meaningful reform. In 1968, under the determined leadership of two Politbureau members (Rezsö Nyers and Jenö Fock), Hungary introduced its New Economic Mechanism. It was quite similar to the ill-fated Czech reform but carefully avoided the three "excesses" that had triggered the Soviet wrath (worker self-management, economic integration with the West, and political liberalization). The Hungarian leaders wholeheartedly accepted the primacy of a unified Communist Party domestically and of the Soviet Union internationally. Thus, the tanks rolled into Prague but not into Budapest, and the Hungarian reform was not renounced. Having originally enacted the reform without the ambivalence exhibited elsewhere, the highest leadership has subsequently shown firm resolve to stick with their reform. They have also, however, shown an unwavering commitment to the U.S.S.R., assuring the Soviets that Hungarian marketization would not be allowed to produce runaway political change.

By the late 1980s, under Kádár's successor, Karoly Grosz, Hungary was the most market-oriented economy inside the Soviet orbit. The role of central planners was sharply limited, mostly to macroeconomic policies. Formerly underground economic activities had been legalized, and private firms were flourishing in trade and services. (Note Close-Up 11.1, "Hungary's March to the Market.") Agriculture had been decollectivized; some 80 percent of its (rapidly growing) output came

---

[1]*The New York Times,* August 21, 1988, p. 16.

from private or genuinely cooperative farms. They provided Hungary with a quarter of its exports. Socialist enterprises were maximizing profits instead of fulfilling output quotas. There were many joint ventures with foreign firms. (One U.S.-Hungarian venture even led to the opening in 1988 of the first school of business administration in Eastern Europe.) In general, prices, including foreign exchange rates, were set by demand and supply in free markets (but the government did fix prices of "highest priority" goods and prescribed price ranges for certain other goods). In addition, Hungarian citizens enjoyed considerably more civic freedoms than their Czech neighbors. Unlike the Czechs, and similar to the Yugoslavs, Hungarians could even travel to the West with relative ease.

## Administrative Decentralization

Several other countries, such as East Germany and Poland, introduced considerably less radical reforms. In general, these reforms reduced (but did not abolish) the giving of instructions by central authorities; they increased (but not very much) the sphere within which enterprise managers could exercise initiative. Ideally, the central planning board concentrated on issuing monetary or less detailed physical input-output instructions, and these were disaggregated for enterprises by new types of cartel-like organizations made up of all enterprises with identical or similar products. Thus, intermediate-level **production associations,** situated in the planning and management hierarchy between the central planning board and individual enterprises, were given many of the powers previously held by the central planning board itself. In short, the bureaucratic hierarchy was reshaped, but the vertical command structure was not given up in favor of horizontal market relations among independent enterprises.

To be sure, each enterprise was "encouraged" to get together with its customers. On the basis of their wishes and the knowledge of its own capabilities, it was to make a consistent and feasible proposal to higher authorities as to what inputs it wanted to get and what, how, and for whom it wanted to produce. However, the higher authorities still had to approve each enterprise plan (to make sure the proposed actions were in the "public interest" and the sum of all such enterprise plans stayed within the national possibilities). There was to be no coordination by the market. In that way, it was argued, higher authorities could selectively approve and disapprove proposed plans. Thus, they could keep direct control over the major proportions of economic activity (private consumption, investment, collective consumption, foreign trade), over the distribution of investment among sectors or regions, and even the output of "principal" products.

The reforms also sought to eliminate the perverse effects of the Stalinist model by reforming price-setting procedures and reshaping the managerial incentive system. Although prices for all scarce things were not to be set by supply and demand in free markets, they were to be "rationalized"; that is, centrally set so as to be in equilibrium. Thus, rates of interest and rent for the use of capital and natural resources (previously set at zero for ideological reasons) were to become positive rates, and all other prices were to be revised thoroughly. Following that, managers were to receive bonuses not based on the production of physical output quantities, but on the basis of some other variable, such as sales or profit.

As a result, many good things were expected to happen: Managers rewarded by profit would think twice about holding on to idle buildings, machines, or inventories, because they would now have to pay interest for the privilege. For the same reason, they would think twice about holding on to idle natural resources, because this would now involve a rental charge. And they would care a great deal about not paying workers for mere attendance. Whether rewarded by sales or profit, finally, managers would think twice before producing the wrong types of goods, shoddy goods, goods without spare parts or servicing, or goods delivered at the wrong time. Such behavior would prevent sales or profit and, thus, the receipt of bonuses, it was argued.

In fact, however, wherever these types of administrative reforms were introduced, the pressures to undo the reforms also were strongest. Often various aspects of the reforms that were mutually supportive were, nevertheless, not introduced simultaneously, ensuring "failure" of the reform. The reform might be introduced in some firms or industries only; or the managerial incentive system might be changed, but the accompanying reform of prices be neglected; or prices might be "reformed" but still be far from their equilibrium values. All this was well designed by the enemies of reform to justify later efforts of recentralization. (As a popular joke had it, "We are going to introduce driving on the left side of the street; to test its desirability, we will try it experimentally first—for buses only.")

In addition, central planners often refused to release their bureaucratic stranglehold over individual enterprises, even when the reform law directed them to give up their "petty tutelage." More often than not, enterprise managers who were now "free" to decide for themselves, found themselves engaged in "direct discussions" with state officials about the meaning of "the public interest." For various reasons, they found the "informal, official guidance" offered them irresistible. Or they found themselves with free investment funds to be spent for any purpose, but also with physical allocations of materials allowing only centrally specified uses. Thus, they continued to be told what numbers and types of workers to use, what quantities and types of products to produce, what types of investments to undertake. . . .

## East Germany

While reform was on the agenda ever since 1953, the time of the East German uprising, official action was only taken in 1963 with the introduction of the *New Economic System*. Yet, this first reform was never fully implemented, and it was totally discredited by the 1968 events in Czechoslovakia (which East Germany helped invade). In the early 1970s, certain central planning functions were indeed passed down the hierarchy to production associations (VVBs), which presided over numerous horizontal mergers of enterprises producing similar products. That reform, however, was superseded by yet another in the late 1970s, which created some 225 vertically integrated groupings of enterprises. These mammoth **combines** (*Kombinate*) were to be partners with the East Berlin planners in drafting and executing the central plan. Unlike the earlier VVBs, the combines were not only *vertically* integrated (containing, say, all enterprises from iron ore mine to steel plant to machinery factory), but they also conducted their own research and were free to arrange their own foreign trade.

By the late 1980s, the limited nature of the East German reforms had become quite obvious. There were some 132 nationwide combines with 25,000 workers on the average; in addition, some 93 regional combines employed an average of 2,000 workers. Most decisions were still based on material balances worked out by East Berlin. Unlike in Hungary, the farm sector remained collectivized, joint ventures with foreigners were out of the question, and the private sector was quite small. Civil freedoms were minuscule; the Berlin Wall continued to symbolize the repressive nature of the regime. See Close-Up 11.2, ''The Wall.'' (Nevertheless, despite the fact that East Germany had only tinkered with the Stalinist model, she suffered less than the Soviet Union from malingering by workers. As a Hungarian observer put it, ''No system has yet been invented under which Germans can be prevented from working.'')

## Poland

Economic reforms have been urged upon the Polish leadership ever since the 1950s by a number of economists of world renown: Wlodzimierz Brus, Michael Kalecki, and Oskar Lange (Biography 8.1). More forcefully, reforms have been induced by the behavior of the population at large—deeply Catholic and traditionally anti-Russian—which included major riots in 1956, 1970, 1976, and 1980. As a result of repeated tinkering with the Stalinist model, there has emerged a significant private sector in the economy: Small private businesses with up to 50 employees are now allowed; over three quarters of the land is privately farmed. On the other hand, there has also occurred a violent suppression of popular aspirations for further reform. Unlike in Yugoslavia where the idea was imposed from the top, Poland's Solidarity union reflected a grass-roots movement for worker control of industry. In 1980, under the leadership of Lech Walesa, the (illegal) union sparked an uprising in the Lenin Shipyards at Gdansk. At the time, workers demanded higher wages, a cut in food prices, and fewer hours of work; before long, amid nationwide scenes of popular enthusiasm, they also demanded a free press, the legalization of opposition parties, and free elections. Predictably, as in Czechoslovakia of 1968, the Soviets drew the line. In 1981, Poland's General Wojciech Jaruzelski crushed the Solidarity Movement by imposing martial law. It was not lifted till 1983 (the year, ironically, when Lech Walesa was awarded the Nobel Peace Prize). In many ways, the Stalinist problems survive; see Close-Up 11.3, ''A Toilet Paper Shortage.''

## Computerization

While central planners in many East European countries were failing to implement reforms designed to dismantle some of their power, they were also busily engaged in experiments designed to increase it. Their hope centered on the mathematical technique of **linear programming,** a direct descendant of input-output analysis (discussed in Chapter 6). Linear programming is a general technique applicable to problems of optimization under constraints (such as production techniques, resource availability, and preferences). It was invented in the Soviet Union in 1939 by Leonid V. Kantorovich (Biography 11.2), but nothing came of it because of Stalin's doctrinaire hostility to the use of mathematics in economic planning. Subsequently, the technique was fully developed in the United States by George B. Dantzig, Tjalling C. Koopmans, and others and reintroduced to the Soviet Union in the 1950s—along with enormous advances in computer technology. This inspired some central planners with an intoxicating vision of a ''computer utopia'' that would rescue central planning from all its errors:

A giant network of high-speed computers might be set up covering the entire country. Through its channels, a hitherto inconceivable volume of information would continually flow to a central ''brain'' in Moscow and similar capitals, coming from each and every enterprise and conveying information of hitherto undreamed-of detail. On instructions by political leaders concerning the desired composition of national output, the central computer would rapidly explore all the implications and issue the perfect plan. In fact, political leaders could contemplate, on paper, the implications of producing many alternative sets of future output, and then choose the one they considered best. How well that would compare to the crude material balance planning of Stalin's days!

In fact, nothing of the sort has happened so far. Nevertheless, it is instructive to note that the dream of administrative centralism is alive and well. Thus, the Ninth Five-Year Plan of the Soviet Union, which ended in 1975, introduced 2,700 automated computer systems at the enterprise level. Eventually, these enterprise computers were to report to regional ones and those, in turn, to a centralized brain. Before long, it was then claimed, this huge brain would be able to supervise some 50,000 industrial firms and a like number of farms. This would become the underpinning, said V. M. Glushkov (head of the Ukrainian Institute of Cybernetics), for the ''scientific regulation of socialist society.'' Thus, it was hoped, the era of the abacus (still widely used in Stalin's days) would give way to the era of electronics. The remainder of this chapter explains what is involved.

## Central planning as a maximization problem*

Let us consider a simple example of central economic planning by means of linear programming. The elements of our hypothetical decision-making problem are laid out in Table 11.1, ''A Maximization Problem.''

---

*Optional Section. This section contains advanced material and can be skipped without loss of continuity. Those who wish to pursue the mathematics involved, however, may also like to try out the relevant computer programs noted at the end of this chapter. The ''Linear Programming'' module enables the interested reader to solve any linear programming problem instantly without having to go through the complicated calculations found on the following pages. The ''Simultaneous Equations'' program can help those who do wish to make the calculations in detail.

**Table 11.1** A Maximization Problem

| Type of Input (0) | Production Activities | | Final Uses | | Unemployment | | | Constraints (Inputs Available) (8) |
|---|---|---|---|---|---|---|---|---|
| | A (1) | B (2) | $D_A$ (3) | $D_B$ (4) | $D_L$ (5) | $D_K$ (6) | $D_T$ (7) | |
| A | −1 | .3 | 1 | 0 | 0 | 0 | 0 | 0 |
| B | .1 | −.9 | 0 | 1 | 0 | 0 | 0 | 0 |
| L | 2 | 3 | 0 | 0 | 1 | 0 | 0 | 180 |
| K | 6 | 5 | 0 | 0 | 0 | 1 | 0 | 500 |
| T | 1 | 3 | 0 | 0 | 0 | 0 | 1 | 90 |
| Planners' Values (rubles): | 0 | 0 | 1 | 4 | 0 | 0 | 0 | — |

*Inputs Needed per Unit of Disposal Activities*

The *row* headings given in column (0) reveal an economy using five types of inputs: intermediate goods A and B, plus the services of human, capital, and natural resources L, K, and T. (We can imagine that all these inputs are measured in convenient physical units, such as tons of fertilizer, tons of wheat, hours of labor, hours of truck use, years of acre use, and so on.)

The *column* headings for columns (1) to (7) indicate that seven types of activities are occurring in this economy (which is why linear programming is also referred to as **activity analysis).** These activities are: (1) producing good A, (2) producing good B, (3) delivering good A to final users (private household consumers, enterprise investors, government consumers, or any type of foreign recipient), (4) delivering good B to final users, (5) delivering human resources into unemployment, (6) delivering capital resources into unemployment, and (7) delivering natural resources into unemployment.

The numbers within any one of these columns indicate the inputs needed if *one unit* of the relevant activity is to be performed; for convenience, output produced is denoted as negative input. Thus, column (1) tells us that the production of 1 unit of good A makes available 1A to the rest of the economy (note the entry of −1), while absorbing from the rest of the economy .1 unit of good B plus 2 units of labor services, L, plus 6 units of capital services, K, plus 1 unit of land services, T (note all the positive entries).

Column (2), similarly, tells us that the production of 1 unit of B absorbs from the rest of the economy .3A, 3L, 5K, and 3T (the positive entries), while making available .9B to the rest of the economy (the negative entry). This implies that the B industry itself is consuming .1B for every 1B it produces.

The interpretation of columns (3) to (7) is child's play: Column (3) says that the delivery of 1 unit of A to a final user (not to be confused with the *production* of 1A shown in column [1]) simply requires the use of 1A, nothing more. Column (4) says, similarly, that the delivery of 1 unit of B to a final user (not to be confused with the *production* of 1B shown in column [2]) requires the use of 1B, nothing else. Likewise, the placement of 1 unit of labor into unemployment (column [5]) requires the use of 1L, nothing else. And the placement of 1 unit of capital resources (column [6]) or of 1 unit of natural resources (column [7]) into unemployment also requires merely the use of 1K or 1T, respectively.

Column (8) lists the constraints under which we imagine our planning problem is to be solved. The first two entries tell us that whatever the *total* production of A or B, its use as intermediate input for making A and B plus its delivery to final users must exactly exhaust production, leaving a zero quantity of each good. The remaining column (8) entries tell us that the *total* use of L, K, or T in production or in unemployment cannot exceed the totals available, which are 180, 500, and 90 units, respectively.

The last row of Table 11.1, finally, reveals the relative preferences of our central planners with respect to the seven possible activities in this economy. These values are not market prices; they are subjective evaluations arbitrarily set. They indicate that our planners attach no value (positive or negative) to the production of A or B as such (columns [1] and [2]) nor to the unemployment of resources (columns [5] to [7]). On the other hand, each unit of A delivered to a final user (rather than consumed, perhaps, as an intermediate good in the process of producing A or B) is considered worth 1 ruble. Similarly, each unit of B delivered to a final user (rather than consumed as an intermediate good) is viewed as four times as valuable as A and considered worth 4 rubles.[2]

We can now state the central planners' task succinctly as a maximization problem: Given production techniques (Table 11.1, columns [1] and [2]), given resource availability (column [8]), and given planners' preferences (last row), find the most highly valued set of economic activities. In our example, where positive values have been placed only on goods delivered to final users, this task amounts to discovering the set of activities that maximizes the GNP.

**The Simplex Method.**    Our central planning problem is simple enough to lend itself to a demonstration of the algebraic solution that would normally be performed by a computer. To begin with, we should note that the information contained in each of the Table 11.1 columns can be written as a **column vector,** which is a

---

[2]In principle, our planners could, however, also assign positive or negative values to the column (1), (2), (5), (6), or (7) activities. What would it mean if these values were not zero as in Table 11.1, but were +1 ruble, −2 rubles, −7 rubles, −4 rubles, and +3 rubles, respectively? This would indicate that planners looked favorably upon the production of A as such (even if none of it ever made it to a final user), while being even more delighted at the unemployment of natural resources (+1 ruble versus +3 rubles). Such valuations might reflect the planners' view that activity A (farming, perhaps) was healthful and good for people's souls and that natural resources should also be preserved for future generations. The negative values (−2, −7, and −4 rubles), on the other hand, would indicate disapproval of the *production* of B (perhaps because it created pollution), regardless of how much B was *consumed,* as well as disapproval of the unemployment of human and capital resources, especially the former.

special kind of matrix consisting of any number of rows and a single column, and which is symbolized by a single capital letter. For example, column (1), (5), or (8) of Table 11.1 can be written as

$$A = \begin{bmatrix} -1 \\ .1 \\ 2 \\ 6 \\ 1 \end{bmatrix} \text{ or } D_L = \begin{bmatrix} 0 \\ 0 \\ 1 \\ 0 \\ 0 \end{bmatrix} \text{ or } C = \begin{bmatrix} 0 \\ 0 \\ 180 \\ 500 \\ 90 \end{bmatrix}$$

In addition, note that the technique of linear programming, as its name suggests, assumes the existence of linear relationships among relevant variables. For example, given vector A, which is the recipe for producing 1 unit of A, it is assumed that 3A can be produced by tripling each of the inputs (that constant returns to scale prevail):

$$3A = 3 \cdot \begin{bmatrix} -1 \\ .1 \\ 2 \\ 6 \\ 1 \end{bmatrix} = \begin{bmatrix} 3 \cdot (-1) \\ 3 \cdot .1 \\ 3 \cdot 2 \\ 3 \cdot 6 \\ 3 \cdot 1 \end{bmatrix} = \begin{bmatrix} -3 \\ .3 \\ 6 \\ 18 \\ 3 \end{bmatrix}$$

This indicates that the production of 3A by the A industry is expected to make available to the rest of the economy 3A, while absorbing inputs from it of .3B, 6L, 18K, and 3T.

We can now designate the central plan by a single equation in which the capital letters denote column vectors, while the letters $a$ through $g$ refer to the unknown levels of the seven possible activities:

$$aA + bB + cD_A + d\,D_B + eD_L + f\,D_K + gD_T = C \tag{11.1}$$

According to this equation, producing $a$ units of good A plus $b$ units of good B, while delivering $c$ units of good A and $d$ units of good B to final users, and while keeping $e$ units of human resources, $f$ units of capital resources, and $g$ units of natural resources unemployed, must exactly meet the constraints of available resources.

Equation 11.1, of course, implies the following:

$$a\begin{bmatrix} -1 \\ .1 \\ 2 \\ 6 \\ 1 \end{bmatrix} + b\begin{bmatrix} .3 \\ -.9 \\ 3 \\ 5 \\ 3 \end{bmatrix} + c\begin{bmatrix} 1 \\ 0 \\ 0 \\ 0 \\ 0 \end{bmatrix} + d\begin{bmatrix} 0 \\ 1 \\ 0 \\ 0 \\ 0 \end{bmatrix} + e\begin{bmatrix} 0 \\ 0 \\ 1 \\ 0 \\ 0 \end{bmatrix} + f\begin{bmatrix} 0 \\ 0 \\ 1 \\ 0 \\ 0 \end{bmatrix} + g\begin{bmatrix} 0 \\ 0 \\ 0 \\ 0 \\ 1 \end{bmatrix} = \begin{bmatrix} 0 \\ 0 \\ 180 \\ 500 \\ 90 \end{bmatrix}$$

This can, in turn, be expanded into five equations, one for each of the Table 11.1 rows:

$$-1a + .3b + 1c + 0d + 0e + 0f + 0g = 0 \tag{11.2}$$
$$.1a - .9b + 0c + 1d + 0e + 0f + 0g = 0 \tag{11.3}$$

$$2a + 3b + 0c + 0d + 1e + 0f + 0g = 180 \qquad (11.4)$$
$$6a + 5b + 0c + 0d + 0e + 1f + 0g = 500 \qquad (11.5)$$
$$1a + 3b + 0c + 0d + 0e + 0f + 1g = 90 \qquad (11.6)$$

These equations are easy to interpret. For example, Equation 11.2 is stated in units of good A. It says that $-1$ times the unknown quantity $a$ of good A produced plus .3 times the unknown quantity $b$ of good B produced (which is the total of A used up in making B) plus 1 times the unknown quantity $c$ of good A delivered to final users must equal zero. Or take Equation 11.4, which is stated in units of labor. It says that 2 times the unknown quantity $a$ of good A produced (which is the amount of labor used by the A industry) plus 3 times the unknown quantity $b$ of good B produced (which is the amount of labor used by the B industry) plus 1 times the unknown quantity $e$ of unemployed labor must equal the 180 units of labor available.

The optimum central plan in our example can be found by solving equations 11.2 to 11.6, *subject to the goal of maximizing the value of economic activities, V,* given the planners' valuations of each. In our example, this goal comes to

$$\text{Maximize V} = 1c + 4d \qquad (11.7)$$

But note that the *five* equations (11.2 to 11.6) contain *seven* unknowns ($a$ through $g$); hence, a huge number of potential solutions must be surveyed to find the one solution that maximizes V. Some of these solutions (namely all those providing negative values for $a$ through $g$) can be ruled out at once as economic nonsense: One cannot produce negative amounts of goods A or B, one cannot deliver negative amounts of A or B to final users, nor can one tolerate negative unemployment of resources (because that would mean using greater quantities than are available). But there does exist a systematic procedure for finding the best solution among all the remaining combinations of zero or positive unknowns. This method is called the **simplex method;** we turn to it now.

**Finding the Basic Feasible Solution.**   The simplex method begins by establishing a **basic feasible solution;** that is, *any* solution of $n$ equations and $n$ unknowns that does not violate the constraints but that need not yet satisfy the goal of maximizing V. If, for example, in Equation 11.1 we arbitrarily set $d$ and $g$ (the delivery of B to final users and the unemployment of natural resources) equal to zero, we are left with five equations and five unknowns, summarized by Equation 11.8:

*Basic feasible solution*

$$a\text{A} + b\text{B} + c\text{D}_\text{A} + e\text{D}_\text{L} + f\text{D}_\text{K} = \text{C} \qquad (11.8)$$

This is equivalent to

$$a\begin{bmatrix} -1 \\ .1 \\ 2 \\ 6 \\ 1 \end{bmatrix} + b\begin{bmatrix} .3 \\ -.9 \\ 3 \\ 5 \\ 3 \end{bmatrix} + c\begin{bmatrix} 1 \\ 0 \\ 0 \\ 0 \\ 0 \end{bmatrix} + e\begin{bmatrix} 0 \\ 0 \\ 1 \\ 0 \\ 0 \end{bmatrix} + f\begin{bmatrix} 0 \\ 0 \\ 0 \\ 1 \\ 0 \end{bmatrix} = \begin{bmatrix} 0 \\ 0 \\ 180 \\ 500 \\ 90 \end{bmatrix}$$

In turn, we can write

$$-1a + .3b + 1c = 0 \qquad (11.9)$$
$$.1a - .9b \qquad = 0 \qquad (11.10)$$
$$2a + 3b + 1e = 180 \qquad (11.11)$$
$$6a + 5b + 1f = 500 \qquad (11.12)$$
$$1a + 3b \qquad = 90 \qquad (11.13)$$

Using any conventional method, we can solve these equations for $a = 67.5$, $b = 7.5$, $c = 65.25$, $e = 22.5$, and $f = 57.5$. Thus, the basic feasible solution can also be written as

$$67.5A + 7.5B + 65.25D_A + 22.5D_L + 57.5D_K = C \qquad (11.14)$$

Given the planners' preferences indicated in the last row of Table 11.1, this set of economic activities is worth 65.25 times 1 ruble, or 65.25 rubles.

**Improving upon the Basic Solution.** Step 2 of the simplex method (see Table 11.2) tests for possible changes in this basic solution. The simplex method, in effect, applies this optimization principle: *Any activity not included in a given solution should be added, and other activities requiring equivalent resources should be deleted, if the net effect is to improve upon the achievement of the goal.* That goal, in our case, is to maximize V.

Consider, for example, adding the delivery of B to final users to the five activities contained in Equation 11.8. To find the amounts of other activities that are equivalent to $1D_B$, we write

$$D_B = vA + wB + xD_A + yD_L + zD_K \qquad (11.15)$$

This, of course, is shorthand for five equations:

$$\begin{bmatrix} 0 \\ 1 \\ 0 \\ 0 \\ 0 \end{bmatrix} = v \begin{bmatrix} -1 \\ .1 \\ 2 \\ 6 \\ 1 \end{bmatrix} + w \begin{bmatrix} .3 \\ -.9 \\ 3 \\ 5 \\ 3 \end{bmatrix} + x \begin{bmatrix} 1 \\ 0 \\ 0 \\ 0 \\ 0 \end{bmatrix} + y \begin{bmatrix} 0 \\ 0 \\ 1 \\ 0 \\ 0 \end{bmatrix} + z \begin{bmatrix} 0 \\ 0 \\ 0 \\ 1 \\ 0 \end{bmatrix}$$

The last expression can be disaggregated as shown in equations 11.16 to 11.20.

$$0 = -1v + .3w + 1x + 0y + 0z \qquad (11.16)$$
$$1 = .1\ v - .9w + 0x + 0y + 0z \qquad (11.17)$$
$$0 = 2\ v + 3w + 0x + 1y + 0z \qquad (11.18)$$
$$0 = 6\ v + 5w + 0x + 0y + 1z \qquad (11.19)$$
$$0 = 1\ v + 3w + 0x + 0y + 0z \qquad (11.20)$$

It follows that $v = 2.50$, $w = -.83$, $x = 2.75$, $y = -2.50$, and $z = -10.83$. Therefore,

$$D_B = 2.50A - .83B + 2.75D_A - 2.50D_L - 10.83D_K \qquad (11.21)$$

**Table 11.2** Simplex Method: Step 2

| Activity That Might Be Added to Program (1) | Equivalent Activities in Present Program (2) | Marginal Benefit of Addition (ruble value of 1) (3) | Marginal Cost of Addition (ruble value of 2) (4) | Marginal Net Benefit of Addition (5) = (3) − (4) |
|---|---|---|---|---|
| A | $1A$ | 0 | 0 | 0 |
| B | $1B$ | 0 | 0 | 0 |
| $D_A$ | $1D_A$ | 1 | 1 | 0 |
| $D_B$ | $2.5A - .83B + 2.75D_A - 2.5D_L - 10.83D_K$ | 4 | 2.75 | 1.25 |
| $D_L$ | $1D_L$ | 0 | 0 | 0 |
| $D_K$ | $1D_K$ | 0 | 0 | 0 |
| $D_T$ | $.75A + .083B + .73D_A - 1.75D_L - 4.92D_K$ | 0 | .73 | −.73 |

Equation 11.21 is nothing else but a complex marginal rate of transformation. Just as a simple *MRT* might tell us that 1 car equals 50 bicycles in the sense that we can produce $+1$ car if we produce $-50$ bicycles, the *MRT* of Equation 11.21 tells us that the delivery of 1B to a final user can be accomplished by *not* doing the kinds of things shown on the right-hand side of the equation; that is, by producing 2.50A less but .83B more while delivering 2.75A less to final users and raising unemployment by 2.50L and 10.83K. (End-of-chapter problem 5 and its answer at the back of the book prove the point.)

The right-hand side of Equation 11.21 is the fourth entry in column (2) of Table 11.2; the remaining entries in that column show analogous equivalences and are similarly calculated. (See end-of-chapter problem 6.)

Given the planners' preferences indicated in the last row of Table 11.1, we can fill in the ruble values of the column (1) entries in column (3) and those of the column (2) entries in column (4). These entries, in turn, show us in column (5) the marginal net benefits to be expected from adding various activities to our basic feasible solution (Equation 11.14).

Because the marginal net benefit from delivering B to final users is largest, the simplex method recommends adding the maximum possible amount of this activity (which we will call $\alpha\, D_B$) to the original (Equation 11.14) program and, of course, deducting amounts of present activities that make equivalent demands on the economy, or $\alpha\, (2.5A - .83B + 2.75D_A - 2.5D_L - 10.83D_K)$. The Equation 11.14 solution, thus, changes to read

$$67.5A + 7.5B + 65.25D_A + 22.5D_L + 57.5D_K + \alpha\, D_B$$
$$- \alpha(2.5A - .83B + 2.75D_A - 2.5D_L - 10.83D_K) = C \quad (11.22)$$

or

$$\alpha\, D_B + (67.5 - 2.5\alpha)A + (7.5 + .83\alpha)B$$
$$+ (65.25 - 2.75\alpha)D_A + (22.5 + 2.5\alpha)D_L$$
$$+ (57.5 + 10.83\alpha)D_K = C \quad (11.23)$$

Since no activity can occur at a negative level, the maximum possible value for $\alpha$ is 23.73—found by comparing $(67.5/2.5) = 27$ with $(65.25/2.75) = 23.73$ and choosing the lower figure. This $\alpha$ value completely eliminates the delivery of A to final users. The new program becomes the:

*Second feasible solution*

$$8.18A + 27.27B + 23.73D_B + 81.83D_L + 314.55D_K = C \quad (11.24)$$

Given the planners' preferences noted in Table 11.1, this set of economic activities is worth $4(23.73) = 94.92$ rubles, or 29.67 rubles more than the basic feasible solution. (The difference reflects the 1.25-ruble marginal net benefit noted in column [5] of Table 11.2, multiplied by 23.73.) Yet, we cannot be certain that Equation 11.24 represents the best of all possible solutions.

**Looking for Further Improvement.**   Once more, the simplex method recommends a test of the net benefit to be gained from expanding any one of our seven activities. Table 11.3 makes the test.

Column (5) of Table 11.3 indicates that no positive marginal net benefits can be reaped by changing the economic program implied by Equation 11.24. The previously calculated value of V = 94.92 rubles is the maximum possible one.

**Interpreting the Optimum Solution.**   It is easy to interpret the optimum solution of Equation 11.24. We can do so most clearly by rewriting the equation as follows:

$$8.18A + 27.27B + 0D_A + 23.73D_B + 81.83D_L + 314.55D_K + 0D_T = C$$
$$(11.25)$$

By making the column vectors explicit, we get

| | A | | B | | $D_A$ | | $D_B$ | | $D_L$ | | $D_K$ | | $D_T$ | | C |
|---|---|---|---|---|---|---|---|---|---|---|---|---|---|---|---|---|
| A | $\begin{bmatrix} -1 \\ .1 \\ 2 \\ 6 \\ 1 \end{bmatrix}$ | | $\begin{bmatrix} .3 \\ -.9 \\ 3 \\ 5 \\ 3 \end{bmatrix}$ | | $\begin{bmatrix} 1 \\ 0 \\ 0 \\ 0 \\ 0 \end{bmatrix}$ | | $\begin{bmatrix} 0 \\ 1 \\ 0 \\ 0 \\ 0 \end{bmatrix}$ | | $\begin{bmatrix} 0 \\ 0 \\ 1 \\ 0 \\ 0 \end{bmatrix}$ | | $\begin{bmatrix} 0 \\ 0 \\ 0 \\ 1 \\ 0 \end{bmatrix}$ | | $\begin{bmatrix} 0 \\ 0 \\ 0 \\ 0 \\ 1 \end{bmatrix}$ | | $\begin{bmatrix} 0 \\ 0 \\ 180 \\ 500 \\ 90 \end{bmatrix}$ |

$8.18 \begin{bmatrix} -1 \\ .1 \\ 2 \\ 6 \\ 1 \end{bmatrix} + 27.27 \begin{bmatrix} .3 \\ -.9 \\ 3 \\ 5 \\ 3 \end{bmatrix} + 0 \begin{bmatrix} 1 \\ 0 \\ 0 \\ 0 \\ 0 \end{bmatrix} + 23.73 \begin{bmatrix} 0 \\ 1 \\ 0 \\ 0 \\ 0 \end{bmatrix} + 81.83 \begin{bmatrix} 0 \\ 0 \\ 1 \\ 0 \\ 0 \end{bmatrix} + 314.55 \begin{bmatrix} 0 \\ 0 \\ 0 \\ 1 \\ 0 \end{bmatrix} + 0 \begin{bmatrix} 0 \\ 0 \\ 0 \\ 0 \\ 1 \end{bmatrix} = \begin{bmatrix} 0 \\ 0 \\ 180 \\ 500 \\ 90 \end{bmatrix}$

Thus, the optimum program implies:

> *For good A:* Producing 8.18A and letting the B industry use all this as an input (27.27 · .3A = 8.18A); no A is delivered to final users.
> *For good B:* Producing 27.27B, of which 8.18 (.1B) = .818B are used by the A industry and 27.27 (.1B) = 2.727B are used by the B industry, while 23.73B are delivered to final users.
> *For human resources, L:* Of 180 units available, the A industry uses 8.18 (2L) = 16.36L, the B industry uses 27.27 (3L) = 81.81L, while 81.83L are unemployed.

**Table 11.3**   Simplex Method: Step 3

| *Activity That Might Be Added to Program* (1) | *Equivalent Activities in Present Program* (2) | *Marginal Benefit of Addition (ruble value of 1)* (3) | *Marginal Cost of Addition (ruble value of 2)* (4) | *Marginal Net Benefit of Addition* (5) = (3) − (4) |
|---|---|---|---|---|
| A | 1A | 0 | 0 | 0 |
| B | 1B | 0 | 0 | 0 |
| $D_A$ | $-.91A + .3B + .36D_B + .91D_L + 3.94D_K$ | 1 | 1.44 | −.44 |
| $D_B$ | $1D_B$ | 4 | 4 | 0 |
| $D_L$ | $1D_L$ | 0 | 0 | 0 |
| $D_K$ | $1D_K$ | 0 | 0 | 0 |
| $D_T$ | $.09A + .3B + .26D_B - 1.09D_L - 2.06D_K$ | 0 | 1.04 | −1.04 |

*For capital resources, K:* Of 500 units available, the A industry uses 8.18 (6K) = 49.08K, the B industry uses 27.27 (5K) = 136.35K, while 314.55K are unemployed.

*For natural resources, T:* Of 90 units available, the A industry uses 8.18 (1T) = 8.18T, the B industry uses 27.27 (3T) = 81.81T, and there is no unemployment.

**Shadow Prices.** We should note that any rearrangement of the Equation 11.25 program—for example, with the intention of eliminating or reducing the unemployment of labor or capital—would *reduce* V, the value of economic activities as measured by the preferences of the central planners.

We should also note that the shaded numbers in Table 11.3 (the last three entries in column [4]) provide central planners with a particularly crucial bit of information. The numbers highlighted there are called **shadow prices;** these are the implicit valuations that always emerge as a by-product of solving a linear programming problem algebraically. Note that an extra unit of labor as well as of capital is designated as worthless in the final solution because the economy has more of each then it can profitably use. On the other hand, the economy's production is in the end limited by the full use of all available natural resources, and this bottleneck input has a positive shadow price of 1.04 rubles. This shadow price indicates that central planners could raise the value of output by 1.04 rubles if they could get another unit of natural resources (which could then be combined with the freely available labor and capital). Such shadow prices are extremely important pieces of information for economic decision makers because they indicate the true scarcity of inputs (which may not be indicated by their official prices). Also note: The value of inputs used, calculated at their shadow prices, always equals the value of the output they produce. In our case, the shadow prices of both labor and capital are zero, but the total value of natural resources employed comes to 90 units times 1.04 rubles per unit, or 93.60 rubles. Except for rounding error, this equals the maximum V associated with the optimum plan of Equation 11.24. ▬▬▬

CLOSE-UP 11.1

## Hungary's March to the Market

Long before the Soviets introduced similar reforms (see Chapter 7), the Hungarians legalized many types of private enterprises. Consider the Budapest taxi driver who delivers packages anywhere in this sprawling capital. Consider the factory worker who now works as a private auto mechanic. Consider the poet who sells eulogies for funerals, or the members of a mountain-climbing club who run a business washing the windows of high-rises.

"We are saying to our ambitious people: Unfold your capacities," declares Miklos Villanyi, Hungary's Deputy Finance Minister. He argues that it is wiser to foster strivings than to have to stop people later from venting frustrations in the streets. "It's quite a natural ambition for all human beings to want more than they had yesterday," he says. "We must give them the chance."

"Not everybody likes what we are doing," concedes Janos Fekete, President of Hungary's National Bank. "They are afraid we are being capitalist. . . ." He continues: "Nothing is holy in our system. Except that we shall be socialist and nothing else. That is holy. But we are flexible."

*Source: The Wall Street Journal,* March 26, 1982, pp. 1 and 16.

## CLOSE-UP 11.2

## The Wall

Some 857 miles of wall—fortified with electrified fencing, barbed wire, minefields, 35,000 automatic shooting devices, 625 watchtowers, 910 concrete bunkers, and 1,000 attack dogs—separate the two Germanies. All that is designed to keep the East Germans at home. No wonder they feel as if they were living in a maximum-security penitentiary. Still, although it seems next to impossible, East Germans try to make a run for it. For every 1 who succeeds, 10 others fail. On the average, some 5,000 prisoners are being held on unlawful-border-crossing charges. The East German government has been "selling" about 1,200 of them a year to the West Germans at $50,000 each.

Among those who try to make it on their own, ingenuity is at a premium. One 24-year-old waiter dug his way out with his bare hands. One family stole a plane and crash-landed it across the border; no one in the group had ever flown an aircraft before. An engineer piloted a glider across. Two families with four children used a home-made hot-air balloon patched together with bedsheets and shower curtains and powered with propane gas designed for camp stoves. Others have made it by hiding in drums used for storing telephone cables, by building a minisubmarine, and even by creating a look-alike U.S. Army vehicle, donning homemade U.S. Army uniforms, and driving across.

*Source: The New York Times,* October 6, 1979, pp. 1 and 8.

## CLOSE-UP 11.3

## A Toilet Paper Shortage

Recently, the Polish Parliament tackled one of the big issues of the times: "When only," a deputy asked, "it it going to end?" She was referring to the fact that people had to stand in line for hours to get simple toilet paper.

The Minister of Chemical and Light Industry acknowledged a 100-million-roll annual shortage and appealed for patience. A new factory was under construction, he said; paper mills were being modernized—all should be well in about three years.

In the meantime, all kinds of goods—ranging from toilet paper to cosmetics, from Scotch whiskey to Japanese radios, from quality watches to auto parts—can be found easily in black markets around the country, in exchange for *bons*. These are an official kind of scrip denominated in dollars and issued by Polish banks in exchange for genuine dollars that some Poles get from American friends. The worse things get in the state-controlled economy the greater is the demand for bons and the higher is their price. While the official exchange rate is 100 zlotys for a dollar, the black market rate can easily be 700 zlotys for an equivalent bon. People call the black market rate the *Jaruzelski index:* The higher it is, the worse things are.

*Sources: Forbes,* February 13, 1984, pp. 45–46; *The Daily Hampshire Gazette,* November 3, 1986, p. 7.

## BIOGRAPHY 11.1   Ota Šik

Ota Šik (1919–     ) was born in Pilsen, Czechoslovakia. He took a job at an electronics firm upon completing school, but soon spent five years in a Nazi concentration camp as a political prisoner. After the war, he studied and taught economics in Prague. In the 1960s, he held numerous important positions in Czechoslovakia, including Director of the Institute of Economics of the CSSR Academy of Sciences, Director of the State Economic Reform Commission, membership in the Central Committee of the Communist Party, and Deputy Prime Minister. As such he became a major spokesman for the "Prague spring" discussed in this chapter. He argued strongly for a market-directed rather than centrally planned economy.

After the Soviet-led invasion of 1968, he was granted political asylum in Switzerland (and was promptly deprived of his Czech citizenship). He is now a professor of economics at the University of St. Gallen and has written numerous books (such as those noted in the "Selected Readings" to this chapter) that advocate a humane and democratic socialism.

*Source: Who's Who in the Socialist Countries* (New York: K. G. Saur, 1978), p. 559.

## BIOGRAPHY 11.2   Leonid V. Kantorovich

Leonid Vitalyevich Kantorovich (1912–     ) was born in St. Petersburg, Russia. His career as a mathematical genius advanced rapidly. At the age of 14, he enrolled at Leningrad University; by the time he was 22, he was a full professor of mathematics. During World War II, he worked at Leningrad's Naval Engineering School; in 1949, he received the Stalin Prize for his work in pure mathematics on functional analysis and computer development. In 1958, he was elected to the prestigious Soviet Academy of Sciences, and he received the 1965 Lenin Prize for his work in mathematical economics (shared with the chief architects of the mathematical revolution in Soviet economics, V. S. Nemchinov and V. V. Novozhilov). In the 1970s, Kantorovich headed the Moscow Institute for the Management of the National Economy. While there, in 1975, he received the Nobel Memorial Prize in Economic Science (jointly with T. C. Koopmans). He is now working at the All-Union Scientific Research Institute for Systems Research.

In the 1930s, the Central Plywood Trust approached Kantorovich with a problem. The producers of plywood were rotating logs in stripping machines that cut off a continuous thin sheet of material. These sheets were then laminated to make plywood. There were many types of logs and many machines with different productivities. How could one match logs to machines so as to process the largest possible volume per unit of time? Kantorovich responded by inventing linear programming. His 1939 Leningrad paper, "Mathematical Methods of Organizing and Planning Production," was the first publication ever to appear on the subject.

By 1943, Kantorovich realized that the national economic plan itself could be viewed as a grandiose linear programming problem. He extended linear programming from a tool for solving short-run planning problems of the firm to one for solving the short-run planning problems of the nation. He noted that the optimum solution of the national planning problem revealed shadow prices for all goods and resources, which could be used to make crucial decisions. As he put it (in the book noted below), "There evolves in the process of plan construction a *sui generis* 'competitive struggle' between different technological paths accompanied by 'price fluctuations,' which help to reveal those whose adoption would be most purposeful." His calculation of positive prices for the use of scarce capital and natural resources, however, clashed with Stalinist ideology (which insisted that such resources be priced at zero under socialism to reflect their common ownership by all the people). As a result of this clash, Kantorovich's book *The Best Use of Economic Resources* was not published until 1959, well after Stalin's death. Since then, Kantorovich has extended his earlier model of optimal short-run national planning to long-run planning as well.

*Sources:* "Selected Readings" on Kantorovich given at the end of this chapter.

## Summary

1. The Stalinist economic system (which was imposed on all of Eastern Europe at the end of World War II) has been plagued by a great variety of problems. No wonder that the economic history of Eastern Europe since Stalin's death has been dominated by a single theme: economic reform. Three ideas have emerged concerning the central planning bureaucracy: (1) that it might be replaced by markets, (2) that it might be improved by a judicious dose of administrative decentralization, and (3) that it might be strengthened through improvements in mathematics and computer technology.

2. In at least two countries, Czechoslovakia and Hungary, there surfaced the idea that much of the central planning bureaucracy could simply be dismantled. A liberal market-oriented Czech reform, however, came to an end with the Warsaw Pact invasion of 1968; a similar Hungarian reform has flourished.

3. Several other countries, such as East Germany and Poland, introduced considerably less radical reforms. Frequently, these reforms involved only an administrative decentralization of central planning board powers to intermediate-level production associations, such as East Germany's VVBs or combines (Kombinate). Many of the Stalinist problems have survived.

4. While central planners in many East European countries have resisted reforms designed to dismantle their powers, they have been busy with experiments designed to increase these powers. One hope has centered on the mathematical technique of linear programming, which is described in detail.

## Key Terms

activity analysis

basic feasible solution

column vector

combines

linear programming

production associations

shadow prices

simplex method

## Questions and Problems*

1. This chapter has focused on the movement for economic reform in Eastern Europe. Turn to some of the "Selected Readings" and find out about the fate of the Stalinist system outside of Europe.

2. East European central planners have typically preferred administrative decentralization to marketization. Can you figure out why?

3. Turn to some of the "Selected Readings" and find out whether other East European countries have ever experienced anything like Stalin's personality cult.

*4. Consider the *basic feasible solution* given in Equation 11.14.
   a. What precisely does it tell us about the country's economic activities?
   b. What are the implied allocations of goods A and B and of the three types of resources?

*5. Consider the complex *MRT* represented by Equation 11.21. Prove that it is correct.

*6. The text explained the calculation of the fourth entry in column (2) of Table 11.2. Similarly explain the calculation of the remaining entries in that column.

*7. Table 11.3 established equivalences between (a) $D_A$ and the activities in the second feasible solution and (b) $D_T$ and the activities in the second feasible solution. Check the calculations.

---

*Questions denoted by an asterisk utilize advanced material presented in optional sections.

**\*8.** Rework the linear programming problem contained in Table 11.1 under the assumption that central planners wish to maximize not the GNP (the value of final goods produced) but a more comprehensive measure of economic welfare, MEW, that evaluates none of the seven activities at zero, but includes the positive and negative valuations given in the footnote on page 316. (Thus, the entries in the last row of Table 11.1 should be imagined to read $+1$, $-2$, $+1$, $+4$, $-7$, $-4$, and $+3$.) Present your answer as a single equation along with the maximum value of MEW.

**\*9.** Present the economic plan found in problem 8 in the form of an input-output table. (Review Chapter 6 as needed.)

**\*10.** Present the economic plan found in problem 8 as a set of material balances. (Review Chapter 7 as needed.)

## Selected Readings

Åslund, Anders. *Private Enterprise in Eastern Europe* (New York: St. Martin's Press, 1985). Focuses on East Germany and Poland.

Berg, Elliot J. "Socialism and Economic Development in Tropical Africa," *The Quarterly Journal of Economics,* November 1964, pp. 549–73. A discussion of socialist ideology in Africa, ranging from Tanganyika's Ujamaa (meaning "familyhood") to Senegal's amalgam of Marxism, Christian socialism, and "negritude" to Guinea's heretical Marxism (which denies the presence of class struggle in Africa) and more.

Bland, Robert G. "The Allocation of Resources by Linear Programming," *Scientific American,* June 1981, pp. 126–44. A superb exposition of the current state of the art.

Bornstein, Morris. *Plan and Market: Economic Reform in Eastern Europe* (New Haven, CT: Yale University Press, 1973). Discusses pressures for, resistance to, and major aspects of economic reforms in Czechoslovakia, East Germany, Hungary, Poland, and Yugoslavia.

Brus, Wlodzimierz. *The Market in a Socialist Economy* (London: Routledge and K. Paul, 1972).

Brus, Wlodzimierz. *The Economics and Politics of Socialism: Collected Essays* (London: Routledge and K. Paul, 1973).

Brus, Wlodzimierz. *Socialist Ownership and Political Systems* (London: Routledge and K. Paul, 1975).

Various works by a major Polish economist.

Dantzig, George M. *A Procedure for Maximizing a Linear Function Subject to Linear Inequalities* (Washington, D.C.: Headquarters U.S. Air Force, 1948).

Dantzig, George M. *Linear Programming and Extensions* (Princeton, NJ: Princeton University Press, 1963).

The original statement of the simplex method, and later developments.

Dorfman, Robert. "Mathematical, or Linear, Programming: A Nonmathematical Exposition," *The American Economic Review,* December 1953, pp. 797–825.

Dubček, Alexander. *Czechoslovakia's Blueprint for "Freedom"* (Washington, D.C.: Acropolis Books, 1968).

Hardt, John P., ed. *Mathematics and Computers in Soviet Economic Planning* (New Haven: Yale University Press, 1967). Chapter 3, written by Benjamin Ward, deals with "Linear Programming and Soviet Planning."

Joint Economic Committee, U.S. Congress (Washington, D.C.: U.S. Government Printing Office). Numerous essays deal with all aspects of East European economies.

 **a.** *Economic Developments in Countries of Eastern Europe* (1970)
 **b.** *Reorientation and Commercial Relations of the Economies of Eastern Europe* (1974)
 **c.** *East European Economies Post-Helsinki* (1977)
 **d.** *East European Economic Assessment,* Parts 1 and 2 (1981)
 **e.** *East European Economies: Slow Growth in the 1980's* (1986)

Kantorovich, Leonid V. "Mathematical Methods of Organizing and Planning Production," *Management Science,* July 1960, pp. 366–422.

Kantorovich, Leonid V. *The Best Use of Economic Resources* (Cambridge, MA: Harvard University Press, 1965).

Kantorovich, Leonid V. "Essays in Optimal Planning," *Problems of Economics,* August-September-October 1976, pp. 3–251.

Translations of the original 1939 article, of his 1943 work not published until 1959, and of 18 essays, with an introduction on the life and work of Kantorovich (Biography 11.2) by Leon Smolinski.

Mrachkovskaia, Irina. *From Revisionism to Betrayal—A Criticism of Ota Šik's Economic Views* (Moscow: Progress Publishers, 1972).

Price, Ralph B. "Ideology and Indian Planning," *The American Journal of Economics and Sociology,* January 1967, pp. 47–64. A discussion of the Congress Party's commitment to building a "socialist pattern of society" (which was alleged best to fit the philosophical foundations of Hinduism).

Šik, Ota. *Plan and Market under Socialism* (White Plains, NY: International Arts and Sciences Press, 1967).

Šik, Ota. *Czechoslovakia, the Bureaucratic Economy* (Greenwich, CN: International Arts and Sciences Press, 1972).

Šik, Ota. *The Third Way: Marxist-Leninist Theory and Modern Industrial Society* (White Plains, NY: International Arts and Sciences Press, 1976).

Šik, Ota. *For a Humane Economic Democracy* (New York: Praeger, 1985).

The former Deputy Premier of Czechoslovakia (Biography 11.1) criticizes the Stalinist system imposed upon his country and presents his "Third Way."

Wilson, Edward O. "The Ergonomics of Caste in the Social Insects," *The American Economic Review,* December 1978, pp. 25–35. A fascinating application of linear programming to the survival of insect colonies.

## Computer Programs

The SYSTEMS personal computer diskette that accompanies this book contains three programs of interest to this chapter:

    **a.** Program 11, "Economic Reform: Variations on a Theme," provides 12 multiple-choice questions about Chapter 11, along with immediate responses to incorrect answers.

    **b.** Appendix B, "Simultaneous Equations," allows you to solve up to 12 simultaneous linear equations.

    **c.** Appendix D, "Linear Programming," allows you to solve any linear programming problem.

# PART 3

# *Capitalist Economic Systems*

The chapters of Part 3 include an idealized version of capitalism: a model of a perfectly competitive market economy in which government plays a crucial but minimal role. This model is contrasted with a real-world economy, that of the United States. A final chapter discusses a trend common to all capitalist countries, the increasing involvement of government in economic affairs.

# CHAPTER 12

# *Market Capitalism: A Model*

In this chapter, we introduce yet another vision of an idealized economic system. It is a vision of those who reject all forms of collectivism but champion individualism. They abhor the conscious direction of society by government toward goals deliberately chosen by it and designed to achieve the common good. They argue, in contrast, that the meaning of the ''common good'' should never be defined by government, however benevolent. In fact, they think that the term has no meaning whatsoever unless one wishes so to designate *whatever* result actually emerges from a multitude of independent choices made by all the individuals in society—provided all of them are free to define their own happiness in their own way and to take whatever actions seem appropriate to achieve it.

Critics, of course, worry about the approach suggested here. In any economy, they say, everything that one person does comes to intermingle with the actions of all others in an endless web. Any one action requires, directly and indirectly, appropriate complementary actions by thousands of other people. Letting millions of people separately select their own economic activities, and refusing to let government coordinate them, is bound to create chaos in the economy.

The advocates of the individualist approach, however, have a ready answer: Coordination of independently decided but interdependent economic activities of millions of people engaged in a division of labor can easily be achieved, they say, by letting self-interested people follow the guidance of *price signals* generated in free markets. They point to the possibility of a **spontaneous coordination** or **market coordination**, to the working of the **Invisible Hand** advocated 200 years ago by Adam Smith (Biography 12.1). Thus, they recommend the very opposite of *deliberate coordination, managerial coordination,* or the *Visible Hand* discussed in

Chapter 6. As they see it, no central economic planner needs to be put in charge of anything (a situation that dooms people, critics argue, to "irrationality" and "enslavement by blind forces"). Under market coordination, they say, people do not cooperate with each other because someone issues commands reinforced, no doubt, by appropriate threats for noncompliance. Gone is the motto of the deliberate order: "You will do what I tell you, or I will do something bad to you." Instead, all individuals make their own plans on the basis of whatever limited knowledge they happen to possess. Then they meet in markets and make conditional offers to one another: "I will do something nice for you, if you do something nice for me."

Coordination of the actions of different people is achieved and maintained by the **price system,** the set of interdependent prices in all the markets for goods and resources. These prices change as long as the independent actions of households and firms are not perfectly coordinated, making households and firms, in turn, change their behavior until coordination is achieved. Prices tell people indirectly what their inability to know everybody and everything intimately keeps them from knowing directly. Being keenly aware of how their welfare is affected by the prices they can get for what they sell and by the prices they must pay for what they want, all people are habitual price watchers. When people look for 16 million tons of apples, while only 8 million are being offered, anxious would-be buyers of apples will compete against each other and drive the price up. In response to these higher prices, two changes will occur: (1) some price-watching households will change their minds and decide to seek fewer apples at the higher price (using, perhaps, oranges instead); (2) some price-watching owners of firms will change their minds, too, and decide to offer more apples at the higher price (producing more apples at the expense of something else, reducing apple inventories, increasing imports, and so on). Before long, a balance will be achieved between the production and consumption of apples. Similar adjustments will occur in all other realms of activity.

In 1845, Frédéric Bastiat, a famous French economist, was considering precisely the same issue:

> On coming to Paris for a visit, I said to myself: Here are a million human beings who would all die in a few days if supplies of all sorts did not flow into this great metropolis. It staggers the imagination to try to comprehend the vast multiplicity of objects that must pass through its gates tomorrow, if its inhabitants are to be preserved from the horrors of famine, insurrection, and pillage. And yet all are sleeping peacefully at this moment without being disturbed for a single instant by the idea of so frightful a prospect. . . .
>
> How does each succeeding day manage to bring to this gigantic market just what is necessary—neither too much nor too little? What, then, is the resourceful and secret power that governs the amazing regularity of such complicated movements, a regularity in which everyone has such implicit faith, although his prosperity and his very life depend upon it?[1]

---

[1]Translated by the author from "Il n'y a pas de principes absolus," in *Sophismes Économiques,* in *Oeuvres Complètes de Frédéric Bastiat,* vol. 4 (Paris: Guillaume, 1907), pp. 94–97. See Bastiat, *Economic Sophisms* (Princeton, NJ: Van Nostrand, 1964) for an English edition.

And Bastiat answered his own question about the secret power that is quite capable of governing the market economy:

> *That power . . . is the principle of free exchange. We put our faith in that inner light which Providence has placed in the hearts of all men, and to which has been entrusted the preservation and the unlimited improvement of our species, a light we term self-interest, which is so illuminating, so constant, and so penetrating, when it is left free of every hindrance. Where would you be, inhabitants of Paris, if some cabinet minister decided to substitute for that power contrivances of his own invention, however superior we might suppose them to be: If he proposed to subject this prodigious mechanism to his supreme direction, to take control of all of it into his own hands, to determine by whom, where, how, and under what conditions everything should be produced, transported, exchanged, and consumed? Although there may be much suffering within your walls, although misery, despair, and perhaps starvation, cause more tears to flow than your warmhearted charity can wipe away, it is probable, I dare say it is certain, that the arbitrary intervention of the government would infinitely multiply this suffering and spread among all of you the ills that now affect only a small number of your fellow citizens.*

Yet, we should not conclude that the advocates of our model would have no room for government. As they see it, government would have to play a crucial although limited role.

## The Crucial Role of Government

A *well-functioning* capitalist market economy, it is argued, requires not only that **economic power,** the capacity to make and enforce decisions on the allocation of resources and the apportioning of goods, is put in the hands of *private* individuals, but also that it is carefully distributed in such a way that all of them have as equal a share of it as possible. For that purpose, government would have to tackle at least three subsidiary tasks:

First, government would have to assign property rights—rights to the exclusive use—for all scarce things. If it did not make clear who could and could not control any scarce thing, chaos would result as people would try to take more of scarce things than was in fact available. Undoubtedly, the strong and cunning would then end up with most scarce resources and goods at the expense of the weak and not so clever; or the usefulness of scarce things would be destroyed by too many people attempting to use them at the same time.

Second, government would have to assign property rights in scarce resources as rarely as possible to itself and as often as possible to private individuals, and it would have to do the latter in such a way that all individuals came to hold, upon reaching adulthood, as nearly equal quantities of resources as possible. As each participant in a fair game of cards receives the same number of cards initially, so every participant in the great game of choice (which scarcity forces upon every society) would thus start with an equal endowment of economic power. This might mean that government, at the time of death of all individuals, would redistribute their holdings of natural and capital resources to other individuals reaching adulthood, and it might mean that opportunities to gain labor skills would be made freely and equally available to all citizens, as in the form of publicly provided health care, general education, and vocational training.

Third, government would have to guarantee to all individuals an equal opportunity to the freest possible use of the property rights it had assigned. Having distributed the cards in the great game of choice, it would have to set up general rules of the game that applied equally to all. Presumably, an appropriate system of laws, enforced by courts and police, would see to it that people in this model world never were coerced into uses of property rights they did not wish to make, unless all others were equally coerced (as in the payment of taxes). Likewise, people could never be prevented from uses of property rights they did wish to make, unless all others were equally prevented (as in the production of heroin). In short, anything one person was allowed to do, all others would have to be allowed to do; anything forbidden to one person, would have to be equally forbidden to all others.

Given these three actions by government, it is argued, all adult individuals would have the maximum possible freedom to promote their own welfare as they saw fit—within the limits of inevitable scarcity and consistent with an equal freedom given to all others. Hence, people could use their resources all alone, hermit-like, without ever relating to others at all. Or they could enter into all sorts of voluntary agreements of cooperation with others, exchanging—at any terms acceptable to all parties concerned—the property rights to resources or to any goods they had made with those resources. Thus, people could be their own master, choose their own path, do their own thing. No one would judge their choices or would have to approve them. People would not be subject to the will of other people; they would not be someone else's unwilling tools. But they would have to face the inevitable consequences of their own voluntary choices. Thus, government would merely set the framework for private choice; it would fix the conditions under which (widely dispersed) resources could be used by their private owners for their private ends.

## The Emergence of the Price System

Under the postulated conditions, it is believed, a multitude of markets would quickly emerge. Many owners of resources and goods would wish to make contact with other people for the purpose of raising their welfare through voluntary (and, therefore, mutually beneficial) exchanges of property rights. Figure 12.1, "The Capitalist Market Economy," pictures the major relations that are expected to emerge.

### An Overview

Consider panel (a) of Figure 12.1. There would exist, pictured by the left-hand box, a multitude of households in whose adult members the property rights in most resources would reside and who would presumably use their property to maximize their personal welfare (or utility). (Clearly, to perform the functions outlined earlier,

**Figure 12.1**   The Capitalist Market Economy

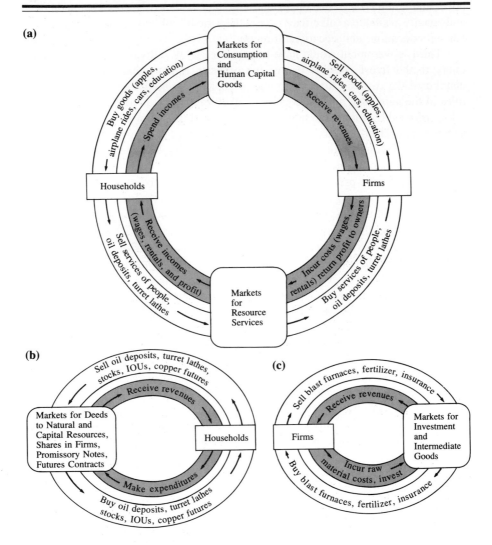

These circular-flow diagrams provide a bird's-eye view of the most important exchange relations likely to emerge among households and firms in the capitalist market economy.

government would also have to hold *some* natural and capital resources: to provide health care, education, and training to all citizens, to handle the assignment of nonhuman resources to them, to keep in check those who would use force or deceit to steal other people's property, to facilitate voluntary exchanges through the provision of money, standards and norms, and a system of courts ready to settle disputes, and more.)

There would also exist, pictured by the right-hand box in panel (a), a multitude of firms—productive enterprises that any adventuresome individual or group would be free to form (and to liquidate) and that, presumably, would seek to maximize profit for their owners. These two types of actors, households and firms, would meet each other in two types of markets. Consider first the lower half of panel (a). Its outer half circle pictures households selling, and firms buying, services of the human, natural, and capital resource stocks that would be owned by households. On a given day, perhaps, a particular household would sell 8 labor hours, 24 oil-deposit hours, and 12 turret-lathe hours—without, of course, giving up ownership of the person, oil deposit, or turret lathe as such. In return for the privilege of being allowed to use these resources temporarily, the firms involved would pay out money in the form of wages and rental payments. This would be a cost to them but income to the households involved. This income stream would be augmented (or decreased) by positive (or negative) profits of those households that were also owners of firms. The shaded half circle in the lower half represents this monetary counterflow to the real flow of resource services.

Now consider the upper half of panel (a). Its outer half circle pictures firms selling, and households buying, consumption goods and human capital goods. As indicated, the consumption goods could be nondurable apples or airplane rides or durable cars; the human capital goods could be educational services. Once more, the shaded half circle represents the monetary counterflow to this real flow of goods.

Panel (a) is fine as far as it goes; it tells the truth but not all of it. If we focused our attention more closely on the household box, we might discover the relationships pictured in panel (b). In a capitalist market economy, frequent exchanges would occur that involved households only. Households could sell outright the stocks of natural and capital resources they owned (instead of just renting them out to firms temporarily), but if they did, other households would come to own them. Similarly, as panel (b) illustrates, households would surely trade corporate stock among themselves; they would lend to and borrow money from each other (which can be viewed as the buying and selling of promissory notes); and they would even trade such strange things as copper futures. Thus, the circular flow in panel (b) adds more detail to our bird's-eye view of the market economy.

Panel (c) adds similar detail about the behavior of firms. Additional frequent exchanges would involve firms only. In particular, firms would sell goods to other firms. Sometimes, these goods would be used up right away by their recipients in the making of other goods (as perhaps the fertilizer or insurance service in our example). Such goods are called *intermediate goods*. Their purchase would give rise to raw material costs on the part of their buyers. At other times, firms would sell goods to one another that would be longer-lasting *investment goods*. The blast furnaces in our example are a case in point. Their purchase would give rise to investment expenditures (financed, perhaps, with a portion of revenues corresponding to depreciation allowances or with the portion of profits not paid out to the owners of firms).

Such would be the major relationships among households and firms in this market economy. However, Figure 12.1 remains a simplification, since it does not show other relationships that would also come into being. Government, for instance, would take away in taxes some of the revenues flowing to firms, or some of the incomes flowing to households. It would use these funds to buy some of the resource services supplied by households (services of judges, teachers, and police officers) and to buy some of the goods supplied by firms (court houses, school buildings, and police cruisers). Recognition of such possible transactions adds further detail to the bird's-eye view provided by Figure 12.1, but it does not invalidate the broad outline of the capitalist market economy that it provides.

## The Equilibrium Price

In the idealized vision discussed in this chapter, it is further imagined that each one of the markets just discussed would possess the features typical of a **perfectly competitive market:**

First, there would be many buyers and many sellers in each market. As a result, no one person would buy or sell a significant percentage of the total traded and be able, acting alone, to influence the price.

Second, all units of the traded item would be viewed as identical by buyers; thus, no buyer would have any reason to prefer one seller over another.

Third, all buyers and sellers would possess full knowledge relevant to trading.

Fourth, all buyers and sellers would be free at any time to enter into or exit from a market.

What would be the nature of events in a typical market under these circumstances? Given all other factors that might influence people's decision to buy or sell, buyers would probably demand a larger quantity at lower prices than at higher ones, and sellers would probably supply a larger quantity at higher prices than at lower ones. This is illustrated by the sloping lines labeled ''demand'' and ''supply,'' respectively, in Figure 12.2, ''A Typical Market.'' And that graph tells us something else. One can expect that the interaction of many buyers and sellers in any one market would come to establish an **equilibrium price** (such as $5 per unit in our graph), at which the quantities demanded and supplied would be just equal to each other (at 34 million units per year in our graph). It is easy to see why.

If the market price were higher than its equilibrium value of $5 per unit, an inconsistency would exist between the choices of buyers and sellers. At $7 per unit, for instance, buyers as a group would wish to buy 20 million units per year (as noted by point *a* in our graph), while sellers as a group would want to sell 48 million units per year (as noted by point *b*). Thus, a *surplus* would emerge of 48 − 20 = 28 million units per year (distance *ab*), and many would-be sellers would be very frustrated. Before long, at least some of them would probably offer to sell the item in question for a somewhat lower price. Immediately, the surplus would diminish: Buyers, moving from *a* to *e,* would buy a larger quantity at the lower price; sellers, moving from *b* toward *e,* would offer a lower quantity. This process of competition among frustrated sellers would continue until price and quantity corresponded to their equilibrium values at point *e*.

**Figure 12.2**   A Typical Market

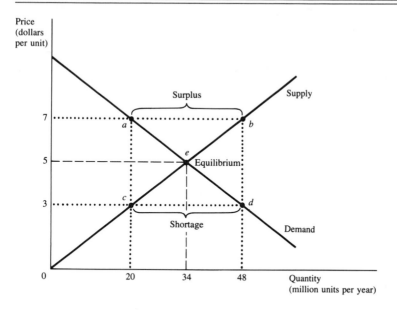

In a perfectly competitive market, the interaction of multitudes of buyers and sellers would establish an equilibrium price (here $5 per unit) at which quantity demanded would just equal quantity supplied (here 34 million units per year).

If the market price were lower than its equilibrium value of $5 per unit, a similar inconsistency would exist between the choices of buyers and sellers. At $3 per unit, for instance, buyers as a group would wish to buy 48 million units per year (as noted by point *d* in our graph), while sellers as a group would want to sell only 20 million units per year (as noted by point *c*). This time a *shortage* would emerge of 48 − 20 = 28 million units per year (distance *cd*), and many would-be *buyers* would be frustrated. Before long, at least some of them would probably offer to buy the item in question for a somewhat higher price. Immediately, the shortage would diminish. Sellers, moving from *c* toward *e,* would sell a larger quantity at the higher price; buyers, moving from *d* toward *e,* would demand a lower quantity. This process of competition among frustrated buyers would continue until price and quantity corresponded to their equilibrium values at point *e*.

Thus, in every market—be it for bushels of apples, scenic airplane rides, or labor hours—an important piece of information would emerge: an equilibrium price at which any buyer could be sure to find a seller and any seller could be sure to find a buyer. The entire system of prices so emerging, furthermore, would serve like a system of telecommunication among all households and firms. It would serve the important function of continually coordinating the independent choices made by them. This is why the price system has often been given a special name: ''The Invisible Hand.''

## The Invisible Hand

To understand what is involved, consider the following. Large numbers of people— all of whom owned resources that they were free to utilize in whatever ways their own concepts of happiness suggested—would face a special problem. They would possess, in their separate minds, many bits of knowledge about technical possibilities and human preferences. They would know that making joint use of such knowledge was likely to be more advantageous to all than an attempt by everyone to live like a hermit. Yet, they would possess no obvious method of arranging this cooperation among themselves! Clearly, they could not sit around a common table and *talk* about which goods each of them could and would like to produce and consume (with whatever types of resources and technical knowledge were available to each and in view of the present tastes of each). But they could utilize an indirect method of communicating and arranging a mutually beneficial cooperation among themselves.

The very competition among sellers or buyers described in the previous section could be accepted as a valuable tool of cooperation. This is so because that competition would generate signals in the form of equilibrium prices that told everyone in condensed form what they could and could not do, if they wished to take part in the joint enterprise of allocating resources and apportioning the goods made with them. Sure enough, buyers would always *prefer* a lower price, and sellers a higher one. But, in the absence of a practical way by which millions of people could sit together and explain to each other why a lower or higher price would not work, the guidance of the equilibrium price could be accepted on blind faith as that of an all-knowing Invisible Hand.

Imagine the task of telling a single consumer why a $5-per-bushel price was the only proper one, if people did not care to produce their own apples in isolation. One might note that there were another 53 million apple buyers who were willing and able to buy 34 million bushels a year at the current price, a quantity that for consistency's sake would have to be equal to supply—supply that was coming from 90,000 orchardists all over the world who happened to be endowed with so many apple trees, who happened to possess certain kinds of technical knowledge, who happened to face certain weather conditions, who happened to be confronted with certain alternative uses of their resources, who had to pay certain wage levels to get people to pick apples rather than produce cars, who would produce fewer apples or none at all at lower apple prices . . . and much more! There would be no way in which such detail could be provided for every buyer and every seller concerning every good and every resource traded in the market. In fact, the market economy would save people the trouble of wasting their time seeking lengthy explanations. The Invisible Hand would send all people who cared to cooperate with other people the most necessary information in capsule form: IF YOU WERE WILLING TO PAY (OR ACCEPT) $5 PER BUSHEL, YOU COULD BUY (OR SELL) ALL THE

APPLES YOU LIKED. A similar message, of course, would be sent to people interested in shoes and airplane rides, or to others wishing to trade the services of people, acres, and turret lathes.

Beyond that, people would be free to follow their self-interest in light of the signals coming from the Invisible Hand. By being continual watchers of price signals, all individuals could fit their own plans in with those of millions of unknown other people. They could sell whatever quantities of their resources they wished, at whatever equilibrium prices markets would dictate to them. In the process, they would earn money income. Since the market price of each good would equal the costs of its production (costs that would be the incomes of all those who contributed resources to the production of the good) plus any profit or loss (which would be income to the owner of the firm producing the good), people would earn, as a group, incomes just equal to the value of goods produced. They could spend that income in any way they wished and, thus, buy up all the goods available for sale at their equilibrium prices. Thus, the spontaneous interaction of people in free markets would produce order rather than chaos; and competition would mean cooperation!

As Adam Smith put it, the individual "stands at all times in need of the cooperation and assistance of great multitudes, while his whole life is scarce sufficient to gain the friendship of a few persons."[2] Yet, though friendship can enlist only the cooperation of a few, one can enlist that of many in a competitive market economy—not by being their friend, but by showing them how it would be to their own advantage to do what one required of them: "It is not from the benevolence of the butcher, the brewer, or the baker that we expect our dinner, but from their regard to their own interest. We address ourselves not to their humanity, but to their self-love, and never talk to them of our own necessities, but of their advantages."

## The Price System at Work*

As was just noted, households and firms in the model capitalist market economy would make their decisions not only by reference to their own particular circumstances, but also by using knowledge beyond their range of vision. This latter information would come to them, as we saw, not in the form of detailed explanations about everything, but in a condensed form that reduced the million and one factors operating in any one market into a single value, called the *price*. As households and firms responded to these prices, they would, in fact, communicate with one another and be invisibly joined together. A mental experiment can help us see the point.

---

*Optional Section. This is a review of material often found in introductory economics classes.
[2]Adam Smith, *An Inquiry into the Nature and Causes of the Wealth of Nations* (Homewood, IL: Richard D. Irwin, 1963/1776), vol. 1, pp. 11–12.

## A Change in the Composition of Demand

Imagine our model capitalist market economy in long-run equilibrium: Each household and firm would be optimizing its activities. Each would be making its decisions on the basis of market-clearing prices, and all firms would be operating at zero profit. And now imagine that households as a group increased their demand for apples, while decreasing their demand for beef. If you were an economic dictator, and nothing could happen without your command (and assuming you knew about and wanted to accommodate the people's wishes), you would have your work cut out for you.

You might begin by making a list of all the extra inputs needed to produce the extra apples people wanted. You would have to come up with extra fertilizer and more pesticides, with more baby apple trees and storage barns, with more human apple pickers, and with more spraying machines. But each of these decisions would require more decisions in turn. Those extra spraying machines would have to be produced too—not only with extra labor, but also with rubber and steel. And extra steel would call for extra coal and iron ore and workers stoking blast furnaces. . . .

You could make a second list showing all the productive inputs *released* if beef production were to be cut by the desired amount. The number of steers could be reduced and that of butchers and ranch hands and veterinarians too. Pastures and feed lots would be set free. Less hay and corn could be produced. And each of these decisions also would lead to further consequences. Less-needed corn would call for fewer silos to be built or maintained, fewer plows and tractors, and less gas to run harvesters. Less gas, in turn, would set free storage tanks and tankers and sailors too. . . .

You would compare the lists, of course, and you would be happy to find that gas saved from running corn harvesters could be used to run orchard spraying machines, that ranch hands could be turned into apple pickers, and pastures into orchards. But you would also meet unpleasant surprises: Butchers and veterinarians may not want to become apple pickers (but their children may); silos may not be convertible into apple storage barns (but the resources that might have kept them in good repair easily may).

Even if you worked out some overall *conversion plan* wherein, for each type of resource, the quantity released (directly or indirectly) from beef production just equaled the additional amount needed (directly or indirectly) in apple production, your work would not be even half finished. You would have to work out the details too. Exactly which individuals would have to switch their jobs and when and where? Exactly which farms would have to cut corn output and by how much and when? Exactly which manufacturer would have to cut harvester production by how much and when so as to make how many extra spraying machines? Millions of details . . .

Every one of these details (and many more) would have to be considered by any economic system. But in our model capitalist market economy, there would be no need for any *human* planner to gather and digest information and then to issue appropriate instructions. Simple changes in prices would constitute coded signals to effect just the right amount of action on the part of just those people of whom it would be required! Three types of effects would be observed: the **impact effect,** or the effect of an initial change in supply or demand on the market concerned; the **spillout effect,** or the effect of this change on other markets; and the **feedback effect,** or the effect of these secondary changes in other markets on the market in which the initial change occurred.

## Impact Effects

**A Lower Demand for Beef.** Panels (a) to (c) of Figure 12.3, "A Fall in the Demand for Beef," depict an original long-run equilibrium in the beef market. The sample household shown in panel (a) consumes three pounds of beef per week at the $2.50-

**Figure 12.3** A Fall in the Demand for Beef

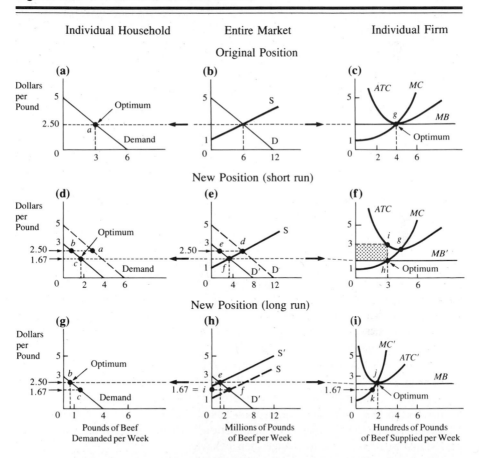

This set of graphs shows some of the adjustments, in a perfectly competitive market economy, to a fall in the demand for beef. If the industry involved is a constant-cost industry, as is assumed, the price of the product is unchanged after the industry has ceased to contract.

per-pound price. That price, at which market demand D and market supply S are just equal in panel (b), is the equilibrium price. This equilibrium price equals the long-run price as shown in panel (c): Our sample firm, which, as always, produces where marginal cost of production equals marginal benefit (or product price), earns zero profit because its minimum average total cost is just equal to price. Thus, there is no incentive for new firms to enter or for existing firms to leave the industry.

Note what would happen if this household's demand for beef fell, as suggested in panel (d), from the dashed to the solid line. As long as price remained unchanged (at $2.50), the household would cut purchases from the old quantity at point *a* to the new one at *b,* which illustrates its fall in demand. If, however, other households were cutting purchases too (and this we assume), market demand for beef would fall, as in panel (e), from D (now dashed) to D'. If the flow of beef from the market to households fell, while the flow of beef from producers to the market continued unabated, a *surplus* would develop at the old $2.50-per-pound price (shown by distance *de*). Storage facilities in the marketplace would fill up and overflow. Competition among sellers would reduce the price to $1.67 per pound (corresponding to intersection *f*). This lower price would be a signal to all involved to change their behavior.

Beef-eating households would, as households always do when the price of a good falls, increase their quantity demanded, as from *b* to *c* in panel (d). Beef-producing firms would, as firms always do when the price of a good falls, decrease their quantity supplied, as from *g* to *h* in panel (f). However, inherent in the situation would be a tendency for further change, because the new $1.67-per-pound equilibrium price would no longer equal the $2.50-per-pound, minimum-average-total-cost, long-run price. Consider how the typical firm would have turned from a zero-profit business into a losing business: Its price would have fallen (from point *g* to *h*), its average total cost would have risen (from point *g* to *i*), and it would then make losses, shown by the dotted rectangle in panel (f).

The losses of firms would induce a predictable kind of change: As soon as they could, firms would reduce their capacities or shut down completely. The particular firm illustrated here is assumed to reduce its capacity, which is why panel (i) cost curves are to the *left* of their original position in panel (f). Compare *ATC'* and *MC'* with *ATC* and *MC*. Other firms, in ever increasing numbers, would also reduce capacity or even shut down entirely. As they did, market supply would fall as from S (now dashed) to S' in panel (h). But if the flow of beef from the producers to the market fell, while the flow of beef from the market to the households continued unchanged, a *shortage* would develop at the new $1.67-per-pound price (shown by distance *fi*). Storage facilities in the marketplace would empty out and, finally, be insufficient to meet demand. Competition among buyers would raise the price to $2.50 per pound (corresponding to intersection *e*). This higher price would be a new signal to all involved to change their behavior.

Beef-eating households would, as households always do when the price of a good rises, decrease their quantity demanded, as from *c* to *b* in panel (g). Beef-producing firms would, as firms always do when the price of a good rises, increase their quantity supplied, as from *k* to *j* in panel (i). Ignoring feedback effects, a final equilibrium would be reached when the firms remaining in the industry, as in panel (i), were again just covering cost with revenue. Their losses would have disappeared because the product price would be back at its old level, while average total cost (which had earlier risen to *i* above its minimum) would in this constant-cost industry again have fallen to that minimum at *j*. In the end, beef producers would have done exactly what households had asked of them: produce less beef.

**A Higher Demand for Apples.**    Panels (a) to (c) of Figure 12.4, "A Rise in the Demand for Apples," again picture an original long-run equilibrium. The household shown in panel (a) consumes three bushels of apples per year at the $12-per-bushel price. The price is the equilibrium price, in panel (b), and is also the long-run price, in panel (c).

Note what would happen if this household's demand for apples rose, as suggested in panel (d), from the dashed to the solid line. As long as price remained unchanged (at $12), the household's higher demand would increase purchases from the old quantity at point *a* to the new one at *b*. If, however, other households were increasing purchases too (and this we assume), market demand for apples would rise, as in panel (e), from D (now dashed) to D'. And if the flow of apples from the market to households rose, while the flow of apples from producers to the market continued unchanged, a *shortage* would develop at the old $12-per-bushel price (shown by distance *de*). Apple storage facilities would empty out in no time, and demand would not be met. Competition among buyers would raise the price to $16-per-bushel (corresponding to intersection *f*). This higher price would be a signal to all involved to change their behavior.

Apple-eating households would, as households always do when the price of a good rises, decrease their quantity demanded, as from *b* to *c* in panel (d). Apple-producing firms would, as firms always do when the price of a good rises, increase their quantity supplied, as from *g* to *h* in panel (f). However, inherent in the situation would be a tendency for further change, because the new $16-per-bushel price would no longer equal the $12-per-bushel, minimum-average-total-cost, long-run price. Consider how the typical firm would have turned from a zero-profit business into a profitable business: Its price would have risen (from point *g* to *h*), its average total cost would have risen less (from point *g* to *i*), and it would now make a profit, shown by the shaded rectangle in panel (f).

The profits of firms would induce a predictable kind of change: As soon as they could, existing firms would expand their capacities and new firms would enter the industry. The particular firm shown here is assumed to expand its capacity, which is why panel (i) cost curves are to the *right* of their original position in panel (f). Compare *ATC'* and *MC'* with *ATC* and *MC*. Other existing firms, in ever increasing numbers, would do the same, and new ones would enter the industry. As they did, market supply would rise as from S (now dashed) to S' in panel (h). But if the flow of apples from the producers to the market rose, while the flow of apples from the market to the households continued unchanged, a *surplus* would develop at the new $16-per-bushel price (shown by distance *fi*). Storage facilities would fill up and overflow. Competition among sellers would lower the price to

**Figure 12.4**    A Rise in the Demand for Apples

| Individual Household | Entire Market | Individual Firm |

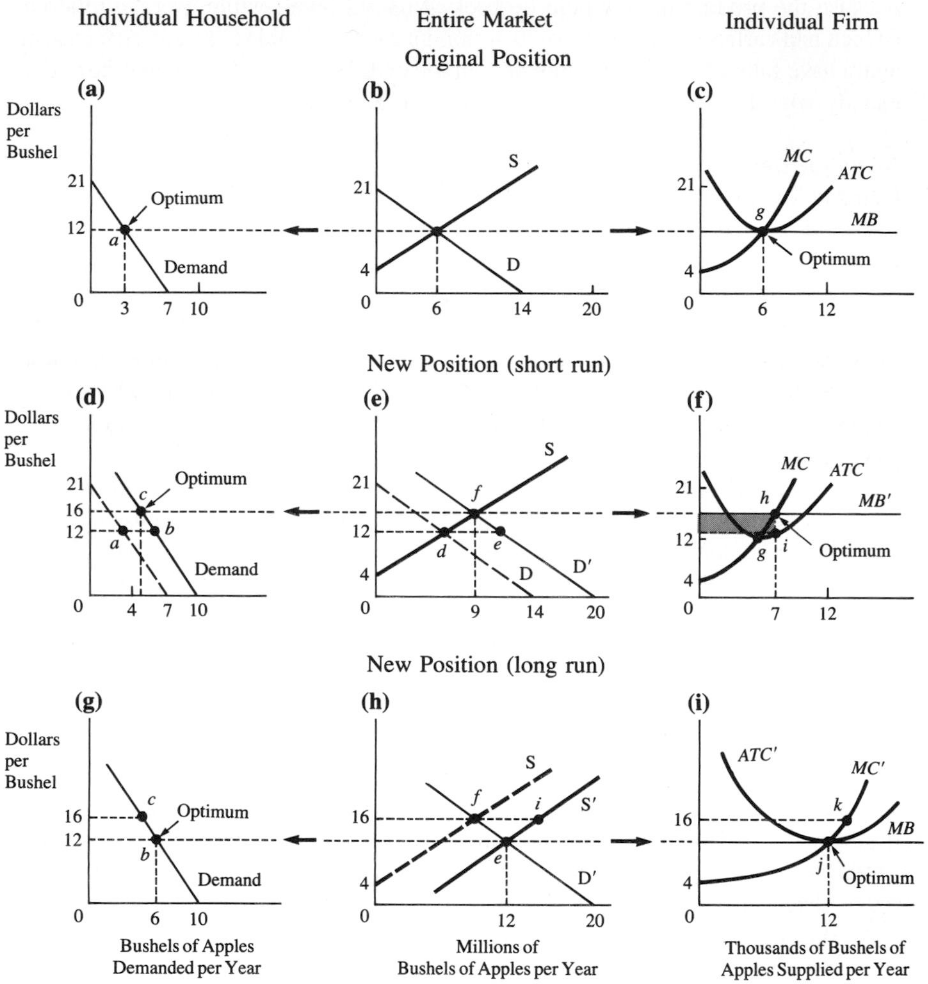

This set of graphs shows some of the adjustments, in a perfectly competitive market economy, to a rise in the demand for apples. If the industry involved is a constant-cost industry, as is assumed, the price of the product is unchanged after the industry has ceased to expand.

$12 per bushel (corresponding to intersection $e$). This lower price would be a new signal to all involved to change their behavior.

Apple-eating households would, as households always do when the price of a good falls, increase their quantity demanded, as from $c$ to $b$ in panel (g). Apple-producing firms would, as firms always do when the price of a good falls, decrease their quantity supplied, as from $k$ to $j$ in panel (i). Ignoring feedback effects, a final equilibrium would be reached when the firms in the industry, as in panel (i), were again just covering cost with revenue. Their profits would have disappeared because the product price would be back at its old level, while average total cost (which had earlier risen to *i* above its minimum) would in this constant-cost industry again have fallen to that minimum at *j*. In the end, apple producers would have done exactly what households had asked of them: produce more apples.

## Spillout Effects

Impact effects like those just described are only a tiny portion of the price system's work. The many firms that would reduce output or entirely leave the beef business in response to a decreasing demand for beef, for instance, would, by their simultaneous actions, reduce the market demand for steers, butchers, ranch hands, veterinarians, pastures, feed lots, hay, corn, silos, harvesters, and much more. These reductions of demand would, by themselves, tend to lower the prices of all these things and send out clear signals to all involved to change their behavior too in ways consistent with the households' desire to have less beef. Thus, cattle breeders and owners of pastureland and makers of harvesters and all the rest would find their incomes falling, and they would have the incentive to put their resources into other, more remunerative fields. To be sure, each individual would be free to buck the trend. Individuals could do just the opposite of what price changes (and resultant income differentials) were asking of them. People could go *into* cattle breeding, pastureland, harvester production, and so on, just when the reverse was in the social interest; if they did, they should not be surprised if they were punished by exceptionally low incomes. Most people, therefore, could be expected to go in the direction pointed out by the Invisible Hand. Once enough inputs had been taken out of these declining fields, these input prices would, of course, go back up, and in the case of constant-cost industries, they would return to their original levels. Then the remaining (and fewer) cattle breeders, pasture owners, harvester producers, and so on would again be receiving their old and higher incomes. The time of famine would be over.

In the same way, many old and new firms that would increase the output of the apple industry in response to increased demand for apples would, by their simultaneous actions, *increase* the demand for fertilizer, pesticides, baby apple trees, storage barns, apple pickers, spraying machines, rubber, steel, coal, iron ore, and much more. These increases in demand would, by themselves, tend to raise the prices of all these things and constitute clear signals to all involved to change their behavior too in ways consistent with the households' desire to have more apples. Thus, producers of fertilizer, human apple pickers, makers of iron ore, and all the rest would find their incomes rising, and they would have the incentive to place more of their resources into such remunerative fields. To be sure, each individual would be free to go against the trend, but those who did go out of fertilizer manufacture, apple picking, iron ore mining, and so on, just when the reverse was in the social interest, would be punished by losing what, at least for a while, would be exceptionally high incomes. Most people, therefore, could be expected to go in the direction pointed out by the Invisible Hand. Once enough new inputs had been put into these expanding fields, these input prices would, of course, go back down, and in the case of constant-cost industries, they would return to their original levels. Then the (greater number) of fertilizer producers, apple pickers, and iron ore miners would again be receiving the lower incomes that once prevailed. The feast would have come to an end.

Finally, many seemingly unrelated effects would occur throughout the economy. Some households, such as the unlucky owners of pastureland, might react to their fall in income by demanding fewer yachts. The owners of profitable orchards might demand more furniture and airplane rides. The producers of corn flakes might supply more of them, because corn would be cheaper once there were fewer steers to be fed. Thus, in a billion unpredictable ways, the price system would tell just those from whom action was required what they should do. It would tell them in un-mistakable ways (that appeal to their self-interests) to move in the direction of the ''carrot'' (higher income) and away from the ''stick'' (lower income). The price system would, thus, become the invisible *governor* of the competitive market economy, spreading its signals throughout.

The decreased demand for beef would reduce also the demand for things required, directly or indirectly, to make beef, as shown in panels (a) to (c) of Figure 12.5, ''How Price Signals Would Spread,'' by a shift of the dashed lines to the solid ones. In the same way, the increased demand for apples would increase also the demand for things required to make apples, as shown in panels (d) to (f). In addition, all kinds of seemingly unrelated effects would occur, as shown in panels (g) to (i). Thus, the original change in household demand, akin to the ripple effect in a pond into which a stone has been thrown, would spread throughout the economy. The arrows in Figure 12.5 highlight the movements of the equilibrium points and the resultant price changes.

## Feedback Effects

Figure 12.5 suggests why owners of iron ore mines, producers of tree fertilizer, human apple pickers, and people giving airplane rides would have higher incomes and would therefore (among many other things) demand more beef. This increase in the demand for beef forces us to reconsider the new long-run position shown in Figure 12.3 (which was based on the assumption of a *decreased* demand for beef by other people).

On the other hand, it is also possible that unlucky butchers, pastureland owners, and producers of corn harvesters or yachts or corn flakes would demand fewer apples. This decrease in demand forces us to reconsider Figure 12.4, which was based on the assumption of an initial *rise* in the demand for apples. All these new and offsetting changes in demand would, in turn, have spillout and feedback effects of their own!

Words and graphs can help illustrate the complexity of the price system's work, but they cannot take us beyond this point. A full analysis would require the use of mathematics that we need not attempt here. ▄▄

**Figure 12.5**   How Price Signals Would Spread

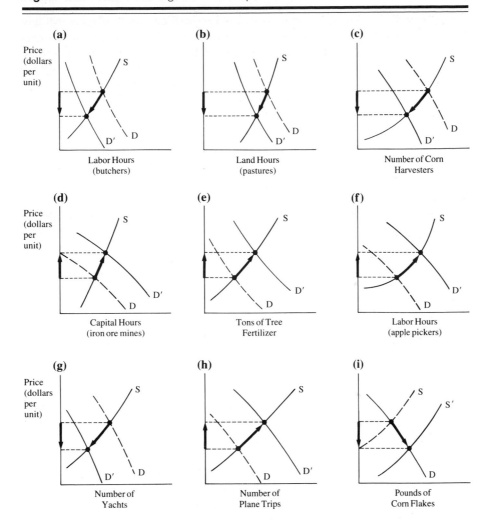

This set of graphs depicts some of the *spillout effects* of a lower demand for beef and a higher demand for apples.

## An Assessment

We are now ready to procecd to an assessment of this model of the capitalist market economy. Because this economy has never existed, we can only speculate on its likely performance. The major goals of economic systems discussed in chapters 2 through 4 can serve as a convenient checklist.

## Full Employment

The advocates of the model economy that has just been described imagine that this economy would produce a full utilization of resources. The meaning of full employment would be defined, however, not by arbitrary government action, nor by public discussion and democratic majority vote, but simply as the undesigned outcome of a multitude of independent decisions of all resource owners. Here is what is expected to happen: All owners of resources would decide separately on the extent to which they would like to have their own resources utilized in the process of production. From these independent decisions, a supply would emerge in each particular resource market, such as the line so labeled in Figure 12.2, "A Typical Market." The slope of this line reflects the likelihood that a given number of resource owners would be likely to offer more units of a resource at a higher than at a lower price.

Equally independently of each other, private owners of firms would decide on the quantities of various resources they wanted to utilize. Thus, a demand would emerge in each particular resource market, such as the line so labeled in Figure 12.2. The slope of the line reflects the likelihood that a given number of firms would be likely to demand more units of a resource at a lower than at a higher price.

Competition among buyers or sellers would then establish some equilibrium price, such as $5 per labor hour (or any other type of resource). Anyone who wished to sell that particular type of labor (or any other resource) at that price could find employment. Involuntary unemployment could only be a temporary phenomenon, it is argued, since it would represent a surplus of the resource on the market. If, in Figure 12.2, the price of labor were $7 per hour, people would indeed offer 48 million hours for sale (point *b*), but firms would hire only 20 million hours (point *a*). The suppliers of some 28 million labor hours could find no job (distance *ab*). A fall in the price of labor to $5 per hour, however, would quickly eliminate this unemployment. As the price fell, firms would hire more labor (a movement from *a* toward *e*), and households would voluntarily withdraw some of the labor previously offered (a movement from *b* toward *e*). The same type of adjustment would occur in all other resource markets. In the end, whatever rate of employment the many resource owners had decided upon as desirable, that rate would come to prevail.

And note: This proposition does not depend on the particular slope of the supply line given in Figure 12.2. If people, for example, insisted on working 48 million labor hours per year regardless of the price of labor (making the labor supply line vertical through points *b* and *d*), a different equilibrium wage would be established (at $3 per hour), but full employment would still come to prevail. Permanent unemployment of a resource could be imagined only if the resource was not scarce; that is, the demand for it, even at a zero price, fell short of its supply. This situation would imply that all firms had so much of the resource in question that use of another unit of it would add nothing to output; hence, its use would not even be worth a penny!

To be sure, critics argue that the full-employment adjustment process might require unbearably large changes in prices or might take an unacceptably long time. To this the model's advocates reply that government would always be free to fight unemployment by using the familiar Keynesian fiscal and monetary policy tools.

## Technical Efficiency

The model's advocates claim that self-interest would drive the owner-managers of firms to minimize the use of inputs for any given level of output and, thus, to maximize output for any given set of inputs. Acting otherwise would not enable them to maximize profits. Critics wonder what would happen if ownership were separated from management. Would nonowner-managers still act reliably to achieve maximum profit and the technical efficiency this implies?

## Economic Efficiency

The advocates of our model economy also imagine that this economy would produce economic efficiency. This result, they argue, would be the accidental consequence of people seeking only their self-interest. Let us see what is involved.

**The First Pareto Condition.** Reconsider our two orchardists from Chapter 2 who were using unskilled labor to produce apples. In our model market economy, both would face identical prices of labor and apples (even though their technical circumstances could differ greatly, as they did in Chapter 2). Market forces might establish an equilibrium price of labor at $5 per unit, and an equilibrium price of apples of $1.61 per unit. Under the circumstances, producer $\alpha$ would never be content being in the kind of situation depicted in part A of Table 2.1, "The Optimum Allocation of a Resource among Producers of the Same Good" (p. 16). Given $\alpha$'s *MRT* of 1x for 2a, the owner of $\alpha$ could clearly increase profit or reduce loss (by $1.78) through releasing a unit of labor (lowering cost by $5) and producing and selling 2 units of apples less (lowering revenue by 2 times $1.61, or $3.22). Thus, self-interest would drive $\alpha$ to do just what Table 2.1 demanded: release labor!

Firm $\beta$, on the other hand, would not be content either in the initial situation depicted in Table 2.1. Given its *MRT* of 1x for 5a, it could increase profit or reduce loss (by $3.05) through hiring an additional unit of labor (raising cost by $5) and producing and selling 5 units of apples more (raising revenue by 5 times $1.61, or $8.05). Thus, self-interest would drive $\beta$ to do just what Table 2.1 demanded: use more labor!

Each firm would continue in this effort until a unit of labor released (in $\alpha$'s case) or a unit of labor added (in $\beta$'s case) changed cost just as much as the resultant change in output was worth. In our case, once loss of a unit of labor at $\alpha$ reduced output by 3.1 units (and hence by 3.1 times $1.61, or $5), and once gain of a unit of labor at $\beta$ raised output by 3.1 units (and hence by $5), further changes would be of no interest to either firm. Thus, they would end up exactly in the position depicted in part C of Table 2.1. Both firms would thus cooperate with each other in a task that was in the social interest: They would help reallocate resources in a fashion that yielded greater output than before and thus reduced overall scarcity. Yet, they would be doing this out of pure self-interest (to get a higher profit or a reduced loss for themselves); they would not even be aware of each other's existence, much less of what they were doing for society!

**The Second Pareto Condition.\***   Now consider our two producers from Chapter 2 who were producing apples and butter. In our model market economy, both would face identical prices of apples and butter, say, of $1.62 per unit of apples and 45¢ per unit of butter. Under the circumstances, producer $\alpha$ would never be content being in the kind of situation depicted in part A of Table 2.2, "The Optimum Specialization of Production among Producers of the Same Goods" (p. 20). Given $\alpha$'s *MRT* of 1$a$ for 2$b$, the owner of $\alpha$ could clearly increase profit or reduce loss (by 72¢) through producing and selling a unit of apples more (gaining revenue of $1.62), while producing and selling 2 units of butter less (losing revenue of 90¢). Since 1 unit of apples, by assumption, employed the same resources as 2 units of butter, $\alpha$'s costs would be unaffected. Thus, self-interest would drive $\alpha$ to do just what Table 2.2 demanded: produce more apples and less butter!

Firm $\beta$, on the other hand, would not be content either in the initial situation depicted in Table 2.2. Given its *MRT* of 1$a$ for 5$b$, it could increase profit or reduce loss (by 63¢) through producing and selling a unit of apples less (lowering revenue by $1.62), while producing and selling 5 units of butter more (raising revenue by 5 times 45¢, or $2.25). Since 1 unit of apples, by assumption, employed the same resources as 5 units of butter, $\beta$'s costs would be unaffected. Thus, self-interest would also drive $\beta$ to do just what Table 2.2 demanded: produce more butter and fewer apples!

Each firm would continue in this effort until an extra unit of apple production changed revenue just as much as did the accompanying change in butter production. In our case, once each firm's *MRT* was 1$a$ for 3.6$b$ (quantities both of which would be worth $1.62), further changes would be of no interest to either firm. Thus, they would end up exactly in the position depicted in part C of Table 2.2. Once more, "private vice" (the pursuit of profit) would have yielded "public virtue" (a reduction in overall scarcity).  ■■■

**The Third Pareto Condition.\***   Consider our pair of producer and consumer from Table 2.3, "The Optimum Composition of Production and Consumption" (p. 22). In our model market economy, both would face identical prices of apples and butter of, say, $1.62 per unit of apples and 45¢ per unit of butter. We have just seen, when discussing the second condition, why firm $\alpha$ would wish to change its position from that shown in part A to that shown in part C of that earlier table.

---

*Optional Section. The achievement of economic efficiency is depicted in an alternative way.

Yet, a similar argument can be made for consumer X. Given X's *MRS* of 1*a* for 5*b*, X could clearly save 63¢ without any change in welfare by consuming 1 more unit of apples (spending an extra $1.62), while consuming 5 units of butter less (spending 5 times 45¢, or $2.25 less). Since 1 unit of apples, by assumption, yielded for X the same welfare as 5 units of butter, X's overall satisfaction would be unaffected. But X could then spend the 63¢ saved on anything and be better off. Thus, self-interest would drive X to do just what Table 2.3 demanded: consume more apples and less butter!

Once again, these changes would continue until α's *MRT,* as well as X's *MRS,* was 1*a* for 3.6*b* (quantities both of which would be worth $1.62). Then further changes would be of no interest to the parties involved. ▬▬

**The Fourth Pareto Condition.**\*   The model capitalist market economy, argue its advocates, would produce an efficient allocation of goods because people would be free to spend their money income as they liked, and all of them would face identical equilibrium prices. Consider the case of the two consumers depicted in Table 2.4, ''The Optimum Allocation of Goods among Consumers of the Same Goods'' (p. 24). Suppose they faced equilibrium prices of $2.90 per unit of apples and $1 per unit of butter. Under the circumstances, neither of them would remain in the position indicated in part A of Table 2.4. Given X's *MRS* of 1*a* for 5*b*, X could clearly save $2.10 by consuming 1 more unit of apples (spending an extra $2.90), while consuming 5 units of butter less (spending 5 × $1, or $5 less). Since 1 unit of apples, by assumption, yielded the same welfare as 5 units of butter, X's overall satisfaction would be unaffected. But X could then spend the saved $2.10 on anything and be better off. Thus, self-interest would drive X to do just what Table 2.4 demanded: consume more apples and less butter!

Given Y's *MRS* of 1*a* for 2*b,* Y could save 90¢ by consuming 1 less unit of apples (saving $2.90), while consuming 2 units of butter more (spending 2 times $1, or $2 more). Since 1 unit of apples, by assumption, yielded for Y the same welfare as 2 units of butter, Y's overall satisfaction would be unaffected. But Y could then spend the saved 90¢ on anything and be better off. Thus, self-interest would also drive Y to do just what Table 2.4 demanded: consume more butter and fewer apples!

Clearly, these changes would continue until the *MRS* of both consumers was 1*a* for 2.9*b* (both quantities being worth $2.90). Then further reallocations of their budgets would be of no interest to the two consumers involved. Obviously, the two consumers would not have to get together and exchange goods with each other. They only would have to be free to spend their money incomes as they liked and be faced with identical prices. Both of these conditions would be met in our model economy. ▬▬

_____

\*Optional Section. The achievement of economic efficiency is depicted in an alternative way.

**All Other Pareto Conditions.** It can be shown that all other Pareto conditions would similarly be fulfilled in a world in which all decision makers faced identical equilibrium prices of resources and goods and were given the freedom to pursue their self-interest. Not surprisingly, this is seen as an enormous advantage of such an economic system by its advocates. Such a system would not require saints to run it; ordinary mortals would do quite well! As Adam Smith put it, "Every individual . . . endeavours . . . to employ his [resources] that [their] produce may be of the greatest value. . . . He generally . . . neither intends to promote the public interest, nor knows how much he is promoting it. . . . He intends only his own security, . . . only his own gain. And he is in this . . . led by an Invisible Hand to promote an end which was no part of his intention. . . . By pursuing his own interest he frequently promotes that of the society more effectually than when he really intends to promote it."[3]

## Economic Growth

The advocates of the model economy discussed in this chapter also imagine that this economy would produce an optimum rate of economic growth. The meaning of optimum growth would emerge, they believe, from a variety of factors:

**Extensive Growth.** For one thing, all income recipients would be free to save part of their income and lend out the funds involved. From the separate saving decisions of all households a supply of loanable funds would emerge, such as the line so labeled in Figure 12.2, "A Typical Market." The slope of this line reflects the likelihood that a given number of households would be likely to offer more loanable funds at a higher than at a lower price (expressed, no doubt, as an interest rate).

Equally independent of each other, owners of firms would decide on the loanable funds they wished to acquire for purposes of exploring for new natural resources or investing in new structures, equipment, and inventories. Thus, a demand would emerge, such as the line so labeled in Figure 12.2. The slope of this line reflects the likelihood that a given number of firms would be likely to demand more loanable funds at a lower than at a higher interest rate.

Competition among lenders or borrowers would then establish some equilibrium rate, such as 5 percent per year. Every dollar lent at that rate would be invested.

Clearly, one cannot predict whether the resultant amount of investment would be a large or a small proportion of national income; whether, over time, people would be using up, just replacing, or rapidly enlarging their stock of capital resources. It is argued that whatever would happen, however, it would be the optimal rate of private capital formation, for it would be the undesigned outcome of all the separate decisions of all the people in society on the issue of foregoing consumption now for future rewards.

---

[3]Adam Smith, *op. cit.*, vol. 2, pp. 22–23.

**Intensive Growth.** Economic growth, as we noted in Chapter 3, is affected by more than the sheer quantities of human, natural, and capital resources placed in the process of production. The quality of resources and the types of recipe utilized in production are at least as important.

As was noted early in this chapter, the advocates of this particular model of capitalist market economy imagine government to collect taxes and to use them to provide all citizens with an equal opportunity for health care, general education, and training. Obviously, one cannot predict the extent to which government would carry this task. Would it tax 5 percent of national income for the purpose of thus creating invisible "human capital"? Would it force people to set aside 25 percent of national income for this purpose? Presumably, the decision would be made by public discussion and vote; thus, it would be "optimal" by definition!

It is equally difficult to predict the likely extent of basic and applied research and of entrepreneurial innovation in this type of economy. Some people suspect that investors in research and innovation would predict a sad ultimate outcome of their gamble: If it was a technical failure (and much money sunk into research and experimenting did not yield that more productive type of apple tree, let us say), the investors alone would have to bear all the cost. If it was a technical success (and a phenomenally more productive apple tree was bred, let us suppose), production costs would be reduced and some profit be made—*in the short run*. But before long, new firms would enter the field imitating the innovator; they would help raise industry supply greatly and, thus, reduce the product's equilibrium price— and eliminate profit. Thus, any long-range, high-cost investment in research and innovation would be discouraged, it is argued.

On the other hand, there are those who are less pessimistic. They think that many important innovations would occur as the result of random tinkering by a multitude of individuals engaged in the productive process. With very little monetary investment, they would raise the yield of apple trees today by applying fertilizer to their roots (rather than spreading it on the ground); they would raise it tomorrow by sprinkling water on apple blossoms when the spring frost was about to kill the year's crop in its infancy. And when other firms imitated their methods and competed away the profit associated with their temporary head start, they would find another way yet to get more apples still from the same resources. Thus, they would once more lower their cost and recreate their profit. By always being a step ahead of everyone else, it is argued, successful innovators could enjoy a permanent profit even when free entry into any field was guaranteed to all. It would just take *repeated* innovations to accomplish the feat, but why should not a minority of successful experimenters appear on the scene, continually teaching others how to do better? Thus, this economy, argue the optimists, would have within it an extremely important source of steady economic growth.

## Economic Equity

It is easy to see that the model capitalist market economy introduced in this chapter would not produce distributive justice. By its very design, there is no agency assigned to the task of distributing output justly among all the people. The distribution of income (and, thus, of output) that would emerge in any one year would, however, be considered eminently fair by the advocates of commutative justice. Their demand—giving all people as equal an opportunity as possible to earn income—would, of course, be one of the very foundation stones of the system under discussion.

All people, for instance, would be equally free to acquire any given skill; and once they had made this decision, they would be morally obliged to live by the consequences. Even then, however, they would be free to retrain and to switch jobs and localities; and if they did not, they should not complain about remaining differences in income. These would then be due to their unwillingness to take advantage of equal opportunities, say the advocates of the system.

Similarly with nonhuman resources: People who had placed their nonhuman resources into beef production when the demand for beef (and beef prices) plummeted should not complain of their low income, as long as they had been free to do anything else with their resources. They would still be free, of course, to switch their resources into the apple industry should demand (and prices) be rising there and higher income beckon.

Nevertheless, critics worry that the type of even-handed initial distribution of resources, which is being assumed throughout, might, in fact, not be carried out. Even if it were attempted, it would be quite difficult to carry out with perfection. (What, for instance, is one to do with the blind, the crippled, and the mentally retarded?) And whatever initial degree of equality in resource endowment was achieved, it would be even more difficult to maintain over time. (Consider how some people would save a lot and others wouldn't, and how that alone would gradually shift the distribution of resource stocks.) Thus, there would emerge, sooner or later, unavoidable differences in people's economic power. In addition, there would be, in any one year, people like our beef producers who would earn little or nothing. True enough, they would have agreed to play the game. True enough, they could eventually escape the sudden and seemingly cruel verdict of the price system by heeding its unmistakable advice to move resources to other uses, to imitate innovations, and so on. Yet, some critics argue, one may wish to help them until then. They urge a compromise between the two conceptions of economic justice: to accept the notion of commutative justice in order to preserve incentives, while reducing the extent of income differentials by guaranteeing to all a certain basic minimum income through a *limited* degree of governmental redistribution.

## Alienation

How, finally, would the model economy presented here perform with respect to the broader aspects of welfare touched upon in Chapter 4? Would people be alienated from themselves, their fellows, and the natural world?

The advocates of this type of economy do not think so. Consider some of the things they have to say.

**From the Self.**   Under what circumstances, they say, could people possibly have a greater chance to develop themselves than under conditions of equal economic power? Here, as nowhere else, all persons would be as free as they could possibly be to discover their best way of living. Here would be a maximum scope for diversity, for differentiation. There would be no one who claimed to know the best way of living, no one who would force others into a preordained mold. Everyone would be free to experiment—to live alone or with a few friends, separated from the rest of humanity; or to join in the division of labor on an equal basis with others who also were hoping to improve their lot by doing so. And anyone would be free, at all times, to learn from failure and to imitate the more successful experimenters in leading a happier life.

**From One's Fellows.**   Similarly, argue the advocates of this model economy, people could hardly be given more power to participate in decisions on an equal basis with all others than in this economy. Naturally, such participation could not take the form of everyone sitting around a table and discussing every issue until a unanimous agreement was reached. But by indirect means, everyone would participate in all decisions on as equal a basis as can be devised. Consider how resources would be continually allocated and reallocated in accordance with the wishes of consumers:

As they freely spent their money incomes, they would determine the demand for various products. Any increased desire on their part for apples and any decreased desire for beef, for example, would raise the demand and the price of apples and lower those for beef. This would instantly make apple production more profitable and beef production less so. Before long, self-seeking apple producers would demand more baby apple trees, more fertilizer, more orchard spraying machines, and more human apple pickers, while equally self-seeking beef producers would demand fewer calves, less hay, less pastureland, and fewer cowboys. All these events would induce further changes in prices: upward wherever resources were being used to help produce apples, downward wherever they were being used to make beef. Eventually, self-seeking resource owners would reallocate their resources. Cowboys would become apple pickers; pastureland would turn into orchards. In the end, the supply of apples would rise (and their price fall again); the supply of beef would fall (and its price rise again), bringing the whole complicated chain of events to a halt.

And note: Consumers, like sovereign voters in a democracy, jointly would have determined the allocation of society's resources through casting their "dollar votes" in the stores. Thus, the system would be one of *consumer sovereignty.*

Note also how in the process just described *worker sovereignty* would be maintained. Sure enough, income differentials would inevitably arise: The wages of apple pickers would rise; those of cowboys fall. These would be the signals of the Invisible Hand, urging people to change their actions in accordance with the expressed desires of their fellows in society. Yet, no one would be *forced* to follow those signals. If you cared to remain a cowboy (or to keep your land as pasture), even if your income fell, you would be free to do so. But then you could hardly blame others for your lower income. It would be the result of your unwillingness to serve your fellow men as they would like to be served!

And how would people experience work in the firms owned by others? It is difficult to say. Would firms be small and, therefore, less likely to give rise to impersonality? Some think so. Would large numbers of people pool their resources to create huge and complex enterprises? It would not be impossible. But, as was noted in Chapter 4, people might very well like to work in complex organizations, as long as they were able to hold the exercise of power over them to account, and such might be much easier to accomplish in a society where the ownership of resources was widely dispersed, and a great many alternative opportunities were available to any one person.

The advocates of our model economy, finally, are equally optimistic about the likely attainment of *citizen sovereignty.* As they see it, it is precisely under central economic planning that citizens are apt to lose their political freedoms. In such an economy, most individuals would be subject to *specific commands,* subject to the will, ultimately, of a single supreme authority. These commands would be addressed to specific individuals, not broadcast, like general laws, to the public at large. They would require unique actions, for they would tell people what to do or not to do and deprive them of the possibility of following their own predilections and using their own judgment. They would call for an unthinking response. Not so in the model suggested here. In the model capitalist market economy, all individuals would be free, within a framework of *general laws,* to make their own choices without coercion by other people. These laws might be set by nature or by people, but they would be alike in the sense of being directed equally to unknown people, abstracted from particular circumstances of time and place. They would enable people to plan their actions with confidence because they could foresee their consequences: If a man built a bonfire in his living room, the law of nature would tell him his house would burn down. If he built the fire in his neighbor's attic, the human law would add, he would go to jail. Thus, everyone could avoid being coerced by other people by refraining from those actions that would be known beforehand to elicit such coercion. And the government would not be involved in detailed economic decision making; thus, it would not be tempted to suppress everyone's freedoms in order to make recalcitrant people obey the central economic plan.

**From the Natural World.**   The advocates of the model capitalist market economy, finally, are quite optimistic about the relationship in their world between people and nature. Take, for instance, the problems of pollution or of the threatened extinction of animal species. Such problems would not arise, they say, because government would perform its first function of assigning property rights in all scarce things.

The absence of property rights in things—be they apples, houses, rivers, or whales—would be fine as long as these things were truly free; that is, as long as demand for their use at a zero price fell short of their supply. No problem at all would arise if, in a given year, a few thousand gallons of sewage were dumped into a clean river (which could assimilate even more without doing harm to anything) or if a few whales were snatched from the vastness of an ocean (which was teeming with millions of such giant mammals). But a problem would arise if these activities were carried on to excess. If the demand at a zero price were to catch up with and overtake the supply, then these resources would, in fact, be scarce, and the continued insistence that they were free could only lead to tragic results. When the dumping of wastes exceeded the environment's capacity to absorb them, or when the hunting of whales exceeded their natural replacement rates, then the usefulness of the resources involved would become impaired or disappear altogether. That is when the government of the model capitalist market economy, say its advocates, would recognize the appearance of scarcity by establishing new types of transferable property rights. The imaginative use of this device would give rise to new kinds of markets through which exclusive use of the resources, newly recognized as scarce, would be channeled to only those who paid the equilibrium prices for their use. Consider part (a) of Figure 12.6, "When Abundance Turns into Scarcity." A river might have the capacity (shown by the vertical line labeled supply) to absorb in a year 4 million tons of sewage without harm to anything—a fact that would be independent of any price charged for the right to dump such sewage. The amount people dumped, however, might vary with the price charged for the privilege. If they had to pay nothing (and were, thus, free to just go ahead and dump sewage whenever they liked), they might dump 2 million tons per year; at a high enough price (say $2,000 per ton), they might dump nothing at all. Under the circumstances pictured in part (a), the river's waste absorption capacity would be a free good. There would be no reason to keep anyone from dumping.

**Figure 12.6**   When Abundance Turns Into Scarcity

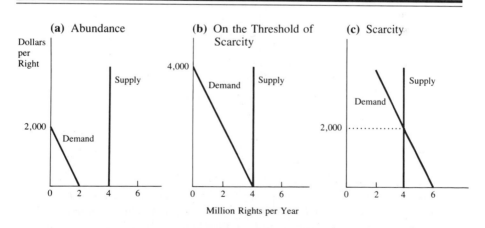

Given supply, rising demand eventually turns abundance into scarcity. Then the government of the model capitalist market economy assigns transferable property rights. As a result, new markets emerge for the scarce things that were once free, and these things are traded at a positive price.

Now suppose, a hundred years hence, population had grown, but as shown in part (b), the river's waste absorption capacity was unchanged at 4 million tons of sewage per year. People might then be dumping 4 million tons into it at a zero price (and it might now take a price of $4,000 per ton to discourage all the dumping). Yet, still, no action would be required. There would just be enough river for everyone!

The familiar problem would appear, as shown in part (c), when people dumped, at a zero price, more than 4,000 tons of sewage, exceeding the river's capacity to absorb. At that point, "No swimming" signs would go up, fish would die, and drinking water would be hard to find. It would be at this point that the government of our model capitalist market economy would establish property rights.

It might simply print up each year 4 million certificates, each of them giving its holder the right to dump 1 ton of sewage into the river during that year. And government might announce that henceforth the river's waste absorption capacity was private property, belonging to the holders of these certificates. If it wished to hold on to the basic philosophy underlying the model economy here discussed, the government could issue these rights in halves, quarters, tenths, and so on, and disperse them widely among all citizens, as by giving each one of them, as a free gift, an equal share on January 1. It is easy to see how, akin to the market for General Motors stock in the real world, a market for dumping rights would spring up at once among those who did and those who did not want to do any dumping. Before long, competition among demanders or suppliers of these rights would push their price to the equilibrium level of $2,000 per right shown in part (c). This process would exclude many would-be dumpers from the scene. Many individuals, firms, and local governments, who would have dumped sewage into the river at a zero price, would then think twice about their behavior. They would suddenly and painfully be confronted—in the form of a price—with the consequences of their action. The price would once more be a coded message: IF YOU WERE WILLING TO PAY $2,000 PER TON, YOU COULD DUMP ALL THE SEWAGE INTO THE RIVER YOU LIKED. Yet, as the sloping demand line indicates, some would find it cheaper to change their behavior (as by treating their sewage instead). Thus, harm to the environment could be prevented because the overall amount of dumping would be restricted to the limited amount the river could absorb (and which was reflected in equally limited amounts of private property rights).

Obviously, a similar procedure could be used to restrict the dumping of fly ash, carbon monoxide, and sulfur dioxide, or even of garbage and noise. And it could be used to restrict the hunting of whales, geese, or zebras, and even the fishing for tuna, sponges, or pearls!

If the hunting of 4 million whales a year, for example, just left their population unchanged, government could issue and distribute just that many hunting rights per year—the moment people overstepped the threshold of scarcity and began to take more than was available at a zero price. Thus, millions of different people would come to own various aspects of the natural environment, just like millions of people in the real world share in the ownership of General Motors. And just like the latter would turn over their GM stock to others only for a price, so the owners of these rights could sell them to would-be hunters of whales or whatever. The fact that only a limited number of rights existed would restrict the total hunt of law-abiding citizens to the socially determined maximum based on natural rates of reproduction.

Thus, argue the advocates of the model capitalist market economy, this society would harness the price system to the task of preserving harmony between people and the natural world. No amount of good will, they say, could by itself convey the essential information to people that the equilibrium prices of dumping rights or hunting rights conveyed: Ability to pay for such a right would be proof that one's contemplated use of nature was all right. In the absence of such a scheme, no individual would know whether the ton to be dumped would easily be absorbed (because it was one of 4 million harmless ones) or whether it was an excess ton destined to cause untold harm. No individual would know whether the killing of a whale would be an acceptable act (because it was akin to harvesting an annual crop) or whether it was an act destined to make whales extinct. Without the property rights in all scarce things, the free markets, and the equilibrium prices of the model capitalist market economy, say its advocates, large numbers of people could not communicate with each other on how each of them should act. There would only be groping in the dark. Thus, human welfare would be smaller than necessary.

## BIOGRAPHY 12.1   Adam Smith

Adam Smith (1723–1790) was born in Kirkaldy, Scotland. He studied at Glasgow and then at Oxford, only to return to Glasgow as a teacher of moral philosophy (economics had not yet been invented as a separate discipline). Smith wrote only two books; both brought him instant fame. His first book, *The Theory of Moral Sentiments,* was published in 1759; his second, *An Inquiry into the Nature and Causes of the Wealth of Nations,* in 1776. The latter book has been called the fountainhead of economic science; it earned Smith the title "father of economics."

The single most important source of the wealth of nations, Smith argues in his later book, is the division of labor. "This division of labor, from which so many advantages are derived," he says, "is not originally the effect of any human wisdom, which foresees and intends that general opulence to which it gives occasion. It is the necessary, though very slow and gradual, consequence of a certain propensity in human nature which has in view no such extensive utility; the propensity to truck, barter, and exchange one thing for another."[a] Throughout his book, Smith emphasizes the importance of economic liberty; that is, of free competition among individuals pursuing their self-interest as they choose to define it. The free, spontaneous interaction of people in the competitive marketplace—all persons having only their own narrow, but not necessarily selfish, ends in mind—brings about, argues Smith,

[a]Adam Smith, *op. cit.,* vol. 1, p. 11.

the general benefit of humanity that nobody intended. In contrast, governmental attempts to guide or regulate the market end up doing more harm than good.

But note: Just as he had no faith in governmental intervention, Smith had none so far as the intentions of businessmen are concerned. Throughout his book, he characterized them as dishonest, mean, oppressive, rapacious, and ruthless. He argued that *competition* was the crucial factor that compelled everyone to adjust their self-interested actions to the needs of fellow men. Under competition only did self-interest produce socially beneficial results.

## Summary

1. This chapter introduces another vision yet of an idealized economic system, a vision that champions individualism. The model of the capitalist market economy seeks to maximize welfare by letting all the adult individuals in society define their own happiness in their own way and take whatever actions seem appropriate to achieve it. Its advocates suggest that coordination of independently decided but interdependent economic activities of millions of people engaged in a division of labor can easily be achieved by letting self-interested people follow the guidance of price signals generated in free markets. They see no need for any central economic planner.

2. Nevertheless, the model's advocates believe that government has to play a limited but crucial role. This role involves the even-handed allocation of *economic power* among private individuals through the definition of property rights in all scarce things, their widest possible distribution, and the establishment of general rules facilitating their free exchange.

3. Under the postulated conditions, it is believed, a multitude of perfectly competitive markets would quickly emerge and an equilibrium price be established in each. The entire system of prices so emerging would serve like a system of telecommunications among all households and firms and (like an Invisible Hand) would continually coordinate the independent choices made by them.

4. The price system's expected work is illustrated with an extended example involving a change in demand from beef to apples. The example considers the impact effects as well as spillout and feedback effects of that change.

5. The likely performance of the model capitalist market economy is assessed with respect to the set of criteria first introduced in chapters 2 through 4. The model's advocates are confident that this economy would perform superbly with respect to all these criteria; some critics are not so sure.

## Key Terms

economic power
equilibrium price
feedback effect
impact effect
Invisible Hand

market coordination
perfectly competitive market
price system
spillout effect
spontaneous coordination

## Questions and Problems*

1. **Mr. A:** Now I have heard everything: People in the market economy are not supposed to coordinate their activities in a rational way, but they should simply submit to the blind forces of the market and all will work out for the good! That's just like announcing, as the fundamental principle of the whole system, that, *"in order to make a perfect and beautiful machine, it is not requisite to know how to make it."* This proposition will be found, on careful examination, to summarize the essential idea of the Invisible Hand. In short, Absolute Ignorance is fully qualified to take the place of Absolute Wisdom.
   **Ms. B:** Poor A, as usual, you don't see what it's all about. Why *not* submit to something that works well, even if you don't understand it rationally? As A. N. Whitehead used to say, "Civilization advances by extending the number of important operations we can perform *without* thinking about them." Knowing full well the limitations of human reason, I vote for the Invisible Hand.
   Evaluate these two opposing positions.
2. "The model capitalist market economy is an ugly society, driven by nothing else but the total selfishness of (utility-maximizing) households and (profit-maximizing) firms alike."
   Evaluate.
3. "Firms should produce for people, not for profit."
   Comment.
4. **Ms. A:** Competition is evil because it pits one person against another. Cooperation is good because people work with each other.
   **Ms. B:** Come on. Can't people cooperate for evil ends? Furthermore, competition *is* cooperation.
   Discuss.
5. "In a perfectly competitive capitalist market economy, the profit-maximizing behavior of firms will lead to the fulfillment of Pareto's first condition."
   Prove it graphically.

*Questions denoted by an asterisk utilize material presented in optional sections.

**\*6.** "In a perfectly competitive capitalist market economy, the profit-maximizing behavior of firms will lead to the fulfillment of Pareto's second condition."

Prove it graphically.

**7. Ms. A:** Competition in the model capitalist market economy can be thought of as an arrangement whereby the people of a society are enabled to discover the cheapest way of producing any given good.
**Ms. B:** You speak well. In fact, just imagine how much less would be the opportunity for making that discovery if there were only one producer or a few or if freedom of entry were denied to newcomers who might enter a market and challenge the ways of existing firms.

Discuss.

**8.** Study the answer to question 7 at the back of the book (page 524). Then depict the story graphically.

**\*9.** "To be a good governor of the economy, the price system must reward people not according to the goodness or badness of their intentions, but on the basis of the objective result of their contribution; and that depends on whether they produced what people wanted most. Hence, it could well be *right* to give someone $100 for 10 bushels of apples produced today, but only $2 for 10 identical bushels produced tomorrow."

Evaluate.

**10.** "Those who advocate the model economy described in this chapter seem to be unaware of government action needed to provide *public goods* that even the most perfect competition will never provide: national defense, interstate highway systems, space programs, beautiful cities, a cure for cancer, and more."

Evaluate.

## Selected Readings

Friedman, Milton. *Capitalism and Freedom* (Chicago: University of Chicago Press, 1962). Argues that a capitalist market economy maximizes human freedom.

Hayek, Friedrich A. "The Price System as a Mechanism for Using Knowledge," *The American Economic Review,* September 1945, pp. 519–30. A classic statement of why decentralized decisions in response to prices determined by market forces can lead to economic efficiency, which central planning cannot.

Hayek, Friedrich A. *The Road to Serfdom* (Chicago: University of Chicago Press, 1944).

Hayek, Friedrich A. *Individualism and Economic Order* (Chicago: University of Chicago Press, 1948).

Hayek, Friedrich A. *The Counter-Revolution of Science* (Glencoe, IL: Free Press, 1952).

Hayek, Friedrich A. *The Constitution of Liberty* (Chicago: University of Chicago Press, 1960).

Hayek, Friedrich A. *Law, Legislation, and Liberty,* vols. 1–3 (Chicago: University of Chicago Press, 1973, 1976, 1979). The 1974 co-winner of the Nobel Prize in Economics (Biography 6.2) maintains that the preservation of a free society depends on a spontaneous economic order emerging within the framework of general laws.

Kohler, Heinz. *Intermediate Microeconomics: Theory and Applications,* 2d. ed. (Glenview, IL: Scott, Foresman and Co., 1986). A detailed discussion of various aspects of the perfectly competitive economy can be found in chapters 3–7, 10, and 12–16.

Nozick, Robert. *Anarchy, State, and Utopia* (New York: Basic Books, 1974). A discussion of the proper role of government.

Smith, Adam. *An Inquiry into the Nature and Causes of the Wealth of Nations* (New York: Modern Library, 1937/1776). A classic, well worth reading today, written by the "father of economics" (Biography 12.1).

## Computer Program

The SYSTEMS personal computer diskette that accompanies this book contains one program of interest to this chapter:

Program 12, "Market Capitalism: A Model," provides 20 multiple-choice questions about Chapter 12, along with immediate responses to incorrect answers.

# CHAPTER 13

# *Market Capitalism: The U.S. Case*

The United States economy resembles the model economy discussed in the previous chapter in some ways, but differs from it in other ways. On the one hand, as in the model, most resources are privately owned by numerous individuals or groups (although the effective controllers; e.g., corporate managers, may differ from the formal owners; e.g., stockholders). In addition, as in the model, the separate decisions made by numerous households and firms are spontaneously coordinated through markets. On the other hand, and contrary to the model, resources are not *evenly* distributed over the whole population, and most of the markets in which people meet are anything but *perfectly* competitive. In many markets, **imperfect competition** rules supreme: The number of buyers or sellers is small, or, when that is not the case, large numbers collude rather than compete; as a result, market participants are not price takers as the model envisions, but can exercise appreciable power over price. Also, differentiated rather than homogeneous products are traded in many markets, and knowledge about market conditions is anything but perfect. Finally, entry into and exit from markets is frequently restricted rather than free.

As a result, many of the expected beneficial results of the capitalist market economy (such as those noted in the previous chapter) do not occur, and critics of the U.S. economy complain about *market failure*. When unemployment, economic inefficiency, "inadequate" economic growth, an "unfair" distribution of income, widespread pollution, or any number of similar evils are observed, critics call upon government to correct these failures of the market system. In the eyes of the advocates of the model capitalist market economy, however, the types of evils just cited are a type of *government failure*. As they see it, these problems arise precisely because the real-world government (when compared to the tasks outlined for it in the previous chapter) fails to do what it should do and acts in ways it shouldn't. Thus, it is said, pollution problems arise when government does not assign property rights in scarce parts of the natural environment, income-distribution problems can be traced in part to the government's failure to disperse resource ownership widely, economic inefficiency and inequity alike can be blamed on the government's failure to smash private tendencies toward monopoly and to ensure the prevalence of perfectly competitive conditions in all markets. Indeed, critics conclude, these government sins of omission are immeasurably compounded by sins of commission: the erection of public barriers to the unrestricted use of property rights by all (as through the granting of exclusive franchises or the creation of government-sponsored cartels, to name just two instances).

There is no need for us to become involved in the semantic debate on whether market failure or government failure is at fault. Let us proceed to describe the major features of the U.S. economy and to assess its performance by the familiar criteria applied throughout this book.

## The Monopoly Game

In the U.S. economy, many people play a "monopoly game": They try to gain control over the prices at which they sell or buy in order to raise their own income at the expense of other people's income. Consider what is involved.

Barring gifts or loans from other societies, Americans *as a group* can increase the yearly flow of goods available to them in only one of three ways:

1. They can utilize the existing stocks of their resources at a higher rate. That is, they can opt for less leisure and less conservation of capital and natural resources.
2. They can increase the size of their resource stocks and then use them at the accustomed rate. For example, they can trade in lowered current consumption for greater investment in human and physical capital.
3. They can increase their productivity. Risk-bearing entrepreneurs, for example, can make innovative changes that coax a larger flow of goods from identical resource flows.

If the American economy contained nothing but perfectly competitive markets, what is always true for Americans as a group would also be true for every individual. Barring the receipt of gifts or loans from other people, every individual who wished to have an increased command over goods would have to do one of the three things just mentioned. Every individual who wished to have a larger piece of the pie and who could not get it through gifts or loans would have to engage in an activity that enlarged the pie itself. In the absence of perfectly competitive markets, on the other hand, there is another way for individuals to increase their command over goods.

When markets are imperfectly competitive, some people can get more goods even from a constant or shrinking pie—*at the expense of other people.* In imperfectly competitive markets, some people can get more goods at others' expense through a cunning alteration of the prices at which exchanges take place. To the extent that individuals can raise the prices of things being sold or reduce the prices of things being bought, purchasing power can be transferred to these manipulators of prices.

If all markets were perfectly competitive, no person would have the power to manipulate prices in such a manner, because trading partners would have plenty of alternatives open to them. If any one seller, for example, tried to dictate a price above the competitive equilibrium level, all buyers would disappear. Buyers could find many other sellers able and willing to supply, at the competitive equilibrium price, as much as they wanted of any good. But now consider this: What if a seller were able to kill off competition in whatever was for sale (and in its close substitutes as well)? What if there were no other sellers or at least no other independently acting ones? In this situation, buyers would be trapped. Instead of finding innumerable sellers, buyers would find only a single seller (or a group of sellers acting as one). Buyers would be confronted by a **monopoly,** a single seller selling a product that has no close substitutes, or by a **cartel,** a group of conspiring sellers acting as one and making joint price-quantity decisions with a view toward earning a larger profit than competition would allow.

## Pure Monopoly

The most successful players of the monopoly game achieve a genuine monopoly. It can originate from a number of technological and legal sources, including increasing returns to scale, exclusive ownership of key resources, patents and copyrights, and exclusive franchises.

### Sources of Monopoly

**Increasing Returns to Scale.**    Consider an industry subject to **increasing returns to scale.** Under such conditions, a simultaneous and equal percentage change in the use of all physical inputs leads to a larger percentage change in physical output. Hence, an increase in scale under conditions of increasing returns shifts average total (and marginal) cost curves not only to the right, but also down. This shift is illustrated, with respect to a hypothetical producer of electric power, in Figure 13.1. "The Natural Monopoly," which depicts a producer who is capable of setting up a multitude of different-sized power plants. Design number 41, for example, yields short-run average-total-cost curve $SRATC_{41}$; design number 71 yields curve $SRATC_{71}$, and so on, until design number 112 produces the optimum plant, the one that has taken advantage of all available economies of scale and yields the lowest possible minimum average total cost (at point $m$). The firm's long-run average-total-cost curve, therefore, is the envelope curve labeled LRATC. Whenever long-run average total cost is in this way declining throughout the range of possible quantities demanded in the market (as shown here by market demand line $AB$), the situation is one of **natural monopoly.**

**Figure 13.1**    The Natural Monopoly

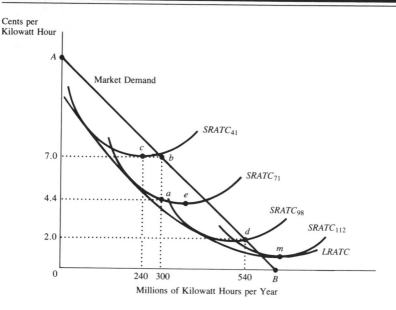

Whenever long-run average total cost is declining throughout the range of possible quantities demanded in the market, the first firm expanding its scale sufficiently to supply the entire market can secure for itself a natural monopoly.

The assumed technical facts—not uncommon for producers of electric power, gas, water, and telephone service—enable a single firm to produce more cheaply than two or more firms. The first firm to recognize and take advantage of such increasing returns to scale can profitably supply the entire market (instead of a negligible fraction thereof), while keeping additional firms out of the market by the certain prospect of losses. Consider how such a firm might design and construct plant number 71, produce 300 million kilowatt hours at 4.4 cents each (point *a*) and sell them at 7 cents each (point *b*). Any potential rival, in order to meet the 7-cents-per-kilowatt-hour price, would have to construct a plant of size number 41 at least and run it at its optimal (minimum average total cost) rate (point *c*). All else being equal, such extra output of 240 million kilowatt hours would raise total quantity supplied to 540 million kilowatt hours, a quantity that could not be sold for more than 2 cents per kilowatt hour (point *d*). This price would inevitably engulf the new and the old firm in losses. (Both *c* and *e*, the minimum average total costs associated with plants 41 and 71, respectively, clearly exceed 2 cents.) These losses would be even larger should the potential newcomer build a plant as large as or larger than number 71, for the resultant market supply could not even be sold at the lowest of all possible average total costs, corresponding to point *m*. This sort of analysis would keep newcomers at bay, or this sort of scenario would, eventually, allow only one firm to survive. Monopoly need not, however, be the result of technical factors.

**Exclusive Ownership of Key Resources.**   Sometimes firms become the only sellers in their industry because they have exclusive ownership of a key resource without which the industry's product cannot be produced. The Aluminum Company of America (Alcoa) once controlled most domestic bauxite deposits (from which aluminum is made), and it also controlled many strategic water power sites capable of generating the massive electric power needed for aluminum ingot production. American Metal Climax once controlled 90 percent of the world's molybdenum (all of it in one Colorado mountain); the International Nickel Company once owned a similar percentage of the world's nickel.

The exclusive ownership conducive to monopoly need not necessarily involve natural resources, however. Consider why New York's Met long held a monopoly in American opera: All the experienced singers available were under long-term contracts to the Met. Professional baseball and football clubs, similarly, sign up all the talented players, making life rather impossible for potential competitors. The same kind of advantage would also accrue to any firm that could sign up all the possessors of some secret production recipe similar, perhaps, to that of making a genuine Stradivarius violin. On that account, however, government today provides a helping hand.

**Patents and Copyrights.**   Government frequently promotes the establishment of monopoly when it issues patents and copyrights. A **patent** is an exclusive right to the use of an invention. It is limited to a period of 17 years and permits the holder to prevent all others from producing a specified product or using a specified process. Patents are, of course, granted in order to encourage the production and disclosure of inventions and to stimulate innovation that is often risky and expensive to undertake but all too easy and cheap for others to copy. Many monopolies in the past have been based on patents, including patents for such products or processes as aluminum, cash registers, cellophane, instant photographic pictures, rayon, scotch tape, shoe machinery, and xerography. Monopolies can, similarly, be created with the help of a **copyright,** the exclusive right to the reproduction, publishing, or sale of a literary, musical, or artistic work. Although patents and copyrights are only granted for limited periods, the seller so favored often acquires an impregnable market position by the time this protection expires.

**Exclusive Franchises.**   The most ancient source of monopoly, and one that often has the most enduring effect, is the **exclusive franchise,** a governmental grant to a single seller of the exclusive right to produce and sell a good. Kings throughout history have granted this privilege to their favored subjects, presumably because it provided a way to enrich them (by enabling them to charge their fellow citizens above-competitive prices) without any drain from the royal purse. For Americans, the monopoly of the British East India Company is, perhaps, of the greatest significance. That monopoly gave rise to the Boston Tea Party.

This type of contrived barrier to competition is common. Consider the exclusive franchises granted by the federal government to the U.S. Postal Service, by state governments to single restaurant chains operating along their turnpikes, and by city governments to cable television companies, garbage collectors, taxi companies, and various concessions (from airport car rentals to food service and parking at sports events).

## Hoped-for Consequences of Monopoly

Whatever their origin, monopolies attempt to create for themselves a situation of permanent profit. Figure 13.2, "A Profit-Making Monopoly," illustrates a successful attempt of this sort. Just like any other firm, this monopoly maximizes profit by selecting an output volume that maximizes the difference, $\pi$, between total revenue, *TR,* and total cost, *TC* (and, therefore, equates marginal revenue, *MR,* with marginal cost, *MC.*) Given the assumed conditions of revenue and cost, this monopoly would maximize profit by producing an output volume of 20 million kilowatt hours per day.

Consider panel (a) of Figure 13.2. It is obvious that any output volume to the left of point *a* or to the right of point *b* would yield losses because total cost would exceed total revenue. All intermediate output levels would yield positive profits, but to varying degrees. The maximum possible profit would be $2.4 million per day (distance *cd*), corresponding to the 20-million-kilowatt-hour total just noted. It is no accident that the slope of the total revenue curve at *c* exactly equals that of the total cost curve at *d*. Between *a* on the one hand and *c* or *d* on the other, total revenue and total cost increasingly diverge from each other; so total profit grows. Between *c* or *d* on the one hand and *b* on the other, total revenue and total cost converge; so total profit declines.

Panel (b) of Figure 13.2 leads to the same conclusion, of course. The ever changing slope, at various potential output volumes, of the total revenue curve is now reflected by the height of the marginal revenue curve. The ever changing slope of the total cost curve, similarly, shows up as the height of the marginal cost curve. The equality of marginal cost and marginal revenue at *F* signifies maximum profit. Consider what would happen if the firm produced the associated 20 million kilowatt hours per day and set a 30-cents-per-kilowatt-hour price to make people demand just this (20-million-kilowatt-hour) quantity (point *B*). Total revenue would then equal rectangle *OABC;* that is, 20 million kilowatt hours times the 30-cents-per-kilowatt-hour price, or $6 million per day, also shown by point *c* in panel (a). Total cost would equal rectangle *OAED;* that is, 20 million kilowatt hours times the 18-cents-per-kilowatt-hour average total cost, or $3.6 million per day, also shown by point *d* in panel (a). Total profit, therefore, would equal shaded rectangle *DEBC;* that is, 20 million kilowatt hours times the 12-cents-per-kilowatt-hour average profit *BE,* or $2.4 million per day, also shown by distance *cd* in panel (a).

Note: The making of positive profit is not inevitable. Given identical demand but less favorable cost conditions, our monopoly could just as well be making zero profit or even a loss.

**Figure 13.2** A Profit-Making Monopoly

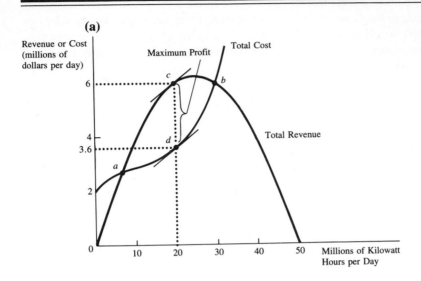

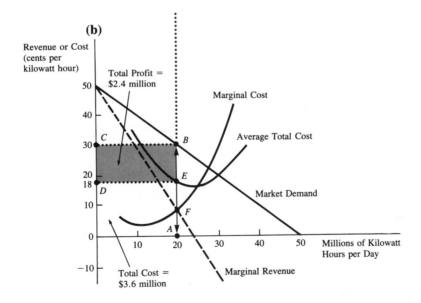

This profit-maximizing monopoly finds its optimal rate of production where its rising marginal cost equals its falling marginal revenue. Given the short-run revenue and cost functions shown here, this equality occurs at points *c* and *d* in panel (a) and at *F* in panel (b). The corresponding optimal rate of production equals 20 million kilowatt hours per day; therefore, a price of 30¢ per kilowatt hour is set. In this example, total revenue exceeds total cost; thus, a positive profit is made that is equal to $2.4 million per day (distance *cd* in the top panel; the shaded rectangle in the bottom panel).

## Private Cartels

It is not difficult to see why firms in an otherwise competitive industry might be tempted to form a cartel. If such firms were lucky enough to imitate the behavior of a profit-making monopoly, their efforts would yield an important prize: permanent economic profit instead of the ever present tendency toward zero profit.

In principle, the formation of a cartel is easy. All it takes is an agreement among all the existing sellers to charge an identical and higher price and to restrict supply until it equals market demand at the cartel price. In practice, however, such would-be monopolists often run afoul of one or more of three obstacles: organizational difficulties, a high price elasticity of demand, or a high price elasticity of supply.

### Organizational Difficulties

There is first the problem of getting all or most existing sellers to join a cartel in the first place. When there are many sellers, this may be a hopeless task. Even when there are few, but they do not get along with each other, the original formation of the cartel may not be possible. But organizational difficulties occur beyond this initial stage. Cartel members must frequently meet and agree on a common price to be charged; they must allocate among themselves the necessary reductions in quantity supplied; they must keep each other from cheating on the agreement. It takes a strong and lasting spirit of cooperation to achieve all this.

Consider, for example, the formation of a private price-fixing and output-restricting agreement among hundreds of thousands of wheat farmers. Their initial circumstances might be those depicted by point *e* in Figure 13.3, "A Cartel." Some 2.5 billion bushels of wheat might be traded in the year prior to the cartel's formation, and wheat might sell at a competitive equilibrium price of $2 per bushel. Yet, a bright organizer might note, a slight restriction of the yearly supply to 2.1875 billion bushels could raise the price to $3 per bushel and benefit all the farmers. How could the organizer persuade all the wheat farmers in the nation to join and to agree on cutting next year's output by 12.5 percent below this year's crop so as to raise the price from the old equilibrium level of $2 to an estimated new level of $3 per bushel? (In 1968, when the National Farmers' Organization tried to organize a *cattle* cartel, only 10 percent of the farmers joined.)

Even if the initial step could be taken, buyers could surely find farmers cheating on the agreement. Imagine yourself to be one of the farmers who has just voted on the above scheme. You used to produce, say, 5,000 bushels, getting $10,000 of gross revenue at the old $2-per-bushel price, Now you know that you will have to cut output by 12.5 percent (as everyone else has to). Then you will sell 4,375 bushels. If the price rises to $3, this will gross $13,125, a clear gain of $3,125. But you know something else. You know that you play an insignificant part in this whole scheme. Nobody would ever notice if you, just you, did not cut your output. Total supply would then be cut, you might figure, from 2.5 billion bushels to only 2.187500625 billion bushels (instead of the agreed-upon 2.1875 billion bushels).

**Figure 13.3** A Cartel

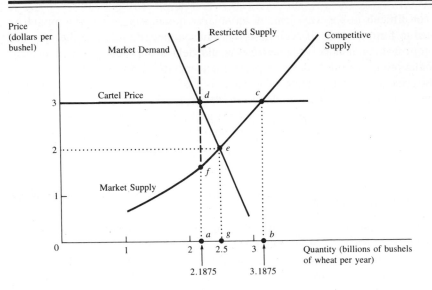

Competitive sellers of a good may improve their welfare at the expense of buyers by conspiring to raise price and by restricting the quantity supplied. If wheat farmers, for example, could agree to restrict supply so that the line going through *f, e,* and *c* was shifted to dashed line *fd,* they could escape the $2-per-bushel competitive equilibrium price (corresponding to *e*) and enjoy the $3-per-bushel cartel price (corresponding to *d*). In the process, they would replace, just as a monopoly does, a price equal to marginal cost (at *e*) with a price (at *d*) above marginal cost (at *f*).

That would surely make no difference. As long as the others stuck to the agreement, price would still rise to $3, or almost that. And then your gross income would rise to almost $15,000, not just to $13,125. Even if you were caught (which would be unlikely), nobody could fine you or throw you in jail. Under the English common law (unwritten law), private conspiracies to fix output and market shares and prices cannot be enforced. It would pay you to cheat! (In 1968, some cattle farmers blew up cattle scales and sat on the roads obstructing cattle shipments by the ''chiselers.'' But many more of them were marketing their cattle; some even used house trailers to conceal their shipments.)

As you might expect, there would be others who would have the same bright idea of cheating as you. There would even be some who were brighter than that. They would *raise* their output in the hope of making a killing when all others cut theirs and caused price to go up. Before long, a surplus of *dc* might appear in the market, putting strong pressure on price to fall. Thus, a privately arranged price-fixing agreement has an excellent chance of breaking down for organizational reasons alone.

## A High Price Elasticity of Demand

Even when the original conspirators are totally loyal to each other and honestly abide by the agreement, a cartel agreement can easily fail. No degree of organizational success can overcome a high price elasticity of market demand. Consider the extreme case of an infinite elasticity where buyers have plenty of good substitutes available for the cartel's product. Under such circumstances, unlike Figure 13.3, any increase in price by the cartel leads to the total disappearance of quantity demanded. Selling nothing at a very high price will satisfy few sellers, indeed.

## A High Price Elasticity of Supply

Finally, a cartel may be wrecked by a high price elasticity of supply. Even if cartel members are loyal and reduce quantity supplied in response to the higher price, newcomers who have no inclination to join the conspiracy may enter the industry, attracted, of course, by the very price rise engineered by the cartel. Thus, former potato farmers may grow wheat to get a piece of the loot. And foreign farmers may ship in huge quantities. These new suppliers may offset or more than offset the supply reduction by the cartel. Then a glut will develop on the market, and buyers will find it easy to be supplied below the cartel price.

# Government-Sponsored Cartels

Given the difficulties encountered by private cartels, it is not surprising that would-be cartel makers have often turned to government for help against reluctant joiners, argumentative members, chiselers, and outsiders. More often than not, such government help has been provided. Typically, it has taken the form of *legislating,* separately or in combination, the setting of a higher price, a cutback in supply, or even an increase in demand.

## Fixing Prices

The U.S. Congress has fixed prices above competitive equilibrium levels either directly or has granted broad powers to specially designed departments of the executive to do such price fixing. Among such executive departments (past or present) are the multitude of federal "alphabet agencies"; the CAB, the FCC, the FMC, the FPC, the FTC, and the ICC, to name just a few! The Civil Aeronautics Board (CAB), now extinct, for many years was responsible for regulating interstate airline service. It set fares at notoriously high levels to accommodate even the highest-cost producers. On identical routes served by CAB-regulated interstate and by nonregulated *intrastate* airlines, the fares of the intrastate lines (such as California's Pacific Southwest and Texas's Southwest) were about 50 percent below the rates of CAB carriers. The Federal Communications Commission (FCC) has performed a similar role for telephone and telegraph companies and radio and television broadcasters. The Federal Maritime Commission (FMC) has done the same thing with respect to ocean shipping, and the Federal Power Commission (FPC) with respect to natural gas and electric power producers. The Federal Trade Commission (FTC) has long kept retail prices high enough to allow high-cost outlets to live side by side with lower-cost chain stores. The Interstate Commerce Commission (ICC) has promoted high prices for interstate barge and ship companies, buses, railroads, and (nonagricultural) truckers. (In the 1980s, however, a number of deregulation acts have severely clipped the powers of the agencies just noted.)

Federal laws setting minimum prices of goods above competitive equilibrium levels have included, most notably, laws fixing prices for agricultural products. These products have ranged from almonds, barley, beans, butter, cheese, corn, cotton, dates, flax seed, honey, milk, lemons, mohair, raisins, sorghum, and oats to peanuts, potatoes, rice, rye, soybeans, sugar beets and cane, tung nuts, tobacco, walnuts, wheat, and wool.

Many state and local governments, in addition, protect sellers beyond the reach of federal laws from the supposed ravages of competition. State liquor commissions set liquor prices; state public utility commissions set electric power and telephone rates. State insurance commissions set insurance rates; city transport commissions set rates on buses, subways, and taxis. For some 38 years prior to 1976 (when a federal law repealed them), states as well as cities promoted minimum retail prices for almost everything. Their so-called **fair-trade laws** allowed any manufacturer to fix a minimum price for a product and, if a single retailer agreed to it, to bind all retailers to it, even those who refused to sign an agreement with the manufacturer. Those selling for less could be enjoined, fined, and even jailed. As recently as 1974, 36 states, from California to New York, still had such laws.

## Cutting Supply

Initial price-fixing moves have to be reinforced by further decrees or laws, as Figure 13.3 also illustrates. When price is raised above its equilibrium level (and kept there by law), a surplus develops because quantity demanded drops (along *ed* in the graph), while quantity supplied rises (along *ec*). To avoid the surplus, a government unwilling to let the price fall must either cut the supply or raise the demand; that is, it must bend the market supply line left until it goes through point *d* or shift the market demand line right until it goes through point *c*.

Supply has often been cut by denying or restricting market entry to new sellers and by forcing existing sellers to reduce their own supply. From its inception in 1938 until recently, for example, the CAB has not allowed the creation of a single new interstate airline, finding such a move "not required by the public interest, convenience, and necessity." The CAB also enforced market sharing or output restrictions among the existing 10 domestic airlines in order to give them "route security" and to avoid "excessive, destructive, and cut-throat competition." The other federal alphabet agencies, as well as their brethren at the lower levels of government, have performed identical supply-restricting functions.

Similarly, agricultural price legislation has been buttressed by restrictions on domestic output and on imports. Domestic farmers have been issued **acreage allotments** that restrict the total acreage planted with particular crops to or below that achieved at a given date in the past. Farmers have also been given **marketing quotas** that set a maximum amount of a product that particular farmers can legally sell. (Marketing quotas were set when farmers with acreage allotments responded by, nevertheless, producing *more,* due to their flooding of the restricted acreage with fertilizer, pesticides, high-yield seeds, and tender, loving care. Close-Up 13.1, ''Orange Uprising,'' provides a fascinating glimpse of the program.) In addition, under the old Soil Bank Program and more recent land-set-asides, farmers have been paid subsidies for taking land entirely out of production. This program has been reinforced by controls on agricultural imports that take the form of either high **tariffs** (import taxes) or low **import quotas** (maximum physical limits on the amounts of goods that may be imported).

The federal government has also helped nonagricultural sellers of goods by such ''protective'' foreign trade legislation. Even though, in many cases, minimum prices have not been legislated, such restrictions on the domestic market supply raise prices indirectly above the level that would otherwise pertain. Thus, the United States has placed tariffs on cars, steel, and textiles; import quotas on baseball mitts, bicycles, and umbrellas; and has persuaded foreign governments to impose, ''voluntarily,'' export quotas on their firms (as in the case of Japanese steel and television sets). The list could easily be lengthened. Indeed, a whole range of other *nontariff* barriers (usually in the form of red tape that discourages foreign trade) has served to accomplish the same goal of reducing alternative sources of supply to the domestic buyer and, thus, enabling favored domestic sellers to charge more.

State governments, similarly, have pushed up the prices of many goods by placing restrictions on the output produced or the number of producers. Under the Prorationing Program in Oklahoma and Texas, for instance, the number of days per month during which existing oil wells may pump is restricted by law (with the exception of offshore wells that are under federal jurisdiction). Every state in the union also requires the licensing of a multitude of ''professions,'' broadly defined to include not just architects, doctors, dentists, lawyers, and psychologists, but also astrologers, barbers, bartenders, dancing instructors, egg graders, morticians, television aerial erectors, and yacht sellers!

## Raising Demand

In addition to reinforcing high prices with cuts in supply, governments can do something for sellers that even the most perfectly organized private cartel would find impossible to do: A government can actually force buyers to buy the same quantity (or even more) at the very time that price is raised. The most common approach is to tax people and then use the money to make purchases from or give outright gifts to the favored sellers. Under the agricultural programs in effect prior to 1974 and again since 1977, for instance, the federal government stands ready to purchase, at the prices officially legislated, butter, peanuts, sugar, wheat, and other products. In Figure 13.3, the government might set the price at $3 per bushel, while letting farmers produce what they like (point *c*) and letting them sell privately what they can (point *d*). The government might then buy the difference (*dc*), spending the taxpayers' money (equal to *abcd*). Taxes finance such purchases as well as the cost of their subsequent storage, destruction, or give-away (be it in the form of school lunches or foreign aid). Close-Up 13.2, "Supporting the Price of Sugar," provides an example. A host of other producers, such as airlines, bus companies, ocean shippers, railroads, and subways, are also subsidized by various levels of government. Thus, taxpayers in all parts of the country who help finance subsidies to airlines or railroads or farmers are, in fact, being forced to "buy" airplane rides and railroad trips and butter without even realizing it. In this way, they are helping to maintain the government-sponsored high prices of air travel or railroad shipping or butter, which, of course, is the object of the monopoly game: for some people to gain at the expense of other people, without making an effort to reduce overall scarcity.

## Oligopoly and Monopolistic Competition

The previous sections have explained why sellers of goods, seeking to gain economic profit on a permanent basis, may wish to eliminate all other sellers in their industry or at least to collude with them. We also noted the major technological and legal foundations on which some firms manage to build successful monopolies or cartels. For many other firms using other approaches, however, complete success remains elusive in this monopoly game.

Some firms, for example, have tried in vain to gobble up their competitors, using such devices as trusts, holding companies, or horizontal mergers. (A **trust** is a combination of several corporations under the trusteeship of a single board of directors that manages their affairs jointly. A **holding company** is a corporation established for the sole purpose of acquiring a controlling stock interest in two or more competing corporations in an industry and then jointly running their affairs. A **horizontal merger** is the direct purchase by one firm of the assets of another firm just like it; consider the merger of two pipeline companies that sell closely related products in the same geographic market.)

Other firms have tried in vain to eliminate their competitors by stealing their customers. This has been attempted through price wars, product differentiation, persuasive advertising, vertical mergers with those customers, the imposition of tying contracts, and more. (In a **price war,** rival firms successively cut their prices below those of competitors and, perhaps, even below their own costs. **Product differentiation** involves the differentiation of the products of one firm from those of other firms in a given industry on the basis of physical aspects [such as color, durability, flavor, octane rating, size, style], legal matters [such as trademarks], and conditions of sale [such as the provision of a store closer to the customers' homes, of free, convenient parking, more business hours per week, more trading stamps, easier credit terms, prompter delivery, better warranties, faster repairs and main-

tenance, and more]. **Persuasive advertising** is advertising designed to divert people's attention from facts to images and make them buy more as a result of imagined
advantages. A **vertical merger** is the direct purchase by one firm of the assets of
another firm that is its supplier or customer; consider the acquisition by an oil
pipeline company of an oil refinery [which henceforth refuses to buy oil from other
pipeline companies]. A **tying contract,** finally, is an agreement by which an aspiring
monopolist forces the customers of its competitors to buy from it alone if they wish
to continue receiving some other product that no one else can deliver.) Finally,
firms have tried to eliminate competitors by stealing their suppliers; consider the
vertical merger of an oil pipeline company that acquires a crude oil producer who
then refuses to sell crude oil to other pipeline companies.

More often than not, these attempts at monopolization are only partially successful; as a result, many firms in the American economy come to inhabit a "twilight
zone," lying somewhere between monopoly or cartel on the one hand and perfect
competition on the other. This middle ground, in which features of monopoly blend
with those of competition, nevertheless involves situations in which individual
sellers face downward-sloping demand curves and, thus, have some measure of
control over price.

The Coca Cola Company, for example, because of its trademark, has a legal
monopoly in this drink. No one else may produce it, and the firm can charge any
price it likes for it. But when it does, it better be aware of its obvious rivals, from
the makers of Pepsi Cola to those of orange juice. Because these rivals produce a
whole range of fairly good substitutes, the Coca Cola Company does not enjoy a
pure monopoly. The suburban corner drugstore, similarly, because of its location,
has a local monopoly of sorts. It, too, can charge any price it wishes for its drugs.
But it better be aware that if its prices get too much out of line, customers will
trade in the advantage of short trips to the neighborhood store for lower prices at
competing drugstores downtown.

Economists have found it useful to classify markets that lie between the extremes
of pure monopoly and perfect competition in two ways. First, they talk of **oligopoly**
when the entry of new firms is difficult and relatively few sellers compete with one
another, while offering either homogeneous products (such as cement, steel, rail
transportation) or differentiated ones (such as cars, cigarettes, soap). Second, they
talk of **monopolistic competition** when the entry of new firms is easy and when
large numbers of sellers compete with one another, while offering differentiated
products.

## Imperfect Competition in Resource Markets

Although it will not be discussed in detail in this book, imperfect competition is
equally rampant in U.S. resource markets. For example, monopoly power on the
selling side of a labor market is frequently exercised by workers who have formed
a cartel for the joint sale of their labor; that is, a **labor union.** Consider how unions,
in typical cartel-like fashion, have tried to raise wages by reducing supply. They

have tried to keep competing workers out by restricting union membership (charging high initiation fees, administering impossible entrance tests, or simply denying access to blacks, females, Jews, or any other easily identifiable group). Consider how they have warded off the threat of nonunion competition by forcing employers to establish **closed shops** (in which only union members are hired) or **union shops** (in which all employees, soon after hiring, have to pay union dues as a condition of continued employment).

On the other hand, it is just as possible for the buyers of resource services to restrict competition. Sometimes there exists only a single buyer, a **monopsony.** Consider a firm that is the only buyer in a labor market. Such a situation is far from unusual. A typical example is the "company town," dominated by a single employer. Think of Seattle and the Boeing Company; Butte, Montana and the Anaconda Copper Mining Company; Hershey, Pennsylvania and the Hershey Chocolate Company; Barstow, California and the Sante Fe Railway. Such dominant employers have "captured" workforces to the extent that such places are inhabited by workers who cannot or will not leave the area (being ignorant of alternatives, unable to find transportation, or reluctant to leave pretty scenery or good friends).

Monopsony need not necessarily be based on the geographic concentration of immobile resources, however. It can also arise when numerous employers agree to act jointly in the hiring of labor and not to compete with each other for workers. Such **antipirating agreements** have been reached on a national basis by major league sports clubs and different departments of the federal government; on a regional basis by coal mining firms and by those manufacturing furniture and garments; and on a local basis by colleges, construction firms, hospitals, hotels, newspapers, and restaurants.

## An Overview of the Economy

What is the relative importance of various market structures in the U.S. economy? To answer the question, we will focus first on the nature of various industries and then on the major sectors of the economy.

### Indexes of Industrial Concentration

To indicate the extent to which particular markets are dominated by a few large firms, economists construct **concentration ratios,** each one of which equals the percentage of industry sales attributable to a given number of the largest firms, usually the 4, 8, 20, and 50 largest companies. Thus a 4-firm concentration ratio of 62 would indicate that the 4 largest firms in the industry accounted for 62 percent of industry sales in a given year.

A 1972 study of 450 U.S. industries revealed that this 4-firm concentration ratio was between 0 and 19 for 87 industries, between 20 and 39 for 168 of them, between 40 and 59 for another 118, and at 60 or above for the remaining 77 industries. Table 13.1, "Concentration Ratios in the United States, 1972," contains much richer detail.

**Table 13.1**   Concentration Ratios in the United States, 1972

| Industry | 4-Firm Ratio | 8-Firm Ratio | Number of Firms |
|---|---|---|---|
| Electron-receiving tubes | 95 | 99 | 21 |
| Motor vehicles, car bodies | 93 | 99 | 165 |
| Primary lead | 93 | 99 | 12 |
| Cereal breakfast foods | 90 | 98 | 34 |
| Electric lamps | 90 | 94 | 103 |
| Turbines and generators | 90 | 96 | 59 |
| Household refrigerators/freezers | 85 | 98 | 30 |
| Cigarettes | 84 | n.a. | 13 |
| Cathode-ray (TV) tubes | 83 | 97 | 69 |
| Household laundry equipment | 83 | 98 | 20 |
| Carbon/graphite products | 80 | 91 | 58 |
| Primary aluminum | 79 | 92 | 12 |
| Household vacuum cleaners | 75 | 91 | 34 |
| Chocolate, cocoa products | 74 | 88 | 39 |
| Calculating/accounting machines | 73 | 89 | 74 |
| Tires, inner tubes | 73 | 90 | 136 |
| Aircraft | 66 | 86 | 141 |
| Metal cans | 66 | 79 | 134 |
| Roasted coffee | 65 | 79 | 162 |
| Sanitary paper products | 63 | 82 | 72 |
| Soap and detergents | 62 | 74 | 577 |
| Storage batteries | 57 | 85 | 138 |
| Glass containers | 55 | 76 | 27 |
| Wine, brandy | 53 | 68 | 183 |
| Malt beverages | 52 | 70 | 108 |
| Pet food | 51 | 71 | 147 |

In many U.S. industries, concentration ratios are high and the number of firms is small.

*Source:* U.S. Bureau of the Census, Census of Manufactures, 1972 *Special Report Series: Concentration Ratios in Manufacturing,* MC72(SR)-2 (Washington, D.C.: U.S. Government Printing Office, 1975).

To some extent, large concentration ratios, such as those of Table 13.1, may even *understate* the market power of firms, for the ratios refer to the nation as a whole. Many markets, however, are effectively limited to a much smaller area because of such factors as prohibitive transportation costs, perishable products, and so on. Suppose there were in a hypothetical industry 1,000 producers, all of equal size. Then the four "largest" companies would ship 4/1,000 of output or .4 percent. If producers competed on a national scale, buyers everywhere would have 1,000 sellers to choose from, and the low concentration ratio might correctly indicate, at least so far as *numbers* are concerned, that perfect competition exists in the industry. Yet, if each firm was the sole supplier in a three-county area and transportation beyond that area was impossible or difficult, each firm would have something close to a monopoly. Because the concentration ratio is calculated on a national basis, it would not reflect this monopoly situation.

However, a high concentration ratio does not necessarily denote imperfect competition. Imports from abroad (of great importance in the case of motor vehicles) may substantially alter the picture. Thus, the four largest firms may account for 100 percent of domestic shipments, yet they may supply only 1 percent of the total sold, if imports are of overwhelming importance. Other perfect substitutes may also be available in large quantities domestically (such as recycled aluminum).

Finally, the meaning of the industry classification must be carefully assessed. "Calculating/accounting machines" (see Table 13.1), for instance, is a broad category. Although the four largest firms supply 73 percent of shipments, we might want to know what these shipments are. It may turn out that each of these firms supplies 100 percent of *particular* machines that have no good substitutes; then the ratio understates what it is supposed to test. Vice versa, "cereal breakfast foods" may be too narrow a category. There are undoubtedly excellent breakfast food substitutes. Even though four companies make 90 percent of shipments, their market power may be much less than the concentration ratio seems to indicate.

## Major Sectors of the U.S. Economy

Industrial organization economists can also tell us much about the U.S. economy as a whole. Consider a recent study by William G. Shepherd that is summarized in Table 13.2, "Trends of Competition in the U.S. Economy, 1939–1980." The first column of numbers in section (A) shows the amounts of 1978 national income that were attributable to the various sectors of the U.S. economy. The sectors are listed in the order in which they appear in government publications. (There are 89 standard industrial classification or SIC categories; agriculture, forestry, and fisheries take categories 0–9; services take categories 70–89.) The numbers in that first column imply that agriculture, forestry, and fishing produced a mere 3.6 percent of national income; mining (including coal, crude oil, metal, natural gas, and nonmetallic minerals) produced another 1.6 percent. Some 5.8 percent of the national income came from construction, but a hefty 30.4 percent from manufacturing activity (involving everything from aircraft engines, breakfast foods, cars, and cement to gasoline, heavy machinery, steel, and soap). Transportation (by air, pipeline, rail, road, and water) and public utilities (electricity, gas, and sanitation services) accounted for 10.7 percent of the total; wholesale and retail trade for another 17.3 percent. Some 13.9 percent of national income, finally, originated in finance, insurance, and real estate, and the remaining 16.7 percent in the service sector (covering anything from auto repair, barbering, domestic service, and entertainment to hotels and restaurants, legal services, and medical care). Table 13.2 tells us more than that.

Using detailed data, Shepherd was also able to classify various economic activities in accordance with the degree of competition prevailing in the relevant markets. He used four categories: An activity was classified as *pure monopoly* when the producer's market share was at or near 100 percent, entry into the market was effectively blocked, and control over price was exercised by the producer. An activity was classified as involving a *dominant firm* when one producer had a market

**Table 13.2** Trends of Competition in the U.S. Economy, 1939–80

| A. Sectors of the Economy | National Income in Each Sector, 1978* | The Share of Each Sector That Was Effectively Competitve | | |
|---|---|---|---|---|
| | | 1939 | 1958 | 1980* |
| | ($ billion) | (%) | (%) | (%) |
| Agriculture, forestry, and fisheries | 54.7 | 91.6 | 85.0 | 86.4 |
| Mining | 24.5 | 87.1 | 92.2 | 95.8 |
| Construction | 87.6 | 27.9 | 55.9 | 80.2 |
| Manufacturing | 459.5 | 51.5 | 55.9 | 69.0 |
| Transportation and public utilities | 162.3 | 8.7 | 26.1 | 39.1 |
| Wholesale and retail trade | 261.8 | 57.8 | 60.5 | 93.4 |
| Finance, insurance, and real estate | 210.7 | 61.5 | 63.8 | 94.1 |
| Services | 245.3 | 53.9 | 54.3 | 77.9 |
| **Totals** | **1,512.4** | **52.4** | **56.4** | **76.7** |

| B. Competition Categories | | The Share of Each Category in National Income | | |
|---|---|---|---|---|
| | | 1939 | 1958 | 1980 |
| | ($ billion) | (%) | (%) | (%) |
| 1. Pure monopoly | 38.2 | 6.2 | 3.1 | 2.5 |
| 2. Dominant firm | 42.2 | 5.0 | 5.0 | 2.8 |
| 3. Tight oligopoly | 272.1 | 36.4 | 35.6 | 18.0 |
| 4. Others: effectively competitive | 1,157.9 | 52.4 | 56.3 | 76.7 |
| **Total** | **1,512.4** | **100.0** | **100.0** | **100.0** |

*1980 figures reflect competitive conditions as of 1980. The industry weights are based on 1978 data for national income, the latest year available.

*Source:* William G. Shepherd, ''Causes of Increased Competition in the U.S. Economy, 1939–1980.'' *The Review of Economics and Statistics,* November 1982, pp. 613–26.

share of between 50 and over 90 percent and had control over price and high profits, and when entry barriers were high. An activity was characterized as *tight oligopoly* when the four-firm concentration ratio exceeded 60 percent, there were medium to high entry barriers, and rigid (cooperatively set) prices existed. Government-regulated firms were included in this category as well, as were firms, such as milk producers, that were actively colluding with the help of government. The remaining economic activities (loosely oligopolistic, monopolistically competitive, and perfectly competitive) were classified as *effectively competitive.* All these had in common a four-firm concentration ratio below 40 percent, low entry barriers and unstable market shares, little collusion, flexible prices, and low profits.

Having made this classification (for the years 1939, 1958, and 1980), Shepherd reached two major conclusions: Roughly three quarters of the U.S. economy in

1980 was effectively competitive (see the last column of section [B]). There has been a major advance in competitiveness since 1958 (see row 4, section [B]). Shepherd attributed this development to vigorous antitrust action, increased import competition, and recent efforts at deregulation.

## The Role of Government

As the earlier section on exclusive franchises and government-sponsored cartels have indicated, government in the United States hardly conforms to the role envisioned for it by the sponsors of the model economy discussed in the previous chapter. Indeed, we might ask: Does government ever counteract the numerous private attempts at creating monopoly? To some extent, it does. Such is the purpose of antitrust laws, of government regulation of natural monopolies, of policies to promote free international trade (which would expose national monopolies to foreign competition). And such is the purpose of "right-to-work" laws (which outlaw the closed and union shops), of antidiscrimination laws, and of affirmative action plans. Frequently, however, such government activities have not been as vigorous as advocates of the model capitalist market economy would hope. Antitrust laws, for instance, have often been badly enforced, the regulation of business to promote competition has often turned into protection of business from competition, and free trade policies have often been counteracted by "escape clauses" and "peril points" set by protectionist interests. Indeed, governmental policies to assure all resource owners of an equal opportunity to use their resources as they like often pale in significance when compared with governmental policies, noted earlier in this chapter, that are designed to aid would-be monopolists.

It is interesting to speculate on why government helps selected people gain extra income by giving them power over prices. Why doesn't it insist, as in last chapter's model world, that people gain income only through productive contributions? Perhaps the answer goes like this.

We are all apt to think of government as the impartial servant of the public good. We like to see government as the instrumentality by which the nation achieves *the national interest*—meaning, perhaps, an overall reduction in the realm of scarcity. But, in fact, the nation does not talk to government officials; individuals do. Within the nation, there are many individuals whose interests conflict with those of other individuals. For each of these individuals, income can be gained more easily by taking it away from other people—given the overall degree of scarcity prevailing—than by making genuine contributions toward reducing the realm of scarcity by working harder, saving more, or making cost-reducing innovations. Is it surprising that some of these individuals want the government to intercede for their *special interest* (which is to gain power to raise the prices of whatever they sell in order to raise their income in the easiest way)? To the extent that government responds to such requests, it does not govern in the national interest; it promotes a coalition of special interests. Sellers use many devices to get government to promote their special interest in above-equilibrium minimum prices, reduced supply, or increased demand for whatever they have to sell.

## The "Capture" of Legislators

Sellers can induce legislators at all levels of government to rig markets directly— or to set up appropriate agencies to do the rigging—by channeling a number of rewards to them. Perhaps the most important reward is campaign contributions.

All legislators must be elected. Those with the "proper" attitude—toward minimum prices (for airplane trips, electricity, insurance, labor, liquor, milk, taxi rides, telephone service, or wheat), toward supply-restricting laws (ranging widely from those concerning cartels, copyrights, exclusive franchising, and immigration to others on import and marketing quotas, mergers, patents, professional licensing, tariffs, and union affairs), and toward demand-raising laws (awarding government contracts or subsidies for anything from peanuts to railroads to the unemployed)— can be rewarded by the beneficiaries of this "proper" attitude. Early rewards come in the form of votes and in the form of funds to finance expensive radio and TV campaigns designed to gather other people's votes. (A federal campaign cost a minimum of $100,000 in the 1980s.) During the early 1970s, for example, major corporations as well as other organizations—ranging from dairy farmers, dentists, and doctors to seafarers, teachers, and truckers—spent more than $100 million on federal election campaigns alone. Following rather aggressive solicitation of funds by top officials in the Nixon administration, many corporations made illegal contributions. Among those who eventually admitted to such contributions publicly were American Airlines, Ashland Oil, Braniff Airlines, Goodyear Tire and Rubber, Gulf Oil, Minnesota Mining and Manufacturing (3M), and Phillips Petroleum.

Once elected, these officials are, of course, expected to show proper gratitude toward their benefactors. They are expected to vote in the "right" way and to lend a ready and sympathetic ear to professional lobbyists who will point out the "national interest" in all types of legislation under consideration, which is really the special interest of those who lobby and whose income position is being advanced by the legislation. Meanwhile, the voices of those whose income position is being eroded by the very same legislation go unheard. The interests of the organized special pleaders are visible and concentrated: Their gain may be $100 million worth of extra revenues that would come to a single firm, or a small group of them, as a result of higher legal prices, a subsidy, or a government contract. On the contrary, the interest of their unorganized victims is invisible and diffuse; their loss may be 50 cents from each of 200 million consumers or taxpayers. The special interest groups can afford to hire full-time professional lobbyists (together with large staffs of lawyers, public relations people, and so on). They can easily inundate the overworked staffs of every single legislator with good advice on the meaning of "sound public policy." They can orchestrate, if necessary, a letter campaign by thousands who have a lot to gain. The millions who lose are silent. Thus, legislators get a nicely biased view of things. By following the "national interest" as represented by special interest groups, the compliant legislators can gather further rewards: more campaign funds in the future, more votes from those with new jobs in new plants built in their home districts by beneficiaries grateful for their help, job offers in case of a lost election, all-expenses-paid vacations, and, perhaps, even gifts of fur coats. Much of this, incidentally, is perfectly legal if financed from people's personal incomes (as in the case of a gift from a high-salaried corporate officer); it is quite illegal if it is financed by corporate funds. Analytical Example 13.1, "The Political Economy of Milk and Housing," provides an interesting case in point.

## The "Capture" of Regulators

Now consider the regulatory bodies set up by the legislative branch of government. Their officials, too, are systematically influenced by those they are supposed to "regulate." They, too, receive rewards for being compliant when approached by the special interests.

Many regulators have strong bonds with the regulated. For example, it is not at all unusual to put doctors on a professional licensing board for practitioners of medicine, to put airline industry officials on the CAB, to place electric power company executives on the FPC. Even when such choices are not dictated by the need for expert knowledge, lobbyists will see to it that this is exactly what happens. (No wonder that regulators are frequently found to own securities and, thus, have a personal financial interest in companies they regulate. In 1974, for example, 19 officials of the FPC, which had raised natural gas prices, held natural gas company stock.)

Even when members of a regulated industry are not the regulators, chummy relations quickly develop. Regulators necessarily have frequent contact with the regulated at formal public hearings before the various commissions involved or at the more than 100,000 nonpublic meetings a year in which specific issues are "informally adjudicated."

The federal alphabet agencies, for instance, employ administrative law judges. They gather evidence, conduct hearings, and make decisions on the government-sponsored cartels about rates charged, the number of firms allowed, and so on. This procedure is typically lengthy and even then any decision can be appealed to the full regulatory commission or challenged in court or both. A recent railroad merger case took 3 years and 275 days of hearings to decide. It produced a veritable paper nightmare of 50,000 pages of transcripts and 100,000 pages of exhibits. There is plenty of occasion for regulators and the regulated to get to know each other not just during hearings, but also during informal contacts over lunch, at business conventions, and at social gatherings. Naturally, the CAB members (who awarded the new route bringing in $100 million in annual revenues) will be invited to the airline's inaugural flight. Naturally, the ICC members (who approved that railroad merger cutting costs by $100 million a year) will go on the inaugural ride, complete with fancy food, liquor, and entertainment. Before long, government officials and industry executives are personal friends. In 1974, the chairman of the CAB was taken on an all-expenses-paid golfing trip to Bermuda by Boeing and United Aircraft

Company officials and journeyed through Europe with a TWA vice-president—all while issues vital to these firms were being decided by the CAB.

Sooner or later, it becomes obvious that friendly regulators (like friendly legislators whose reelection bids fail) can expect future jobs from those they now regulate. In 1971, for example, 12 of 24 former CAB members were employed by the firms they used to regulate. Could it be any clearer why government underwrites the monopoly game?

## An Assessment

To assess the performance of the American economy, we once again employ the criteria of chapters 2 through 4.

### Full Employment

As in last chapter's model, the definition of full employment in the United States is left to each private resource owner. Unlike in the model, however, resource prices are not always free to adjust, or to adjust quickly enough, to their equilibrium levels. When labor unions insist on, or governments prescribe, minimum wages above equilibrium, for example, a surplus of labor develops. As a result, all kinds of people who would like to work at the going wage (of, say, $7 per hour) find themselves involuntarily unemployed (as those represented by distance *ab* in Figure 12.2, "A Typical Market," on page 339). Since a decline in the wage is impossible, their unemployment persists. Scarcity is greater than it has to be.

This situation can be overcome, however, even if downward wage flexibility cannot be restored, by an increase in the demand for labor (which, in Figure 12.2, might shift the demand line to the right until it passed through point *b*). Recognition of this fact lies at the heart of the Keynesian theory—born in the Great Depression of the 1930s. Keynes noted that an increase in overall spending on newly produced goods in an economy would increase the demand for labor and, thus, reduce involuntary unemployment. This basic insight has since been incorporated into the official policies of the U.S. government. When involuntary unemployment appears, the federal government attempts to stimulate overall spending through the cutting of household and business taxes, the raising of governmental spending, or the lowering of interest rates to encourage borrowing (and spending) by households, businesses, and other levels of government. These policies have helped prevent any recurrence of the Great Depression, but they have worked far from perfectly. True enough, the labor unemployment rate has on average been substantially below the experience of the Great Depression (25 percent of the civilian labor force was involuntarily unemployed in 1933, and the rate never went below 14 percent until 1940). Since that time, the unemployment rate has fluctuated between 1 percent (1944) and 10 percent (1982), equaling about 7 percent in the late 1980s. As a result of involuntary unemployment of their resources, Americans have lost (at 1958 prices) an annual average of over $25 billion of goods since the turn of this century.

The degree of success in fighting involuntary unemployment depends on a variety of factors. Among these are the nature of the policy-making mechanism, which determines the speed and accuracy with which demand-raising policies can be pursued. If it takes a year to debate a tax cut in the U.S. Congress and then the cut ends up being too small or too large, one should not be surprised about a less-than-perfect result. Or if government raises its spending on new goods, but these goods are produced in one region while all the unemployment is concentrated in another one, one should not wonder why the unemployment persists (unless people are also given relocation assistance). And if spending is raised on new goods produced with one set of skills, while all the unemployed possess a different set of skills, one should not wonder why the unemployment persists (unless people are also given opportunities to retrain).

## Technical Efficiency

Estimates of technical inefficiency in the U.S. economy are highly controversial. As is noted in the "Selected Readings" at the end of this chapter, there are some economists who have come to view technical inefficiency as all pervasive and as much more significant in scope than economic inefficiency, but others disagree.

The former group believes that firms with **monopoly power,** the power to raise the selling price above the perfectly competitive level, not only incur considerable expenses in obtaining, strengthening, and defending that power (as discussed in an earlier section), but they are generally lax on cost control because they do not face intense competitive pressure. Before long, such extravagances as lavish offices, high entertainment budgets, and long coffee breaks push costs to unnecessary levels.

This type of conclusion has been confirmed by a number of investigations. One recent study investigated electric power producers.[1] In 49 U.S. cities that had two or more competing companies, average total cost was 11 percent lower, all else being equal, than in cities without such competition. Another study focused on banks.[2] In 34 U.S. metropolitan areas, banks with little competition had larger staffs and higher labor costs, all else being equal, than banks located in places with competition. Indeed, business newspapers, magazines, and trade journals—from the *Wall Street Journal, Barron's, Business Week, Forbes,* and *Fortune* to *Computerworld* and *Iron Age*—fill their pages with sad stories of sleeping giants stuck in old modes of operation, lacking new ideas, lethargic, and inbred. Yet, it is difficult to interpret such anecdotal evidence and even more difficult to confirm the claim of some that technical inefficiency may cost the U.S. as much as 12 percent of national product annually.[3]

---

[1]Walter J. Primeaux, "An Assessment of X-Efficiency Gained Through Competition," *Review of Economics and Statistics,* February 1977, pp. 105–08.

[2]Franklin R. Edwards, "Managerial Objectives in Regulated Industries: Expense-Preference Behavior in Banking," *Journal of Political Economy,* February 1977, pp. 147–62.

[3]William S. Comanor and Harvey Leibenstein, "Allocative Efficiency, X-Efficiency, and the Measurement of Welfare Losses," *Economica,* August 1969, pp. 304–09.

## Economic Efficiency

In light of Pareto's guidelines, it is unlikely that the U.S. economy produces economic efficiency, but the extent of the resultant welfare loss is difficult to estimate.

**The First Pareto Condition.**   Consider again the first Pareto condition illustrated in Table 2.1, "The Optimum Allocation of a Resource among Producers of the Same Good" (p. 16). When the prices of all goods and resources are not given to individual buyers and sellers (as a result of being determined by unrestricted competition among multitudes of buyers or sellers in every market), it is conceivable for producers $\alpha$ and $\beta$ to be quite content in the situation depicted in part (A) of that earlier table. Imagine that both firms $\alpha$ and $\beta$ faced a union-set wage of $500 per week of labor (with labor input being represented by symbol $x$ in the table). Imagine that $\alpha$ was producing 50 electric motors per week (represented by symbol $a$), and was selling them at $1,000 each. Firm $\alpha$ might, indeed, be able to release a unit of labor (and save itself $500), while producing 2 electric motors less than before. If it did, it might even be able to raise its product price to $1,030 per motor (if that cut quantity demanded down to the lower quantity now supplied). But why should $\alpha$ do such a thing? Its weekly revenue would go from 50 times $1,000, or $50,000, to 48 times $1,030, or $49,440, a reduction of $560. Having reduced its cost by only $500 a week, this would *reduce* its profit by $60 a week! Nor might $\alpha$ have any reason to use *more* labor: An additional unit would cost an extra $500 a week, but the additional 2 motors produced might be salable only if product price was cut to $970 each (and customers were lured away from $\beta$). Hence, weekly revenue would go from 50 times $1,000, or $50,000, to 52 times $970, or $50,440. Having raised its cost by $500 a week, this would also reduce profit by $60 a week.

Firm $\beta$ might, similarly, have no incentive to change its behavior. Its weekly output of 80 electric motors might be selling at $980 each. (Yet, $\alpha$'s 50 customers may be convinced that the objectively identical product of $\alpha$ was worth the slightly higher price. This might be an illusion; or there might be good reasons: an outlet closer by; free, convenient parking; friendlier clerks; easier credit terms; prompter delivery; better warranty; faster repair and maintenance.) Firm $\beta$ might, indeed, be able to hire another unit of labor (for another $500), while producing 5 electric motors more than before. If it did, it might have to lower its price to $927 each (to lure some customers away from $\alpha$). Hence, weekly revenue would go from 80 times $980, or $78,400, to 85 times $927, or $78,795. Having raised its cost by $500 a week, this would reduce its profit by $105 a week. Nor might $\beta$ have any reason to use *less* labor: Using a unit less per week would save cost of $500, but 5 fewer motors would be produced. This might enable $\beta$ to raise product price to $1,035 each (if that just cut quantity demanded to the lower quantity supplied). But note: $\beta$'s weekly revenue would then go from 80 times $980, or $78,400, to 75 times $1,035, or $77,625. Having cut its cost by $500 a week, this would also reduce its profit, by $275 a week.

Under the circumstances, both α and β might be perfectly content with their situation, and the inefficiency depicted in part (A) of Table 2.1 would continue unabated.

**The Second Pareto Condition.***   A similar result might occur with respect to the case illustrated in Table 2.2, "The Optimum Specialization of Production among Producers of the Same Goods," on page 20. All we have to imagine is the not infrequent case of two producers who are the sole producers in their industry. Suppose α and β produced refrigerators (good *a*) and washing machines (good *b*), but different advertising campaigns had convinced some customers that α's products were inferior (contrary to objective facts). Under the circumstances, α might be able to sell its products only at $180 and $90, respectively, while β might be able to sell its units at $500 and $100, respectively. Given the *MRT*s shown in part (A), it is easy to see why neither α nor β would have any reason whatsoever to reallocate their resources. So inefficiency would persist.  ▬▬

**The Third Pareto Condition.***   Now consider Table 2.3, "The Optimum Composition of Production and Consumption," on page 22. A position of inefficiency, as that illustrated in part (A), might be perpetuated to the extent that producers and consumers faced different prices. All we have to do is imagine the not infrequent case of government levying differential taxes on the sales prices of particular products. Then firm α might receive $20 per unit of good *a,* but consumer *X* pay $50 for it (with the government collecting a $30 tax). And α might receive, and *X* pay, $10 per unit of good *b*. As a result, neither party would have the slightest incentive to change its behavior. Inefficiency would persist.  ▬▬

**The Fourth Pareto Condition***   Except in special circumstances (such as wartime rationing or price discrimination), the U.S. economy is likely to allocate goods efficiently among consumers. The reasons correspond to those spelled out in the corresponding section in the previous chapter: People are generally free to spend their money incomes as they like, and different consumers typically face identical prices.  ▬▬

**All Pareto Conditions.**   One can easily imagine circumstances under which all the Pareto conditions might be violated in the U.S. economy. However, the preceding discussion has deliberately focused on the negative. It is also likely for these conditions to be fulfilled wherever the existing circumstances correspond to those imagined in the Chapter 12 discussion of economic efficiency. Obviously, the real world is somewhat of a mixture—providing efficiency here, violating it there. Most

---

*Optional Section. The possible failure to achieve economic efficiency is depicted in an alternative way.

observers believe, however, that any losses in welfare as a result of economic inefficiency are likely to be slight (and smaller by far than the losses associated with the less-than-full utilization of resources).

## Economic Growth

In the view of most observers, the U.S. economy has exhibited a remarkable rate of economic growth in the long run. Measured in 1982 prices, real output has grown at an average annual rate of 3.2 percent since the turn of this century, raising total real output 16-fold, and per capita real output 5-fold, in a mere 88 years. Just compare the typical American's life today with that of your ancestors not too long ago. Note how the masses today enjoy good and varied food, clothing, housing, and education; how appliances and tools make life easy for them at home and on the job; how they enjoy long lives and generally healthy ones; how they have much leisure filled with many forms of recreation. And then picture the days, not so long ago, when life was "nasty, brutish, and short": Most people had insufficient and monotonous diets and no fancy clothing, they lived in drafty, crowded houses (with cold privies out back and muddy streets in front), had little education, were tied to backbreaking work in those "satanic mills" or spent the day scrubbing laundry and stoking the cookstove, all the while being sick, isolated from the world, and dying young! What has brought on this dramatic change in the living standard of large numbers of people?

**Extensive Growth.**    Karl Marx, capitalism's most ardent critic, had this to say on the subject: "The bourgeoisie . . . has been the first to show what man's activity can bring about. It has accomplished wonders far surpassing Egyptian pyramids, Roman aqueducts, and Gothic cathedrals. . . . The bourgeoisie, during its rule of scarce one hundred years, has created more massive and more colossal productive forces than have all preceding generations together."[4] Indeed, voluntary private saving and investing (by individuals and corporations) have been a major source of this economic growth. All along, such private efforts have been reinforced by governmental ones (ranging from easy monetary policies to the granting of tax credits to direct public investment). In the United States, the capital stock (private and public) has increased more than sixfold since the turn of this century. As a result, studies by Edward F. Denison show this: From 1909 to 1929, some 26 percent of the observed rate of growth of real U.S. output can be attributed to the growth of capital (and another 39 percent to more labor hours performed by a larger population); from 1929 to 1969, the respective figures were 15 and 27 percent.[5] What explains the remaining 35 and 58 percent, respectively, of economic growth?

---

[4]Karl Marx and Friedrich Engels, *Manifesto of the Communist Party,* in David McLellan, ed., *Karl Marx: Selected Writings* (Oxford: Oxford University Press, 1977), pp. 224–25.

[5]Edward F. Denison, *The Sources of Economic Growth in the United States and the Alternatives Before Us* (New York: Committee for Economic Development, 1962) and *idem, Accounting for United States Economic Growth 1929–1969* (Washington, D.C.: Brookings Institution, 1974).

**Intensive Growth.**  A significant part of real economic growth has resulted from improvements in the general levels of health, education, and training, as well as from a rapid pace of technical advance. The latter has become increasingly important over time.

In the past, great inventions and innovations were the result of hard work by gifted individuals, by a few dreamers and tinkerers, who, driven by curiosity, worked with little assistance and few resources. Think of the invention of the incandescent light bulb, the reaper, the telegraph. But by now technological advance is a major societywide effort, supported by fantastically expensive facilities set up by government and large corporations. The first industrial research laboratory in the United States, for example, was set up by Thomas Edison, as late as 1876. By now, there are hundreds of them, spurred on by favorable tax treatments and relentless competition among the corporate giants.

It is interesting to speculate about the relationship between market structure and the extent of intensive growth. Economists have been of two minds. The late Joseph Schumpeter, for example, claimed that firms that are large and hold monopoly power are likely to have a larger cash flow and more borrowing ability than smaller and competitive firms. Because the large firms with monopoly power would be able to count on a broader and more durable market, they would engage in more research and product development (R&D). They would innovate more, introducing the assembly line today and computers and robots to run it tomorrow; giving consumers ballpoint pens or instant photos today and space settlements or doubled lifetimes tomorrow. Competitive firms, on the other hand, even if they could find the funds, would shy away from R&D and entrepreneurial innovation. If their R&D were a technical failure (and much money sunk into research and experimenting did not yield that more productive type of apple tree, let us say), the investors alone would have to bear all the cost. If it were a technical success (and a phenomenally more productive apple tree were bred), the investors would have to share the gain with the world at large: Production costs would be reduced and some profit would be made—*in the short run* (as illustrated in Figure 12.D on page 527). But before long, new firms would enter the field imitating the new; they would help raise industry supply greatly and would reduce the product's equilibrium price—eliminating profit. Thus, any long-range, high-cost investment in research and innovation on the part of such firms would be discouraged.

Schumpeter's argument, however, can also be reversed. Might monopolistic giants not be lethargic? Might they not be run by "abominable no-men" who veto every innovative move because there are no competitors who pose a threat? Might not a multitude of important innovations occur precisely under perfect competition, as the result of random tinkering by a multitude of individuals engaged in the productive process? With very little monetary investment, such people might raise the yield of apple trees today by applying fertilizer to their roots (rather than spreading it on the ground). They might raise it tomorrow by sprinkling water on apple blossoms when the spring frost is about to kill the year's crop in its infancy. And when other firms imitated their methods and competed away the profit associated with their temporary head start, they might find another way yet to get more apples still from the same resources! Thus, they might once more lower their cost and recreate their profit. By always being a step ahead of everyone else, such successful innovators could enjoy a permanent profit even when free entry into their field was guaranteed to all. Such innovators would just have to come up with *repeated* innovations to accomplish the feat, but that very necessity would produce a better performance on the intensive-growth front than imperfect competition ever could. Who is right? Is imperfect or perfect competition more conducive to economic growth?

Economists have amassed a great deal of empirical evidence, which does not clearly corroborate either of the two hypotheses just discussed. Data show that the major force promoting research and development and subsequent innovation is not to be found in the absolute size of firms nor in the degree of firm concentration in their industry. The R&D expenditures of U.S. firms, for instance, when measured per dollar of sales, rise up to a point with the size of firms, then level off, and even decline. The output resulting from R&D, as measured by inventions, is clearly not concentrated in the hands of giant firms, nor in those operating in highly concentrated industries. The majority of inventions are, in fact, made by individuals and small firms. Innovations, in turn, are often made by small and competitive firms (but then frequently imitated by larger ones). The secret seems to be this: Intensive growth is advanced by the existence of moderately high barriers to entry into an industry. Where the entry of new firms is very easy, fear of rapid imitation seems to discourage significant R&D and innovation, regardless of the prevailing size or number of firms. Where entry is next to impossible, the lack of any competitive threat seems to dull the incentive of existing firms to push technical advance. Yet, where entry barriers are moderate (which is typical of many sectors of the U.S. economy), strong R&D and innovative activity is observed—carried out either by newcomers or by existing firms wishing to keep out newcomers. Thus, a blend of small and large firms (which are neither perfect competitors nor monopolies) seems most conducive to technical progress.

## Economic Equity

Before we can assess its fairness, we must study the objective facts about the U.S. distribution of income. Table 13.3, "The Distribution of Money Income Before Taxes among U.S. Families in 1985," contains typical data on the subject. The table shows a highly unequal distribution of income. Note how the poorest 20 percent of all families (with 1985 incomes under $13,193) received only 4.6 percent of that year's aggregate family income, while the richest 5 percent of families (with incomes above $77,707) received 16.7 percent of the total. Quite often, the extent of this income inequality is also pictured graphically.

**A Graphic Exposition.**    The **Lorenz curve** is a favored graphical device that shows the way in which income is apportioned among the members of any group and highlights the extent of equality or inequality among them. Figure 13.4, "The Lorenz Curve," shows how to graph the data in Table 13.3 by drawing a square

**Table 13.3**    The Distribution of Money Income Before Taxes among U.S. Families in 1985*

| Income Class (1) | Percent of Families in Class (2) | Percent of Total Income Received by Families in Class (3) | Percent of Families in Class or Lower Ones (4) | Percent of Total Income Received by Families in Class or Lower Ones (5) |
|---|---|---|---|---|
| Under $13,193 | 20 | 4.6 | 20 | 4.6 |
| $13,193–$22,725 | 20 | 10.9 | 40 | 15.5 |
| $22,726–$33,040 | 20 | 16.9 | 60 | 32.4 |
| $33,041–$48,000 | 20 | 24.2 | 80 | 56.6 |
| $48,001–$77,706 | 15 | 26.7 | 95 | 83.3 |
| $77,707 and over | 5 | 16.7 | 100 | 100.0 |

*In 1985, some 2,093.9 billion of aggregate family income was distributed in the highly uneven fashion shown here among 64 million U.S. families (An additional 486.1 billion of income went to some 31 million individuals not living in families.)

*Source:* U.S. Bureau of the Census, *Current Population Reports,* Series P-60, No. 156, "Money Income of Households, Families, and Persons in the United States, 1985" (Washington, D.C.: U.S. Government Printing Office, 1987), pp. 4, 37, and 38.

measuring percentage of total money income received on the vertical axis and the percentage of families on the horizontal axis. Families are arranged from left to right from the one with the lowest to the one with the highest income.

The straight line that has been drawn from the bottom left corner at 0 to the top right corner at *e* is the **line of perfect equality,** because it represents the hypothetical position of the Lorenz curve if the same amount of money income went to each family. If all families in the country shared total income equally, 20 percent of the families would share 20 percent of total income (at *a*), 40 percent of all families would share 40 percent of total income (at *b*), and so on, until 100 percent of all families shared 100 percent of total income (at *e*).

Note: This line of perfect equality should not be called one of perfect *equity,* or *justice,* for there is no objective way of defining what apportionment of income is perfectly just. One can, however, determine objectively whether income is apportioned perfectly equally, be that considered just or not.

At the other extreme, if one family received all the money income while all the others received none of it, what would the Lorenz curve look like? If we arranged the families on the horizontal axis as before on the basis of income, we would find that the poorest 20 percent of all families received 0 percent of total income (at *g* rather than at *a*), that the poorest 40 percent of all families similarly shared 0 percent of total income (at *h* rather than *b*), and so on. Even 99 percent of all families would still share 0 percent of total income ( just a little bit to the left of *f* rather than to the left and below *e*). Yet, when we considered all families, including the

**Figure 13.4**  The Lorenz Curve

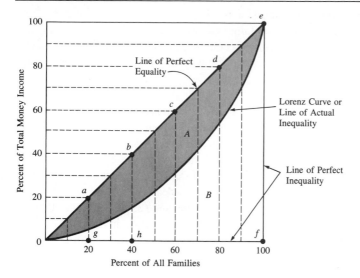

This Lorenz curve is a representation of the way in which money income was apportioned among U.S. families in 1985. The ratio of area *A* to *A* + *B* is the *Gini coefficent*. (The data used to plot this graph were taken from the fourth and fifth columns of Table 13.3.)

one having all the income, we would find that 100 percent of families had 100 percent of income (at *e*). Thus, we could call the line 0*fe* a **line of perfect inequality,** because it represents the hypothetical position of the Lorenz curve if all the income went to one family and none of it to all the others.

In reality, 1985 money income in the United States was distributed neither perfectly equally (as would be shown by the line of perfect equality) nor perfectly unequally (as shown by the line of perfect inequality). Plotting the data of columns (4) and (5) of Table 13.3 reveals the actual Lorenz curve or the **line of actual inequality.** Like a loose string fastened to points 0 and *e*, this line hanging below the line of perfect equality (0*e*), and above that of perfect inequality (0*fe*), provides a visual representation of actual income inequality in the United States. Any increase in equality would shift it toward 0*e*, any decrease toward 0*fe*. In fact, the extent of income inequality has been unchanged for many decades, if one looks at the data at given points in time. (But consider Analytical Example 13.2, "Income Dynamics," for another perspective.)

**A Numerical Summary.**  Economists often summarize the extent of personal income inequality with the help of the **Gini coefficient,** the ratio of shaded area *A* (between the lines of perfect equality and actual inequality) to areas *A* + *B* (between the lines of perfect equality and perfect inequality). The Gini coefficient can hypothetically range from 0 (perfect equality) to 1 (perfect inequality), but in the

United States it typically lies in the .35 to .45 range. Whether one considers such a distribution fair or not depends entirely on which criterion of equity one wishes to embrace. (Recall the relevant discussion in Chapter 3.) Advocates of the absolute-equality type of distributive justice certainly cannot find comfort in these statistics. Whether the proponents of other forms of economic justice are able to do so cannot be answered until we take a closer look at the way in which the observed income inequality is being generated.

**The Causes of Income Inequality.**    Except for any possible redistribution of income through government, households in the U.S. economy receive money income in return for supplying to the process of production the services of human, natural, and capital resources that they own. Thus, the money income earned by any one household (and the share of output it can claim) depends on three things: (1) on the (size and quality of the) stocks of resources owned, (2) on the rate at which these stocks are placed in the process of production, and (3) on the prices that are established in the resource markets for the use of the resources involved. Thus, the principle of income distribution that the U.S. market economy follows is: *"From each according to his or her ability and willingness to contribute resources to the process of production, to each according to the market's objective evaluation of the output produced by these resources."*

**The Ability to Contribute.**    Differences clearly exist with respect to the ability of different households to contribute resources to the process of production. Households own vastly different quantities and qualities of human, natural, and capital resources—and not only because different households contain different numbers of people. As a result of differences in biological inheritance and differential rates of resource acquisition after birth (due, in turn, to differences in effort or luck), people come to own different stocks of human capital and of physical capital and natural resources as well. Those advocates of commutative justice who would endow people with as nearly equal stocks of resources as possible will find little to cheer about here.

The U.S. government certainly has failed to disperse the private ownership of resources as widely and as equally as is called for by the model discussed in the previous chapter. Although inheritance laws impose estate taxes on natural and capital resources at the time of death of their owners, these taxes are far from confiscatory. More often than not, they can also be escaped, or their impact can be softened, by a variety of legal means, such as the establishment of personal trusts or the making of gifts during one's lifetime. Governmental policies aimed at placing natural and capital resources into the hands of those holding few of them, such as the minority capitalism program, have had minimal impact. As a result, the private ownership of natural and capital resources tends to be highly concentrated in the hands of a few. At the end of 1962, for example, the most unfortunate quarter of all U.S. households held wealth (including, but not confined to natural and capital resources) of less than $1,000 each, while the most fortunate 17 percent of households held wealth of over $25,000 each. While the former group held 0.5 percent of total wealth, the latter one owned 74 percent of it.[6]

The advocates of commutative justice will find government action more to their liking in the area of human resources, however. Considerable governmental efforts clearly exist to make general education, vocational training, and health care widely available. Consider the availability of free elementary and high school education for all. Consider the subsidization of selected individuals to enable them to acquire college or vocational training, food, or medical care. True enough, publicly provided services are not always of the same quality for all recipients, and higher-income households can provide their offspring with additional privately provided education, training, and health care, but the current trend is clearly one of making the ownership of human resources more widely and more equally available than ever before.

**The Willingness to Contribute.**    There is a second reason why household money incomes differ. Households often exhibit differential willingness to contribute resource services to the process of production. Not only do some household members stay out of the labor force entirely, but even those who do work do so for varying numbers of hours per year, simply because they differ from other people when it comes to choosing between leisure and the goods its sacrifice can bring. Similar differences in voluntary choice occur with respect to nonhuman resources. The advocates of cummutative justice would find nothing to worry about here.

**Rates of Pay.**    A third reason for income differences is that households receive differential rates of pay for the resource services they do offer, and this is true both in perfectly and imperfectly competitive markets.

*Perfectly competitive markets.*    Consider the sale of labor services for wages. In the short run, certainly, wage differentials can exist even under perfect competition. Market demand and market supply for janitors and truck drivers, for example, might just happen to intersect at different wage levels, as in panels (a) and (b) of Figure 13.5, "Wage Differentials." Yet, if people were alike and jobs were alike, the free mobility found in perfectly competitive markets would eliminate such differentials eventually. Janitors would leave their occupations; supply, S, in panel (a) of our graph would shift to the left. Given demand, D, janitorial wages would rise. As ex-janitors turned into truck drivers, supply, S*, in panel (b) of our graph would shift to the right. Given demand, D*, truck driver wages would fall. These changes would continue until the wage differential had disappeared.

But people are not alike; nor are jobs. That is why wage differentials could persist even in a world of perfectly competitive labor markets.

*Differences in people.*    There exist certain biological differences among people. People differ in physical strength, in size, and in intelligence. Some have a

---

[6]Dorothy S. Projector and Gertrude S. Weiss, *Survey of Financial Characteristics of Consumers* (Washington, D.C.: Board of Governors of the Federal Reserve System, 1966).

**Figure 13.5** Wage Differentials

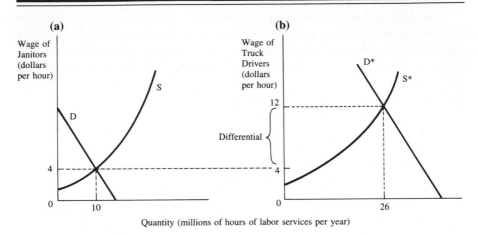

Quantity (millions of hours of labor services per year)

In perfectly competitive labor markets, the wage differential depicted here could not persist if all people and all jobs were alike. By the same token, biological differences in people and differences in the attractiveness of jobs can produce permanent wage differentials even when labor markets are perfectly competitive.

natural talent for athletics, music, or science; others are utterly inept in these fields. To the extent that these personal qualities cannot be acquired after birth, low-priced janitors cannot enter the occupations making use of these talents, and wage differentials can persist even in the long run.

*Differences in jobs.* While people can sell the services of their natural and capital resources without being present when they are used, a seller of labor power must personally accompany what is being sold. For this reason, nonmonetary aspects of jobs become a crucial consideration. Jobs differ in a million ways: Some have to be performed in harsh northern climates; others in the humid South. Some must be done in urban areas; others in the countryside. Some can be carried out in small firms; others only in giant ones. Some jobs have regular hours; others require overtime, work on weekends and holidays, or even at night. Some provide opportunities for advancement, responsibility, prestige, and power. Some are physically tiring, dirty, smelly, and noisy; others are boring, dull, and lonely. Some must be preceded by long periods of training and income foregone; others involve risks to health and life.

The list could be lengthened, but this much is clear: People have different preferences with respect to job characteristics. Some people like the northern climate; others hate it. Some love cities; others abhor them. Some seek out responsibility; others run from it. To the extent that monetary wage differentials only offset nonmonetary differences in the perceived attractiveness of jobs, differentials can persist. Such wage differentials are then called **equalizing wage**

**differentials** or **compensating wage differentials.** If all the janitors depicted in Figure 13.5 believed that they would rather lead a peaceful life than get paid $8 per hour more risking their lives on the highways, no shifts of supplies would occur in the two markets. Thus, people who are free to move among jobs may fail to do so in spite of permanent wage differentials. Such wage differentials may be seen to equalize nonmonetary aspects of jobs, and such differentials cause income differences for the same number of hours worked. Similar differential returns can arise when people exhibit different attitudes toward risk taking with their nonhuman resources. Consider how some people will operate in the stock market, gamble in casinos, speculate in futures markets, and undertake risky innovations, while others will not. Inevitably, differences in monetary returns will arise as a result. Consider, finally, how perfectly competitive markets are not always in equilibrium.

*Market disequilibrium.*   Multitudes of people who are engaged in similar activities jointly determine the values of the activities involved, and these values can change. Today, all the people demanding apples (or beef) and all the people supplying these goods may jointly determine that apples are worth $12 per bushel (and beef is worth $5 per pound). All the people demanding the services of apple pickers (or pastureland) and all the people supplying these resource services may jointly determine that such service is worth $4 per hour per apple picker (and $100 per year per acre of pastureland). Now consider how a sudden change in taste could raise the demand for apples and lower that for beef, how the wages of apple pickers and the rents of orchard land would suddenly rise (together with the price of apples), while the wages of butchers and the rents of pastures would plummet (together with the price of beef). Through no fault of their own, those contributing resources to the apple industry would suddenly find a pot of gold in their laps. Those contributing resources to the beef industry (and working just as hard as ever before) would suddenly find themselves being punished. This scenario illustrates the price system's way of encouraging people to reallocate resources: to make butchers become apple pickers, to make pastureland owners grow apple trees. Temporarily, though, their rates of return would surely differ. The advocates of commutative justice wouldn't mind. They would, however, object to differential rates of pay arising from the use of monopoly power.

*Imperfectly competitive markets.*   In the presence of imperfectly competitive markets, otherwise temporary differences in returns to resources can become permanent ones and can then contribute to permanent differences in income, which people cannot escape by appropriate resource reallocations. The market price of beef may turn out to be $10 per pound (instead of $5 per pound) if government helps beef producers form a cartel and helps defend the cartel against would-be intruders by restricting imports, along with new domestic production. The market price of butchers may turn out to be $20 per hour (instead of $4 per hour) if government helps these workers restrict their numbers (with the help of labor unions or "professional" licensing boards or immigration quotas) and, thus, prevents other workers who earn less from becoming butchers and thereby eliminating the artificial wage differentials.

Indeed, economists have in recent years spent much effort trying to determine how successful monopoly power has been in restricting resource mobility, in raising the prices of favored resources, and, thus, in redistributing income towards the holders of such power. Table 13.4 summarizes the results obtained by two researchers. As the table shows, monopoly power (as measured by concentration ratios and entry barriers) has indeed raised profit rates. Consider how, in the 1936–1940 study, high concentration always produced higher profit rates than moderate concentration, while higher entry barriers, given identical concentration ratios, did the same.[7]

***Conclusion.***    The observed inequality of income in the U.S. market economy is clearly not the result of any deliberate distribution according to need or hours worked, and it directly contradicts the ideal of absolute income equality. Thus, the advocates of all three types of distributive justice discussed in Chapter 3 also are bound to see economic injustice. However, one should also note that government in the United States has been increasingly involved in outright redistribution of income through taxes and subsidies. By the late 1980s, cash transfer payments by governments at all levels came to 8 percent of the gross national income. While the oldest of these programs of income redistribution toward the poor went back to the Revolutionary War, most of them were born since the 1930s: social security for the aged; aid to the blind, disabled or injured; aid to families with dependent children, to the unemployed, to the sick, and more. All these were enacted, however, in response to particular emergencies, without any master plan. Thus, they leave much to be desired in the eyes of those wishing to establish some type of distributive justice, who are looking forward to the time when a comprehensive program of income redistribution is enacted, such as the negative income tax scheme that would guarantee, perhaps, that no citizen will end up with income less than 80 percent or higher than 120 percent of the national average. And they are also looking forward to a time when government enforces national standards of behavior that put an end to the endless inflationary spiral that now expresses the struggle over

---

[7]Note that these results are controversial. Other economists have attributed the apparent correlation between profitability and monopoly power in Table 13.4 to a number of errors: the use of accounting instead of economic profit, the failure to account for absolute size of firms studied (large ones being more prevalent in concentrated industries and earning high profit for being technically more efficient), the subjective definitions of ''high'' and ''moderate'' concentration, the subjective classification of entry barriers, the use of too small a sample of industries, the use of time periods in which profits were abnormally high, and more. See, for instance, Yale Brozen, ''Bain's Concentration and Rates of Return Revisited,'' *Journal of Law and Economics,* October 1971, pp. 351–69; ''Concentration and Profits: Does Concentration Matter?'' *Antitrust Bulletin,* Summer 1974, pp. 381–99; and Harold Demsetz, ''Are Large Corporations Inefficient?'' in M. Bruce Johnson, ed., *The Attack on Corporate America* (New York: McGraw-Hill, 1978), pp. 245–51. Also see, David J. Ravenscraft, ''Structure-Profit Relationships at the Line of Business and Industry Level,'' *Review of Economics and Statistics,* February 1983, pp. 22–31, who analyzed the unusually rich and detailed data of the 1975 Federal Trade Commission *line-of-business* survey (which broke the operations of any given firm down into 3,186 potential lines of business, while actual firms surveyed had between 1 and 47 such lines). This study found no positive relationship between profitability and concentration, but a powerful one between profitability and market share (higher returns to advertising?) and vertical integration (lower average total costs?).

**Table 13.4**   Profit Rates versus Concentration and Entry Barriers:
U.S. Manufacturing

| Concentration | Entry Barriers | | |
|---|---|---|---|
| | Low to Moderate | Substantial | Very High |
| **1936–1940 (20 industries)** | | | |
| High | 10.5 | 10.2 | 19.0 |
| Moderate | 5.3 | 7.0 | — |
| **1947–1951 (20 industries)** | | | |
| High | 15.4 | 14.0 | 19.0 |
| Moderate | 10.1 | 12.5 | — |
| **1950–1960 (30 industries)** | | | |
| High | 11.9 | 11.1 | 16.4 |
| Moderate | 8.6 | 12.2 | — |

Studies by Bain and Mann related average profit rates on stockholders' equity to industrial concentration and entry barriers. An 8-firm concentration ratio of 70 or more was considered "high," a lower one "moderate." Entry barriers were defined as "very high" when firms could hold prices 10 percent or more above minimum average total cost without inducing new entry. Bain included industries making automobiles, cigarettes, high-quality fountain pens, liquor, tractors, and typewriters in this group. Barriers were defined as "substantial" when prices could be held 5–9 percent above minimum $ATC$; such industries included copper, complex farm machines, petroleum refining, high-quality men's and specialty shoes, soap, and steel. Industries that could keep price only 1–4 percent above minimum $ATC$ had "low to moderate" barriers and included producers of canned fruits and vegetables, cement, simple farm machinery, flour, low-quality fountain pens, gypsum products, meat packing, metal containers, rayon, women's and low-quality men's shoes, tires, and tubes.

*Sources:* Joe S. Bain, *Barriers to New Competition* (Cambridge, MA: Harvard University Press, 1956), pp. 192–200. H. Michael Mann, "Seller Concentration, Barriers to Entry, and Rates of Return in Thirty Industries," *Review of Economics and Statistics,* August 1966, pp. 296–307.

the pie among powerful groups in the economy (and that devalues the purchasing power of those who are unable to raise their money income as rapidly as the general level of prices, while raising that of others who are able to raise their money income more rapidly).

## Alienation

Does the U.S. economy produce alienation? Consider once more the three forms most frequently cited.

**From the Self.**   Certainly many people do not own nonhuman resources. So they are forced to join with others in the division of labor. Thus, they do end up working in central workplaces, with many machines, following rigid schedules. And they do, more often than not, relate to even more machines in their leisure time. But are they, as a result, unhappy? Do they fail to develop any of their inherent talents? It would be difficult to argue thusly.

Survey after survey indicates that 85 percent of American workers, for example, are well satisfied with their jobs. And their behavior indicates the same. Why else do people work overtime and even moonlight (when they could clearly get along just fine with the goods their regular jobs provide)? Why else are rates of absenteeism and labor turnover so low? Why else are strikes so rare? Why else don't workers regularly burn down their factories and riot in the streets? Why don't they go off to join communes and live "the simple life" (which they are certainly free to do)? And isn't it true that they do engage in a multitude of creative activities in their leisure time? Isn't it true that nobody forces them to acquire all those machines that fill their leisure time (but which they are all too eager to use)?

**From One's Fellows.**    Certainly the relationships of most people with most other people are indirect, impersonal, businesslike, and cold, rather than direct, personal, intimate, and warm. As has been noted before, however, this is inevitable in any large grouping. Large numbers of people, who do not care to place themselves under a personal dictator but wish to make joint decisions, have no alternative but to signal each other in indirect ways that are impersonal and seem businesslike and cold. Hence, they decide what goods to produce by casting dollar votes (rather than having loving, warm, intimate discussions about it all). But critics are right when they say that the number of votes people can cast differs among them for unjustifiable reasons. But they are almost certainly wrong when they claim that people are so brainwashed by advertisers that they cannot *help* casting their votes as producers want them cast. Indeed, the *limited* power of the alleged Madison Avenue "manipulators" over people's tastes is evidenced by the manipulators' preoccupation with market surveys, their failure to launch at all between 80 and 90 percent of all technically successful new products (because they do not survive market research), and their withdrawal of a third to a half of those products that are launched (because they fail to sell sufficiently during the first year). And the thoughtful appraisal of people's own choices is evidenced by their subscriptions to consumer magazines, the seeking of disinterested advice, and their refusal to make repeat purchases when dissatisfied with a product.

Nor are large numbers of people who join together as members of labor unions or employees of large corporations able to escape impersonal bureaucracy (and establish loving relationships with everyone) any more than they are able to do so in their role as citizens of the United States. But does this have to spell unmitigated unhappiness? This too can be doubted.

Citizens can and do hold their government officials to account for their actions. In the same way, workers can and often do control their own unions democratically; and authentic unions, in turn, help them establish procedures by which workers can hold the exercise of power by their bosses to account. As a result, more often than not, they are protected from tyranny on the job. They cannot be arbitrarily reassigned, laid off, or dismissed. They cannot be discriminated against in promotions with respect to age, race, or sex. They can point out stupidity on their supervisor's part and do it with impunity. They are free to quit and find another job. Thus, their morale is high.

**From the Natural World.**   Most certainly, the U.S. government has often failed to perform the model role laid out in the previous chapter. As a result of its not assigning property rights in such scarce things as the air, rivers, lakes, or oceans, for example, everybody has used such resources freely for any purpose, even after the age of abundance has turned into one of scarcity. Thus, a host of problems have arisen, such as the one illustrated in panel (c) of Figure 12.6, ''When Abundance Turns into Scarcity'' (p. 359). Too many people, for example, want to use the same airspace to fly in it at the same time, or to send signals through it, or to use it as a dumping site. Or too many people, at the same time, want to use the same lake for swimming, or waterskiing, or boating, or fishing, or the dumping of their wastes. Or too many people want to hunt whales or seals, catch tuna or herrings, dive for pearls or sponges, or use the oceans for mining nickel and oil. So they have come into conflict with others seeking to do the same thing or who wish to pursue a different goal (such as simply breathing pure air or drinking pure water).

Yet, in the last two decades, various levels of government have responded to the popular concern with the preservation of nature. Beginning in the early 1970s, for example, the state of Vermont introduced fees for waste disposal in its waterways (a practice long used in Europe), and Vermont introduced deposit fees for the disposal of bottles and cans. Before long, the federal government banned the use of DDT, several states banned phosphates in laundry detergents, several cities the spraying of fire-proofing asbestos. Since passage of the National Environmental Policy Act and the establishment of the Environmental Protection Agency, a variety of standards have been set to limit the disposal of many types of pollutants. Close-Up 13.3, ''Of Bubbles, Offsets, and Banks,'' indicates how much things have changed in recent times.

## ANALYTICAL EXAMPLE 13.1

## The Political Economy of Milk and Housing

In many real-world markets, government intervention will not allow the equilibrium price to be established. In 1982, for example, the U.S. government had legislated an above-equilibrium minimum price for milk (and milk products) such as that shown in the accompanying graph. The predictable result was a surplus (such as *ab*) for butter, cheese, and milk; the government spent $2.4 billion to purchase it, and thereby spent more on otherwise unwanted dairy products than on numerous other programs deemed important by many. (The dairy subsidy was eight times larger than federal spending on the arts and humanities, three times larger than spending on the National Park Service, twice as large as spending on the National Science Foundation, and also twice as large as the Agency for International Development's spending on Third World development projects.) The program was rationalized as an aid to poor farmers, but, in fact, most of the money went to the biggest and richest

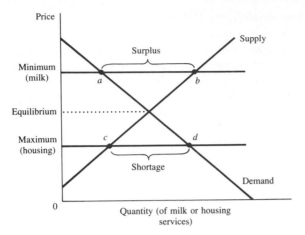

farmers who had most of the milk to sell, while the higher price of dairy products hurt most the consumers with low incomes. Was there an explanation? Of course. The mere 500 dairy farmers per Congressional District were impressively organized and spent $1.8 million on 1982 federal election campaigns—given the $2.4-billion return, not a bad investment.

Or consider a typical government intervention at the local level. In many communities in the United States and abroad, rent controls have been imposed since World War II, such as the below-equilibrium maximum price for housing services in the accompanying graph. The predictable result is a shortage (such as *cd*). The result has been long waiting lists (in the late 1950s, it took 40 months to get an apartment in Stockholm) and a deteriorating housing stock (in New York landlords spend half as much on repairs of rent-controlled apartments as on repairs of similar noncontrolled units). Typically, the rationale (landlords are rich, renters are poor) is not supported by the facts, but the policy is explained by the organized use of political power.

*Sources:* John D. Donahue, "The Political Economy of Milk," *The Atlantic Monthly,* October 1983, pp. 59–68; S. Rydenfelt, "Rent Control Thirty Years On," *Verdict on Rent Control* (London: Institute for Economic Affairs, 1972), p. 65; G. Sternlieb, *The Urban Housing Dilemma* (New York Housing and Development Administration, 1972), p. 202.

ANALYTICAL EXAMPLE 13.2

## Income Dynamics

Data on the personal distribution of income, such as those embodied in Table 13.3 or Figure 13.4, can easily be misleading, and not only for the obvious reason that money-income measures neglect income in kind. More importantly, such data are likely to be misleading because most individuals go through a *cycle* of earning low incomes during their youth, growing incomes thereafter (with a peak just before retirement), and lower incomes late in life. Thus, it is *possible* for every individual to have the same lifetime income, while income-distribution statistics look precisely as in Table 13.3, year after year. The apparent income inequality, then, reflects nothing more than the age distribution of the population! Each year, x percent of the population seems to live in poverty, and y percent seems to enjoy great riches, *but the people who are poor or rich at one time are frequently not the same people who are poor or rich at another time.* Surely, we would want to know whether this hypothetical scenario is applicable to the United States.

Fortunately, a group of researchers at the University of Michigan's Survey Research Center has been working diligently for the past 17 years on the first truly adequate study of income dynamics in the United States. Under the direction of James N. Morgan and Greg J. Duncan, researchers associated with the Panel Study on Income Dynamics (PSID) have conducted lengthy, yearly interviews with the heads of 5,000 American families—the *same* families—in order to track the changes of their economic fortunes. (The original sample was indistinguishable from the American population as a whole and has been studied ever since 1968, including families that split off, such as children living alone or starting their own families, widows and widowers, separated and divorced partners, and so on. By 1983, the panel included 6,500 families and 16,000 people.) The results to date are remarkable. They show that the "freeze-frame" character of yearly income-distribution data (such as Table 13.3) makes for a real distortion and causes us to miss the importance of mobility in the U.S. economy and, thus, muddles our thinking about poverty, equality, and economic justice.

**Dynamic Poverty.**    Surely, if a significant proportion of the people poor in 1988 were not poor in 1987 and will not be poor in 1989, then the character of American poverty is radically different from what it would be if there were no turnover in the poverty population. The PSID study for the first time made it possible to distinguish among families poor for a single year, a multi-year spell, or persistently. As Table A indicates, while nearly a quarter of the families were poor at least during one year of the 1969–1978 period, only 5 percent were poor for five or more years, and fewer than 1 percent were poor during the entire decade. The most surprising result is that such a large proportion of American families (a proportion demographically indistinguishable from the population as a whole) falls below the poverty level at *some* time. This

**Table A**    Percent of Individuals in Families with Incomes Below Official Poverty Level, 1969–78

| | |
|---|---|
| Poor in 1978 | 6.8% |
| Poor one or more years | 24.4% |
| Poor five or more years | 5.4% |
| "Persistently poor" (eight or more years) | 2.6% |
| Poor all ten years | 0.7% |

**Table B**   Changes in Family Income, 1971–1978

| Family Income Quintile, 1971 | Family Income Quintile, 1978 | | | | | |
|---|---|---|---|---|---|---|
| | *Highest* | *Second* | *Third* | *Fourth* | *Lowest* | *Total* |
| Highest | 48.5 | 29.5 | 14.0 | 4.5 | 3.5 | 100% |
| Second | 22.0 | 31.5 | 25.5 | 15.0 | 6.0 | 100% |
| Third | 14.0 | 18.5 | 30.5 | 23.5 | 13.5 | 100% |
| Fourth | 9.0 | 13.5 | 21.5 | 34.5 | 21.5 | 100% |
| Lowest | 6.0 | 7.0 | 9.5 | 22.0 | 55.5 | 100% |

is caused not by some long-term problem, such as lack of education, but by short-term occurrences, such as divorce, death, layoffs, or returning to school. A second result of significance is the small percentage of the persistently poor. Clearly, all this has important implications for public policy.

**Dynamic Equality.**   The PSID study also shows an astonishing degree of movement within the American income distribution. Consider the stunning changes indicated in Table B. The table shows the percentage of people in family income quintiles that remained in the same (1971) quintile and the percentage that rose or fell to another. Thus, of those who were either at the top or the bottom levels in 1971, only about half remained in those relative positions by 1978. Change in the middle income groups was even more dramatic: Only about a third remained in the same place; the rest rose or fell. (If there were no mobility in the American economy, the encircled numbers in Table B would be 100 percent; as can be seen, none is higher than 56 percent.) Given these persistent changes, the "half-life" of the American income distribution (as measured in quintiles) is at most seven years!

**Dynamic Justice.**   The PSID study also makes it possible to compare the economic status of a large group of people with that of its parents. Consider Table C, which makes this comparison for those who formed new households by 1981. As one can

**Table C**   Intergenerational Economic Mobility, 1969–1981

| Parents' Average Family Income Quintile | Young Adult's Average Family Income Quintile | | | | | |
|---|---|---|---|---|---|---|
| | *Highest* | *Second* | *Third* | *Fourth* | *Lowest* | *Total* |
| Highest | 36 | 23 | 19 | 13 | 9 | 100% |
| Second | 25 | 26 | 22 | 17 | 10 | 100% |
| Third | 17 | 26 | 23 | 23 | 11 | 100% |
| Fourth | 15 | 19 | 19 | 24 | 23 | 100% |
| Lowest | 2 | 9 | 18 | 27 | 44 | 100% |

see, only just over a third of young adults with parents in the highest income group ended up in the same group, while fewer than half of those with parents in the lowest group remained there. (Again, if there were no mobility in the American economy, the encircled numbers in Table C would be 100 percent.) It may well be that the strong intergenerational mobility indicated here (which, no doubt, has something to do with the greater degree to which *equal opportunity* is realized in the United States compared to other countries) leads to long-term equality of *results.*

Economists can learn a great deal from this study, not least of all that the "movie" of an open economy is not simply the sum of the "still shots" they are used to studying.

*Source:* Mark Lilla. "Why the 'Income Distribution' Is So Misleading." *The Public Interest,* Fall 1984, pp. 62–76. For a first report on the study itself, see Greg J. Duncan et al., *Years of Poverty, Years of Plenty: The Changing Fortunes of American Workers and Families* (Ann Arbor, MI: University of Michigan Institute for Social Research, 1984).

## CLOSE-UP 13.1

## Orange Uprising

To Jacques Giddens, grower of navel oranges in Orange Cove, California, the federal marketing quotas were "crazy." Each year, he said, they forced him to throw away perfectly good food merely to hold up prices. In 1976, he rebelled.

After selling 3,441 cartons of oranges above his Department of Agriculture quota, Mr. Giddens was fined $12,620 by the government. He declined to pay, sued the government, and lost. He was broke but not broken. In fact, after his revolt, the rancher managed to exceed his marketing quota by leasing some of his trees directly to consumers at $16 apiece. He guaranteed each lessee 120 pounds of fruit. His ranch did the picking and packing; the lessee paid the shipping.

"This is exempt from the marketing order," Mr. Giddens explained, "because when you lease a tree from me, that's your tree, and all I do is ship you the fruit from it. I take care of it for you. It's not covered by the quota."

At the time, he said, he was the only orange grower in the country who leased trees.

More recently, other farmers have joined the fight, using petitions and lawsuits to put an end to "1930s-bred socialism." Federal marketing orders prevent them from harvesting millions of oranges all across California's San Joaquin Valley; as one grower put it, "Even the Communists don't do what we're doing—destroying good food."

*Source:* Richard Haitch, "Orange Uprising," *The New York Times,* May 11, 1980, p. 37; *The Wall Street Journal,* June 17, 1987, pp. 1 and 13.

## CLOSE-UP 13.2

### Supporting the Price of Sugar

As the rain pelted the leaky old warehouse one summer day in 1978, a mysterious substance as viscous as lava and as dark as motor oil oozed under the doors and into a street in Riviera Beach, Florida, attracting swarms of flies and bees. The warehouse was filled with raw sugar acquired by the federal government under its new 1977 price support program; the scene was repeated in many places all over the United States.

Under the new program, sugar growers could borrow money (at 14.73¢ a pound) from the government but had to turn over their crops as collateral. If later market prices were higher, they could reclaim the sugar; if they were not, they forfeited their crops. Taxpayers, through the government, became the reluctant owners of the sugar. The stakes were large. At a time when the world price of sugar was less than 8¢ a pound, each penny increase in price added $224 million to the American sugar growers' revenue, but (as they said) this would "only" cost the average American one extra dollar per year.

Note: The world market price of sugar has fluctuated wildly, from 65¢ a pound in 1974 to 8¢ a pound in 1977 to 42¢ a pound in 1980 to 7¢ a pound in 1982. In the latter year, U.S. taxpayers were paying an average of $215,000 in support money to U.S. sugar producers—far more than the analogous amount going to the average dairy farmer ($11,250) or the average wheat farmer ($475).

*Sources:* William Robbins, "Conflicting Interests over Sugar Create Unwanted U.S. Surpluses," *The New York Times,* January 14, 1979, pp. 1 and 48; *idem,* "Lobbyists Worked Off Stage to Shape Sugar Laws," *The New York Times,* January 15, 1979, pp. A1 and D4; and *idem,* "Powerful Rivals Clash over Sugar Price Supports," *The New York Times,* January 16, 1979, pp. A1 and D11; July 18, 1982.

## CLOSE-UP 13.3

### Of Bubbles, Offsets, and Banks

As Analytical Example 8.1, "A Market for Pollution Rights" (p. 232) has shown, uniform pollution standards (which require every firm or even every plant to reduce waste emissions by the identical percentage) are almost certain to achieve a given degree of environmental quality at a higher-than-necessary total cost. A number of studies have confirmed this theoretical insight. One study considered the case of 53 municipalities in Wisconsin that were ordered to reduce their 20,800-pounds-per-day discharge of phosphorus into Lake Michigan by 85 percent each.[a] The compliance cost was $4,880 per day, but it would have been only $3,920 per day if discharge

[a]Randolph M. Lyon, "Auctions and Alternative Procedures for Allocating Pollution Rights," *Land Economics,* February 1982, pp. 16–32.

rights for 3,120 pounds per day (15 percent of the above figure) had been handed out, along with the right for subsequent trade. The same study cited the case of five towns and six paper producers along the Willamette River in Oregon. Their discharges reduced the dissolved oxygen in the river excessively; they were ordered to cut their biochemical oxygen demand (BOD) by about 70 percent each to a total of 168,000 pounds per day. The compliance cost was $9,840 per day, but it could have been $8,500 per day under a marketable pollution rights scheme.

Another study of 102 duPont plants found that duPont, if it had been allowed to achieve a given environmental quality goal in the cheapest possible way, could have reduced its compliance cost by 60 percent if trades among duPont plants had been allowed (one plant cutting emissions a lot, another one very little, for example, rather than all plants making an identical percentage cut) and by 85 percent if similar trades between duPont and other area firms had been allowed.[b] This sort of evidence led the Environmental Protection Agency to the adoption of a more flexible policy.

**Bubbles.** The new "bubble" policy treats all sources of waste emissions that come from a given factory, firm, or geographic area as if they were contained in a bubble and constituted a single emission source. As long as the bubble as a whole meets pollution standards, each source within it is considered to be in compliance with the law. As a result, a firm can find the cheapest way of achieving an environmental goal; for example, by cutting one source of emission down to 5 percent and another one not at all, while still meeting the goal of, say, a 50-percent overall reduction. The number of such bubble trades has been growing rapidly; here are some examples:

1. The Narraganset Electric Company has two generating stations in Providence, Rhode Island. Under the bubble policy they were allowed to use high-sulfur oil (2.2 percent sulfur) at one plant when the second plant was burning natural gas or was not operating, instead of being required to burn 1-percent sulfur oil at both plants. This action resulted in a savings of $3 million annually, reduced the use of imported oil by 600,000 barrels per year, and reduced sulfur emissions by 30 percent.
2. The duPont Corporation was allowed to control five major sources of volatile organic compounds to more than 97-percent efficiency in exchange for relaxed controls on more than 200 difficult-to-control sources of fugitive emissions. The expected savings include $12 million in capital costs plus several million dollars in recurring operating costs.
3. Manufacturers of cans were allowed to comply with existing laws for each can-coating line by averaging emissions of volatile organic compounds on a daily basis so long as the source did not exceed the total allowable plant-wide emissions per day. This is expected to save the industry $107 million in capital expenditures, $28 million per year in operating costs, and 4 trillion BTUs of natural gas per year, chiefly because expensive add-on pollution-control equipment that would have been energy-consuming is no longer necessary.

[b]M. T. Maloney and Bruce Yandle, "The Estimated Cost of Air Pollution Control under Various Regulatory Approaches," Working Paper, (Clemson, SC: Clemson University Department of Economics, 1979).

**Offsets.** The new "offsets" policy allows new or existing polluters to make deals with other polluters in order to achieve a given environmental standard in the cheapest way. Instead of spending $50 million to control annual waste emissions of 50,000 tons at its new plant, the firm in question might, for example, pay less than $50 million to another firm so that the latter reduces its emission by 50,000 tons per year more than required by law. If the latter firm has a low marginal cost of pollution abatement (and can do so for $50 million or less in our example), a mutually profitable deal is possible, without adversely affecting environmental quality. Among recently concluded offset transactions are these:

1. A cement company in Texas entered into an agreement with another local company providing for that company to install dust collectors. The cement company paid for the equipment, while the other company agreed to accept the maintenance costs, which were negligible.
2. The emissions from a 90-megawatt refuse-burning powerplant to be operated by the city of Columbus, Ohio, were offset at the city's expense by installing pollution controls at two privately owned asphalt plants and by increasing the height of a smokestack at a third company.
3. A company wanting to build an oil terminal to handle 40,000 barrels a day in Contra Costa County, California, was granted a permit when it acquired, for $250,000, an offset created when a local chemical company shut down.
4. In the mid-1970s the state of Pennsylvania created an offset by altering its road-paving practices—which served to reduce hydrocarbon emissions—and used this offset to successfully induce the Volkswagen Corporation to locate its first American production facility in a depressed region in that state.

**Banks.** In anticipation of bubble or offset deals, polluters can also cut waste emissions more than required and get credit for this action at a new emissions "bank." These credits can be used later or sold to others. Recently concluded transactions include these:

1. In Louisville, Kentucky, General Electric acquired several hundred tons of hydrocarbon emission credits from International Harvester. The price was $60,000; this allowed GE to meet standards without having to spend $1.5 million for an incinerator that would have been worthless two years hence (because hydrocarbons would not be emitted thereafter).
2. The Pacific Gas and Electric Company sold its credits to pump 1,092 tons of nitrogen oxides and 176 tons of sulfur dioxide into the air for $18 million.
3. B. F. Goodrich sold credits to 25 tons of hydrocarbon emissions for $62,500.

*Sources:* Philip Shabecoff, "New Policy Widens Pollution 'Sales,' " *The New York Times,* April 3, 1982, p. 7; Richard Greene, "Selling Dirt," *Forbes,* May 24, 1982, p. 120; Tom Tietenberg, *Environmental and Natural Resource Economics* (Glenview, IL.: Scott, Foresman and Co., 1984), pp. 306–07.

# Summary

1. As in the model of market capitalism described in the previous chapter, most resources in the U.S. economy are privately owned and the separate decisions made by numerous households and firms are spontaneously coordinated through markets. Contrary to the model, however, resources are not *evenly* distributed over the whole population and most markets are *imperfectly* competitive.

2. Many people in the U.S. economy play a "monopoly game": They try to gain control over the prices at which they sell or buy in order to raise their own income at the expense of other people's income.

3. One approach involves the formation of a pure monopoly. It can originate from technological or legal sources, including increasing returns to scale, exclusive ownership of key resources, patents and copyrights, and exclusive franchises. Owners of monopolies hope to achieve permanent profit for themselves; in fact, monopoly profit can be positive, zero, or even negative.

4. A second approach involves the formation of privately organized cartels. Firms establish cartels also in the hope of reaping permanent profit. The success of privately established cartels, however, is often elusive because of organizational difficulties, a high price elasticity of demand, or a high price elasticity of supply.

5. A third approach yet involves the establishment of government-sponsored cartels. Numerous successful examples exist. Typically, they involve *legislating,* separately or in combination, the setting of a higher price, a cutback in supply, or even an increase in demand.

6. Sellers who fail to achieve monopoly or successful cartels often find themselves in market situations lying in between the extremes of monopoly/cartel and perfect competition. Examples include (a) oligopoly, in which the entry of new firms is difficult and relatively few sellers compete with one another, offering either homogeneous or differentiated products, and (b) monopolistic competition, in which the entry of new firms is easy and large numbers of sellers compete with one another, offering differentiated products.

7. The previous examples referred to goods markets, but imperfect competition is equally widespread in U.S. resource markets, as the existence of labor unions or business monopsonies illustrates.

8. An overview of the importance of various market structures in the U.S. economy can be gained by examining indexes of industrial concentration as well as data on the prevalence, in the major sectors of the economy, of monopoly, oligopoly, and the like. (These data suggest a trend toward more competition since the 1950s.)

9. Government in the United States hardly conforms to the role envisioned for it by the sponsors of the model economy discussed in the previous chapter. Although there are attempts to promote a competitive

environment (consider antitrust laws or free trade legislation), such policies often pale in significance when compared with those designed to aid would-be monopolists. Many observers explain this schizophrenic behavior of government by the ''capture'' of legislators and regulators alike by special interests.

**10.** The performance of the U.S. economy is assessed by all of the criteria introduced in chapters 2 through 4.

## Key Terms

acreage allotments
antipirating agreements
cartel
closed shops
compensating wage differentials
concentration ratio
copyright
equalizing wage differential
exclusive franchise
fair trade laws
Gini coefficient
holding company
horizontal merger
imperfect competition
import quotas
increasing returns to scale
labor union
line of actual inequality
line of perfect equality

line of perfect inequality
Lorenz curve
marketing quotas
monopolistic competition
monopoly
monopoly power
monopsony
natural monopoly
oligopoly
patent
persuasive advertising
price war
product differentiation
tariff
trust
tying contract
union shops
vertical merger

## Questions and Problems

**1.** The text claims that, unlike Figure 13.2, ''A Profit-Making Monopoly,'' a monopoly could just as well end up with zero profit. Illustrate the possibility graphically.

**2.** Rework problem 1, but for a monopoly that is incurring losses.

**3.** ''The text claims that government aids in the setting up of cartels so as to enrich some people at the expense of other people. Surely, there must be other and better reasons.'' Can you think of any?

**4.** Have another look at Figure 13.3, ''The Cartel.'' How do we know that raising the price from $2 to $3 will raise profit?

**5. Ms. A:** ''When government helps firms gain monopoly power, it hands them a valuable asset.''

**Mr. B:** "And when government destroys monopolies, it destroys valuable assets."

Evaluate this exchange.

6. The text discusses governmental price fixing in the goods market. Is there anything equivalent in resource markets?

7. A section of Chapter 7 discusses the underground economy of the Soviet Union. Is there anything equivalent in the United States?

8. Choose any one Pareto condition. Illustrate the possible economic inefficiency of imperfectly competitive markets graphically.

9. How do you think one might *measure* the overall impact of economic inefficiency? (This *is* a difficult question; some of the "Selected Readings" may help you find an answer.)

10. The advocates of distributive economic justice always argue for a more vigorous policy of governmental income redistribution. Can you think of instances in which such a policy might do more harm than good?

# Selected Readings

Berle, Adolph A., Jr. *Power Without Property* (New York: Harcourt Brace Jovanovich, 1959).

Berle, Adolph A., and Gardner C. Means. *The Modern Corporation and Private Property* (New York: Commerce Clearing House, 1932).
Argues that in large American corporations control is exercised by managers, not stock-holding owners.

Buchanan, James M., et al. *Toward a Theory of the Rent-Seeking Society* (College Station, TX: Texas A&M University Press, 1980). The winner of the 1986 Nobel Prize in Economics argues that the gradual accumulation of special interest legislation is changing the nature of private property rights and of the American economy.

Domar, Evsey D. "Poor Old Capitalism: A Review Article," *Journal of Political Economy,* November/December 1974, pp. 1301–13. A critical review of the first edition of Edwards, Reich, and Weisskopf, noted below.

Edwards, Richard C., Michael Reich, and Thomas E. Weisskopf. *The Capitalist System: A Radical Analysis of American Society,* 3d ed. (Englewood Cliffs, NJ: Prentice-Hall, 1986). A view of American capitalism from the perspective of radical economists.

Elliott, John E., and John Cownie, *Competing Philosophies in American Political Economics* (Pacific Palisades, CA: Goodyear, 1975).

*Forbes,* 70th Anniversary Issue, July 13, 1987. The entire issue is devoted to the history and nature of capitalism, mostly in the United States.

Galbraith, John K. *The New Industrial State* (Boston: Houghton Mifflin, 1971).

Galbraith, John K. *The Affluent Society* (Boston: Houghton Mifflin, 1958).
Argues, among other things, that consumer tastes in the U.S. economy are

strongly manipulated by an industrial *technostructure* (which leads the economy to produce a "wrong" set of goods).

Heilbroner, Robert L., *Business Civilization in Decline* (New York: Norton, 1976). A pessimistic view of the future of American capitalism.

Kohler, Heinz. *Intermediate Microeconomics: Theory and Applications,* 2d ed. (Glenview, IL: Scott, Foresman and Co., 1986). Chapters 8, 9, and 11 provide detailed treatments of imperfectly competitive goods and resource markets, and Chapter 12 deals with the economic inefficiency of such markets and reports on measurements of welfare losses from economic inefficiency. Chapters 17 through 19 focus on the role of government in the U.S. economy, in particular on antitrust policy, regulation, externalities, and public goods.

Kwoka, John E., and Lawrence J. White, eds. *The Antitrust Revolution* (Glenview, IL: Scott Foresman and Co., 1989). Thirteen case studies illustrate the most recent revolution in U.S. antitrust policy.

Schumpeter, Joseph A. *Capitalism, Socialism, and Democracy,* 3d ed. (New York: Harper & Row, 1950). A classic work on American capitalism and its future.

Sommers, Albert T. *The U.S. Economy Demystified,* revised ed. (Lexington, MA: D.C. Heath, 1988). Discusses the meaning of the major types of economic statistics.

Sowell, Thomas. *Essays and Data on American Ethnic Groups* (Washington, D.C.: The Urban Institute, 1978). A superb analysis of the fate of various ethnic groups in America, focusing on Blacks, Chinese, Japanese, Irish, Italians, and Jews.

Sowell, Thomas. *Markets and Minorities* (New York: Basic Books, 1981). The careful and intelligent examination of a wide range of evidence provides a breath of fresh air on a topic that is generally the subject of unreasoning passion, emotion, and prejudice.

## Computer Program

The SYSTEMS personal computer diskette that accompanies this book contains one program of interest to this chapter:

Program 13, "Market Capitalism: The U.S. Case," provides 20 multiple-choice questions about Chapter 13, along with immediate responses to incorrect answers.

# CHAPTER 14

# *Government Intervention: Variations On A Theme*

The previous chapter has characterized the U.S. economy as a capitalist market economy with a significant degree of government intervention. The same can be said of many countries throughout the world that clearly do not fit any of the categories of socialism described in Part 2 of this book. Consider Western Europe or the Far East. In countries such as France, Great Britain, Sweden, West Germany, or Japan (countries on which this chapter will focus), most resources continue to be privately owned and the economic activities of millions of people continue to be coordinated by markets. Yet, the role of government in these countries, too, is considerably more pervasive than envisioned in the Chapter 12 model of the capitalist market economy.

Frequently the governments of the countries of "regulated capitalism" have been inspired by socialist thought, but not necessarily that of Karl Marx. Consider the influence of François Babeuf, Louis Blanc, Étienne Cabet, Charles Fourier, or Henri de Saint-Simon on the French, of Robert Owen or the Fabians (Annie Besant, George Bernard Shaw, Beatrice Webb, Sidney Webb) on the British. These "utopian" socialist thinkers of long ago, nevertheless, provide the driving force behind present-day demands for government action designed to achieve greater equality in wealth, income, and economic power.

Yet, unlike in Eastern Europe, the political parties that articulate these demands in the countries studied here are committed to the maintenance of political democracy. They stress popular control of the government by the people, along with the protection of civil liberties. They want to reform and "humanize" capitalism, but only in ways acceptable to the majority. They opt for peaceful and gradual change, not for violent revolution. That is why continental European countries such as

France, Sweden, or West Germany often refer to themselves as **social democracies,** which the British Labor Party prefers to call **democratic socialism.** Even the Communist parties in Western Europe, often referred to as "Eurocommunists," condemn the Soviet-style dictatorship and the associated repression of civil liberties.

The stress on democracy in the countries to be discussed in this chapter has two consequences. First, there exists a great diversity in the approaches different governments take when they intervene in the economy. Some have fairly elaborate planning bureaucracies; others don't. Some seek to equalize wealth, income, and economic power by nationalizing private businesses; others eschew that approach but impose heavy taxes to finance elaborate government programs of education, health care, income transfers, and more. Others still prefer to promote the power of organized labor or to issue a million regulations that limit the power of private business. While this chapter will not attempt to provide a complete description of the economic institutions or the economic histories of the social democracies, it will provide examples of all these approaches.

Second, the stress on democracy inevitably leads to frequent changes in governmental philosophy. When a labor or socialist party is thrown out of office and a bourgeois or conservative party is elected, we should not be surprised if the entire thrust of governmental intervention in the economy is halted or even reversed. We will see examples of this as well.

## The Nature of Governmental Planning

Consider some of the variations in governmental planning found in our five-country sample.

### France

In France, the governmental direction of economic affairs has a long tradition. It goes back at least to Louis XIV (1643–1715), whose Finance Minister, Jean Baptiste Colbert, instituted the export-promoting and import-impeding policy of *mercantilism.* The interventionist tradition continued under Louis xv, whose personal physician, François Quesnay, turned from the study of blood circulating through the human body to that of goods and resources circulating through the economy. Indeed, Quesnay's famous 1758 sketch of the economy, known as the *tableau économique,* was a forerunner of Leontief's input-output table, discussed in Chapter 6. Interestingly, some two and a half centuries later, the French embraced input-output analysis as a framework for central economic planning.

Ever since the end of World War II, the French have set up central economic plans of the type illustrated in Table 6.2, "The Plan Document," on page 93. But, unlike Soviet-style central plans the fulfillment of which is *commanded* by the government, French plans have been of an entirely different nature. They have not carried the force of law; the French "toothless" plans have in fact been elaborate forecasts indicating to all concerned what the government expected to happen during the plan period, given its own actions and those likely to be taken by private parties. That is why Soviet planning has been called **imperative planning,** while French planning, in contrast, has been termed **indicative planning.**

Modern French planning originated during World War II when plans were made for postwar reconstruction. In 1946, a General Planning Commissariat (Commissariat Général au Plan) was set up under Jean Monnet. It has issued a series of multiyear plans ever since: a First Plan for 1947–1950, a Fifth Plan for 1966–1970, and so on. Each plan has been based on an explicitly stated "optimum" rate of economic growth and a set of major objectives. (The First Plan, for example, sought to expand and modernize certain *basic sectors,* including coal, electric power, steel, cement, agricultural machinery, and transportation. The Second Plan, similarly, called for certain *basic actions* throughout the economy, including stepped-up research, increases in productivity, marketing reforms, and more.) The major objectives of each plan have been translated into final demands (such as the column (4) through (7) entries in Table 6.2 on page 93) and have been placed in a fairly aggregative input-output table. Finally, with the help of the Leontief inverse and technical coefficients derived from past experience, the Commissariat has filled in the remainder of each table, thereby completing each plan of future input-output flows.

While the Commissariat has employed only a small group of people (140 persons in a recent year), its work has been aided by a number of *planning commissions* made up of enterprise executives as well as representatives of labor unions and government. In a recent year, there were 31 such commissions with a total of 2,095 members. Some 25 of these commissions were "vertical"; they were organized on an industry basis (chemicals, energy, mining, steel, transportation, etc.) and concerned with a single sector exclusively. The 6 remaining commissions were "horizontal"; they dealt with issues common to the whole economy (production equilibrium, financial equilibrium, manpower equilibrium, balanced regional development, etc.).

What has been the purpose of plans that the government cannot enforce? The purpose has been to eliminate the boom and bust of the business cycle by making the future path of the economy "transparent" to all, by reducing uncertainty and, thus, the errors potentially associated with it. Some have described the French plan as a generalized piece of market research simultaneously made available to all suppliers and customers. All of them are free to make their own decisions, but they can do so with a knowledge of the intentions of the rest of the economy. (Thus, a steel industry executive can compare the company's production and investment plans with the authoritative government forecast of national steel demand and can foresee, say, a potential slippage in the company's market share. This ability to foresee the future, it has been argued, promotes private actions that help achieve the national growth target.)

More than that! The government has not been entirely powerless to promote its plan: Consider, for example, the planned volume and composition of investment. The government clearly has direct control over the public enterprise sector and is free to carry out the portion of the national investment plan affecting that sector.

It can, in addition, affect the volume and composition of private investment by selectively imposing credit controls, providing tax breaks, withholding factory building permits, and more. And French governments have "persuaded" private businesses in purely verbal ways as well to conform to its plan. These ways have included threats of nationalization and many informal government-business get-togethers. The latter have been designed to instill faith in the inevitability of the plan and have been carried on amid an atmosphere that some have likened to "revivalist prayer meetings."

## Great Britain

The British Labor Party, just like its utopian socialist forerunners, has long been arguing against a society based on individualism and supported by governmental laissez-faire. It has consistently denounced the "blind forces of the market" and argued in favor of a "collective organization of the economy by enlightened people" who would seek to attain a "social purpose." Yet, compared to France, the machinery of governmental planning in Great Britain has been primitive. A 1944 White Paper merely called for Keynesian full employment measures. Since World War II, successive Labor governments have restlessly created and destroyed governmental planning agencies, setting up a new institution today, reorganizing it tomorrow, and eliminating it the next day. Never has there been a master input-output plan.

The closest thing to a central planning board that has ever been created has been the National Economic Development Council. First set up in 1962 and quickly nicknamed "Neddy," the council brought together some 20 business executives, labor leaders, and government officials to engage in "planning by consent." An early goal was "maximum economic development" (originally defined as a real GNP growth rate of 4 per cent per year), consistent with "soundness" of the economy. Later goals included the modernization of industry, the retraining of labor, and the abatement of inflation. As in France, only indirect means of promoting these goals have been used.

## Sweden

Swedish central economic planning, if one can call it that, also has been less specific than that of the French. A Royal Planning Commission has been instrumental in involving representatives of business, labor, and government in various cooperative endeavors. The goal has been a "created harmony" of interests. A most important example, perhaps, has been the Centralized Wage Bargain, a national collective bargaining agreement reached periodically between the Swedish Employers' Confederation (SAF) and the Swedish Trade Union Confederation (LO). Ever since 1938, the wages of about half the labor force have been negotiated centrally in this way. (There has been much stress on "wage solidarity." Workers in highly profitable industries have been asked to show wage restraint in favor of workers not so situated. There has also been an unusual emphasis on economic literacy, on making sure that negotiators gain realistic insights into the world's complexities and then control their emotions to negotiate like "statesmen" with cool heads.

The Swedish government has also pioneered, even prior to Keynes, in macro-economic stabilization policy. This has included the standard tools of monetary and fiscal policy as well as a number of special tools. One of these has involved direct intervention in the labor market via government subsidies to firms that maintain employment during business-cycle downswings or that promote early retirement programs for workers. Another special feature has been the **investment reserve.** Private firms have been allowed to set aside 40 percent of pretax profits in the Central Bank for future investment. While the firms have been free to invest these funds in any project of their own choosing, a Labor Market Board has had the power to decide *when* these frozen funds are released. As a result, the board has been able to control the most volatile component of aggregate demand, private investment.

Overall, the Social Democratic Party has stressed group action over individual action and has attempted to instill in people the highest regard for the expert, technician, and bureaucrat who might guide such group action.

## West Germany

The West Germans, once again, do not have an elaborate central planning bureaucracy. The government has, however, been concerned with the establishment of a socially responsible market economy (*soziale Marktwirtschaft*). As the Social Democrats have put it, "as much competition as possible, as much planning as necessary." Thus, competitive markets have been promoted by such measures as the 1957 Law Against Constraints of Competition, membership in the European Common Market, and the official encouragement of small and medium-sized firms (through subsidized research, preferential government contracts, and the like). On the other hand, the self-regulation of the economy on the micro level has always been supplemented by governmental steering on the macro level. Thus, Keynesian stabilization polices have always been pursued vigorously, as prescribed by a 1967 Law on the Promotion of Economic Stability and Growth.

## Japan

Japan has developed a fairly intensive form of central economic planning despite the fact that the government's statutory powers in this regard are severely limited. After World War II, the U.S. occupation forces broke up the *zaibatsu* (literally, "financial cliques"), which were vast economic empires subject to the highly personalized control of some 20 families. The breakup of these diversified conglomerates, run by the Furukawas, Mitsubishis, Mitsuis, Sumitomos, and the like, went hand in hand with the enactment of strict antimonopoly laws and a weakening of central government powers.

Yet somehow, from nebulous foundations and without appropriate legislation, strong governmental powers emerged in later years. The old zaibatsus reconstituted themselves as *keiretsus,* confederations of formally independent enterprises, and these new industrial groupings engaged in an extraordinary amount of "consultation" with government, making no major decisions without it. The reverse has also been true: The government has continually deferred to the wishes of a potent lobby of some 700 large corporations that make up the Federation of Economic Organizations (Keidanren) and whose chairman is referred to as the Prime Minister of Japanese industry.

On the government's side, the Ministry of International Trade and Industry (MITI) has been particularly important in drawing up indicative central plans (similar to those of the French) and in devising numerous strategies to ensure their fulfillment. When necessary, the antimonopoly laws have been interpreted leniently, and all kinds of vertical and horizontal groupings of firms have been permitted. Firms have also been protected from foreign competition through import quotas and tariffs; they have been aided to compete abroad by subsidies, governmentally financed market research, and more. Private investment has been made to conform to the national plan through cheap loans, grants, tax breaks, governmental advice on optimal production scale or technology, and the creation of government-sponsored cartels. Thus, in the 1970s, in response to a worldwide excess capacity, MITI pushed Japanese shipbuilders into forming a cartel and cutting their capacity by a third. And, in the 1980s, MITI guided Japanese industry into forming a consortium of companies to gain world supremacy in computer technology by developing the "fifth-generation computer" (which can see visual images, respond to the spoken word, and even engage in syllogistic reasoning).

## The Nationalization of Resources

Just as there are major variations in governmental planning institutions, our sample countries reveal considerable differences in governmental policies. In this section, we consider the extent to which they have tried to promote the fulfillment of national goals through an expansion of the public enterprise sector.

### France

The French have a long history of nationalizing privately owned resources. In the 1890s, some railroads were taken over by the government; in the 1930s, armament manufacturers. Even during several decades of conservative party rule following World War II, there were nationalizations of electric power and gas companies, coal and oil producers, insurance firms, telecommunications, transportation enterprises (Air France), some manufacturing companies (Renault autos, tobacco products, steel), and more. By the mid-1950s, 17 percent of the labor force was employed in public enterprises, but the percentage varied widely from 83 percent for utilities and 69 in transportation/communications to 8 percent in manufacturing/mining and 5 in commerce/finance.

The election in 1981 of a socialist-communist government under François Mitterrand (Biography 14.1) gave considerable new impetus to nationalization. Changes occurred at a breathtaking speed. By the beginning of 1982, a third of industry had been nationalized and half the French labor force worked in firms that the government owned outright or in which it had at least a 51-percent ownership stake. Newly nationalized were almost all the banks and insurance companies plus 11 key industries, ranging from aerospace, armaments, chemicals, and electronics to pharmaceuticals, steel, and textiles.

What were the reasons for this socialist rearrangement of property relations? First, it was argued that the private ownership of natural and capital resources had been too concentrated and that this unequal distribution of *wealth* had to be corrected. (Critics pointed out that wealth would be even more highly concentrated—in the hands of a single government rather than numerous private owners.) Second, and closely related, was the argument that nationalization would help correct an all-too-unequal distribution of *income* in that it would remove interest, rent, and profit income from the affected wealth holders. (Critics pointed out that no such effect would occur because nationalization was being carried out not by expropriation but with full compensation. Thus, the former capitalists would hold other forms of wealth—government bonds rather than an auto plant, say—and could earn in interest what they had previously earned in dividends.) Third, it was argued that nationalization would more widely distribute the *power of decision making*. Indeed, public enterprises were to be run by tripartite boards composed of workers, consumers, and government officials. (In practice, however, government ministries have appointed managers who have exercised true power, while the supervisory boards have discussed trivia.) Fourth, nationalization has been viewed as an ideal means to promote the goals set in the national plan, but critics have scoffed at this approach. For example, in order to achieve full employment, companies close to bankruptcy have been nationalized (the steel and textile industries provide examples) and have then been infused with government subsidies. This was to save jobs at any cost, "even if corporate balance sheets suffer." (This approach has been ridiculed as "lemon socialism.") Similarly, nationalization has been viewed as a means to promoting extensive and intensive economic growth. Thus, tax receipts have been used directly for investments in public enterprises. And the nationalized banks and insurance companies, many of which hold *equity* positions in private firms, have been used to approve or deny credit selectively, depending on whether private firms intended to carry out the types of technology-advancing projects encouraged by the national economic plan. (In 1982, the French government controlled 85 percent of credit allocations in this way.)

## Great Britain

Whenever the Labor Party has been in charge, nationalizations (with compensation) have been carried out, typically for the same reasons as in France. Some of these actions were taken before World War II (the national electric grid, radio and television, the London passenger transport system, British Overseas Airways), but most of them occurred after 1945. Early on, this policy affected electric and gas companies, coal and steel producers, the transportation sector (airlines, buses, railroads, long-distance trucking), and the Bank of England. Eventually, firms throughout the economy were affected, ranging from aerospace, electronics, and machine tools to health services, newspapers, and shipbuilding. Frequently, the government has engaged in "lifeboat operations," bailing out near bankrupt enterprises, such as Rolls Royce (a maker of cars and jet engines) and British Leyland (another automaker). By the mid-1960s, about 25 percent of the British labor force worked for the government, but the percentage varied widely from 87 percent in personal services and 70 in utilities/transportation/communications to 9 percent in manufacturing and 8 in construction.

## Sweden

The Swedish Social Democrats, like their French and British counterparts, have presided over a limited degree of nationalization as well. In many cases, beginning with the Lapland iron ore mines in World War I, the government has ended up as a co-owner of once private firms. Thus, a state-owned holding company, *Statsforetag,* has participated in a variety of industries, ranging from iron ore, petrochemicals, and shipbuilding to printing, publishing, textiles, and more. By the mid-1960s, some 20 percent of the labor force worked in government enterprises, but the percentage varied from 71 percent in utilities and 56 in personal services to 53 percent in transportation/communications, 12 in construction, and 4 in manufacturing/mining.

In addition, the Swedes have stressed the establishment of **consumer cooperatives,** usually retail stores owned and run by their customers. This trend goes back at least a century. Members (who refer to each other as "brothers" and "sisters") have sought to provide themselves with consumer goods at lower prices than profit-seeking private stores. Success, however, has been elusive. Lower prices have usually been short-lived and have been paid for with a great deal of free labor that members had to provide to keep the enterprise afloat. In addition, the co-ops have only been able to focus on bare necessities; they have provided neither "luxury" goods nor service nor credit. And they have had no funds for expansion because any "profit" has been paid back to members in the form of a year-end rebate (in accordance with the recipients' annual purchase volume). As a result, most consumers have been attracted to private retailers who provide a greater variety of goods, along with credit, service, and no hassle. In a recent year, only about 15 percent of retail stores were co-ops.

## West Germany

The prevalence of government enterprise in West Germany has been somewhat less than in the countries discussed so far. In the mid-1960s, only 9 percent of the labor force worked in such enterprises, but this percentage was 74 in the transportation/communications sector (mostly railroads, radio, telephone, and television), 43 for utilities (electricity, gas, water, sanitation), and 33 in personal services. The percentage was negligible in manufacturing and mining, where the state sometimes participated in ownership. (The federal government, for example, owned 20 percent of Volkswagen and a state government, Lower Saxony, another 20 percent, but these government shares were later sold to the public.)

## Japan

Some government enterprises have existed in Japan ever since the Meiji Restoration, but their overall importance, as in West Germany, has remained low. In the mid-1960s, only 10 percent of the labor force worked for the government; the percentage was 42 in transportation/communications (airlines, railroads, telephones), 40 in personal services, 20 for utilities, and 14 in construction. It was near 0 in manufacturing and mining (except for a state monopoly in alcohol, tobacco, and salt).

## The Welfare State

Over many decades, many political parties in capitalist countries have striven to create a more equal distribution of income by means of a more direct route than the nationalization of nonhuman resources. They have tried to create societies of "fairness" and "generosity" and "human warmth" and "solidarity," as they have put it, by guaranteeing a certain minimum income (continuously redefined) to every citizen, regardless of that citizen's personal contribution to current production. For this purpose, they have pursued policies of providing governmentally financed general education, vocational training, and health care (to disperse income-earning opportunities widely) and they have created elaborate systems of direct income payments (for children or young mothers, for the disabled, sick, or unemployed, for the poor, the retired, and more). In the process, they have created the modern **welfare state**—a capitalist society in which government pledges to protect people not only from the rigors of the marketplace but, quite literally, from all types of misfortunes that might befall them on their lifelong travel from cradle to grave. This is, of course, a costly commitment, and no single measure, perhaps, can better illustrate the significance of the welfare state than the percentage of the gross domestic product collected in taxes. In all capitalist countries, this percentage has risen significantly since World War II. By 1985, it equaled 46 percent in France, 38 in Great Britain, 51 in Sweden, 38 in West Germany, and 28 in Japan. (It was 29 percent in the United States.)[1] Let us consider a few cases in greater detail.

### Great Britain

In Great Britain, the Labor Party has long pushed for an expansion of social programs designed to create a "minimum practicable inequality of income." While recognizing that *some* income inequality is useful (in that it provides incentives for those

---

[1]U.S. Bureau of the Census, *Statistical Abstract of the United States: 1988* (Washington, D.C.: U.S. Government Printing Office, 1987), p. 810.

who work harder than the rest), Party platforms have consistently stressed solidarity with the poor and unfortunate.

No one, they have said, should be so much richer or poorer than his or her neighbors as to be unable to mix with them on equal terms. Income differences are important to make the economic machine work without the need for bureaucratic central planning. But the highest rewards must not be inordinately high, exceeding what any civilized person should need, nor must the lowest ones be inhumanly low, far less than what any civilized person should have to endure.

Party economists have looked with disdain at economic efficiency (discussed in Chapter 2) and have stressed economic equity (discussed in Chapter 3). The former, they have said, may well provide a fancy cigarette lighter for the man driving a Rolls Royce, along with steak for his dog—while denying other people decent homes, medical care, education, and contentment in old age. Thus, an increase in taxes and government spending "to reallocate resources in accordance with ethical standards" should be viewed as a matter of national pride. Government activity to wipe out poverty, distress, and social squalor, they have said, should never be squeezed by petty prejudice and greed. Indeed, Party economists have noted that Adam Smith, commonly regarded as the apostle of self-interest, had highest praise for unselfishness: "To feel much for others, and little for ourselves . . . to restrain our selfish and to indulge our benevolent affections, constitutes the perfection of human nature and can alone produce among mankind that harmony of sentiments and passions in which consists their whole grace and propriety."[2]

Thoughts such as these produced Great Britain's massive social security system, reaching literally from womb to tomb and including everything from state-financed education and health care to income transfers and counseling in the face of personal need to tax breaks (for children and housing), price fixing (for food, rent, agriculture, transportation), and much more.

But critics have argued that the welfare state has undermined people's self-reliance and self-respect, has led to eternal fighting over the pie (as evidenced by persistent inflationary pressure or long waiting lines for the "free" services), and—above all—has produced marginal tax rates so high as to kill off incentives to work, save and invest, or innovate. The latter, critics claim, has produced "the British disease" (slow economic growth) and has reduced Great Britain's per capita real gross domestic product relative to other countries. (From 1950 to 1985, for example, the per capita real GDP of Great Britain—measured in 1983 prices—grew from $4,548 to $9,278, while that of France grew from $3,891 to $12,020, that of Sweden from $5,470 to $13,337, that of West Germany from $3,343 to $12,972, that of Japan from $1,336 to $11,941, and that of the United States from $7,536 to $14,386.)[3]

---

[2]Adam Smith, *The Theory of Moral Sentiments* (Oxford: Oxford University Press, 1976), 1.i.5.5.
[3]H. Stephen Gardner, *Comparative Economic Systems* (Chicago, IL: Dryden Press, 1988), p. 454.

## Sweden

Sweden is usually cited as the most advanced example of the welfare state. The impression may well be correct. Consider the fact, noted earlier, that the government collects more than half of the country's gross domestic product in taxes. As the Social Democrats like to put it, in Sweden "the capitalist produces, the state distributes."

The reasoning is the same as in Great Britain, and the womb-to-tomb welfare programs cover any type of personal need one can imagine. Besides programs of education (at all levels) and health care (physical and mental) and housing, there are generous cash payments for children, day care, disability, sickness, survivors, old age, unemployment, and much more.

Once again, critics argue that the high marginal tax rates (up to 85 percent) discourage all initiative and have turned Sweden into "a nation of hustlers" who absent themselves from their jobs for an average of 22 days a year (at full pay) and devote themselves to underground economic activities hidden from the tax collector. As Close-Up 14.1, "Team Work in Sweden," illustrates, private firms have taken extraordinary measures to fight the problem of labor absenteeism.

Some even argue that the omnipresent paternal state depresses the Swedes and makes them profoundly unhappy (as evidenced by unusually high suicide rates). Others, such as the world-renowned Swedish economist Gunnar Myrdal (Biography 14.2) scoff at these suggestions.

## The Role of Labor

In most capitalist countries, governments have taken steps to strengthen the hands of workers vis-à-vis business, usually by protecting labor unions as well as by a variety of laws reducing the rights of business. The percentage of workers organized in unions varies widely. In the mid-1980s, it varied from 20 percent in France and 44 in Great Britain to 80 in Sweden, 22 in Japan, and 35 in West Germany. (It was 20 in the United States.)[4]

## France

Unlike American unions, labor unions in France have traditionally pursued their goals not so much at the bargaining table as at the ballot box. In the 1980s, during the early days of the Mitterrand presidency, legislation was passed to let the workers of state-owned firms elect a third of the firms' directors. This was hailed as an important step toward **industrial democracy,** the state of affairs in which workers participate in all enterprise decisions affecting their employment, incomes, and

---

[4]Central Intelligence Agency, *The World Factbook 1983*. (CR83-11300, 1983).

psychic or physical welfare. Yet, the practical consequences of the legislation were modest. The story of the giant Rhone-Poulenc chemical firm is typical. When the government manager wanted to cut the size of the firm's labor force (then 645,000 workers), labor union leaders objected: "This is a nationalized company. We represent the workers. Now we'll decide what's going to be." Said the manager: "You represent workers, but I represent 50 million Frenchmen, and my job is to run a modern factory." The labor force was cut, just as planned by management.[5] The incident clearly illustrates the fears of those who oppose industrial democracy: that it will severely impair the technical efficiency of the affected enterprises and, hence, the ability of the economy in the long run to maintain and raise the level of welfare already attained.

## Great Britain

Whenever the Labor Party has been in power, numerous measures to strengthen labor unions have been enacted. The Party has always insisted that workers be treated with "proper respect for their dignity," that they are not just "hired hands to be manipulated at work," and that they must have participatory control over their working lives.

Thus, Labor governments have encouraged aggressive unionism to get the "unearned income" (interest, rent, profit) of the capitalists and to gain control not only over wages but also over wage differentials among workers, over hours worked, hirings, promotions, layoffs, and firings, the organization of work, and more. As a result, British labor unions since World War II have accumulated enormous power, usually at the local level. And these local unions have preferred to make gains through bargaining rather than through participation in management.

Critics have charged that union militancy has contributed to slow economic growth by retarding productivity growth. They have pointed to numerous make-work rules, high absenteeism, sloppy work, ubiquitous sabotage, and incessant strikes as the real reason for "the British disease." (Indeed, in the 1970s, British managers spent about 50 percent of their time dealing with local labor disputes, about 10 times as much as their American or West German counterparts.)

## Sweden

As was noted in an earlier section, collective bargaining in Sweden is carried on at the national level between an Employers' Confederation and a Trade Union Confederation. In addition, however, a 1977 Law on Codetermination in Working Life assures workers of a significant amount of decision-making power at the level of the shop floor. In each plant, workers elect a **work council** that has the legal right to be informed and consulted on company affairs. The work council can confine itself to expressing its opinions, or it can compel management to negotiate

---

[5]*The Wall Street Journal,* April 18, 1985, p. 1.

on any subject of interest until the workers' consent is obtained. Pertinent subjects include decisions on working hours, methods of pay, shop rules, safety conditions. They include fringe benefits and vacation schedules, matters of hiring, firing, layoff. They include the classification of workers and their transfer among tasks or plants. They even extend to plant closings, company production and investment plans, mergers, and manpower training. Observers note that work councils have significantly reduced labor-management tensions and have improved mutual understanding, but they have also slowed down managerial decision making considerably.

In addition, Swedish workers have attempted to extend their powers by taking on the stockholders themselves. In 1975, a prominent trade union economist, Rudolph Meidner, formulated a plan through which workers, via their trade unions, would gain ownership of the means of production—an approach he considered vastly superior to workers gaining such control via governmental nationalization. As he saw it, workers can trust their trade unions to defend their interests; as the Soviet and East European experience had shown, they cannot trust their government to do so. In fact, the **Meidner Plan,** as it came to be called, was adopted by the Swedish Trade Union Confederation (LO) in 1976, and it became part of the Social Democratic Party platform in 1979. According to the plan, all companies with 50 or more employees would be forced to capitalize 20 percent of their annual pretax profit in the form of a new stock issue that would be handed to a union-controlled **wage earners' fund.** Over an estimated period of, perhaps, 6 years, the funds would come to gain effective control of 75 percent of all enterprises and over 20 years would come to hold the majority of all outstanding stock and would wrest company control from the original stockholders.

Opposition to the plan was fierce, so much so that in 1976 the Social Democrats, led by Olof Palme, lost their first election since 1932. (Among other things, critics noted, the plan would penalize the most innovative and successful companies: Stockholders owning the most profitable companies would lose control over their companies the fastest.)

Nevertheless, a watered-down version of the Meidner Plan was in place by the mid-1980s: Instead of one wage earners' fund per company, five regional funds were established. They are administered by boards containing a majority of union representatives but a minority of others. Each year, the funds receive the proceeds of a special profits and wage tax, which are invested in equities. No fund, however, is allowed to acquire more than 8 percent of a single corporation's stock. Thus, the five funds as a group cannot acquire more than 40 percent of a given corporation's stock.

## West Germany

The most significant feature of labor relations in West Germany was created by a series of **codetermination laws.** Some of these laws created work councils, as in Sweden. Others were designed to put workers representatives in the corporate boardroom.

In German corporations, stockholders elect *supervisory boards,* which, in turn, appoint and supervise corporate managers. A 1951 law affected the mining, iron, and steel industries; it gave 50 percent of all seats on these boards to labor union representatives. A 1952 amendment extended the law to all corporations and gave labor 33 percent of supervisory board seats. Finally, in 1976, the labor directors were increased to 50 percent in all corporations with over 2,000 employees.

Some labor critics of this supposedly pro-labor approach have, however, argued that the codetermination laws were a trap, not a beachhead. They have seen labor become part of management and, thus, having been paralyzed at the bargaining table (because labor sits on both sides of it). Indeed, examples abound. In major steel negotiations in 1978, for example, the labor directors sided with management and ruled *against* the steelworkers' demand for a 35-hour work week.

## Japan

Unlike those in Great Britain, business-labor relations in Japan are anything but adversarial. Although a quarter of Japanese workers are union members, the unions are *cooperating* with management to produce a hardworking and disciplined labor force. The unions are company unions; their life is embedded in a universally accepted framework of thinking that looks to the *paternalistic family* as a model for business-labor relations. The head of the business firm is seen as the father— not a tyrannical but a benevolent father—who is responsible for the well-being of his family. The workers are viewed as loyal and obedient children. Each is tied to the other in a web of mutual obligations.

This unique system of business-labor relations (called *nenkō seido*) rests on three pillars: employment security, compensation, and promotion.

**Employment Security.**   About a third of the Japanese labor force enjoys guaranteed lifetime employment in large industrial enterprises (a situation not unlike the tenure system for professors at American universities). Typically, companies recruit workers directly from schools, provide them with on-the-job training, weed them out during a trial period, and then guarantee lifetime employment to the remainder. These permanent employees of a company tend to be the cyclically justifiable minimum, however. Large companies provide themselves with flexibility by subcontracting a part of their work to numerous small-scale firms (which do not have the kind of arrangement noted here and which bear the brunt of business-cycle downswings). In addition, large firms hire numerous temporary workers on a casual basis. Finally, as business conditions change, companies shift their lifetime workers among company divisions, possibly retraining them repeatedly. Given their internalized cultural values, Japanese workers accept such changes willingly (unlike their British or American counterparts, who would be out on strike in no time at all). Close-Up 14.2, "Guaranteed Employment in Japan," tells more of the story. But note: Most of the workers favored by lifetime employment are male; most of those not so favored, female.

**Compensation.**  The wages of workers are determined by a number of factors: Length of service and age play a dominant role, while time spent, the intensity of work, output produced, and level of education and skill play minor roles only. As within the family, age is accorded great respect; it is also preferred as a compensation criterion because it is an objective, publicly known piece of information and leaves no room for arbitrary discrimination (as, for example, payment according to ability easily might). The weak emphasis on performance-related criteria (such as paying workers by the piece or giving managers a percentage of profit) also reflects a cultural abhorrence of shaming individuals for personal mistakes (as low hourly ouput or annual company losses may appear to be).

In addition to the basic wage, Japanese lifetime workers receive fringe benefits vastly exceeding in scope those of American or West European workers. Many of these benefits, in fact, incorporate those provided by *governments* in other countries. This accounts for the relatively low tax burden in Japan noted earlier (28 percent of GDP versus 51 percent in Sweden) and the description of Japan as a land of **welfare corporatism** (because the private business corporation takes on many of the functions of the welfare state).

Consider some of the fringe benefits revealed by a survey of Japan's 1,000 largest firms:

1. Some 83 percent of the firms provided rent-subsidized company housing for married workers, some 91 percent for unmarried workers. (One is again reminded of similar faculty housing at American universities.)
2. Most companies provide numerous other types of subsidized goods: food service at work, transportation, discount stores, medical care, savings plans, cultural and recreational facilities.
3. Most companies pay a semi-annual bonus of about 25 percent of regular wages. (This is designed to elicit worker interest in company growth enhanced by high-quality work.)
4. Almost half of all companies provide additional training for those who want to advance their skills.
5. All companies provide generous retirement pay. (There is a tendency to underpay the young and overpay the old. This provides an additional incentive for workers to stay with a given company for life and give that company their best. It explains in part the unusually low rates of absenteeism and labor turnover and the rarity of strikes in Japan.)

**Promotion.**  As they advance in age, the lifetime employees can expect that they will also advance in authority. As experience and skills accumulate, promotions are sure to come. This helps explain the high degrees of work motivation and work satisfaction reported. Indeed, unlike anywhere else in the world, the distinction between working time and private time is blurred, because Japanese workers do not view work as a punishing routine to be escaped as soon as possible.

## Reversals

In recent years, some capitalist countries have experienced reversals in the trends described in this chapter so far. Voters have become disenchanted with the policies of Big Government and Big Labor alike, which have failed to fulfill promises of full employment, price stability, and rapid increases in real incomes for all. Accordingly, voters have elected conservative governments determined to put an end to nationalization, to shrink the welfare state, and to clip the power of labor unions. Consider the 1976 election of Thorbjorn Fälldin in Sweden, the 1979 election of Margaret Thatcher in Great Britain, the 1986 election of Jacques Chirac in France. Let us focus on the British example.

## The British Example

By the 1970s, almost everyone agreed that the British economy was in shambles. Consider some of the titles of books appearing at the time: *Why England Sleeps* (John Cockcroft), *The Stagnant Society* (Michael Shanks), *Can Britain Survive?* (D. E. Bland and K. W. Watkins), *Slow Growth in Britain* (Wilfred Beckerman), *The British Disease* (George C. Allen), and *The Future That Doesn't Work: Social Democracy's Failures in Britain* (R. Emmett Tyrrell, Jr., ed.) Journal articles at the time were no more complimentary; for example: "Is the British Sickness Curable?" (*Fortune,* May 1974), and "Why Nothing Works in Britain" (*Business Week,* February 1975).

In May 1979, Margaret Thatcher (Biography 14.3), leader of the Conservatives, won a decisive victory. She proceeded forthwith to reverse Labor Party policies.

**Privatization.** Large numbers of government enterprises, generally viewed as badly managed and technically inefficient, were sold to private buyers. Among others, the denationalization affected the iron and steel industry and long-distance trucking. It included such well-known enterprises as British Aerospace, British Airways, British Telecom, and Rolls Royce. The government also sold a million publicly owned rental apartments to their occupants and encouraged private home and stock ownership via tax breaks. And it turned inner-city redevelopment programs over to private developers and away from labor-dominated local governments.

**Shrinking the Welfare State.** The government proceeded to defuse the "social security time bomb" by shrinking government spending and taxes. A sweeping review of the National Health Service (scandalized by run-down facilities, equipment shortages, and long waiting lists even for the desperately ill) led to plans for (1) quintupling the role of private health care and (2) putting an end to the principle of free health care for all. And the government moved to control runaway health care costs by ordering competitive bids for hospital cleaning, laundry, and catering services.

**Putting a Leash on Labor.** The power of labor unions (which were blamed for runaway cost-push inflation and widespread inefficiency) was considerably reduced. The defeat of a 1984–85 coal miners' strike was symbolic of the new era. Thus, new legislation required unions to use secret ballots when electing officials and before calling a strike. It also restricted picketing, outlawed sympathy strikes by those not involved in a dispute, and more. It gave government the power to sequester

## CLOSE-UP 14.1

## Team Work in Sweden

Critics have blamed generous income maintenance payments and high marginal tax rates for the fact that Swedish enterprises face the world's highest rates of labor turnover and absenteeism. Whatever the reason, in 1974, the Volvo Car Corporation decided to fight the problem once and for all. It built a new plant at Kalmar, specifically designed to make life more pleasant for the workers and, eventually, to create a labor force that was stable, well-trained, and highly motivated. This would, in turn, the argument went, yield more and higher-quality cars per labor hour.

The Kalmar plant dispensed with Henry Ford's notorious assembly line along which thousands of highly specialized workers perform the same task over and over again as cars move by them at a predetermined speed. The new plant was constructed with many separate rooms, each with a separate entrance and large windows to the world outside. Old union job classifications were abolished, along with the common practice at conventional plants of workers standing idly by while waiting for a fellow worker with the "proper" classification to perform a narrowly specified task. Instead, all workers were treated as interchangeable, and each room was given to a *team* of 15 to 25 workers who were made jointly responsible for performing, in a specified time, a broadly defined task, such as electric wiring, door assembly, fitting upholstery, or installing an exhaust system. In each room, there might be 60 different things to do to finish the assigned task, and workers were free to decide how to do it and who did what and when. (This also reduced the need for lower-level management, such as foremen.) Once the task was done, the car would move on to the next team, being carried about the plant on computer-controlled trolleys.

Given a greater variety of work and greater responsibility, Volvo figured, workers would have a chance to be creative as well. They would be happier at work and be less likely to quit or pretend to be sick. (Indeed, the Kalmar plant was designed to improve the workers' mood by being airy, light, and quiet; and each team's work room had easy access to nearby saunas and lounges, complete with overstuffed chairs, coffee, and telephones.) In addition, the absence of any one worker forced the remaining team members to work harder, so there was social pressure for everyone to be there and do his or her fair share.

It is not surprising that the Kalmar plant has had a steady stream of visitors from all over the world. Here are some of the early reactions:

*Peugeot:* No chance whatsoever that the experiment will be emulated. Kalmar's investment as well as operating costs are 30 percent higher than those at a conventional plant in France.

*General Motors:* No desire to copy. The American Lordstown, Ohio, plant can produce 400,000 cars per year; Kalmar 30,000.

*Ford:* The experiment will at best have a gradual impact in America.

*A group of American autoworkers:* We do not like it at all. Team work requires constant attention. On the assembly line, one can do a routine job and daydream, blocking out the drudgery of work.

Yet, in the long run, Volvo's gamble paid off. Productivity increased sharply. By 1987, Volvo was constructing another plant at Uddevalla, taking the team concept to its ultimate conclusion: Each team would assemble a *complete* car by itself.

Note: The Japanese have long used a similar approach to motivating workers. (As an unbelieving visitor recently reported, when the buzzer sounded to indicate the end of the working day at a Japanese auto plant, the workers went to a nearby room to play Japanese chess. Could one even imagine a similar scene in the United States?) As it turns out, the Japanese have brought the team approach to America via the recent Toyota-GM venture in Fremont, California. In no time at all, the new Japanese managers took workers previously described as "difficult and sloppy" and persuaded them to produce top-quality cars in teams. By 1987, the plant produced the same number of cars with 2,500 workers that GM had produced with 5,000 workers.

General Motors, meanwhile, persuaded the United Auto Workers to give up rigid job classifications in exchange for greater employment security. At its plant in Lansing, Michigan, the team concept was introduced as well. Workers were forced to rotate jobs within a team to fight off blue-collar blues; they could also transfer to other teams to broaden their skills. In the mid-1980s, similar changes were being made at Chrysler plants, at the Xerox Corporation, and at the National Steel Corporation. (In the latter case, the labor hours per ton of steel were dramatically reduced from over 5 to 4, with a further reduction to 3 likely.) On the other hand, Ford workers went on strike in 1988 to protest the company's attempt to introduce "Japanese-style work practices."

*Sources: The New York Times,* March 1, 1977, pp. 1 and 36; March 24, 1978, pp. A1 and D3; June 23, 1987, pp. D1 and 5; December 29, 1987, pp. D1 and 5; and February 14, 1988, p. F7.

## CLOSE-UP 14.2

## Guaranteed Employment in Japan

Large Japanese firms must cope with economic unheavals as severe as their American and West European competitors, yet they do not resort to layoffs. How do they do it?

The story of Toray Industries is instructive. Ever since 1970, this leading producer of synthetic fibers was faced with rapidly declining demand due to a variety of factors, including competition from China, Korea, and Taiwan as well as the existence of a "voluntary" export quota with respect to the United States. An American firm would have cut production and laid off workers—not so here.

First, the company sought and received governmental permission to form a "depression cartel" with its domestic competitors. The cartel arranged a joint cut in production and increase in prices to maintain profits and buy time for longer-range solutions. Second, the company instituted a policy of not replacing retiring workers. Third, the company arranged for the transfer of workers to different in-house jobs. Thus, a factory worker went to the sales department, an engineer into public relations. (Japanese unions give management complete flexibility in this regard; they do not establish narrow job descriptions and insist on maintaining them.) Fourth, the company transferred workers to affiliated companies in the 120-company Toray group (which included spinners and weavers and hotels and travel agencies, for example). Fifth, the company increased its research and development effort mightily, seeking to find alternative uses for its synthetic fiber technology. Eventually, the effort transformed the synthetic fiber company completely. By 1987, the company was producing polyester film for audio and video tape and floppy disks; carbon-polyacrylonitrile fiber resistant to fatigue, corrosion, and radar signals (and sought by the aerospace industry); optical fibers and soft contact lenses; imitation suede, silk, and mink; membranes for water desalinators and artificial kidneys; feed additives for livestock; and a drug (beta-interferon) for the treatment of melanoma and hepatitis.

Between 1970 and 1987, employment in the original synthetic fiber plant fell from 25,000 to 11,000; yet, not a single worker was laid off!

Note: Similar stories abound. A leading producer of electric appliances, the Matsushita Electric Industrial Company, for example, used to produce color TVs, microwave equipment, refrigerators, washing machines, and VCRs. When the VCR boom ended, it switched to producing copiers, semiconductors, optical memory disks, personal computers, and robotics.

*Source: Fortune,* July 13, 1987, pp. 84–88 and 372–74.

## BIOGRAPHY 14.1    François Mitterrand

François Maurice Marie Mitterrand (1916–      ) was born in Jarnac, France. He studied at the University of Paris and served in the military during World War II, was taken prisoner, but escaped back to France where he was active in the resistance movement. Toward the end of the war, he became secretary-general of the Organization for P.O.W.s, War Victims, and Refugees. He was elected to the National Assembly repeatedly between 1946 and 1978 and held numerous governmental positions (Minister for Ex-Servicemen, Minister for Overseas Territories, Minister of the Interior, Mayor of Château-Chinon, and many more). In 1971, he became First Secretary of the Socialist Party. In 1981, he was elected President of France, ending 23 years of conservative rule reaching back to Charles de Gaulle.

At the time, there was great popular enthusiasm about France's tilt toward socialism, but all that changed within a few years. As promises of full employment, price stability, and rapid income growth failed to materialize, Mitterrand's portraits disappeared from the union halls and 1984 polls rated him as the most unpopular president since World War II. Before long, strikes erupted all over the country; 10,000 coal miners marched on Paris, and truck drivers created a nationwide traffic jam, mocking the failed government's policy of raising everyone's income by chanting: "Let them eat rats."

Mitterrand, who had once talked of the "cruelty of the forces of capitalism" and had empathized with "men and women sacrificed to the law of profit," turned to once reviled business executives to "modernize France." As he put it, "We did not recognize the realities of economics; we could order the economy to disburse, but not to produce." And a 1984 government spokesman added: "This is our hardest hour, the time of realistic awakening. . . . All the illusions were shared by the directors of the Socialist Party. We were carried along by them and there was a departure from the laws of reality."

By 1984, the Communists left the government, and two years later, the electorate turned against the socialist experiment. While Jacques Chirac, a conservative, became Prime Minister and took over the often unpopular tasks of day-to-day government, Mitterrand presided over everyone in kingly aloofness. He abandoned ideology and became content with "softening capitalism's harsh face." In 1988, on a platform promising a market economy "with social justice," he was reelected. Soon, he named free-market advocate Michel Rocard to be Prime Minister. Rocard continued the privatization of state-owned companies in preparation of a unified Europe in 1992. Mitterrand's critics accused him of "changing his politics like he changes his shirts."

*Sources: The International Who's Who, 1982–83* (London: Europa Publications, 1982), p. 902; *The New York Times,* December 26, 1984, p. A8; *The Wall Street Journal,* March 9, 1988, pp. 1 and 21, and May 11, 1988, p. 7.

## BIOGRAPHY 14.2    Gunnar Myrdal

Karl Gunnar Myrdal (1898–1987) was born in Gustafs, a small village in central Sweden where his father was a railroad worker. He studied law and economics at Stockholm University, so impressing his teachers that he was named to the faculty upon graduation. In addition to teaching, he became a government advisor on financial and social questions and achieved world renown through an investigation for the Carnegie Corporation on the status of the American Negroes, published as *An American Dilemma: The Negro Problem and Modern Democracy* (1944). Eventually, this book helped to destroy the "separate but equal" racial policy in the United States. (The book literally became a footnote to history—the famous footnote 11 to the U.S. Supreme Court's 1954 ruling that segregation in public schools was unconstitutional. Listing sources to prove that schools could not be "separate but equal" because separation implied and enforced inferiority, the Court cited Myrdal's book.) After the Second World War, Myrdal held numerous government and United Nations positions, and he published many books on macroeconomics, international trade, and economic development, including the three-volume *Asian Drama: An Inquiry into the Poverty of Nations* (1968). In 1974, he was the co-winner of the Nobel Prize in Economics (with Friedrich von Hayek, Biography 6.2). His wife, Alva Myrdal, a leading feminist, pacifist, and diplomat, was the co-winner of the 1982 Nobel Peace Prize for her efforts to promote world disarmament.

Just as he did in the United States, Myrdal left his mark on Sweden, where he drafted many economic and social programs that made him into one of the leading architects of the welfare state. Myrdal faced head-on those critics (like Hayek) who warned that the welfare state was but the first step toward socialist tyranny. Said Myrdal:[a]

> *In the Western countries, one of the least informed and least intelligent controversies of our time has concerned the question whether we should have a "free" or a "planned" economy. This controversy has always been unrealistic and is becoming ever more so. . . . People generally tend to keep themselves unaware of how far they have proceeded from a "free" economy; how very much regulatory intervention by organized society there actually is in their countries, and important national economic planning of a pragmatic, non-comprehensive type has in fact become. . . . Anybody who makes a plea for the ideals of a "free" economy and . . . who from these goes on to characterize what we are indulging in as "creeping socialism" and warns that we might be on the "road to serfdom," can be sure of a sympathetic audience. . . . While the actual development in our countries has continually been towards more and more planning, the anti-planning attitudes have remained respectable and popular ones. . . . My value premises are the long-inherited ones of liberty, equality, and brotherhood. . . . The trend towards economic planning has broadly implied an ever fuller realization of these ideals.*

Myrdal was proud of the fact that poverty and slums had disappeared from Sweden, and he was scornful of suggestions that affluence and security had made Swedes bored, depressed, frustrated, and even suicidal. "This is a fantastic lie," he said. "Why in hell should the protection of your life from economic disasters and from bad health, opening education for young people, pensions for old people, nursery care for children—why should that make you frustrated?" But he did acknowledge that the welfare state had its problems: The high rates of labor turnover and absenteeism and the large underground economy, he said, were the result of generous social services combined with high marginal tax rates that were turning Swedes "into a nation of hustlers" and were corrupting such traditional values as honesty (to get ahead on long waiting lists or escape taxes).

---

[a]Gunnar Myrdal, *Beyond the Welfare State* (New Haven, CT: Yale University Press, 1960), pp. 3, 11–13, and 15–16.

*Sources: The International Who's Who, 1982–83* (London: Europa Publications, 1982), p. 937; *The New York Times,* October 3, 1976, p. 6, and May 18, 1987, pp. A1 and D14; Kurt Dopfer, "In Memoriam: Gunnar Myrdal's Contribution to Institutional Economics," *Journal of Economic Issues,* March 1988, pp. 227–31.

## BIOGRAPHY 14.3  Margaret Thatcher

Margaret Hilda Thatcher (1925–    ) was born in Grantham, England. She was educated at Somerville College, Oxford, worked as a research chemist, then a lawyer. In 1959, she became a member of Parliament, eventually Secretary of State for Education and Science and leader of the Conservative Party. In 1979, she was elected Prime Minister. She was reelected in 1983 and again in 1987. The feat of serving three consecutive terms in that position was unprecedented in the 20th century.

Thatcher's announced goal was to turn Great Britain from the "sick man of Europe" into a "property-owning democracy." As she put it, "My long-term goal is to see an England free of socialism." In 1987, she unveiled a "radical manifesto" announcing her determination to apply the free market principles of her economic policy to education, health, housing, inner-city development, and other aspects of the welfare state. Her goals included the financing of schools according to their ability to attract students, partial privatization of the National Health Service, and the transfer of rental housing and urban rehabilitation programs from government to the private sector. This would bring about, she argued, a more cost-effective delivery of social services. Government, she said, ought to operate for the convenience of the tax-paying "consumers" of its services, not for that of the "producers," the millions of workers on government payrolls. Thatcher's critics have countered that she was dismantling the welfare state and promoting "an ethos of sleazy selfishness at the heart of what was heretofore one of the world's most humane, altruistic cultures."

*Sources: The International Who's Who, 1982–83* (London: Europa Publications, 1982), p. 1313; *The New York Times,* May 13, 1987, p. A3; *The New York Times Magazine,* May 31, 1987, pp. 18–82.

## Summary

1. Many capitalist countries throughout the world have one thing in common: a significant degree of government intervention in the economy. Inspired by socialist thought, this government action is often designed to achieve greater equality in wealth, income, and economic power. Yet, unlike in Eastern Europe, the political parties that articulate such demands in countries such as France, Great Britain, Sweden, West Germany, or Japan are committed to the maintenance of political democracy. Given the stress on democracy, it is not surprising that there exists a great diversity in the approaches different governments take when they intervene in the economy.

2. The nature of governmental planning, for example, differs widely. It ranges from the fairly elaborate indicative planning of the French that uses input-output tables to traditional Keynesian macroeconomic policies coupled with numerous regulations at the micro level.

3. Just as there are major variations in governmental planning institutions, so there are considerable differences in policies designed to achieve chosen goals. Some countries, notably France and Great Britain, have attempted to do so by the *nationalization* of privately owned resources and a corresponding expansion of the public enterprise sector.

4. Many more countries have taken the route of heavy taxing and government spending, designed to create a *welfare state* in which government pledges to protect people not only from the rigors of the marketplace but, quite literally, from all types of misfortunes that might befall them on their lifelong travel from cradle to grave.

5. In many capitalist countries, governments have, in addition, taken steps to strengthen the hands of workers vis-á-vis business and to promote *industrial democracy*. Some governments have promoted aggressive unionism; others have strengthened labor through codetermination laws. The Japanese system of paternalistic business-labor relations, however, is unique.

6. As one would expect in democracies, trends described in this chapter are not necessarily permanent. As some political parties are thrown out of office and replaced by others, institutions are changed and policies reversed. Great Britain's shift from Labor Party to Conservative Party rule in recent years provides the most spectacular example.

## Key Terms

codetermination laws
consumer cooperatives
democratic socialism
imperative planning
indicative planning
industrial democracy
investment reserve

Meidner Plan
social democracies
wage earners' fund
welfare corporatism
welfare state
work council

## Questions and Problems

1. **Mr. A:** "The work of the French planning commissions described in this chapter provides an ideal opportunity for business collusion with respect to investment, output, exports, and so on."
   **Ms. B:** "Of course. The essence of French planning is the planning of each industry's activities by its own members who act as a cartel, but with the government sitting in on the monopoly game."
      Comment.

2. With the help of sources such as those listed in this chapter's "Selected Readings," set up a table comparing *labor unemployment rates* for

France, Great Britain, Sweden, West Germany, Japan, and the United States during any post–World War II 20-year period.

3. Review the answer to question 2. Can you see any problem with the international comparisons made?

4. With the help of sources such as those listed in this chapter's "Selected Readings," set up a table comparing *real GNP growth rates* for France, Great Britain, Sweden, West Germany, Japan, and the United States during any post–World War II five-year period.

5. Review the answer to question 4. Can you see any problem with the international comparisons made?

6. Once again review the answer to question 4. Can you think of any reason why even the intertemporal comparisons of growth rates for a *given* country may be problematic?

7. With the help of sources such as those listed in the "Selected Readings" of chapters 7, 11, or 14, compare the *absolute GNP values* among selected capitalist and socialist countries for any given year.

8. Review the answer to question 7. Can you see any definitional problem with the international comparisons made?

9. Review the answers to questions 7 and 8. Can you think of any reason why the interspatial comparisons of national outputs may remain problematic even after the definitional adjustments noted in answer 8 have been made?

10. With the help of sources such as those listed in the "Selected Readings," prepare statistics on the *post-tax income distribution* among households in France, Great Britain, Japan, Sweden, West Germany, and the United States for any recent time period.

## Selected Readings

Allen, G. C. *A Short Economic History of Modern Japan* (New York: St. Martin's Press, 1983).

Childs, Marquis W. *Sweden: The Middle Way on Trial* (New Haven, CT: Yale University Press, 1980). A critical discussion of the Swedish compromise between individualism and collectivism.

Cole, Robert E. *Japanese Blue-Collar: The Changing Tradition* (Berkeley, CA: University of California Press, 1971). Analyzes the unique system of industrial relations in Japan.

Crosland, C. A. R. *The Future of Socialism* (New York: Schocken, 1963).

Crosland, C. A. R. *The Conservative Enemy* (London: Jonathan Cape, 1962). Presents the Labor Party view favoring the welfare state.

Drucker, Peter F. *The Unseen Revolution: How Pension Plan Socialism Came to America* (New York: Harper and Row, 1976). Argues that socialism arrives through the back door when worker pension funds acquire corporate shares.

Eatwell, John. *Whatever Happened to Britain? The Economics of Decline* (New York: Oxford University Press, 1982). Sees the freedon of the marketplace as a "deadly trap" and argues for exerting stronger government control over "destabilizing market forces."

*Economic Report of the President* (Washington, D.C.: U.S. Government Printing Office). Published annually in February; contains U.S. as well as comparative international statistics.

Estrin, Saul, and Peter Holmes. *French Planning in Theory and Practice* (Boston: Allen and Unwin, 1983). Surveys the literature on indicative planning.

Fleisher, Frederic. *The New Sweden: The Challenge of a Disciplined Democracy* (New York: McKay, 1967). A sympathetic description.

Garson, G. David, ed. *Worker Self-Management in Industry: The West European Experience* (New York: Praeger, 1977). Discusses the increasing power of workers on the shop floor and on the corporate board of directors.

Huntford, Roland. *The New Totalitarians* (New York: Stein and Day, 1972). Argues that Aldous Huxley's *Brave New World* and George Orwell's *1984* have arrived— in Sweden's welfare state.

Johnson, Chalmers. *MITI and the Japanese Miracle* (Stanford, CA: Stanford University Press, 1982).

Knott, Jack K. *Managing the German Economy* (Lexington, MA: D.C. Heath, 1981).

Kuisel, Richard F. *Capitalism and the State of Modern France* (New York: Cambridge University Press, 1981). A historical survey.

Laidler, Harry W. *History of Socialism* (New York: Thomas Y. Crowell, 1968). A detailed description of socialist movements in many lands, including France, Germany, Great Britain, Sweden, and more. Contains an excellent bibliography.

Lundberg, Erik. "The Rise and Fall of the Swedish Model," *Journal of Economic Literature,* March 1985, pp. 1–36. A general survey.

Meade, James E. *The Theory of Indicative Planning* (Manchester, England: Manchester University Press, 1970). A superb theoretical work, written by the 1977 co-winner of the Nobel Prize in Economics.

Organization for Economic Cooperation and Development (OECD), *Economic Survey* (Paris), *National Accounts of OECD Countries* (Paris). Numerous studies of individual member countries, published annually. (In 1988, there were 25 members, including France, Great Britain, Japan, Sweden, West Germany, and the United States.)

Pollard, Sidney. *The Wasting of the British Economy* (New York: St. Martin's, 1982).

Schollhammer, Hans. "National Economic Planning and Business Decisions: The French Experience," *California Management Review,* Winter 1969, pp. 74–88. Based on interviews of about 400 firms; identifies positive and negative effects of indicative planning.

Shonfield, Andrew. *Modern Capitalism* (London: Oxford University Press, 1965). A perceptive study of government planning in many countries.

United Nations, *Statistical Yearbook*. A compilation of data submitted by member countries.

U.S. Bureau of the Census. *Statistical Abstract of the United States* (Washington, D.C.: U.S. Government Printing Office). Published annually; a final section usually contains comparative international statistics.

Wilson, Thomas, and Dorothy J. Wilson. *The Political Economy of the Welfare State* (London: Allen and Unwin, 1982). A thorough examination of the British welfare system.

## Computer Program

The SYSTEMS personal computer diskette that accompanies this book contains one program of interest to this chapter:

Program 14, "Government Intervention: Variations on a Theme" provides 12 multiple-choice questions about Chapter 14, along with immediate responses to incorrect answers.

# PART 4

# *Special Topic*

## 15.  *The Legacy of Marx*

This final part of the book summarizes the teachings of Karl Marx and explores a fascinating puzzle about their relationship to the world's economic systems today.

# CHAPTER 15

# *The Legacy of Marx*

The doctrines of Karl Marx (Biography 15.1), it is often alleged, now dominate a major part of the globe. Indeed, Soviet leaders from Lenin to Stalin, from Khrushchev to Gorbachev, have called themselves *Marxists*. So have Mao Zedong and Deng Xiaoping, Ho Chi Minh and Pol Pot, Castro and Tito, and many more. The common claim by so many—all of whom are seemingly engaged in constructing their society "along Marxist lines"—leaves us, however, with a puzzle: How can the leaders of societies with institutions and policies as diverse as those found in Pol Pot's Cambodia, Castro's Cuba, Mitterrand's France, Tito's Yugoslavia, or even Mugabe's Zimbabwe *all* be implementing the blueprint of socialism supposedly laid out by the identical man? And whom are we to believe when these same leaders accuse one another of having misunderstood or even betrayed what the great prophet has had to say? This last chapter of the book is intended to answer these questions. We begin by looking at the teachings of Marx.

## The Teachings of Marx

We turn first to a key feature of Marxism that derives from the writings of the German philosopher G. W. F. Hegel (whose ideas dominated thinking at the University of Berlin when Marx attended it).

### The Dialectical Approach

As he turned to study the world around him, Marx adapted Hegel's **dialectical approach.** This method of study rejects the uncritical acceptance of existing empirical *appearances* and seeks to discover inner "contradictions" that hold the key to understanding the *essence* of things. It holds that the world cannot be understood when seen merely as a static collection of things; true understanding requires discovery of the dynamic process that makes all things continually evolve. All things are seen to contain inner pressures and stresses, inherent conflicts, opposing forces, or what Marx liked to call inner "contradictions." These inner forces become a driving force that produces eternal change, metamorphosis, development, or "revolution." (When reading Marx, it is important to remember that *contradictions* do not denote "logical impossibilities" but "inner tension," while *revolution* usually refers to a metamorphosis brought about by contradictions and not necessarily to fighting in the streets.)

Consider, for example, any isolated observable fact, such as a tadpole swimming in a pond. An uncritical observer focuses on the outward appearance, sees it as a fixed thing, describes it in all detail perhaps, and, yet, paints a misleading picture of reality. A follower of the dialectical approach focuses on the inner essence, sees but a transitory stage of an unfolding reality, and paints a complete picture of what is being observed. True enough, the tadpole is real—the outward appearance is not a delusion. Yet, the inner essence is present as well; there are already unseen forces at work to produce development, not only quantitative growth (a bigger tadpole, perhaps), but also qualitative transformation (an inexorable change into a frog).

In the same way, the follower of the dialectical approach looks beyond the acorn to see the inner "contradictions" already at work that will produce the oak, sees the butterfly in the caterpillar and tomorrow's apple tree in today's apple blossom. Marx insisted on applying the same approach to social phenomena. Unlike what he termed the "vulgar economists" of his day (who dealt with outward appearances only), he sought to lay out the inner essence of social arrangements as well. The capitalist system of his day, for instance, was not an eternally fixed arrangement for Marx; he looked on it as he would at an apple blossom—destined to become apple and apple tree.

This approach, it should be noted, implied for Marx the supreme ethical principle of **historical justification.** According to this principle, no fixed ethical conclusions can be drawn concerning any given social phenomenon. In an ever evolving world, the very thing that is acceptable and even necessary at one stage of history can be unacceptable after "revolution" (generated by inner tension, and not by a coup from without) has ushered in the next stage of history.

## Philosophic Materialism

Marx also placed himself in the tradition of **philosophic materialism,** which views the material world as the ultimate reality and rejects the notion that spiritual forces could be behind the world perceptible to our senses. (This stand clearly must not be confused with the popular meaning of materialism that pictures greedy people preoccupied with material possessions.) To Marx, this philosophic view implied a humanistic ethics: Ethical norms were not derived from God, but were derivable by thinking about human happiness—what made people happy was "good"; what made them unhappy was "bad."

In addition, Marx also concluded that human thinking and behavior were molded by their material environment, the significance of which we all see presently.

## A Theory of History

Using the dialectical approach and based on the materialist assumptions just noted, Marx developed a sweeping vision of the entire history of mankind, reaching back into the distant past and forward to the indefinite future. He was not interested in describing given states of being (tadpoles) but in explaining the continual transformation of societies from one era to the next (tadpoles becoming frogs).

The ultimate causes of all social and political changes, he argued, lay not in the minds of men, in their increasing insight into eternal truth and justice, but in *changes* in the mode of production and exchange. Technological changes changed the way people were organized for production and, ultimately, changed their "thinking" (a term used in the broadest possible sense to include art, law, politics, science, and other products of the mind).

As Marx saw it, the process of social change always involved a **class struggle** between social groups internally held together by a common ideology, such as devotion to existing institutions or an interest in changing existing institutions. Marx argued that he had, thus, discovered a *scientific law* of historical change, and he was most interested in applying it to his own times.

In the mid-19th century, he argued, two social classes were pitted against one another: the capitalist class or **bourgeoisie,** which owned all the natural and capital resources, and the **proletariat,** which had only labor to sell. In appearance, the workers were free; in essence they were not. In order to live, they *had* to sell their labor to the capitalists. The latter used their economic power to force workers (a) into producing much more than their own subsistence and (b) into handing the surplus product above subsistence over to the capitalists. As a result, the bourgeoisie accumulated ever more capital, but it was also creating the weapon of its own destruction—a proletariat that was growing in size and unity while becoming ever more impoverished. Ultimately, the proletariat, overworked and underpaid, would expropriate the bourgeoisie. Thus, Marx confidently predicted, the inner forces at work in capitalism would *inevitably,* regardless of the will of men, destroy capitalism and replace it with communism.

## The Labor Theory of Value

Marx did more than present a grand vision of historical change. He also worked out an intricately detailed argument to support his vision of capitalism's doom. His labor theory of value was part of this argument.

Marx distinguished three types of value: one subjective type and two objective types. First, he talked of **use value,** the satisfaction or utility subjectively experienced when a person consumes a good. This value cannot be measured and presumably differs from person to person and from one time to another. According to Marx, use value is the only type of value that exists in simple societies wherein people produce articles only for their own, direct use. Marx called such articles **products.**

In complex societies wherein people engage in a division of labor, however, people mostly produce articles with a view toward market exchange, to be used by others. Marx called these articles **commodities.** Commodities, Marx argued, have to be capable of delivering use value or they cannot be exchanged, but they also have two types of objective values. One of these is the *market price,* the number of monetary units for which a unit of the commodity can be traded in the market, such as $2 per loaf of bread. This type of exchange value, argued Marx, is the only one of interest to the "vulgar economist," who cannot see below the surface of things and always focuses on appearance rather than essence. A second type of objective value is much more important, said Marx. It is the **true exchange value** that reflects the essence of things, *the fact that all commodities are produced with human labor.* This value, argued Marx, is determined by the labor time expended in the process of production. True exchange value, Marx argued, is frozen or congealed labor time "embodied" in a commodity.

The time in question, he said, can be objectively determined and is equal to the time *socially necessary* to produce the commodity in question. He defined **socially necessary labor time** as the time required to produce a commodity that is in demand when production occurs under "normal conditions"—using labor of average skill and average intensity and equipped with up-to-date machinery.

Thus, if it takes 1 hour of socially necessary labor (1H) to produce a loaf of bread and 10 such hours (10H) to produce a pair of shoes, the objectively correct exchange rate is 10 loaves for 1 pair of shoes because each of these quantities embodies 10H. Indeed, according to this Marxian **labor theory of value,** the true exchange value of *anything* can be measured by the socially necessary labor time required to make it. What, for example, is the true exchange value of the labor power of a man working for a day? If the man's labor power can be reproduced by providing him, say, with a loaf of bread, a sausage, a yard of cloth, and a day's worth of shelter and if these goods, in turn, require a total of 5 socially necessary labor hours for *their* production, the true exchange value of the man's labor power is 5H as well. It is, in short, the labor needed to produce the man's subsistence.

## The Theory of Exploitation

The **theory of exploitation,** according to which capitalists routinely steal part of the output produced by workers, became the next building block in the Marxian edifice. Exploitation was traced to the fact that not all of the labor socially necessary to produce a given commodity was necessary to provide the livelihood of the workers who made that commodity. Consider, Marx argued, the typical relationship between capitalists and workers. The capitalists, let us assume, own a factory full of machines, stores of raw material to be processed, as well as all kinds of consumer goods needed by workers (food, clothing, housing, and the like). The workers own nothing but their labor power. The capitalists need the workers to produce output (factories, machines, raw materials, and the like produce *nothing* by themselves);

the workers need the capitalists to make a living. A deal is struck: The workers come to the factory and process the raw materials on the machines; in return, they receive the consumer goods they so desperately need.

Marx called the structures, machines, and raw materials used up in the process of production **constant capital, c.** By Marxian reckoning, its value is measured by the socially necessary labor time embodied in it. Thus, if a factory was produced with 10,000 hours of such labor time (H) and lasts 5,000 days, letting workers use the factory for a day amounts to endowing them with constant capital worth (10,000/5,000) = 2H. Similarly, if the machines were produced with 8,000H and last 2,000 days, their use for a day amounts to additional constant capital of (8,000/2,000) = 4H. And if the raw materials used up in a day were themselves produced with 20H, the total of constant capital handed to workers comes to c = 2H + 4H + 20H = 26H (a figure that modern accountants would measure in monetary units and call depreciation and raw material expenses). According to Marx, the use of c = 26H during a day represents the use of past or "dead" labor and automatically imparts an *equal* value to the day's product, giving it a true exchange value of at least 26H.

In addition, Marx held, the capitalists "advance" to the workers consumer goods equal to the true exchange value of the workers' labor power. Calculated in the fashion noted in the previous section, this set of goods may be worth 5H per working day. Marx called this real income paid workers the **variable capital, v.** Thus, if 10 workers are hired for a day and their daily labor power is worth 5H each, they receive v = 50H (a figure that modern accountants would measure in monetary units and call wages).

Yet, argued Marx, the 10 workers in question may be made to work for 16 hours each, or a total of 160H. What, then, is the true exchange value, T, of the day's product? According to Marx, it equals the sum of "dead" and "live" labor expended during the day's production, or T = 26H + 160H = 186H in our example. Having advanced c = 26H plus v = 50H, the capitalists end up holding output worth T = 186H. Marx called the difference between (1) a commodity's true exchange value (the socially necessary dead plus live labor expended on its production) and (2) the constant plus variable capital advanced by the capitalists during its production by the term **surplus value, s.** In our example, surplus value comes to

$$s = T - (c + v) = 186H - (26H + 50H) = 110H$$

(a figure that modern accountants would measure in monetary units and call by such names as rent, interest, and profit).

The foregoing implies that we can figure the Marxian true exchange value of any commodity as

$$T = c + v + s$$

or, in our case, as

$$186\ H = 26H + 50H + 110H$$

the sum of constant capital, variable capital, and surplus value.

Marx attributed the appearance of surplus value to a built-in feature of capitalism: Because capitalists own the means of production and workers don't, capitalists can *exploit* workers by forcing them to work more hours than would be necessary to reproduce the expended labor power. In our example, a worker can produce a subsistence real income in a mere 5 hours, yet the worker is made to work 16 hours. Thus, according to Marx, 11 hours' worth of product is stolen from the worker (which accounts, in our 10-worker example, for the value of s = 110H).

Note: Marx argued that exploitation occurs in the "sphere of production" (in the factory, for example), not in the "sphere of circulation" (in the market). Thus, capitalists may pay workers in the *labor market* precisely what labor power is worth by Marxian reckoning (the value of v = 50H in our case). They may sell the output produced in the *goods market* precisely for what it is truly worth according to Marx (the value of T = 186H in our case). Yet, exploitation occurs as long as s is greater than zero. And Marx accused fellow economists who could not detect fraudulent behavior in labor or goods markets of being blinded by appearances, of missing the essence of things—of engaging in **commodity fetishism,** a tendency to focus on surface relations among commodities rather than deeper relations among men.

## The Marxian Ratios

Building further upon his argument so far, Marx defined three crucial concepts: the organic composition of capital, the rate of surplus value (or of exploitation), and the rate of profit. The **organic composition of capital** is the ratio, c/v, of constant capital to variable capital. It measures the capital intensity of production and is expected to vary among industries, as exemplified in Table 15.1. Note in the table how capitalists "advance" the same total of capital (worth 100H) in each of five industries, A to E. Industry A is least capital intensive or most labor intensive; the reverse is true for industry E.

**Table 15.1**   True Exchange Values Versus Market Prices (measured in socially necessary labor time)

| | | | | | Rate of Profit | | |
| | | | | | before equalization | after equalization | |
| | *Constant Capital,* $c$ | *Variable Capital,* $v$ | *Surplus Value,* $s$ | *True Exchange Value,* $T = c + v + s$ | $p' = \dfrac{s}{c+v}$ | $p^* = $ *average* $p'$ | *Market Price* $M = c + v + (100p^*)$ |
|---|---|---|---|---|---|---|---|
| *Industry* | *(1)* | *(2)* | *(3)* | *(4)* | *(5)* | *(6)* | *(7)* |
| A | 50 | 50 | 50 | 150 | .50 | .30 | 130 |
| B | 60 | 40 | 40 | 140 | .40 | .30 | 130 |
| C | 70 | 30 | 30 | 130 | .30 | .30 | 130 |
| D | 80 | 20 | 20 | 120 | .20 | .30 | 130 |
| E | 90 | 10 | 10 | 110 | .10 | .30 | 130 |
| Total | 500 | | 150 | 650 | | | 650 |

The **rate of surplus value** or **rate of exploitation** is the ratio, s/v, of surplus value to variable capital. In the Table 15.1 example, the ratio is 1 or 100 percent in all of the industries, which implies (as Marx put it) that workers are made to produce two hours' worth of product for every one hours' worth of product they are paid. Marx argued that this rate would become equal among industries through the migration of workers when rates diverge.

The **rate of profit** is the ratio, s/(c + v), of surplus value to the sum of constant capital plus variable capital. As Table 15.1 shows, given different organic compositions of identical capitals and identical rates of exploitation, rates of profit differ among industries. Marx argued that capital migration would equalize the rates as shown in column (6). As a result, individual market prices (equal to M = c + v + *average* s) can diverge from the exchange values (and the outward appearance can hide the inner essence postulated by Marx: that relative labor inputs explain relative exchange values). Yet, the *sum* of all exchange values always equals that of all market prices (650H in our example).

## The Marxian Tendencies

Marx wrote much about *tendencies* and when he did, he was not necessarily talking about any actual or predicted course of events. Rather, he was talking about a cause that *would* produce a given effect if it were unimpeded (but that was in fact often checked or weakened by counteracting forces). For example, Marx talked about a tendency for a declining rate of profit as well as another tendency for an increasing misery of workers. The two were not unrelated.

**The Tendency for a Declining Rate of Profit.**   Over time, argued Marx, as more and more capital is being accumulated, the organic composition of capital rises. Given a constant rate of exploitation, the rate of profit tends to decline. Indeed, this conclusion is a truism, as a review of Marx's *definition* of the profit rate indicates.

Marx defined the profit rate as $p' = s/(c+v)$, but this expression can be rewritten as

$$p' = \frac{\dfrac{s}{v}}{\dfrac{c}{v} + \dfrac{v}{v}} = \frac{\dfrac{s}{v}}{\dfrac{c}{v} + 1}$$

The numerator now equals the rate of exploitation, s/v; the denominator contains a measure of the organic composition of capital, c/v. Clearly, if s/v does not change, a rise in c/v must decrease $p'$.

All this can also be visualized with the help of Table 15.1. Let the data illustrate not differences in the organic composition of capital among industries at a given time, but changes in that composition over time, moving from row A to row E.

Given a constant ratio of s/v (columns [3] and [2]), an increase in the ratio c/v (columns [1] and [2]) is associated with a decline in the profit rate (column [5]).

There was a reason for Marx's interest in the tendency just noted: He thought it would call forth numerous reactions on the part of capitalists designed to forestall its realization. Thus, he thought, capitalists would do everything in their power to raise the rate of exploitation, s/v, by raising s or lowering v. They might raise s by lengthening the working day or increasing the intensity of work. They might lower v by reducing male workers' pay and forcing them to put wives and children to work in order to survive. Indeed, the spread of machinery would make it ever easier to employ physically weaker population groups. On the other hand, some capitalists, Marx thought, might temporarily turn back the clock and shift production to poorer countries (as from England to its colonies) where the organic composition of capital was still low, profit rates were still high, and, in addition, workers were available who were used to a lower level of living.

All these developments and more Marx greeted with joy: They would intensify the class struggle and bring closer the day of revolution!

**The Tendency for an Increasing Misery of Workers.** The forces just noted, argued Marx, would over time produce a worsening in the real income of workers, either absolutely or relative to the capitalists. In addition, workers would increasingly be crippled by the stultifying effect of routine work. The lifelong repetition of the identical trivial operation would reduce workers to mere fragments of men. Even if their pay should rise absolutely and relatively, their lot in life would grow worse.

## Marxian Economic Crises

Marx identified another reason yet for the eventual downfall of capitalism: cyclical swings in aggregate economic activity that appeared "as regularly as the comets" and which he termed "crises." He attributed the reason for these *business cycles* (as they were later to be called) to the fact that the capitalist economy was not directed by human consciousness but was instead operating "at the mercy of chance." As he saw it, numerous capitalists are separately undertaking production for market sale and are, thus, jointly allocating the nation's overall working time among the various branches of industry. If errors are made and the subsequently appearing demand does not correspond to the composition of production, *ex post* corrections have to be made: Once 2 million coats have been produced and only 1 million coats are demanded, it becomes obvious belatedly that half of the "socially necessary labor" allocated to coat production had not been socially necessary at all. Coat prices fall, the value of labor in coat making is "discounted," and labor is real-located. As Marx's collaborator, Friedrich Engels, put it, "Only through the undervaluation or overvaluation of products is it forcibly brought home to the individual commodity producers what things and what quantity of them society requires or does not require."[1] According to Marx, every five to seven years, the "crisis of

---

[1]Karl Marx, *The Poverty of Philosophy* (New York: International Publishers, 1963), p. 19.

disproportion'' goes into a violent phase. It brings about fearful devastations that, like earthquakes, cause the bourgeois society to tremble to its foundations.

Once again, however, Marx looked upon such events with glee. As he saw it, successive crises would widen in scope, become ever more universal, spread to more sectors, to more countries. Each time, more capitalists would become impoverished and join the proletariat. Fewer and fewer capitalists would own larger and larger firms. This ''centralization'' and ''concentration'' of capital would make the ultimate revolution easier and easier.

## The End of Capitalism

The inner forces at work in capitalism, argued Marx, will eventually cause its demise. On the one hand, increasing misery will incite workers to think about their fate and to join together in order to improve it. On the other hand, there will be larger and larger concentrations of capital owned by fewer and fewer people. It would be easy to expropriate the few and usher in a new era in which workers not only use the means of production jointly but own them jointly as well.

In the 1840s, Marx imagined that the end would come in the form of a violent, armed uprising that would sweep away the capitalists. Later in his life, although he never renounced the path of violence, he also contemplated the real possibility of a peaceful transformation of society, of a revolution from within. As the franchise spread, Marx looked to workers making revolution through the ballot box. He envisioned a mass movement of workers who would over the decades gain experience and theoretical insights and win the battle of *democracy*. The numerical superiority of the proletariat would turn the democratic republic into a *dictatorship of the proletariat,* but in the sense that a majority always exercises authority over the minority in a democratic state. As a ruling class, the proletariat would bring about the general conditions necessary for a noncapitalist society. But Marx envisioned a society that would maintain democracy and cherish human freedom, and he imagined that his revolution would occur first in the most advanced industrialized countries (such as Germany or Great Britain).

## The Communist Future

As Marx envisioned it, the postcapitalist phase of history would be *communism,* a classless society in which the means of production would be owned and used in common. But Marx said next to nothing beyond this generality; he refused to outline the future society's specific features or, as he put it, ''to prepare recipes for the cookshops of the future.'' In fact, Marx ridiculed the socialists of his day who spent their time spinning ideal future utopias out of their heads. He rejected as unscientific any attempt to imagine the future in detail. Marx did talk of a ''lower stage'' of communism (which Lenin later called *socialism*) in which the ''anarchy'' of the market would give way to conscious planning but the *attitudes* of workers would still be influenced by their experiences in the old society. Thus, workers would still have to be rewarded according to their contribution to production (such as hours worked) and there would still be income inequality. Eventually though, a "higher stage" of communism would arrive, which would have no defects at all. It would be an industrialized, classless, and nonexploitative society. Above all, the lower transition stage would have produced a dramatic change in the outlook of people. A "new person" unlike the present ones would have emerged, who would contribute freely and gladly to the well-being of all, being neither coaxed by material incentives nor by bureaucratic commands. The abundance created by economic growth and the lack of egoism exhibited by the new type of human being would make possible a new principle of production and distribution: "From each according to his ability, to each according to his need."[2]

## The Consequences of Marx

Having summarized the teachings of Marx in the preceding sections, we now turn to a final question: What, in the end, have been the consequences of his life?

The answer, perhaps, is this: Marx has offered to mankind a dramatic and fascinating vision of social change. The vision simultaneously *explains* the harshness of life experienced by many and *promises* a brighter future, a future that is "bound to come." On the one hand, the millions who are suffering from intense scarcity are told that their misfortune is not the result of natural circumstances or personal failings, but is due to their *exploitation* by greedy capitalists. Regardless of the facts, this simple explanation has great appeal. On the other hand, these same people are urged to compare the all-too-real defects of their actual society with a vague picture of an assuredly better future. Marx virtually hands people a blank page on which to draw their own outlines of the new society that is to be built on the ruins of the old. They can fill that blank page with any and all of their dreams. Thus, Marx has handed to the disenchanted of the world something like a Rorschach inkblot into which the fondest dreams can be read. How can one possibly reject *that* future?

It does not matter that hardly anyone ever *reads* the massive works of Marx. Nor does it matter that serious scholarship often rejects his arbitrary postulates, his reasoning, and his conclusions. What does matter is the simple fact that the Marxian message noted in the preceding paragraph has *worked,* again and again, to help self-styled Marxists mobilize the underprivileged with the promise of a better life. Thus, Marxism has in the end become *a mighty instrument for the acquisition and maintenance of political power.* In many cases, as we well know, the humane creed of Marx has quickly been forgotten by the new holders of power, who have not hesitated to install brutal dictatorships in the name of Marx and, almost certainly, contrary to his spirit.

Given the fact that Marx analyzed capitalism and had almost nothing to say about socialism, the common habit of socialist societies to characterize themselves

---

[2]Karl Marx, *Critique of the Gotha Program,* in Robert C. Tucker, ed., *The Marx-Engels Reader,* 2d ed. (New York: Norton, 1978), p. 531.

as "the living practice of Marxism" is patently absurd. The Soviet Union provides but one of numerous examples. Neither the revolution itself (in a peasant country) nor the institutions or policies instituted afterward are clearly deducible from the teachings of Marx. Yet, Marxism has served the function of post-hoc rationalization, of legitimizing any and all government actions after the fact. The works of Marx have been a wonderful source of (out-of-context) quotations to justify actions taken on practical grounds. Naturally, contrary or inconvenient Marxist sayings have been ignored, suppressed, or reinterpreted. Precisely the same has been occurring in all the other "Marxist" countries studied in this book.

## BIOGRAPHY 15.1 Karl Marx

Karl Marx (1818–1883) was born in Trier, Germany. His father was a prosperous lawyer who had descended from a long line of rabbis. Marx adored him, but hated his Dutch mother (who, unlike his father, would not support his lifelong tendency to live off others: his parents, his in-laws, his friends).

Since Jews were not permitted to study at the local school, Karl's father baptized him into the Christian faith on his sixth birthday, which allowed him to attend a Jesuit school. From there he went on to the universities of Bonn and Berlin, supposedly to study history, law, and philosophy. But he didn't study much. By all accounts, he led a wild student life, carousing and drinking and engaging in fist fights and duels and sinking heavily into debt. Instead of studying, he wrote poems that were filled with themes of destruction and savagery and, like the following, often contained apocalyptic visions (long before he discovered capitalism as their focus).

> *Then I will wander godlike and victorious*
> *Through the ruins of the world*
> *And, giving my words an active force,*
> *I will feel equal to the creator.*[a]

> *But who advances here full of impetuosity?*
> *It is a dark form from Trier, an unleashed monster,*
> *With self-assured step he hammers the ground with his heels*
> *And raises his arms in all fury to heaven*
> *As though he wished to seize the celestial vault and lower it to earth.*
> *In rage he continually deals with his redoubtable fist,*
> *As if a thousand devils were gripping his hair.*[b]

[a] David McLellan, *Karl Marx: His Life and Thought* (New York: Harper and Row, 1973), p. 22.
[b] *Ibid.*, pp. 32–33.

Eventually, Marx moved on to Jena (a well-known diploma mill), earned a doctoral degree in philosophy, then worked as a newspaper editor. His newspaper work brought trouble with the Prussian authorities and forced him to emigrate to France, then Belgium, and, finally, England. In London, he was part-time correspondent for *The New York Daily Tribune* for a decade; his meager earnings were supplemented by Friedrich Engels, who owned factories in Germany and England and was a lifelong friend and collaborator. Marx spent much time in the British Museum studying and writing. Through his writings, he came to influence the thought of generations; today, over a third of the world's population lives in countries calling themselves Marxist. Many espouse his teaching with religious fervor.

The major works of Marx include *Economic and Philosophical Manuscripts* (1844), *The Communist Manifesto* (1848), *The Grundrisse* (1857–58), *Theories of Surplus-Value* (1861–1863), and *Capital: A Critique of Political Economy* (vols. 1–3, 1867–1880, edited by Engels, 1883–1894), and more.

Marx provided a grandiose vision of historical evolution. As he saw it, *economic conditions* (the ways in which resources are owned and used and newly produced goods are apportioned) shape people's attitudes and actions and, ultimately, history. Capitalism, for example, is characterized by the crucial fact that natural and capital resources are owned by a small minority of the population—the capitalist class, or *bourgeoisie.* The vast majority of people own only their bodies, and have only their labor to sell. They are the working class, or *proletariat.* By virtue of their economic position, and independent of individual volition, argued Marx, these classes are antagonistic to each other. Inevitably, they struggle over the *economic surplus,* the difference between the total of goods produced and the portion needed to maintain and reproduce the capital and human resources who helped produce that total. To the extent that the bourgeoisie keeps the economic surplus, said Marx, it *exploits* the proletariat. This exploitation does not arise from individual circumstances, occasionally and accidentally, but from the logic of the capitalist system—unavoidably and independently of individual intention.

Equally unavoidable is revolution. Workers will expropriate the bourgeois exploiters and seize political power. A new era of *communism* will be ushered in; workers will enjoy ownership of nonhuman resources and will be the masters of the productive process rather than its slaves. "Let the ruling classes tremble. . . . The proletarians have nothing to lose but their chains. They have a world to win. WORKING MEN OF ALL COUNTRIES, UNITE!"[c]

It is interesting to note that the Communist Manifesto from which the above lines are taken was written not for a mass movement of industrial workers but for a small group of radical intellectuals and professionals—all under the age of 30 and the offspring of privilege calling themselves the proletariat. Marx's ideas have had a special appeal to the same kind of people throughout history: the intellectuals and the disaffected young.

[c] Karl Marx and Friedrich Engels, *Manifesto of the Communist Party,* in Robert C. Tucker, ed., *The Marx-Engels Reader,* 2d ed. (New York: Norton, 1978), p. 500.

## Summary

1. The teachings of Karl Marx are of special interest because the leaders of numerous countries around the globe have claimed and continue to claim that they are Marxists.

2. Marx adopted Hegel's *dialectical approach,* a method of study that rejects the uncritical acceptance of existing empirical *appearances* and seeks to discover inner "contradictions" that hold the key to understanding the *essence* of things. The approach led Marx to develop a sweeping vision of the entire history of mankind as a history of class struggles. In his own time, under capitalism, he argued, the class struggle raged between the bourgeoisie (which owned all the means of production) and the proletariat (which had only its labor to sell). Inevitably, he predicted, the struggle would end by destroying capitalism and ushering in communism.

   Marx did more than present this grand vision of historical change. He also worked out an intricately detailed argument to support his vision of capitalism's doom. This argument is summarized in this chapter as well.

3. What has been the ultimate consequence of Marx's life? He has offered to mankind a dramatic and fascinating vision of social change that simultaneously *explains* the harshness of life experienced by many and *promises* a brighter future. The explanation (that people are poor because they are being exploited by others) is appealing to many. The promise is equally appealing because it is vague enough to let all read into it their most cherished dreams.

   In the end, Marxism has turned out to be nothing more nor less than a mighty instrument for the acquisition and maintenance of political power. The common habit in current socialist countries of characterizing themselves as "the living practice of Marxism" is nothing else but a monstrous pretense.

## Key Terms

bourgeoisie
class struggle
commodities
commodity fetishism
constant capital, c
dialectical approach
historical justification
labor theory of value
organic composition of capital
philosophic materialism
products

proletariat
rate of exploitation
rate of profit
rate of surplus value
socially necessary labor time
surplus value, s
theory of exploitation
true exchange value
use value
variable capital, v

## Questions and Problems

1. Look through some of the works of Marx listed in the "Selected Readings" and find an original statement on the theory of history according to which changes in the *economic base* in turn change people's *thinking*.

2. Look through some of the works of Marx listed in the "Selected Readings" and find an original statement on the *true exchange value* of commodities in general and of labor power in particular.

3. Look through some of the works of Marx listed in the "Selected Readings" and find an original statement on *surplus value*.

4. Look through some of the works of Marx listed in the "Selected Readings" and find an original statement on the *increasing misery* of the proletariat.

5. Look through some of the works of Marx listed in the "Selected Readings" and find an original statement on the *class struggle* and the *end of capitalism*.

6. Look through some of the works of Marx listed in the "Selected Readings" and find an original statement on *income distribution* in the *two stages of communism*.

7. Marxism has been likened to a *religion*. Do you think that makes sense? Explain.

8. Can you think of instances in which Marxian teachings have had a direct effect on Soviet practice? Explain.

9. Can you find any questionable postulates in Marx's teachings? Explain.

10. In recent years, there have been those who have argued that the socialist and capitalist economic systems discussed in this book are becoming ever more similar over time.

    a. Can you think of arguments to support this *convergence hypothesis?*
    b. Can you think of counterarguments?
    c. How might one measure convergence empirically?

## Selected Readings

Böhm-Bawerk, Eugen von. *Karl Marx and the Close of His System: A Criticism* (New York: Macmillan, 1898). A severe early criticism of Marx's work.

Bowles, Samuel, and Richard Edwards. *Understanding Capitalism: Competition, Command, and Change in the U.S. Economy* (New York: Harper and Row, 1985). A Marxist view.

Engels, Friedrich. *Socialism: Utopian and Scientific* (New York: International Publishers, 1935).

Engels, Friedrich. *Anti-Dühring: Herr Eugen Dühring's Revolution in Science* (Moscow: Progress Publishers, 1969).

Freedman, Robert. *Marx on Economics* (New York: Harcourt Brace Jovanovich, 1961). A systematic compilation of Marx's writings.

Hunt, E. K., and Howard J. Sherman. *Economics: An Introduction to Traditional and Radical Views,* 5th ed. (New York: Harper and Row, 1986). An introductory textbook written from the Marxist perspective.

Laidler, Harry W. *History of Socialism* (New York: Crowell, 1968). Chapters 13 through 16 provide a detailed discussion of Marx and Marxism.

Lindbeck, Assar. *The Political Economy of the New Left: An Outsider's View,* 2d ed. (New York: Harper and Row, 1977). A prominent Swedish economist and Social Democrat critically looks at the New Left in the United States; includes New Left responses.

Marx, Karl. *Economic and Philosophic Manuscripts of 1844* (Moscow: Foreign Languages Publishing House, 1961).

Marx, Karl. *A Critique of the Gotha Programme* (New York: International Publishers, 1938).

Marx, Karl. *A Contribution to the Critique of Political Economy* (Chicago: Charles H. Kerr and Co., 1904).

Marx, Karl. *Grundrisse* (New York: Vintage Books, 1973).

Marx, Karl. *Capital: A Critique of Political Economy,* vols. 1–3 (Chicago: Charles H. Kerr and Co., 1906).

Marx, Karl. *Theories of Surplus Value* (New York: International Publishers, 1952).

Marx, Karl, and Friedrich Engels. *Selected Correspondence* (New York: International Publishers, 1942).

Marx, Karl, and Friedrich Engels. *Manifesto of the Communist Party* (New York: International Publishers, 1932).

McLellan, David. *Karl Marx: His Life and Thought* (New York: Harper and Row, 1973).

*The Monthly Review.* A socialist magazine published in the United States.

Nove, Alec. *Marxism and "Really Existing Socialism"* (Chur, Switzerland: Harwood Academic Publishers, 1986). Examines the relationship between Marxist ideas and Soviet reality.

*Review of Radical Political Economics.* A journal published by the New Left in the United States, a group of Marxists who reject Soviet-style Marxism.

Samuelson, Paul A. "Marxian Economics as Economics," *The American Economic Review,* May 1967, pp. 616–23. The 1970 winner of the Nobel Prize in Economics assesses Marx as an economist on the 100th anniversary of *Capital.*

Samuelson, Paul A. "Understanding the Marxian Notion of Exploitation: A Summary of the So-Called Transformation Problem Between Marxian Values and Competitive Prices," *Journal of Economic Literature,* June 1971, pp. 399–431; March 1973, pp. 58–68; March 1974, pp. 51–77.

Schumpeter, Joseph A. *Capitalism, Socialism, and Democracy* (New York: Harper and Row, 1950). One of this century's great economists also predicts the demise of capitalism, but for entirely different reasons than those given by Marx.

Schumpeter, Joseph A. *Ten Great Economists from Marx to Keynes* (New York: Oxford University Press, 1951). Views Marx as "the greatest social scientist who ever lived."

Sowell, Thomas. *Marxism: Philosophy and Economics* (New York: Morrow, 1985).
A compellingly readable exposition of Marx that shatters many interpretations
of Marx that have become standard through sheer repetition rather than scholarship.

Tucker, Robert C. *The Marx-Engels Reader,* 2d ed. (New York: Norton, 1978). An
excellent anthology of the writings of Marx and Engels.

## Computer Program

The SYSTEMS personal computer diskette that accompanies this book contains
one program of interest to this chapter:

Program 15, "The Legacy of Marx," provides 12 multiple-choice questions
about Chapter 15, along with immediate responses to incorrect answers.

# Glossary

(Chapter numbers appear in parentheses.)

**acceptance method**   a Soviet method of transferring bank balances between enterprises that is initiated by the payee rather than the payor, as in the case of checking accounts (7)

**acreage allotments**   legal restrictions to the total acreage that can be planted with particular crops (13)

**activity analysis**   another name for the mathematical technique of **linear programming** (11)

**adjoint matrix**   in matrix inversion, the transposed matrix of cofactors (6)

**agency problem**   the problem arising in every large organization of getting *agents* (who are supposed to implement decisions made at the top) to obey *principals* (who are in charge) (7)

**agricultural procurement prices**   prices set by the Soviet government and paid to collective farmers when delivering commanded quantities of agricultural products to the government (7)

**alienation**   a state in which people are estranged from themselves, their fellow human beings, and the natural world (4)

**allocative efficiency**   see **economic efficiency** (2)

**allocative inefficiency**   see **economic inefficiency** (2)

**antipirating agreements**   agreements among employers to act jointly in the hiring of labor and not to compete with each other for workers (13)

**applied research**   the application to a particular problem of the knowledge gained in basic research (3)

**assortment problem**   a persistent problem in the Soviet Union, arising from the fact that bonus-seeking managers (who are rewarded by total output) disregard the wishes of customers as to the composition of output (7)

**average total cost**   the ratio of total cost (fixed plus variable) to total output (8)

**basic feasible solution**   in linear programming, any solution of $n$ equations and $n$ unknowns that does not violate the constraints (11)

**basic organizations of associated labor (BOALs)**   small groups of workers within the Yugoslav socialist firm who can be distinguished from other such groups by the nature of their tasks and whose output is, thus, distinguishable from that of such other groups (9)

**basic research**   scientific inquiry not directed toward any specific "useful" discovery (3)

**bourgeoisie**   Marx's capitalist class that owns all the natural and capital resources (15)

**brigade contract system**   in the Soviet Union, a procedure by which collective farm workers are divided into small groups, called brigades, which contract to produce a set amount on a given piece of land and are rewarded accordingly (7)

**capital resources**   productive ingredients made by people, including structures, equipment, and inventories (1)

**capitalism**   an economic system in which the formal ownership of natural and capital resources resides predominantly in private individuals (5)

**cartel**   a group of conspiring sellers acting as one and making joint price-quantity decisions

459

with a view toward earning a larger profit than competition would allow (13)

**central plan** a document that precisely specifies the economic activities to be performed by every individual in a society during a future period (6)

**central plans** systematic programs of allocating resources and apportioning output, designed to achieve objectives chosen by the government (7)

**centralized socialism** a socialist economic system in which the economic activities of different people are coordinated by central government commands (5)

**citizen sovereignty** a state of affairs in which all citizens share the power to control their political leaders and, thus, to assure themselves such precious individual liberties as the right to free speech and press, to peaceful assembly, to privacy in their homes, to habeas corpus, to a speedy trial by jury, and more (4)

**class struggle** the antagonism between social groups that are internally held together by a common ideology; according to Marx, this struggle explains the movement of history (15)

**closed shops** firms operating under a collective bargaining agreement that forbids the hiring of nonunion workers (13)

**codetermination laws** laws in Western Europe giving workers the power to participate in the control of their workplaces (14)

**coefficient of relative effectiveness** the reciprocal of the **payback period** (7)

**cofactor** a lower-order determinant associated with a particular element of a higher-order determinant; equals the element's minor with an appropriate sign: *plus,* if the sum of the element's subscripts is even; *minus,* if that sum is odd (6)

**collective farm markets** in the Soviet Union, markets in which collective farmers may sell privately produced goods at unregulated prices to anyone (7)

**collective farms (*kolkhozy*)** large farms first created during Stalin's collectivization drive; officially formed by the voluntary pooling of separate land and livestock holdings of numerous peasant households, but in fact compulsory producer cooperatives (7)

**collectivization** the forced elimination of agricultural private property, such as land, buildings, equipment, inventories, and livestock, and its transferral to government-controlled institutions, such as state farms, collective farms, and machine-tractor stations (7)

**column vector** a special kind of matrix consisting of any number of rows and a single column (11)

**combines** vertically integrated groupings of enterprises in East Germany, created during the course of administrative decentralization (11)

**commodities** physical objects—solid, liquid, or gaseous (1); in Marx, articles produced by people with a view toward market exchange, to be used by others (15)

**commodity fetishism** according to Marx, a tendency to focus on surface relations among commodities rather than deeper relations among men (15)

**communal socialism** a socialist economic system in which the economic activities of different people are coordinated through the internal incentive of love (5)

**communes** institutions in which people live and work together and usually own jointly all means of production and consumption; see also **intentional community** (10)

**communism** the perfect society that Marx expected to emerge at the end of a long historic development, after the demise of both capitalism and socialism; a moneyless society in which all resources are owned in common and selfless people contribute to the best of their ability to the process of production, while only taking according to their needs (7)

**communities of interest** in Yugoslavia, voluntary organizations of producers and consumers that provide all kinds of public goods (9)

**commutative justice** a situation in which goods are apportioned among people as a result of free choices by all people, all of whom enjoy as nearly equal opportunities as possible in the process of allocating resources to the production of goods (3)

**compensating wage differentials** wage differences that offset nonmonetary differences in the perceived attractiveness of jobs (13)

**concentration ratio** the percentage of industry sales attributable to a given number of largest firms, usually the 4, 8, 20, and 50 largest companies (13)

**conflict curve** another name for the **contract curve** in the **Edgeworth box diagram,** so called because people in economically efficient positions on the curve can make utility gains only at the expense of other people who will resist the attempt (3)

**constant capital, c** in Marx, the structures, machines, and raw materials used up in the process of production (15)

**constant-cost industry** an industry with a horizontal long-run supply curve; in such an industry, the output price is unchanged after the industry has ceased to expand (in response to higher demand and temporary profits) or has ceased to contract (in response to lower demand and temporary losses) (8)

**consumer cooperatives** retail stores owned and run by their customers (14)

**constant returns to scale** a characteristic of the production function such that a simultaneous and equal percentage change in the use of all physical inputs leads to an *identical* percentage change in physical output (6)

**consumer sovereignty** a state of affairs in which all consumers share the power to decide what types of goods are being produced (and consumed) (4)

**consumption indifference curve** a graph showing all the combinations of two goods that, in the opinion of a given consumer, yield the same utility total and among which the consumer, therefore, is indifferent (2)

**contract curve** the locus of all the economically efficient points in the **Edgeworth box diagram,** so called because people in economically inefficient positions not on the curve can make mutually beneficial contracts to achieve economic efficiency on the curve (3)

**control by the ruble** in the Soviet Union, a form of external auditing of enterprises by the State Bank (7)

**control figures** in the Soviet Union, the tentative material balances set up by Gosplan in the process of plan construction (7)

**coordination problem** the problem of fitting the specialized activities of all the people engaged in the division of labor into a well-coordinated whole (6)

**copyright** the exclusive right to the reproduction, publishing, or sale of a literary, musical, or artistic work (13)

**decreasing-cost industry** an industry with a downward-sloping long-run supply curve; in such an industry, the output price is lower after the industry has ceased to expand (in response to higher demand and temporary profits); it is

higher after the industry has ceased to contract (in response to lower demand and temporary losses) (8)

**decreasing returns to scale** a characteristic of the production function such that a simultaneous and equal percentage change in the use of all physical inputs leads to a *smaller* percentage change in physical output (6)

**demand for a good** all the alternative quantities of the good people would buy in a period at all the good's possible prices—all else being equal (1)

**democratic socialism** a predominantly capitalist country with a significant degree of government intervention in the economy but committed to the maintenance of political democracy (14)

**depreciation** the shrinkage through wear and tear of buildings and equipment from the capital stock during a period (7)

**desire for a good** the one quantity of the good people would take in a period if they could have it for nothing (1)

**determinant** a number of elements arranged in rows and columns to form a square and that can be evaluated, yielding a single number (6)

**dialectical approach** a method of study that rejects the uncritical acceptance of existing empirical *appearances* and seeks to discover inner "contradictions" that hold the key to understanding the *essence* of things (15)

**distributive justice** a situation in which goods are apportioned by an authority seeking to act justly, usually by consulting a personal characteristic (such as need or hours worked) that measures the recipient's merit (3)

**draft plan** in the Soviet Union, the revised control figures (or material balances) set up by Gosplan after discussions with subordinate planning agencies and enterprise managers, ready to be submitted to parliament (7)

**economic efficiency** a situation in which it is *impossible,* through some reallocation of resources or goods among different productive enterprises or households, to make some people better off (in their own judgment) without making others worse off (in *their* own judgment) (2)

**economic equity** a situation in which the apportionment of goods among people is considered fair (3)

**economic growth** a sustained expansion over time in a society's ability to produce goods (3)

**economic imperialism** a relationship between two countries in which the dominant country obtains involuntary favors from the weaker country (7)

**economic inefficiency** a situation in which it is *possible*, through some reallocation of resources or goods among different productive enterprises or households, to make some people better off (in their own judgment) without making others worse off (in *their* own judgment) (2)

**economic power** the capacity to make and enforce choices on the allocation of scarce resources and the apportionment of scarce goods (5, 12)

**economic systems** the set of arrangements through which people in a society make choices about the allocation of their scarce resources and the apportionment of their scarce goods (5)

**Edgeworth box** a diagram that highlights the crucial distinctions between economic efficiency and inefficiency and between economic efficiency and economic equity (3)

**empire building** the tendency of Soviet officials who are in charge of ministries, regions, or enterprises to make them as self-sufficient as possible (7)

**enterprise director** in the Yugoslav socialist firm, an official appointed by the management board, responsible for carrying out the day-to-day management of the enterprise under the immediate supervision of the management board (9)

**enterprise managers** in the Lange model of market socialism, government officials, distinct from **industry managers,** who run individual socialist enterprises and are charged with following specific rules of behavior (8)

**enterprise wholesale prices** prices set by the Soviet government for interenterprise transactions involving nonagricultural products; equal to an industry branch's planned average total cost (until recently, wages, raw material costs, and depreciation) plus planned profit (7)

**entrepreneurship** risky, innovating activity involving the process of production (3)

**equilibrium price** the price at which quantity demanded equals quantity supplied (12)

**equalizing wage differentials** wage differences that offset nonmonetary differences in the perceived attractiveness of jobs (13)

**exclusive franchise** a governmental grant to a single seller of the exclusive right to produce and sell a good (13)

**extensive economic growth** an expansion of a society's production possibilities resulting from the availability of more units of the very types of resources previously available, technology being unchanged (3)

**external incentives** stimuli coming from other people (such as criticism and punishment or praise and money rewards) that motivate people to take or not to take an action (10)

**fair-trade laws** laws allowing manufacturers to fix minimum prices for their products and, if a single retailer agrees to it, to bind all retailers to it (13)

**feedback effect** the effect of secondary changes in other markets on the market in which an initial change in supply or demand occurred (12)

**final goods** goods produced by domestic producers during a period and *not* used up (as intermediate goods are) by the same or other domestic producers during the same period in the making of other goods (6)

**financial capital** claims (such as money, stocks, deeds, or bonds) against real resources (1)

**flow** a quantity per unit of time (1)

**free goods** goods available in larger quantities than all people would want to take if the goods could be had for nothing (1)

**Gini coefficient** the ratio of two areas in the Lorenz curve graph that summarizes the extent of income inequality; the ratio of the area between the line of perfect equality and actual inequality to the area between the line of perfect equality and the line of perfect inequality (13)

**goods** commodities and services that people desire because they consider them likely to enhance their welfare (1)

**Gosplan** the Soviet agency in charge of central economic planning (7)

**Great Leap Forward** the period in Chinese history from 1957 to 1962, during which an attempt was made to create abundance by the destruction of egoism and the creation of a new type of human being (10)

**Great Proletarian Cultural Revolution** the period in Chinese history from 1966 to 1969, during which a repeated attempt was made to create a new type of human being, free of egoism (10)

**gross investment** the addition of newly produced buildings and equipment to the capital stock during a period, plus the change in producer inventories (7)

**historical justification**  a Marxian ethical principle according to which no fixed ethical conclusions can be drawn concerning any given social phenomenon; the same action can be acceptable in one stage of history but unacceptable in another (15)

**holding company**  a corporation established for the sole purpose of acquiring a controlling stock interest in two or more competing corporations in an industry and then jointly running their affairs (13)

**horizontal merger**  the direct purchase by one firm of the assets of another firm just like it (13)

**household contract and responsibility system**  a feature of China's post-Mao economic reforms that has effectively decollectivized agriculture (10)

**human capital**  the health care, general education, and training "embodied" in people (1)

**human resources**  people able and willing to participate in the process of production (1)

**identity matrix**  a square matrix that consists of 1s along the main diagonal, all other elements being zero (6)

**impact effect**  the effect of an initial change in supply or demand on the market concerned (12)

**imperative planning**  the central planning in Soviet-style economies that carries the force of law (14)

**imperfect competition**  a situation in which the conditions defining a **perfectly competitive market** are violated (13)

**import quotas**  maximum physical limits on the amounts of goods that may be imported (13)

**imcreasing-cost industry**  an industry with an upward-sloping long-run supply curve; in such an industry, the output price is higher after the industry has ceased to expand (in response to higher demand and temporary profits); it is lower after the industry has ceased to contract (in response to lower demand and temporary losses) (8)

**increasing returns to scale**  a characteristic of the production function such that a simultaneous and equal percentage change in the use of all physical inputs leads to a *larger* percentage change in physical output (3, 6, 13)

**indicative planning**  the central planning of the French that does not carry the force of law but merely suggests a desired or likely course of events (14)

**industrial democracy**  a state of affairs in which workers participate in all enterprise decisions affecting their employment, incomes, and psychic or physical welfare (14)

**industry managers**  in the Lange model of market socialism, government officials, distinct from the managers of individual enterprises, who have the task of creating new enterprises in profitable industries and closing down existing enterprises in loss-making industries (8)

**inflation**  see **open inflation** and **repressed inflation**

**input norms**  in centralized socialism, verbal commands—addressed to the manager of each productive enterprise—to use designated maximum quantities of various inputs per unit of designated outputs (6)

**input-output analysis**  a mathematical technique designed to visualize the internal structure of an economy and to study interdependencies in it (6)

**input-output table**  a table that lists the flows of all newly produced goods and of resource services between all their suppliers and recipients and, thus, illustrates the web of interrelationships in the economy (6)

**intensive economic growth**  an expansion of a society's production possibilities resulting from the availability of better methods of production and higher-quality resources (3)

**intentional community**  a voluntary and deliberate association of people who value togetherness above all and seek to extend intimate, sharing relationships beyond the immediate family (10)

**intermediate goods**  goods produced by domestic producers during a period and then used up by the same or other domestic producers during the same period in the making of other goods (6)

**internal incentives**  stimuli arising within people (such as feelings of joy or guilt) that motivate people to take or not to take an action (10)

**internal rate of return**  the average annual rate of return on an initial investment expenditure over the years of the project; equals the interest rate that makes the net present value of an investment project just equal to zero (7)

**inverse matrix**  that matrix which, when multiplied by an original matrix, yields an identity matrix (6)

**investment reserve**  a special macroeconomic policy tool used in Sweden (14)

**Invisible Hand**  see **spontaneous coordination** (12)

**isoquant**   a graph showing all the combinations of two resources that, under current technology, yield the same maximum output total (2)

**knowledge problem**   in a large group of people, the difficulty of making use jointly of all the knowledge relevant to the achievement of economic efficiency, given the fact that this knowledge is not available to a single mind in its totality but is found, in billions of dispersed fragments, in the minds of countless separate individuals (6)

**labor-managed market economy**   a socialist market economy proposed by Vanek in which enterprises are managed by the workers working in them (8)

**labor theory of value**   the Marxian theory according to which the true exchange value of anything can be measured by the socially necessary labor time required to make it (15)

**labor union**   a cartel among workers for the joint sale of their labor (13)

**law of declining marginal utility**   given the quantities of all other goods being consumed, and given tastes, successive additions of equal units of a good to the process of consumption eventually yield ever smaller additions to total welfare or utility (2)

**law of diminishing returns**   given the quantities of all other inputs being used, and given technical knowledge, successive additions of equal units of a resource to the process of production eventually yield ever smaller additions to total output (2)

**Leontief inverse matrix**   a table showing, for those goods of which a portion of output is used up in the process of production itself, the total outputs ultimately required if one unit of such a good is to be delivered to final users (6)

**Leontief matrix**   in output-output analysis, the difference between an identity matrix and the upper portion of a technical-coefficients matrix (6)

**line of actual inequality**   see **Lorenze curve** (13)

**line of perfect equality**   the hypothetical position of the **Lorenz curve** if the same amount of income went to each member of the group in question (13)

**line of perfect inequality**   the hypothetical position of the **Lorenz curve** if all of income went to one member of a group and none of it to other members (13)

**linear programming**   a mathematical technique for optimization (maximization or minimization), given constraints such as production techniques, resource availability, and preferences (11)

**Lorenz curve**   a graphical device that shows the way in which income is apportioned among the members of any group and highlights the extent of equality or inequality among them (13)

**machine-tractor stations (MTS)**   state-owned enterprises first created during Stalin's collectivization drive (but abolished in 1958); they held the agricultural implements of the formerly independent peasants who were forced into collective farms (7)

**main diagonal**   in a square matrix, all the elements running from the upper left to the lower right corner (6)

**management board**   in the Yugoslav socialist firm, a group of worker representatives charged with appointing and overseeing the enterprise director (9)

**managerial coordination**   the coordination of the separate economic activities of people engaded in a division of labor by means of the deliberate application of reason on the part of a central planner or manager, followed by the subsequent issuance of verbal managerial directives to subordinates (6)

**marginal conditions**   a set of conditions, first stated by Pareto, that must be met if **economic inefficiency** is to be avoided and **economic efficiency** is to achieved (2)

**marginal cost**   the change in total cost associated with a one-unit change in output (8)

**marginal output-to-capital ratio**   the extra output produced with the help of extra capital during a period, divided by that extra capital (7)

**marginal physical product**   the change in total physical product associated with a one-unit change in one input, all other inputs and technology being held constant (8)

**marginal rate of substitution (MRS)**   the rate at which a consumer is willing to exchange, as a matter of indifference, a little bit of one variable (say, the consumption of apples) for a little bit of another variable (say, the consumption of butter) (2)

**marginal rate of technical substitution (MRTS)**   the rate at which a producer is able to exchange, without affecting the quantity of output produced, a little bit of one input (say, labor) for a little bit of another input (say, capital) (2)

**marginal rate of time preference** a marginal rate of substitution between current and future consumption goods: the additional units of future consumption goods a consumer would have to get in order to be indifferent about a one-unit sacrifice of current consumption goods (3)

**marginal rate of time productivity** a marginal rate of transformation between current and future consumption goods: the additional units of future consumption goods a producer could produce if a one-unit sacrifice of current consumption goods were made (and the resources thus saved were used for investment that made the added production of future consumption goods possible) (3)

**marginal rate of transformation (*MRT*)** the rate at which a producer is technically able to exchange, in the process of production, a little bit of one variable (say, labor or butter) for a little bit of another variable (say, apples produced with the help of that labor or produced in place of that butter) (2)

**marginal value product** marginal physical product multiplied by output price (8)

**market capitalism** a capitalist economic system in which the economic activities of different people are coordinated through monetary incentives established in markets (5)

**market coordination** see **spontaneous coordination (12)**

**market socialism** a socialist economic system in which the economic activities of different people are coordinated through monetary incentives established in markets (5)

**marketing quotas** maximum amounts of a product that farmers can legally sell (13)

**material balance** a Soviet central planning tool, listing in physical units (such as tons) all the prospective sources and uses of a given "material" (such as steel) and making certain that these sources and uses are equal to each other and, thus, "balance" (7)

**matrix** any rectangular array of numbers (6)

**measure of net normative output** in the Soviet Union, a managerial success indicator, similar to value added (7)

**Meidner Plan** a Swedish plan through which workers might gain ownership control of their workplaces (14)

**minor** a lower-order determinant associated with a particular element of a higher-order determinant; equals the portion of the higher-order determinant that remains after the element's row and column is deleted (6)

**monopolistic competition** a market structure in which the entry of new firms is easy; large numbers of sellers compete with one another, offering differentiated products (13)

**monopoly** an industry that has only a single seller the product of which has no close substitutes (13)

**monopoly power** the power to raise the selling price above the perfectly competitive level (13)

**monopsony** a buyer who is the only buyer in the market (13)

**natural monopoly** a situation in which long-run average total cost is declining with higher output throughout the range of possible quantities demanded in the market (13)

**natural resources** productive ingredients not made by people and as yet untouched by them: the gifts of nature in their natural state (1)

**net investment** the net change in the capital stock during a period, equal to gross investment minus depreciation (7)

**net present value** the sum of the present values of the negative and positive components of an investment project (7)

**New Economic Policy (NEP)** a policy initiated by Lenin in 1921 and terminated by Stalin in 1928 that permitted a heavy dose of "capitalism under communism" in the Soviet Union (7)

**nomenklatura system** the appointment system operated by the Central Committee of the Communist Party in the Soviet Union and used to fill the most significant jobs throughout society (7)

**norm of relative effectiveness** an arbitrarily selected **coefficient of relative effectiveness** (7)

**oligopoly** a market structure in which the entry of new firms is difficult and relatively few sellers compete with one another, offering either homogeneous or differentiated products (13)

**open inflation** a sustained increase over time in the general level of prices (3)

**organic composition of capital** in Marx, the ratio of **constant capital** to **variable capital,** or c/v (15)

**output quotas** in centralized socialism, verbal commands—addressed to each producing enterprise, household, and administrator of the means of production—to supply, during a given period, designated minimum quantities of goods or resource services, respectively, to designated recipients (6)

**Pareto optimum**   a situation in which all the marginal conditions of economic efficiency are fulfilled simultaneously (2)

**participatory economy**   a socialist market economy proposed by Vanek in which enterprises are managed by the workers working in them (8)

**Party directives**   directives specifying in broad terms the desired composition of the future GNP, sent by the leadership of the Communist Party to Gosplan, the central planning agency (7)

**patent**   an exclusive right to the use of an invention (13)

**payback method**   a criterion for selecting investment projects that rejects all projects the (undiscounted) returns of which require more than a predetermined length of time to repay the initial investment outlay (7)

**payback period**   the number of years it takes for initial investment outlays to be paid back by (undiscounted) future receipts (7)

**perfectly competitive market**   a market in which there is a large number of independent buyers and also of sellers, all units of the traded item are viewed as identical, all buyers and sellers possess full knowledge relevant to trading, and nothing impedes entry into and exit from the market (12)

**performance criteria**   criteria (such as full employment, technical efficiency, economic efficiency, economic growth, and more) that can be used to assess the performance of economic systems and, thus, their success in dealing with the scarcity problem (2)

**persuasive advertising**   advertising that is designed to divert people's attention from facts to images and make them buy more as a result of imagined advantages (13)

**philosophic materialism**   a view that sees the material world as the ultimate reality and rejects the notion that spiritual forces could be behind the world perceptible to our senses (15)

**plan law**   in the Soviet Union, the revised control figures of the **draft plan** after approval by the Supreme Soviet, the final set of **material balances** that people are asked to obey (7)

**political factories**   in Yugoslavia, socialist firms established as a result of political pressure with the aim of providing local employment or prestige, but that are economic mistakes (9)

**pollution**   excessive waste disposal into the natural environment that makes its subsequent uses harmful to life (4)

**pollution right**   a transferable certificate that allows the holder to dump one unit of a specified waste into a specified environment (8)

**positive-sum game**   a game at which no one wins at someone else's expense and the sum of (positive) winnings and (nonexisting negative) losses is positive (3)

**price system**   the set of interdependent prices in all the markets for goods and resources, which changes as long as the independent actions of households and firms are not perfectly coordinated, making households and firms, in turn, change their behavior until coordination is achieved (12)

**price war**   a situation in which rival firms successively cut their prices below those of competitors (and perhaps even below their own cost) (13)

**priority principle**   a Soviet procedure that assigns different levels of priority to different production targets and, if it beomes necessary during plan execution, sacrifices low-priority targets for high-priority targets (7)

**process of production**   the set of activities deliberately designed to make goods available to people where and when they are wanted (1)

**product differentiation**   the differentiation of the products of one firm from those of other firms in a given industry on the basis of physical aspects, legal matters, or conditions of sale (13)

**production associations**   cartel-like groupings of enterprises in East European countries, based on product-relatedness or geographic proximity and intervening between the central planning board and individual enterprises (7,11)

**production brigades**   in China's communes, groups of about 10 production teams or 500 families (10)

**production function**   the technical relationship that shows the alternative *maximum* quantities of an output that are associated, under current technology, with all conceivable combinations of inputs (2)

**production possibilities curve**   a graph showing all the combinations of two goods or groups of goods that a producer is able to produce, under current technology, by using a given set of resources fully and in technically efficient ways (1,2)

**production teams**   in China's communes, groups of about 50 families (10)

**products**   in Marx, articles produced by people only for their own, direct use (15)

**proletariat** Marx's working class, which has only its labor to sell (15)

**property right** the exclusive (but variously qualified) right to the use of something scarce (5)

**rate of exploitation** in Marx, the ratio of **surplus value** to **variable capital**, or s/v (15)

**rate of profit** in Marx, the ratio of **surplus value** to the sum of **constant capital** plus **variable capital**, s/(c + v) (15)

**rate of surplus value** in Marx, the ratio of **surplus value** to **variable capital**, or s/v (15)

**regional economic councils (*sovnarkhozy*)** in the Soviet Union, a set of about 100 regional planning organs that under Khrushchev briefly replaced the ministries in the planning hierarchy (7)

**residual income** in the Yugoslav socialist firm, total revenue minus nonlabor costs (9)

**resources** ingredients used in the process of production: human, natural, or capital (1)

**scarce goods** goods available in smaller quantities than all people would want to take if the goods could be had for nothing (1)

**scarcity problem** the basic economic problem, arising from the fact that in all nations on earth today the limited flow of goods that can be produced in a period is insufficient to fulfill the combined desire for goods by all the people (1)

**self-management agreements (SMAs)** in Yugoslavia, agreements among groups of workers within enterprises (**BOALs**) or among different enterprises that spell out their mutual obligations to one another (9)

**services** temporary uses of commodities or people (1)

**shadow prices** implicit valuations emerging as a by-product of solving a linear programming problem (11)

**simplex method** a mathematical routine for solving complicated linear programming problems (11)

**social compacts** (SCs) in Yugoslavia, consensual statements on macroeconomic policy objectives that establish people's mutual obligations if specified goals are to be reached (9)

**social democracies** capitalist countries with a significant degree of government intervention in the economy but committed to the maintenance of political democracy (14)

**social dividend** in the Lange model of market socialism, a (supposedly equal) government payment to each citizen that distributes the interest, rent, and profit income collected by the government from all the socialist enterprises that are owned by the people as a whole (8)

**socialism** an economic system in which the formal ownership of natural and capital resources resides predominantly in groups of people, possibly even in all of a society's people as a group (5)

**socially necessary labor time** in Marx, the time required to produce a commodity that is in demand when production occurs under "normal conditions"—using labor of average skill and average intensity and equipped with up-to-date machinery (15)

**spillout effect** the effect of a change in supply or demand on markets other than the one in which it occurs (12)

**spontaneous coordination** the coordination by price signals of the separate economic activities of people engaged in a division of labor; also called the system of the **Invisible Hand** (12)

**state farms (*sovkhozy*)** huge farms owned by the people as a whole, first created during Stalin's collectivization drive (7)

**state retail prices** prices set by the Soviet government at which consumer goods are offered for sale at state retail stores (7)

**stock** a quantity in existence at a *moment of time* (1)

**storming** in the Soviet Union, regular seasonal spurts in production activity designed to fulfill or overfulfill the output plan by the quarterly accounting deadline (7)

**success criteria** criteria (such as full employment, technical efficiency, economic efficiency, economic growth, and more) that can be used to assess the performance of economic systems and, thus, their success in dealing with the scarcity problem (2)

**sucrophilia** the "liking of sugar," referring to the Cuban leaders' attempt, since 1964, to promote Cuban economic growth by reliance on sugar production and export (10)

**sucrophobia** the "disliking of sugar," referring to the Cuban leaders' attempt, until 1964, to rid Cuba of its dependence on sugar (10)

**surplus value, s** in Marx, the difference between a commodity's true exchange value, on the one hand, and the constant plus variable capital advanced by the capitalists during its production, on the other hand (15)

**system of eonomic accountability (*khozras-chet*)** in the Soviet Union, a process of internal enterprise auditing, designed to encourage ''businesslike behavior'' (7)

**tariff** a tax on imports (13)

**technical coefficients** numbers showing the quantity of inputs producers in an industry require on the average per unit of output (6)

**technical efficiency** a concept applying to a single productive enterprise and describing a situation in which the inputs actually being employed by this enterprise *cannot*, under current technology, yield a larger quantity of output than is in fact being produced; this situation of actual output equaling maximum possible output implies that current technology does not allow the enterprise to produce its actual quantity of output with less of at least one input without having to increase other inputs (2)

**technical inefficiency** a concept applying to a single productive enterprise and describing a situation in which the inputs actually being employed by this enterprise could, under current technology, yield a larger quantity of output than is in fact being produced; this situation of actual output below maximum possible output implies that current technology allows the enterprise to produce its actual quantity of output with less of at least one input without having to increase other inputs (2)

**technology** the set of known methods of production (1)

**theory of exploitation** the Marxian theory according to which capitalists routinely steal part of the output produced by workers (15)

**true exchange value** in Marx, the value of a commodity as determined by the socially necessary (dead plus live) labor time expended in its production; $T = c + v + s$ (15)

**trust** a combination of several corporations under the trusteeship of a single board of directors that manages their affairs jointly (13)

**tying contract** an agreement by which an aspiring monopolist forces the customers of its competitors to buy from it alone if they wish to continue receiving some other product that no one else can deliver (13)

**underground economy** in the Soviet Union, a wide spectrum of semilegal and clearly illegal activities through which people enhance their own welfare by allocating resources and acquiring goods in ways not sanctioned by the central plan (7)

**union shops** firms in which all employees, within 30 days after hiring, must become union members or at least pay union dues as a condition of continued employment (13)

**use value** in Marx, the satisfaction or utility subjectively experienced when a person consumes a good (15)

**utopia** the good place that is no place; an imaginary place in which people could lead a perfectly fulfilling existence (10)

**variable capital, v** in Marx, the real income paid workers (15)

**vertical merger** the direct purchase by one firm of the assets of another firm that is its supplier or customer (13)

**Visible Hand** see **managerial coordination (6)**

**wage earners' fund** in Sweden, a union-controlled fund of corporate shares designed to promote worker control of the means of production (14)

**War Communism** a period of ''planless command'' in Soviet history (mid-1918 to early 1921), characterized by civil war and an abortive attempt to establish communism (7)

**welfare corporatism** the state of affairs, exemplified by Japan, in which the private business corporation takes on many of the functions of the welfare state (14)

**welfare state** a capitalist society in which government pledges to protect people not only from the rigors of the marketplace but, quite literally, from all types of misfortunes that might befall them on their lifelong travel from cradle to grave (14)

**work council** a West European instrument of worker codetermination at the level of the shop floor (14)

**workers' council** in the Yugoslav socialist firm, a group of worker representatives responsible for basic policy decisions (9)

**worker self-management** a system in which each socialist enterprise is managed collectively by the workers employed in it (9)

**worker sovereignty** a state of affairs in which all workers share the power to decide what type of labor is being supplied and under what conditions it is rendered (4)

**X-inefficiency** a form of technical inefficiency caused by people who are inadequately motivated to do a good job (2)

**zero-sum game** a game in which the winnings of some are exactly matched by the losses of others and the sum of (positive) winnings and (negative) losses is zero (3)

# Comments on Questions and Problems

## Chapter 1

1. Figure 1.A depicts a typical demand schedule: All else being equal, the monthly quantity of milk demanded equals 0 gallons at a price of 80¢ per gallon (point *a*), 10 gallons at a price of 60¢ per gallon (point *b*), 20 gallons at a price of 40¢ per gallon (point *c*), 30

**Figure 1.A**

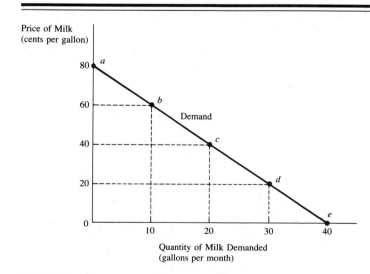

gallons at a price of 20¢ per gallon (point *d*), and 40 gallons at a price of 0¢ per gallon (point *e*). Thus, the entire line from *a* to *e* represents *demand*. Yet the *desire* for milk—measured as the quantity people would take if milk could be had for nothing—is represented by a single point, *e,* and equals 40 gallons.

2. Given the text and glossary definition of *natural resources,* sand at a beach not yet discovered by people, sunshine, and a school of tuna in the ocean would always be classified in that category. A highway, a college building, and a can of peas would never be so classified (the first two being real capital resources and the can of peas being a consumption good, if owned by a household, or real capital, if part of a firm's inventory). The 100 cubic feet of coal, cow, and acre of land might be classified as natural resources if the coal was unmined, the cow was a wild animal, and the land was virgin. They might be capital resources if the coal sat in the factory yard, the cow was domesticated and used on a farm, and the land was cultivated. Indeed, they might even be considered consumption goods if a household, say, had purchased the coal and was keeping the cow as a pet and the land for private enjoyment.

3. Given the text and glossary definition of *capital resources,* an automobile assembly plant, unsold refrigerators held by an appliance dealer, and an inventory of groceries held by a food store would always be classified in that category. Ford Motor Company stock, a natural waterfall, and a truck driver would never be so classified (although Ford stock may be called *financial* capital and the truck driver may be said to embody *human* capital). A toy truck, a horse, and a wristwatch might be classified as real capital if the toy truck and wristwatch were part of a store's inventory and the horse was domesticated and used on a farm. Yet, the toy truck, horse, and wristwatch might also be consumption goods if purchased by and used within a household, and the horse might even be considered a natural resource if it were a wild animal.

4. a. Figure 1.B illustrates the case of abundance: Production possibilities exceed the desire for goods.

   b. Figure 1.C illustrates a society on the threshold between abundance and scarcity: Production possibilities precisely equal the desire for goods.

## Figure 1.B

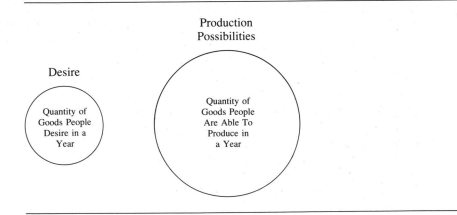

Production Possibilities

Desire

Quantity of Goods People Desire in a Year

Quantity of Goods People Are Able To Produce in a Year

**Figure 1.C**

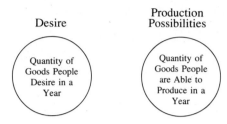

Desire

Quantity of
Goods People
Desire in a
Year

Production
Possibilities

Quantity of
Goods People
are Able to
Produce in a
Year

5. In Figure 1.D, let people in fact produce combination *A* on their production possibilities frontier, while their desire for goods equals combination *D*. Then panel (a) depicts scarcity, panel (b) depicts abundance, and panel (c) depicts the threshold situation.

6. Consider the three panels of Figure 1.E. Because the issue of scarcity versus abundance revolves around the relationship of what is available (*a*) and what is desired (*d*) *at a zero price,* we should focus on the position of points *a* and *d* on the horizontal axis. Thus, panel (a) depicts scarcity because, at the zero price, the quantity desired (*d*) exceeds that available (*a*). Panel (b) depicts abundance because, at the zero price, the quantity desired (*d*) falls short of that available (*a*). Panel (c) depicts the threshold situation because, at the zero price, the quantity desired (*d*) precisely equals that available (*a*).

7. The supply line in each panel might represent the 60 hourly take-off or landing slots available at an airport. Panel (a) might depict the demand for these slots on a busy Friday afternoon between 5 and 6 P.M. Note how the scarcity of slots shows up as a *shortage at a zero price* (*d* > *a*). Panel (b) might depict the demand for the same slots on Tuesday night between 2 and 3 A.M. Note how the abundance of slots shows up as a *surplus at a zero price* (*a* > *d*). Panel (c) might depict the demand for the same slots

**Figure 1.D**

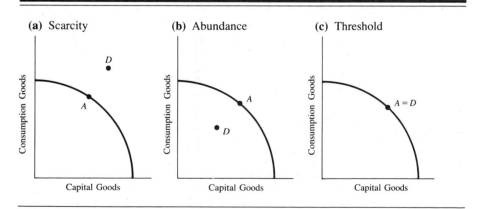

**(a)** Scarcity          **(b)** Abundance          **(c)** Threshold

**Figure 1.E**

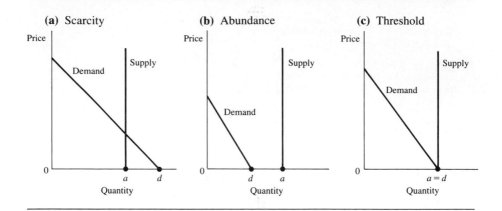

**(a)** Scarcity    **(b)** Abundance    **(c)** Threshold

at some other time—say, Wednesday between 3 and 4 P.M. Note the absence of shortage as well as surplus at a zero price ($a = d$).

8. The two sets of concepts should not be used as synonyms. To be sure, as answer 7 shows, one can identify the presence of scarcity by noting the existence of a shortage *at a zero price,* and one can identify the presence of abundance by noting the existence of a surplus *at a zero price.* However, traditionally, the term *shortage* describes a situation in which quantity demanded exceeds quantity supplied at some *positive* price, while the term *surplus* describes an analogous situation in which quantity supplied exceeds quantity demanded at some positive price.

   Consider Figure 1.F.

**Figure 1.F**

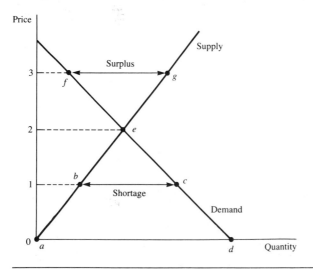

This demand and supply diagram clearly concerns a good that is *scarce* (because, at a zero price, *d* exceeds *a*). A free market might establish an equilibrium price of $2, equating demand and supply at *e*. Yet, it is also possible for there to be a surplus *or* a shortage of this *scarce* good. A government price floor of $3 would create a surplus of *fg,* for example. A government price ceiling of $1 would create a shortage of *bc.*

9. Natural resources in many places were once free, and are now scarce. Reconsider Figure 1.E and let the supply line represent the waste absorption capacity of some major river. Many years ago, the demand for this resource was small, as in panel (b). Gradually, over time, as population—and the desire to dump wastes—grew, panel (b) changed into (c) and, ultimately, into (a). The pollution problem was born.

   There are plenty of answers to the second question. The answer to problem 7 is one example; here are others: Consider the use of a zero-toll highway. If the service desired by a user involved travel near New York City, at 55 miles per hour, the good may indeed be free to this user between 3 and 5 A.M. on Mondays. Yet, from 8 to 9 A.M. on Mondays, in city-bound lanes, this desired service may not be available because too many people desire it at the same time. Then the free good would become scarce, and unless it was rationed (through physical highway access controls or pricing) the quality of the good would deteriorate. In this case, 55-mph travel from 8 to 9 A.M. on Mondays in city-bound lanes might become totally unavailable and 10-mph travel become the closest substitute. Similarly, the use of air space is now free to users at some times or places (it is now free at any time in rural Iowa), but scarce at other times or places (from 4 to 6 P.M., Mondays to Fridays, over New York City).

10. One may be tempted to dismiss the statement out of hand. Because this book aims to discuss and compare different economic systems *now,* one fact alone matters: Scarcity is their common problem now; it is irrelevant whether abundance ruled supreme in mankind's past or will so rule in mankind's future.

    On the other hand, it is interesting to speculate on whether scarcity is mankind's eternal companion. Consider the past. Surely, scarcity has been present in all of recorded history. Yet, many societies treasure myths of earlier days in which people lived in pre-economic paradise, in a Garden of Eden, in a land of plenty wherein all goods were free, peace reigned supreme, and even life was eternal. For a fascinating discussion of the Biblical myth, see the article by Hamblin in this chapter's "Selected Readings."

    What about the future? Consider the famous 1932 prophesy of Keynes, also noted in this chapter's "Selected Readings":

> What can we reasonably expect the level of our economic life to be a hundred years hence? Assuming no important wars and no important increase in population, the economic problem *may be solved, or be at least within sight of solution, within a hundred years. This means that the economic problem is not—if we look into the future—the permanent problem of the human race. . . .*
>
> *If, instead of looking into the future, we look into the past, we find that the economic problem, the struggle for subsistence, always has been hitherto the primary, most pressing problem, of the human race. . . . If the economic problem is solved, mankind will be deprived of its traditional purpose. . . . Thus for the first time since his creation man will be faced with his real, his permanent problem, how to use his freedom from pressing economic cares, how to occupy his leisure, which science and compound interest will have won for him, to live wisely and agreeably and well. (pp. 360, 365–67)*

Yet, not all economists are equally impressed by the possibilities inherent in the recent growth in output, leisure, and life expectancy. Consider Kenneth E. Boulding, *Economics as a Science* (New York: McGraw-Hill, 1970):

*These projections of the developmental process into a society of effortless abundance in which economics . . . has withered away are fantasies arising from a rather naive extrapolation of what may eventually be seen historically as a rather brief period in the history of man. It is true, of course, that for the last two hundred years man, especially in the temperate zones of the world, has been getting very much richer than he was before, as measured by per capita real income. His provisions have increased in quantity and variety to the point where the scale of human life by comparison with anything that has gone before has become reasonably ample in regard to such provisions as food, clothing, shelter, information inputs, and travel. This is true for about a third of mankind; two-thirds of the human race remain in the condition of severely limiting poverty in which man has lived for most of his history. There is little doubt that short of catastrophe this process of development will continue and expand to more and more people. Nevertheless, it is a process which will not go on indefinitely. . . . Growth at a constant rate cannot go on forever, or even for very long. Otherwise, there would soon be only one thing in the universe. Every growth curve exhibits a declining rate of growth as the thing that is growing increases in size. . . . The economic growth which has been characteristic of the last two hundred years is no exception to this rule. (pp. 142–43)*

Finally, note the Linder and Weisskopf citations in the "Selected Readings." They suggest that the Keynes–Boulding controversy about the growth of available *goods* ultimately does not matter; scarcity is bound to persist, unless people (as in the Garden of Eden) can also gain unlimited *time;* that is, immortality!

# Chapter 2

1. Of course, there are other costs besides goods foregone (but these other costs are not what this chapter is about). Consider the involuntary unemployment of human resources; it can inflict wounds that tear apart civilized society. In the United States, the most dramatic instance of this was the Great Depression of the 1930s. This is a period with which most readers of this book will be only faintly familiar, for fewer than 10 percent of today's population were adults in 1930. But try to imagine what it must have been like living in a country in which millions, many millions, were involuntarily unemployed for years on end. To be sure, initially their unemployment may almost have seemed a welcome vacation. Hopefully and vigorously went the search for a new job. But when employment did not come soon, the vacation-type atmosphere quickly vanished. Job hunting turned desperate. Week after week, month after month, there was no luck. Then the clothes wore out, the few valuables were sold to feed the family, the food became less, and worse. Human skills began to erode for lack of use. Despair began to move in, followed by stark poverty. By the thousands, people were evicted from their apartments, lost their houses, and were pushed off their farms. Think how they must have felt, living with friends, making a few rooms serve a dozen people, shivering through a winter, and listening to their children cry for bread.

Think of the mental anguish of men or women in this position, unable to look at their family because they felt so guilty, frightened at their own inability to help them, irritable because they disliked the stigma of charity, angry because their society denied them the opportunity to earn their own living. There just was no place for them and those they loved! No wonder the parks and streets were filled with people in shabby clothes, refusing to even move. No wonder others, by the thousands, wandered through the countryside, aimlessly, scraping by on almost nothing, pursued by the police and "respectable" citizens who wanted nothing to do with them.

Yet, we need not dwell in the 1930s. What may seem like ancient history to you can be found in the midst of contemporary society (although of lesser scope and intensity). Recent studies show that few events are as traumatic as involuntary unemployment and that there is a close connection not only between such unemployment and poverty (the lack of goods), but also between unemployment and alcoholism, drug addiction, heart disease, mental illness, suicide, crime, family breakdown, and more.

2. This is an important question, with no simple answer. Indeed, Leibenstein's critics, noted in this chapter's "Selected Readings," argue that the elimination of X-inefficiency (by any of the indicated means) may well be so costly as to make it not worthwhile in light of the expected output gains. The issue of incentives will be taken up again in later chapters of this book. See the subject index under *incentives*.

3. The task has already been accomplished in text Figure 2.2, "Economic Inefficiency." Note that the $MRT_{x,a}$ is nothing else but the slope of the production-function graph.

4. The second Pareto condition (Table 2.2) can most easily be illustrated with the help of production possibilities curves, as in Figure 2.A. Each curve shows all the combinations of good $a$ and good $b$ that a given productive enterprise is able to produce with current technology by using fixed quantities of resources fully and in technically efficient ways. Note that the $MRT_{a,b}$ is nothing else but the slope of such a curve.

**Figure 2.A**

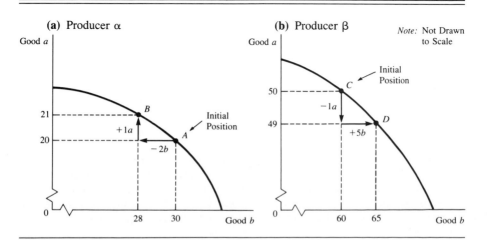

5. Soviet Union *MRT:* 1 fishing vessel for 1,000 sewing machines. Bulgaria: 1 fishing vessel for 5,000 sewing machines. *Specialization:* If the Soviet Union produced 1 more fishing vessel (and, therefore, 1,000 fewer sewing machines), while Bulgaria produced 1 less fishing vessel (and, therefore, 5,000 more sewing machines), world output would clearly be up by 4,000 sewing machines (without the use of any additional resources). *Trade:* If the Soviet Union then exported to Bulgaria 1 extra fishing vessel in exchange for 4,000 sewing machines, both countries would be better off (even though the gain from specialization would not be shared equally). The Soviet Union would have the same number of fishing vessels as before (output $+1$; export $+1$), but 3,000 more sewing machines (output $-1,000$; import $+4,000$). Bulgaria would have the same number of fishing vessels as before (output $-1$; import $+1$), but 1,000 more sewing machines (output $+5,000$; export $+4,000$).

Bonus question: Planners would need data on *marginal* costs of production, because marginal rates of transformation between goods could be inferred from marginal cost ratios. Unfortunately, planners often did not have such data and used instead average cost or price data, both of which were poor indicators of marginal costs. In fact, specialization decisions made on the basis of price ratios that do not reflect marginal cost ratios could easily *reduce* world output. Use, for example, the following price set, while assuming as correct the marginal rates of transformation given above:

|  | *Fishing Vessels* | *Sewing Machines* |
|---|---|---|
| **Soviet Union** | 1,000 rubles | 100 rubles |
| **Bulgaria** | 1,000 leva | 200 leva |

These prices suggest the ability of the Soviet Union to exchange 1 fishing vessel for 10 sewing machines and that of Bulgaria to exchange 1 fishing vessel for 5 sewing machines. Specializing on the basis of this false opportunity cost signal (fishing vessels in terms of sewing machines appear cheaper in Bulgaria) leads to the change in actual output (based on the true marginal rates of transformation) given below. Apparently, this type of result often occurred but was masked by a lower-than-possible rate of economic growth.

| | | |
|---|---|---|
| **Soviet Union** | $-1$ fishing vessel; | $+1,000$ sewing machines |
| **Bulgaria** | $+1$ fishing vessel; | $-5,000$ sewing machines |
| **Combined** | No change | $-4,000$ sewing machines |

6. The third Pareto condition (Table 2.3) can most easily be illustrated by juxtaposing a production possibilities curve (as in problem 4) and a consumption indifference curve (which shows all the combinations of good *a* and good *b* that, in the opinion of a given consumer, yield the same total of welfare or utility and among which the consumer, therefore, is indifferent). See Figure 2.B and note that the $MRT_{a,b}$ is the slope of the production possibilities curve, while the $MRS_{a,b}$ is the slope of the consumption indifference curve. Also note: While the producer moves from *A* to *B*, the consumer (who would be indifferent about moving along indifference curve $I_0$ from *C* to *D*) in fact moves from *C* to *E* (and ends up with higher utility on indifference curve $I_1$).

**Figure 2.B**

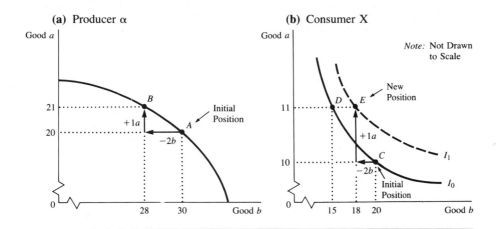

**(a)** Producer α

**(b)** Consumer X

*Note:* Not Drawn to Scale

7. The fourth Pareto condition (Table 2.4) can most easily be illustrated with consumption indifference curves of the type introduced in problem 6. See Figure 2.C and observe that the $MRS_{a,b}$ is nothing else but the slope of such a curve. Note: While consumer X would be indifferent about moving along indifference curve $I_0$ from $A$ to $B$, the consumer actually moves from $A$ to $C$ (and ends up with higher utility on indifference curve $I_1$). At the same time, while consumer Y would be indifferent about moving along indifference curve $I_2$ from $D$ to $E$, the consumer actually moves from $D$ to $F$ (and ends up with higher utility on indifference curve $I_3$).

8. Table 2.A here is an adaptation of text Table 2.4 to show the optimum allocation of resources among users of the same resources. Firm α might initially produce 100 bicycles

**Figure 2.C**

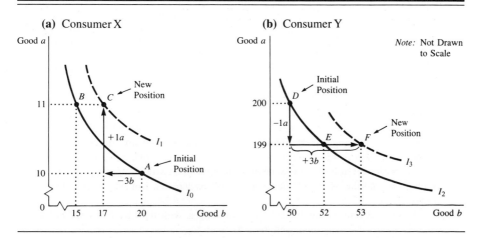

**(a)** Consumer X

**(b)** Consumer Y

*Note:* Not Drawn to Scale

**Table 2.A**

| Resource Services Consumed Per Year | MRTS | Assessment |
|---|---|---|
| **(A)** *Initial Situation* | | |
| Producer $\alpha$    10x and 20y | 1x for 5y | |
| Producer $\beta$    200x and 50y | 1x for 2y | |
| 210x and 70y | | Economic inefficiency exists; it is advisable for |
| **(B)** *New Situation* | | $\alpha$ to use more x (and less y) and for $\beta$ to use |
| Producer $\alpha$    11x and 17y | 1x for 4.8y | more y (and less x) |
| Producer $\beta$    199x and 53y | 1x for 2.1y | |
| 210x and 70y | | |
| **(C)** *Final Situation* | | |
| Producer $\alpha$    20x and  2y | 1x for 2.9y | Economic efficiency has been reached; no |
| Producer $\beta$    190x and 68y | 1x for 2.9y | further changes are desirable |
| 210x and 70y | | |

per day, while using 10 units of labor (x) plus 20 units of capital services (y). Firm $\beta$ might initially produce 300 bicycles (or, significantly, 300 lawnmowers), while using 200 units of identical labor (x) plus 50 units of identical capital services (y). Given the divergent marginal rates of technical substitution of part (A), the new situation (B) implies higher outputs for both firms (11x and 15y would have produced the same output for $\alpha$; 199x plus 52y, the same output for $\beta$). . . .

9. The new Pareto condition (Table 2.A) can most easily be illustrated with *equal-product curves* or *isoquants* (each of which shows all the combinations of resource x and resource y that, under current technology, yield the same maximum output total). The slope of isoquants, which look just like consumption indifference curves, equals the $MRTS_{x,y}$. Consider Figure 2.D and note how it equals Figure 2.C, except for labels. Note also that the isoquants have been labeled with cardinal output numbers (100 bicycles, 120 bicycles, etc.). Unlike the utility totals of Figure 2.C indifference curves, which can only be ranked by ordinal numbers—1st, 2nd, etc., output totals can be measured cardinally.

10. Pareto has plenty of critics. For example, his (and our) definition of economic efficiency is based on a number of value judgments. Some economists do not share these values. They do not consider economic efficiency, as defined by Pareto and in this book, a worthy goal to be pursued.

   First, Pareto defines total economic welfare in terms of the welfare of all the individuals comprising society. Total economic welfare is somehow the sum of individual welfares; it is not a separate concept independent of these individual building blocks. Pareto's critics often look upon society as an entity independent of the individuals that compose it, and they talk of "the social good" as separate from the sum of individual welfares.

   Second, Pareto assumes that adult individuals (with the rarest of exceptions) are the best judges of their own welfares. An increase or decrease in the welfare of an individual is counted as such only when the affected individual so testifies. Pareto's

**Figure 2.D**

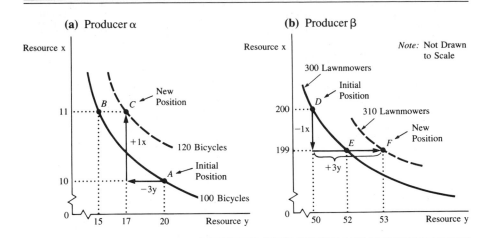

**(a)** Producer α                    **(b)** Producer β

*(a)* Resource x — New Position, B, C, +1x, 120 Bicycles, Initial Position, 11, 10, A, −3y, 100 Bicycles, 0, 15, 17, 20, Resource y

*(b)* Resource x — *Note:* Not Drawn to Scale, 300 Lawnmowers, Initial Position, D, 200, −1x, 310 Lawnmowers, New Position, E, F, 199, +3y, 0, 50, 52, 53, Resource y

critics often believe that the preferences of some people are superior to those of others and that everybody's welfare should be judged on the basis of these superior tastes.

Third, as noted in Biography 2.1, Pareto assumes, contrary to Bentham, that the welfare of one individual cannot be compared with that of another. As a result, Pareto is willing to make pronouncements about changes in *total* economic welfare only when the welfares of all individuals (in their own judgments) have remained unchanged or moved in the same direction. Pareto remains silent on all other comparisons. Thus, if a million people said they were better off as a result of a reallocation of resources or goods, if even a single person claimed to be worse off, this would lead Pareto to assert ignorance about the effect on *total* economic welfare.

As a consequence, the Pareto optimum, unlike Bentham's welfare maximum, is not a unique situation. Many possible situations would be considered optimal by the Pareto criterion. For example, the situation in part (C) of Table 2.4 is economically efficient because the Pareto condition concerning equality of the marginal rates of substitution is satisfied. According to Pareto, no further changes could be recommended by economists because such changes would not increase total economic welfare *with certainty.* But now consider a situation in which the two individuals consumed completely different shares of the total quantities of the goods available. Suppose X as well as Y each consumed 105$a$ and 35$b$. If the marginal rates of substitution were still equal (at whatever rate), this situation would be equally efficient as the one depicted in part (C). Again, the Pareto criterion would not endorse any change because, again, such change would not raise total economic welfare *unambiguously.*

Yet, the two situations would almost surely differ by a Benthamite measure of welfare (which measured and added together each person's welfare with the help of a cardinal number). Quite possibly, Pareto's critics assert, making poor X richer at the expense of rich Y would raise the total of economic welfare by giving, say, 300 units of extra satisfaction to poor X, while taking 20 units from rich Y. Yet, Pareto, crippled by his own assumptions, would support the status quo and refuse to endorse any change in the (legitimate) fear that poor X might gain 300 and rich Y lose 800 units of satisfaction in the process. Since we cannot measure these changes in satisfaction but can only speculate about them, Pareto refuses to make a judgment. Any distribution of goods among consumers that is associated with equal marginal rates of substitution is, therefore, considered equally acceptable by his efficiency criterion, which exasperates Pareto's critics.

Nor is this all. Even those who approve of Pareto's approach wonder whether there might not exist a real problem with *implementing* moves away from economic ineffi-ciency: The required adjustments (like switching resources from the production of one good to the production of another or rearranging which consumer consumes what) are surely not costless. They take time and effort at the least. Might this not discourage people from carrying out such changes? And what about envy, they ask? Even if two parties wanted to get together and make themselves better off, third parties (who would become no worse off by objective standards) might interfere because they would *feel* worse off. After all, most people look at their own welfare *relative to* that of others. They rejoice when others become worse off, and they resent it when others become better off, these critics fear. Hence, they reason, envious people will do their best to obstruct any Pareto-like changes that improve the lot of their fellows. What do *you* think?

# Chapter 3

1. The flow of human resources in a given period can be increased in two ways. First, one can use a larger stock of resources at an unchanged rate: By using 125 million people for 8 hours per day instead of 100 million people for 8 hours per day, one has 1,000 million instead of 800 million hours of labor per day. Second, one can use an unchanged stock of resources at a higher rate: By using 100 million people for 10 hours per day instead of 100 million people for 8 hours per day, one also has 1,000 million instead of 800 million hours of labor per day. (The same approach can, of course, be used with respect to natural and capital resources. And the result is the same too: A greater resource flow translates into a greater flow of goods.)

The stock of human resources might be increased by encouraging births (as hap-pened in Nazi Germany, France, Czechoslovakia) with the help of such devices as propaganda, medals for mothers, measures against infant mortality, provision of ma-ternity pay, child care centers, children's allowances, and—on the negative side—outlawing abortions and contraceptives. The stock can also be increased by promoting immigration on a permanent or temporary basis (as evidenced by Turkish, Greek, and Yugoslav "guest workers" in West Germany, Polish workers in Czechoslovakia and East Germany, Mexican workers in the United States, Bulgarian and Vietnamese workers in the Soviet Union). At the same time, emigration can be discouraged or forbidden (as in many places, ranging from Afghanistan, Cuba, and East Germany to Kampuchea and the Soviet Union). In addition, the labor force participation rate can be increased, as by drawing housewives, students, and the elderly back into the process of production (as has happened in China and the Soviet Union).

Finally, of course, the number of hours worked per year by any given person can be increased in numerous ways: fewer holidays, longer working days, and more.

2. Answers can vary, but here is one: The entrepreneur might discover, and then take advantage of, the fact that an enterprise's production function exhibits *increasing returns to scale*. This is a situation in which a simultaneous and equal percentage change in the

use of all physical inputs leads to a *larger* percentage change in physical output. Triple all inputs, for example, and output more than triples. Thus, output *per unit* of input is up. Why should the average products of all inputs rise when scale is increased and, therefore, fall when scale is reduced? A number of possible reasons can be cited. Most important among these are the advantages inherent in a specialization of inputs and the operation of certain physical laws.

As the scale of production becomes larger, the process of production can be broken down into a multitude of ever narrower tasks, and more and more people and machines can specialize in performing these different tasks. As a result, people who have different inherent talents can concentrate on what they can do best. In an apple orchard, for example, the person with a knack for mechanics can work full time fixing orchard-spraying machines when the orchard is large and there are 300 of them but could hardly make a full-time job out of fixing just one. At the same time, other people can specialize in accounting, financing, marketing, apple picking, bee keeping, research, or perhaps even in worker dental care. Even when talents are not inherent, it is easier to create and then maintain skills in people when each person's work is reduced to a simple and repetitive operation: "Practice makes perfect." This advantage is lost to the jack-of-all-trades who must pass from operation to operation, moving, possibly, among many different locations of work, using ever different sets of tools, and all the while losing valuable time in between tasks or while "warming up" for a new one.

The very simplicity and repetitiveness of narrowly specialized, large-scale operations encourages, in turn, the invention and use of machines. When only 900 bushels of apples are produced per year, who would think of installing an assembly line to sort and wash them? The introduction of all kinds of specialized capital equipment, from electric turbines and internal combustion engines to computers and servo-mechanisms, testifies to the endless possibilities of increasing productivity through the use of specialization.

The operation of certain physical laws is also responsible for increasing returns to scale. Consider a box that is 1 foot long, 1 foot wide, and 1 foot high. It has a surface area of 6 square feet and a volume of 1 cubic foot. If one quadruples the length, width, and height, the surface area becomes 96 square feet, and the volume grows to 64 cubic feet. A 16-fold increase in surface area produces a 64-fold increase in volume! Frequently, the input quantities needed to construct "containers," such as cargo ships, office buildings, or pipelines, depend on their surface area, but their output depends on their volume. Larger scale, therefore, yields more output per unit of input. Many similar examples can be cited.

3. For a continuation of Table 3.1, see Table 3.A. *Comment:* Compared to low-growth strategy I, strategy II sacrifices total consumption of 18 (periods 2 to 9), but delivers higher consumption from period 11 onwards forever. Strategy III sacrifices total consumption of 46 (periods 2 to 10), but delivers higher consumption than Strategy I from period 12 onwards and higher consumption than Strategy II from period 13 onwards. According to Horvat, this shows that a maximum growth strategy is best for human welfare in the long run. Yet, one wonders: Does it make sense to assume an eternally constant marginal-output-to-investment ratio of $\frac{1}{3}$? Does it make sense to add up consumption sacrifices (or consumption gains) of different years and treat them as equals, without employing the discounting process? In short, can one justify ignoring how people *feel* about losing 1 unit of consumption now and gaining 2, 3, or more units back 50 years hence?

**Table 3.A.**

| Period | Strategy I | | | | Strategy II | | | | Strategy III | | | |
|---|---|---|---|---|---|---|---|---|---|---|---|---|
| | Output $Q$ | Saving = Investment | | Consumption $C = Q - S$ | Output $Q$ | Saving = Investment | | Consumption $C = Q - S$ | Output $Q$ | Saving = Investment | | Consumption $C = Q - S$ |
| | | % of $Q$ | Amount $S = I$ | | | % of $Q$ | Amount $S = I$ | | | % of $Q$ | Amount $S = I$ | |
| 11 | 163 | 15 | 24 | 139 | 188 | 25 | 47 | 141 | 214 | 35 | 75 | 139 |
| 12 | 171 | 15 | 26 | 145 | 204 | 26 | 53 | 151 | 239 | 37 | 88 | 151 |
| 13 | 180 | 15 | 27 | 153 | 222 | 27 | 60 | 162 | 268 | 39 | 105 | 163 |
| 14 | 189 | 15 | 28 | 161 | 242 | 28 | 68 | 174 | 303 | 41 | 124 | 179 |
| 15 | 198 | 15 | 30 | 168 | 265 | 29 | 77 | 188 | 344 | 43 | 148 | 196 |

4. Imagine an economy that at every moment in time wasted 12 percent of its resources by incurring unnecessary costs (X-inefficiency) and by violating Pareto's conditions of economic efficiency. If that economy's output, because of the very circumstances that produced X-inefficiency and economic inefficiency, grew at a rate of 6 percent per year, while it would grow at only 3 percent per year if it managed to avoid the aforementioned inefficiencies, Schumpeter would advise us to embrace inefficiency as the price of superior growth performance. That economy's output would not grow at 3 percent a year, as the series

$$100\text{-}103\text{-}106.09\text{-}109.27\text{-}112.55\text{-}115.93 \ldots$$

It would grow instead from its lower inefficient base at a rate of 6 percent a year, such as the series

$$88\text{-}93.28\text{-}98.88\text{-}104.81\text{-}111.10\text{-}117.76 \ldots$$

Note: After a mere five years, the people in the latter economy would have overcome their output handicap. Forevermore, they would be better off than the people in the former economy (which would always avoid Leibenstein's and Pareto's inefficiency alike).

As Schumpeter put it, "A system . . . that at every given point of time fully utilizes its possibilities to the best advantage may yet in the long run be inferior to a system that does so at *no* given point of time, because the latter's failure to do so may be a condition for the level or speed of long-run performance."[1] But, as in problem 3, once again the question arises: Who should decide whether a sacrifice of goods in one year is or is not worth more goods in the future?

5. This can be debated at length, but note that not all concepts of economic justice require the kinds of utility comparisons alluded to by the two speakers here. Consider commutative justice. Consider the hours-worked variant of distributive justice. Note also that Ms. B's situation could arise even under the absolute-income-equality variant of distributive justice. What if the people who lacked insulin or milk had the same income as those owning planes or yachts but had spent it all on furniture and vacation trips? What if the people who owned planes or yachts had the same income as those lacking insulin or milk but, unlike the latter, had starved themselves of all kinds of other goods in order to indulge their hobby?

6. See Figure 3.A for Mr. A's comment. Picture a very large initial deviation from equality at *D* or *F*, respectively. Moving from *D* to *E*, person A gains utility of $a + b$, person B loses $b$, making for a net *gain* of $a$ (shaded). Moving from equally likely *F* to *E*, person B gains utility of $f + g + d$, person A loses $g + d + c$, making again for a net *gain* of $(f - c)$. In this example, there is *certainty* of gain from a move to equality. For further discussion, see John Bennett, "The Probable Gain from Egalitarian Redistribution," *Oxford Economic Papers*, March 1981, pp. 165–69.

So far as Ms. B is concerned, comments will vary. But note: Figure 3.C in problem 8 pictures her "efficient pleasure machine" (as a person named Smith).

---

[1]Joseph A. Schumpeter, *Capitalism, Socialism, and Democracy*, 3d ed. (New York: Harper & Row, 1950), p. 83. A similar sentiment is expressed in Peter Wiles, "Growth vs. Choice," *Economic Journal*, June 1956, pp. 244–55.

**Figure 3.A**

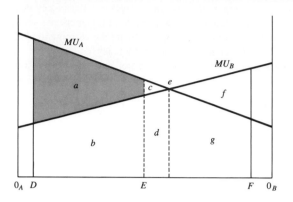

7. Consider the case of two persons (or groups of persons), P and R. Let P be poor and have no earning capacity at all (or a low one). Let R earn $20 per hour and be rich. We would not be surprised if R, when taxed to support P (and when, thus, receiving an effectively lower wage), were (1) to reduce hours worked and (2) to reduce hours worked all the more the higher was the tax. Some of the possibilities are shown in Table 3.B. In this example, society's income is maximized (at $160) if R is not taxed at all and P receives nothing, as in row A. In row D, society's income is cut in half (to $80) if a tax rate of 50 percent is introduced and P and R are given identical incomes (of $40 each). Yet, in row C a less strict goal that maintains some income inequality enables P as well as R to be better off (with $48 and $72, respectively). This, presumably, is what Rawls' exception is all about. Figure 3.B, which is based on columns (4) and (5) of Table 3.B, illustrates the discussion graphically.

8. a. From *E*, Jones and Smith could move to any point within shaded, lens-shaped area *EDAC*, including points on the indifference curves enclosing this area. From *F* or *G*,

**Table 3.B** Hypothetical Income Redistribution

| | Tax Rate on R (1) | Hours Worked by R (2) | Pre-Tax Income of R (3) = (2) × $20 | Tax Revenue and Transfer to P (4) = (1) × (3) | After-Tax Income of R (5) = (3) − (4) |
|---|---|---|---|---|---|
| **(A)** | 0% | 8 | $160 | $ 0 | $160 |
| **(B)** | 20% | 7 | 140 | 28 | 112 |
| **(C)** | 40% | 6 | 120 | 48 | 72 |
| **(D)** | 50% | 4 | 80 | 40 | 40 |
| **(E)** | 60% | 2 | 40 | 24 | 16 |
| **(F)** | 80% | 0.5 | 10 | 8 | 2 |
| **(G)** | 100% | 0 | 0 | 0 | 0 |

Redistributive taxation that changes extreme income inequality, in row A, to absolute equality, in row D, may well produce disincentive effects so strong that all people are worse off than would be possible under some degree of inequality, as in row C.

**Figure 3.B**   The Limits of Redistribution

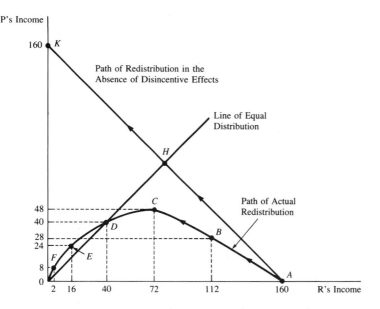

It may be impossible to redistribute income from rich R to poor P along line *AHK* (which implies an unchanged income total). It may only be possible to redistribute along line *ACF* (because the very act of redistribution has disincentive effects that reduce the income total). Under the circumstances, any attempt to redistribute a *given* income from a position of extreme inequality (*A*) to absolute equality (*H*) is bound to fail; an equal distribution of a *lower* income is possible (*D*), but this makes all people worse off than would be possible while maintaining some degree of inequality (*C*). The difference between *C* and *D* illustrates the exception to the Rawlsian absolute-equality rule.

they could move to any point within a similar lens-shaped area formed by the two persons' indifference curves (not shown) going through *F* or *G*.

b. A cross-cut of the utility mountain above the contract curve is shown by the top line in Figure 3.C, wherein the horizontal axis represents the straightened-out contract curve. Note how various points on the contract curve along the path from $O_J$ to $O_S$ (such as *K*, *D*, *C*, and *H*) appear in this graph as well. Obviously, Jones's total utility rises along the path from $O_J$ toward $O_S$, while that of Smith rises from $O_S$ toward $O_J$, as ever higher indifference curves are reached. If utility were not only measurable, but also interpersonally comparable, one could construct the top line of social utility, $U_J + U_S$. Caution: Do not confuse this graph with text Figure 3.3, "The Equal Income Argument," which measures *marginal* utility (of income).

c. Yes, as long as the two consumers' marginal rates of substitution diverged (and they were, thus, positioned off the contract curve).

9. This rather cryptic statement does allude to an important issue. Open inflation—a sustained increase over time in the general level of prices—can have a number of deleterious effects, unless it happens to be perfectly anticipated and perfectly balanced (all prices move by the same percentage and *relative* prices are, thus, unchanged). Unanticipated

**Figure 3.C**

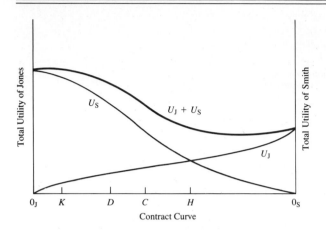

inflation, for example, capriciously redistributes people's income and wealth and, thus, affects the degree of equity achieved. (People whose money income rises less rapidly than the general price level or who hold financial assets are hurt; others whose money income rises more rapidly than the general price level or who hold real assets are helped.) Such inflation is likely to make people feel angry, cheated, mistrustful, and belligerently active in trying to preserve their ''rightful'' share of the pie. Under certain circumstances, such inflation can also reduce the size of the pie itself (for example, when a market economy collapses entirely into a complex network of barter); it can even put an end to social and political institutions.

10. The answer depends on how equity is defined. But consider high-income individuals in, say, the United States or Japan. What are they likely to do with, say, a $5 million income per year? To consume it, they would have to spend on consumption goods nearly $14,000 *per day*—an unlikely feat. More likely than not, a large share of their income is invested and, thus, contributes to economic growth. What if someone now pursued equity in the sense of equal incomes for all? Almost certainly, many of the low-income beneficiaries would increase consumption rather than save and invest. The rate of economic growth would fall. A similar story could be told about any centrally planned economy in which the government was initially receiving (and investing) a large share of the nation's income.

# Chapter 4

1. One is tempted to agree with the statement (exceptions to the contrary notwithstanding). Consider how Bushmen individually embody all of their society's knowledge, can produce all they need, and can survive in complete isolation from their fellow tribesmen. Not so with Americans. As individuals, they know, perhaps, how to wire a single type

of appliance but little else: They do not know how to grow food, how to catch game, or how to clothe or house themselves; nor do they know how to make or repair most of the gadgets surrounding them and used by them daily! It is easy to see why. When the productive process becomes fragmented, each person must concentrate on playing a small part in one of its many stages. Everyone is productive only in the most indirect way; no one can point to a complete product that he or she has made. And people become tied to helping produce, in the most roundabout way, a single type of product only. As a result, they can realize only a minimum of the vast repertoire of abilities slumbering within them.

2. This is a pretty arrogant argument, often heard. Clearly, there is a fine line between the speaker's belief that our wants are created artificially by others and the assertion that the speaker's tastes are superior to those of others.

    Sure enough, people are born with very few innate desires, with wants that are *theirs* in the ultimate sense that they are fixed in their genes. Thus, it is inevitable that most preferences beyond the liking of mother's milk and the disliking of loud noises and such are learned from other people, such as parents, teachers, and peers. Yet, one can question whether individual firms that advertise thereby create wants. They merely identify wants already existing, and they try to get people to satisfy them in a particular way. They "create" wants merely in this trivial sense. Thus, all people at all times and in all places want food. Although the "manipulators" have nothing to do with this fact, they might try to channel such a basic desire toward ice cream, and Häagen Dazs ice cream at that. Similarly, all people want clothing, but they might be induced to satisfy this basic want with Robert Hall coats. And people want beauty, cleanliness, and excitement; mobility, shelter, and sex. The "manipulators" do not create these desires either, but they do their best to direct them: toward RCA Beethoven records, Sweet Life herbal essence shampoo, and scenic rides in Schweizer sailplanes; toward Ford Escort stationwagons, American Barn homes, and *Playboy* magazines. Indeed, in the United States, the *limited* power of the alleged manipulators is evidenced by their preoccupation with market surveys, by their failure to launch 80 to 90 percent of all technically successful new products at all (because they do not survive market research) and by their withdrawal of a third to a half of those products that are launched (because they fail to sell sufficiently during the first year). At the same time, the *thoughtful* appraisal of their own choices by consumers is evidenced by their refusal to make repeat purchases where their basic desires have not been satisfied by a specific product, by their purchase of disinterested advice (an appraiser's, before buying a house, and a mechanic's, before buying a used car), and by their subscription to consumer magazines. Perhaps we better accept people's spending decisions as expressions of their "true" wants and dismiss those who would do otherwise as would-be dictators who would love to impose their own tastes on others.

3. Those who are concerned about the alienation of people from other people seek to eliminate the coercion of people into *involuntary* choice. Such coercion should not be confused (as it is in this statement) with the painful consequences of *voluntary* choice. Those who take a job voluntarily thereby choose its advantages (such as pay) as well as its disadvantages (such as having to be at work by 8 AM). The mere existence of such disadvantages does not indicate the presence of coercion.

4. Like so many other things in life, jobs have advantages and disadvantages. Workers want the former and gripe about the latter. There certainly is no known way to quantify

the degree of alienation resulting, say, from any violation of worker sovereignty. Perhaps one should take American workers at their own word: A recent U.S. government study reports that 85 percent of American workers do not complain about dehumanizing work and are well satisfied with their jobs. To assess the presence of alienation, one could, however, also consider more objective indicators of the type mentioned by A and B: American workers clearly do not stay home from work in droves, they do not burn down their workplaces, they do not riot in the streets. They can choose their occupation, their geographic location, their employer. Through unions and government, they do influence the incidence of industrial accidents or occupational diseases, and more.

5. Mr. A is dreaming. In an enterprise employing many hundreds of thousands of workers (which is true of G.M.) impersonal relationships are inevitable and there is nothing sinister about it: The human mind cannot cope with complex relationships. Not everyone can directly participate in all decisions in a large group because of the sheer impossibility of running the switchboard of communications! In a group of three people, there are 6 possible relationships (three 1:1 relations, plus three involving a couple versus one person). In a group of four people, these possible links rise to 25. And things skyrocket from there. In a large organization, therefore, many potentially warm relationships must be nipped in the bud and be replaced by an impersonal nexus of money or command lest everything grind to a halt.

However, as Ms. B implies, there is nothing inevitable about workers being organized by a management elected by private stockholders. For example, General Motors could be run by a management elected entirely by the firm's own workers, or by a combination of stockholders and workers or by all kinds of other combinations, such as stockholders and workers and customers and even neighbors and local government officials. Conceivably, workers who thus had a voice in the establishment of power over them (and who could periodically replace those in power) would enjoy a greater degree of worker sovereignty and have less reason to be alienated.

6. The statement is essentially correct. Genuine labor unions that are truly responsible to their members only and are not the tool of someone else (such as private employers or a government central planning board) routinely help draw up and enforce contracts protecting workers from tyranny on the job. This is true in the United States. Far from being considered a hated means of oppression, such contract rules, explicit and equally applicable to all, are *liked* by workers because they protect workers from the arbitrary whim of the boss with respect to hiring, work assignment, layoff, recall, promotion, disciplinary action, dismissal, physical working conditions, and much more. As a result, just as citizens at large can criticize their government, American workers can point out stupidity on the foreman's part and do it with impunity. More likely than not, their morale is *high*.

7. A matter of opinion. This case clearly indicates how the goals people pursue (and which are discussed in chapters 2 through 4 of this book) may well be contradictory. Thus, if the pursuit of economic growth calls for the construction of a canal, the avoidance of alienation from nature may well counsel abandonment of the project. Indeed, the same issue created the great Everglades jetport controversy of 1969:* There had been plans to build in the Florida Everglades a new giant jetport serving Miami, together with

*This section is based in part on Philip Wylie, "Against All Odds, the Birds Have Won," *The New York Times,* February 1, 1970, section 10, pp. 1 and 11.

industrial and residential developments. Thirty-nine square miles had been purchased, $13 million spent on one landing strip, when federal funds for the jetport were withdrawn and an agreement was reached to locate it elsewhere. All this, furious critics pointed out, to save a 5,000-square-mile superswamp full of alligators, poisonous snakes, clouds of mosquitoes, and huge biting flies! Why *not* pave it all over?

The reason given by ecologists was simply this: Here, south of Lake Okeechobee's 700 square miles of shallow fresh water, was a vast wetland composed of three swamps. At first sight, this area may indeed seem useless. First, there is the Big Cypress Swamp. Second, there is the sawgrass region or prairie of brownish ''grass'' standing in shoal water (really consisting not of grass but of an abrasive sedge that quickly strips a visitor of clothing and then of skin). Third, there is the largest mangrove forest on earth, impenetrable with tentacle-like roots and stiff, entwined branches standing in slow-moving water that becomes brackish, then salty, and then the sea. This area harbors more than alligators and mosquitoes. It is the home of egrets and ibises, of ducks and turkeys, of panthers and foxes, of deer and bears, of herons and otters, of orchids and flowers. Because of its uniqueness, Congress established part of the area in 1934 as Everglades National Park. The construction of the jetport and its satellite developments would doom the area because it would change the flow of water and would pollute. And this is the problem, ecologists pointed out. Since we do not know what life forms are essential for man's survival, we cannot afford to let the Everglades die. Since we know so little about the intricate living understructure supporting humanity, we cannot risk losing *any* form of life. A single break in the planetary, life-sustaining system can become fatal for all life. For example, all organisms build protein basically from hydrogen, oxygen, sulfur, carbon, and nitrogen. If people were to destroy any of a half dozen types of bacteria involved in, say, the nitrogen cycle, all life on earth could end.

When these arguments won out over commercial interests, for the first time in U.S. history, people's dependence on nature, however indirect, was explicitly recognized to have priority over economic growth.

8. Once again, the conflict noted in answer 7 comes to the surface, but this time the issue of equity arises as well. Without doubt, pollution avoidance involves an opportunity cost, and someone has to bear it. Considering the law of declining marginal utility, the rich may be more willing to sacrifice goods for the preservation of nature than the poor. Yet, depending on the method of pollution avoidance that is employed (see answer 10), the actual sacrifice might have to be made by the rich or the poor.

9. Many critics of economic growth view mankind as travelers on a spaceship called Earth that has embarked on a long voyage with no end in sight. When life is viewed in this way, a natural corollary is that mankind should be proud of its activities only if the spaceship and all the human bodies traveling on it were kept in perfect shape. Therefore, an ever growing quantity of goods would be a true source of pride only if it were produced each year with renewable resources and recyclable wastes. Otherwise, the human space travelers would be destroying the ultimate source of their lives. They would be acting no differently than the mad bombers who are about the blow up the airplane on which they are flying.

10. Answers can vary, but here are some of the policies that might be pursued in the context of the U.S. economy: moral suasion; banning polluting activities outright; setting input, emission, or ambient standards; taxing waste dumping; subsidizing waste abatement; marketing pollution rights. For a detailed discussion of all these alternatives, see the Kohler citation noted in this chapter's ''Selected Readings.''

# Chapter 5

1. Answers can vary, but here are two possibilities (based on Vaclav Holesovsky, *Economic Systems: Analysis and Comparison* [New York: McGraw Hill, 1977], pp. 49–50, 76–77, and 81–83):

   **Feudalism.**   This economic system prevailed in medieval Europe, beginning between the 7th and 10th centuries. It had two main features.
   a. The formal "ownership" of land was vested in a class of feudal lords (suzerains, nobles, church dignitaries, monasteries) who formed a hierarchy reaching from the king on top to his vassals, then to vassals' vassals of successively lower ranks. Land, however, was held by a given lord as a grant or fief from his superior in the hierarchy and, unlike modern private property, was encumbered by obligations of loyalty, payment of tribute, and military service. Hence the quotation marks above.
   b. At the bottom of the hierarchy stood the laborers who actually cultivated the land. These bondsmen or serfs received a piece of land for their own use but had to pay tribute to their lord and provided the labor (corvée) on the lord's own domain (demesne). Unlike slaves, serfs had *some* rights: the custody of their land, the right to a family, the right to their product above the tax in kind. They were not mobile, however, being tied to the land. (Interestingly, until 1975, the Soviet collective farm peasant was also legally bound to the collective farm where he was born.)
      A system similar to European feudalism existed in Indian villages (the *jajmani* system) in which high-caste landowning families called *jajmani* faced subordinate castes of *kamins* who specialized in different occupations.

   **Fascist Regimentation.**   The National Socialist (Nazi) regime in Germany (1933–1945) introduced a unique system of universal compulsory cartelization that combined formal private ownership of the means of production with central government regimentation. Private business interests were supposed to "dissolve in the organic unity of the nation and be subordinated to the organizing will of the state." The state took over crucial managerial decisions on prices, wages, dividends, finance, investment, and more. Every enterprise was made a member of a "branch group"; "branch groups" were tied into "economic groups" (31 in industry), and "economic groups" were headed by "national groups" (7 altogether). The pyramid was topped by the Ministry of the Economy.
      Note: For further readings on these systems, see Frederic L. Pryor, "Feudalism as an Economic System," *Journal of Comparative Economics,* December 1980, pp. 56–77, and Arthur Schweitzer, *Big Business in the Third Reich* (Bloomington, IN: Indiana University Press, 1964). The "Selected Readings" at the end of this chapter contain a number of sources dealing with other extinct economic systems; note the selections by Baudin, Dalton, Firth, Malinowski, and Wittvogel.

2. Others are doing better. Consider chemistry and the periodic table of Dmitri Mendeleyev (1834–1907). Consider biology and the classification of all forms of life by Carolus Linneaus (1707–1778). In the latter's scheme, we find a division into flora and fauna (the kingdoms of plants and animals); then a division of the animal kingdom into monocellular and multicellular animals; the latter into animals without organs (like sponges) and with organs (like chordates); chordates into nonvertebrates and vertebrates; vertebrates into fishes, amphibians, reptiles, birds, and mammals; mammals into orders,

then families, then genera, then species, then subspecies. Take any concrete individual (your housecat Morris, perhaps) and it can be fitted into all the successive categories containing each other, from cats to fauna.

For a detailed listing, see the *Larousse Encyclopedia of Animal Life* (London: Hamlyn, 1967), pp. 614–17.

3. The speaker doesn't appreciate the *continuum problem:* In the real world, the ownership characteristic in question is not manifested in discrete fashion (100 percent government ownership or 0 percent); instead, as official statistics show, such government ownership ranges anywhere *between* 0 percent and 100 percent, depending on the country in question. See Table 5.A, which considers government to be the owner if it holds title to at least 50 percent of the assets of any establishment (which in itself is a debatable point).

4. Once again, the continuum problem noted in answer 3 arises. In the real world, *economic power* (the capacity to make and enforce choices on the allocation of scarce resources and the apportionment of scarce goods) does not rest with government either 100 percent or 0 percent. Everywhere, we find a *mixture* of government direction and market direction of economic affairs. Consider Table 5.B, which offers an informed guess. Note that the first two countries are usually referred to as capitalist; the latter two, as socialist.

**Table 5.A**   The Relative Importance of Government Ownership

| | | Ratio of Economically Active Population in Enterprises and Facilities Owned by the Government to Total Economically Active* | | |
|---|---|---|---|---|
| Country | Year | Total | Total Material Production[†] | Total except Agriculture, Forestry, Fishing | Total Material Production except Agriculture, Forestry, Fishing |
| West Germany | 1950 | 9% | 7% | 12% | 10% |
| Japan | 1960 | 10 | 5 | 14 | 9 |
| Switzerland | 1960 | 11 | 8 | 12 | 9 |
| United States | 1960 | 15 | 5 | 16 | 6 |
| France | 1954 | 17 | 10 | 22 | 15 |
| Sweden | 1960 | 20 | 6 | 22 | 7 |
| Israel | 1959 | 24 | 8 | 28 | 11 |
| United Kingdom | 1962 | 25 | 17 | 26 | 19 |
| Yugoslavia | 1953 | 30 | 18 | 75 | 80 |
| Austria | 1966 | 31 | 27 | 33 | 30 |
| Finland | 1965 | 34 | 25 | 36 | 26 |
| Bulgaria | 1956 | 37 | 27 | 92 | 88 |
| Poland | 1960 | 48 | 40 | 84 | 86 |
| Soviet Union | 1959 | 59 | 49 | 96 | 95 |
| East Germany | 1964 | 71 | 69 | 80 | 84 |

*Source:* Frederic L. Pryor, *A Guidebook to the Comparative Study of Economic Systems* (Englewood Cliffs, NJ: Prentice-Hall, 1985), p. 19.

*"Economically active" refers to all men and women who participate in the labor force or who are looking for employment.

[†]"Material production" refers to total production excluding services.

**Table 5.B**   Public Planning and Administration of the Economy

| Public Planning and Administration of the Economy | Examples |
|---|---|
| Low | United States in early 1980s |
| High | Nazi Germany; many wartime economies |
| High | Soviet Union in early 1980s |
| Low | Yugoslavia in late 1960s |

*Source:* Frederic L. Pryor, *A Guidebook to the Comparative Study of Economic Systems* (Englewood Cliffs, NJ: Prentice-Hall, 1985), p. 24.

Note also that "government direction" is a vague term. Are we talking of complete centralization wherein all decisions, from the most general to the most minute, emanate from a central decision maker, while all other people obediently and passively carry out the central will? Are we contemplating a disaggregated form of central command wherein broad decisions are made at the top of a hierarchy, then travel down to other people who make more specific choices that are implied by the broader ones? Or are we, perhaps, thinking of a government that directs the economy in indirect ways: by taxing and spending, by import quotas, price fixing, and more? The latter type of activities surely are present in many economies under "market direction."

5. Once again, the continuum problem noted in answer 3 arises. Government expenditures (presumably as a percentage of gross national product, GNP) can and does take on all kinds of sizes. Which is "high," which "low"? Consider Table 5.C for an interesting compilation.

**Table 5.C**   Public Consumption Expenditures in Western and Eastern Europe in 1962

| Country | Public Consumption Expenditures as Percent of GNP | Country | Public Consumption Expenditures as Percent of GNP |
|---|---|---|---|
| West Germany | 30% | East Germany | 33% |
| Austria | 28 | Czechoslovakia | 30 |
| Ireland | 18 | Hungary | 17 |
| Italy | 28 | Poland | 20 |
| Greece | 20 | Bulgaria | 22 |
| Unweighted average | 24.8% | Unweighted average | 24.4% |

*Note:* Public consumption expenditures are expenditures at all levels of government (central and local) that are financed by taxes or governmental borrowing. In this table these expenditures include the following eight functions: political administration, diplomacy and foreign aid, military, internal security, education, health, welfare, and research and development. These data exclude all private expenditures for these eight functions.

*Source:* Frederic L. Pryor, *A Guidebook to the Comparative Study of Economic Systems* (Englewood Cliffs, NJ: Prentice-Hall, 1985), p. 25.

6. Consider an informed assessment, as in Table 5.D. Note that all four countries are commonly considered socialist.

7. Imagine applying the performance criteria of chapters 2 through 4 to various model economic systems. Given that these systems do not exist, one cannot *measure* their performance; one can only speculate about their likely performance, and this procedure *is* vulnerable to the assessor's ideological bias. One must try, of course, to avoid such bias.

   The comparison of actual systems can be just as biased because one can select countries for comparison in such a way as to favor one's predilections: Compare a capitalist country that happens to have 2 percent unemployment with a socialist country that happens to have 20 percent unemployment, if one wants capitalism to look good— even though contrary examples abound.

   *Note:* One should never attempt to mix models with actual cases when making comparative assessments, but people often do just that to score debating points. Example 1: Pick *one* of many versions of capitalism (say, nonexisting laissez-faire) and compare it with *one* of many versions of socialism (say, Kampuchea under murderous Pol Pot); capitalism comes out smelling like a rose. Example 2: Pick 19th-century Britain with seven-year-old children toiling in horrid factories and compare it with a 20th-century blueprint of a small commune, filled with loving brothers and sisters; socialism comes out smelling like a rose.

8. Both speakers are apt to be correct.

   As to Mr. A, imagine a mother *paying* her child for speaking the truth, a husband paying his wife for each smile, a boss paying the secretary for each letter typed, a government paying the citizens for each dollar of revenue collected. . . . These thoughts should be sufficient to elicit other examples of human interaction that involve command or love alongside a preponderance of monetary incentives. And consider the importance, in the real world, of unconscious habits according to which people conform voluntarily to certain moral principles. Such firmly established patterns of conduct as those involving courtesy, honesty, punctuality, and the keeping of confidences and promises clearly reveal deeply ingrained moral beliefs. They might be classified under the rule of "love." Much of the orderliness of the world, in both U.S.-type market economies and Soviet-type command economies, depends on the presence of such "love," which makes people voluntarily observe moral rules without being paid or commanded to do so.

**Table 5.D**   The Relative Importance of Material Incentives

| Importance of Material Incentives | Examples |
| --- | --- |
| High | Soviet Union in early 1980s |
| High | Yugoslavia in late 1960s |
| Low | Cuba during mid-1960s, almost any army |
| Low | China during Cultural Revolution in mid-1960s |

*Source:* Frederic L. Pryor, *A Guidebook to the Comparative Study of Economic Systems* (Englewood Cliffs, NJ: Prentice-Hall, 1985), p. 26.

As to Ms. B, one can, similarly, find examples of human interaction that involve monetary incentives or love alongside a preponderance of command: Note how soldiers fight not only for fear of jail or the firing squad, for also for money, love of country, or their buddies. Or note how citizens soften the impact of bureaucracy by bribing officials or trading in black markets and how pure command systems are overthrown in revolt.

9. The speaker is apt to be correct. Note how (some) earthly fathers issue commands and threaten to withhold their children's allowance, how the Heavenly Father issues commandments and threatens damnation. Consider why (some) communes end up distributing goods according to "points" members have earned by work. . . . These thoughts should be sufficient to elicit other examples of human interaction that involve monetary incentives or command alongside a preponderance of love. For example, consider the marriage relationship (or the teacher-student relationship) as one dominated by love, with a strong supplementary dose of monetary incentives. How long would a spouse (or teacher) maintain the relationship without some *quid pro quo?* Yet, note how quickly the relationship would wither if one formalized the monetary aspects: Can you imagine a marriage contract detailing the exchange of money for dishwashing, vacuum cleaning, sex, housepainting, baby-minding, or cooking supper? How about teachers billing students separately for classes, office consultations, and friendly chats over lunch? In both these relationships money certainly plays a role, but we keep it in the background because the relationships involve much more than mere exchange. Those who forget this destroy the relationship.

10. Note the Holesovsky citation in the "Selected Readings" of this chapter; it agrees with both of our speakers. Holesovsky refused to accept customary labels as guides for classification of systems. The fact that a political regime declares its economic system to be "socialism," he argued, is not sufficient reason for nodding obligingly and doing the same. He wanted to revive the crucial distinction between self-serving label and substance. He paraphrased Lenin: Can anything more "shallow" be imagined than this judgment of an economic system based on nothing more than what the representatives of that system say about themselves? (V. I. Lenin, "What Is to Be Done?" *Collected Works* [London: Lawrence and Wishart, 1961], vol. 5, p. 357). And he quoted Friedrich Engels: "The more productive forces [the state] takes over, placing them under its ownership, the more does it turn into a true integral capitalist, the more citizens does it exploit. Workers remain wage earners, proletarians. The capitalist relationship is not abolished; rather, it is pushed to the extreme." ("Anti-Dühring," *Marx-Engels Werke* [Berlin: Dietz, 1968], p. 260.) Accordingly, Holesovsky renamed Soviet-type economies as economies of *state capitalism*.

    This suggestion is not being followed in this book (although it was tempting to do so) because the whole world is referring to Soviet-type economies as socialist; changing that label now can only contribute to confusion.

# Chapter 6

1. a. One would normally not expect any of the column (4) entries to be negative. Consider Table 6.1, "The Input-Output Table." A negative entry in rows A through C of column (4) would indicate that electric power, steel, or corn previously delivered to households

were being taken away from households in this period. This would be technically impossible in the case of electric power. Negative entries in rows D through F of column (4) are logically impossible: One cannot take away resource services stored up in a previous period, since they cannot be stored.

b. Still considering Table 6.1, the monetary sums of the rows would indicate the dollar receipts of the sellers listed on the left from all the buyers listed on top. Thus, row A, column (8), would denote the receipts of electric power producers; row D, column (8), the receipts of the sellers of labor, and so on. *Note:* The sum of the sums of rows D through F would measure the gross national income.

The monetary sums of the columns would indicate the dollar expenditures of the parties listed on top for all the items listed on the left. Thus the sum of column (1) would indicate the expenditures by electric power producers on raw materials (electric power, steel, corn) and on primary inputs (labor, land, capital); the sum of column (4) would indicate personal consumption expenditures by all households, and so on. *Note:* The sum of the sums of columns (4) through (7) would measure the gross national expenditure $(C + I + G + NX)$.

2. a. Interpreting the Rows

We see from row A, column (8) that truck producers are producing 20 million trucks this year. Some 6 million trucks are being delivered to domestic producers (columns [1] to [3]), but these trucks are *completely used by* their recipients in this very year in the making of other goods. Thus, they are labeled "intermediate goods." While domestic households receive no trucks at all (column [4]), domestic producers receive another 7 million trucks (column [5]), which are not used up in the making of other goods by the time the current year comes to an end. Those trucks, therefore, are "final goods." So are another 2 and 5 million trucks, which are delivered to domestic government or foreigners.

Row B shows this country producing 50 million barrels of fuel oil during this year (column [8]). However, another 663 million barrels are being imported from abroad (negative entry in column [7]), bringing domestic supplies to 713 million barrels. Of this total, 13 million barrels are delivered to and completely used up by domestic producers of trucks, fuel oil, and corn (columns [1] to [3]). Domestic households and government receive another 400 and 100 million barrels (columns [4] and [6]), while domestic producers increase their inventories of fuel oil by the remaining 200 million barrels (column [5]). As in the case of trucks, the receipt by domestic producers of current output that is not used up in this year, thus increasing the capital stock, is listed in column (5).

Row C shows the country's farms producing 300 million tons of corn during this year (column [8]). However, another 261 million tons are taken out of inventories accumulated in previous years (negative entry in column [5]), bringing domestic supplies to 561 million tons. Of this total, 31 million tons are delivered to and completely used up by domestic producers (columns [1] to [3]). Domestic households and government receive another 20 and 10 million tons (columns [4] and [6]), while 500 million tons are exported (column [7]).

Row D shows 700 million labor hours being performed this year (column [8]). Some 231 million hours are being worked making trucks, fuel oil, and corn (columns [1] to [3]); another 100 and 300 million hours provide services directly to domestic households and governments (colunns [4] and [6]). Even foreigners receive some of this country's labor (column [7]), perhaps by visiting as tourists or by employing migrant workers. Note that the entry in column (5) must always be zero for rows showing services flowing from the country's stock of resources. Consider how it is impossible for domestic producers to receive labor hours during this year and not use them up at the same time. Unlike trucks, fuel oil, and corn, which can be used up during the period of receipt (columns [1] to [3]) *or* stored for later use (column [5]), human services must be used up when performed. For reasons of logic they must appear in columns (1) to (3) when going to producers. The same is true for services coming from the stocks of natural or capital resources. Hence row E and row F entries must also be zero in column (5). The remaining entries correspond to those of row D.

b. Interpreting the Columns

The columns of our table have, of course, been discussed by implication. Columns (1) to (3) show all the inputs used by the three types of producers while producing the output totals given in column (8) of rows A to C. Truck producers, for instance, produce in this year 20 million trucks (row A, column [8]) by completely using up the inputs shown in column (1): 1 million trucks, 2 million barrels of fuel oil, 1 million tons of corn, 200 million labor hours, 800 million acre hours, and 400 million machine hours. It is easy to interpret these data: The 1 million trucks might be used up through testing or by carrying oil, corn, and workers; the 2 million barrels of oil might be used up running machines, including the above trucks; the 1 million tons of corn might be used to make plastic parts used in the truck cabins; the 200 million labor hours might represent 100,000 workers working somewhat under 6 hours a day for the entire year. . . .

Columns (4) to (7) list the detailed composition of this country's real GNP: Column (4) shows the receipt of final goods by households, ranging from fuel oil and corn to, perhaps, the services of barbers and piano teachers (row D), of building lots and garden plots (row E), and of jetliners and taxicabs (row F). Column (5) shows the country's investment during the period, the addition to the capital stock of 7 million trucks and 200 million barrels of oil, and the loss from it of 261 million tons of corn. Column (6) shows the receipt of final goods by government, ranging from trucks, fuel oil, and corn to, perhaps, the services of soldiers and typists (row D), city parks and national seashores (row E), and garbage trucks and police cruisers (row F). Column (7) accounts for foreign trade: Thus, imports are deducted, but exports are added to the final goods received by domestic households, producers, and governments in order to measure properly the total production of final goods by *this* country's resources. Conceivably, units of all the commodities and services listed in our six rows are being exported and imported at the same time. Column (7) lists the *net effects:* Imports of fuel oil (row B), but exports of everything else, ranging from trucks (row A) and corn (row C) to, perhaps, services provided to foreign visitors by waiters, national parks, and rental cars (rows D to F).

3. See Table 6.A.

4. See Table 6.B.

The Leontief inverse is a table showing, for those types of goods of which a portion of output is regularly used up by producers in the process of production itself, the total outputs ultimately required if one unit of such a good is to be delivered to final users. This category of goods includes trucks, fuel oil, and corn in our example. The inverse applicable to Table 6.A (and, thus, to text Table 6.6) is Table 6.B here. Consider column (1). It tells us that the recipients of final goods could get one truck, provided total truck output equaled 1.0583 trucks and fuel oil output equaled .1189 barrel and corn output equaled .0588 ton. Such production levels would ensure sufficient raw materials at all the various stages of production (too complex to be grasped by our minds) to accom-

**Table 6.A**   Technical Coefficients

| | Inputs Required by Average Producer to Make | | |
|---|---|---|---|
| | 1 Truck (1) | 1 Barrel of Oil (2) | 1 Ton of Corn (3) |
| **(A) Trucks** (number) | $\frac{1}{20} = .05$ | $\frac{2}{50} = .04$ | $\frac{3}{300} = .01$ |
| **(B) Fuel oil** (barrels) | $\frac{2}{20} = .1$ | $\frac{5}{50} = .1$ | $\frac{6}{300} = .02$ |
| **(C) Corn** (tons) | $\frac{1}{20} = .05$ | $\frac{0}{50} = 0$ | $\frac{30}{300} = .1$ |
| **(D) Labor** (labor hours) | $\frac{200}{20} = 10$ | $\frac{1}{50} = .02$ | $\frac{30}{300} = .1$ |
| **(E) Land** (acre hours) | $\frac{800}{20} = 40$ | $\frac{550}{50} = 11$ | $\frac{930}{300} = 3.1$ |
| **(F) Capital** (machine hours) | $\frac{400}{20} = 20$ | $\frac{50}{50} = 1$ | $\frac{150}{300} = .5$ |

**Table 6.B**   The Leontief Inverse

| | Total Output Required If Delivery to Final Users Is to Equal | | |
|---|---|---|---|
| | 1 Truck (1) | 1 Barrel of Oil (2) | 1 Ton of Corn (3) |
| **(A) Trucks** (number) | 1.0583 | .0470 | .0128 |
| **(B) Fuel oil** (barrels) | .1189 | 1.1164 | .0261 |
| **(C) Corn** (tons) | .0588 | .0026 | 1.1118 |

modate the ultimate delivery of one truck to a final user. In addition, of course, the services of people, land, and capital would also be needed.

Note how easily someone looking at the technical-coefficients table only could have come to incorrect conclusions: Providing some final user with one more truck, such a person might have figured, would directly require the production of one more truck (that is common sense), and it would indirectly require the production of another .05 truck, .1 barrel of fuel oil, .05 ton of corn, etc. (as the column [1] entries of Table 6.A seem to say). Yet, this person would be wrong! Giving someone another truck does not require the extra production of 1.05 trucks plus .1 barrel of oil plus .05 ton of corn (as we just figured), but it requires the extra production of 1.0583 trucks plus .1189 barrel of oil plus .0588 ton of corn (as the column [1] entries of the inverse tell us). Thus, the inverse makes us aware not only of the direct extra output requirements and the most obvious indirect ones, but also of others that are far from obvious. Check your understanding of this by imagining that we wanted to give a final user another barrel of oil. Looking at the technical coefficients only (column [2], Table 6.A), you might call for an additional output of .04 truck, 1.1 barrels of oil (including the barrel to be given to that final user), and no corn at all. Yet, the true figures, taking account of *all* the ramifications, are different. They are found in column (2) of Table 6.B.

5. See Table 6.C.
   You could use Table 6.B, ''The Leontief Inverse,'' to fill in the top three entries of Table 6.C, column (8): Note how you are to deliver next year $7 + 20 + 5 = 32$ million trucks to final users. Multiplying each of the Table 6.B, column (1) entries by 32 million, therefore, yields the total production levels of trucks, fuel oil, and corn that could accommodate this goal.

   However, there is the other goal of delivering $400 + 200 + 100 - 100 = 600$ million barrels of oil to final users. Multiplying each of the Table 6.B, column (2) entries by 600 million, therefore, yields *additional* production levels of trucks, fuel oil, and corn that are needed to accommodate this second goal.

   Finally, there is the third goal of delivering $20 + 100 + 10 + 500 = 630$ million tons of corn to final users. Multiplying each of the Table 6.B, column (3) entries by 630 million, yields *further* production levels of trucks, fuel oil, and corn that are needed to accommodate this third goal.

   If you performed the calculations and added the results, you would get the top three entries in column (8) of Table 6.C, ''The New Plan.''

   At this point, columns (1) to (3) of Table 6.C, as well as the lower half of column (8), would still be blank. You could now proceed to fill in the rest of the table: Since you would now know the total output requirements for the three products (top half, column [8]), you could utilize Table 6.A, ''The Technical Coefficients,'' to calculate all the inputs required by each type of producer (still assuming, of course, that technical relationships that hold in the present on the average will hold in the future!). Multiplying the 70.1296 million total of truck output by all the column (1) entries of Table 6.A yields the column (1) entries of ''The New Plan.'' Multiplying the 690.0878 million barrel total of fuel oil output by all the column (2) entries of Table 6.A yields the column (2) entries of ''The New Plan.'' Finally, multiplying the 703.8756 million ton total of corn output by all the column (3) entries of Table 6.A yields the column (3) entries of ''The New Plan.''

   At this point, a quick accuracy check can be made. Do the column (8) totals of rows A to C, which were independently derived, really equal the sum of all the entries in their respective rows? Except for minor rounding errors, this is, indeed, true.

   At this point only three cells of the table would be blank, the boxed totals of rows D to F. They can be found, of course, by simple addition of all the numbers in the respective rows. If the total flows of human, natural, and capital resources shown in these boxes could be squeezed from available resource stocks, the new document of Table 6.C would represent a well-coordinated *and feasible* plan of future economic activity.

6. Central planning would get even more complicated. The technical-coefficients table would change as the scale of operations was altered. In the case of increasing returns to scale, for instance, the entries in that table would decrease as output was expanded and increase as it was contracted. The opposite would happen in the case of decreasing returns to scale.

**Table 6.C** The New Plan.

| Recipients / Suppliers | Of Intermediate Goods | | | Of Final Goods | | | | Total |
|---|---|---|---|---|---|---|---|---|
| | Truck Producers (1) | Fuel Oil Producers (2) | Corn Producers (3) | Domestic Households (4) | Domestic Producers (5) | Domestic Government (6) | Foreigners (7) | (8) |
| **(A) Truck Producers** (Millions of trucks) | 3.5065 | 27.6035 | 7.0388 | 0 | 7 | 20 | 5 | 70.1296 |
| **(B) Fuel Oil Producers** (million barrels of oil) | 7.0130 | 69.0088 | 14.0775 | 400 | 200 | 100 | -100 | 690.0878 |
| **(C) Corn Producers** (million tons of corn) | 3.5065 | 0 | 70.3876 | 20 | 100 | 10 | 500 | 703.8756 |
| **(D) Labor Force** (million labor hours) | 701.2960 | 13.8018 | 70.3876 | 100 | ✕ | 300 | 0 | 1,185.4854 |
| **(E) Landowners** (million acre hours) | 2,805.1840 | 7,590.9658 | 2,182.0143 | 100 | ✕ | 500 | 0 | 13,178.1641 |
| **(F) Capital Owners** (million machine hours) | 1,402.5920 | 690.0878 | 351.9378 | 200 | ✕ | 20 | 0 | 2,664.6176 |

7. The equations are:

$$-.95T_A + .04T_B + .01T_C + OT_D + OT_E + OT_F = -32$$
$$.10T_A - .90T_B + .02T_C + OT_D + OT_E + OT_F = -600$$
$$.05T_A + OT_B - .90T_C + OT_D + OT_E + OT_F = -630$$
$$10T_A + .02T_B + .1T_C - 1T_D + OT_E + OT_F = -400$$
$$40T_A + 11T_B + 3.1T_C + OT_D - 1T_E + OT_F = -600$$
$$20T_A + 1T_B + .5T_C + OT_D + OT_E - 1T_F = -220$$

If one solves these six equations for the six unknowns, one derives almost precisely the row A to F totals given in Table 6.C, "The New Plan" (slight differences being due to rounding):

$T_A = 70.1506$                 $T_D = 1,185.6980$
$T_B = 690.1032$             $T_E = 13,179.2400$
$T_C = 703.8973$             $T_F = 2,664.0650$

8. This is very true. The failures of real-world central planning often stem from the neglect of such knowledge. Thus, central planners may insist on sowing wheat in province X because their *scientific* knowledge convinces them it is possible. (They may know, from last year's technical-coefficients table, that it takes so much seed, fertilizer, land area, labor hours, truck hours, and so on to produce a ton of wheat; and they may have provided in the plan for the timely delivery of all these inputs.) Yet, the plan may still go awry because central planners lack the *nonscientific* knowledge of the specific circumstances of time and place only people on the spot can have. (Thus, some 10 billion wasps may have appeared on the scene, clogging up truck engines to the point of making them useless and rendering the harvesting of wheat impossible. Or a cyclone may have turned all the roads into rivers of mud. . . .) Thus, the failure of central planners to know these nonscientific kinds of things can be just as troublesome as would be their insistence on using the wrong kind of scientific knowledge—applying, say, the technical coefficients for steel production when planning the production of wheat.

*Note:* In a market economy, the people on the spot would have had decision-making powers. They would not have sown wheat, in the full knowledge that it could not be harvested, and might have concentrated on making furniture instead. It is interesting to note that the low morale of agricultural workers in real-world centrally planned economies often stems from experiences of this type: being ordered to so something that is bound to fail (as only those commanded know).

9. This might be true because it might still be impossible to *handle* the vast amount of information, to issue the vast number of appropriate commands, and to verify their execution. In short, the attempt to fulfill Pareto's marginal conditions might still founder on the problem of information overload. An infinite amount of information—all of which is relevant to economic efficiency and all of which is continually changing—simply might not be digestible in one central place. Any single individual (or group of individuals), even with fancy computers, has a limited attention span and a limited capacity for comprehension or for weighing alternatives. When told absolutely everything, even if it were possible, planners might simply not be able to handle all the information received. Thus, an economic commander could not help but ignore much that is relevant for the achievement of economic efficiency.

10. This is easily explained. All the entries in Table 6.2, "The Plan Document," were derived on the assumption that technical coefficients were unchanged. See the section "Planning Input Requirements of Intermediate Goods." So, naturally, the calculation of a new technical-coefficients table from Table 6.2 would yield the old technical-coefficients table.

Mathematically, the row A, column (1) entry in Table 6.3, "Technical Coefficients," was calculated by dividing the row A, column (1) entry in Table 6.1, "The Input-Output Table," by that table's row A, column (8) entry: (40 / 400) = 0.10.

Later, the row A, column (1) entry in Table 6.2, "The Plan Document," was calculated by multiplying 0.10 by that table's row A, column (8) entry of 488.624. It was noted that

$$0.10 \times 488.624 = 48.8624$$

Naturally, therefore,

$$( 48.8624 / 488.624 ) = 0.10$$

# Chapter 7

1. See Tables 7.A and 7.B.

2. All these events can be explained by the perverse incentive system:
   a. In one year, the output target was stated in square feet; in the other year, in tons.
   b. The output target of the construction enterprise was stated in terms of gross value of output (*val*). The fence was erected in order to fulfill the plan, which called for so many rubles' worth of construction.
   c. The output plan was stated in *val;* saving material and labor would decrease the value of production both for the supplier of slabs and the engine factory. If it made the

**Table 7.A**  A Material Balance for Corn (in millions of tons)

| Sources | | Uses | | |
|---------|---|------|---|---|
| Production | 1,171.818 | Electric power producers | 48.862 | Intermediate |
| Inventory decrease* | 110.000 | Steel producers | 88.592 | |
| Imports[†] | 50.000 | Corn producers | 234.364 | |
| | | Households | 500.000 | Final |
| | | Inventory increase* | 210.000 | |
| | | Government | 200.000 | |
| | | Exports[†] | 50.000 | |
| Total Sources | 1,331.818 | Total Uses | 1,331.818 | |

*The detail is arbitrary here, but the net change in inventories must equal +100, as in row C, column (5) of Table 6.2.
[†]The detail is arbitrary here, but net exports must equal zero, as in row C, column (7) of Table 6.2.

**Table 7.B.** A Material Balance for Labor (in millions of labor hours)

| Sources | | Uses | | |
|---|---|---|---|---|
| New domestic labor | 2,608.628 | Electric power producers | 4.886 | Intermediate |
| Imported labor* | 100.000 | Steel producers | 885.924 | |
| | | Corn producers | 1,171.818 | |
| | | Households | 50.000 | Final |
| | | Government | 400.000 | |
| | | Exports* | 196.000 | |
| Total Sources | 2,708,628 | Total Uses | 2,708.628 | |

*Labor cannot be added to or taken from inventories, so that category is missing here. Labor can, however, be traded with foreigners. The detail is arbitrary here, but net exports must equal 96, as in row D, column (7) of Table 6.2.

same parts with less material, the part itself would be cheaper and the factory would be penalized for failing to fulfill its plan.

    d. When asked why they were performing an obviously useless task, they said: "We must fulfill the weeding plan."

3. The Soviet Union has experienced both open and repressed inflation. Official statistics show retail price increases of 8,000 percent from 1917 to 1921, of 700 percent between 1928 and 1937, yet claim zero inflation for 1955–1975, with more recent increases of less than 1 percent annually. Western analysts distrust the official statistics: The included products are not representative of goods bought, goods sold in free markets are excluded, and enterprises routinely hide price increases by reclassifying products as higher-quality items. Above all, there is plenty of *repressed* inflation, as evidenced by queues, waiting lists, growing savings accounts forced upon people by shortages in the state retail sector, and the flourishing underground economy.

4. Mr. A's view reflects the ancient fear that "strategic materials" might fall into the wrong hands and pose a danger to the seller. Such reasoning gave rise to the U.S. Export Control Act of 1949, the Trading with the Enemy Act of 1950, the Battle Act of 1952, the Johnson Act of 1964. Indeed, there are those who would practice maximum trade denial on the grounds that *all* goods are "strategic," even food. (If the Russians couldn't have our wheat, they would have to shift their resources from armaments to pipelines and fertilizer plants lest their population starve and overthrow the government. . . .)

    In contrast, there are those who advocate "judicious" trade, using trade to gain concessions. (In 1974, the United States linked the granting to the Soviet Union of long-term credits and of most-favored-nation status to freer emigration from the Soviet Union.) Finally, there are those who fear that autarchy enhances and economic interdependence decreases a nation's ability to wage war. They would go full steam ahead with trade. Have your pick!

5. From 1950–1969, Soviet capital inputs grew rapidly (at annual rates between 7.9 and 12.6 percent); labor inputs grew much more slowly, if at all (at annual rates from −1.3 to +5.8 percent). As one input rose relative to the other, the effect was the same as if it had risen while the other was constant: Diminishing returns set in. Output increases based on further capital accumulation decreased. (See Martin L. Weitzman, "Soviet

Postwar Economic Growth and Capital-Labor Substitution," *American Economic Review,* September 1970, pp. 676–92.

6. The GNP equals 500 million rubles originally; net investment of 35 million rubles occurs. Given a marginal output-to-capital ratio of .09 for residential housing, investment in that sector would raise the GNP by .09 (35 million rubles) = 3.15 million rubles. The GNP increase from 500 to 503.15 million rubles would equal .63 percent.

   Given a marginal output-to-capital ratio of .65 for chemicals, investment in that sector would raise the GNP by .65 (35 million rubles) = 22.75 million rubles. The GNP increase from 500 to 522.75 million rubles would equal 4.55 percent.

7. In a nutshell, here is the story of Lake Baikal. It is the largest and deepest freshwater body on earth, containing twice the volume of Lake Superior. It is 20 million years old, and its highly transparent water harbors 1,200 species, 700 of which (including the celebrated omul and freshwater seals) are found in few places on earth or nowhere else.

   Yet, the bulk of numerous factories along the Selenga (Baikal's chief tributary) discharge wastes raw into the river. These range from sulfates to chlorides, from nitrates to magnesium hydroxide. In addition, the farming of ever steeper slopes in the mountainous region has led to disastrous earth crumblings and landslides and increasing silt flow. In 1966, the first of several pulp and paper mills along the lake was constructed at Baikalsk and began dumping into the lake. Logs were rafted on the lake, and since 10 percent sink on the way, began rotting in it. Huge alkaline sewage islands began appearing on the lake. Although the lake and its basin were a "protected zone" from 1950, economic considerations won out. In spite of much publicity, a second mill was constructed in 1971 at Selenginsk. . . .

8. See the accompanying table.

| Project | (a) Net Present Value at Zero Percent Discount | (b) Payback in Years | (c) Net Present Value at 9-Percent Discount | (d) Internal Rate of Return |
|---|---|---|---|---|
| A | $-500 + (40 \times 90) = 3{,}100$ | $(500/90) = 5.56$ | 468.16 | 18% |
| B | $-100 + (25 \times 80) = 1{,}900$ | $(100/80) = 1.25$ | 685.81 | 80% |
| C | $-100 + (20 \times 90) = 1{,}700$ | $(100/90) = 1.11$ | 721.57 | 90% |
| D | $-800 + (50 \times 50) = 1{,}700$ | $(800/50) = 16.00$ | $-251.92$ | 5.9% |
| Ranking: | | | | |
| 1st | A | C | C | C |
| 2nd | B | B | B | B |
| 3rd | C = D | A | A | A |
| 4th | C = D | D | D | D |

9. This may well be true. In a sense, the underground economy grafted onto the Stalinist system has long been a sort of spontaneous surrogate for the official reforms. The former has flourished; the latter have failed again and again. Note these words of Nikolai Shmelyov, a Soviet economist writing on the 1987 reforms: "Just as we did in 1953 and 1965, we are again dooming ourselves to half-hearted measures. And half-heartedness, as we all know, is often worse than inactivity." (*The New York Times,* June 4, 1987, pp. A1 and 6)

10. This is an old argument, also made by the Nazi followers of Hitler. "In a large organization," it is said, "orders emanate at the very top. Even if the crimes perpetrated by the organization are enormous, one can't assign responsibility to any individual except the one at the very top."

    Yet, one can surely disagree with this assessment. One can argue that subordinates who implement commands are guilty if: (a) They know what it is all about and yet cooperate (few follow orders *blindly*); or (b) they follow orders with *zeal* (perhaps, so as to improve their own status and income); or (c) they even show entrepreneurship, falling all over themselves to take the initiative, to come up with an even better way to achieve the chosen end.

    These thoughts and more are discussed in Albert Breton and Ronald Wintrobe, "The Bureaucracy of Murder Revisited," *Journal of Political Economy,* 5, 1986, pp. 905–26. See also Stanley Milgram, *Obedience to Authority: An Experimental View* (New York: Harper and Row, 1974), who reports on "obedience experiments" in which a high percentage of perfectly normal people quickly become voluntary agents in a destructive process even though the consequences of their actions are entirely apparent and they have nothing to gain by their cooperation.

## Chapter 8

1. *At A:* Total Revenue (1,000 bu. × $5) = $5,000. Fixed Cost ($15,000) + Variable Cost (1 × $5,000) = Total Cost ($20,000). Thus, Profit = −$15,000.

    Profit would be higher at position *B:* Total revenue (3,000 bu. × $5) = $15,000. Fixed Cost ($15,000) + Variable Cost (2 × $5,000) = Total Cost ($25,000). Profit = −$10,000.

    *At H:* Total Revenue (10,000 bu. × $5) = $50,000. Fixed Cost ($15,000) + Variable Cost (8 × $5,000) = Total Cost ($55,000). Thus, Profit = −$5,000.

    Profit would be higher at position *G:* Total revenue (9,800 bu. × $5) = $49,000. Fixed Cost ($15,000) + Variable Cost (7 × $5,000) = Total Cost ($50,000). Profit = −$1,000.

2. *At B:* Total Revenue (3,000 bu. × $5) = $15,000. Total Cost = $25,000. Profit = −$10,000.

    Profit would be higher at position *C:* Total revenue (6,000 bu. × $5) = $30,000. Total Cost = $30,000. Profit = 0.

    *At G:* Total Revenue (9,800 bu. × $5) = $49,000. Total Cost = $50,000. Profit = −$1,000.

    Profit would be higher at position *F:* Total revenue (9,500 bu. × $5) = $47,500. Total Cost = $45,000. Profit = $2,500.

3. The effects would correspond to those described in the text section "An Illustration." The higher taxes would reduce household demand for all kinds of goods, the effects being similar to those described in Figure 8.8, "A Decreased Demand for Refrigerators." The increased government demand for all kinds of (identical or other) goods would have effects similar to those described in Figure 8.7, "An Increased Demand for Bicycles." (The industries affected, of course, need not be constant-cost industries.) In addition, there would be numerous effects on the resource markets that need not be mutually offsetting: An increased taxation of $50 billion, for instance, may cut consumer demand

by $43 billion (and saving by the difference), while raising government demand by $50 billion. Even if the same types of goods were affected (fewer typewriters bought by households and more typewriters bought by government), which is unlikely, there may well be net changes in the demand for particular types of resources leading to a change in their equilibrium prices and, ultimately, in income distribution. (For example, the wages of some types of workers may rise; those of other types of workers fall. Or wages in general may fall, but rents rise, along with subsequent social dividends.)

4. Consider Figure 8.4, ''The Input Decision'' (and the underlying Table 8.1). An increased supply of labor would lower labor's equilibrium price (column [6] of Table 8.1) and— all else being equal—raise the quantity of labor employed by enterprises (whose additional use of labor would lower labor's marginal physical product and, therefore, bring the marginal value product down to the new price of labor).

   An analogous story could be told with the help of Figure 8.5, ''The Output Decision'' (and the underlying Table 8.2). The lower price of labor would lower the marginal cost curves of enterprises (column [7] of Table 8.2) and—all else being equal—raise their output volumes (a result implied by the increased use of labor noted above).

   But caution is advised: The preceding discussion only illustrates the initial effects. The socialist market economy (like a large system of simultaneous equations) is an intricately interdependent system; millions of other effects would occur: The very lowering of marginal cost curves would also shift output supply curves to the right; the very hiring of more labor at lower wages may alter total household income and, thus, overall household demand for goods, and more.

5. Consider Figure 8.A. Panels (a) and (d), respectively, depict free markets for apples and butter in which prices of $5 per unit of apples and 27.8¢ per unit of butter have been established. These prices would become the givens to the managers of all firms, including α and β, depicted in panels (b) and (e) or (c) and (f), respectively. According to the output rule, each manager would choose that output quantity at which the output's rising marginal cost, $MC$, just equaled its price, $P$. Thus, firm α would choose to produce 27 units of apples (intersection $a$) and 11 units of butter (intersection $b$). Firm β would choose to produce 43 units of apples (intersection $c$) and 91 units of butter (intersection $d$). As a result, the marginal cost of producing apples in one firm (distance $A$) would exactly equal that in the other firm (distance $B$).

$$MC_a^\alpha = \$1 = MC_a^\beta$$

The same would be true with respect to the marginal cost of butter (distance $C = D$).

$$MC_b^\alpha = 27.8¢ = MC_b^\beta$$

By implication, one firm's marginal cost ratio ($A/C$) would also equal that of the other ($B/D$), each being equated with the identical ratio of output prices.

$$\left(\frac{MC_a}{MC_b}\right)^\alpha = \frac{\$1}{27.8¢} = \frac{3.6}{1} = \left(\frac{MC_a}{MC_b}\right)^\beta$$

Yet, the reciprocal of the marginal cost ratio of two goods is nothing else but Pareto's marginal rate of transformation between them. If, at the margin, it costs 3.6 times as

## Figure 8.A.

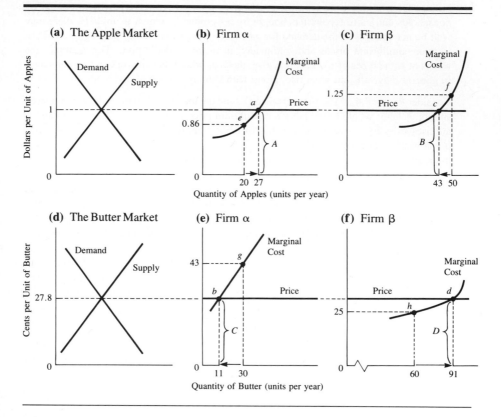

**(a)** The Apple Market

Dollars per Unit of Apples

Demand

Supply

1

0

**(b)** Firm α

Marginal
Cost

Price

0.86

*a*

*e*

*A*

0

20  27

Quantity of Apples (units per year)

**(c)** Firm β

Marginal
Cost

1.25

Price

*f*

*c*

*B*

0

43  50

**(d)** The Butter Market

Cents per Unit of Butter

Demand

Supply

27.8

0

**(e)** Firm α

Marginal
Cost

43

*g*

*b*    Price

*C*

0

11    30

Quantity of Butter (units per year)

**(f)** Firm β

Marginal
Cost

Price

25

*h*

*d*

*D*

0

60    91

much to produce a unit of apples as to produce a unit of butter, one can transform 1
unit of apples into 3.6 units of butter. Thus, the above implies

$$MRT_{a,b}^{\alpha} = 1a \text{ for } 3.6b = MRT_{a,b}^{\beta}$$

Obedience to the rules in the Lange economy, therefore, would keep α and β away
from the kind of choices that spell economic inefficiency for the economy, which are
depicted in part (A) of Table 2.2 on page 20 and by points *e* through *h* in Figure 8.A.

6. Consider Figure 8.B. Panels (a) and (d), respectively, depict the establishment of equilibrium prices of $2.90 per unit of labor and $1 per unit of capital services. These prices
   would become the givens to the managers of all firms, including α and β, depicted in
   panels (b) and (e) or (c) and (f), respectively. According to the input rule, each manager
   would choose that input quantity at which the input's falling marginal value product,
   *MVP*, just equaled its price, *P*. Thus, firm α would choose to use 20 units of labor
   (intersection *a*) and 2 units of capital services (intersection *b*). Firm β would choose to
   use 190 units of labor (intersection *c*) and 68 units of capital services (intersection *d*).

## Figure 8.B

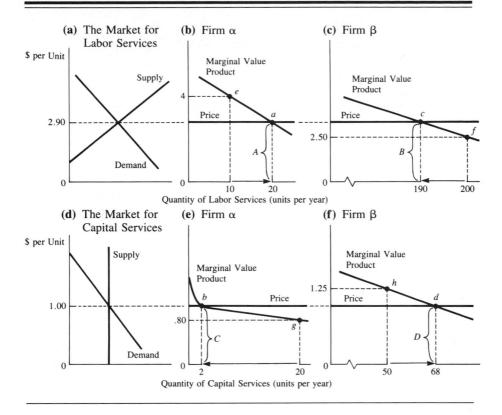

As a result, the marginal value product of using labor in one firm (distance *A*) would exactly equal that in the other firm (distance *B*).

$$MVP_x^\alpha = \$2.90 = MVP_x^\beta$$

The same would be true with respect to the marginal value product of capital services (distance *C* = *D*).

$$MVP_y^\alpha = \$1 = MVP_y^\beta.$$

By implication, one firm's marginal value product ratio (*A/C*) would also equal that of the other (*B/D*), each being equated with the identical ratio of input prices.

$$\left(\frac{MVP_x}{MVP_y}\right)^\alpha = \frac{\$2.90}{\$1.00} = \left(\frac{MVP_x}{MVP_y}\right)^\beta$$

Furthermore, because the marginal value product equals the marginal physical product times output price, it would also be true that

$$\left(\frac{MPP_x \cdot P_o}{MPP_y \cdot P_o}\right)^{\alpha} = \frac{\$2.90}{\$1.00} = \left(\frac{MPP_x \cdot P_o}{MPP_y \cdot P_o}\right)^{\beta}$$

and that

$$\left(\frac{MPP_x}{MPP_y}\right)^{\alpha} = \frac{2.9}{1} = \left(\frac{MPP_x}{MPP_y}\right)^{\beta}$$

Yet, the reciprocal of the marginal physical product ratio of two inputs is nothing else but Pareto's marginal rate of technical substitution between them. If, at the margin, a unit of x produces 2.9 times as much as a unit of y, one can technically substitute 1 unit of x for 2.9 units of y and still produce the same output. Thus, the above implies

$$MRTS_{x,y}^{\alpha} = 1x \text{ for } 2.9y = MRTS_{x,y}^{\beta}$$

Obedience to the rules of the Lange economy, therefore, would keep $\alpha$ and $\beta$ away from the kind of choices that spell economic inefficiency for the economy, which are depicted in part (A) of Table 2.A on page 478 and by points $e$ through $h$ in Figure 8.B.

7. True. Figure 8.C is one possible illustration of the situation. If the central planning board set a price of $10 per unit, quantity demanded (at $a$) would fall short of quantity supplied (at $b$); the price would be lowered, eventually reaching $e$. But producing 500 million units would entail a loss of $ce$ per unit, causing the industry manager to close down the firm.

**Figure 8.C**

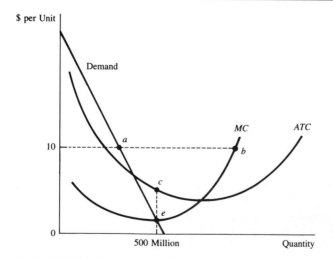

8. See Figure 8.D. Assume there exist only two firms, α and β. Their horizontally combined marginal cost curves constitute the legal supply. In the absence of managerial cheating, an equilibrium price of $5 per unit would emerge (point *e*). Firm α would produce 100 million units according to the $MC = P_o$ equality at *a;* firm β would produce 150 million units according to the $MC = P_o$ equality at *b*. Given the *ATC* curves, neither firm would have any profit ($ATC = P_o$ at *a* as well as *b*). If both firms colluded and supplied half their legal volume no matter what the price, the illegal supply line in part (a) would emerge. The shortage of *ce* would drive the price to $13 per unit (point *d*). Firm α would sell 50 million units at $13 each (point *f*) but produce them at lower *ATC* (point *g*), making a profit of *fg* per unit. Firm β would produce 75 million units at $13 each (point *h*) but produce them at lower *ATC* (point *i*), making a profit of *hi* per unit. The total profits are shown by the shaded areas.

　　Note, incidentally, the economic inefficiency implied by diverging marginal costs $(A \neq B)$.

9. Both speakers do have a point. A consideration of their arguments should help eliminate strange notions about "nonlabor" incomes financing nothing but the luxury consumption of rich capitalists under capitalism; hence, socialism is needed to "correct" the distribution of income. More likely than not, workers who gained control of all incomes other than wages would not be able to raise their private consumption levels noticeably. They would have to use most of their added income to finance the same activities most of this income finances under capitalism: maintenance and enlargement of the means of production, and governmental services. Any other policy would be disastrous in the long run.

10. Surely, Lange exaggerated greatly. Given the complexity of any national economy, even today's super computers would need a long time to solve a general-equilibrium problem involving millions of equations. But a more important point is this: Nobody has even the tiniest fraction of the data needed to specify the equations in question; thus, nobody

## Figure 8.D

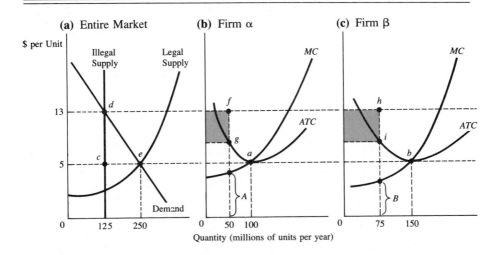

is able to feed them into a computer. For a discussion of this issue, see Paul A. Samuelson and William D. Nordhaus, *Economics,* 12th ed. (New York: McGraw-Hill, 1985), p. 685.

# Chapter 9

1. The commune is able to tax and can, thus, literally create its own returns. Beyond that, there are nonmonetary returns: an increase in local employment opportunities, an enhancement of the personal standing of local officials, a sense of pride, and more. In addition, the commune participates in the appointment of the enterprise director and can subsequently exert all kinds of pressure on the director to influence the firm's actions. Frequently, communes bail out enterprises about to go bankrupt.

2. See Table 9.A. Note that the assumed output price was 5; the assumed fixed input cost was 15,000.

3. Figure 9.A is a graph of columns (4) and (5) of Table 9.A.

4. a. Total revenue equals 24,000 dinars (point *d*) times 40 workers, or 960,000 dinars. Total costs equal 15,000 dinars (point *c,* the sum of per-worker labor costs at *a* and nonlabor costs at *b*) times 40 workers or 600,000 dinars. Thus, profit equals *cdef,* the shaded area; that is, 9,000 dinars (*cd*) times 40 workers, or 360,000 dinars.
   b. The residual income per worker is 20,000 dinars (*AB*); thus, the total worker income is 20,000 times 25 = 500,000 dinars.
   c. The residual income per worker is 14,000 dinars (*bd*); thus, the total worker income is 14,000 times 40 = 560,000 dinars.

5. a. The inefficiency argument could be wrong if workers' councils did not distribute the residual income equally among all workers. If a newcomer in α could be paid the

## Table 9.A

| Number of Workers (1) | Output (bushels) (2) | Total Revenue (dinars) (3) = 5 · (2) | Total Revenue per Worker = Average Value Product of Labor (4) = (3)/(1) | Nonlabor Cost per Worker (5) = $\frac{15,000}{(1)}$ | Residual Income per Worker (6) = (4) − (5) |
|---|---|---|---|---|---|
| 1 | 1,000 | 5,000 | 5,000 | 15,000 | − 10,000 |
| 2 | 3,000 | 15,000 | 7,500 | 7,500 | 0 |
| 3 | 6,000 | 30,000 | 10,000 | 5,000 | 5,000 |
| 4 | 8,000 | 40,000 | 10,000 | 3,750 | max. (6,250) |
| 5 | 9,000 | 45,000 | 9,000 | 3,000 | 6,000 |
| 6 | 9,500 | 47,500 | 7,917 | 2,500 | 5,417 |
| 7 | 9,800 | 49,000 | 7,000 | 2,143 | 4,857 |
| 8 | 10,000 | 50,000 | 6,250 | 1,875 | 4,375 |

**Figure 9.A**

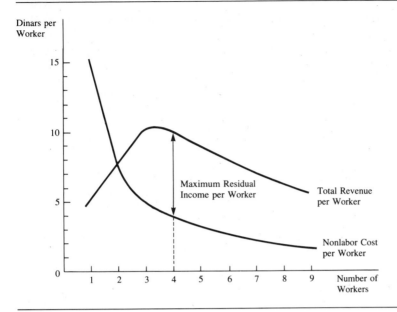

marginal value product or even less (rather than the same as all the other workers), such a worker might be lured away from β. See, for example, James E. Meade, "The Theory of Labor-Managed Firms and of Profit Sharing," *Economic Journal,* Supplement, March 1972, pp. 402–28.

    b. The disparity could grow if α workers invested more than β workers (in physical or human capital). Then *AVP* might shift up rapidly in α and less in β, possibly widening the residual-income difference between α and β.

6. Answers may vary. More likely than not, workers in both circumstances will be interested in their *own* welfare. If the system in question is a competitive market system, capitalists can only make profit by directing workers to produce goods pleasing to customers; thus, they "serve the community." Similarly, self-managed workers can only maximize their personal income by doing likewise.

7. If the model underlying Figure 9.1 on page 250 can be believed, this is true. The increased product price shifts upward labor's curves of marginal value product and average value product. An intersection such as *a* moves to the right; thus, the autocratic firm increases employment. Yet, the maximum residual income per worker (*AB*) may well be found at the same or even a lower employment level.

8. Possibly true. Since labor is not priced in a market (and the category of wages is *gone*), one cannot determine the best labor-capital input mix by comparing wage and capital costs.

9. This may be true if workers' councils pay all workers an equal share of residual income. Old-timers have contributed much more than newcomers to the firm's capital stock

through past saving and investment. Why should they share the current return to their past sacrifices with the newcomers?

10. It is true enough that workers have many goals besides money income—stable employment, interesting work, promotion, congenial supervisors and co-workers, good working conditions, fringe benefits, plenty of vacations, participation in decision making—the list goes on. As a result, each worker will rank the firm's income-distribution options differently. Worker 1 may rank reinvestment (R) before collective consumption (C) and that before private consumption (P). Workers 2 and 3 may have different rankings. Thus,

$$\#1 : R > C > P$$
$$\#2 : C > P > R$$
$$\#3 : P > R > C$$

Yet, they may all agree that it is wise to maximize the pot from which the distribution is to be made; that is all the theory assumes.

An interesting sidelight: The preferences of director and staff typically equal those of #1; the preferences of middle-aged and skilled workers often equal those of #2; the preferences of the young and unskilled often equal those of #3.

And note: The *order* of voting can easily determine the outcome. In our three-person case, voting first R versus C, R wins; voting then R versus P, *P wins*. Voting first R versus P, P wins; voting then P versus C, *C wins*. Voting first C versus P, C wins; voting then C versus R, *R wins*.

# Chapter 10

1. Answers can vary. One is tempted to agree with both speakers. The objectives of many utopias are only vaguely specified as "the common purpose" or "the common good" or "the general interest"—terms that carry no meaning whatsoever. Yet, people are often asked to take the utopia's superior performance for granted, without any concern for proof. As a result, the identical society may turn out to be a heaven for one person and a hell for another, depending on the type of life preferred by each.

2. Answers can vary. One is tempted to agree with Mr. A. Mr. B's first point is an age-old statement made by dictators of all kinds (who have plenty to gain, even if only the joy of exercising power over others). Contrary to B's second point, people usually do have much to lose from leaving. In the case of the Bruderhof, people stay as long as the benefit of moving (the value of escaping tyranny) falls short of the cost of moving (the value of staying with one's friends in familiar circumstances).

3. This is often true. History abounds with examples. Consider how the gentle teachings of Jesus gave rise to the Inquisition; the humanism of Marx, to the bloody dictatorship of Stalin, then Mao, then Castro.

4. Answers can vary. One writer (Fairfield) put it this way:
   a. Back to basics: minimal living quarters; no more ticky-tacky tract houses, dehumanizing apartments, nor multi-garaged, gadget-filled suburban mansions—instead, self-individualized dress and hair style—healthful, natural, additive-free, balanced, inexpensive food—*shared* furniture, TV sets, cars (hence, less hard work, more spiritual growth).

    b. Back to the land: soil underfoot, fresh air, sun on bodies, growing things, no more cities, congestion, pollution.

    c. Back to people: sitting on the floor, touching one another, singing and yelling; no more separateness, isolation, nuclear-family loneliness.

    d. Back to the self: realizing one's potential as a fully functioning, sensitive human; no more chasing after college degrees, good jobs, settling down, raising a family.

5. Maoists had a great preference for people who did practical work that served the masses directly and immediately, rather than work that served them only indirectly, and in the nebulous future. Some people who recognized the error of their ways were forgiven, just as in the Bruderhof.

6. There are plenty of parallels. Consider the dislike of private property in the means of production and consumption, of egoism and external incentives, of markets, money, exchange; as well as the advocacy of taking according to need, contributing to the best of one's ability, internal incentives, a unifying ideology, thought reform, criticism and self-criticism, continual struggle to be born anew, and much more.

7. Answers can vary. Here is one possibility:

    Much of the reservoir construction work was destructive of the soil, the regular functioning of rivers, and of existing irrigation systems. The whole program lacked adequate geological surveying, technical backup, and consistent planning. The hasty, uninformed, and haphazard building of dams, reservoirs, and canals (many of which leaked, resulting in a 40- to 60-percent water loss) turned much good soil into alkaline or swampy soil over a wide area.

    In addition, "bourgeois science" was dismissed as "a pile of garbage" as a campaign for invention and innovation by "the untutored but intuitive masses" was promoted. Its aim was an increase in productivity through the improvement of tools and production methods. But the hastily made improvements were often only locally applicable; their instant emulation on a vast scale often produced disastrous results. See Jan S. Prybyla, *The Political Economy of Communist China* (Scranton, PA: International Textbook Company, 1970), pp. 264–65 and 269–74.

8. Answers can vary. Here is one possibility:

    When he was alive, Chinese propaganda pictured Mao as abiding by a classless vow of poverty: eating cups of plain rice, wearing simple dress, sleeping on a wooden plank. Since his death, his former associates have painted a different picture of Mao inside the old imperial pleasure grounds: living in a spacious villa, complete with swimming pool, fancy baths, massage parlors, and numerous servants who prepared elaborate meals, shined his shoes, and even squeezed toothpaste onto his brush.

    Similarly, the Party, military, and government elite has been described as living in luxury behind the walled compounds, enjoying multi-bedroom houses with modern kitchens, flush toilets, pianos, color TVs, parquet floors, along with many other amenities not available to ordinary citizens: shopping in special stores, traveling by air, sending children to study abroad, riding soft-berth railroad cars or chauffeured limousines, and more.

9. Answers can vary. Here is one possibility:

    The Chinese have a long history of concern with the issue. As early as the first century B.C., the Record of Rites of the Elder Tai warned against man's polluting his environment. Throughout history, down to the teachings of Mao Zedong, Chinese writers

have emphasized sensitivity to nature and curative measures of afforestation, land re-
clamation, and water conservancy by those who would exploit nature. One of the "black
deeds" of Liu Shaoqi was, in fact, not only his stress on economic growth, but his
views on industrial wastes as so much garbage to be thrown out. This was branded a
"counterrevolutionary, revisionist approach."

But these were words. Is China really a showpiece of a nonpolluting society, as
Maoist propaganda would have it? Although data are scarce, China's pollution problems
in the early Mao years were relatively minor, but this was due to lack of industrialization
and not due to the presence of "new men." Most of China's wastes were still agricultural
and organic, as is typical in all poor countries. And there was very little pollution
connected with the transportation system. In 1969, for instance, China had only 0.8
vehicles (counting trucks, buses, and cars) per mile of roads. However, where there
were industrial plants, pollution problems were no less serious than elsewhere. Visitors
reported downtown Beijing under a pall of pollution that blotted out the sun. Anshan,
Manchuria, where China's biggest steel mill is located, was described as more polluted
than any steel city in the West. And the river and mountain scenery at Kweilin in
southwest China, of which generations of poets have sung, was described as fouled with
sewage and industrial wastes and hidden by thick orange factory smoke.

What were Mao's policies? In the 1950s, there were 10 "comprehensive expedi-
tions" to explore and inventory the natural environment and to plan for exploitative *and
curative* environmental management. This was followed by great efforts to improve the
health conditions of workers. Emphasis was placed on vaccination and environmental
sanitation, with the aim of stamping out typhus, typhoid fever, cholera, plague, and
dysentery; thus, the disposal of human wastes into lakes and rivers was reduced, the
proper construction of latrines and wells was emphasized, and sewage was transported
to the country for fertilization and irrigation.

So far as industrial wastes were concerned, two types of policies were pursued,
recycling and relocation. Recycling was stressed as "a serious political assignment,"
notably a transformation of industry's "four wastes" (materials, water, gas, and heat)
into "treasures." Many plants made multipurpose use of wastes. Take the Kiangmen
sugarcane plant, for instance. It processed its cane scrap into paper, and the waste from
that was used to fire a small blast furnace to make crude steel. Fly ash was made into
cinder blocks. Syrupy remnants from sugar refining were fermented into alcohol or
turned into animal fodder and even growth hormones. The carbon dioxide given off by
the production of alcohol was, in turn, chilled into dry ice. Lime, another waste from
refining sugar, was turned into cement.

As an alternative, there was much emphasis on transporting industrial wastes,
together with sewage, to the country—for fertilization and irrigation or just to get them
away from cities. This was done by tying their disposal into vast irrigation systems and
by relocating industry downwind and downriver from cities. Both of these were not
pollution-avoidance measures at all but rather a means to relocate pollutants. (Ecolog-
ically, the use of industrial wastes for fertilization and irrigation may have catastrophic
consequences, since there is no evidence of any scientific analysis of these wastes prior
to such use.)

By 1980, things had gotten much worse. There were ubiquitous reports of serious
air and water pollution. Visiting officials of the U.S. Environmental Protection Agency
measured the extent of particle pollution and found it to be 120 parts per million (ppm)
in Beijing and 400 ppm in Wuhan. (For comparison, the highest count ever recorded
in Washington, D.C., was 50 ppm, and the U.S. "safe" standard equals 25 ppm.) Most

of China's 400,000 factories had no antipollution devices. China's major rivers were heavily polluted with oil, chemicals, and more. More often than not, the fish were dead, and former fishermen carried large doses of mercury in their bodies. Mao's campaign to "take grain as the key link" (which had led to the plowing up of prairie land) ultimately enlarged China's deserts by 25,000 square miles. . . .

There were also, however, some signs of governmental concern: In 1979, an Environmental Protection Office was established. It initiated a number of health studies, issued a set of emission standards, and fined some polluters. An ambitious program of afforestation (building a Green Wall parallel to the famous Great Wall made of stone) was underway as well. (See *The New York Times,* April 6, 1980, pp. 1 and 14, and April 7, 1980, p. 12.)

10. Answers can vary. Castro's reversal was, of course, a compromise with the stubbornness of old attitudes. For a comparison, review the way the Bruderhof communities and the Israeli kibbutzim deal with dirty work, such as dishwashing.

# Chapter 11

1. Answers can vary, but most socialist countries outside Europe that had adopted the Stalinist system have also sought to reform it. In recent years, the march toward more market-oriented economies has been almost universal.

   Consider *Vietnam:* A sweeping economic reform in 1987 (called the Council of Ministers' Decision No. 217) practically abandoned central economic planning. Decision-making powers were transferred to enterprise managers within the state sector. The Vietnamese economy was to be "renovated" through the use of unorthodox methods, including strict cost accounting, wages tied to productivity, shareholding, private retail and service businesses, and more. (*The New York Times,* December 29, 1987, p. A4.)

   Consider *Angola:* Also in 1987, Angola decided to abandon the Soviet model in favor of free markets. The central planning experience had been disastrous, involving precipitous declines in all types of output, often to 1940s levels, affecting everything from coffee, diamonds, and iron ore to batteries, bicycles, and shoes. Collectivization had put an end to a thriving agricultural sector, requiring major food imports from Europe and America. While state stores were empty, commerce had thrived in *candongas,* open air markets at the edge of towns. There one could find anything one's heart desired, batteries and oranges, soap and tomatoes, meat and vegetables. The official currency had become worthless; in the black markets, people had invented a new medium of exchange: imported beer. The 1987 government decree denationalized many industrial and agricultural enterprises. It called on the private sector to take over farming, cattle raising, construction, retail trade, road transport, and food services. (*The New York Times,* December 29, 1987, p. A6.)

   Other and similar examples include Kampuchea, São Tomé and Principe, and Guinea. In *Kampuchea,* the Khmer Rouge under Pol Pot once erected a death camp in every village to eliminate the enemies of socialism, and they murdered 3 million of the country's 7 million people. (See Haing Ngor, *A Cambodian Odyssey* (New York: Macmillan, 1988.) More recently, under Vietnamese occupation, "renovation" has swept the country. In *São Tomé and Principe,* independence from Portugal in 1975 went hand in hand with the nationalization of cocoa plantations; by 1987, the output of the country's chief product had fallen by 75 percent. The government privatized the industry. In *Guinea,* independence from France in 1958 led to large-scale nationalization and precipitous output declines. After the death of President Ahmed Sékou Touré in 1984, the Socialist economy was dismantled: state companies were privatized, prices decontrolled, foreign investments encouraged. Production soared.

2. Administrative decentralization is a sort of socialist putting-out system: It divides among many agencies a task that used to be done by one agency. There is still government planning; it simply occurs in many places instead of a single place. The planners' jobs are shifted about but not eliminated (as they would be in a market system).

3. Answers can vary, but Stalin was not the only case in point. Consider Rumania's President Nicolae Ceausescu. This ruthless and power-hungry despot maintained the Stalinist system even in the late 1980s and showed great hostility even to the Gorbachev reforms. He practically made his position "hereditary" by installing his wife, Elena, as second in command and placing his son in a top leadership position as well. In 1987, major riots erupted, leading to the looting of the special stores reserved for the Party elite and the public burning of Presidential portraits. In characteristic fashion, Ceausescu responded with attack dogs, tear gas, and tanks. He also razed 8,000 of the country's 13,000 villages and proceeded to herd the population into 500 towns where they could be more easily supervised. Some 50,000 Rumanians fled to Hungary.

4. Equation 11.14 tells us the following
   a. 67.5 units of good A are to be produced plus 7.5 units of B. Final users are to get 65.25 units of A and no B. Unemployment involves 22.5 units of labor, 57.5 units of capital, but no land.
   b. Combining equation 11.14 with the information given in Table 11.1, the following is implied.
      *Good A:* Production 67.5 units, use by B industry .3 (7.5) = 2.25 units, delivery to final users 65.25 units.
      *Good B:* Production 7.5 units, use by A industry .1 (67.5) = 6.75 units, use by B industry .1 (7.5) = .75 units, delivery to final users zero. Note: The B industry coefficient of $-.9$ can be viewed as the sum of $-1$ and $+.1$: for each unit of B produced, .1B is used up in the B industry, making .9B available outside B industry.
      *Labor:* Available 180 units, use by A industry 2 (67.5) = 135 units, use by B industry 3 (7.5) = 22.5 units, unemployment 22.5 units.
      *Capital:* Available 500 units, use by A industry 6 (67.5) = 405 units, use by B industry 5 (7.5) = 37.5 units, unemployment 57.5 units.
      *Land:* Available 90 units, use by A industry 1 (67.5) = 67.5 units, use by B industry 3 (7.5) = 22.5 units, unemployment zero.

5. The left-hand side of the equation (delivering 1B to a final user) is made possible by *not* doing the kinds of things shown on the right-hand side:
   *Good A:* If A production is cut by 2.5A, while B production is raised by .83B (which requires .3 times .83 = .25 extra A as input), there is a deficit of 2.75A; hence, final users must get 2.75A less.
   *Good B:* If B production is raised by .83B (which implies an extra use of .083B as B industry input), while A production is cut by 2.5A (which requires .1 times 2.5 = .25B less as input), there is a 1B surplus; hence, final users can get 1B more.
   *Labor:* Use in A industry declines by 2 (2.5) = 5L, use in B industry rises by 3 (.83) = 2.5L; hence, unemployment rises by 2.5L.

*Capital:* Use in A industry declines by 6 (2.5) = 15K, use in B industry rises by 5 (.83) = 4.15K; hence, unemployment rises by 10.85 K.

*Land:* Use in A industry declines by 1 (2.5) = 2.5T, use in B industry rises by 3 (.83) = 2.5T, no change in unemployment.

6. a. $A = vA + wB + xD_A + yD_L + zD_K$

$$
\begin{bmatrix} -1 \\ .1 \\ 2 \\ 6 \\ 1 \end{bmatrix} = v \begin{bmatrix} -1 \\ .1 \\ 2 \\ 6 \\ 1 \end{bmatrix} + w \begin{bmatrix} .3 \\ -.9 \\ 3 \\ 5 \\ 3 \end{bmatrix} + x \begin{bmatrix} 1 \\ 0 \\ 0 \\ 0 \\ 0 \end{bmatrix} + y \begin{bmatrix} 0 \\ 0 \\ 1 \\ 0 \\ 0 \end{bmatrix} + z \begin{bmatrix} 0 \\ 0 \\ 0 \\ 1 \\ 0 \end{bmatrix}
$$

Hence, $v = 1$, $w = 0$, $x = 0$, $y = 0$, $z = 0$.

  Thus, $A = 1A$.

b. $B = vA + wB + xD_A + yD_L + zD_K$.

$$
\begin{bmatrix} .3 \\ -.9 \\ 3 \\ 5 \\ 3 \end{bmatrix} = v \begin{bmatrix} -1 \\ .1 \\ 2 \\ 6 \\ 1 \end{bmatrix} + w \begin{bmatrix} .3 \\ -.9 \\ 3 \\ 5 \\ 3 \end{bmatrix} + x \begin{bmatrix} 1 \\ 0 \\ 0 \\ 0 \\ 0 \end{bmatrix} + y \begin{bmatrix} 0 \\ 0 \\ 1 \\ 0 \\ 0 \end{bmatrix} + z \begin{bmatrix} 0 \\ 0 \\ 0 \\ 1 \\ 0 \end{bmatrix}
$$

Hence, $v = 0$, $w = 1$, $x = 0$, $y = 0$, $z = 0$.

  Thus, $B = 1B$.

c. $D_A = vA + wB + xD_A + yD_L + zD_K$.

$$
\begin{bmatrix} 1 \\ 0 \\ 0 \\ 0 \\ 0 \end{bmatrix} = v \begin{bmatrix} -1 \\ .1 \\ 2 \\ 6 \\ 1 \end{bmatrix} + w \begin{bmatrix} .3 \\ -.9 \\ 3 \\ 5 \\ 3 \end{bmatrix} + x \begin{bmatrix} 1 \\ 0 \\ 0 \\ 0 \\ 0 \end{bmatrix} + y \begin{bmatrix} 0 \\ 0 \\ 1 \\ 0 \\ 0 \end{bmatrix} + z \begin{bmatrix} 0 \\ 0 \\ 0 \\ 1 \\ 0 \end{bmatrix}
$$

Hence, $v = 0$, $w = 0$, $x = 1$, $y = 0$, $z = 0$.

  Thus, $D_A = 1D_A$.

d. $D_L = vA + wB + xD_A + yD_L + zD_K$.

$$
\begin{bmatrix} 0 \\ 0 \\ 1 \\ 0 \\ 0 \end{bmatrix} = v \begin{bmatrix} -1 \\ .1 \\ 2 \\ 6 \\ 1 \end{bmatrix} + w \begin{bmatrix} .3 \\ -.9 \\ 3 \\ 5 \\ 3 \end{bmatrix} + x \begin{bmatrix} 1 \\ 0 \\ 0 \\ 0 \\ 0 \end{bmatrix} + y \begin{bmatrix} 0 \\ 0 \\ 1 \\ 0 \\ 0 \end{bmatrix} + z \begin{bmatrix} 0 \\ 0 \\ 0 \\ 1 \\ 0 \end{bmatrix}
$$

Hence, $v = 0$, $w = 0$, $x = 0$, $y = 1$, $z = 0$.

  Thus, $D_L = 1D_L$.

e. $D_K = vA + wB + xD_A + yD_L + zD_K$.

$$
\begin{bmatrix} 0 \\ 0 \\ 0 \\ 1 \\ 0 \end{bmatrix} = v \begin{bmatrix} -1 \\ .1 \\ 2 \\ 6 \\ 1 \end{bmatrix} + w \begin{bmatrix} .3 \\ -.9 \\ 3 \\ 5 \\ 3 \end{bmatrix} + x \begin{bmatrix} 1 \\ 0 \\ 0 \\ 0 \\ 0 \end{bmatrix} + y \begin{bmatrix} 0 \\ 0 \\ 1 \\ 0 \\ 0 \end{bmatrix} + z \begin{bmatrix} 0 \\ 0 \\ 0 \\ 1 \\ 0 \end{bmatrix}
$$

Hence, $v = 0$, $w = 0$, $x = 0$, $y = 0$, $z = 1$.
  Thus, $D_K = 1D_K$.
f. $D_T = vA + wB + xD_A + yD_L + zD_K$.

$$\begin{bmatrix} 0 \\ 0 \\ 0 \\ 0 \\ 1 \end{bmatrix} = v \begin{bmatrix} -1 \\ .1 \\ 2 \\ 6 \\ 1 \end{bmatrix} + w \begin{bmatrix} .3 \\ -.9 \\ 3 \\ 5 \\ 3 \end{bmatrix} + x \begin{bmatrix} 1 \\ 0 \\ 0 \\ 0 \\ 0 \end{bmatrix} + y \begin{bmatrix} 0 \\ 0 \\ 1 \\ 0 \\ 0 \end{bmatrix} + z \begin{bmatrix} 0 \\ 0 \\ 0 \\ 1 \\ 0 \end{bmatrix}$$

Hence, $v = .75$, $w = .083$, $x = .725$, $y = -1.75$, $z = -4.917$.
  Thus, $D_T = .75A + .083B + .725D_A - 1.75D_L - 4.917D_K$.

7. a. $D_A = vA + wB + xD_B + yD_L + zD_K$.

$$\begin{bmatrix} 1 \\ 0 \\ 0 \\ 0 \\ 0 \end{bmatrix} = v \begin{bmatrix} -1 \\ .1 \\ 2 \\ 6 \\ 1 \end{bmatrix} + w \begin{bmatrix} .3 \\ -.9 \\ 3 \\ 5 \\ 3 \end{bmatrix} + x \begin{bmatrix} 0 \\ 1 \\ 0 \\ 0 \\ 0 \end{bmatrix} + y \begin{bmatrix} 0 \\ 0 \\ 1 \\ 0 \\ 0 \end{bmatrix} + z \begin{bmatrix} 0 \\ 0 \\ 0 \\ 1 \\ 0 \end{bmatrix}$$

Hence, $v = -.91$, $w = .30$, $x = .36$, $y = .91$, $z = 3.94$.
  Thus, $D_A = -.91A + .30B + .36D_B + .91D_L + 3.94D_K$.
b. $D_T = vA + wB + xD_B + yD_L + zD_K$.

$$\begin{bmatrix} 0 \\ 0 \\ 0 \\ 0 \\ 1 \end{bmatrix} = v \begin{bmatrix} -1 \\ .1 \\ 2 \\ 6 \\ 1 \end{bmatrix} + w \begin{bmatrix} .3 \\ -.9 \\ 3 \\ 5 \\ 3 \end{bmatrix} + x \begin{bmatrix} 0 \\ 1 \\ 0 \\ 0 \\ 0 \end{bmatrix} + y \begin{bmatrix} 0 \\ 0 \\ 1 \\ 0 \\ 0 \end{bmatrix} + z \begin{bmatrix} 0 \\ 0 \\ 0 \\ 1 \\ 0 \end{bmatrix}$$

Hence, $v = .09$, $w = .30$, $x = .26$, $y = -1.09$, $z = -2.06$.
  Thus, $D_T = .09A + .30B + .26D_B - 1.09D_L - 2.06D_K$.

## Table 11.A

| Recipients / Suppliers | Of Intermediate Goods and Primary Resources | | Of Final Goods and Primary Resources | Total |
|---|---|---|---|---|
| | A Industry | B Industry | | |
| Good A | 0 | $7.5(.3) = 2.25$ | 65.25 | 67.5 |
| Good B | $67.5(.1) = 6.75$ | $7.5(.1) = .75$ | 0 | 7.5 |
| Human Resources | $67.5(2) = 135$ | $7.5(3) = 22.5$ | 0 | $180 - 22.5 = 157.5$ |
| Capital Resources | $67.5(6) = 405$ | $7.5(5) = 37.5$ | 0 | $500 - 57.5 = 442.5$ |
| Natural Resources | $67.5(1) = 67.5$ | $7.5(3) = 22.5$ | 0 | 90 |

Note: Entries in each row are measured in respective physical units, such as tons of good A, hours of labor, etc.

8. The single equation is

$$67.5A + 7.5B + 65.25D_A + 22.5D_L + 57.5D_K = C$$

The maximum MEW is $-269.75$ rubles, which is the sum of $67.5(1) + 7.5(-2) + 65.25(1) + 22.5(-7) + 57.5(-4)$.

9. The input-output table is Table 11.A.

10. The material balances are based on the Table 11.A rows. The breakdown of the final uses data is arbitrary (see asterisks).

## Good A

| Sources | | Uses | |
|---|---|---|---|
| Production | 67.5 | Intermediate uses | |
| Inventory decrease* | 10.0 | B industry | 2.25 |
| Imports* | 5.0 | Final uses | |
| | | Households* | 33.25 |
| | | Inventory increase* | 15.00 |
| | | Government* | 20.00 |
| | | Exports* | 12.00 |
| Total | 82.5 | Total | 82.5 |

\* = arbitrary breakdown.

## Good B

| Sources | | Uses | |
|---|---|---|---|
| Production | 7.5 | Intermediate uses | |
| Inventory decrease* | 5.0 | A industry | 6.75 |
| Imports* | 10.0 | B industry | .75 |
| | | Final uses | |
| | | Households* | 4.00 |
| | | Inventory increase* | 8.00 |
| | | Government* | 2.00 |
| | | Exports* | 1.00 |
| Total | 22.5 | Total | 22.5 |

\* = arbitrary breakdown.

## Human Resources

| Sources | | Uses | |
|---|---|---|---|
| Supplied from labor force | 180 | A industry | 135 |
| | | B industry | 22.5 |
| | | Unemployment | 22.5 |
| Total | 180 | Total | 180 |

Capital Resources

| Sources | | Uses | |
|---|---|---|---|
| Supplied from capital stock | 500 | A industry | 405 |
| | | B industry | 37.5 |
| | | Unemployment | 57.5 |
| Total | 500 | Total | 500 |

Natural Resources

| Sources | | Uses | |
|---|---|---|---|
| Supplied from natural resource stock | 90 | A industry | 67.5 |
| | | B industry | 22.5 |
| Total | 90 | Total | 90 |

# Chapter 12

1. Answers can vary. One is tempted to vote with Ms. B. Mr. A's statement, incidentally, paraphrases an early book review, in the *Athenaeum,* of Charles Darwin's *On the Origin of Species.* The reviewer could not accept the notion of evolution, which to him meant accepting a universe under the rule of Absolute Ignorance. He preferred belief in a Master Artificer, endowed with Absolute Wisdom, who created and maintained the universe by reason.

2. *Utility Maximization*

   The utility maximization assumption is often misunderstood. Economists who use it are not imagining that all people are totally selfish and driven only by self-love. The utility maximization assumption is perfectly consistent with people being selfish, selfless, or a mixture of both. Totally selfish people, who have no use for other people unless they can get something out of them, might maximize their utility by working their resources to the utmost and then spending their incomes on an army of gadgets that give pleasure to them alone: cars and snowmobiles; vacuum cleaners and refrigerators; power saws and electric toothbrushes. Yet other people, equally selfish, might prefer a minimum of work and money income and then to maximize their utility by sleeping late, swinging in hammocks, lolling at the beach, and spending hours each day in lonesome meditation. Perfect altruists, on the other hand, might spend lives of hard work, only to give away most of their incomes to the church, to the college of their choice, or to the victims of the latest drought, hurricane, or war. They, too, would be maximizing their utility. Their happiness would not be derived from the pleasurable use of gadgets or free time, but from the pleasure of contemplating the help they had given to the sick, crippled, orphaned, or college students who, thanks to their scholarships, need not toil in factory and field. These same altruistics could, of course, like our selfish friends, forego work and income and monetary charity, maximize their leisure time, and give their *personal* attention to those they cared to help. In each of these very different cases, people are maximizing their utility. When citing this goal as the basic motivation of households, economists only assume that people will attempt to make as much progress toward their goals in life as they possibly can, whatever these goals might be. Presumably, this is as important to the egotist as to the altruist.

*Profit Maximization*

Economists expect that people setting up and running firms consider a high money income very important for achieving their particular goals in life. Economists attribute to the owners of firms the hope that the revenues they derive from the sale of goods will exceed, as much as possible, the costs they must incur during the production of these goods. In a world of uncertainty, running a firm clearly amounts to taking a chance: hoped-for profits may fail to materialize. Losses may take their place if lower-than-expected revenues or higher-than-expected costs appear, at which point owners of firms may note belatedly that it would have been better not to have gone into business at all. It does not seem unreasonable, therefore, to assume that those people who nevertheless go into business—and by that very fact indicate a desire to increase their money incomes beyond what they would otherwise be—will conduct that business in such a fashion as to get the greatest possible profit. For this reason, advocates of the model capitalist market economy assume that owners of firms keep a sharp eye on business affairs, are personally involved in their businesses, and are always ready to exploit whatever opportunity presents itself to increase profit to the maximum possible level.

But once more, a word of warning is in order. Economists are not assuming that all owners of firms must be selfish and exploitative, nor are they approving of such orientation. Nor are they assuming that those who make profits (rather than losses) will use their higher money incomes to promote selfish purposes. There is nothing to prevent the monetarily successful owners of a firm from using their profits to help the poor or to do any one of a million "unselfish" things. Nor is there anything, of course, to force profit makers into doing any of these "socially responsible" things. Just like wage income, profit can be large or small (and unlike wage income, it can even be negative); just like wage income, it represents power to pursue *whatever* goals the recipients wish to pursue.

3. In the context of the model capitalist market economy, this is a stupid statement. Profit serves as the inducement for an industry to expand when people demand more of its product, and to keep expanding as long as productive capacity has not risen sufficiently to supply the increased demand of people at the lowest possible average total cost. Thus, producing for profit *is* producing for people. Higher prices are signals, and resultant profits are inducements, for producers to undertake the very actions desired by people (such as producing more apples). Without such a mechanism, how would just the right people know how much to do of what and when? By what other mechanism, for example, might a greater demand for apples be satisfied? Should people write letters to their congressmen, who might set up a central planning agency to order greater apple production (and all this implies)?

   In the same way, profit-seeking firms that incur losses (as in the text example of the beef industry) and, therefore, *reduce* production are also doing what people want.

4. Students often misunderstand the nature of the competitive process by which equilibrium would be reached in the model capitalist market economy. From their own experience

with competitive sports, they are apt to visualize competition as personal rivalry, as a situation of strife and conflict in which one party endeavors to gain what another endeavors to gain at the same time. Hence, the success of one party is believed to involve the failure of the other. One party would win what the other lost. Yet, this view is quite inapplicable here. The process of competition in the model capitalist market economy would be an *impersonal* one, and it would serve to ferret out possibilities that allowed everyone to win at the same time.

Personal rivalry requires that the rivals know each other and have the power to affect each other. But in the model capitalist market economy there would be so many market participants that few would even know each other, and no one would carry a sense of personal power. Since market participants would feel so personally impotent vis-à-vis market prices (set, as they would be, by the collective actions of so many), they would have no reason to ascribe great power to others, either. Each buyer and seller would, rather, look upon other buyers and sellers the way you would look at them when shopping for apples. Do you know all those millions competing for apples with you? Even if you met one in the store, would you regard this "competitor" as a personal enemy whose existence made life immeasurably harder for you?

More importantly, this impersonal competition in the model capitalist market economy, far from creating a win-lose situation, would establish the conditions necessary for giving full reign to cooperation and mutual aid. Obviously, in a world of scarcity, this cannot possibly mean that everyone can have everything, as sellers could by charging infinite prices and buyers could by paying zero prices. It can only mean searching for those deals whereby one party benefits itself by simultaneously benefitting the other. The equilibrium price identifies these possibilities. All who could gain from trading at this price are assured that they can so trade, that they are not reaching for the impossible, and that their wishes are consistent with those of others who would also gain. The establishment of the equilibrium price, furthermore, would also determine how the common gain would be shared. Consider Figure 12.A. In it we imagine all potentially traded bushels of apples as tokens in a game called *Exchange*. We might line up, on the horizontal axis, each one of the bushels demanded according to the maximum price someone would be willing to pay for it. A bushel for which someone most eager for apples would be willing to pay \$21 would be first in line, next to the vertical axis. A bushel for which someone else (or the same person) would only be willing to pay \$18 (or \$6) would be placed further to the right (at *a* or *b*, respectively). We might, similarly, line up horizontally bushels potentially supplied according to the minimum price someone would be willing to accept for them. A bushel someone would be willing to supply for the least amount, say \$3, would be first in line for trading (*c*). A bushel someone else (or the same firm) would be willing to supply for a higher price (say \$15) would appear further to the right (at *d*) with less of a chance to be traded. Then we open up the game: All mutually beneficial trades are made, and all trades that would cause one party to lose are rejected. Interestingly, a *vertical* line drawn through the equilibrium point *E* discriminates between the trades made and those rejected. And a *horizontal* line drawn through point *E* shows us how the traders would split their joint gain!

Notice how those bushels that would have been bought for the equilibrium price or more (such as *a*) would be traded (at the equilibrium price). To the extent that their buyers were willing to pay more, they each would reap a little bit of a net benefit; the total net benefit to all buyers is shown by the dotted triangle *BEC*. Those bushels that would have been sold for the equilibrium price or less (such as *c*) would be traded too (at the equilibrium price). To the extent that their sellers were willing to accept less,

## Figure 12.A

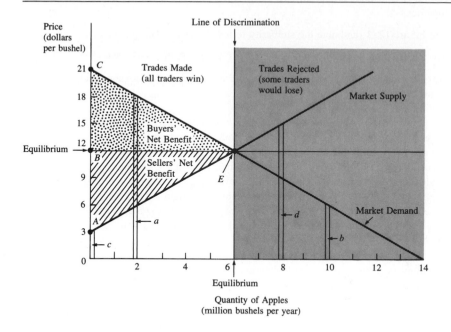

An age-old conflict between buyers and sellers must be resolved in each market. Buyers always want lower prices; sellers always want higher ones. Competition becomes the arbiter, setting the equilibrium price as the only correct indicator of the degree of scarcity prevailing. Thus, the potential quantity traded in each market is split into two groups (note the vertical line of discrimination). Units that can be traded at a clear gain to both buyer and seller involved are, in fact, traded (unshaded). Units that could be traded only if buyer or seller lost by the deal are not traded (shaded). Those people who do trade do so at a clear gain to themselves (note triangle *AEC*). The level of the equilibrium price determines how that gain is split among them (the dotted portion goes to buyers, and the dashed one goes to sellers).

they would each reap a little bit of a net benefit too; the total net benefit of all sellers is shown by the cross-hatched triangle *BEA*. Thus, all those bushels lined up in the unshaded area would be traded, and at a clear gain to all buyers and sellers involved! The equilibrium price would determine how buyers and sellers would share the total gain from trade (triangle *AEC*).

On the other hand, all potential bushels (such as *b*) that only would have been bought below the equilibrium price would not be traded. The same holds for the potential bushels (such as *d*) that would only have been sold for more than the equilibrium price. All the bushels lined up in the shaded area would not be traded at all, because such trade would require one of the trading parties to lose. In a world of scarcity, such discrimination concerning who can and cannot participate in an economic activity is inevitable. The higher-cost suppliers and less eager demanders alike must be left out of the game. This avoids the chaos that would result if everyone tried to do what cannot possibly be done. Note that among the potential traders in the shaded area there is not a single supplier who could cover costs, even when getting paid the highest price an excluded demander offered to pay. So no *voluntary* exchange would get these people together.

5. See Figure 12.B (and note the similarity to text Figure 8.4 on page 213).

6. See Figure 12.C (and note the similarity to Figure 8.A on page 506).

7. Answers can vary, but here are some thoughts about technical innovation and its dispersal throughout the economy:

*The Incentive to Innovate*

Imagine you were running one of those *zero-profit* businesses (part i, Figure 12.4, page 346) created by the expansion of your industry. With sad memory you would recall the good old days, transient as they were, when you had a profitable business (part f, Figure 12.4). And one thought would continually occupy your mind: Even though you could not, by any action of your own, raise the price of apples (shift up the *MB* line back to *MB'* or beyond), perhaps, just perhaps, you could lower your costs (shift down the *ATC'* line). If you succeeded in doing that, you would open up a gap between price and average total cost (just as in part f of Figure 12.4), and you would recreate that lovely profit: So you would think and think and think. Day in and day out.

You could not, of course, lower cost by depressing the prices of fertilizer or spraying machines or pesticides or even human apple pickers, for that matter. In those markets you would be just as powerless as in the market for apples when it comes to affecting price. But you might lower your average total and marginal costs at all possible output

## Figure 12.B

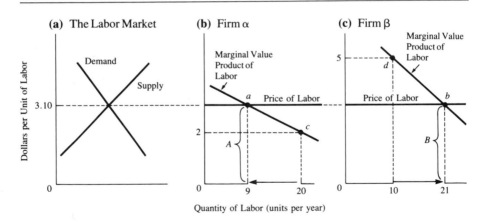

**(a)** The Labor Market    **(b)** Firm α    **(c)** Firm β

Quantity of Labor (units per year)

Perfectly competitive firms maximize profit by buying input quantities at which an input's declining marginal value product, $MVP_i$, just equals the input's price, $P_i$ (points a and b). Because all firms face the identical input price, any input's marginal value product comes to be the same in all firms ($A = B$). Because an input's marginal value product, in turn, equals its marginal physical product, $MPP_i$, multiplied by output price, $P_o$ and because output price is the same for all firms, any input's marginal physical product comes to be the same in all firms as well. This equality fulfills Pareto's first condition because the marginal physical product of an input is the marginal rate of transformation of the input into output.

## Figure 12.C

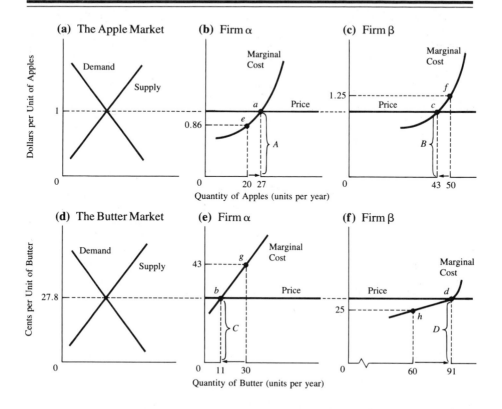

Perfectly competitive firms maximize profit by producing output quantities at which rising marginal cost, *MC*, just equals output price, *P* (points *a* through *d*). Because they face the identical output prices in any given market, all firms in effect equate each other's marginal costs of producing any good (*A* = *B* and *C* = *D*.) As a result, firms equate the marginal cost ratio of any two goods *A/C* = *B/D*. This equality fulfills Pareto's second condition because each marginal cost ratio is a marginal rate of transformation of one good into another.

levels by raising productivity; that is, by raising physical output from *given* physical inputs.

You might think of a new way to breed apple trees that would yield more or bigger fruits. You might experiment with the timing of fertilizer or pesticide applications. You might replace people by machines or put different ones in their hands. You might reorganize the way your workers were going about their daily tasks. And you might be lucky! But whether you would be or not, one thing would be certain in the model market economy: If it were humanly possible, in some way, to squeeze more physical output from given physical inputs (and, thus, to lower costs at each and every output level), someone, sooner or later, would think of it and try it. This is so because economic power would be so widely dispersed and market freedom would be ensured. Therefore, those who thought of a way to lower cost would have about as much power as anyone else to try out their scheme (using their own money or that borrowed from others) and no one would prevent them from trying. If they were successful, they would, of course, end up with a profitable business. Profit would be their reward for performing a risky venture for society that might very well have ended in personal losses. But this would also set up the powerful incentive for others to imitate them.

*The Imitators*

There would be many imitators, for in the model capitalist market economy no one could be kept from going into a particular line of business. So the successful innovator would soon experience the very same sequence of events discussed in panels (g) to (i) of Figure 12.4. At first, a few others would adopt the new way of doing things (and shift down their cost curves to reap the profits to be made). Then more . . . and more. Gradually, market supply would rise and product price would fall. This would quickly force *everyone* into line, even the most timid. A time of showdown would have arrived: Those using the old way of doing things (and, like everyone else, operating a zero-profit business) would experience losses as product price fell. They would have to shape up or ship out. They would have to adopt the new lower-cost methods (shift down the old *ATC* to the new lower level proven to be possible) or go out of business. In this way, the price fall would continue until it reached the minimum of the new and lower average total cost! At that point, once more, the expansion would come to a halt. Everyone would be using the latest production technique, everyone would again be making zero profit, and consumers would ultimately have reaped the reward of technical progress.

8. Answers can vary, but here is one possibility: Consider Figure 12.D, beginning with panels (a) and (b). They represent a long-run equilibrium of the apple market in the model capitalist market economy. Now suppose the firm pictured in panel (b) succeeded in raising productivity. Panel (b) would turn into panel (d), with the original cost curves (*ATC'* and *MC'*) replaced by new and lower ones (*ATC\** and *MC\**). As long as overall market conditions were unchanged (that is, graph *c* equaled graph *a*), the innovator would, indeed, reap the reward for the risky service done for society. Even at the $9.10-per-bushel price (which gave no profit before), there would now be a profit (shaded rectangle). This would be so because *ATC\** in graph *d* was below *ATC'* in graph *b*. But sooner or later, imitators would appear on the scene. Market supply would increase significantly, lowering the equilibrium price, perhaps to $6.50 per bushel, corresponding to *E\** in part *e*. Panel (c) would turn into panel (e). Our innovator, now producing 12,300 bushels per year (panel f), would be in the same boat as before, making zero profits (just as in panel a).

People as a whole, though, would be better off. They would pay less for apples than before: the new and lower long-run price! This, again, would be a message to everyone: YOUR FREEDOM TO HAVE WHAT YOU WANT HAS JUST BEEN IN-CREASED. And true it would be. Since the same resources could now produce more apples than before (and all producers would, in fact, be using this new method) scarcity would be less severe than it used to be. People could have more apples without having less of other things. If they preferred, they could also have more of other things and the same amount of apples, for fewer resources would now be needed to produce the same amount of apples.

**Figure 12.D**

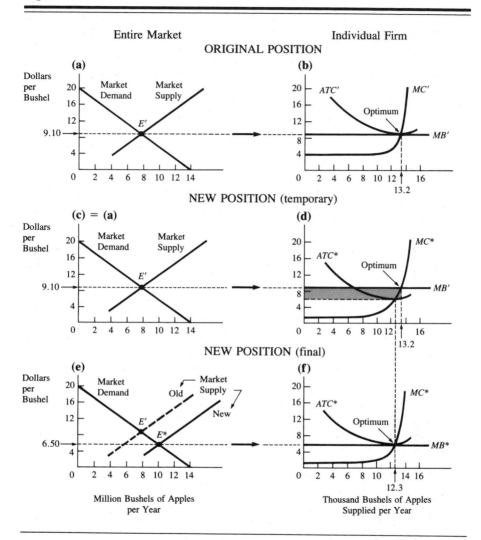

Entire Market                      Individual Firm

ORIGINAL POSITION

(a) ... (b) ... NEW POSITION (temporary) ... (c) = (a) ... (d) ... NEW POSITION (final) ... (e) ... (f)

Million Bushels of Apples
per Year

Thousand Bushels of Apples
Supplied per Year

9. The advocates of this chapter's model and of commutative justice would strongly *agree* with this statement. Those who favor distributive justice would probably dissent.

10. Although public goods were not discussed in this chapter, the model advocates are not denying that the provision of true public goods requires action by government. Even Adam Smith emphasized this fact. For a detailed discussion of public goods, see chapter 19 of Kohler, listed in "Selected Readings" of this chapter.

# Chapter 13

1. See Figure 13.A.

2. See Figure 13.B.

**Figure 13.A**   A Zero-Profit Monopoly

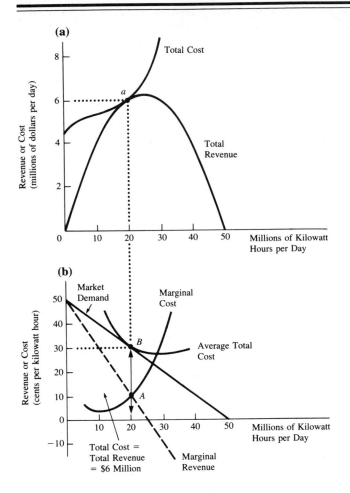

This profit-maximizing monopoly finds its optimal rate of production where its rising marginal cost equals its falling marginal revenue. Given the short-run revenue and cost functions shown here, this equality occurs at point *a* in panel (a) and at *A* in panel (b). The corresponding optimal rate of production equals 20 million kilowatt hours per day; therefore, a price of 30¢ per kilowatt hour is set, but zero profit is made: total cost just equals total revenue (point *a*); average cost just equals average revenue (point *B*). Any other production volume would yield losses.

**Figure 13.B**    A Loss-Incurring Monopoly

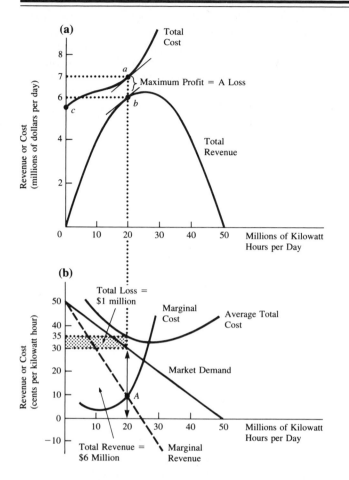

This profit-maximizing monopoly finds its optimal rate of production where its rising marginal cost equals its falling marginal revenue. Given the short-run revenue and cost functions shown here, this equality occurs at points *a* and *b* in panel (a) and at *A* in panel (b). The corresponding optimal rate of production equals 20 million kilowatt hours per day; therefore, a price of 30¢ per kilowatt hour is set, but a loss is incurred: total cost exceeds total revenue by $1 million per day (distance *ab* in the top panel; the dotted rectangle in the lower panel). Any other production volume would yield larger losses. Note: This monopoly would cease to exist in the long run and would produce at the indicated output level in the short run only as long as its loss fell short of fixed cost, as is the case here. (Remember that fixed cost can be read off at the point where the total cost curve intercepts the vertical axis, as at *c*.)

3. True enough, government often claims to be aiding the formation of cartels for reasons unrelated to the monopolistic consequences here discussed. Federal government programs relating to agriculture, for example, have been enacted for purposes of equity in order to maintain *parity,* defined as the 1910–1914 relationship between the prices received by farmers for agricultural goods and the prices paid by them for nonagricultural goods. But regardless of the ''good'' intent, such policies have promoted monopoly, and that alone is our concern in this chapter. (The wisdom of the parity program can be questioned on other grounds. In 1910–1914, the bushels-per-acre yields of U.S. farmers equaled, for example, 14.3 in wheat, 26 in corn, 200.3 in cotton. By 1972–1976, these yields were 30.6, 86.7, and 477.2, respectively. Thus, even substantial reductions in prices per bushel need not imply reduced farm income.)

  State programs that have promoted monopoly, similarly, have often been enacted for other reasons. Consider the Texas restrictions on oil production. They emerged because oil is *fugacious;* it will migrate underground heedless of surface boundary lines. Prior to the state's prorationing law, landowners would produce as fast as possible, especially along the boundaries of their tracts, lest their neighbors drain away their oil. This runaway production dissipated underground pressure too rapidly; oil was bypassed by water and permanently lost. Thus, the law was enacted to prevent this physical waste.

  State and local licensing provisions, finally, have the admirable goal of certifying the competency of sellers to buyers. But they also restrict the number of practitioners unnecessarily. Examples abound, but here is just one: Of 2,149 aspiring general contractors who took the Florida construction industry licensing board exam in 1973, all failed. Another reason why licensing can be seen as a device to restrict trade rather than to protect the public from unscrupulous charlatans is that state licensing usually evaluates novices only at the start of their careers. Short of outright criminality, they are rarely unlicensed, even if they turn out to be undependable, incompetent, or senile! As the saying goes, the road to hell is paved with good intentions.

4. Total revenue *rises* from $2 per bushel (2.5 billion bushels), or $5 billion, to $3 per bushel (2.1875 billion bushels), or $6.5625 billion. Total cost *falls* by area *agef.* Hence, profit rises.

5. This is quite true. As we know, economic profits in a perfectly competitive industry tend toward zero in the long run. Suppose, however, that the producers in an industry, say taxi drivers, perhaps with the help of government, restricted industry output below the perfectly competitive level and thereby gained the power to raise price above the competitive level. Such *monopoly power* might enable each member of the cartel to reap permanent economic profits of, say, $50,000 a year. If the current interest rate were 10 percent, this prospective profit stream is equivalent to that which one could derive from owning a $500,000 bank account (because, at the assumed 10-percent interest rate, the owner of the account could also earn $50,000 a year forever). Hence, those who hold monopoly power effectively own a valuable asset (equal to the present value, such as our $500,000 above, of the extra future incomes derivable from that power), and, not surprisingly, this asset can be sold in the market. Table 13.A indicates recent market prices people have paid in order to acquire monopoly power from its holders.

6. Certainly. Consider the legislating of above-equilibrium minimum wages. Thus, a federal minimum wage was set at 25¢ per hour under the Fair Labor Standards Act of 1938; this minimum wage had risen to $3.35 per hour by 1984. The original law did not by any means apply to all workers; employees of state and local governments, farm workers,

**Table 13.A**

| Sources of Monopoly Power | Market Price | Year |
|---|---|---|
| Boston taxicab licenses | $23,000 | 1967 |
| Chicago taxicab licenses | $10,000–18,000 | 1968 |
| New York taxicab licenses | $68,000 | 1980 |
| American Baseball League franchises | $20–25.3 million | 1981 |
| National Baseball League franchises | $6–11 million | 1971 |
| National Basketball League franchises | $1–3 million | 1971 |
| Commodity Futures Exchange seats | $200,000–325,000 | 1980 |
| New York Stock Exchange seats | $82,000–212,000 | 1979 |
| Television station licenses | $2–50 million | 1979 |
| Tobacco growing rights (per acre) | $1,500–3,000 | 1960 |
| Trucking operating rights (per route) | $5,000–2.5 million | 1979 |

Note: If the government were to auction off monopoly rights at the time of their creation at the kind of prices indicated in the table, government would thereby recoup for its citizens as a group the present value of money to be taken from them in the future through the exercise of monopoly power. If government fails to do this initially (as is usuallly the case), it cannot easily do it later. Once the initial recipient of a monopoly right has sold it to someone else, the purchaser of this right will not make economic profits because cost will be so much higher. In New York City, for example, someone may pay $78,000 for a taxi, only $10,000 of which is for the physical car, the remainder going for the medallion needed to run it. If the present value of future monopoly profits equals the medallion's $68,000 market value, extra profit and extra cost just offset each other. Secondary owners of monopoly rights, therefore, would justifiably resent it if they suddenly had to pay the government for these rights.

The same facts make it difficult to deregulate an industry that was government-regulated in the past. Thus, the impact of the Motor Carrier Act of 1980 on the balance sheets of trucking firms was swift and massive. The size of suddenly worthless monopoly route privileges, carried as intangible "operating rights" assets on the books, ranged from a low of $3 million (Cooper-Jarrett) to a high of $34.9 million (Yellow Freight System).

*Sources:* Edmund W. Kitch et al., "The Regulation of Taxicabs in Chicago," *The Journal of Law and Economics,* October 1971, pp. 285–350; David A. Andelman, "New York's Taxi Industry Thriving on Some Controversial Economics," *The New York Times,* March 13, 1980, pp. A1 and B8; R. G. Noll, ed., *Government and the Sports Business* (Washington, D.C.: Brookings, 1974); Laurel Sorenson, "Seats on Major Exchanges These Day Are Bringing Sellers Some Record Sums," *The Wall Street Journal,* September 3, 1980, p. 38; Karen W. Arenson, "New York Stock Exchange Faces Challenge," *The New York Times,* Octobeer 29, 1979, pp. A1 and D3; R. G. Noll et al., *Economic Aspects of Television Regulation* (Washington, D.C.: Brookings, 1973); Ronald Alsop, "Once-Shaky UHF Stations Lure Viewers, and Surging Profits Attract Eager Buyers," *The Wall Street Journal,* January 8, 1980, p. 46; F. H. Maier et al., "The Sale Value of Flue-Cured Tobacco Allotments," *Technical Bulletin* 148 (Agricultural Experiment Station, VPI, April 1960); M. Kafoglis, "A Paradox of Regulated Trucking," *Regulation,* September-October, 1977, pp. 27–32; Thomas Baker, "Reality Takes the Wheel," *Forbes,* October 27, 1980, pp. 133–34: *The New York Times,* June 17, 1981, p. 1.

and household workers, for example, were excluded. Over the years, as Congress has raised the minimum with clocklike regularity, however, it has also extended the coverage of the law. Subsequent to its enactment in 1938, the federal minimum wage, for example, has been increased 15 times between 1939 and 1984; it has been extended to new groups of workers 16 times. One economist, Yale Brozen, conducted a careful study of the actual employment effects of these minimum-wage changes.*

Brozen found that, because the overwhelming majority of workers have always enjoyed wages exceeding the legislated minimum, most people's wages and jobs have not been affected by changes in the statutory minima. The effects of minimum-wage laws have been primarily on the wages and employment of low-skilled workers. The largest single category of such workers are teenagers. Brozen noted that the monthly change in teenage unemployment, for some 20 years covered by his data, was down 123 times, up 111 times, zero 6 times. Yet, each time the minimum rose, teenage unemployment rose as well. Brozen was unable to attribute this relationship to coincidence.

In addition to these immediate increases in teenage unemployment, Brozen found a long-term upward trend in teenage unemployment relative to that of other people. This trend occurred despite a rising average level of education in this group and a declining rate of labor-force participation. For example, before the $1.15-per-hour minimum wage went into effect, unemployment among teenagers was 2.5 times the unemployment rate of the total labor force. In the year following the increase, it was 2.7 times as large. When the minimum wage rose further to $1.25 per hour, the teenage unemployment rate rose further to 3.1 times the general incidence of unemployment; by the time the minimum stood at $1.60 per hour, the multiple had risen to 3.6.

The minimum wage has affected employment opportunities more adversely even for non-white teenagers than for teenagers in general. For example, while the ratio of the incidence of general teenage unemployment to the unemployment of all workers rose by 64 percent from 1949–1968, that for nonwhite teenage unemployment rose by 154 percent.

Brozen concluded that minimum-wage statutes, at the time of their imposition, have increased the incomes of some workers—namely, those who did not lose their jobs. These increases would, however, have come anyway within two to five years, as evidenced by studying the wage rates of noncovered workers, such as private household and agricultural workers. These rates have been rising 4 percent per year since 1949 despite the wage-depressing effects of additional workers looking for jobs in this sector after having been forced out of jobs covered by minimum wages. Apparently, successive amendments to the minimum-wage statute have raised wages particularly rapidly in the first year in the affected occupations, with very slow rises occurring thereafter. The total increase in the long run has differed little in covered and not-covered occupations. According to Brozen:

*If all that happened as a result of the minimum-wage statute was a change in the timing of wage rate increases, there would be little to concern us. However, in the interval between the time that the minimum wage is raised and the time that productivity and inflation catch up with the increase, thousands of people are jobless, many businesses fail which are never revived, people are forced to migrate who would prefer not to, cities find their slums deteriorating and becoming overpopulated, teenagers are barred*

---

*Yale Brozen, "The Effect of Statutory Minimum Wage Increases on Teenage Employment," *The Journal of Law and Economics*, April 1969, pp. 102–22.

*from obtaining the opportunity to learn skills which would make them more productive, and permanent damage is done to their attitudes and their ambitions. This is a large price to pay for impatience.*

Brozen's study does not stand alone. Numerous later ones have confirmed significant adverse effects of minimum wages on teenage employment.* Apparently, the attempt to help the working poor has proven to be the most effective way yet to keep teenagers idle. Because of their healthy propensity to test their abilities and opportunities, teenagers have always switched jobs more often than adults and, therefore, have always experienced higher rates of unemployment. Laws that have legislated teenage wages above teenagers' productivity, however, have given their jobs to more productive adults or to machines. Such laws have, thus, eliminated many traditional *entry-level jobs* that require little training or experience and allow untrained and inexperienced job seekers to find employment, gain experience, and depart these stepping-stones for better jobs.

What, finally, has the minimum wage done to relieve the incidence of poverty? Next to nothing, studies show. Here are some of the reasons: About half of all low-wage workers (especially teenagers) live in middle- and upper-income families; about one third of the poor do not work because they are elderly and retired. The law fixes the *nominal* wage; even if it rises and a worker remains employed, employers can keep the real wage unchanged by reducing fringe benefits, such as low-cost meals, housing, or health insurance. The law is not strictly enforced and penalties for breaking it are small; apparently 30–50 percent of eligible workers work at illegally lower wages.†

7. Yes. Consider people who cheat on their taxes by understating their income, the waiter who reports only half his tips, the plumber who gives customers a break if they pay cash, the gambler or the babysitter who keeps no records at all. Estimates of the size of the U.S. underground economy vary from a conservative 3 percent to an astounding 20 percent of the GNP. About two thirds of the underground economy consists of income that, if reported, would be legitimate; one third is derived from criminal activities. In 1985, unreported legal income was perhaps $332 billion; unreported income from illegal sources, $163 billion. The latter included (in billions) drugs $59, stolen goods $26, prostitution $20, bribery $20, fraud $13, pornography $8, gambling and loan sharking $8, and more (*Source:* Ralph T. Byrns and Gerald W. Stone, *Economics,* 3d ed. [Glenview, IL: Scott, Foresman and Co., 1987], p. 138.)

8. Answers can vary; Figure 13.C is one possibility. Figure 13.C represents the profit-maximizing behavior of two firms that are imperfect competitors in the markets for two

---

*As a partial listing only, *see* Thomas G. Moore, "The Effect of Minimum Wages on Teenage Unemployment Rates," *Journal of Political Economy,* July August 1971, pp. 897–902; Douglas K. Adie, "Teen-Age Unemployment and Real Federal Minimum Wages," *Journal of Political Economy,* March-April 1973, pp. 435–41; Finis Welch, "Minimum Wage Legislation in the United States," *Economic Inquiry,* September 1974, pp. 285–318; Jacob Mincer, "Unemployment Effects of Minimum Wages," *Journal of Political Economy,* August 1976, pp. S87–S104; James F. Ragan, "Minimum Wages and the Youth Labor Market," *The Review of Economics and Statistics,* May 1977, pp. 129–36; Robert Swidinsky, "Minimum Wages and Teenage Unemployment," *Canadian Journal of Economics,* February 1980, pp. 158–71; and Robert H. Meyer and David A. Wise, "The Effects of the Minimum Wage on the Employment and Earnings of Youth," *Journal of Labor Economics,* no. 1, 1983, pp. 66–100. (According to the latter study, the 1973–1978 employment of out-of-school men, aged 16–19, would have been 7 percent higher in the absence of the minimum wage.)

†Orley Ashenfelter and Robert S. Smith, "Compliance with the Minimum Wage Law," *Journal of Political Economy,* April 1979, pp. 335–50.

**Figure 13.c**    Imperfect Competition and Pareto's Second Condition

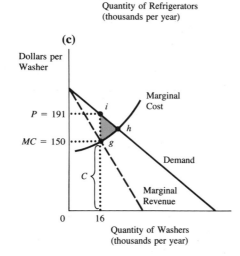
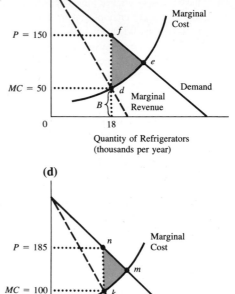

Sellers that have monopoly power maximize profit on the goods they sell by producing output quantities at which rising marginal cost just equals falling marginal revenue (points *a, d, g, k*). Under such circumstances, firms are unlikely to equate their marginal costs. Note how, in this example, $A \neq B$ and $C \neq D$. Because the marginal rate of transformation between any two goods is, in turn, closely linked to the ratio of marginal production costs, the *MRT*s are also unlikely to be the same for any two firms producing the same goods. This inequality of the *MRT*s violates Pareto's second condition.

goods. Such firms would equate their marginal costs of production with marginal revenue. Firm α would do so at intersections *a* and *g;* firm β at intersections *d* and *k*. Accordingly, α would produce 10,000 refrigerators and 16,000 washers per year, while β would produce 18,000 and 26,000 units, respectively.

Note: Unlike in Figure 12.C on page 525, which illustrates the *fulfillment* of the second condition in the case of perfect competition, the two firms' marginal costs, as well as their ratios, would now diverge ($A \neq B$, $C \neq D$, and $A/C \neq B/D$). Realizing that these ratios are closely linked to the marginal rates of transformation between the two goods (and denoting refrigerators by $r$ and washers by $w$), a clear violation of Pareto's second condition can be observed:

$$\left(\frac{MC_r}{MC_w}\right)^{\alpha} = \frac{\$150}{\$150}$$

Hence, $MRT_{r,w}^{\alpha}$ is $1r$ for $1w$.

$$\left(\frac{MC_r}{MC_w}\right)^{\beta} = \frac{\$50}{\$100}$$

Hence, $MRT_{r,w}^{\beta}$ is $1r$ for $.5w$. Therefore, $MRT_{r,w}^{\alpha} \neq MRT_{r,w}^{\beta}$. In spite of this violation, neither firm would have any incentive to change its behavior because each would be maximizing profit. Thus, economics inefficiency would persist.

9. Arnold Harberger, about 30 years ago, made the first attempt to measure the welfare loss implied by economic inefficiency.[*] Harberger focused on the fact, visible in Figure 13.C, that firms with monopoly power in the goods market usually choose output levels at which price exceeds marginal cost. (A price-discriminating firm might be an exception.) As a result, units of output that potential consumers would value more highly than other goods are not produced, and potential welfare is unnecessarily foregone. Note in Figure 13.C how firm $\alpha$ could push the production of refrigerators and washers beyond the chosen quantities to higher levels corresponding to points $b$ and $h$, respectively. Each one of these extra units would be valued (along demand line segments $cb$ or $ih$) more highly than the resources needed to make them (as measured along marginal cost line segments $ab$ or $gh$). The height of marginal cost reflects, in turn, the most highly valued alternative goods that could be produced with the resources involved. The shaded "triangles" thus measure the loss of potential consumer welfare. They are a measure of the inefficiency caused by monopoly power. (For firm $\beta$, of course, "triangles" *def* and *kmn* can be similarly interpreted.)

    When Harberger set out to measure the extent of economic inefficiency, however, he made a number of special assumptions (for which he was later severely criticized). Harberger assumed that demand was unit-elastic, that producers did not engage in price discrimination, and that long-run average total cost was constant (and, therefore, equal to long-run marginal cost) for both firms and industries.

    Using data for 1924–1928, Harberger calculated the deadweight welfare loss imposed by monopoly power (and shown by the shaded "triangles" in Figure 13.C) for each of 73 U.S. manufacturing industries. He summed the results to $26.5 million. Expanding his sample result to all of manufacturing, he reached an estimate of $59 million, equal to about .1 percent of the gross national product (GNP).

10. A significant amount of governmental redistribution can destroy the important incentives the price system creates. Consider the example in the previous chapter of a change in

---

[*]Arnold C. Harberger, "Monopoly and Resource Allocation," *The American Economic Review,* May 1954, pp. 77–87. Note also the discussion on pp. 88–92.

demand from beef to apples (figures 12.3 and 12.4). If one taxed suddenly rich apple pickers and orchardland owners and subsidized suddenly poor butchers and pastureland owners, why should butchers still move to become apple pickers? Why should pastureland owners bother about planting apple trees? The attempt to be "fair" would take the heart out of the price system's message. Instead of telling people that they could recapture the once higher incomes only by doing what sovereign dollar-voting consumers had decreed (taking resources out of the beef industry and putting them into the apple industry instead), people would be getting quite a different message: *"No matter whether you produce apples or beef, your income will be, more or less, the same."* Of course, people would then have little reason to change their behavior; resources would *not* be used efficiently for the purposes most wanted by households.

In short, as long as the payment of income is tied to contributions made to society's output, *differential* payments are necessary based not on effort put in, but on the objective result achieved; that is, based on whether the right kind of output is produced. Without differential payments, there couldn't be rewards and penalties to entice required changes in behavior.

The incentive problem is even greater if the tie between income received and contribution is broken entirely. Suppose all persons were guaranteed, through an appropriate program of government taxation and subsidies, an exactly identical income, independent of their contribution to production. Such a policy would effectively countermand *all* the orders of the price system with this single message: *"No matter what you do, your income will, ultimately, be the same!"* Under such circumstances, people may wonder about working only three hours a day, if at all. The nation's production possibilities frontier would suddenly collapse on itself. Everyone would be contributing fewer resources for use in the process of production. Society's output and, therefore, society's total money income would fall. Like children fighting over a pie and spilling half of it on the floor, our egalitarian crusaders would have destroyed the very thing they wanted to distribute. The latest message to all, printed above in italics, would turn out to have been a classic Delphic oracle indeed. Everyone's income would ultimately be *the same* all right, but the same *as everyone else's* (and close to zero), not the same *as before!*

Many thoughtful economists, therefore, are hesitant to recommend creating perfect income equality and breaking the link between income and productive contribution. They recognize that people generally must be given rewards in order to contribute to the process of production at all. Without such rewards, the world's work simply would not get done. They also recognize that people must be given differential rewards if the right things are to be done. Most economists do not rule out, of course, a limited redistribution to offset income differences arising from factors beyond people's control, such as inheritance or monopolistic practices.

The answer to Chapter 3, problem 7 (pp. 484–85) illustrates the fairness-incentive problem graphically.

# Chapter 14

1. One is tempted to agree. Indeed, French government officials have admitted the anti-competitive dangers noted here, but they argue that such collusion would happen anyway, even without the plan. Better to have it happen in full view of the planning authorities

and in the context of an attempt to achieve faster economic growth, they say. (For more on the issue, see the article by Schollhammer in the "Selected Readings.")

2. Answers can vary. See Table 14.A.

3. There could be a serious problem if the concept of "unemployment" were defined differently in different countries or if the survey methods used by statisticians differed. Then the identical facts might be measured as a 1.2-percent rate in one country but as a 5.3-percent rate in another. Consider how the measurement is made in the United States.

**Table 14.A**   Unemployment Rates (percent of civilian labor force)

| Year | France | Great Britain | Sweden | West Germany | Japan | United States |
|------|--------|---------------|--------|--------------|-------|---------------|
| 1960 | 1.6 | 2.2 | n.a. | 1.1 | 1.7 | 5.5 |
| 1961 | 1.4 | 2.0 | 1.4 | .6 | 1.5 | 6.7 |
| 1962 | 1.3 | 2.7 | 1.5 | .6 | 1.3 | 5.5 |
| 1963 | 1.2 | 3.3 | 1.7 | .5 | 1.3 | 5.7 |
| 1964 | 1.3 | 2.5 | 1.5 | .4 | 1.2 | 5.2 |
| 1965 | 1.4 | 2.1 | 1.2 | .3 | 1.2 | 4.5 |
| 1966 | 1.7 | 2.3 | 1.6 | .3 | 1.4 | 3.8 |
| 1967 | 1.8 | 3.3 | 2.1 | 1.3 | 1.3 | 3.8 |
| 1968 | 2.4 | 3.2 | 2.2 | 1.1 | 1.2 | 3.6 |
| 1969 | 2.2 | 3.1 | 1.9 | .6 | 1.1 | 3.5 |
| 1970 | 2.5 | 3.1 | 1.5 | .5 | 1.2 | 4.9 |
| 1971 | 2.7 | 3.9 | 2.6 | .6 | 1.3 | 5.9 |
| 1972 | 2.8 | 4.2 | 2.7 | .7 | 1.4 | 5.6 |
| 1973 | 2.7 | 3.2 | 2.5 | .7 | 1.3 | 4.9 |
| 1974 | 2.9 | 3.1 | 2.0 | 1.6 | 1.4 | 5.6 |
| 1975 | 4.2 | 4.2 | 1.6 | 3.4 | 1.9 | 8.5 |
| 1976 | 4.5 | 5.9 | 1.6 | 3.4 | 2.0 | 7.7 |
| 1977 | 5.0 | 6.4 | 1.8 | 3.5 | 2.0 | 7.1 |
| 1978 | 5.4 | 6.3 | 2.2 | 3.4 | 2.3 | 6.1 |
| 1979 | 6.0 | 5.4 | 2.1 | 3.0 | 2.1 | 5.8 |
| 1980 | 6.4 | 7.1 | 2.0 | 2.9 | 2.0 | 7.1 |
| 1981 | 7.5 | 10.5 | 2.5 | 4.1 | 2.2 | 7.6 |
| 1982 | 8.3 | 11.4 | 3.1 | 5.9 | 2.4 | 9.7 |
| 1983 | 8.5 | 11.9 | 3.5 | 7.4 | 2.7 | 9.6 |
| 1984 | 9.9 | 11.7 | 3.1 | 7.8 | 2.8 | 7.5 |
| 1985 | 10.4 | 11.3 | 2.8 | 7.9 | 2.6 | 7.2 |
| 1986 | 10.5 | 11.6 | 2.7 | 7.6 | 2.8 | 7.0 |
| 1987 | 11.1 | 10.0 |  | 7.2 |  | 6.2 |

*Sources: Economic Report of the President: January 1987* (Washington, D.C., U.S. Government Printing Office, 1987), p. 367; *February 1988,* p. 373; U.S. Bureau of the Census, *Statistical Abstract of the United States* (Washington, D.C.: U.S. Government Printing Office, 1979, p. 902, 1986, p. 848, 1987, p. 830, 1988, p. 812).

## The Problem

Measuring the involuntary unemployment of people, like measuring the nation's output of goods, is not an easy task. Just imagine the kind of decisions *you* would have to make if you had to figure out who among all Americans was involuntarily unemployed. What would you do about the 15-year-old who hated school or the convict who hated prison or the surgical patient who hated the hospital, all of whom would rather be out having a paying job? Would they be involuntarily unemployed? What about the crippled old man who hated his infirmities, or the woman tied down with small children at home, both of whom would rather have a paying job? What about the soldier who wished he were back in civilian clothes, the son working without pay in his father's store, or the farmer stuck inside because of the rain and snow? What about the young man laid off until next week or his sister out on strike, at home with the flu, or fresh out of college? Indeed, what about the woman with a 3-hour-per-week job (but looking for a 40-hour one), or her neighbor who could get unlimited work (typing at $1 per page), but who insists on $1,000 per page (and, needless to say, earns nothing at all)? These are the kinds of situations you would find out there in the real world; all kinds of people in all kinds of different circumstances. Unless you drew some pretty arbitrary boundary lines about who was or who was not entitled to be called *involuntarily unemployed,* you could measure nothing at all! Naturally, others might disagree with the lines you would draw, but you would have to draw them nevertheless. The federal government must and does do the same thing.

## The Official Definition

In the United States, measurements of human unemployment are being made by the Bureau of the Census and the Bureau of Labor Statistics. They publish monthly data on the *unemployment rate,* expressing the number of people who are involuntarily unemployed as a percentage of the civilian labor force. Consider Figure 14.A, "U.S. Population, Labor Force, and Unemployment." It presents official estimates for 1987, based on the averaging of data gathered in 12 monthly surveys. The average U.S. population in that year, which came to 243.8 million persons, is represented by the height of the first block.

The official data-gatherers first eliminated from the population figure all people who were *unable* to work for pay. Among the 59.3 million persons so excluded in 1987 were 56.0 million persons under 16 years of age (considered too young to work or required to go to school) as well as all those institutionalized (notably in hospitals and in prisons). Deducting those considered unable to work from the population yielded the *potential labor force* (of some 184.5 million people in 1987).

Many potential workers, however (some 62.9 million in 1987), were *unwilling* to work for pay. This is evidenced by the fact that they were neither working at nor looking for a job requiring their skill and paying the going wage. They were considered to be in *voluntary unemployment.* Among these were youngsters going to school beyond age 16, college students, housewives, and retired people. Similarly classified were persons making unreasonable demands, such as an untrained teenager looking for a job as a heart surgeon or an unemployed accountant making no job-hunting efforts at all, but eagerly waiting for a delegation from General Motors to offer the firm's presidency. Deducting those considered voluntarily unemployed from the potential labor force yielded the *total labor force* (of some 121.6 million people in 1987).

**Figure 14.A** U.S. Population, Labor Force, and Unemployment (1987, millions of persons)

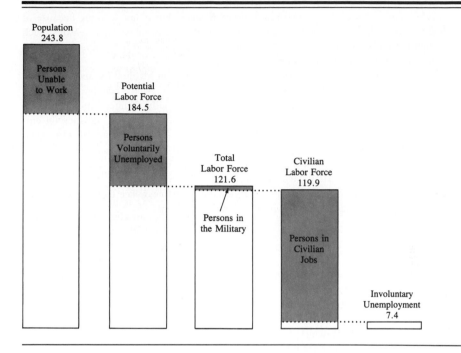

Excluding the members of the armed forces (some 1.7 million in 1987) yielded, finally, the official measure of the *civilian labor force* (of 119.9 million persons in 1987). It was divided into two segments, the employed (112.5 million in 1987) and the involuntarily unemployed (7.4 million in 1987). The latter figure, as a percentage of the civilian labor force, was the official rate of involuntary unemployment (6.2 percent in 1987).

## The Monthly Survey

The employment-unemployment status of the members of the civilian labor force is derived through a monthly sample survey of about 50,000 households. These households are interviewed, and interviewers use the following guidelines: Any noninstitutionalized civilian, aged 16 or above, who is not working *at all* during the week in which statistics are gathered, is considered in *involuntary unemployment* if he or she is currently available for work (even if perhaps temporarily ill) and if he or she (1) had made specific efforts to find a job in the preceding 4 weeks or (2) has not made such efforts because he or she is (a) temporarily laid off subject to recall or (b) scheduled to begin a new job within 30 days. "Making specific efforts to find a job," furthermore, can take many forms, such as going to the employment service, applying directly to an employer, answering a want ad, being registered on a union or professional listing, checking with friends, and so on.

On the other hand, any noninstitutionalized civilian aged 16 or above, who is working at least 1 hour for pay or profit during the survey week, is regarded as having *employment*. So is a person who has a job or business but is not working because of bad weather, illness, vacation, a labor-management dispute, or personal reasons (such as hunting for a different job). And so is a family member who is working at least 15 hours per week in a family enterprise without pay.

You can see immediately why the official statistics on involuntary unemployment give an absolute minimum measurement of the problem. Many people, who would consider themselves involuntarily unemployed, are officially counted among the employed or among the voluntarily unemployed. For instance, official statistics on employment include all those people working only part time, but desiring full-time jobs. Similarly, official statistics on voluntary unemployment include *discouraged workers;* that is, persons who want a job but have stopped looking because they consider it hopeless to find a job. They have experienced so much rejection that they refuse even to search for work. So, naturally, the interviewing guidelines place these people in the same category as students, housewives, and retired persons.

## Conclusion

The foregoing discussion makes clear why any meaningful international comparison of unemployment rates requires a careful study of how the data are derived. Consider just this example: A U.S. worker on three-months' layoff and waiting for recall would be counted among the involuntarily unemployed (and would be collecting unemployment benefits from the government). An identical Swedish worker would remain on the firm's payroll and be counted as employed (and would be collecting regular wages for which the employer would be reimbursed by the government).

4. Answers can vary. See Table 14.B.

5. Answers can vary. It is certainly possible, for numerous reasons, that the data are not comparable internationally. One would want to know whether the concept of the *gross national product* is the same in all these countries and one would care about the measurement error associated with the data.

   Consider just this example: If real output were to grow precisely the same in countries A and B, but a large underground economy existed in A but not in B, an identically defined GNP (which ignores the underground economy) would appear to grow faster in B. On this subject see, for instance, Carol S. Carson, "The Underground Economy: An Introduction," *Survey of Current Business,* May 1984, pp. 21–37. As a percentage of the official GNP, she estimates the size of the underground economy from 9 to 10 percent in France, from 1 to 15 percent in Great Britain, from 1 to 17 percent in Sweden, from 2 to 12 percent in West Germany, from 4 to 15 percent in Japan, and from 3 to 33 percent in the United States.

6. Answers can vary, but one possible problem is the *index-number problem*. This problem emerges whenever an attempt is made to compare heterogeneous aggregates of output over time. Heterogeneous outputs of apples, blast furnaces, medical care, and steel, for example, cannot be compared directly; they have to be added together using the common denominator of money. To yield meaningful results, the same price weights must be applied to the lists of quantities produced in two different periods, but one can use the prices of one year just as easily as those of another. If (as is likely) relative prices come to differ over time, different results can emerge.

**Table 14.B**   Real GNP Growth Rates (percent per year)

| Year | France | Great Britain | Sweden | West Germany | Japan | United States |
|------|--------|---------------|--------|--------------|-------|---------------|
| 1961–1954 | 5.9 | 3.2 | | 4.7 | 6.8 | 4.6 |
| 1966–1970 | 5.4 | 2.5 | | 4.2 | 11.2 | 3.0 |
| 1971–1975 | 4.0 | 2.2 | | 2.1 | 4.7 | 2.2 |
| 1976–1980 | 3.3 | 1.7 | | 3.4 | 5.0 | 3.4 |
| 1981–1985 | 1.2 | 1.7 | 1.8 | 1.2 | 4.0 | 2.4 |
| 1986 | 2.1 | 2.3 | 2.3 | 2.5 | 2.5 | 2.9 |
| 1987 | 1.6 | 3.5 | | 1.7 | 3.6 | 2.9 |

*Sources: Economic Report of the President: January 1987* (Washington, D.C.: U.S. Government Printing Office, 1987), p. 368; *February 1988,* p. 374; U.S. Bureau of the Census, *Statistical Abstract of the United States: 1987* (Washington, D.C.: U.S. Government Printing Office, 1986), p. 825.

**Table 14.C**

| Type of Output | 1928 | | 1937 | |
|----------------|------|------|------|------|
| | Quantity | Price | Quantity | Price |
| Food | 100 | 1 | 90 | 2 |
| Machinery | 50 | 1 | 300 | 0.5 |

Raymond P. Powell once attempted to measure the growth of Soviet GNP from 1928 to 1937, a time during which the Soviets industrialized their economy. Measured in 1928 prices, the average annual growth rate was 11.9 percent, but measured in 1937 prices, it was 6.2 percent.* Neither answer is more correct than the other. The hypothetical example in Table 14.C. highlights the problem. Evaluate each year's physical output at earlier 1928 prices and aggregate output is seen to have risen from (100 × 1) + (50 × 1) = 150 rubles to (90 × 1) + (300 × 1) = 390 rubles—at an average rate of more than 11 percent per year. Now evaluate each year's physical output at later 1937 prices and aggregate output can be seen to have risen from (100 × 2) + (50 × 0.5) = 225 rubles to (90 × 2) + (300 × 0.5) = 330 rubles—at an average rate of less than 5 percent per year. There is no logical way to escape the problem. And precisely the same problem arises when one wants to measure the real GNP growth of France, Great Britain, or any other country!

7. Answers can vary. See Table 14.D.

8. Of course. It is possible that the *national product* is defined differently from one country to the next. As a matter of fact, Western capitalist countries tend to measure their national

---

*Raymond P. Powell, "Economic Growth in the U.S.S.R.," *Scientific American,* December 1968, pp. 17–23. Reprinted in Heinz Kohler, *Readings in Economics,* 2nd ed. (New York: Holt, Rinehart, & Winston, 1969), pp. 629–39.

**Table 14.D**   GNP (in billions of 1982 dollars)

| Country | 1975 | 1980 | 1983 |
|---------|------|------|------|
| United States | 2,573.8 | 3,066.2 | 3,163.9 |
| | | | |
| France | 450.2 | 531.5 | 541.4 |
| Great Britain | 435.2 | 472.3 | 486.9 |
| Japan | 770.6 | 989.0 | 1,091.6 |
| Sweden | 92.9 | 98.2 | 98.4 |
| West Germany | 562.0 | 670.0 | 670.6 |
| | | | |
| Bulgaria | 46.6 | 48.9 | 50.6 |
| China | 239.8 | 319.1 | 384.7 |
| Czechoslovakia | 102.3 | 113.7 | 115.7 |
| East Germany | 127.8 | 143.2 | 147.0 |
| Hungary | 62.0 | 68.5 | 70.3 |
| Poland | 202.5 | 209.5 | 204.3 |
| Romania | 83.9 | 101.6 | 104.3 |
| Soviet Union | 1,475.9 | 1,651.6 | 1,768.6 |
| Yugoslavia | 45.2 | 60.5 | 59.1 |

*Source:* U.S. Bureau of the Census, *Statistical Abstract of the United States: 1987* (Washington, D.C.: U.S. Government Printing Office, 1986), p. 824.

outputs according to the U.S. definition of the GNP, as the sum of the market values of all final goods produced from the country's resources during a period.

Eastern socialist countries, on the other hand, tend to follow the Soviet concept of output, called the *gross social product,* or GSP. It differs from the GNP in two ways. First, following a distinction made by Adam Smith and later by Karl Marx, the Soviets differentiate two types of labor. All human effort put forth in the agricultural, construction, and industrial sectors (including services of white-collar and transportation workers in these fields) is termed *productive labor.* All other types of human effort, such as providing personal services (as in barber shops, doctors' offices, or restaurants) or services in the government sector (as in administration, defense, or education) are termed *unproductive labor.* This has nothing to do with calling one type of work useful and the other useless. It only indicates that one kind of work brings forth something we can see (a *product*); the other does not. Based on this distinction, the Soviet measure of output is much *narrower* than the U.S. one, counting only what has been produced by "productive" labor, but not what has been made by "unproductive" labor.

Second, the Soviets do not eliminate multiple counting of production. If 100 rubles of wheat is produced by the people, land, and capital employed by firm A, it is counted as output. If this wheat is taken over by firm B to be transported to firm C and sold to it for 120 rubles, another 120 rubles of output is counted. If firm C holds the wheat for a year, finally selling it to firm D for 130 rubles, another 130 rubles of output is counted. If firm D turns the wheat into flour, selling it to firm E for 215 rubles, another 215 rubles of output is counted. And so it goes. At this point, we would have recorded an output (Soviet definition) of $100 + 120 + 130 + 215 = 565$ rubles, having counted the value added by A four times (100 rubles), the value added by B three times (20 rubles), the value added by C twice (10 rubles), and the value added by D once (85 rubles). The U.S. definition of output (value added) would have only yielded a total of $100 + 20 + 10 + 85 = 215$ rubles. The Soviet measure is much *broader* now.

Thus, a meaningful international output comparison requires that the same definition is used throughout. Western scholars often translate Soviet GSP data into GNP figures. Thus, they add services not counted in the GSP to Soviet output figures, and they take the multiple counting out of the GSP.

9. The index-number problem, first noted in answer 6, can invalidate comparisons over space just as easily as over time. Consider a comparison of U.S. with Soviet output for a *given* year. At the least, this requires recalculating U.S. output in terms of a GSP definition or recalculating Soviet output in terms of the GNP concept. In either of these cases, two further possibilities exist: adding individual outputs together with the help of a set of Soviet prices or with the help of U.S. prices. Thus, we could compare Soviet and U.S. outputs in four different ways, comparing (a) GSPs in Soviet prices, (b) GSPs in U.S. prices, (c) GNPs in Soviet prices, and (d) GNPs in U.S. prices. Not all of these will give the same result. According to (a), Soviet output may be 29 percent of U.S. output. According to (b), it may be 44 percent; according to (c), 39 percent; and according to (d), 50 percent.

A hypothetical example based on Table 14.E can illustrate the problem: Evaluate each country's physical output at U.S. prices, and Soviet output is seen to equal $(44 \times 1) + (200 \times 1) = 244$ dollars as opposed to U.S. output of $(200 \times 1) + (200 \times 1) = 400$ dollars; hence, Soviet output is 61 percent of U.S. output. Now evaluate each country's physical output at Soviet prices (which is just as logical), and Soviet output is seen to equal $(44 \times 1) + (200 \times 100) = 20,044$ rubles as opposed to U.S. output of $(200 \times 1) + (200 \times 100) = 20,200$ rubles; therefore, the Soviet output is 99 percent of the U.S. output. Both statements cannot be true at the same time.

10. Answers can vary. See Table 14.F. It shows, for example, that the 10 percent poorest households in 1970 France received 1.4 percent of total after-tax income, while the richest 10 percent received 30.5 percent of the total. But caution is advised: These data do not show the subsequent impact of government welfare programs.

# Chapter 15

1. Consider Karl Marx, *A Contribution to the Critique of Political Economy* (Chicago: Kerr, 1904), Preface.

*In the social production which men carry on they enter into definite relations that are indispensable and independent of their will; these relations of production correspond to a definite stage of development of their material powers of production. The sum total of these relations of production constitutes the economic structure of society—the real foundation on which rise legal and political superstructures and to which correspond definite forms of social consciousness. The mode of production in material life determines*

## Table 14.E

| Type of Output | 1975 United States | | 1975 Soviet Union | |
|---|---|---|---|---|
| | *Quantity* | *Price (dollars)* | *Quantity* | *Price (rubles)* |
| Food | 200 | 1 | 44 | 1 |
| Machinery | 200 | 1 | 200 | 100 |

**Table 14.F**    Size Distribution of After-Tax Personal Income Based on
                  Standardized Household Size

| Country | Year | 1 | 2 | 3 | 4 | 5 | 6 | 7 | 8 | 9 | 10 |
|---------|------|---|---|---|---|---|---|---|---|---|----|
| | | | | | | | *Deciles* | | | | |
| France | 1970 | 1.4 | 2.8 | 4.2 | 5.5 | 7.4 | 8.8 | 9.7 | 13.1 | 16.6 | 30.5 |
| Great Britain | 1973 | 2.4 | 3.7 | 5.3 | 6.9 | 8.5 | 9.9 | 11.1 | 12.9 | 15.4 | 23.9 |
| Japan | 1969 | 2.7 | 4.4 | 5.7 | 6.7 | 7.8 | 9.0 | 10.1 | 11.6 | 14.1 | 27.8 |
| Sweden | 1972 | 2.6 | 4.7 | 6.3 | 7.8 | 9.0 | 10.0 | 11.6 | 13.1 | 16.4 | 18.6 |
| West Germany | 1973 | 2.8 | 3.7 | 4.6 | 5.7 | 6.7 | 8.2 | 9.8 | 12.1 | 15.7 | 30.6 |
| United States | 1972 | 1.7 | 3.2 | 4.6 | 6.3 | 7.9 | 9.6 | 11.4 | 13.2 | 16.0 | 26.1 |

*Source:* OECD, *OECD Economic Outlook, Occasional Studies, Income Distribution in OECD Countries,*
July 1976, p. 19.

> *the general character of the social, political and spiritual processes of life. It is not the consciousness of men that determines their existence, but, on the contrary, their social existence determines their consciousness. At a certain stage of their development the material forces of production in society come in conflict with the existing relations of production, or—what is but a legal expression for the same thing—with the property relations within which they had been at work before. From forms of development of the forces of production these relations turn into their fetters. Then comes the period of social revolution. With the change of the economic foundation the entire immense superstructure is more or less rapidly transformed.*

2.  Consider Karl Marx, *Capital* (Chicago: Kerr, 1906), vol. 1, pp. 45ff. and 187ff.

> *We see then that that which determines the magnitude of the value of any article is the amount of labour socially necessary, or the labour-time socially necessary for its production. Each individual commodity, in this connexion, is to be considered as an average sample of its class. Commodities, therefore, in which equal quantities of labour are embodied, or which can be produced in the same time, have the same value. The value of one commodity is to the value of any other, as the labour-time necessary for the production of the one is to that necessary for the production of the other. "As values, all commodities are only definite masses of congealed labour-time."*
>
> *The value of labour-power is determined, as in the case of every other commodity, by the labour-time necessary for the production, and consequently also the reproduction, of this special article. So far as it has value, it represents no more than a definite quantity of the average labour of society incorporated in it. Labour-power exists only as a capacity, or power of the living individual. Its production consequently presupposes his existence. Given the individual, the production of labour-power consists in his reproduction of himself or his maintenance. For his maintenance he requires a given quantity of the means of subsistence. Therefore the labour-time requisite for the production of labour-power reduces itself to that necessary for the production of those*

*means of subsistence; in other words, the value of labour-power is the value of the means of subsistence necessary for the maintenance of the labourer.*

3. Consider Karl Marx, *Capital* (Chicago: Kerr, 1906), vol. 1, pp. 206, 212ff, 232.

*The labour-process, turned into the process by which the capitalist consumes labour-power, exhibits two characteristic phenomena. First, the labourer works under the control of the capitalist to whom his labour belongs; the capitalist taking good care that the work is done in a proper manner, and that the means of production are used with intelligence, so that there is no unnecessary waste of raw material, and no wear and tear of the implements beyond what is necessarily caused by the work.*

*Secondly, the product is the property of the capitalist and not that of the labourer, its immediate producer. Suppose that a capitalist pays for a day's labour-power at its value; then the right to use that power for a day belongs to him, just as much as the right to use any other commodity, such as a horse that he has hired for the day. . . . We assumed, on the occasion of its sale, that the value of a day's labour-power is three shillings, and that six hours' labour are incorporated in that sum; and consequently that this amount of labour is requisite to produce the necessaries of life daily required on an average by the labourer. . . .*

*We know, however, from what has gone before, that the labour-process may continue beyond the time necessary to reproduce and incorporate in the product a mere equivalent for the value of the labour-power. Instead of the six hours that are sufficient for the latter purpose, the process may continue for twelve hours. The action of labour-power, therefore, not only reproduces its own value, but produces value over and above it. This surplus-value is the difference between the value of the product and the value of the elements consumed in the formation of that product, in other words, of the means of production and the labour-power.*

4. Consider Karl Marx and Friedrich Engels, *Manifesto of the Communist Party* (New York: International Publishers, 1932), pp. 9ff, and Karl Marx, *Capital* (Chicago: Kerr, 1906), vol. 1, p. 708.

*Hitherto, every form of society has been based, as we have already seen, on the antagonism of oppressing and oppressed classes. But in order to oppress a class, certain conditions must be assured to it under which it can, at least, continue its slavish existence. The serf, in the period of serfdom, raised himself to membership in the commune, just as the petty bourgeois, under the yoke of feudal absolutism, managed to develop into a bourgeois. The modern labourer, on the contrary, instead of rising with the progress of industry, sinks deeper and deeper below the conditions of existence of his own class. He becomes a pauper, and pauperism develops more rapidly than population and wealth. . . .*

*. . . [T]hey mutilate the labourer into a fragment of a man, degrade him to the level of an appendage of a machine, destroy every remnant of charm in his work and turn it into a hated toil; they estrange from him the intellectual potentialities of the labour-process in the same proportion as science is incorporated in it as an independent power; they distort the conditions under which he works, subject him during the labour-process to a despotism the more hateful for its meanness; they transform his life-time into working-time, and drag his wife and child beneath the wheels of the Juggernaut of capital.*

5.  Consider Karl Marx and Friedrich Engels, *Manifesto of the Communist Party* (New York: International Publishers, 1932), pp. 9ff, and Karl Marx, *Capital* (Chicago: Kerr, 1906), vol. 1, pp. 836–37.

> *The history of all hitherto existing society is the history of class struggles.*
>
> *Freeman and slave, patrician and plebeian, lord and serf, guild-master and journeyman, in a word, oppressor and oppressed, stood in constant opposition to one another, carried on an uninterrupted, now hidden, now open fight, a fight that each time ended, either in a revolutionary reconstitution of society at large, or in the common ruin of the contending classes. . . .*
>
> *Our epoch, the epoch of the bourgeoisie, possesses, however, this distinctive feature: It has simplified the class antagonisms. Society as a whole is more and more splitting up into two great hostile camps, into two great classes directly facing each other—bourgeoisie and proletariat. . . .*
>
> *Hand in hand with this centralisation, or this expropriation of many capitalists by few, develop, on an ever extending scale, the co-operative form of the labour-process, the conscious technical application of science, the methodical cultivation of the soil, the transformation of the instruments of labour into instruments of labour only usable in common, the economising of all means of production by their use as the means of production of combined, socialised labour, the entanglement of all peoples in the net of the world-market, and this, the international character of the capitalistic regime. Along with the constantly diminishing number of the magnates of capital, who usurp and monopolise all advantages of this process of transformation, grows the mass of misery, oppression, slavery, degradation, exploitation, but with this too grows the revolt of the working-class, a class always increasing in numbers, and disciplined, united, organised by the very mechanism of the process of capitalist production itself. The monopoly of capital becomes a fetter upon the mode of production, which has sprung up and flourished along with, and under it. Centralisation of the means of production and socialisation of labour at last reach a point where they become incompatible with their capitalist integument. This integument is burst asunder. The knell of capitalist private property sounds. The expropriators are expropriated.*

6.  Consider Karl Marx, *A Critique of the Gotha Programme* (New York: International Publishers, 1938), pp. 8ff.

> *What we have to deal with here is a communist society, not as it has* developed *on its own foundations, but, on the contrary, as it* emerges *from capitalist society; which is thus in every respect, economically, morally and intellectually still stamped with the birthmarks of the old society from whose womb it emerges. Accordingly the individual producer receives back from society—after the deductions have been made—exactly what he gives to it. . . . [N]othing can pass into the ownership of individuals except individual means of consumption. But, as far as the distribution of the latter among the individual producers is concerned, the same principle prevails as in the exchange of commodity-equivalents, so much labour in one form is exchanged for an equal amount of labour in another form. . . .*
>
> *In spite of this advance, this* equal right *is still stigmatised by a bourgeois limitation. The right of the producers is* proportional *to the labour they supply; the equality consists in the fact that measurement is made with an* equal standard, *labour.*
>
> *But one man is superior to another physically or mentally and so supplies more labour in the same time, or can labour for a longer time; and labour, to serve as a*

*measure, must be defined by its duration or intensity, otherwise it ceases to be a standard of measurement. This* equal *right is an unequal right for unequal labour. It recognises no class differences, because everyone is only a worker like everyone else; but it tacitly recognises unequal individual endowment and thus productive capacity as natural privileges.* It is therefore a right of inequality in its content, like every right. *Right by its very nature can only consist in the application of an equal standard; but unequal individuals (and they would not be different individuals if they were not unequal) are only measurable by an equal standard in so far as they are brought under an equal point of view, are taken from one* definite *side only, e.g., in the present case are regarded* only as workers, *and nothing more seen in them, everything else being ignored. Further, one worker is married, another not; one has more children than another and so on and so forth. Thus with an equal output, and hence an equal share in the social consumption fund, one will in fact receive more than another, one will be richer than another, and so on. To avoid all these defects, right, instead of being equal, would have to be unequal.*

*But these defects are inevitable in the first phase of communist society as it is when it has just emerged after prolonged birth pangs from capitalist society. Right can never be higher than the economic structure of society and the cultural development thereby determined.*

*In a higher phase of communist society, after the enslaving subordination of individuals under division of labour, and therewith also the antithesis between mental and physical labour, has vanished; after labour, from a mere means of life, has itself become the prime necessity of life; after the productive forces have also increased with the all-around development of the individual, and all the springs of co-operative wealth flow more abundantly—only then can the narrow horizon of bourgeois right be fully left behind and society inscribe on its banners: from each according to his ability, to each according to his needs!*

7. It makes quite a bit of sense. Consider just some of the similarities with established religions:
   a. There is a Force that is moving history. (The Inexorable Laws of History take the place of God.)
   b. There is a Fall of Man in the distant past (Marx envisions an early period of "primitive communism" in which private property did not exist, then a later period when the strong and the clever, "by hook and by crook," appropriated natural resources. One can liken that moment of sin to the eating of the apple in the Garden of Eden.)
   c. There is a great prophet. (Marx like Moses, Jesus, or Mohammed.)
   d. There is a promise of salvation. (The communist society of the future versus heaven after death.)
   e. There are sacred writings, rarely read by anyone. (The works of Marx versus Bible or Koran.)
   f. There are excesses of fanatics. (Stalin's slaughter of millions of kulaks, Pol Pot's genocidal rule, KGB torture versus Crusades, the slaughter of infidels or torture by the Inquisition.)
   The list could be lengthened.

8. Examples exist; most of them have been harmful:
   a. Because Marx condemned *interest* as stolen surplus value, the concept of interest was long banned, leading to economic inefficiency. (See Analytical Example 7.1, "Soviet Investment Criteria.")

    b. Because the Marxian labor theory traced true exchange value to labor input, natural resources (which are gifts of nature and not the products of human labor) were deemed not to have any exchange value. Hence, the concept of *rent* was long banned, leading to economic inefficiency.

    c. Soviet prices have long been set according to the Marxian formula T = c + v + s, adding depreciation, raw material expenses, wages, and profit or taxes. The neglect of other costs (such as interest and rent) and the neglect of demand have caused no end of troubles.

    d. Soviet measurements of national output have utilized Marxian concepts of "productive" and "unproductive" labor. Note the Chapter 14 discussion of the GSP concept (pp. 542–43).

    e. The Marxian espousal of philosophic materialism has caused myriad troubles in Soviet biological science because it was interpreted to mean that the environment was more important than genes. (See Close-Up 7.4, "The Lysenko Tragedy.")

9. One can; here are some:

    a. "Labor (past or present, dead or live) creates all of output (but doesn't get all of it, hence is exploited)."

        The truth is more complicated than this. Although capital and natural resources *by themselves* produce nothing, labor *by itself* doesn't, either. Output is the result of a complex interaction of all resources. (Surely, people's saving and investing and innovating are also productive.)

        Consider an analogy: "People are only alive because of their hearts." Superficially, this "heart theory of life" seems to be true because people would surely be dead without their hearts. Yet, we can substitute "liver" for heart and many other organs still. Each of these new theories seem to be true as well. In the end, we must recognize that a complex interaction of all organs is required for life. In the same way, a complex interaction of many resources produces output. This makes Marx's simple-minded exploitation theory highly suspect.

    b. "Migration of workers among industries will equalize the rate of exploitation, s/v."

        Why should workers care about the *rate* of exploitation rather than the *absolute* value, v, of their real income?

    c. "Migration of capitals among industries will equalize the profit rate, s/(c + v)."

        Capitalists never relate profit to c + v as defined by Marx (that is, to depreciation plus raw material expenses plus wages). They relate profit to *total capital invested*. Marx is confusing the annual *flow* of depreciation with this much larger *stock*.

10. a. The convergence hypothesis has great intuitive appeal and, of course, dramatic ideological implications. Those who favor the hypothesis have contrasted "creeping capitalism" in socialist countries with "creeping socialism" in capitalist countries. On the one hand, they have argued, there are the economic reforms in the East (a political rather than geographic designation). They point to a gradual dismantling of central government controls in favor of greater autonomy of enterprises, use of market forces and monetary incentives, international joint ventures, and more.

        On the other hand, there has been increasing government intervention in Western capitalist economies to promote full employment, growth, the welfare state, and more. This has been accompanied by a dilution of enterprise decision-making rights through government regulation, worker participation, and the like.

    b. Critics reject the types of arguments just noted as superficial. (Many economic "reforms" in the East, for example, have quickly been abandoned.) They see just as many *divergent* trends. For further discussion, see Jan Tinbergen, "Do Communist and Free Economies Show a Converging Pattern?" *Soviet Studies,* April 1961, pp. 333–341; Knud Erik Svendsen, "Are the Two Systems Converging?", *Øst-Økonomi,* December 1962, pp. 195–209; Peter Wiles, "Will Capitalism and Communism Spontaneously Converge?" *Encounter,* June 1963, pp. 84–90; H. Linnemann, J. P. Pronk, and Jan Tinbergen, "Convergence of Economic Systems in East and West," in Emile Benoit (ed.), *Disarmament and World Economic Interdependence* (New York: Columbia University Press, 1967), pp. 246–260, reprinted in Morris Bornstein (ed.), *Comparative Economic Systems: Models and Cases,* 3d ed. (Homewood, IL: Irwin, 1974), pp. 493–510; and James R. Millar, "On the Theory and Measurement of Economic Convergence," *Quarterly Review of Economics and Business,* Spring 1972, pp. 87–97. For a Soviet assessment that rejects the hypothesis as a myth thought up by the enemies of socialism, see L. Leontiev, "Myth about 'Rapprochement' of the Two Systems," *Reprints from the Soviet Press,* Feb. 9, 1967, pp. 3–11.

c. One attempt involves the "spectrum model" that defines two extreme poles with respect to some variable, such as the percentage of natural and capital resources publicly owned:

0% _____100%

It then repeatedly locates individual countries along the spectrum and notes how their position changes over time. However, it is next to impossible to select a "meaningful" list of variables to measure convergence and then to weight them to arrive at an overall measure. Nevertheless, it has been tried. See, for example, Carmelo Mesa-Lago, "A Continuum Model to Compare Socialist Systems Globally," *Economic Development and Cultural Change,* July 1973, pp. 573–90. Mesa-Lago sets forth 17 ideological, political, social, and economic characteristics by which economic systems can be compared across space and time. The framework is applied to five socialist economies (China, Cuba, Czechoslovakia, the Soviet Union, and Yugoslavia) but can be applied to other countries as well. It vividly illustrates the difficulties involved in determining the existence of "convergence."

# Name Index

# Subject Index

## A

abundance 6, 9, 10, 33–34, 39–40, 359, 470–74
acceptance method 146
acreage allotments 377
activity analysis 315–23, 325–30
adjoint matrix 98
administrative decentralization 311–13, 327, 516
agency problem 32, 142–51
agricultural procurement prices 144
Albania 27, 77, 127, 308
alienation 56–66, 114–16, 169–72, 230–34, 253–55, 356–61, 401–403, 486–89, 503–504
allocative efficiency 15, 25; *see also* economic efficiency
Angola 515
antipirating agreements 380
antitrust policy 414
applied research 36
assortment problem 148–49
auditing 145–46
autarky 287, 289
autocratic firm 250, 262, 264

## B

bargaining 246–48, 256–59, 263
basic research 35–36
basic feasible solution 318, 327
basic organization of associated labor 247, 249, 258–59
birth control 295–98, 480
black markets 130, 153; *see also* underground economy
bond market 283
bonus system 147–49, 179, 200; *see also* incentives

bourgeoisie 444, 453
brigade contract system 181
Bruderhof 267–71, 303, 305, 512–13, 515
bubbles 409
Bulgaria 27, 127, 308, 476, 480, 491–92, 542

## C

capital budgeting 189–92, 201, 203
capital resources 4–5, 9, 69–72, 163–64, 470
capitalism 71–72, 74–75, 82–84, 331–457, 520–49
capitalism under communism 131–32
cartel 368, 373–78, 412, 530
central economic planning 86–126, 133, 135, 138–203, 206–207, 273–74, 285–86, 288–91, 311–13, 315–23, 325–28
centralized socialism 75–76, 85–203, 241–42
China 77, 84, 127, 272–84, 292–300, 303, 305–306, 480, 493, 513–15, 542, 549
circular-flow diagrams 206, 237, 336
citizen sovereignty 61–62, 114–15, 121, 126, 128–31, 134, 143, 171, 231, 255, 280, 284, 290–91, 306, 309–11, 313, 324–25, 327, 358, 364–65, 402, 416, 439, 487, 515
class struggle 300, 444, 453, 455, 546
classifying economic systems 67–84, 490–94
closed shops 380
Club of Rome 55
codetermination laws 427
coefficient of relative effectiveness 192
coercion *see* citizen sovereignty
cofactor 97
collective farm markets 145, 151, 275, 290, 302
collectivization 72, 136–38, 142, 144–45, 241, 243, 273, 490, 515
column vector 317
combines 312